914.233

ENGLISH PLACE-NAME SOCIETY. VOLUME LII
FOR 1974–1975

GENERAL EDITOR
K. CAMERON

THE PLACE-NAMES OF DORSET

PART I

ENGLISH PLACE-NAME SOCIETY

The English Place-Name Society was founded in 1923 to carry out the survey of English place-names and to issue annual volumes to members who subscribe to the work of the Society. The Society has issued the following volumes:

The volumes for the following counties are in preparation: *Cheshire* (Part 5), *Dorset, Kent, Leicestershire & Rutland, Lincolnshire, the City of London, Shropshire, Staffordshire.*

All communications with regard to the Society and membership should be addressed to:

THE HON. DIRECTOR, English Place-Name Society, School of English Studies, The University, Nottingham, NG7 2RD.

ENGLISH PLACE-NAME SOCIETY. VOLUME LII

THE PLACE-NAMES OF DORSET

By

A. D. MILLS

PART I

THE ISLE OF PURBECK,
THE HUNDREDS OF ROWBARROW, HASLER, WINFRITH,
CULLIFORD TREE, BERE REGIS, BARROW,
PUDDLETOWN, ST GEORGE

ENGLISH PLACE-NAME SOCIETY

1977

Published by the English Place-Name Society

Library of Congress Catalogue Card Number: 72–75303

ISBN: 0 904889 02 5

Printed in Great Britain
at the University Press, Cambridge

The collection from unpublished documents of material for all the
Dorset volumes has been greatly assisted by generous grants
received from the British Academy.

CONTENTS

MAPS

PREFACE

This first volume of *The Place-Names of Dorset* deals with the place-names of the eight Hundreds in the south-east of the county, an area which includes the Isle of Purbeck, the valleys of the Frome, the Piddle or Trent, and the Wey, and the towns of Wareham, Weymouth and Dorchester. Subsequent volumes, to be published as they are ready, will deal with the place-names of the east, the north, and the west of the county, in that order. The concluding volume will deal with the county-name, the river-names and road-names, and will also contain the Introduction, notes on the phonology, the analyses of elements and personal names, a section on the Old English charter boundaries, and the index.

The only survey of the names of this county that has previously appeared is Anton Fägersten's doctoral dissertation, *The Place-Names of Dorset*, Uppsala 1933. This is an excellent pioneer work, combining sound material with scholarly interpretation, but having the limited scope of the earliest of the EPNS volumes in being mainly restricted to the major names. For the present survey all the sources both printed and unprinted used by Fägersten have been re-examined, a considerable number of sources not seen by him have been gone through, and coverage of the county's names (minor names, field-names and street-names as well as major names) is as nearly comprehensive as is practically possible. But in spite of this increased scope, and even though a good many of the etymologies of the major names have had to be modified in the light of later knowledge or fuller material, it is a pleasant duty to be able to pay tribute to the excellence of Fägersten's book, and in so doing I recall warmly a friendly meeting with Dr Fägersten in Uppsala in 1961, soon after I had agreed to prepare these volumes for the English Place-Name Society, and his good wishes then for the successful continuation of his work.

It is a great pleasure to record my personal gratitude, and the thanks of the English Place-Name Society, to the many people who have helped, directly or indirectly, in the preparation of this survey.

I owe a great debt to many scholars in this field of study. The late Professor A. H. Smith, formerly Honorary Director of the Survey of English Place-Names, as my tutor and supervisor first kindled and encouraged my interest in the subject, and has remained an inspiration to me ever since. Mr John McN. Dodgson, formerly my teacher and supervisor, now my colleague and friend, has been a constant source of generous help, advice and encouragement, and many are the improvements in etymology and interpretation which have resulted from his comments and suggestions. Professor Kenneth Cameron has taken a friendly and lively interest in the project throughout, and as present Honorary Director of the Survey has given unstintingly of his time and expertise in editing my manuscript for publication, as well as in making many helpful contributions to the text. The Society's Honorary Vice-Presidents in Scandinavia, the late Dr Olof von Feilitzen and Professor Mattias Löfvenberg, have read over the work in typescript and have provided detailed and valuable comments on individual names. Professor Kenneth Jackson, a Vice-President of the Society, has examined the Celtic material in typescript, and has suggested important corrections and improvements. Professor Dorothy Whitelock, President of the Society, and Dr Margaret Gelling have both read over the work in proof and have made valuable suggestions. To all these scholars I am deeply grateful for the way they have so generously put at my disposal their time, their learning and their expertise.

I would also like to thank many other scholars in this and related fields for help and advice, either in conversation or through correspondence, on individual points or on more general matters, among them Dr Gillian Fellows Jensen, Professor H. C. Darby, Professor Lewis Thorpe, Dr Dafydd Evans, Mr Peter McClure, Mr Oliver Padel, Dr J. H. P. Pafford, the late Professor Melville Richards, Miss Ann Oxenham, Mr A. N. Willson, and Mrs Veronica Smart.

I am grateful to the many archivists and librarians who have generously given their help and advice over the years while the material for this work was being collected, to the staff of the British Museum, the Public Record Office, the Bodleian Library, the National Register of Archives, Somerset Record Office, Cornwall Record Office, Cambridge University Library, Bury St Edmunds and West Suffolk Record Office, Hampshire Record Office, Wiltshire Record Office, Devon Record Office, Dorset County Library, Poole Central Library, and the Duchy of Cornwall Estate Office. In particular I would like to extend my thanks to Miss Margaret Holmes, County Archivist at the Dorset Record Office, for her willing co-operation, valuable advice and personal kindness during my visits to Dorchester, and for reading parts of my typescript, also to her colleague Mr James Smart and to her assistants past and present for their friendly interest in the project. My best thanks are also due to Mr Roger Peers, Curator of Dorset County Museum, for his help in affording me access to books and other material in his care, for reading parts of my typescript, and for his generous gesture in lending me over a number of years a set of Hutchins's *History of Dorset* (3rd edition) interestingly annotated by the Rev. James Cross.

As well as to the many individuals and bodies whose collections are now in the keeping of the Dorset and other record offices, estate offices, and firms of solicitors (fuller details of which are given in the bibliography), I must also extend my grateful thanks to those who have allowed access to the documents still in their possession, among them Lord Salisbury, Major J. C. Mansel, Colonel Sir John Carew Pole, Mr G. D. Roper, the Dean and Chapter of Salisbury, Eton College, Winchester College, the University of Nottingham, and King's College, Cambridge.

I am pleased to be able to express my gratitude to the many Dorset people, local historians and others, who in correspondence and conversation have given me the benefit of their knowledge of particular districts or subjects, among them Mr K. G. Knight, Mrs R. J. Tennent (who also kindly excerpted field-names from Tithe Awards), Mr R. F. J. Chiplen, Dr T. B. Anderson, Mr W. Stuart Best, Mr R. J. Saville, Mr J. Stevens Cox, Mrs A. Rainey, Mr W. H. P. Comben, Mr H. J. S. Clark, Mr D. Lewis, and Mr J. Whatmoor. Most especially I would like to thank Miss Barbara Kerr for kindly providing information concerning the modern field-names of several parishes, for giving me the benefit of her deep understanding of agricultural and social history, and for letting me see a list of current field-names collected by members of the Dorset Women's Institutes in 1974 in response to her questionnaire.

I am greatly indebted to many younger scholars for their help with the collection of material for this survey. Miss Patsy Khaliq, Mrs Joy Jenkyns (née Hubble), Miss Celia Parker and Miss Helen Thomas, past and present Research Assistants to the English Place-Name Society, have given me much valuable assistance, especially in the transcription and checking of Tithe Awards. Mr Richard Samways also helped with the transcription of Tithe Awards, and Miss Monica Ory, formerly of Dorset Record Office, transcribed documents in the Public Record Office and in the Henry E. Huntington Library, California. In particular I acknowledge my great debt to Mr Alex Rumble, formerly Research Assistant to the Society, without whose extensive, accurate and scholarly transcription from documents in the British Museum and the Public Record Office, as well as in other archives offices and in private hands, the completion of this survey would have been delayed by some years.

My former teachers and colleagues at University College London, Professor Arthur Brown and Mr G. I. Needham, my former colleagues at the University of Uppsala, Professor Erik Tengstrand, Dr K. I. Sandred, Professor Erik Frykman and Dr Rune Forsberg, and my present and former colleagues at Queen Mary College London, the late Dr B. J. Timmer, Professor Norman Callan, Professor S. S. Hussey, Professor Eric Stanley, Mr Peter Dixon, Dr Rima Handley, Mr Terry Hoad, and Professor Nigel Alexander, have given me all kinds of help in many different ways, and I thank them for their friendship and encouragement.

I am indebted to Mr Roy Versey for drawing the excellent maps. The late Mrs E. Garbutt and Miss Pat Winterflood helped me by typing out lists of field-names. In particular my best thanks are due to Mrs M. D. Pattison of Nottingham for her careful and accurate typing of my difficult manuscript notebooks, and to Mrs Kathleen Cameron for her kind and patient help with the checking of the typescript.

I would like to record my gratitude to my wife Solvejg and to my daughters Karen and Susan for helping in numerous practical ways but most of all for their unfailing love and devotion during the long preparation of this work without which it could not have been finished.

Finally, it is a pleasure to acknowledge the financial assistance of the Central Research Fund of the University of London towards the expenses of the collection of unpublished material for this survey.

A. D. MILLS

Queen Mary College London
July 1976

ABBREVIATIONS AND BIBLIOGRAPHY

Abbreviations printed in roman type refer to printed sources and those in italic to manuscript sources. For abbreviations of parish names, *v.* Index of Dorset Parishes at the end of this volume.

a	*ante.*
a.	*anno.*
Abbr	*Placitorum Abbreviatio* (RC), London 1811.
AC	*Ancient Charters* (PRSoc 10), 1888.
acc.	accusative.
Acct	J. S. Drew, 'Early Account Rolls of Portland, Wyke and Elwell', DoNHAS **66** 31–45, **67** 34–54.
AD	*Catalogue of Ancient Deeds* (PRO), London 1890 and in progress.
AD	Ancient Deeds in PRO.
Add	Additional MSS in BrMus.
AddCh	Additional Charters in BrMus.
AddRoll	Additional Rolls in BrMus.
adj.	adjective.
adv.	adverb.
AFr	Anglo-French.
Almack	T. F. Almack, *A Village Heritage: the story of Blandford St Mary*, Dorchester.
als.	*alias*, otherwise.
alt. app.	altered apportionment of a Tithe Award.
Altmt	Allotment.
Ampthill	Deeds deposited by Lord and Lady Ampthill in DRO (D 71).
AN	Anglo-Norman.
Anderson	O. S. Anderson, *The English Hundred-Names, The South-Western Counties*, Lund 1939.
Angl	Anglian dialect of OE.
ANInfl	R. E. Zachrisson, *Anglo-Norman Influence on English Place-Names*, Lund 1909.
AntIt	*Itinerarium Antonini Augusti*, ed. G. Parthey and M. Pinder, Berlin 1848; A. L. F. Rivet, 'The British Section of the Antonine Itinerary', *Britannia* **1** 34–82 (includes an appendix on the Place-Names by K. Jackson).
AOMB	Augmentation Office Miscellaneous Books in PRO.
Arkell	W. J. Arkell, 'Some Topographical Names in South Dorset', DoNHAS **62** (1940) 39–49; 'Further Notes on Topographical Names in South Dorset', ib **63** (1941) 33–40.
art.	article.
ASC	*The Anglo-Saxon Chronicle*, ed. B. Thorpe (RS) 1861; *Two of the Saxon Chronicles Parallel*, ed. C. Plummer, 1892–9.
ASCharters	*Anglo-Saxon Charters*, ed. A. J. Robertson, Cambridge 1939.
ASCoins	*Anglo-Saxon Coins: Studies presented to F. M. Stenton*, ed. R. H. M. Dolley, 1961.
Ass	Extracts from Assize Roll for 1244 in Fees II 1386–8; *Assize Rolls*, typescript vols. in DCM by E. A. Fry.
Ass	Assize Rolls in PRO.

Asser Asser's *Life of King Alfred*, ed. W. H. Stevenson, 1904, new impression 1959.

ASWills *Anglo-Saxon Wills*, ed. D. Whitelock, Cambridge 1930.

ASWrits *Anglo-Saxon Writs*, ed. F. E. Harmer, Manchester 1952.

AthelC *Two Cartularies of the Benedictine Abbeys of Muchelney and Athelney* (SoRecSoc 14), ed. E. H. Bates, London 1899.

Ave Avenue.

Bach A. Bach, *Deutsche Namenkunde*, Heidelberg 1952–6.

Banco *Placita de Banco 1327–8* (PRO Lists and Indexes 32), 1909; *De Banco Rolls*, typescript vols. in DCM by E. A. Fry.

Bardsley C. W. Bardsley, *Dictionary of English and Welsh surnames*, London 1901.

Barnes William Barnes, *A Glossary of the Dorset Dialect with a Grammar*, Dorchester 1886; reprinted by Toucan Press 1970.

Bartelot Documents deposited by Dr R. Bartelot in DRO (LL and KF).

Batten Documents deposited by Miss M. M. Batten in DRO (D 13).

Battiscombe Documents deposited by Mrs Y. E. Battiscombe in DRO (D 239).

Bayly J. Bayly, *A Map of Dorsetshire*, 1773.

BCS *Cartularium Saxonicum*, ed. W. de G. Birch, London 1885–93.

Bd Bedfordshire; with page reference, PN BdHu.

bdy boundary.

Bede *Historia Ecclesiastica* in *Venerabilis Baedae Opera Historica*, ed. C. Plummer, Oxford 1896.

Bent Court roll of Wootton Glanville deposited by Sir P. Benthall in DRO (D 220).

Berkeley J. Berkeley, *Lulworth and the Welds*, Gillingham 1971.

Bettey[1] J. H. Bettey, *The Island and Royal Manor of Portland*, Bristol 1970.

Bettey[2] J. H. Bettey, *Dorset*, Newton Abbot 1974.

Bk Buckinghamshire; with page reference, PN Bk.

B.K. Spellings and information supplied by Miss Barbara Kerr; with page reference, B. Kerr, 'Dorset Fields and their Names', DoNHAS **89** 233–256.

BlandF *Blandford Forum from 705 A.D.–1873 A.D.*, Blandford 1923.

Bldg, Bldgs Building(s).

BM *Index to the Charters and Rolls in the Department of Manuscripts, British Museum*, 2 vols., London 1900–12.

BMFacs *Facsimiles of Royal and other Charters in the British Museum*, London 1903.

BNF *Beiträge zur Namenforschung*.

Bodl Documents in the Bodleian Library, Oxford.

Boswell Edward Boswell, *The Civil Division of the County of Dorset*, Sherborne 1795.

Bowen E. Bowen, *Map of Dorset*, 1755.

BPR *The Register of Edward the Black Prince* (PRO), London 1930–3.

BRA Publications of the British Records Association.

BRA Documents deposited by BRA in DRO (D 233).

Bracton *Henricus de Bracton, Note Book*, ed. F. W. Maitland, London 1887.

Brad	Cartulary of Bradenstoke Priory in BrMus (Cotton Vit. A XI).
BrEll	Typewritten calendar of Dorset documents in the Bridgewater and Ellesmere Collection in the Henry E. Huntington Library, California, prepared by Miss Monica Ory.
Bret	Breton.
Brid	*Catalogue of the Records of Bridport Borough* (typescript calendar in DRO).
Brid	Municipal Records of Bridport in DRO.
Brit	British.
Brk	Berkshire; with page references, PN Brk.
BrMus	(Documents preserved in) the British Museum.
Brock	J. Brocklebank, *Affpuddle*, 1968.
BRS	Publication of the British Record Society.
Brunner	K. Brunner, *Altenglische Grammatik nach der Angelsächsischen Grammatik von Eduard Sievers*, Halle 1942.
BrutC	Bruton Cartulary in *Two Cartularies of the Augustinian priory of Bruton and the Cluniac priory of Montacute*, ed. C. H. Maxwell Lyte and T. S. Holmes (SoRecSoc 8), London 1894.
BRW	Deeds deposited by Messrs Brundrett, Randall & Whitmore, solicitors, in DRO (D 118).
BT	*An Anglo-Saxon Dictionary* (based on the collections of J. Bosworth) by T. N. Toller, Oxford 1898.
BTAdd	*Enlarged Addenda and Corrigenda* to BTSuppl, by A. Campbell, Oxford 1972.
Btm	Bottom.
BTSuppl	*Supplement* to BT, by T. N. Toller, Oxford 1921.
Bülbring	K. D. Bülbring, *Altenglisches Elementarbuch*, Heidelberg 1902.
Bundy	Court Book of Mappowder deposited by R. Bundy, Esq., in DRO (D 261).
BurgHid	The 'Burghal Hidage' in ASCharters 246–9.
byn.	byname.
c.	*circa.*
C	Cambridgeshire; with page reference, PN C.
Camd	W. Camden, *Britannia*, London 1590, and later editions.
Cameron	K. Cameron, *English Place-Names*, London 1961.
CampbCh	Campbell Charters in BrMus.
Campbell	A. Campbell, *Old English Grammar*, Oxford 1959.
Cantor & Wilson	L. M. Cantor and J. D. Wilson, 'The Medieval Deer-Parks of Dorset, I-IX', J. D. Wilson, 'The Medieval Deer-Parks of Dorset, X-XIV', DoNHAS **83–96** (referred to as Cantor & Wilson **1–14**).
CarP	Typewritten calendar in DRO of Carew Pole MSS in Cornwall Record Office, cf. *Pole.*
CartAnt	*The Cartae Antiquae Rolls 1–20* (PRSoc NS 17 and 33), 1939 and 1960.
Cary	J. Cary, *A Map of Dorsetshire*, 1789.
Cecil	Documents in the possession of the Earl of Salisbury at Hatfield House.
CecilMap	Map in the possession of the Earl of Salisbury at Hatfield House.
Celt	Celtic.
cent.	century.

Cerne	'The Cartulary of Cerne Abbey', ed. B. F. Lock, DoNHAS **28** 65–95, **29** 195–224.
cf.	compare.
Ch	*Calendar of Charter Rolls* (PRO), 6 vols., 1903–27.
Ch	Cheshire; with page reference, PN Ch.
CH	Court rolls for Cranborne hundred, survey of Tincleton, etc. deposited by Messrs Curtler & Hallmark, solicitors, in DRO (D 172, D 202).
ChancP	*Calendar of Proceedings in Chancery in the reign of Queen Elizabeth* (RC), London 1827–32; *Index of Chancery Proceedings* (PRO Lists and Indexes 7, 24, 30), London 1896.
ChancR	Variant readings from the Chancellor's copy of the Pipe Rolls, as noted in PRSoc vols., and the Chancellor's Roll for 1196 (PRSoc NS 7).
ChancW	Calendar of Chancery Warrants (PRO), 1927 and in progress.
Chatwin	C. P. Chatwin, *The Hampshire Basin and adjoining areas*, 3rd ed., London 1960.
Chessell	H. Chessell, *A Portrait of Lyme*, 1969.
ChR	*Calendarium Rotulorum Chartarum* (RC), London 1803.
ChrP	Cartulary of Christchurch Priory in BrMus (Cotton Tib. D VI).
Cl	*Calendar of Close Rolls* (PRO), in progress.
Cl	Close (in field-names).
Clegg	A. L. Clegg, *A History of Dorchester, Dorset*, London 1972.
CleggWim	A. L. Clegg, *The History of Wimborne Minster*, 1960.
ClR	*Rotuli Litterarum Clausarum* (RC), London 1833–44.
Cmn	Common.
Co	Cornwall.
Cock	Court Book of Hillfield deposited by Mrs E. Cockburn in DRO (D 128).
Coin, Coins	Spellings taken from the legends of coins, ex inf. Mrs Veronica Smart.
Coker	J. Coker, *Survey of Dorset*, London 1732 (now attributed to Thomas Gerard).
CollA	Deeds deposited by the College of Arms in DRO (D 299).
Collingwood & Myres	R. G. Collingwood and J. N. L. Myres, *Roman Britain and the English Settlements*, Oxford 1937.
Collins	Capt. G. Collins, *Great-Britain's Coasting Pilot*, London 1753.
Comm	Exchequer Special Commissions in PRO.
comp.	comparative.
ContGerm	Continental German(ic).
Coram	*Coram Rege Rolls*, typescript vols. in DCM by E. A. Fry.
CoramR	*Placita coram domino Rege 25 Ed i* (BRS 19), 1898.
Corn	Cornish.
CoRO	Document in Cornwall Record Office, Truro.
Cott	Cotton MSS in BrMus.
CottCh	Cotton Charters in BrMus.
Crawf	*The Crawford Collection of Early Charters*, ed. A. S. Napier and W. H. Stevenson, Oxford 1895.
Croft-Murray	Document deposited by E. Croft-Murray, Esq., in DRO (D 79).
Ct	Court Rolls in PRO.

Ctg, Ctgs	Cottage(s).
Cu	Cumberland; with page reference, PN Cu.
Cur	*Curia Regis Rolls* (PRO), in progress.
Cur(P)	Curia Regis Rolls in PRSoc 14, 24 and NS 31.
CurR	*Rotuli Curiae Regis* (RC), London 1835.
CW	Various printed churchwardens' accounts.
CW	Various unpublished churchwardens' accounts.
D	Devon; with page reference, PN D.
dat.	dative.
Db	Derbyshire; with page reference, PN Db.
DB	Domesday Book; ed. A. Farley and H. Ellis, London 1783–1816; ed. and transl. of Do section in VCHDo 3.
DBGazetteer	H. C. Darby & C. R. Versey, *Domesday Gazetteer*, Cambridge 1975.
DBGeography	*The Domesday Geography of South-West England*, ed. H. C. Darby and R. Welldon Finn, Cambridge 1967.
DCM	Dorset County Museum.
DCM	Documents in DCM collections now in DRO.
DCMCt	Court Rolls in DCM collections now in DRO.
DCMDeed	Card index of deeds in DCM collections now in DRO; G. D. Squibb, 'A Calendar of XVIth Century Dorset Deeds', DoNHAS **69** 68–107; other calendars of Dorset deeds in DoNHAS **32, 43, 49, 50, 53, 54, 55, 56, 57** and **58**.
DCMDeed	Deeds in DCM collections now in DRO.
DCMMap	Map or photocopy of map in DCM collections now in DRO.
DCMRent	Rentals in DCM collections now in DRO.
DCMSurv	Surveys in DCM collections now in DRO.
Deed	Form taken from an original deed.
def.	definite.
DEPN	E. Ekwall, *The Concise Oxford Dictionary of English Place-Names*, 4th ed., Oxford 1960.
dial.	dialect(al).
Digby	Records of the Sherborne Castle Estate and of the Digby family in DRO (KG).
DLComm	Duchy of Lancaster Special Commissions in PRO.
DLCt	Duchy of Lancaster Court Rolls in PRO.
DLMB	Duchy of Lancaster Miscellaneous Books in PRO.
DLRent	Duchy of Lancaster Rentals in PRO.
Do	Dorset.
DoIpm	*Abstracts of Dorset Inquisitiones post mortem, Charles I*, ed. E. A. Fry and G. S. Fry, London 1894.
DoNHAS	*Proceedings of the Dorset Natural History and Archaeological Society*.
DorB	*Catalogue of the Records of Dorchester Borough* (DRO typescript calendar).
DoRecSoc	Dorset Record Society publications.
DorM	*Plan of Dorchester*, 1610, facing p. 91 in DorR.
DorR	*The Municipal Records of the Borough of Dorchester*, ed. C. H. Mayo, Exeter 1908.
Douce	Douce Charters in the Bodleian Library, Oxford.
Douch	R. Douch, *A Handbook of Local History, Dorset, with A Supplement of Additions and Corrections to 1960*, Bristol 1962.

Drax	Drax Papers in custody of Messrs Preston & Redman, Bournemouth.
Drew	Col. C. D. Drew's manorial index in DCM.
DRO	(Documents preserved in) Dorset Record Office; collections in DRO are given their call numbers/letters (e.g. *Ampthill* D 71, *Digby* KG, etc.).
DRO	Miscellaneous documents in DRO (e.g. 19th cent valuation lists).
DROCt	Court Rolls in DRO.
DROMap	Printed maps and plans in DRO.
DROMap	Unpublished maps and plans in DRO.
DROSurv	Surveys in DRO.
Du	County Durham; with page reference, PN NbDu.
Du	Dutch.
DuCo	Documents in Duchy of Cornwall Estate Office.
Dugd	W. Dugdale, *Monasticon Anglicanum*, London 1817–30.
Dun	Dunster Castle MSS in Somerset Record Office.
e	early; in dates, with a number for the century, indicates the first third, e.g. e13 is 1200–1233; eOE is early OE, etc.
E	East(ern).
EAngl	East Anglia(n).
ECy	East Country.
ed.	edition; edited by.
Ed 1, Ed 2 etc.	Regnal date, t. Edward I, t. Edward II etc; Ed 1 1272–1307, Ed 2 1307–27, Ed 3 1327–77, Ed 4 1461–83, Ed 5 1483, Ed 6 1547–53.
EDD	J. Wright, *The English Dialect Dictionary*, Oxford 1898–1905.
EDG	J. Wright, *English Dialect Grammar*, Oxford 1905.
EENS	*Early English and Norse Studies, Presented to Hugh Smith in honour of his Sixtieth Birthday*, ed. A. Brown and P. G. Foote, London 1963.
EETS	Publications of the Early English Text Society.
Eg	Egerton MSS in BrMus.
EgCh	Egerton Charters in BrMus.
Ekwall	*v.* DEPN, Ln, OEDials, OE wīc, PN -ing, RN, Studies[1], Studies[2], Studies[3].
el.	place-name element.
EL	*Deeds in Exeter City Library* (typescript calendar in DRO).
Eliz	Regnal date, t. Elizabeth 1, 1558–1603.
eME	Early Middle English.
EMidl	East Midland(s).
eModE	Early Modern English.
EnclA	Unprinted Enclosure Awards in DRO.
EPN	A. H. Smith, *English Place-Name Elements*, Parts 1 and 2 (EPNS 25, 26), Cambridge 1956.
EPNS	Publications of the English Place-Name Society.
ERO	Surveys of Corscombe and Halstock presented to DRO by Essex Record Office.
E & S	*Essays and Studies by Members of the English Association.*
esp.	especially.
Ess	Essex; with a page reference, PN Ess.
ESt	*Englische Studien.*
et freq	*et frequenter*; and frequently (thereafter).

et seq	*et sequenter*; and subsequently.
Eton	*Eton College Records*, volume 2 (typescript calendar in DRO).
Eton	Eton College Records.
Evison	V. I. Evison, *The Fifth Century Invasions South of the Thames*, London 1965.
Exon	The Exon (Exeter) Domesday; editions as for DB.
Ext	Ancient Extents in PRO.
Eyton	R. W. Eyton, *A Key to Domesday ... an Analysis and Digest of the Dorset Survey*, London 1878.
f, ff	following page(s).
f., ff.	folio(s).
FA	*Feudal Aids* (PRO), London 1899–1920.
Fägersten	A. Fägersten, *The Place-Names of Dorset*, Uppsala 1933.
Fd, Fds	Field(s).
Fees	*The Book of Fees* (PRO), London 1920–31.
Feilitzen	O. von Feilitzen, *The Pre-Conquest Personal-Names of Domesday Book*, Uppsala 1937.
Fellows Jensen	G. Fellows Jensen, *Scandinavian Personal Names in Lincolnshire and Yorkshire*, Copenhagen 1968.
fem.	feminine.
Feth	Documents deposited by Commander R. Fetherstonhaugh-Frampton, R.N. in DRO (D 29).
FF	*Full Abstracts of the Feet of Fines relating to Dorset*, ed. E. A. Fry and G. S. Fry (Dorset Records 5 and 10), London 1896 and 1910.
Field	J. Field, *English Field Names, A Dictionary*, Newton Abbot 1972.
Finberg	H. P. R. Finberg, *The Early Charters of Wessex*, Leicester 1964.
Fine	*Calendar of Fine Rolls* (PRO), in progress.
FineR	*Excerpta e rotulis finium* (RC), London 1836.
Flg, Flgs	Furlong(s).
Fm	Farm.
fn.	footnote.
f.n., f.ns.	field-name(s).
foll.	the following place-name.
For	Forest Proceedings in PRO.
Forde	Cartulary of Forde Abbey (by kind permission of G. D. Roper, Esq.).
ForReg	Regard of Forest in BrMus (Add 22934 ff. 110–111).
Forsberg	R. Forsberg, *A Contribution to a Dictionary of Old English Place-Names*, Uppsala 1950.
ForsbergCh	R. Forsberg, 'Topographical notes on some Anglo-Saxon Charters', NoB 30 150–8.
Forssner	T. Forssner, *Continental-Germanic Personal-Names in England*, Uppsala 1916.
Förstemann	E. Förstemann, *Altdeutsches Namenbuch: Personennamen* (PN), *Ortsnamen* (ON), 3rd ed. by H. Jellinghaus, Bonn 1913–16.
FörsterKW	M. Förster, *Keltisches Wortgut im Englischen*, Halle 1921.
FörsterTh	M. Förster, *Der Flussname Themse und seine Sippe*, München 1941.
Fort	Fortescue Papers in Cornwall Record Office.
Foster	Foster Muniments in Lincolnshire Record Office.

Fowler	J. Fowler, *Medieval Sherborne*, 1951.
Fr	French.
France	*Calendar of Documents preserved in France* (PRO), London 1899.
Fransson	G. Fransson, *Middle English Surnames of Occupation*, Lund 1936.
freq, *freq*	*frequenter*, frequent(ly).
Fris	Frisian
Fry	Documents deposited in DCM by E. A. Fry, now in DRO.
FW	Florence of Worcester; *Florentii Wigorniensis monachi Chronicon ex Chronicis*, ed. B. Thorpe, London 1848–9.
G	German.
Gdn, Gdns	Garden(s).
GeldR	Dorset Geld Rolls preserved in Exon, VCHDo 3 115–149.
gen.	genitive.
Germ	Germanic.
Gerv	Gervase of Canterbury; *Gervasius Cantuarensis, Mappa Mundi* (RS), London 1867–9.
Gibbons	A. O. Gibbons, *Cerne Abbas*, Dorchester 1963.
GillCt	Gillingham Court Rolls in DRO (D 407).
Gir	Giraldus Cambrensis; *Giraldi Cambrensis Opera* (RS), London 1861–91.
Gl	Gloucestershire; with page reference, PN Gl.
Glast	*The Great Chartulary of Glastonbury*, ed. Dom A. Watkin (SoRecSoc 59, 63, 64), 1947, 1952, 1956.
Glast	Glastonbury Cartulary in the Bodleian Library, Oxford (Bodley MS Wood empt i).
GlastC	Quire from e14th century Glastonbury Cartulary in BrMus (Add 22934 ff. 114–125).
GlastE	Extents of Manors belonging to Glastonbury Abbey in BrMus (Egerton MS 3321/f).
GlastF	*A Feodary of Glastonbury Abbey* (SoRecSoc 26), ed. F. W. Weaver, London 1910.
GlastR	*Rentalia et Custumaria Michaelis de Ambresbury 1235–1252 et Rogeri de Ford 1252–1261 Abbatum Monasterii Beatae Mariae Glastonicae* (SoRecSoc 5), ed. C. I. Elton, London 1891.
Glouc	Deeds deposited by Gloucester City Library in DRO (D 107).
Glyn	Documents deposited by Sir Richard Glyn in DRO (D 54).
GM	Geoffrey of Monmouth, *Historia Regum Britanniae*, ed. J. Hammer, Cambridge (Mass.) 1951.
Good	R. Good, *The Old Roads of Dorset*, Bournemouth 1966.
Goth	Gothic
Gough	Gough MSS in the Bodleian Library, Oxford.
GoughMap	*Facsimile of the Ancient Map of Great Britain in the Bodleian Library*, Oxford, A.D. 1325–50 (O.S.), 1935.
Gr	Greek.
Grd, Grds	Ground(s).
Gre	C. and J. Greenwood, *Map of Dorset*, 1826.
Grundy	G. B. Grundy, 'Saxon Charters of Dorset', DoNHAS **55–61** (referred to as Grundy **1–7**).
Gt	Great.

GW	Deeds deposited by Messrs Gibson & Weldon, solicitors, in DRO (D 145).
Ha	Hampshire; Mr J. E. B. Gover has permitted the consultation of his unpublished typescript on the place-names of Hampshire.
Hardy	W. M. Hardy, *Old Swanage or Purbeck Past and Present*, Dorchester 1908.
HaRecSoc	Hampshire Record Society Publications.
Harl	Harleian MSS in BrMus.
HarlCh	Harleian Charters in BrMus.
HarlRoll	Harleian Rolls in BrMus.
HaRO	Documents in Hampshire Record Office.
Hart	C. Hart, 'Some Dorset Charter Boundaries', DoNHAS **86** 158–63.
Hastings	Court roll for Newton Montague in the Hastings Collection in the Henry E. Huntington Library, California (ex inf. Miss Monica Ory).
HBr	Documents deposited by Hunter Bruce Ltd in DRO (D 247).
Hd	Hundred.
He	Herefordshire; with page reference, PN He.
Hen[1]	Hengrave MSS in Bury St Edmunds and West Suffolk Record Office.
Hen[2]	Hengrave Hall MSS in Cambridge University Library.
Heref	Documents deposited by Hereford Public Library in DRO (D 111).
HH	*Henrici Huntendonensis Historia Anglorum* (RS), London 1879.
Higden	Ranulph Higden's *Polychronicon* (RS), London 1865–86.
Hine	Documents deposited in DCM by Mrs R. Hine, now in DRO (LN).
HMC	(Report of) the Historical Manuscripts Commission.
Ho	House.
Hosp	*The Knights Hospitallers in England*, ed. L. B. Larking (Camden Society 65), 1857.
HospCG	*Cartulaire général de l'ordre des hospitaliers de S. Jean de Jérusalem* 1100–1310, ed. J. D. le Roulx, Paris 1894–1906.
Hr	Higher.
Hrt	Hertfordshire; with page reference, PN Hrt.
HTax	*Dorset Hearth Tax Assessments* 1662–1664, ed. C. A. F. Meekings, Dorchester 1951.
Hthr	Hither.
Hu	Huntingdonshire; with page reference, PN BdHu.
Hutch[1]	J. Hutchins, *The History and Antiquities of the County of Dorset* (1st edition), 2 vols., London 1774.
Hutch[3]	J. Hutchins, *The History and Antiquities of the County of Dorset* (3rd edition), 4 vols., ed. W. Shipp and J. W. Hodson, 1861–70.
Hutchings	M. Hutchings, *Inside Dorset*, Sherborne 1965.
Hy 1, Hy 2 etc.	Regnal date, t. Henry I, t. Henry II etc.; Hy 1 1100–35, Hy 2 1154–89, Hy 3 1216–72, Hy 4 1399–1413, Hy 5 1413–22, Hy 6 1422–71, Hy 7 1485–1509, Hy 8 1509–47.
Hyde	*Liber Vitae, Register and Martyrology of New Minster and Hyde Abbey*, ed. W. de Gray Birch (HaRecSoc), 1892.
HydeC	Cartulary of Hyde Abbey in BrMus (Cotton Domit. A. xiv).

ib, *ib*	*ibidem.*
Icel	Icelandic.
IE	Indo-European.
Ilch	Documents deposited by the Earl of Ilchester in DRO (D 124).
Ilchester	*Plaintiff's Documents of Title in the lawsuit The Earl of Ilchester v. Raishley and Others in the High Court of Justice*, 1888.
inf.	infinitive.
Inq aqd	*Calendarium Inquisitionum ad quod damnum* (RC), London 1803; *Inquisitions ad quod damnum* (PRO, Lists and Indexes 17, 22), London 1904, 1906.
intrans.	intransitive.
Ipm	*Calendar of Inquisitions Post Mortem* (PRO), in progress.
IpmR	*Calendarium Inquisitionum post mortem* (RC), London 1802–28.
IPN	*Introduction to the Survey of English Place-Names* (EPNS 1, i), Cambridge 1924.
Jackson	K. Jackson, *Language and History in Early Britain*, Edinburgh 1953.
Jas 1, Jas 2	Regnal date, t. James I, t. James II; Jas 1 1603–25, Jas 2 1685–88.
JEPN	*The English Place-Name Society Journal.*
Jervoise	E. Jervoise, *The Ancient Bridges of the South of England*, London 1930.
JervoiseSh	E. Jervoise, *Shaftesbury, Dorset: The Streets, Roads and Lanes*, Shaftesbury 1950.
John	Regnal date, t. John, 1199–1216.
Jordan	R. Jordan, *Handbuch der Mittelenglischen Grammatik*, Heidelberg 1934.
K	Kent; with page reference, PN K.
Karlström	S. Karlström, *Old English Compound Place-Names in -ing*, Uppsala 1927.
KCC	Documents in King's College Cambridge.
KCD	J. M. Kemble, *Codex Diplomaticus Ævi Saxonici*, London 1839–48.
Kelly	*Kelly's Directory of Dorsetshire*, 1939.
King's Works	*The History of the King's Works. The Middle Ages*, ed. R. A. Brown, H. M. Colvin and A. J. Taylor, 1963.
Kip	W. Kip, *Map of Dorset*, 1610.
Kirkby	'Kirkby's Inquest', in Hutch[3] 4 lxxi–lxxvi.
Kluge	F. Kluge, *Nominale Stammbildungslehre der Altgermanischen Dialekte*, 3rd ed. by L. Sutterlin and E. Ochs, Halle 1926.
KockF	'Studia germanica tillägnade Ernst Albin Kock', *Lunder germanistische Forschungen* 1, 1934.
Kökeritz	Review by H. Kökeritz of A. Fägersten, *The Place-Names of Dorset*, Uppsala 1933, in SNPh 6 120–131.
KPN	J. K. Wallenberg, *Kentish Place-Names*, Uppsala 1931.
Kt	Kentish.
l	late; in dates, with a number for the century, indicates the last third, e.g. l13 is 1267–1299; lOE is late OE, lME is late ME.
l.	line.
L	Lincolnshire.
La	Lancashire; with page reference, PN La.
Laʒamon	Laʒamon's *Brut*, ed. F. Madden, London 1847.
Lane	Documents deposited by Mrs J. M. Lane in DRO (D 60).

Lang & Arber	W. D. Lang and M. A. Arber, 'Names of the West Dorset Cliffs', SoDoNQ **23** 278–81.
Lansd	Lansdowne MSS in BrMus.
Lat	Latin.
LatAdd	B. Dickins, 'Latin additions to Place- and Parish-Names of England and Wales', in *Proceedings of the Leeds Philosophical and Literary Society* (Literary and Historical Section, **3**, vi), Leeds 1935, 334–41.
Ld, Lds	Land(s).
Legg	R. Legg, *Purbeck Island*, Milborne Port 1972.
Lei	Leicestershire.
Leland	*The Itinerary of John Leland*, ed. L. Toulmin Smith, London 1906, reprinted 1964.
Lewes	*The Lewes Chartulary*, ed. W. Budgen and L. F. Salzman (Sussex Record Society), 1943.
LG	Low German.
LHyda	*Liber Monasterii de Hyda*, ed. E. Edwards, London 1866.
Lib	*Calendar of Liberate Rolls* (PRO), in progress.
LibR	*Rotuli de liberate ac de misis et praestitis* (RC), London 1844.
LN	*Liber niger Scaccarii*, ed. T. Hearne, Oxford 1728.
Ln	London; with page reference, E. Ekwall, *Street-Names of the City of London*, Oxford 1954.
LodersC	*Cartulaire de Loders, Prieuré dépendant de l'Abbaye de Montebourg*, ed. L. Guilloreau, Evreux 1908, also in *Revue Catholique de Normandie* **17–19** (1907–9).
Löfvenberg	M. T. Löfvenberg, *Studies on Middle English Local Surnames*, Lund 1942.
LP	*Letters and Papers Foreign and Domestic, Henry VIII* (PRO), London 1864–1932.
Lr	Lower.
LRMB	Land Revenue Miscellaneous Books in PRO.
Lt	Little.
Luick	K. Luick, *Historische Grammatik der Englischen Sprache*, Leipzig 1914–40.
LVD	*Liber Vitae Dunelmensis* (Surtees Society 136), Durham 1923.
LymeR	*Lyme Regis Borough Archives* (typescript calendar in DRO).
LymeR	Borough archives of Lyme Regis.
Lysons	D. and S. Lysons, *Magna Britannia*, London 1816.
m.	membrane.
m	mid; in dates, with a number for the century, indicates mid-century, e.g. m13 is 1234–1266.
Mansel	*Catalogue of documents in possession of Major J. C. Mansel* (HMC).
Mansel	Documents in possession of Major J. C. Mansel.
Map	Various printed maps and plans.
Map	Various unpublished maps and plans.
Margary	I. D. Margary, *Roman Roads in Britain*, Vol. I, London 1955; revised one volume ed. 1967 (page references to this ed.).
Marten	Documents deposited by Hon. Mrs M. A. Marten in DRO (D 84).
masc.	masculine.
Maslen	Deeds deposited by T. F. Maslen, Esq., in DRO (D 9).
MCorn	Middle Cornish.

Md	Mead.
MDu	Middle Dutch.
Mdw, Mdws	Meadow(s).
ME	Middle English.
MED	*Middle English Dictionary*, ed. H. Kurath, University of Michigan, Ann Arbor, in progress.
MedArch	*Medieval Archaeology.*
MedLat	Medieval Latin.
Mem	*Memoranda Rolls* (PRO), in progress.
Memo	*Memoranda Rolls* (PRSoc NS 11, 21, 31), 1933, 1943, 1953.
Merc	Mercian dialect of Old English.
M.H.	Spellings and information supplied by Miss M. E. Holmes, Dorset County Archivist.
MHG	Middle High German.
Midd	Middleton MSS at University of Nottingham.
Midl	Midland(s).
Milne	Survey of Moreton (c. 1300) deposited by Dr. J. F. Milne in DRO (D 303).
MiltC	Customary of Milton Abbey in BrMus (Add 40886).
MiltRoll	Roll of Milton Abbey in DRO (D 357).
MinAcct	Ministers' Accounts in PRO.
Misc	*Calendar of Inquisitions Miscellaneous* (PRO), in progress.
MLG	Middle Low German.
ModE	Modern English.
ModEdial.	Modern English dialect(al).
ModWelsh	Modern Welsh.
Mon	Monmouthshire.
Mont	Court Book for Chickerell, etc. deposited by V. Montague, Esq., in DRO (D 45).
MontC	Montacute Cartulary in *Two cartularies of the Augustinian priory of Bruton and the Cluniac priory of Montacute*, ed. C. H. Maxwell Lyte and T. S. Holmes (SoRecSoc 8), London 1894; extracts in T. Bond, 'Holme Priory', DoNHAS 11 142–7.
Mow	Documents deposited by A. R. Mowlem, Esq in DRO (D 65).
MP	Documents deposited by H. P. M. Mansel-Pleydell, Esq in DCM, now in DRO (MR).
MS, MSS	Manuscript(s).
Mx	Middlesex; with page reference, PN Mx.
n.	note.
(n)	new place-name element, not in EPN.
N	North(ern).
Names	*Names* (Journal of the American Name Society).
NatT	Documents deposited by the National Trust in DRO (D 102).
Nb	Northumberland; with page reference, PN NbDu.
NCPN	B. G. Charles, *Non-Celtic Place-Names in Wales*, London 1938.
NCy	North Country.
n.d.	undated.
NED	*A New English Dictionary*, ed. J. A. H. Murray and others, Oxford 1888–1933.
neut.	neuter.
Nf	Norfolk.

NI	*Nonarum inquisitiones* (RC), London 1807; some forms taken from Hutch[3].
NichHosp	MS at St Nicholas Hospital, Salisbury (ex inf. Chr. Wordsworth, Master in 1919).
NoB	*Namn och Bygd.*
nom.	nominative.
Norw	Norwegian.
NQ	*Notes and Queries.*
NRA	The National Register of Archives; *Report of the National Register of Archives*, in progress.
NS	New Series.
Nt	Nottinghamshire; with page reference, PN Nt.
NTCB	M. Gelling, W. F. H. Nicholaisen and Melville Richards, *The Names of Towns and Cities in Britain*, London, 1970.
Nth	Northamptonshire; with page reference, PN Nth.
Nthr	Nether.
NWMidl	North-West Midland(s).
O	Oxfordshire; with page reference, PN O.
O&N	*The Owl and the Nightingale*, ed. E. G. Stanley, London 1960.
obl.	oblique case.
Obl	*Rotuli de Oblatis* (RC), London 1835.
OBret	Old Breton.
obs.	obsolete.
OCorn	Old Cornish.
ODan	Old Danish.
OE	Old English.
OEBede	*The Old English Version of Bede's Ecclesiastical History*, ed. T. Miller (EETS 95–6, 110–11), 1890–8.
OEDials	E. Ekwall, *Contributions to the Study of Old English Dialects*, Lund 1917.
OE wīc	E. Ekwall, *Old English wīc in Place-Names*, Lund 1964.
OFr	Old French.
OFris	Old Frisian.
OG	Old German.
Ogilby	J. Ogilby, *Itinerarium Angliae*, London 1675.
OIIG	Old High German.
OIcel	Old Icelandic.
ON	Old Norse.
ONFr	Old Northern French.
Orchd, Orchds	Orchard(s).
Ord	Ordericus Vitalis, *Historia Ecclesiastica*, ed. A. le Prévost (Société de l'Histoire de France), Paris 1838–55.
orig.	original document.
Orig	*Originalia Rolls* (RC), London 1805–10.
O.S.	The Ordance Survey.
OS	First edition of 1″ Ordnance Survey map.
OS	Original Series in a run of periodicals or publications.
OSax	Old Saxon.
OScand	Old Scandinavian.
Osm	*Vetus registrum Sarisberiense: the register of St Osmund*, ed. W. H. R. Jones, London 1883–4.
OSwed	Old Swedish.
OWelsh	Old Welsh.

p.	page.
p	*post.*
(p)	place-name used as a personal name or surname.
P	*Pipe Rolls* (PRSoc), in progress.
pa.	past.
Pap	*Calendar of Papal Registers* (PRO), in progress.
pa. part.	past participle.
par., pars.	parish(es).
ParlSurv	Parliamentary Surveys in PRO.
par.n.	parish-name.
Pars	Documents purchased from G. Parsons, Esq in DRO (D 355).
part.	participle.
Pat	*Calendar of Patent Rolls* (PRO), in progress.
PatR	*Rotuli Litterarum Patentium* (RC), London 1835.
Pavey	R. W. J. Pavey, *Notes on Charmouth*, Charmouth 1969.
Pce	Piece.
Pdk	Paddock.
pers.n., pers.ns.	personal name(s).
Petre	Petre MSS in Devon Record Office.
P.H.	Public House.
Phonol.	Phonological section in the concluding volume of the Dorset survey.
Pick	Documents deposited by W. A. Pickard-Cambridge, Esq in DCM, now in DRO (OA).
Pigot	Pigot & Company, *London and Provincial New Commercial Directory for 1823–4.*
Pitfield	F. Pitfield, *Bere Regis*, Sherborne 1974.
Pitt	Pitt Papers in BrMus (Add 29976).
pl.	plural.
Plant., Plants.	Plantation(s).
PlR	Pleydell-Railston MSS in DRO.
p.n., p.ns.	place-name(s).
PN BdHu	A. Mawer, F. M. Stenton, *The Place-Names of Bedfordshire and Huntingdonshire* (EPNS 3), Cambridge 1926.
PN Bk	A. Mawer, F. M. Stenton, *The Place-Names of Buckinghamshire* (EPNS 2), Cambridge 1925.
PN Brk	M. Gelling, *The Place-Names of Berkshire*, Parts 1–3 (EPNS 49–51), Cambridge 1973–5.
PN C	P. H. Reaney, *The Place-Names of Cambridgeshire and the Isle of Ely* (EPNS 19), Cambridge 1943.
PN Ch	J. McN. Dodgson, *The Place-Names of Cheshire*, Parts 1–4 (EPNS 44–7), Cambridge 1970–2.
PN Cu	A. M. Armstrong, A. Mawer, F. M. Stenton, B. Dickins, *The Place-Names of Cumberland*, Parts 1–3 (EPNS 20–2), Cambridge 1950–2.
PN D	J. E. B. Gover, A. Mawer, F. M. Stenton, *The Place-Names of Devon*, Parts 1 and 2 (EPNS 8, 9), Cambridge 1931–2.
PN Db	K. Cameron, *The Place-Names of Derbyshire*, Parts 1–3 (EPNS 27–9), Cambridge 1959.
PN Ess	P. H. Reaney, *The Place-Names of Essex* (EPNS 12), Cambridge 1935.
PN Gl	A. H. Smith, *The Place-Names of Gloucestershire*, Parts 1–4 (EPNS 38–41), Cambridge 1964–5.

PN He	A. T. Bannister, *The Place-Names of Herefordshire*, Cambridge 1916.
PN Hrt	J. E. B. Gover, A. Mawer, F. M. Stenton, *The Place-Names of Hertfordshire* (EPNS 15), Cambridge 1938.
PN -ing	E. Ekwall, *English Place-Names in -ing*, 2nd ed., Lund 1962.
PN K	J. K. Wallenberg, *The Place-Names of Kent*, Uppsala 1934.
PN La	E. Ekwall, *The Place-Names of Lancashire*, Manchester 1924.
PN Mx	J. E. B. Gover, A. Mawer, F. M. Stenton, S. J. Madge, *The Place-Names of Middlesex* (EPNS 18), Cambridge 1942.
PN NbDu	A. Mawer, *The Place-Names of Northumberland and Durham*, Cambridge 1920.
PN Nt	J. E. B. Gover, A. Mawer, F. M. Stenton, *The Place-Names of Nottinghamshire* (EPNS 17), Cambridge 1940.
PN Nth	J. E. B. Gover, A. Mawer, F. M. Stenton, *The Place-Names of Northamptonshire* (EPNS 10), Cambridge 1933.
PN O	M. Gelling, *The Place-Names of Oxfordshire*, Parts 1 and 2 (EPNS 23, 24), Cambridge 1953-4.
PN Sa	E. W. Bowcock, *The Place-Names of Shropshire*, Shrewsbury 1923.
PN Sf	W. W. Skeat, *The Place-Names of Suffolk*, Cambridge 1913.
PN Sr	J. E. B. Gover, A. Mawer, F. M. Stenton, A. Bonner, *The Place-Names of Surrey* (EPNS 11), Cambridge 1934.
PN St	W. H. Duignan, *Notes on Staffordshire Place-Names*, London 1902.
PN Sx	A. Mawer, F. M. Stenton, J. E. B. Gover, *The Place-Names of Sussex*, Parts 1 and 2 (EPNS 6, 7), Cambridge 1929-30.
PN W	J. E. B. Gover, A. Mawer, F. M. Stenton, *The Place-Names of Wiltshire* (EPNS 16), Cambridge 1939.
PN Wa	J. E. B. Gover, A. Mawer, F. M. Stenton, F. T. S. Houghton, *The Place-Names of Warwickshire* (EPNS 13), Cambridge 1936.
PN We	A. H. Smith, *The Place-Names of Westmorland*, Parts 1 and 2 (EPNS 42, 43), Cambridge 1967.
PN Wo	A. Mawer, F. M. Stenton, F. T. S. Houghton, *The Place-Names of Worcestershire* (EPNS 4), Cambridge 1927.
PN Wt	H. Kökeritz, *The Place-Names of the Isle of Wight*, Uppsala 1940.
PN YE	A. H. Smith, *The Place-Names of the East Riding of Yorkshire & York* (EPNS 14), Cambridge 1937.
PN YN	A. H. Smith, *The Place-Names of the North Riding of Yorkshire* (EPNS 5), Cambridge 1928.
PN YW	A. H. Smith, *The Place-Names of the West Riding of Yorkshire*, Parts 1-8 (EPNS 30-7), Cambridge 1961-3.
Pole	Papers of the Pole family in the possession of Col. Sir John Carew Pole, Bt. of Antony House, Cornwall; cf. CarP.
Poll	Deeds deposited by Miss J. Pollard in DRO (D 87).
Polyolbion	M. Drayton, *Poly-Olbion*, London 1612.
Poole	*Poole Borough Archives* (typewritten calendar in DRO).
Poole	Documents in Poole Central Library.
Poor	Bere Regis Poor Rates (ex inf. Miss B. Kerr).
Poul	Poulett MSS in Somerset Record Office.
Pr	Primitive.

PR   *Magnus rotulus scaccarii 31 Henry I*, ed. J. Hunter, London 1833; *The Great Roll of the Pipe 2, 3, 4 Henry II* (RC), ed. J. Hunter, London 1844.

PrCelt   Primitive Celtic.

prec.   the preceding place-name.

prep.   preposition.

pres.   present.

PrGerm   Primitive Germanic.

Prideaux   NRA calendar of documents formerly deposited by Miss I. Prideaux in DRO (D 68).

Prideaux   Documents deposited by W. A. Prideaux, Esq in DRO (D 4).

PRO   (Records preserved in or published by) the Public Record Office, London.

PrOE   Primitive Old English.

PRSoc   The Pipe Roll Society.

PrWelsh   Primitive Welsh.

Ptolemy   *Claudii Ptolemaei Geographia*, ed. G. Parthey and M. Pinder, Berlin 1860, ed. C. Müller, Paris 1883.

Queens   Queens MSS in the Bodleian Library, Oxford.

q.v.   *quod vide.*

QW   *Placita de Quo Warranto* (RC), London 1818.

R   Rutland.

R.   River.

R1, R2 etc.   Regnal date, t. Richard I, t. Richard II, etc.; R1 1189–99, R2 1377–99, R3 1483–5.

Rav   *Ravennatis Anonymi Cosmographia*, ed. G. Parthey and M. Pinder, Berlin 1860; I. A. Richmond and O. G. S. Crawford, 'The British Section of the Ravenna Cosmography', *Archaeologia* **93** 1–50.

Rawl   Documents deposited by Mrs S. Rawlins in DRO (D 151).

RB   Romano-British.

RBE   *The Red Book of the Exchequer* (RS), London 1896.

RC   Record Commission publications.

RC   *Rotuli Chartarum* 1199–1216, London 1837.

RCHM(Do)   Royal Commission on Historical Monuments, *Dorset*, Volumes 1–5, 1952–70, in progress.

Rd   Road.

Reaney   P. H. Reaney, *A Dictionary of British Surnames*, London 1958.

Reaney OES   P. H. Reaney, *The Origin of English Surnames*, London 1967.

Redin   M. Redin, *Studies on Uncompounded Personal Names in Old English*, Uppsala 1919.

Rent   Rentals in PRO.

RES   *Review of English Studies.*

RGl   *The Metrical Chronicle of Robert of Gloucester* (RS), London 1887.

RH   *Rotuli Hundredorum* (RC), London 1812–18.

RHistS   The Royal Historical Society.

R.J.S.   Spellings and information supplied by R. J. Saville, Esq.

R.J.T.   Spellings and information supplied by Mrs R. J. Tennent.

r.n., r.ns.   river-name(s).

RN   E. Ekwall, *English River-Names*, Oxford 1928.

RNs.   Section on River-Names in the concluding volume of the Dorset survey.

Robinson	C. E. Robinson, *A Royal Warren, or Picturesque Rambles in the Isle of Purbeck*, London 1882.
RomK	R. E. Zachrisson, *Romans, Kelts and Saxons in ancient Britain*, Uppsala 1927.
Roscoe	*The Marn'll Book*, ed. E. H. Roscoe, Gillingham 1952.
Roy	Royal MSS in BrMus.
RoyMap	Map in Royal MSS in BrMus.
RoyRoll	Royal Rolls in BrMus.
RS	Rolls Series.
Russ	Russell papers in Devon Record Office.
Ryder	Survey of Wareham deposited by D. Ryder, Esq in DRO (D 86).
S	South(ern); with number, Sawyer (in references to forms from Anglo-Saxon charters).
s.a.	*sub anno.*
Sa	Shropshire; with page reference, PN Sa.
Saints	*Die Heiligen Englands*, ed. F. Liebermann, Hanover 1889.
Salis	Documents in the Diocesan Record Office at Salisbury.
SalisT	Glebe terriers in the Diocesan Record Office at Salisbury.
Salkeld	Documents deposited by Lt. Col. P. E. Salkeld in DRO (D 281).
Sandison	A. Sandison, *Trent in Dorset*, Dorchester 1969.
Sandred	K. I. Sandred, *English Place-Names in -stead*, Uppsala 1963.
Sarum	*Sarum Charters and Documents* (RS), London 1891.
Sawyer	P. H. Sawyer, *Anglo-Saxon Charters*, London 1968; this list is also referred to as S in citing forms from Anglo-Saxon charters, e.g. S 534 (1) = charter no. 543, MS 1, in Sawyer's list.
Saxton	Saxton's *Map of Dorsetshire*, 1575.
sb.	substantive.
Sc	Scottish.
SC	*The Minute Books of the Dorset Standing Committee, 1646–1650*, ed. C. H. Mayo, Exeter 1902.
Scand	Scandinavian.
SCat	Sale catalogues in DRO, etc.
SCy	South Country.
SD	*Symeonis monachi Opera Omnia* (RS 75), London 1882–5.
SE	South-East(ern).
Searle	W. G. Searle, *Onomasticon Anglo-Saxonicum*, Cambridge 1897.
Seymer	Documents deposited by Lt. Col. V. H. Seymer in DCM, now in DRO (JP).
Seymer	Forms from card index of deeds in above collection in DRO.
Sf	Suffolk; with page reference, PN Sf.
sg.	singular.
Shaft	Cartulary of Shaftesbury Abbey in BrMus (Egerton 3135).
ShaftMR	*The Municipal Records of the Borough of Shaftesbury*, ed. C. H. Mayo, Sherborne 1889.
ShaftR	Shaftesbury Register in BrMus (Harley 61).
Sheen	Inventory of muniments of Sheen Priory in BrMus (Cotton Otho B. xiv).
Shepherd[1]	Documents deposited by Mrs M. Shepherd in DRO (D 217).
Shepherd[2]	Court Book for Holnest and Long Burton deposited by Mrs M. Shepherd in DRO (D 12).

Sher	Archives of the Almshouse of St John the Baptist and St John the Evangelist, Sherborne, in DRO (D 204).
SherC	Cartulary of Sherborne Abbey in BrMus (Add 46487).
Sheridan	Documents deposited by Mrs J. L. M. Sheridan in DRO (D 51).
Short	B. C. Short, *The Isle of Purbeck*, Poole 1967.
SloaneCh	Sloane Charters in BrMus.
Smith	H. P. Smith, *The History of the Borough and County of the Town of Poole*, 2 vols., Poole 1948, 1951.
SMSp	*Studia i Modern Språkvetenskap.*
s.n.	*sub nomine.*
SNPh	*Studia Neophilologica.*
So	Somerset; Dr. A. G. C. Turner has permitted the consultation of his unpublished Ph.D. thesis *The Place-Names of North Somerset.*
SoDoNQ	*Notes and Queries for Somerset and Dorset.*
SoRecSoc	Somerset Record Society publications.
SOSÅ	*Sydsvenska Ortnamnssällskapets Årsskrift.*
SPDom	State Papers Domestic in PRO.
Speed	J. Speed, *The Theatre of the Empire of Great Britain*, 1611–12; *Map of Dorset*, 1610.
Sq	Square.
Sr	Surrey; with page reference, PN Sr.
SR	*The Dorset Lay Subsidy Roll of 1332* (DoRecSoc 4), ed. A. D. Mills, Dorchester 1971; P. N. Dawe, 'A Dorset Lay Subsidy Roll, 1525', SoDoNQ **26** 204–13, 225–30, **27** 11–15, 25–30, 54–7, 73–5, 92–3, 108–110.
SR	Lay Subsidy Rolls in PRO.
SRO	Documents in Somerset Record Office.
St	Saint.
St	Staffordshire; with page reference, PN St.
St.	Street.
StdE	Standard English.
Stenton	F. M. Stenton, *Anglo-Saxon England*, 3rd ed., Oxford 1971.
Steph	Regnal date, t. Stephen, 1135–54.
st.n., st.ns.	street-name(s).
StoweCh	Stowe Charters in BrMus.
str.	strong.
StRO	Document in Staffordshire Record Office.
Strode	Strode family papers in DCM collection, now in DRO (MW).
Studies[1]	E. Ekwall, *Studies on English Place- and Personal-Names*, Lund 1931.
Studies[2]	E. Ekwall, *Studies on English Place-Names*, Stockholm 1936.
Studies[3]	E. Ekwall, *Etymological Notes on English Place-Names*, Lund 1959.
superl.	superlative.
surn.	surname.
Surv	Surveys in PRO.
s.v.	*sub voce.*
SW	South-West(ern).
Swan	Documents deposited by Swanage Urban District Council in DRO (D 37).
Swed	Swedish.

SWMidl	South-West Midland(s).
Sx	Sussex; with page reference, PN Sx.
SxAS	Deeds deposited by Sussex Archaeological Society in DRO (D 250).
Sydenham	L. Sydenham, *Shaftesbury and Its Abbey*, Lingfield 1959.
Sym	Deeds deposited by A. A. Symonds, Esq in DRO (D 90).
t.	*tempore.*
TA	Tithe Awards in PRO and in DRO.
TAMap	Maps accompanying Tithe Awards.
Tax	*Taxatio Ecclesiastica Angliae et Walliae c. 1291* (RC), London 1802.
Tayl	I. Taylor, *Map of Dorset* 1765, 2nd ed. 1795.
Taylor	C. Taylor, *Dorset*, London 1970.
T.B.A.	Spellings and information supplied by Dr T. B. Anderson.
Templar	*Records of the Templars in England*, ed. B. A. Lees, London 1935.
Tengstrand	E. Tengstrand, *A Contribution to the Study of Genitival Composition in Old English Place-Names*, Uppsala 1940.
Tengstrand MN	E. Tengstrand, 'Marginal Notes to the Place-Names of Dorset', SNPh 6 90–103.
Tengvik	E. Tengvik, *Old English Bynames*, Uppsala 1938.
Tennent	R. J. Tennent, *A Purbeck Parish through the Ages: Church Knowle*, Dorchester 1963.
TGuide	Various modern town guides.
Thorpe	B. Thorpe, *Diplomatarium anglicum ævi Saxonici*, London 1865.
Thuresson	B. Thuresson, *Middle English Occupational Terms*, Lund 1950.
Timperley & Brill	H. W. Timperley and E. Brill, *Ancient Trackways of Wessex*, London 1965.
TopCh	Topham Charters in BrMus.
TPlan	Various modern town plans and maps.
trans.	transitive.
transl.	translated by; translation.
TRE	*tempore Regis Edwardi*, the DB term for 'on the day that King Edward the Confessor was alive and dead'.
Tres	R. Treswell, *Map of Purbeck*, c. 1586 (in Hutch³ I facing p. 463), *Plan of the Town and Castle of Corfe*, 1585–6 (in Hutch¹ I facing p. 177, in Hutch³ I between pp. 482 and 483).
TRMB	Treasury of the Receipt Miscellaneous Books in PRO.
TRW	*tempore Regis Willelmi*, the DB term for 'during the days of King William I.'
UD	Documents deposited by unknown donor in DRO (D 36).
Udal	J. S. Udal, *Dorsetshire Folk-Lore*, Hertford 1922, reprinted 1970.
Upr	Upper.
v	*verso.*
v.	*vide.*
Val	Valuation and sale of Crown Lands in BrMus (Harley 606–608).
Vaux	Cartulary of the College of St Nicholas de Vaux, Salisbury in BrMus (Add 28870).
vb.	verb.

VCHDo   *The Victoria History of the County of Dorset*, Vol. 2 ed.
             W. Page, London 1908; Vol 3 ed. R. B. Pugh, Oxford 1968.
VE   *Valor Ecclesiasticus* (RC), London 1810–34.
v.l.   *varia lectio.*
W   West(ern).
W   Wiltshire; with page reference, PN W.
Wa   Warwickshire; with page reference, PN Wa.
Wal   Documents deposited by Lord Walpole in DRO (D 39).
Waller   Court Book of Shaftesbury deposited by Mrs N. J. Waller in
             DRO (D 42).
Wardle   Document deposited by D. B. Wardle, Esq in DRO (D 8).
Warne   C. Warne, *Ancient Dorset*, Bournemouth 1872.
WCy   West Country.
Wd   Wood.
We   Westmorland; with page reference, PN We.
Weld[1]   Documents deposited by Col. J. W. Weld in DRO (D 10).
Weld[2]   Documents deposited by Col. H. J. G. Weld in DRO (D 16).
Wells   Dean and Chapter of Wells MSS in Somerset Record Office.
WeyM   *Weymouth and Melcombe Regis Minute Book 1625–1660*
             (DoRecSoc 1), ed. M. B. Weinstock, Dorchester 1964.
WeyR   H. J. Moule, *Descriptive Catalogue of the Charters, Minute
             Books and other Documents of the Borough of Weymouth and
             Melcombe Regis, 1252–1800*, Weymouth 1883.
WFris   West Frisian.
WGerm   West Germanic.
Whil   Deeds deposited by G. M. Whiley, Ltd in DRO (D 240).
W.H.P.C.   Spellings and information supplied by W. H. P. Comben,
             Esq.
WI   List of current f.ns. collected by Dorset Women's Institutes,
             1974.
Widén   B. Widén, *Studies on the Dorset Dialect*, Lund 1949.
Williams   G. S. Williams, 'Streets and Lanes in Wareham at the end of
             the XVIIIth Century and some of their Inhabitants',
             DoNHAS **64** 92–109.
Wim   Wimborne Minster archives in DRO (P 204).
WimCW   Wimborne Minster churchwardens' accounts in Hutch[3] **3**
             255–267.
Winch   Winchester College Muniments.
WinchCath   *Chartulary of Winchester Cathedral*, ed. A. W. Goodman,
             Winchester 1927.
wk.   weak.
Wm 1, Wm 2   Regnal date, t. William I, t. William II; Wm 1 1066-87, Wm 2
             1087–1100.
WM   *Willelmi Malmesbiriensis Monachi de gestis regum Anglorum
             libri quinque* (RS), London 1887–9.
WMidl   West Midland(s).
WMP   *Willelmi Malmesbiriensis de Gestis Pontificum Anglorum* (RS)
             London 1870.
Wo   Worcestershire; with page reference, PN Wo.
WRO   Documents in Wiltshire Record Office.
WSax   West Saxon.

Wt	The Isle of Wight; with page reference, PN Wt.
WW	T. Wright, *Anglo-Saxon and Old English Vocabularies*, ed. R. P. Wülcker, London 1884.
Wyld	H. C. Wyld, *A Short History of English*, London 1929.
Yd	Yard.
YE	The East Riding of Yorkshire; with page reference, PN YE.
YN	The North Riding of Yorkshire; with page reference, PN YN.
YW	The West Riding of Yorkshire; with page reference, PN YW.
Zachrisson DTR	R. E. Zachrisson, 'Meaning of the Place-Names of Dorset in the light of the Terminal Rule', SNPh 6 133–163.
Zachrisson EPP	R. E. Zachrisson, 'English Place-Name Puzzles', SNPh 5 1–69.
Zachrisson ETT	R. E. Zachrisson, 'Meaning of English Place-Names in the light of the Terminal Theory', SNPh 6 25–89.
1″	Ordnance Survey 1″ maps, 7th series, 1960.
6″	Ordnance Survey 6″ maps, editions of 1902–1938.
*	a postulated form.
~	cognate with, related to.
×	times (e.g. 4× =4 examples).

Key to hundreds and parishes

7 Poxwell
8 East Stoke
9 Wareham Lady St Mary
& St Martin
10 Warmwell
11 Watercombe
12 Winfrith Newburgh
13 Woodsford
14 Wool

I Rowbarrow
1 Corfe Castle
2 Langton Matravers
3 Studland
4 Swanage
5 Worth Matravers

II Hasler
1 Arne
2 East Holme
3 Kimmeridge
4 Church Knowle
5 Steeple
6 Tyneham

III Winfrith
1 Chaldon Herring
2 Coombe Keynes
3 East Lulworth
4 West Lulworth
5 Moreton
6 Owermoigne

IV Culliford Tree
1 Bincombe
2 Broadwey
3 Chickerell
4 West Knighton
5 Osmington
6 Portland
7 Preston
8 Radipole
9 West Stafford
10 Upwey
11 Weymouth & Melcombe
Regis
12 Whitcombe
13 Winterborne Came
14 Winterborne Herringston
15 Winterborne Monkton
16 Wyke Regis

V Bere Regis
1 Bere Regis
2 Milborne Stileham
3 Winterborne Kingston

VI Barrow
1 Affpuddle
2 Turners Puddle

VII Puddletown
1 Athelhampton
2 Burleston
3 Dewlish
4 Milborne St Andrew
5 Piddlehinton
6 Puddletown
7 Tincleton
8 Tolpuddle

VIII St George
1 Bradford Peverell
2 Broadmayne
3 Charminster
4 Dorchester St Peter
& All Saints
5 Stinsford
6 Stratton
7 Winterborne St Martin

South-east Dorset: Hundreds and Parishes

PHONETIC SYMBOLS

p	pay	j	you	ɔ	pot
b	bay	x	loch (Scots)	ɔː	saw
t	tea	h	his	ɔi	oil
d	day	m	man	e	red
k	key	n	no	ei	mate
g	go	ŋ	sing	ɛ	jamais (Fr)
ʍ	when	r	run	ɛː	there
w	win	R	bird (WCy)	i	pit
f	foe	l	land	iː	bead
v	vote	tʃ	church	ou	low
s	say	dʒ	judge	u	foot
z	zone	ɑː	father	uː	boot
ʃ	shoe	ɑu	cow	ʌ	much
ʒ	azure	a	mann (German)	ə	ever
þ	thin	ai	fly	əː	bird
ð	then	æ	cab	?	water (Cockney, glottal stop)

Phonetic symbols are enclosed in square brackets, thus ['swɔnidʒ] Swanage, ['djuːliʃ, 'duːliʃ] Dewlish. The sign ' indicates that the following syllable is stressed. The sign ː indicates that the preceding vowel is long.

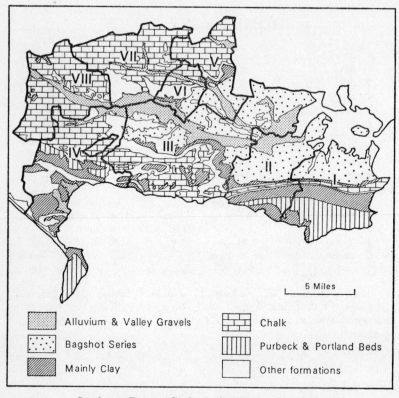

5 Miles

Alluvium & Valley Gravels

Bagshot Series

Mainly Clay

Chalk

Purbeck & Portland Beds

Other formations

South-east Dorset: Geology, also showing Hundreds

NOTES ON ARRANGEMENT

(1) The names in these volumes are arranged topographically in the old Hundreds, starting with the south-east of the county (this Part), followed by the areas of the county to the north and then by those to the west (subsequent Parts). Regional names (e.g. Isle of Purbeck) are dealt with in their appropriate topographical place. The civil parishes are arranged in alphabetical order within each Hundred, and each Part is provided with a map of the Hundreds and parishes dealt with in that Part. The parish boundaries are those shown on the 1902–4 edition of the O.S. 6″ map, but a note on older or more recent boundary changes (if any) is placed at the beginning of each parish. The Hundreds are those found in Speed, Bowen, Boswell, Hutch³, Kelly, etc., except that, for convenience, liberties and boroughs have been incorporated into topographically appropriate Hundreds. A note on such modifications, as well as on historical changes, is placed at the beginning of each Hundred.

(2) Most of the modern spellings of the place-names in these volumes (printed in small capitals) are taken from the 1902–4 edition of the O.S. 6″ map, but some are from the 1925 and 1929–30 editions.

(3) Each parish name is printed in bold type as a heading. Within each parish section the names are arranged as follows: (i) the parish name; (ii) other major names (i.e. names of sizeable settlements and names of primary historical or linguistic interest), each treated separately in alphabetical order; (iii) all minor names (i.e. the remaining names on the O.S. 6″ map and other recent maps, as well as some names that are 'lost' or 'local', v. infra), treated in alphabetical order in a single paragraph; (iv) field-names (which include other unidentified minor names) in small type, (a) modern field-names recorded since c. 1750 (with any older spellings of these names) printed in lower case roman type, (b) medieval and early modern field-names recorded only before c. 1750, printed in lower case italic type, the names in either group being arranged alphabetically. Street-names when they occur are treated as a separate section in small type immediately after the parish name; existing street-names (including some taken from modern town plans and other recent large-scale maps) are printed in small capitals. As a rule, street-names

not recorded before c. 1850 are excluded unless they bear some particular local interest or allusion.

(4) Place-names no longer current (that is, those not recorded on the editions of the 1″ and 6″ O.S. maps used) are marked '(lost)'. This does not mean that the site to which the name refers is unknown. Such names are normally printed in italic when referred to elsewhere in these volumes and in the index.

(5) Place-names marked '(local)' are those not recorded on modern maps but still current locally.

(6) Full grid references are given to parish names and other major names after the main heading for each name.

(7) The local and standard pronunciations of a name, when of interest and not readily suggested by the spelling, are given in phonetic symbols in square brackets after the map reference.

(8) In explaining the various place-names and field-names summary reference is made, by printing the elements in bold type, to the analysis of elements in the final volume, and more particularly (except when marked '(n)' in the list of elements) to *English Place-Name Elements* (EPNS 25, 26). In many of the minor names and field-names the meaning is so obvious as to need no comment or so uncertain as not to warrant it. For personal-names which are cited without authority, reference should be made for Old English names to Redin, Searle and Feilitzen, for Old (Continental) German to Förstemann PN and Forssner, and for English surnames to Bardsley and Reaney.

(9) Unprinted sources of the early spellings of place-names are indicated by printing the abbreviation for the source in italics. The abbreviation for a printed source is printed in roman type. The exact page, membrane or folio reference is only given where the precise identification of an entry may be a matter of further debate.

(10) Where two dates are given for a spelling, e.g. 1285 (1450), the first is the date at which the document purports to have been composed, and the second is the date of the copy that has come down to us. Sources whose dates cannot be fixed to a particular year are dated by century (e.g. 12, 13 etc.), by regnal date (e.g. Ed 1, Hy 2 etc.), or by a range of years (e.g. 1475–1510), although this last form of date may alternatively mean that the spellings belong to particular years within the limits indicated.

(11) The early spellings of each place-name are presented in the order 'spelling, date, source'.

(12) The sign '(p)' after the source indicates that the particular spelling given appears in that source as a person's surname, not primarily as a reference to a place.

(13) When a letter or letters in an early place-name form are enclosed in brackets, it means that spellings with and without the enclosed letter(s) occur. When only one part of a place-name spelling is given as a variant, it means that the particular spelling only differs in respect of the cited part from the preceding or following spelling. Occasional spellings given in inverted commas are usually editorial translations or modernisations and whilst they have no authority linguistically they have chronologically. Affixes are usually given after the basic place-name form, and a hyphen is usually placed before or after to indicate whether the affix is suffixed or prefixed.

(14) Cross-references to place-names in other parishes are given by the name of the parish with *supra* or *infra* (e.g. *v.* Salterne in Studland par. *infra*); *supra* refers to a name dealt with earlier in this Part, *infra* to a name dealt with later in this Part or to appear in a subsequent Part (*v.* Index of Dorset parishes). Where no parish name is given (e.g. cf. Redhorn *supra*), the reference is to a place-name in the same parish as the one in question. In subsequent volumes, cross-references back to names dealt with in an earlier Part will be made by Part number and page (e.g. **1** 53).

(15) Putative forms of personal names and place-name elements which will appear asterisked in the analyses in the concluding volume are not always asterisked in the text, although the discussion will often make it clear which are on independent record and which are inferred.

(16) In the lists of modern field-names, in order to save space, 'Acre' names of the type 'Twenty Acres' are printed '20 Acres' where the spelling is unremarkable, but the alphabetical order has been kept. In the same lists, 'and' is used when it is an integral part of a single name or entry (e.g. '5 and 20 Acres'), '&' when two separate names or entries are combined to save space (e.g. 'North Hill & Plot', representing 'North Hill' and 'North Plot').

DORSET

ISLE OF PURBECK

pars telluris Purbicinga 948 (15) *ShaftR* (S 534 (1))
Porbi 1086 DB, Exon
Hundret Porbiche 1086 DB, *Porbich* 1129 CartAnt, 1190 (1332) Ch
Purbica 1100–35 (1496) Pat, *-bic* c. 1170 MontC, 1200 Cur (p),
    1208, 1209 P both (p), 1214 Cur (p), 1275 RH (p)
Porbica 1107 (1300) Ch, *-bic* 1214 Cur (p)
Purebica 1154–89 (1496) Pat (p), *-bic* 1214 Cur, 1237, 1240 Lib,
    foresta de — 1240 Cl
Purbik(e), *-byk(e)* c. 1170 MontC, Hy 3 (14) Cerne, 1221 Cur (p),
    1223 ib (p), 1239 Lib, 1250 ib ('the forest of —'), 1257 Cl
    (*foresta de* —), 1258 ib (*warenne de* —) *et freq* to 1482 Cl ('—
    forest'), 'the King's warren at —' 1315 Cl, 'the chace of —'
    1324 ib, 1330 Fine, 1354, 1359 Pat, 'the king's free chace of —'
    1333 ib, *Estpurbyk*, *-bik(e)* 1357, 1382 Fine, 1397 Pat *et freq* to
    1456 Fine, 'the isle of *Purbyk*' 1385, 1415 Pat, *the Ile of Purbyke*
    c. 1500 *RoyRoll*, *ilond of Purbike* 1541 Hutch[3], (*the*) *Ile of*
    Purbycke, *-bicke* 1554 Mansel, 1614 *AddCh*
Purbek(e) c. 1170 MontC, c. 1500 *Eg*, 1535–43 Leland (— *Forest*),
    -bec 1206, 1207 P both (p)
Purbich 1189 (1313) Ch, 1199 Cur (p), n.d. (1372) *ChrP*
Porbik(e), *-byk(e)* 1249 Cl, 1268 *Ass*, 1320, 1334 Pat, 1406 Fine,
    p1483 *Sheen*
Purebik 1272 Pat (p)
Purbygge 1344 Pat ('the king's free chace of *Corfe* and of —')
Purpyk 1356, 1358, 1360 Pat
Pir-, *Pyrbyk* 1377 *Ass*
Purbek 1380 Pat ('the isle of —'), 1402, 1403 ib ('the forest of —')
et freq to 1512 *Ct*, 'the warren of —' 1486 Pat, *The Isle of* —
    1575 Saxton, *Purbeck* 1381 (16) *Pitt*, 1407 (1410) Pat, 1422 ib
    ('— forest'), 1513 *Ct*, 1551 AD III ('island of —') *et passim*,
    insulam de Purbecke 1584 DCMDeed, *the Ile of Purbecke* 1636
    Ilch, 1664 *GW*
Pourbyke 1399 Cl
Purbuyk 1414 Pat, 1462 ib ('the Isle of —')

Purby 1456 *Weld*[1]
Porbek forest ground 1535–43 Leland
Purbeyke 1563 *Mansel*
th'yle of Purbak l16 Hutch[3]

The first el. of this difficult name is probably OE pūr 'a bittern (or snipe)' as suggested by Ekwall (DEPN and Studies[3] 81–3) and accepted by Smith (EPN 2 75). The second el. is probably OE *bic or *bica 'a bill or beak', used in some such transferred topographical sense as 'beak-like projection' as proposed by Löfvenberg, ESt xliii 40, cf. Ekwall, Studies[3] 81–3. The name would then refer to the prominent central chalk ridge which crosses the Isle of Purbeck from W to E; the W part of this ridge where it crosses the pars. of Steeple and Tyneham *infra* is called Purbeck Hills (6″), *Purbeck Hill* 1811 OS. The meaning of the name might then be 'ridge which resembles a bittern's (or snipe's) beak' or 'beak-shaped ridge frequented by the bittern (or snipe)'. There is in fact much uncertainty about the exact species of bird the pūr was (cf. NED s.v. *purre*[1]), but at any rate various kinds of both bittern and snipe were not uncommon in Do (cf. Hutch[3] 4 cxxii–cxxiii, DoNHAS 67 111, 121), and the presence of bitterns in Purbeck, at least in the marshy N area, is attested by the f.n. Bitters Gall in Arne par. *infra*.

The OE charter form *pars telluris Purbicinga* 'part of the land of the men of Purbeck' occurs as a description of eight hides granted in Corfe C. par. *infra*; on this use of -ingas to form a folk-name from a p.n., *v.* EPN 1 300. For the DB and Exon spellings showing loss of final -c, *v.* ANInfl 27 note 1, Feilitzen 110, and for the AN spellings in -ch(e), *v.* ANInfl 32 ff, Feilitzen 107. The DB form *Hundret Porbiche* is used in an entry describing an estate '7 hides less ½ virgate' thought to be Langton Mat. par. *infra* (VCHDo 3 95, cf. Rowbarrow hundred *infra*).

The name Purbeck for the ridge was probably extended at a very early date to describe the whole area now known as the Isle of Purbeck, so called (from c. 1500) because it is a peninsula almost surrounded by water, *v.* ile 'island', alternating with ēg-land and insula. It is bounded on the N by R. Frome and Poole Harbour, on the S and E by the Channel, and on the W partly by Luckford Lake, a tributary of R. Frome (*v.* RNs. *infra*). It consists of the two hundreds of Rowbarrow and Hasler *infra*, and its bounds are still those described in

1381 (16) *Pitt* (ff. 65, 71), 1381 Misc (also printed in Hutch³ 1 496) and c. 1586 Tres.

There is frequent mention of the 'forest' of Purbeck between 1240 Cl and 1482 ib, and this is also referred to as a 'warren' between 1258 Cl and 1541 Hutch³, and as a 'chace' between 1324 Cl and 1359 Pat (*v.* forest, wareine, chace). An alternative name for the forest of Purbeck (or perhaps for only part of it) is *war(r)enna (d'ni Reg')* *de Corf(f)* 1232 Cl *et freq* to 1266 ib, 1280 *Ass*, '(King's) warren (and forest) of *Corf(e)*' 1232 Ch *et freq* to 1283 Pat, '(the king's) (free) chace of *Corf(f)(e)*' 1276 Cl *et freq* to 1344 Pat, 'king's forest of *Corf*' 1285 Cl, *v.* Corfe C. par. *infra*, cf. 'the king's free chace of *Corfe* and of *Purbygge*' 1344 Pat, and the inquisition of 1381 by which it was found that the whole Isle of Purbeck was a warren of the king and pertained to the castle of Corfe (Hutch³ 1 496). The forest was divided into two districts, no doubt coterminous with the two hundreds of Hasler and Rowbarrow respectively (Hutch³ 1 463), referred to as *la Westbayl(l)y(e)*, *-baillie*, *-bailly* 1402 Pat *et freq* to 1482 Cl, 'the Westbailiwick' 1422 Pat, *the West-baillywike* 1541 Hutch³, and as *the Est-baillywike* ib, *v.* la, west, ēast, baillie 'the district of a bailiff', bailiwick, cf. *Estpurbyk*, *-bik(e)* 1357 Fine, etc. which must also refer to the E half (i.e. Rowbarrow hundred). The three principal lodges of the forest were at Creech Barrow in Ch. Knowle par., at Slepe in Arne par., and in Swanage par. (all *infra*, *v.* Hutch³ 1 463). Names which may allude to hunting in this royal game preserve (although some are doubtful and others may be recent) include Deer Fold, Fox Grd, Game Copse, Keeper's Copse, and Warren all in Corfe C. par., The Warren Wd in Studland par., Hartland Moor in Arne par., and King's Standing in Steeple par., all *infra*.

I. ROWBARROW HUNDRED

Rowbarrow hundred consists of the E part of the Isle of Purbeck *q.v. supra*. Corfe C. was once a borough and is now a hundred in itself (Kelly), but parts of it were earlier always included in this hundred: Afflington, Kingston, Ower and Rollington lay in this hundred in 1327 *SR*, 1332 SR, 1664 HTax and 1795 Boswell, and likewise Rempstone in 1664 HTax and 1795 Boswell. The remaining parts of Corfe C. outside the borough (Blashenwell and Encombe) were included in Hasler hundred in 1327 *SR*, 1332 SR, 1664 HTax and 1795 Boswell, but for convenience the whole of Corfe C. is included here. Langton Wallis in Langton Mat. was included in Hasler hundred in 1327 *SR*, 1332 SR. For a reconstruction of this hundred as it was in c. 1086 GeldR, *v.* VCHDo 3 136-7.

Aileveswode hundret c. 1086 GeldR
Hundret Porbiche 1086 DB
Rugebergahundredum 1183, *-berg'* 1198 P
Ruggebergahundredum 1184 P, *-bergh* 1244 *Ass*
Ruberge(hundredum) 1195, 1199 P, *-ber'* 1275 RH, *-bergh'* 1288
   Ass, 1379 *MinAcct*, *Ruebergh(e)* 1265 Misc, 1280 *Ass*
Rugheberg' 1244, *-bergh(e)* 1268 *Ass*, 1303 FA, 1342 Pat, *-burgh*
   1289 Orig, 1290 Fine, Pat, *Rowgh'barough* n.d. (e15) *MiltRoll*,
   Roughburgh 1461 Pat, *Rughborowe* 1509 BrEll
Rougeberghe 1244, *Rogborwe* 1268, *Rogeberwe* 1280 all *Ass*
Rou(e)burh 1268, *-berue*, *-berewe* 1280 *Ass*, *-bergh* 1288 ib, 1307
   Ipm *et freq* to 1425 Cl, *-b(u)rgh* 1346 FA, *-berg* 1399 Ipm,
   -bargh 1425 IpmR, 1428 FA, *-borgh* 1431 ib, *Row(e)berge*,
   -berwe 1278 QW, *-berue* 1280 *Ass*, *-bergh(e)* 1288 *ib*, 1412 FA,
   -borowe 1492 Pat, *-barrowge* 1546 *Ct*, *-burgh* 1548 Pat, *-boroughe*
   1550 ib, *Rouweberu(w)e* 1280 *Ass*, *Ruweberyce* (sic) 1296 Ipm,
   Robergh 1346 FA, *-bargh* 1428 ib
Routheber 1280 *Ass*, *Rouzberwe* 1303 FA, *Rousebergh* 1316 ib

The two 11th-cent. names for this hundred are taken from Ailwood in Corfe C. par. *infra* and from the Isle of Purbeck *supra*. Rowbarrow is 'rough hill or barrow', *v.* rūh (wk. obl. *rūgan*), beorg, a name common in the OE charters for Do, e.g. (*on*) *Ruanberghe* 891 (14) *Bodl* (S 347 (2)), cf. also Rowbarrow in Ch. Knowle par. *infra* and Roborough hundred D 222. According to Hutch[3] 1 629 'near Tapers or Talbot's Hill in Woolgarston, and south of it, is a lane called Rowbarrow Lane, and in a ground near it the Hundred Court was formerly held', *v.* Tabbit's Hill, Woolgarston, and Rowbarrow Lane, all in Corfe C. par. *infra*. Tabbit's Hill is only just over ½ mile SW of Ailwood, and as Anderson 123 points out, it is therefore probable that the meeting-place of the hundred was not changed, but that the hundred was called Ailwood because its meetings were held at Rowbarrow near the place or in the wood called Ailwood. For the name *Estpurbyk*, *-bik(e)* which must refer to an area coterminous with Rowbarrow hundred, *v.* Isle of Purbeck *supra*.

LOST OR UNIDENTIFIED PLACE-NAMES IN ROWBARROW HUNDRED: *Avercomb*
1560 Hutch³, cf. William (*H*)*avercombe* 1539 *Ct*, 1560 Hutch³ (perhaps
hæfera 'oats', hæfer¹ 'a he-goat', or, as Professor Löfvenberg suggests,
ME *aver* 'a draught horse' (MED s.v.), with cumb; possibly in or near
Worth Mat. par. *infra*); *Torne* 1086 DB (2 ×), *Torna* Exon (2 ×) (*v.* þorn
'thorn-tree', possibly in a collective sense 'place where thorn-trees grow,
thorn copse'; the two small DB manors of this name, each consisting of only
one hide, are listed between entries concerning Worth Mat. par. and
Brenscombe in Corfe C. par. Eyton 111–12 places them in this hundred, and
identifies them with Durnford in Langton Mat. par. *infra*, but formally this
is not possible, a more likely formal identification being with *La Thorne*
in the same par. However, it is possible that *T*(*h*)*orne* was an earlier name
for the estate later called Durnford, *v.* discussion under Durnford and *La
Thorne infra*. A different identification of the DB manors of *Torne*, with
Thornham in Ch. Knowle par. *infra*, is proposed by DBGazetteer 127.

Corfe Castle

Corfe Castle was a borough by prescription, but was not incorporated
until 1576, after which it remained a borough until 1883 (Kelly). It is
now a hundred in itself (ib) and is very occasionally referred to as such
earlier, though usually it is described as *burgus* or *ville* (for a description
of the extents of 'the liberties of the Towne of Corff', *v.* 1381 (16) *Pitt*
(ff. 67–8), 1381 Misc and Hutch³ 1 497–8). Blashenwell and Encombe
earlier lay in Hasler hundred, whilst Afflington, Kingston, Ower, Rollington,
and Rempstone were earlier included in Rowbarrow hundred. Kingston,
formerly a parochial chapelry, has been a separate ecclesiastical par. since
1877 (Kelly). Three small tenements on the shores of Poole Harbour –
Goddins, Greenland and Phillips – were part of Corfe C. in 1795 Boswell
but are now in Studland par. *infra*; likewise, at the same date, Knaveswell
now in Langton Mat. par. *infra*, and Swalland now in Kimmeridge par.
infra. Ailwood and Westwood were formerly (1795 Boswell) in the manor
of *Langton Wallis* in Langton Mat. par. *infra*.

CORFE CASTLE (SY 961820)
> *at Corf* 955 (14) *ShaftR* (S 573), *ad*, *to Corf* 956 (14) *ib* (S 632),
> *Corf* 1162, 1202, 1203, 1210 P, 1213 (1320) Ch, 1219, 1223 Cur
> *et freq* to 1456 Fine, *Corfe* 1241 Pat *et passim*, *Corfe alias Corfe
> Castle* 1636 *Ilch*
> (*æt*) *Corfesgeate* 11 ASC (D), (*at*) *Corf geate* e12 ib (F), *in loco qui
> dicitur Porta Corf* e12 ib (F, Lat), (*æt*) *Corfes geate* 12 ib (E) all
> s.a. 979, *Corvesgeate* e12 FW, 12 SD, -*gate* 12 HH, e15 LHyda
> *Chorf* 12 King's Works
> *Corff*(*e*) 1217 Pat, 1227 Lib *et freq* to 1636 *Ilch*, *Corffe in Purbyk*
> 1383 Cl

Corf(*f*)(*e*) *Castel*(*l*), -*castel*(*l*)(*e*) 1302 Pat, 1305, 1309 FF, 1327
   SR et freq to 1575 Saxton, -*castle* 1545 *Ct et passim*, -*Chastle*
   1632 *Pitt*
Crof' 1320 Pat, *Croffe* 1535 Hutch[3], 1566 *Rent* (-*Castell*)
Corft 1399 Cl, 1427 Pat
Hundred of Corff 1381 (16) *Pitt, hundredos de Corff Castell vocat'*
   le Inne Hundred et le Out Hundred 1547 *ib*

'A cutting, a gap, a pass', *v.* corf, with geat 'an opening, a gap'
(replaced in one instance by Lat *porta*) and castel(l) 'castle', cf. Isle
of Purbeck *supra*. The name aptly describes the gap in the central
ridge of the Purbeck Hills at this place. *Corf*(*es*) *geat* probably means
'the gap called *Corf'*, *v.* -es[2], cf. Tengstrand xxvii; for the same
combination, though non-genitival, *v.* Corscombe par. *infra* and
Coryates in Portisham par. *infra*. For specific references to the castle,
v. Corfe Castle *infra*, and for Corfe Castle as a hundred, cf. note under
par. heading *supra*, *v.* in 'inner', ūt 'outer'. Three sets of bounds
describing Anglo-Saxon estates mainly in the southern half of the
present par. occur in 948 (15) *ShaftR* (S 534 (1)), 955 (14) *ib* (S 573),
and 956 (14) *ib* (S 632).

STREET-NAMES: EAST ST., 1697 *DCMDeed*, 1774 Hutch[1], *East Streete de
Corff* 1603 *Swan*, *v.* ēast; WEST ST., 1584 *Swan*, 1716 *DCMDeed*, *Westrete*
1546 *Ct*, *v.* west. Buildings include *Town hall* 1774 Hutch[1], *Ship Inn* 1844
TA, *Greyhound Inn* 1882 Robinson.

AFFLINGTON FM (SY 971801)

Alveronetune, Alvronetone, Alvretone (2 ×), *Alfrunetone* 1086 DB,
   -*tona* Exon
Alurinton 1244 *Ass*, -*ynton* 1323 *MinAcct*
Alfrin(*g*)*ton*(*e*), -*yn*(*g*)- 1244 *Ass*, 1264 Ipm, 1281 Hutch[3], 1288
   Ass, 1309 Hutch[3], 1315 Ipm, 1318 FF *et freq* to 1546 *Ct*,
   Alfringeton 1381 (16) *Pitt*, *Al*(*l*)*f*(*f*)*rington*, -*yng*- 1512 *Ct*,
   1525 *AOMB*, 1537, 1545 *Ct*, *Alfrengton* 1586 Hutch[3]
Alfre(*s*)*ton* 1288 *Ass*
Alfington 1307 Pap
Affryn(*g*)*ton* Ed 3 *Surv*, 1399 Cl, *Affrunton* p1483 *Sheen*
Alrington, -*yng*- 1348 *MinAcct et freq* to 1510 Hutch[3], — or *Alurunt*
   1427 Pat, — *in Purbyke* p1483 *Sheen*
Aldryngton otherwyse called Alfryngton 1545 *Whil, Aldrington alias
   Alfrington* 1545 Hutch[3], *Aldringtons alias Alsington alias
   Alfringtone* 1599 *Pitt*

Aflington c. 1586 Tres, *Afflington* (*Farm*) 1795 Boswell, 1811 OS,
Afflington, Alfrington or Addlington 1861 Hutch³

'Ælfrūn's farm', from the OE fem. pers.n. *Ælfrūn* and tūn. A lady
of this name (*Alueron*) held the manor TRE (DB). The name shows
analogical development of medial *-ing-* and assimilation of *-lfr-* to
-fl-. There was formerly a chapel here, called 'the chantry of
Alryngton' 1428 Pat, 'the free chapel of *Aldrington*' 1545
Hutch³.

AILWOOD (SY 994812) ['eilud]
   Aleoude 1086 DB
   Ailewud 1222 ClR (p), *Ayl(e)wo(o)d(e)* 1409 Hutch³, 1423 *Midd*,
      1426 Hutch³, 1435 *Midd*, 1811 OS
   Aylethewode 1304 Ipm, 1305 Cl
   Aileworth 1585 Hutch³
   Aylywood c. 1586 Tres
   Arlwood Farm (sic) 1844 *TA*

'Æðelgifu's wood', from the OE fem. pers.n. *Æðelgifu* and wudu,
as the form *Aileveswode hundret* c. 1086 GeldR cited for Rowbarrow
hundred *supra* shows in spite of the analogical gen. *-s, v.* -es². Later
forms show confusion or alternation with the OE fem. pers.n.
Æðelgȳð. For both pers.ns., the first of which occurs in independent
use in DB as *Ailueua*, the tenant TRE of three virgates in Morden
par. *infra, v.* Feilitzen 183, and for AN loss of intervocalic ð in
Æðel-, reduction of *-gifu*, and loss of w in *-wudu, v.* Feilitzen 76,
102, 260.

ARFLEET MILL (lost, SY 962828) ['æfliːt]
   Alflode 1286 *Ass* (p)
   Alfledesmuthe 1288 *Ass* (p)
   Alfledesmulle 1309 Hutch³, 1318 FF
   Alfletemell 1384 FF, *-mill* 1426 IpmR, *-mulle* 1435 FF, *Alflete*
      1431 FA, 1510 Hutch³ ('mill at —')
   Alfletmill(e) 1408, 1413 IpmR, *-mulle* 1421 Fine, 1423 Cl
   Aflet Milne 1585, *-Mills* c. 1586 Tres, *Afflett Mill(s)* 1774
      Hutch¹, 1795 Boswell, *Affleet Mill* 1586 Hutch³, *Affleet* 1765
      Tayl
   Arfleet Mill 1811 OS, *-Mills* 1844 *TAMap*

The first el. is probably OE ǣl 'eel'. The second would seem to be an OE *flēd or *flēde '(intermittent) stream', related to OE flōd 'flow of water, stream' and flōde 'channel, gutter' and postulated by Löfvenberg 66 to explain Fleed So. The earliest form *Alflode* may either be an error for *Alflede* or contain the unmutated flōd or flōde; the later -*flet(e)*- probably shows association or confusion of the second el. with OE flēot 'inlet, stream'. *Alflede* was no doubt an earlier name for (the part of) the Corfe River (*v.* RNs.) on which the mill was situated; *Alfledesmulle* means 'mill at *Alflede*', *v.* -*es*², myln. In the form from 1288 *Ass*, -*muthe* may represent OE mūða 'mouth, estuary', though since this roll (214) has many dubious forms, it may be an error for -*mulle*.

BLASHENWELL FM (SY 952803) ['blæʃənwel]

  at *Blechenhamwelle* 955 (14) *ShaftR* (S 573), to *Blechenenwelle*, on *Blechene*, of *þanne welle* 956 (14) *ib* (S 632), *Bleche(ne)well(e)* 1288 *Ass*
  at *Blachenwelle* 956 (14) *ShaftR* (S 632), *Blachen(e)well(e)* 1218, 1232 Hutch³, 1285 FA, 1376 Pat (p), *Ass* (p), 1381 (16) *Pitt* (-*Bridge, the runninge water of*-), 1539 *Ct*, 1861 Hutch³, -*woll(e)* 1332 SR, 1376, 1377 *Ass* both (p), *Blachyn(g)well* 1316 FA, 1512 *Ct*, -*in*- 1513 *ib*, *Blashenwell Fm* 1844 *TA*
  Blakenwelle (rubric) 956 (14) *ShaftR* (S 632), *in Blacanawilla* n.d. (15) *ShaftR*, *Blackene*- 1227 FF, *Blackenwell* 1795 Boswell
  Blauethewolle (probably for *Blaneche*-) 1327 SR, *Blanchinwell* c. 1586 Tres
  Black Knowl 1811 OS
  Blatch Nowl 1826 Gre

The first el. may be an OE noun *blǣcen 'bleaching', as suggested by Fägersten 118–19, with hamm 'enclosure, river-meadow' and well(a) (WSax wyll(a)) 'spring, stream'. Professor Löfvenberg points out that an OE *blǣcen presupposes a PrGerm *blaikīniz, an abstract noun derived from *blaikīian (whence OE blǣcan 'to bleach'), and that the name would refer to a place where cloth was bleached. *Blechenenwelle* may be a reduced form of *Blechenhamwelle* ('(spring or stream at) the bleaching enclosure') or a scribal error for *Blechenwelle* ('bleaching spring or stream'). The charter bdy form *Blechene* (956), used as the name of the spring or stream, may be a back-formation or the abstract noun used in a concrete sense (cf. EPN s.v.

-en[1] (iv)); in the description of the bdy, *Blechene* could be taken to refer either to the calcareous spring near Blashenwell Fm described in Hutch[3] **1** 526 and DoNHAS **17** 67 ff (springs are marked 6″), or to the stream flowing NNE from the farm into the now unnamed tributary of the Corfe River (*v. Hollwysshe water* in RNs.). The sporadic forms in *Bla(c)k-*, *Blac-* are probably due to influence from the OE adj. blāc 'pale, white' (cf. thc OE variation *blāc: blǣc* and *blācian* 'to turn pale': *blǣcan* 'to bleach') or even the OE adj. blæc 'black'. The form *Blanchinwell* (c. 1586) may contain the noun *blanching* 'the action of making white' (1600 NED). The 19th-cent. forms with -(*k*)*nowl* have no doubt been influenced analogically by Bucknowle and Cocknowle in the adjacent par. of Ch. Knowle *infra*. For -*bridge*, *v.* brycg.

BRENSCOMBE FM (SY 977824) [ˈbrinskəm]

    Brunescume 1086 DB, Exon, -*cumb* 1219 FF, *Brunnescorne* (sic) 1301 Pat, *Brunscombe* 1449 Fine
    Brundescumb 1244 *Ass* (p)
    Bryncescomb 1286 Abbr, *Bronchys-* 1443 IpmR, *Brenshyscomb* 1463 FF
    ?*Bramescumb* 1318 FF, *Branscombe* 1664 Hutch[3]
    Brynnescombe 1376 Pat, *Ass*
    Brenscomb(e) 1509 Hutch[3], -*farme*, -*alias Bremescombe* 1636 *Ilch*, *Bremescombe* 1586 Hutch[3]
    Bryans- 1795 Boswell, *Brianscomb(e)* 1811 OS, 1861 Hutch[3]

v. cumb 'valley'. The first el. is probably the OE pers.n. *Brȳni* (Redin 121), alternating with *Brȳnic* (ib 149, 165), cf. Brinscombe Sx 53 which is also from *Brȳni* and cumb. There is mention of a 'church house and schoole house in Branscombe' in 1664 Hutch[3].

BURBERRY LANE (SY 953805), 1783 *DROMap*, named from *Burbarrow* 1545 Hutch[3], 1774 Hutch[1], 1861 Hutch[3], cf. *Burberry Ctg*, *Hr & Lr Burberry Md* 1844 *TA*, 'hill with a cottage', *v.* būr[1], beorg, cf. Burbarrow Lane in Gl **3** 69. Hutch[3] **1** 526 describes *Burbarrow* as 'a small tenement in West Lynch, on the north side of the south hill between Kingston and Blachenwell'.

BUSHEY (SY 981835), 1861 Hutch[3], *Burshawe* 1299 Banco, *Bursewe* 1550 *Midd*, *Burshew(e)* 1586, *Bershew* 1623 Hutch[3], *Bushy or Burshews* 1700 (c. 1774) *DCMDeed*, *Bushy* 1740 Hutch[3], *Bushey or*

Buckshaw 1774 Hutch[1], *Bushaw* 1811 OS, possibly 'small wood or copse with a cottage', from bŭr[1] and sc(e)aga, if the 13th-cent. form can be trusted, but the first el. may alternatively be (ge)būr 'a peasant'. A chapel here mentioned by Hutch[3] 1 535 is referred to in *Bushew Churchyard, Church Cl* 1844 *TA*.

CHALLOW FM (SY 964821) & HILL, 1844 *TA*, *Chalwyll* 1510 Hutch[3], *Challway downe, -Farm* 1716 *DCMDeed, Challows* 1774 Hutch[1], 1861 Hutch[3], *Callows* 1795 Boswell, *Challow (Hill)* 1811 OS. The forms are late and discrepant and there is perhaps more than one name among them; *Chalwyll* may mean 'cold spring or stream', *v.* c(e)ald, wella, with reference to the small stream shown (6") as rising near Challow Fm; *Challway* may mean 'chalk way', *v.* c(e)alc, weg, and refer to the old track from Corfe C. which skirts Challow Fm and leads W up Challow Hill (part of the chalk ridge) towards Rempstone *infra* (cf. Hutch[3] 1 530), but *Chall-* in this form may only be a reduced form of *Chalwyll*; *C(h)allow(s)* is probably for *Challway(s)* with loss of stress in the second syllable, the *-s* being elliptical or pseudo-manorial.

COOMBE BOTTOM (SY 968785), *on þanne cumb, þonne an lang cumbe* 948 (15) *ShaftR* (S 534 (1)), *la Combe* Ed 3 *Surv, Bottam* c. 1825 Map, cf. *E, Green, Heathy, Middle & W Coombe, Coombe Md* 1844 *TA, v.* cumb 'valley', botm. The bdy point in the OE charter cited is probably identical with *on struthgeardes cum* 955 (14) *ShaftR* (S 573), 'to Strūtheard's valley', cf. the nearby points *onne strut heardes paþe, of þane paþe* 948 (15) *ib* (S 534 (1)), *on struthherdes wege, of þane wege* 955 (14) *ib* (S 573), 'to, from Strūtheard's path, way', from an OE pers.n. *Strūtheard* with cumb, pæð and weg; for the pers.n., *v.* Street Ashton Wa 114, Tengstrand 309–10.

CORFE CASTLE (remains of) (SY 959823), *castellum Warham* 1086 DB, *castello quod dicitur Chorf* l12 RCHM, *castellum-, castrum de Corf(f)(e)* 1196 ChancR *et freq* to 1435 *Midd, castellum de Coruo* 1199, 1200 P, *castrum de Corft* 1288 *Ass, Ruins* 1844 *TAMap, v.* castel(1), giving its name to the par. The description of the castle as *castellum Warham* 'the castle of Wareham' (*v.* Wareham par. *infra*) appears in the DB entry for the manor of Kingston *infra*, which was held by the Abbey of Shaftesbury, as follows: 'The King has 1 hide of the manor of Kingston in which he built the castle of Wareham

and (in exchange) for this he gave to St Mary (Shaftesbury) the
church of Gillingham with what belongs to it' (VCHDo **3** 83); the
identification is made certain by the fact that in 1212 Fees (91) the
Abbey held the advowson of Gillingham church *in escambium pro
terra ubi castellum de Corf positum est.* Other similar references to the
castle at Corfe include *into þam castele to Wærham* 12 ASC (E) s.a.
1113, *castellum de Warham* 12 King's Works, 'the castle of Wareham'
1130 ib, cf. King's Works **1** 27, **2** 852, Castle Close in Wareham
par. *infra.*

Various parts of the castle are recorded as follows: in 1235 Cl
turris de Corf 'tower of Corfe'; in 1255 Cl *capella castri regis de
Corf* 'chapel of the royal castle of Corfe' (cf. *capella de Corf* 1236
Hutch³, 'the three chapels of *Corf*' 1241 Lib, 'chapel in the castle
of Corfe' 1269 Pat, 'the chapel of St Mary' 1282 Hutch³); in 1280
Hutch³ 'the tower called *Butavaunt*' (*Butavant* 1280–1285 King's
Works, 1282 Hutch³, 'chamber called *Botevant, -le Botavant*',
'prison *del Botavant*' 1356 King's Works; Professor Lewis Thorpe
and Dr D. H. Evans point out that this is from OFr *bo(u)ter* 'to
thrust' and OFr *avant* (AN *avaunt*) 'forward', and compare the
Fr p.n. *Boutavent* (Oise); Hutch³ **1** 484 suggested that *Butavaunt*
was another name for Dungeon Tower (*v. infra*), and in fact the
meaning 'that which sticks out' would aptly describe the position
of this tower at the W extremity of the castle; the name also occurs
in Do as the surname of John *Botevant* 1321 *Winch* (Osmington),
-Boteuaunt 1332 SR (Owermoigne), cf. also *botevaunt* 'an article of
furniture', from 1306–7 MED), 'the chamber called *Gloriette*'
(*camera regis juxta coquinam in la Gloriet* 1356 King's Works, 'a
certain new tower called *la Gloriet*' 1379 ib, *v.* gloriette 'a highly
decorated chamber' (NED)), 'prison called *Malemit*' (1285 King's
Works; Dr D. H. Evans suggests that this could be a poor spelling
for OFr *malmis*, pa.part. of *malmetre* 'to illtreat, torture, etc';
Professor Lewis Thorpe compares the second part of the name with
Fr argot *mit(t)e* (masc. or fem.) 'gaol' (< argot *cachemitte* < *cachot*)
attested from c. 1800, and takes *Male-* to represent OFr *mal* adj.
'evil' with a fem. ending or with a vocalic glide between *l* and *m*;
Professor Löfvenberg suggests that *Malemit* is possibly an error for
OFr *maledit* 'cursed, accursed'), 'prisons called *Swalwe*' (*Swaluwe*
1281 King's Works, *v.* swalg 'a pit'); in 1280–1285 King's Works
'tower called *Cocaygne, -Cokayne*' (*Cokayngue, Cokaygne* 1282,
Cocagnue 1325, *Cokayne* 1356, *Cokeyn* 1367 all Hutch³, *v.* cokaygne

'an imaginary land of abundance and bliss' (MED from ?a1325 (a1300)), 'tower called *Plentey*' (*Plante, Plente(y)* 1282 Hutch[3], *Plente* 1282 King's Works ('chamber called —'), 1367 Hutch[3], *v.* plente 'abundance'), 'tower called *Sauveray*' (Dr von Feilitzen suggests that this may be AN *salverei, sauverei* 'save the king'); in 1303 Cl 'the bridge of the king's castle of *Corf*' (*the Bridge* (2 ×) 1586 Tres, 'a stately bridge of four very high, narrow, round arches', 'the second bridge of one arch' 1774 Hutch[1], *v.* brycg); in 1325 Hutch[3] 'the gate which is called *Middelghete*' (*v.* middel, geat, probably = Gateway 6″), 'chamber called *Le Parlour*' (*v.* parlour); in c.16 Hutch[3] *the Barbigan* (*v.* barbican); in 1585 Tres *ye base courte* ('the lower courtyard'); in 1586 ib *The Castle diche* (*v.* dīc), *a Courte* (2 ×), *The Dungen towre* (*v.* dongoun 'keep, prison', = Dungeon Tower 6″, cf. *Butavaunt supra*), *ye Kingestowre* ('the King's tower', = King's Tower 6″), *The Kitchen, Newe Bulwark* (*v.* bulwerk 'rampart'), *ye Queenes Towre* ('the queen's tower', = Queen's Tower 6″), *a stable, the Steare leading up into ye Kinges Towre* (*v.* stæger[1], cf. 'the chamber *ultra staeriam*' 1282 Hutch[3]), *a Vaute* (freq), *the Firste, Seconde, Thirde & Fourth Warde* (*v.* ward 'division'), *ye Well* (2 ×) (sites of both marked 6″). Two other towers, both built in the 13th cent., are now referred to as the Horseshoe Tower (RCHM **2** 65, so called from its semicircular shape), and the Plukenet Tower (ib **2** 66, from its bearing the shield-of-arms of Alan *de Plukenet*, constable of the castle 1269–70).

In 1549 Hutch[3] the demesne lands of the castle included *Castle Borough* (*v.* burh), *Castle Down* (1586 Tres, *v.* dūn), and *Castle Hayes* (*v.* (ge)hæg). The hill on which the castle stands was called *Castle hil(l)* in 1585 Tres; also named from the castle are North Castle and Castle Lease *infra*. For the circular earthwork ¼ mile SW of the castle, *v.* The Rings *infra*.

ENCOMBE (SY 944786) (FM), *Hen(n)ecumbe* 1244 Ass (p), *Henycumbe* 1280 ib, *Henna cumba* n.d. (15) ShaftR, *Enecumbe* 1285 FA, 1288 Ass, *-comb(e)* 1327 SR, 1332 SR, *Encombe* 1489 Ct et passim, 1590 Mansel (*Farme of —, — Hedde*), 1599 Pitt (*mannor and ferme of —*), *— House* 1811 OS, probably 'hens' valley', from henn (gen.pl. *henna*) and cumb, with ferme and hēafod (perhaps with reference to the high spur N of Encombe); alternatively Professor Löfvenberg suggests that the first el. may be ēan (gen.pl. *ēana*) 'lamb' or the OE pers.n. *Ēana*, cf. Ekwall, Studies[2] 70–1.

FELBACK (lost), 1774 Hutch[1], 1861 Hutch[3], -ba(c)ke 1540, 1547 ib, cf. *Filbanks Mdw, Towns End Md or Hr Filbanks* 1844 *TA*, situated near Town's End *q.v. infra*, possibly 'ploughed hill', *v.* felh, bæc.

FITZWORTH COPSE, FM (SY 990866), HEATH & POINT, *Fitoure* 1545 Hutch[3], *Vytower* 1617 ib, *Fitzoure* 1661 Hutch[1], *Vitt-Ower* 1774 ib, *Vittower* 1795 Boswell, *Fit-, Fytworth* 1561, *Phitworth* 1586, *Fitzworth* 1571, 1633 all Hutch[3], (— *Heath*) 1811 OS, — *or Vitt-Ower* 1861 Hutch[3]. The second el. is OE ōra[1] 'bank, shore' as in Ower *infra* which lies 1 mile SE in a very similar position on a small cape on the S shore of Poole Harbour. The first el. is probably OE fitt 'fight, contest', so that the name would mean 'shore subject to dispute', cf. Fitmoor Gl 1 215. There is perhaps some reflection of this in the fact that at least part of Fitzworth was parcel of the manor of Worth Mat. *infra* in 1561 and 1571 (Hutch[3] 1 662, 692). This association may also explain the remarkable replacement of *-ower* by *-worth* as well as that of *Fit-* by *Fitz-*, for the Fitz Paynes held knight's fees in the manor of Worth Mat. from at least as early as 1212 until c. 1346 (not to mention the wife of Hugh Fitz Grip who had 3 virgates of land there in 1086 DB and the Fitz Alans who inherited the manor c. 1379) (Hutch[3] 1 692).

FOX GROUND (SY 997830), FOXGROUND PLANT., *Foxland* 1545, 1562 Hutch[3], 1599 Pitt, 1774 Hutch[1], 1861 Hutch[3], *-ground* 1545 *Ct*, 1697 (c. 1734) DCMDeed, (*East-*) 1844 *TA*, 'plot of land frequented by foxes', *v.* fox, land, grund. *Foxland* and *Foxground* seem to be alternative names for the same property, cf. the description of *Foxland* in Hutch[3] 1 535 as 'some grounds adjoining to the east side of Rempston' (*v.* Rempstone *infra*). Fox Ground lies close to the par. bdy.

FURZEY ISLAND (SZ 011871), (*island called*) *Fursey* 1545 Hutch[3] *et freq* to 1795 Boswell, *Fursey Insul* 1575 Saxton, c. 1586 Tres, *Fusey* (sic) 1597 DROMap, *Bursey Island* (sic) 1610 Speed, *Furze I(sle)* 1773 Bayly, 1811 OS, 'furze island', *v.* fyrs, ēg, with later explanatory ēg-land, ile and insula.

GREEN ISLAND (SZ 006866) (LAKE), *tres* (*hidas terræ*) *apud Fromemuthe apud insulam quæ dicitur la Ye* 843 for 934 (17) BCS 739, *atte Fromemouþe. atte yle ðan ye* 843 for 934 (eME) ASCharters, *Fromouthe quod dicitur Insula Sc̄e Elene* 1310 Inq aqd, 'at Fromemouthe, which is called the Island of St. Helen' 1311 Pat, *Insula S'ce Elene infra Warennam d'ni Regis de Purbyk* 1409 (e15) MiltRoll,

Seynt Helenyslond 1423 (e15) *ib, Insula S̄c̄ē Helene in Purbyke* 1535
VE, *(island called) St. Helen's* 1545 Hutch³, 1795 Boswell, *Scti
Elyns Insul* 1575 Saxton, *St. Elins Insul* c. 1586 Tres, *Sent Kleres*
(probably for *Elenes*) 1597 DROMap, *Green I(sle)* 1773 Bayly,
1811 OS, *-Island* 1844 *TA, St. Helen's, now called Green or Stony
Island* 1774 Hutch¹, 1861 Hutch³. This small island in Poole Harbour
was at first known simply as 'the island at the estuary of the Frome',
v. ēg, ile, insula, mūða, R. Frome (RNs. *infra*). The later name *St
Helen's (is)land* is from the dedication of the former chapel here
(Hutch³ 1 538), called *capella S'ce Elene* 1409 (e15) *MiltRoll, v.*
land, ēg-land, cf. The Hermitage *infra*. Green Island Lake is a small
channel in Poole Harbour, *v.* grēne¹, lacu.

HOLLISH (lost, about SY 955806)

> *oþ olle discan, of olle discan* 948 (15) *ShaftR* (S 534 (1)), *on olle
> discan* 956 (14) *ib* (S 632)
> *on alle þiscan, of alle discan* 948 (15) *ShaftR* (S 534 (1))
> *on holen wicken* 955 (14) *ShaftR* (S 573)
> 'meadow called *Holewich'* 1291 Hutch³, *(prat' voc') Holwiche*
> 1513, 1514 *Ct*
> a mede called *Hollwyssh, Hollwysshe water* 1381 (16) *Pitt*
> *Holles* 1545 *Ct*
> *Hollish Furlong* 1700 (c. 1774) *DCMDeed*, 1844 *TA, Bailiff's
> Hollish* 1783 DROMap, *Bailiffs Hollish Md, Long Hollish* 1844
> *TA*
> *Hawlish* 1861 Hutch³

Probably 'Olla's marshy meadows', from the OE pers.n. *Olla*
found in Owlpen Gl 2 245 and wisc, with mǣd, wæter; the OE forms
in *-an*, as Professor Löfvenberg points out, probably represent a
dat.pl. in *-um*. However, Dr von Feilitzen considers *Olla* an unlikely
first el. in view of the consistent ME forms with initial *H-* and prefers
hol² 'hollow' on the basis of *holen-* 955 and *Hole-* 1291. The forms
in *-discan, -þiscan* from the ME copies of the two earliest OE
charters are probably due to scribal confusion of *w* (*p*), *þ*, *ð* and *d*
(cf. *-forð* for *-ford* in *ShaftR* (S 534 (1)), and *dis* for *þis, nord* for
norð, saþendune possibly for *sawendune* (q.v. *infra*) in *ib* (S 632));
-wicken in *ShaftR* (S 573) has probably been influenced by the
wi(c)ken spellings in this charter for the r.n. Wych (earlier the name
of the Corfe River, *v.* RNs.); *alle-* in *ShaftR* (S 534 (1)) probably

shows confusion of the rare OE pers.n. *Olla* with the common OE pers.n. *Alla*, and *holen-* in *ib* (S 573) may have been influenced by *on þa holendich* and *on þat holenbedde* (both dealt with *infra*) in the same charter. The fields called *Hollish* are water meadows situated along the S bank of the stream (referred to once as *Hollwysshe water* but now unnamed) which rises near Downshay Fm in Worth Mat. par. *infra* and flows WNW to meet the Corfe River near the Corfe C.–Ch. Knowle bdy. *Bailiff's Hollish* belonged to 'the Bailiff of Corfe' (1783 *DROMap*), cf. Bayleys Cowleaze *infra*.

KINGSTON (SY 957797), c. 1586 Tres, *Chingestone* 1086 DB, *ad Kinghestunam, Kyngest(o)un* n.d. (15) *ShaftR, Kingeston* 1212 Fees, 1266, 1270 Pat, 1280, 1288 *Ass*, 1575 Saxton, *Kyng(g)eston* 1270 (1371) Pat, 1288 *Ass*, 1316 FA, 1327 *SR et passim* to 1545 *Ct, Kyngeston Abbatisse* 1297 FF, *Kyngston* 1512 *Ct*, 'the king's farm', *v.* cyning, -es[2], tūn. In 948 *ShaftR* (S 534 (1)) King Eadred granted land here (referred to as *pars telluris Purbicinga, v.* Isle of Purbeck *supra*) to the religious woman Ælfðryð who was apparently then abbess of Shaftesbury; Kingston belonged to Shaftesbury Abbey until the dissolution, hence *Abbatisse.* According to Hutch[3] 1 511 Kingston was 'sometimes called South Kingston, and Kingston Abbess, to distinguish it from the other Kingstons in the county' (there are at least six examples of this name in Do).

LYNCH FM (SY 960800) & LODGE, WEST LYNCH
>*on anne linc reawe, of þane linche* 948 (15) *ShaftR* (S 534 (1)), *on þane hlinc, anlang hlinkes* 956 (14) *ib* (S 632)
>*La Linche* 1254 FF, 1285 FA (p), *atte Lynch(e)* 1327 *SR* (p), 1332 SR (p)
>*Lynch(e), Linch* 1545, 1562, 1576 Hutch[3], 1590 *Mansel, the Linches* Eliz Hutch[3], *ye Lynches* c. 1586 Tres, *East Linch, -Lynch* 1652 Hutch[3] *et freq* to 1861 Hutch[3], *West Lynch, -Linch* 1700 (c. 1774) *DCMDeed et freq* to 1861 Hutch[3], *Linch Fm* 1811 OS, *Lynch Fm* 1844 *TA.*

'The ridge or bank', *v.* hlinc, with rǣw 'row (of trees, etc)', la, atte; as Professor Löfvenberg notes, the OE compound *hlinc-rǣw* may denote 'the boundary line formed by a bank' (BTSuppl) or may simply mean 'line or row of linches', cf. *stān-rǣw* 'line of stones' (BTSuppl). *The Linches* refers to *East Lynch* (now Lynch Fm) and

West Lynch, both farms situated on the 200' contour about ¼ mile apart on the N slope of a ridge which reaches 500' ½ mile S and which is referred to as 'the south down' by Hutch³ 1 527, cf. Norden *infra*. *Lynch Lane* 1783 *DROMap* leads N from Lynch Fm.

NEW MILLS (SY 963839) (HEATH), *Neumulle* 1334 Hutch³, *pons co'is apud le Nuwemulle* 1423, *marisco d'ni iuxta le Nuwemulle* 1428, *Newmylle* 1550 all *Midd*, *-mull* 1586 Hutch³, *-Mill* 1795 Boswell, *New(e)myll(e)s*, *-Mills* 1586 Hutch³ *et freq* to 1861 ib, *New Mills Heath* 1844 *TA*, 'new mill(s)', *v.* nīwe, myln. The place is situated on the Corfe River, but there is no mill here now, nor is there a bridge (*pons*). The marsh (*mariscus*) probably refers to New Mills Heath (marshland marked 6").

NORDEN FM (SY 950829), 1844 *TA*, *Northdon* 1291, *Nordone* 1381 Hutch³, *-don* c. 1586 Tres *et freq* to 1861 Hutch³, *-den* 1381 (16) *Pitt*, 1795 Boswell, 'north hill', *v.* norð, dūn, the latter el. confused with denu 'valley'. Although Norden Fm itself lies low, it takes its name from the ridge which reaches 300' ¼ mile S and is called *Norden Hill* 1844 *TA*, cf. Hutch³ 1 527 who says that the farm 'takes its name from the north down...so called from its situation relatively to the south down at Kingston', cf. Kingston, Lynch *supra*.

OWER FM (SY 998855), OWER (1") [ˈauə]
    (*apud*) *Ore* 843 for 934 (17) BCS 739, (*æt*) *Ore* 843 for 934 (eME) ASCharters, *Ore* 1288 *Ass*, 1291 Tax, Hutch³, 1310 Inq aqd, 1311 Pat, *Ora* 1086 DB, Exon, 1280 Hutch³, *Hore* 1212 Fees, 1288 *Ass*, *Ere* 1332 SR (sic)
    Oure 1316 FA, 1327 *SR*, 1381 Hutch³, n.d. (e15) *MiltRoll* (*-apud Fromemouth in Purbyk*), *Owre* 1512 *Ct*, 1575 Saxton, c. 1586 Tres, 1617 Hutch³, *Ower(e)* 1512 *Ct et passim*, (*E & N*) *Ower* 1844 *TA*

'(At) the bank or shore', *v.* ōra¹, cf. Fitzworth and Green Island *supra*, Goathorn in Studland par. *infra*. The place lies on a small promontory on the shore of Poole Harbour and was at one time a port, cf. Ower Passage *infra*. The bounds of Ower are given in n.d. (e15) *MiltRoll* m. 4r.

REMPSTONE (HALL) (SY 992824)
    Rameston(') 1280 *Ass* (p), 1376 Pat (p)
    Remston' 1288 *Ass* (p), *Remyston* 1376 Pat (p), *Remeston* 1384 ib

(p), 1535 VE, *Rempston* 1435 *AD* (p), 1454, 1489, 1498 *Ct*, 1795 Boswell, — *Ho*. 1811 OS, *Rempstone* (*Hall*) 1844 *TA* *Rymeston*(') 1288 *Ass* (p), 1363 Pat (p), *Rymston* 1362 ib (p), *Rympston'* 1399 *AddCh* (p)

Probably 'farm where wild garlic grows', from hramsa, hramse and tūn, as suggested by Professor Löfvenberg who, for the forms in -*e*-, compares OE *Hremesleage* for Romsley Sa (DEPN) and MLG *remese* by the side of *ramese*. However, it may also be possible that the name means 'stone near the boundary', from rima, *rioma, *reoma 'rim, edge, boundary' and stān 'stone', perhaps in allusion to the Stone Circle (6″) which lies 200 yds from the present par. bdy ¼ mile SW from Rempstone Hall, *v*. Noggets in Studland par. *infra* and Rempstone Gate in Tyneham par. *infra*, cf. Remenham Brk 66–7. On the other hand, the preponderance of forms used as personal names among the early spellings may in fact suggest that Rempstone is a transferred name, as was supposed by Fägersten 120.

ROLLINGTON FM (SY 969827)

Ragintone 1086 DB, -*tona* Exon

Radelinton 1236 Fees, -*ington*, -*yngton*(*e*) 1256 FF (p), 1288 *Ass*, 1290 Cl, FF, 1309 ib, 1421 IpmR, 1426 Cl, 1431 FA, — *juxta Corfe Castle* 1290, 1309 Hutch³, — *in Purbik* 1420 Fine, '— *by Corfcastelle*' 1421, 1426 Cl, *Radling*-, -*yngton* 1268 *Ass* (p), 1399 Cl, 1412 FA, 1586 Hutch³ (— *alias Rollington*), -*yngdon* 1316 FA, -*in*-, -*yntone* 1334 Ipm, Cl, *Radlengton-juxta-Corfe* 1399 Hutch³

Rodlington 1242–3 Fees, *Rothelington* 1288 *Ass*

Redlyngton(*e*) 1291 Hutch³, 1306 FF, 1332 SR, *Redelyngton* 1401 Cl, -*ington juxta Corfe Castle* 1449 Hutch³

Rydelington (v.l. *Rikelinton*) 1303 FA, *Ridelyngton* 1327 SR, *Ryadelyngton* 1346, *Rykelyngton* (sic) 1428 FA, *Ridlington otherwise Rowlington* 1828 DCMDeed

Rudelington 1422 IpmR

Rollyngton 1435 FF, 1486 (— *otherwise called Radlington*), 1510, 1529 Hutch³, 1543, 1546 *Ct*, -*ington* 1512 ib, c. 1586 Tres *et passim*

Possibly 'farm called after Rǣdel or Rǣdla', from the OE pers.n. *Rǣdel* or *Rǣdla* and -*ingtūn*, as suggested by Fägersten 121, cf. Redlingfield Sf (DEPN s.n.). Both pers.ns. are short forms of names in *Ræd-*; *Rædel* is found as the name of a moneyer (Redin 139) and *Rædla* would correspond to OHG *Rātilo*; the DB, Exon form *Rag-* is probably for *Rad-* (cf. ANInfl 117), thus representing the pers.n. stem *Ræd-* without the *-el* or *-la* suffix. However, in view of the ME forms with *-o-*, *-i-*, and *-u-*, Professor Löfvenberg suggests that the name may mean 'farm belonging to a place called *Hrēodlēah*' ('reed clearing', *v.* hrēod, lēah); for the early *a*-forms, cf. Radipole par. *infra*, Redwick Gl **3** 136–7. For the additions *juxta Corfe* and *in Purbik*, *v.* Corfe C. and Isle of Purbeck *supra*. There is mention of a water mill here in 1529 Hutch³.

ST EDWARD'S BRIDGE (SY 959824), *St. Edward's or King Bridge* 1774 Hutch¹, 1861 Hutch³, cf. *cursus aque apud Seint Edwardis-wateryng* 1429 Midd, *St. Edward's Fountain* 1861 Hutch³, named after King Edward the Martyr who was murdered at Corfe in 978 (ASC s.a.) and to whom the church (*v.* foll.) is dedicated, *v.* **brycg**, **wateryng** 'watering-place for horses and cattle' (c. 1386 NED, sense 15b), perhaps also 'well, spring' (1600 ib, sense 16), cf. St Thomas Watering Sr 5. *Kyngebrigge* 1318 FF may also belong here. For a traditional account of Edward's death and the miracles that followed it, *v.* Hutch³ **1** 499–500 and cf. C. E. Fell, *Edward King and Martyr*, Leeds 1971. *St. Edward's Fountain* is a spring with healing properties in which the body is said to have lain; St Edward's Bridge is where the road out of Corfe towards Wareham, where the body was later taken (cf. The Priory in Wareham par. *infra*), crosses the Corfe River (cf. St Edward's Ctg in Arne par. *infra* which is also on this road near the Corfe–Arne bdy); *Seint Edwardiswateryng* may refer to the Corfe River at this spot, or to the spring. An earlier name for a bridge here (or near here) is *Spadeforde Bridge* 1381 (16) *Pitt*, perhaps from **spadu**, **spada**, **-e** 'spade' in some concrete or figurative sense, cf. the use of scofl 'shovel' in p.ns., with ford, brycg. An even earlier name for a river crossing here occurs as an important bdy point in all three OE charters relating to Corfe: *from wicanforð*, *to Wikenforde* 948 (15) *ShaftR* (S 534 (1)), *on Wickenford, on lang Wikenforde* 955 (14) *ib* (S 573), *of Wikenforde, on Wichenford* 956 (14) *ib* (S 632), 'the ford over the River Wych', *v.* Wych Channel & Lake in RNs. *infra*, **ford**.

ST EDWARD THE MARTYR'S CHURCH (SY 961820), *ecclesiam de Corf* 1259 Cl, 'the (parish) church of *Corf(f)(e) (Castel(l))*' 1259 Pat *et freq* to 1467 ib, *ecclesiam Sancti Edwardi de Corf(f)* 1288 Ass,

Corff church 1585 Tres, cf. *the Church Ho* 1861 Hutch[3], *v.* cirice and for the dedication *v.* prec.

SCOLES FM (SY 964799), *the crofte which Rob't Scovile holdethe* 1381 (16) *Pitt, Skoules* 1473, *Skovylys* 1510, *Scovell* 1528, *Scolles* 1618, *Scowles* 1623 all Hutch[3], 1774 Hutch[1], 1861 Hutch[3], *Sc(h)oles Fm* 1735, 1773 *DCMDeed*, cf. *Scoles Hill* 1844 *TA*, from the family of *Scovill* who probably originated from Escoville in Normandy and who were here at least as early as the 13th cent.: William de *Scouill* occurs under Rowbarrow hundred in 1244 *Ass*, John de *Scovill* possessed land in *La Linche* (now Lynch Fm *supra* ¼ mile W) in 1254 Hutch[3] 1 525 (cf. also 1254 FF p. 101), and William *Scovile, -uyle* was taxed in Afflington tithing in 1327 *SR* and 1332 SR.

SWYRE [ˈswaiə] HEAD (SY 934783) *&* WD, *uppe on swuren, þwert ouer swuran* 955 (14) *ShaftR* (S 573), *Swyer hill* 1590 *Mansel, Swyer* 1717 (c. 1734) *DCMDeed, Swyres* p1795 *Mansel, Swyre Head* 1811 OS, *Swyre Hill & Wd* 1844 *TA*, 'a neck of land, a col', *v.* swēora (late WSax swīra, swȳra, swūra), with hēafod 'hill, ridge, promontory', cf. Swyre Head in Chaldon H. par. *infra* and Swyre par. *infra*.

WEST MILLS (SY 957823), *molend' voc' le Westmyll* 1512 Ct, *West Mill* 1585 Tres, *v.* west, myln, cf. *Mill Close* 1549 Hutch[3], 1585 Tres, *Myll Close,* — *Mead* 1603 Swan, *West Mill Bridge* 1791 Boswell, *v.* clos(e), mæd. The place is situated W of the castle on the Corfe River. The mill here may be identical with the water mill at Corfe mentioned in 1291 Hutch[3], 1435 Ct, *AD*, 1549 Hutch[3] and may also have given name to Henry de *Molendino* 1270 Hutch[3], John *atte Mille* 1325 ib, and John *Miller* 1549 ib to whom a water-mill and the demesne lands of the castle were demised. According to Hutch[3] 1 550 the hundred court for Hasler hundred *infra* was held here ('in a cotage called the West Mill, near Corfe').

WESTWOOD FM (SY 987808), *Westwode* 1332 SR (p), *Westwood (Fm)* 1774 Hutch[1], 1811 OS, 'west wood', *v.* west, wudu. The farm lies in the E of the present par. but lies W of *Langton Wallis* in Langton Mat. par. *infra*, to which manor it formerly belonged (Boswell 18, Hutch[3] 1 533).

(Lt) WOOLGARSTON (SY 985814) ['wulgəstən, 'wu(:)sən]

Orgarestone 1086 DB

Wulgar(e)ston 1213 Cur, 1288 *Ass* (p), 1498 *Ct*, 1510 Hutch[3], -*graston* 1544 *DCMDeed*, -*gerston* 1546 *Ct*, c. 1586 Tres, *Wlgareston* 1256 FF, 1268 *Ass* (p)

Wolgar(e)ston 1256 Hutch[3], 1280 FF, 1285 (1372) *ChrP et freq* to 1636 *Ilch* with affixes -*in Purbyck* n.d. (1372) *ChrP, East-* 1443 Hutch[3], *West-* 1599 ib; *Wolger(e)ston* 1264 Ipm, 1383, 1404 IpmR, 1429 *Midd*, 1443 IpmR, -*gariston* n.d. (1372) *ChrP*, -*gurston* 1599 *Pitt, East-, West Woolgarston* 1700 Hutch[3], *Woolgarston or Wo(o)lston* 1795 Boswell, 1861 Hutch[3], *Wo(o)lgorston* 1811 OS

Walgarston 1264 (e15) *MiltRoll, Walgareston* 1285 FF

Wlmareston n.d. (1372) *ChrP*

Wolgeston 1404 Cl

Est Wolston 1528 Hutch[3], *Wolston* als. *Wolgarston* 1677 *DCMDeed, Woolson Fm, Lt Woolston Md* 1844 *TA*

Wurgerston 1546 *Ct*

'Wulfgār's farm', from the OE pers.n. *Wulfgār* and tūn. For the same pers.n., cf. the lost *Este and Weste Wolgarslond infra*. For the DB spelling, cf. ANInfl 121. The form *Wlmareston* contains the OE pers.n. *Wulfmǣr*. *East* and *West Woolgarston* were presumably earlier names for Woolgarston and Lt Woolgarston (½ mile W) respectively, *v.* ēast, west. For -*in Purbyck, v.* Isle of Purbeck *supra*.

WYTCH FM (SY 979855), ?*terra de Wicha* R 1 (1372) *ChrP, man' de Hich'* (sic) 1280 *Ass, Wych(e)* 1498 *Ct*, 1661 Hutch[1], — *Fm* 1811 OS, *Viche* c. 1586 Tres, cf. *Witch Ho* 1844 *TA*, from the r.n. Wych, the old name for the Corfe River, *v.* Wych Channel & Lake in RNs. *infra*.

AFFLINGTON BARN, 1811 OS, from Afflington *supra*. AFFLINGTON WD, *Alfryngton's Wodde, le Croffte under le Wodde* 1525 *AOMB*, cf. prec., *v.* wudu, croft. AILWOOD COPSE, from Ailwood *supra*. AILWOOD DOWN, 'hill of *Aylethewode*' 1305 Cl, *regiam viam subt' montem de Aylewode* 1423 *Midd, Aylewood Down* 1586 Hutch[3], *Ail-, Arlwood Down(s)* 1844 *TA*, cf. prec., *v.* dūn. ALMSHOUSES, 1844 *TA*, cf. 'the almshouse of Corfe Castle' 1621 Hutch[3], 'an almshouse

in E. Street' 1774 Hutch[1], cf. Almshouse Hawes *infra*. ASHEY COPSE,
cf. *Ayssehayes* 1546 *Ct*, *Ash Coppice* 1844 *TA*, *v.* æsc, (ge)hæg.
BATRICK'S PLANT., cf. John *Batterick* 1664 HTax (Ch. Knowle).
THE BELT, *v.* belt. BIG WD, *Great Wd* 1844 *TA*, adjacent to Little
Wd *infra*. BREACHES LANE, *Breach* — 1844 *ib*, cf. *la Breche* 1389
Pat, *brechedich*, *the northerbrechedych* n.d. (e15) *MiltRoll*, *le Breche
juxta Corfe Castle* 1510 Hutch[3], (*Hr & Lr*) *Breach* 1844 *TA*, *v.*
brēc, dīc, norðerra. BRENSCOMBE HEATH, HILL & (LITTLE) WD,
1844 *ib*, from Brenscombe *supra*. BROADLEY WD, *Broad Lead* (*Wd*)
1844 *ib*, probably 'wide watercourse', *v.* brād, lǣd, explained by the
statement in Hutch[3] 1 520 that 'Encombe [300 yds W] was much
improved by the late Earl of Eldon, who, at great cost, tunnelled the
eastern hill and brought from a spring in the adjacent valley a more
copious supply for the piece of water in front of the mansion', cf.
Fish Pond *infra*; the second el. has been confused with lēah. THE
BUNGALOW. BURNBAKE (PLANT.), *v.* burnbake. HR & LR BUSHEY
FM, *Hr & Lr Bushew* (*Fm*) 1844 *TA*, from Bushey *supra*. BUSHEY
LANE & WD (*Bushew* — 1844 *ib*), cf. prec. CASTLE INN. CHAFFEY'S
(local), a house. CHETTLE WD, 1844 *ib*, cf. Chettle par. *infra*. CLAY
WASHING PITS, near *Clay Pits* 1844 *TAMap*, perhaps so called from
the washing of clay, or because used as sheep-washes, *v.* washing.
CLEAVEL POINT, 1811 OS, a promontory, *v.* point, perhaps from the
family named (*de*) *Clavil(l)e, -vell* which held lands at various places
in Corfe C. from 1086 DB (Hutch[3] 1 527 ff), cf. Clavel Tower in
Kimmeridge par. *infra*. COMMON CLOSE CTGS, cf. *Common Close(s
Altmt*) 1844 *TA*. CORFE COMMON, *Corf(f)e Com(m)on* 1585 Tres,
1735 DCMDeed, *Corfe Commons*, (*Great & New*) *Common* 1844 *TA*,
marked as *Heath* 1826 Gre, cf. *Comans londe* 1525 *AOMB*, *v.*
common, land. COUNTESS POINT, a small promontory, *v.* point, perhaps from some lady of this title such as Hy 7's mother, the Countess
of Richmond, for whom Corfe Castle was repaired although she
never seems to have resided there (Hutch[3] 1 494), *v.* contasse.
COW LEAZE COPSE, cf. *Middle & North* — 1735 DCMDeed, *South
Cow Leaze* 1773 *ib*, *Cowleaze* (freq), *Cowleaze Md & Pieces* 1844
TA, *v.* cū, lǣs. CRABTREE COPSE. CROSS (remains) (Kelly), *the
crosse of Corff* 1381 (16) *Pitt*, *the Corffe Cross* c. 16 Hutch[3], *v.* cros.
CUCKOO PEN, usually a jocular (field) name alluding to the folk-tale
(told of the men of Gotham) of 'penning the cuckoo' to prevent the
passing of summer, common in O 438, Gl 1 43, etc., cf. Udal 295,
Cuckoo Pound in Langton Mat. par. *infra*, and Go Croft in Arne

par. *infra*; but possibly the allusion is to cuckolding, cf. Cuckolds
Parlor *infra*. EAST HILL, 1844 *TA*, *the Hill* 1585 Tres, E of the
castle, *v.* hyll, cf. West Hill *infra*. EGMONT BIGHT, locally also called
Egmont Pond, Cove, Pool or Bay. *v.* byht, **cove**; Egmont must remain
unexplained in view of the absence of early spellings. EGMONT POINT,
Encombe — 1811 OS, a promontory near prec., *v.* point, Encombe
supra. ELDON SEAT, one of several inscribed man-made seats in
lofty places round Encombe, from the Earls of Eldon (from Eldon
Du) who bought the estate in 1807 (Hutch[3] 1 513, 517), cf. the f.n.
Eldon *infra*. FISH POND (2 ×), both S of Encombe, *v.* Broadley Wd
supra. FIVE ACRE COPSE, cf. *Five Acres* (*Mdw*) 1844 *TA*. FLASHET
PLANT., 'place characterised by swampy grassland', *v.* flasshett
(flasshe, -ett), cf. Flashett in Swanage par. *infra*. The place lies low
beside a stream, and marsh is marked nearby (6″). FOREST LANE
is tree-lined and leads into woodland. FRESHWATER STEPS, 1861
Hutch[3], cf. *Freshwater* 1811 OS, *Fresh Water* 1844 *TA*, from a
stream and waterfall marked 6″, *v.* fersc, wæter, cf. Freshwater Bay
in Portland par. *infra*, Freshwater (Bay) Wt 122, with the term **step**
used no doubt in its geological sense of 'a fault or dislocation of
strata'. GAME COPSE, *v.* game, perhaps in the sense 'wild animals or
birds such as are hunted'. GOLDEN BOWL, *the* — 1774 Hutch[1], a
nickname for productive land; 'the hilly part [of Encombe]...from
its fertility, has been distinguished by the name of the Golden
Bowl' (Hutch[1] 1 186). GREEN POND. HR *&* LR GROVE, cf. *Hr Grove
Plant.*, *Lr Grove Coppice*, *Middle Grove*, *Grove Cowleaze Md* 1844
TA, *v.* grāf(a). THE GWYLE, cf. foll. N *&* S GWYLE, *Guile* 1717
(c. 1734), *Goil* 1734 DCMDeed, *South Guile Withy Bed* 1844 *TA*,
v. goyle, cf. prec. HALVES CTGS (local), from the f.n. Hawes *infra*.
THE HERMITAGE, on Green Island *supra*, perhaps with reference to
the former chapel there. HIGH LEDGE (local), cf. Kimmeridge Ledges
in Kimmeridge par. *infra*. HILL BOTTOM PLANT., from Hill Bottom
in Worth Mat. par. *infra*. HILL COPPICES, below West Hill *infra*.
HOUNSTOUT CLIFF, *Hounstout* (*Cliff*) 1844 *TA*, — *Clift* 1844 *TAMap*,
a high cliff (500′), possibly from tōte 'look-out hill', with **hund**
'hound' or the OE pers.n. *Hund*; alternatively Professor Löfvenberg
suggests that the second el. may be stūt 'hill' for which *v.* Brimpts
D 192, EPN 2 165. JACK GREEN'S COPSE, *Jacks Green Coppice*,
Cowleaze & Md 1844 *TA*, perhaps from the pers.n. or surname *Jack*.
KEEPER'S COPSE, perhaps from the surname *Keeper* or from **keeper**
'a gamekeeper', possibly also 'one employed at a keep or castle'.

THE KENNELS. KIMMERIDGE HILL COPSE, *Kimmeridge Hill* 1844 *TA*, probably from Kimmeridge par. *infra*. KINGSTON BARN & HILL, from Kingston *supra*. KINGSWOOD DOWN, from King's Wd in Studland par. *infra*. LADY CAROLINE'S CLUMP, doubtless from Lady Caroline Katharine Montagu who married John Hales Calcraft of Rempstone in 1828 (Hutch³ 1 534), *v.* clump. (OLD) LIMEKILN, cf. (*Hr*) *Lime Kiln, Lime Kiln Cl* 1844 *TA*. LITTLE CLUMP, 1844 *ib*, cf. *Long Clump* 1844 *ib*, *v.* clump. LITTLE COPPICE, 1844 *ib*. LITTLE WD, 1844 *ib*, cf. Big Wd *supra*. LONDON DOOR QUARRY, perhaps so called from the use of stone quarried here in London buildings. LONG ISLAND, 1774 Hutch¹, — *I(sle)* 1773 Bayly, 1811 OS. LONG WD, 1844 *TA*. THE MANSE, *v.* manse. MEADUS'S LANE & PLANT., from the Do surname *Meadus*. MIDDEN (remains of); finds indicate a prehistoric settlement here, *v.* RCHMDo 2 511. MIDDLE PLANT. MILFORD CTG (lost), near Ower *supra* (Legg 79), cf. *aquam vocat' Myll'vord* n.d. (e15) *MiltRoll* in bounds of Ower, *v.* myln, ford. MOLLY'S GDN (local), the thorny undercliff of Hounstout Cliff *supra*. MORTON'S HO, *Dacombs* 1882 Robinson, earlier *The Manor House* (Kelly), cf. *Moreton Plot* 1844 *TA*, from the family of *Dac(k)omb*, *Dack(h)am* here 16th–17th centuries and the family of *Morton* here 17th–18th centuries (Hutch³ 1 510). MOUNT COPSE, cf. *Mount* 1844 *TA*, near a small hill, *v.* mont. NATH POINT, *Neas Point* 1811 OS, a small promontory, *v.* hnop, nesu, cf. The Nothe in Weymouth par. *infra*. NELSON PLANT., cf. John *Nelson* of Fordington who owned the tenement of *Burbarrow* (*v.* Burberry Lane *supra*) in 1744 (Hutch³ 1 526). NEW RD. NEWTON BAY, 1844 *TA*, from Newton in Studland par. *infra*. NORDEN COMMON (1844 *ib*), HEATH, PLANT. & WD (1844 *ib*), from Norden *supra*. NORTH CASTLE, 1585, 1586 Tres, — *or 12 Acres* (*Coppice*), *North Castle Cl, Hill & Plot* 1844 *TA*, originally a close or tenement north of the castle, *v. supra*. NURSERY. OWER BAY (*Owre Bay* 1661 Hutch¹), HEATH (cf. (*Close at*) *Ower* (*North*) *Heath* 1844 *TA*) & LAKE (1811 OS, a small channel in Poole Harbour, *v.* lacu), from Ower *supra*. OWER PASSAGE, 1811 OS, cf. *the way or passage to Owre Key* 1698 Hutch³, *Key Fd* 1844 *TA*, *v.* Ower *supra*, passage 'river-crossing, ferry', key 'quay', and cf. Wytch Passage *infra*; Ower Passage lies c. 700 yds N of Ower Fm on Poole Harbour; according to Hutch³ 1 538 'Ower seems to have been formerly the chief port in the Isle of Purbeck, and it was the principal, if not the only, quay for the exportation of stone and marble', the volume of this traffic being suggested by 'the remains of deep tracks and roads leading across the heath from Ower towards the town of Corfe', cf. Peppercorn Lane *infra*. PARSONAGE COPPICE, cf. *Parsonage 5 Acres, Hill & Wd* 1844 *TA*, near Rectory *infra*. PEPPERCORN LANE (local), a track once used for carting stone from Corfe to Ower Passage *supra*, formerly kept open by the payment of a peppercorn rent (Legg 17, cf. Udal 111). THE PLANTATION, cf. *Plantation* 1844 *TA*. POUND, v. pund. QUARRY WD, cf. *lapides de quareria* 1280 *Ass, E & W Quarry Cl, Quar-, Quarries-, Quarry Grd, -Plant.* 1844 *TA, v.* quarrere. RAMSHORN LAKE, *Rams Horn* 1811 OS, a small channel in Poole Harbour, perhaps so named because it curves in a manner resembling a ram's horn, *v.* ramm, horn, lacu, but cf. Goathorn Point and Redhorn Quay in Studland par. *infra* which are promontories and have different second els., and Ramshorn Down D 466 (a hill). RANDALL'S PLANT., cf. *-Mdw* 1844 *TA*. RECTORY, *Ye Parsonage* c. 1586 Tres, *Parsonage* 1826 Gre, *the mansion of the person of ye Churche of Corff* 1381 (16) *Pitt, v.* Parsonage Coppice *supra*. REMPSTONE FM (*Rempston-* 1811 OS), HEATH (1844 *TA, Rempston-* 1811 OS) & WD (1844 *TA, boscu' d'ni apud Rempston* 1454, 1489, 1498 *Ct*), from Rempstone *supra*. RICKETT'S COPSE & FM, cf. *Ricketts Cmn* 1844 *TA*, John *Rickets* 1732 Hutch[3]. THE RINGS, a circular siege earthwork thrown up by Stephen in 1139 and still known as 'Stephen's Rings' (King's Works **1** 42), *v.* hring; called *Cromwells Battery* 1844 *TA*, probably in allusion to the siege of Corfe castle by Cromwellian forces in 1643–5 (Hutch[3] **1** 504–9), *v.* ModE **battery** 'platform or fortified work on or within which artillery is mounted', cf. Battery Bank in E Stoke par. *infra*. The field in which the earthwork is to be found was called *Castle Close* 1291, 1381 Hutch[3], 1585 Tres, either from the earthwork itself or from the present castle, *v.* castel(l), clos(e). ROLLINGTON HILL (cf. *Rollington Down Eweleaze* 1844 *TA*) & WD (1844 *ib*), from Rollington *supra*. ROUND CLUMP, *v.* clump. ROUND ISLAND, 1774 Hutch[1], *-I(sle)* 1773 Bayly, 1811 OS. ROWBARROW LANE (lost), 1774 Hutch[1], 1861 Hutch[3], near Woolgarston *supra, v.* Rowbarrow hundred *supra*. ST JAMES'S CHURCH, cf. 'the chapel of Kingston' 1547 Hutch[3], 'a chapel dedicated to St. James' 1861 ib, *v.* Kingston *supra*. SALTINGS, freq on the shores of Poole Harbour near Wytch Fm, Fitzworth Fm and Ower Fm (all *supra*), cf. the thirteen salt-makers (*salinarii*) at Ower in 1086 DB (DBGeography 111–12, VCHDo **3** 79), and the several salterns mentioned in connection with Wytch and Fitzworth in 1545 Hutch[3] **1** 538; for other references to the Purbeck

salt industry, *v.* Salterne in Studland par. *infra*, Salterns Copse in
Arne par. *infra*, and VCHDo **2** 327, **3** 22–3. SANDY HILL FM (1844
TA, *Sandy Hills* 1664 HTax, — *Hill* 1774 Hutch[1]) & LANE, SANDY-
HILLS COPSE (*Sandy Hill Coppice* 1844 *TA*), cf. *Sandy Hills Down*
1844 *ib*, *v.* sandig, hyll. SARGENT'S PLANT. SCOLES GATE CTG (*Scholes
Ctg* 1844 *TA*), SCOLES LANE COPSE (cf. *Scholes Lane* 1844 *ib*), from
Scoles Fm *supra*. SCOTLAND, 1774 Hutch[1], *v.* scot 'tax, payment',
land. SHARFORD BRIDGE, 1811 OS, *Sherford Bridge* 1575 Saxton,
1586 Hutch[3], 1597 *DROMap*, cf. (*terr' in*) *Sherford(e)* 1550 *Midd*,
1586 Hutch[3], *Sharpford* 1621 ib, on the par. bdy where a track crosses
the Corfe River, *v.* sc(e)aru 'boundary', ford, brycg, cf. Sherford in
Morden par. *infra* although this has a different origin; however
Sharpeford 1285 FA, and *aqua currens apud Sheppeford ex parte
boriali crucis ibidem* 1423 *Midd*, may also belong here, the first of
which together with *Sharpford* 1621 would suggest instead a first el.
scearp 'sharp, steep'. SHARFORD CTG, from prec. SHOTOVER MOOR,
low marshy ground on the shore of Poole Harbour near Ower Fm
supra, no doubt to be connected with *Shottewade* n.d. (e15) *MiltRoll*,
Shotwood Bay 1661 Hutch[1]. *Shottewade* occurs in the bounds of
Ower; -*wade* is probably (ge)wæd 'ford', later confused with wudu;
-*over* may represent ōfer[1] 'bank, shore'; the first el. of both names
may be sc(e)ota 'trout' or a wk. form of the OE pers.n. *Scēot*
suggested by DEPN for Shoreston Nb, cf. Henry *S(h)ot* 1327 *SR*,
1332 *SR*, Mary *Shott* 1664 HTax (all Ch. Knowle). SNAG FM,
perhaps ModE snag (NED 1577) 'tree stump, sharp projection,
obstacle, etc.', but cf. Do dial. *snag* 'the small peabig variety or
species of sloe' (Barnes 102); the farm lies on low marshy ground in a
bend of the Corfe River; probably analogous are Snag Lane in
Milborne S. par. *infra* (running down to a stream) and the f.n.
Snaghill in W Lulworth par. *infra*. SOUTH DEEP, 1811 OS, *South
Deeps* c. 1770 DCMMap, *South-deep channel* 1774 Hutch[1], in Poole
Harbour, *v.* dēope. SQUARE PLANT. TABBIT'S COPSE, — HILL FM &
— HILL LITTLE WD, *Terra Talebotte* 1264 (e15) *MiltRoll*, *Tabbote's
Hill* 1586 Hutch[3], *Tapers Hill* 1774 Hutch[1], 1811 OS, *Tabbits
Coppice*, *Tabbits Hill Barn*, — *Barton*, — *Cmn*, — *Fm* & — *Md*,
Coppice Tabbits Hill 1844 *TA*, *Tabbett's Hill or Talbot's Hill*,
Talbot's Hill Meads 1861 Hutch[3], cf. also *Tappet's Hay* 1619 ib,
from the *Talbot* family of Godlingston in Swanage par. *infra*, a
younger branch of which had a small tenement here (Hutch[3] 1 532,
663, 713), *v.* hyll, barton, (ge)hæg. THRASHER'S CTG, HEATH,

PIT & LANE, *Threshers & 4 Acres*, (*Inclosure in*) *Threshers Heath* 1844 *TA*, cf. Stephen *le Threscher* 1332 SR (Poole). TINKER'S COPSE, 'copse where tinkers camped', *v.* tynkere, or from the surname *Tinker.* TOWN'S END, the S extremity of the village, *v.* toun, ende[1], Felback *supra.* VERGER'S MD, *Verges* — 1844 *TA*, cf. Thomas *Verge junr'* 1664 HTax (Swanage), Thomas *Devirges* 1664 ib (Corfe C.). THE VINEYARD, *Vineyard, Hr & Lr part* 1844 *TA*, *grounds called The Vineyards* 1861 Hutch[3], *v.* vinȝerd. WARREN (lost, about SY 986862), 1811 OS, *v.* wareine, cf. Isle of Purbeck *supra.* WEST HILL, 1826 Gre, *the pasture upon the hill* 1381 (16) Pitt, *The Hill* 1586 Tres, W of the castle, cf. East Hill *supra.* WESTHILL FM, *West-Hill* 1774 Hutch[1], *West Hill Fm* 1811 OS, on the westerly of two hill spurs, but perhaps from West Hill in Worth Mat. par. *infra.* WESTHILL WD, cf. *West Hill Plant.* 1844 *TA*, from prec. LOWER WESTHILL, below Westhill Fm *supra.* WILLWOOD CTGS, LIMEKILN & (LT) PLANT., cf. *E & W Will Wood* (*Coppice*) 1844 *TA*, first el. possibly well(a) (WSax will(a)) with reference to the small stream (6″) flowing N from Willwood Ctgs. WITHY BED (2×), cf. *le Wythybere* Ed 3 *Surv*, 1603 *Swan, the Wythye* 1381 (16) Pitt, *Willow Beds* 1717 (c. 1734) DCMDeed, *With(e)y Bed* 1844 *TA* (*freq*), *v.* wiðig, bearu, bedd. WOOLGARSTON COPSE, from Woolgarston *supra.* WYTCH FIR POUND, from Wytch Fm *supra* or Wych Channel and Lake (*v.* RNs. *infra*), no doubt an old cattle pound planted with firs, *v.* pund, cf. Fir Pound Plot in Studland par. *infra.* WYTCH HEATH (1844 *TA*, *Wych* — 1811 OS) & MOOR, cf. prec. WYTCH PASSAGE, *Wych* — 1811 OS, cf. *Wytch Passage Ho, South Md belonging to the passage, Passage Ho Grd, Witch Quay* 1844 *TA*, described by Hutch[3] I 538 as 'at the head of the channel of the same name...and...used as... [the] point of embarcation...for passage by water to Poole', *v.* passage, key and cf. prec., Ower Passage *supra.*

FIELD-NAMES

The undated forms are 1844 *TA* 70. Spellings dated 948 (15) are *ShaftR* (S 534 (1)), 955 (14) *ib* (S 573), 956 (14) *ib* (S 632), n.d. (15) *ib*, 1280 *Ass*, 1324 (17), 1381 (16), 1599 *Pitt*, 1326 *Ext*, 1327 *SR*, 1332 SR, Ed 3 *Surv*, 1357, 1382, 1423 *Fine*, 1381[2] *Misc*, n.d. (e15) *MiltRoll*, 1435, 1550 *Midd*, 1455 *Weld*[1], p1483 *Sheen*, 1489, 1498, 1512, 1513, 1514, 1539, 1543, 1545, 1546 *Ct*, c. 1500 *RoyRoll*, 1525 *AOMB*, 1566, 1584, 1603, 1614 *Swan*, 1585, 1586 Tres, 1648 *AddCh*, 1664 HTax, 1700 (c. 1774), 1704, 1716, 1717

(c. 1734), 1734, 1735, 1745, 1773, 1821 *DCMDeed*, 1776, 1783 *DROMap*, 1791, 1795 Boswell, and the rest Hutch[3].

(*a*) Afflington Hill (from Afflington *supra*); All Grams; Almshouse Hawes (cf. Almshouses *supra*, Hawes *infra*); Arable Fd; Arfleet Md (*Allflete Meade* 1546, from Arfleet *supra*, *v.* mǣd); Arlwood Cowleaze & Md (cf. *campo de Aylewode* 1435, from Ailwood *supra*); Bakers Md (cf. *ye ditche...of John Baker of Hom'well* 1381 (16), John *Baker* 1599, cf. *le Bakehowse infra*); Bankes Md (from the *Bankes* family, here from 17th cent., *v.* Hutch[3] 1 470–1, 538, 547); Barn Barton; (Old) Barn Cl (cf. *South Mead or Barn Close* 1735); Barn Plot; Barns Wood 4 Acres, 10 Acres & Mdw, Furzy Barns Wood (*v.* fyrsig); Bartholemew Mdw; Barton; Bayleys Cowleaze (cf. *Phil(l)ip Bayley(s house)* 1664, 1667, but possibly a reference to the bailiffs of Corfe Castle, *v.* baillie, cf. Hollish *supra*); Bean Closes; Bee Md & Plot (*v.* bēo); Blacklands (*The Black Lands* 1717 (c. 1734), *v.* blæc, land); Blashenwell Down (from Blashenwell *supra*); Blensfield Mdw (first el. possibly a reduced form of a surname such as *Blind*, but cf. Blynfield Fm in Cann par. *infra*); Blinklakes (*v.* discussion under Blynfield Fm *loc. cit.*); Bog Grd; Bonds Mdw; Bottom Cl, Grd & Md, Long Bottom Mdw (*v.* botm); Gt Brickneck (*Gt & Lt Breakneck* 1783, no doubt a nickname for a steep or rough field, cf. Break neck in Steeple par. *infra*); Broad East; Broad Md; Burying Grd; Bushborn Md; Busheu Down (from Bushey *supra*); (Lr) Bushew Heath (*Burshew* — 1821, cf. prec.); Calves Cl; Castle Lease 1861, Castle Lease Gdn, Castle Leaze Fd ((*pastur' vocat') Castel(l)ese* 1326, 1381[2], from Corfe Castle *supra*, cf. *Leseditche* 1381 (16), *v.* lǣs, dīc); Church Fd (from St James's Church *supra*); Churchill's Fd; Clay Fd; Cliff (Md) (cf. *Cliff(e) Ground(s)* 1717 (c. 1734), 1734, *v.* clif); Cockrams (Md, Ho & Plot) (from the *Cockram* family here e18, *v.* Hutch[3] 1 526, 532, 538, 713); Common Grd, E & W Common Plot (cf. Corfe Common *supra*); Copper Bridge Md (*Copper Bridge* 1776, *Cooper's Bridge* 1791, possibly a surname, but perhaps so called from a toll, with copper in the sense of 'copper money' (NED s.v. sense 2), cf. Pennybridge Sx 383, though copper could alternatively have some attributive sense such as 'of small value' or 'copper-coloured' (NED s.v. senses 9c, 9d), cf. Copper Mead in Ch. Knowle par. *infra*; the field is situated near the confluence of a small unnamed stream with the Corfe River SSW of the castle at SY 955816); Coppice, Copse Cl (cf. *Copps Wood Land* 1717 (c. 1734), *v.* copis); Corn Fd; Cotterells Mdw; Gt & Lt Cow Closes; Cow Nas (or Coppice) (a small promontory on Poole Harbour, *v.* næss, cf. Nath Point *supra*, perhaps so named from its resemblance in outline to a cow's head); Croft Ridge (*Crate Rudge* 1717 (c. 1734), *v.* croft, hrycg); Croombs Plot (cf. Joseph *Croomes* 1757 (Ch. Knowle)); Crowders Mdw; Cuckolds Parlor (a small field, perhaps a humorous name for a secluded place where some woman cuckolded her husband or where a cuckold hid in shame, cf. another instance in Gl 2 182 and Cuckoo Pen *supra*); Culls Apes Coppice, Culls Grd (cf. Harry *Cull* of Langton Mat. c. 1500, John & Mary *Cull* 1740, 1770; *Apes* is probably from æpse (the metathesized form of æspe) 'aspen-tree, white poplar')); Culliford (perhaps from the *Culliford* family (of Culliford D) who had land in Corfe

3   M D T

C. from 16th cent., v. Hutch³ I 516, 517); Dandy hay (the surname *Dandy*, v. (ge)hæg); Deer Fold (v. dēor-fald); Dial Cl (v. dial); Diffey's Md & Plot (the Do surname *Diffey*); Gt & Lt Dips (perhaps dip in the sense 'hollow' (NED from 1789)); Drove (Way) (v. drove); Dun Lease, — Leaze (probably 'the pasture lower down', v. dūne, læs); N & S Dunsley (perhaps 'Dun's wood or clearing' from the OE pers.n. *Dun(n)* and lēah); East Fd (*in campo orientali de Alryngton* p1483, le (*Nether*) *Est Fylde* 1525, v. ēast, feld, cf. Afflington *supra*); (Lt) East Grd; East Md (*le Est Meade* 1525, v. ēast, mæd); (E, Middle & W) 8 Acres (Coppice); 18 Acres; Eldon (a high spur pointing seawards at SY 956776 on which ancient field systems are marked I", so probably 'hill long used or formerly used for agriculture', v. (e)ald, dūn, cf. *La Eldedo(u)n(e)* in Langton Mat. par. and Swanage par. *infra*); Enclosure Plot; Encombe Lodge Fd (from Encombe *supra*); N & S Ew-leaze; Field; 15 Acres; 5 Acres (Mdw); Fir Plant.; Flat Bridge 1776; 4 & 14 Acres; (Gt) Franklands (Md) (cf. Roger *Frankelayn* 1270; for development to -*land*, v. Franklin's Fm W 316); French Grass Fd (v. french grass); Froghole Md (v. frogga, hol¹); Gt Furzemans (Md(w)), Lt Furzemans (cf. Anthony *Furzeman* 1655); Furzey Cl (Grd & Marsh), Furzey Grd & Plot (cf. *Furze Close* 1700 (c. 1774), v. fyrs, fyrsig); Garden (Altmt & Plot); Georges Plot (cf. William *George* 1664); Gooks Ho (the surname *Gook*, ME *goke* 'cuckoo', cf. Go Croft in Arne par. *infra*); Goose-ham (v. gōs, hamm); Gore Cl (v. gāra); Goulds Plot (cf. John *Goulde* 1332); Grain Grd (probably ModE grain 'corn, seed of wheat, etc'); Grants Md; Graves Md; Great Bridge 1791; Great Cl; Great Md(w) (*South Great Mead* 1603, (*the*) *Great Mead(ow)* 1735, 1773); Green Fd Cowleaze; Green Plot; Green's Acre (from John *Green* n.d., v. Hutch³ I 544); Grimberry (Md & 3 Acres) (probably 'barrow or mound haunted by a spectre or goblin', v. grima², beorg); Hr Grotton (v. græd-tūn 'stubble field (on which animals are turned out after the harvest)', cf. Do dial. *grotten* 'a sheep-slade; a run or pasture for sheep' (Barnes 67)); Groves Mdw (cf. *Thomas Groues house* 1664); Guys (cf. Stephen *Guy* 1664); Ham(s) (v. hamm); Harden's 1861 (from John *Harden* 1786); Dollands, Middle, Vicars & West Hawes (*The Vicars Hawes* 1586, *Vicaryes Hawes* 1716, *West Hawes* 1585, 'enclosures', v. haga¹, cf. Halves Ctgs *supra*, William *Dolling*, *Edward Dollins house* 1664, v. vicare, vicarie 'vicar', west); Haycrate (*le Haycrofte* Ed 3, *le Heygh Craffte* 1525, v. hēg, croft); Hayward Plot (cf. Robert *Hayward* 1435); Heath (Grd & Pce); Higher Fd (cf. *le Heygh Fylde* 1525, v. hēah, feld); Higher Md; Highlands; Hilly Md; Gt & Lt Home Fd; Home Grd, Md (— *Meadow* 1717 (c. 1734)) & Plot; (E & W) Horse Cl; N & S Horse Croft (*Horse Crates* 1717 (c. 1734), v. croft); Horse Grd & Plot; House Grd; Howard Mdw (*Howard's* — 1861); Hundred Acres (a nickname for a small field); Hunger Hills (a nickname for poor land, v. hungor); Ilchester Pce (from the Earls of Ilchester, v. Hutch³ I 535); Island Gdn (from an island in the now unnamed stream (formerly Byle Brook, v. RNs. *infra*) SE of the castle; the island is clearly marked on 1585 Tres); Joiners Md; Jones Mdw (cf. *Richard Jones* (*house*) 1664); Kents Cl, Grd & Md; King Acre Mdw (cf. Robert *le Kynge* p1483); Kingston Cmn (— *Fm* 1861) & Md (cf. *Kingston Fds* 1735, from Kingston *supra*); Kit Cl (possibly the pers.n. or

surname *Kit(t)*, or cyte 'cottage', cf. Salterns Copse in Arne par. *infra*);
Kitchen Gdn & Md; (K)nappy Grd (*v.* cnæppig, cf. Nappy Pce *infra*);
(Gt & Lt K)naps (*v.* cnæpp); Gt Knowles (*v.* cnoll); Laines (*v.* leyne);
Lannings Md (cf. Nicholas *Laning* 1664); The Large Mdw; Lawn (*v.* land
or launde); (North) Leaze (cf. *le Northe* —, *le Sougthe New(e) Lease* 1525,
Inlease 1717 (c. 1734), *v.* læs, norð, sūð, nīwe, in 'inner'); Leg (*v.* leg);
Little Bridge 1791; Little Mead(s Orchd & Lane) (*Litle Mede* 1381
(16), *v.* lȳtel, mǣd); Little Plot; (Coppice in) Long Cl (*Long Close*
1586, *v.* lang[1], clos(e)); Long Furlands (*v.* furlang); Long Grd; Long
Md(w) (cf. William *Langmede* 1514, *v.* lang[1], mǣd); Long Wd; Loops Md
(cf. the *Loop* family which had Bucknowle in Ch. Knowle par. *infra* in
16th and 17th centuries, *v.* Hutch[3] I 584); Lynch 5 Acres, Lynch Md 8 & 10
Acres, E Lynch Mdw (cf. *East Linch Lane* 1735, named from Lynch *supra*);
Marsh (*v.* mersc); Marsh's Plot (cf. *terr' nup' Merche*, Thomas *Marsshe*
1546); Matchams Mdw; Mead behind the House; Meadow (to the North);
(Gt & Lt) Merry Fd, Merry Fd Mdw (*Meryfilde* 1566, *Myrrifield* 1584,
Merrefeild 1614, cf. Robert *Meryfylde* 1543, 'pleasant field', or possibly
'field used for merry-making', *v.* myrge, feld, cf. Dr von Feilitzen's note
in Ch 3 177, and Merry Fd in Arne par. *infra*); Middle Cl, Fd, Grd & Md;
Milking Barton (*v.* milking); Millers Md (cf. John *Myller* 1539); Moor
(Mdw) (cf. *Moor Mead(e)* 1549, 1585, *v.* mōr, mǣd); Hr & Lr Moors (*v.*
mōr); Morgans Plot (cf. *Morgan* Kydwelly 1486, *Morgan* Jenkins 1664);
Mount Pleasant, late Henry Browns & Galleys Mds (complimentary nickname for productive land, with the surnames *Brown* and *Galley*); Mower
Md (from ME mowere 'one who mows' or the surname derived from this);
Mulberry Md; Nap Grd (*v.* cnæpp); Nappy Pce (*v.* cnæppig, cf. (K)nappy
Grd *supra*); New Cl (1704, 1717 (c. 1734)); New Grd; (N & S) New Inclosure; New Md(w) & Plant.; 9 Acres; Noggetts (identical with Noggets
in Studland par. *infra q.v.*); North Closes (& Bottom) (*v.* botm); North Fd
(*le Northe Fylde* 1525, *v.* norð, feld); North Hill (1717 (c. 1734)); North
Md(w) (*Northmead* 1603, *v.* norð, mǣd); Norths Plot; Notleys Md (from
the Do surname *Notley*); (Lr) Orchard, Orchard Md (cf. *the North Orchard*
1773); Osmonds Plot (cf. Sarah *Osmund* 1765); Ox Cl; Paddle Dock (no
doubt identical in origin with Puddledock Sx 485 (1697) and Puddle Dock
Ess 135 (*Puddleduck Farm* 1777), for which no explanation has been offered;
the field lies beside the Corfe River just above New Mills *supra*, so perhaps
'muddy pool where a boat could rest', *v.* puddel, dock, cf. Puddle Mill in
Ch. Knowle par. *infra*; for another Do instance of this name, *v.* Puddle
Dock Dairy Ho in Preston par. *infra*); Pain's Fd, Paines Md, John Paines
Moor (cf. Margery *Pagan* Hy 3, John *Payn* 1332); Park Md (cf. *the Park
(Meadow)* 1717 (c. 1734), *v.* park); Peach's Cl (cf. Bartholomew *Peche*
1253); Peaked Cl & Grd (cf. *Peaked Mead* 1718, *v.* peked); Pepper Md (*v.*
pepper); Picked Cl (*v.* piked or picked); Plantation; Plot; Point Grd; Pond
Cl (cf. *Po(u)nd Close* 1717 (c. 1734), 1734, *v.* ponde or pund); Poole Mdw
(*v.* pōl); Poor Ho & Gdn, Poors Grd, Md & Cmn (cf. *the Poor Land* 1795,
bought 'for the benefit of the poor of the parish' (*v.* Hutch[3] I 533)); Pyke's
Tenement 1861; Rawles Mdw; Red Lane Md (cf. *vico voc' Redlayne* 1513,
v. rēad, lane (with the early spelling influenced by leyne)); Rempstone

Down (from Rempstone *supra*); Rick Barton; (Plot) Rick Pound (*v.* pund);
Roe's Plot 1861; Rough Grd, Pasture & Plot; Round Grd; Rushy Grd,
Marsh & Plot; Sampfords Mdw (cf. *Sanpfordes land* 1585, John *Sampforde*
1539); Serrels Md (the surname *Serrel*(*l*), a family of which name acquired
Lynch Fm *supra* in e18, *v.* Hutch³ 1 526); (The) 7 Acres (or Peaked Cl)
(*v.* peked); Sheeps Sleight (*v.* slæget); E, Gt & W Shop Hayes (cf. *Schape
Haye West Fyld* 1525, *v.* scēap, (ge)hæg, cf. West Fd *infra*); Shorts Fd;
(Hr & Yonder) 6 Acres; 6 and 7 Acres; Smiths Cmn, Fd, Grd & Md
(cf. *Henry Smith in Dionis Smiths house* 1664); Sour Md (*v.* sūr); South
Down; Gt & Lt South Fd (*le Sowthe Fylde* 1525, *v.* sūð, feld); South Md
(cf. *South Mead or Barn Close* 1735); Spears Plot (cf. Edward *Speare* 1625);
Spencers Fd & Grd (cf. Robert *Spencer* 1803); Spring Cl (*v.* spring);
Stable Plot; Steart (*v.* steort); Stot Fd (*Stotfield* 1717 (c. 1734), possibly
from stot 'horse, ox', but more probably to be associated with the bdy point
oþ þane ealden stodfald 948 (15), *onne þo alde stodfald, of þanen falde* 956 (14),
'the old studfold, horse enclosure', *v.* ald (wk. obl. *aldan*), stōd-fald, and
with *one þe stod dic* 956 (14), *one þat northene stod dich, of þare dich* ib, 'the
(northern) stud ditch', i.e. 'ditch of a stud-fold', *v.* norðerne, stōd, dīc;
Stot Fd may represent the earlier stōd-fald, with feld 'field' having replaced
fald, or it may simply be 'field where a herd of horses is kept'); Straps (*v.*
strap); Streets Mdw (cf. *Henry Street*(*s house*) 1664); Strouds Gdn & Grd
(cf. William *Strowde* 1546); Swalland Eweleaze & Md (from Swalland in
Kimmeridge par. *infra*); Tanhouse (*v.* tanhouse); (Rocky & W) 10 Acres
(*Tenacres* 1745); 13 Acres; (E & W) 30 Acres; Thornmoor (*v.* þorn, mōr);
3 Acres; 3 Cornered Piece; Tidburys Mdw (cf. Thomas *Tydbury* 1514);
Toaps Cl (cf. Robert *Toop* 1623); Trims Grd (cf. Henry *Trym de West
Criche* 1512, cf. W Creech in Steeple par. *infra*); 12 Acre(s); (E, W & Yonder)
20 Acres, 20 Acre Md; (Lt & W) 2 Acres; The Two and Half Acres; E &
W Two Gates; Vincents Md (cf. Robert *Vincent* 1562); Viver's Tenement
1861; Wash Pond Cmn (*v.* wæsce, cf. foll.); Washing Plot (*v.* washing,
cf. prec.); Water Md(w); Way Cl (*v.* weg); Weasses (Coppice) (cf. Peter
Weys 1664); Webber's Tenement 1861; Well Cl & Grd (*v.* wella); Westall
(probably 'west nook of land', *v.* west, halh); West Fd ((*le*) *West Fyld*(*e*)
1525, *v.* feld); Wheelers or Lannings Md (cf. Jonathan *Wheeler* a1743, *v.*
Lannings Md *supra*); West Grd & Md(w); Wills Md & Plot; Wimborne
Md (part of a 17th-cent. charitable endowment for the benefit of ten poor
persons of Wimborne (M.H.)); Witch Furland, Hr & Lr Witch Mdw,
Wytch Mdw, Plot near Wytch Wares (*Hr & Middle Witch* 1783, from
Wytch *supra*, *v.* furlang, ware 'sheep walk', cf. Ware in Swanage par. *infra*);
Wood, Wood (Cl) Md (*Wood Md* 1717 (c. 1734)); Woodlands; Woolgres-,
Woolgraston Down (*Woolgarston Down* 1700, from Woolgarston *supra*);
Woolgraston Gdn & Hill (cf. prec.); Yonder Fd & Plot.

(*b*) on *Alfricheswelle, of þane welle* 955 (14) ('Ælfrīc's spring or stream',
from the OE pers.n. *Ælfrīc* and wella); on *Alfstanes þaþ* 956 (14) ('Ælfstān's
path', from the OE pers.n. *Ælfstān* and pæð); on *auenes broc, of þane broke*
955 (14), on *aueres* [sic] *broc, adune anlang brokes* 956 (14) ('the stream called
Avon', a r.n. *Avon* (*v.* aβon), *v.* -es², brōc; for the use of the gen. -*es* here,
v. RN 22, Tengstrand xlix note 1); *le Bakehowse* 1539 (*v.* bæc-hūs); *le*

Barghey ad castrum de Corff 1435 ('the enclosure at the hill or mound', *v.* beorg, (ge)hæg, cf. Corfe Castle *supra*); *le Bawse Haye* 1525 (perhaps a ME surname *Baw* from the OE pers.n. *Bēaw, v.* (ge)hæg); *on beam broc, an ðonnen an lang broke* 948 (15), *uppen irichte on beambroc, swo up anlang streames, of þane streame* 955 (14) ('beam brook, brook with a tree-trunk across it', *v.* bēam, brōc, with strēam 'current, stream', cf. Bamford La 54, RN 27); *oþ-, of þane bige* 956 (14) (*v.* byge[1] 'bend (of a river)'); *Boure Mill (Bridge)* 1510, *molend' voc' Borismylle* 1512, *Boremill Bridge* 1791 (*v.* būr[1] 'cottage' or (ge)būr 'peasant', myln, brycg); *Bursice Wodde* 1525 (cf. Walter *Bursey* 1324 (17), *v.* wudu).; *Chaunterelleslond* a1427 (cf. Edward *Chaunterell* ib, *v.* land); *on þane clif upward* 948 (15), *oþe clif* 956 (14) (*v.* clif); *Corfhayes* 1381 (*v.* (ge)hæg, cf. Henry *de la Haye* 1270, 1280); *Corffe way* 1603 ('the road to Corfe' (from Swanage?), *v.* weg, cf. *W(h)ar(h)am(m)eswey(e) infra*); *Couhayes* 1381 (16) (*v.* cū, (ge)hæg); *on þone-, of þane crundel* 955 (14) (*v.* crundel); *le cutte* 1539 ('the channel', *v.* cut); *Derby lands* 1621 (cf. *ten' terr' nup' Rob' Derby* 1546, *v.* land); *oþ þa-, of þare dich* 948 (15), *on anne dich, of þare-, on-, anlang dich* ib, 955 (14), 956 (14), *on þa ealdene dich, anlang dich* 955 (14) (*v.* ald, dīc); *on ða ealdene hege rewe, anlang þare hege rewe* 948 (15) (*v.* ald, hege, rǣw); *one þo ealde rode, onlang rode* 956 (14) (*v.* ald, rod[1], rodu); *on þane ealde weg, and lang weies* 955 (14) (*v.* ald, weg); *East Hills* 1718; 'close called *Eastover*' 1700 (probably 'east slope or hill', *v.* ofer[2]); *on ecge, ford* (for *-forð*) *be ecge* 955 (14) (*v.* ecg); *be eficlif* 956 (14) (perhaps 'ivy-covered bank', *v.* īfig (cf. the adj. derivative īfede, eofede), clif); *be euisc* 956 (14) (*v.* efisc 'edge, border'; for this variant of efes, *v.* Tengstrand 35); *Fryeres Heye* 1525 (frere 'friar', perhaps used as a surname, *v.* (ge)hæg); *Harmar's Croft* 1700; *on hecgan sled, of þane slede* 955 (14) ('valley with a hedge', *v.* hecge, -an, slæd); *on ðone-, of þen-, on þare-, of þanne herepaþ(e)* 948 (15), 956 (14), *on þene richte herepath* 948 (15) ('the (straight) highway', *v.* riht[2], here-pæð); *de la Hide* 1327 (p), 1399 (p), *de la Hyde* 1332 (p) (*v.* hīd); *on þen hirnen* 948 (15) (*v.* hyrne); *crucem vocat' Hoggyscroys* n.d. (e15) (the surname Hogg, *v.* cros); *on þat holenbedde, of þat holnebedde* 955 (14), contiguous with *on þare holne stoke, of þane stocke* ib ('holly bed', and 'holly stump' or 'outlying farmstead characterised by holly', *v.* holegn, bedd, stocc or stoc); *on þa holendich, an lang dich* 955 (14) ('the hollow ditch', *v.* hol[2] (wk. obl. *holan*), dīc); *Hyldbury or Hyldeway juxta Corfe Castle* 1510 (cf. Stephen — 1327, Richard —, Roger *Huldewey(e)* 1332, 'road on a slope', *v.* hielde, weg; *-bury* may mean 'manor house', *v.* burh (dat. sg. *byrig*)); 'the pasture called King's Doune' 1291, *pastur' q' vocat' Kyngestoune* 1326, *Kyngesdoune* 1357, 1382, 'a wood called *Kemsdon*' 1545 ('hill belonging to the king', *v.* cyning, dūn, cf. Kingston *supra*); *Lane Hill Meadow* 1717 (c. 1734); *lansshoredych* n.d. (e15) (in the bounds of Ower *supra, v.* land-scoru 'boundary', dīc); *little Mary Mead* 1603 (probably the fem. pers.n. *Mary*, but cf. Merry Fd *supra, v.* lȳtel, mæd); *Merkewey* n.d. (e15) (in the bounds of Ower *supra, v.* mearc 'boundary', weg); *ouer þane merse* 948 (15) (*v.* mersc 'marsh'); *Mochecroft* 1498 ('large enclosure', *v.* micel, croft); *on anne mor adune anlang mores* 956 (14) (*v.* mōr); *Porters Mead(e)* 1549, 1585 (the surname Porter, *v.* mæd); *on (þane) (i)richt wei, -wege, of þan(n)e weie, -i wege* 955 (14), 956 (14) 'the straight road', *v.* riht², **weg**); *on þane rupemor, of þane mor* 955 (14) (probably for *ruwe-* from *rūwan* wk. obl. of rūh 'rough', *v.* mōr); *ut on sce, of sa* 948 (15) (*v.* sǣ); *le Safkynse heye* 1525 (probably the surname *Sawkin(s)*, *v.* (ge)hæg); *anlang safundune* 948 (15), *anlang saþendune* (possibly for *sawen-*) 956 (14) (*v.* dūn 'hill'; Professor Löfvenberg suggests that the first el. may possibly be OE *safene, safine* 'savine' (a kind of juniper); for the possible scribal confusion of þ and *w* in the second form, cf. Hollish *supra*); *Schapcrofte* Ed 3 (*v.* scēap, croft); *on seuen willes þry, anlang streames* 955 (14) (probably identical with *on þane broc, þonne anlang stremes* 948 (15), *Sufewella* n.d. (15), 'seven springs or streams', *v.* seofon, **wella**, with þrūh (dat. sg. þrȳh) 'trough', *v.* strēam); *Slutes hole* 1585 (Professor Löfvenberg points out that this is apparently an early instance of *slut('s)-hole* 'a place or receptacle for rubbish' (1862 NED s.v. *slut*), cf. Löfvenberg 191 for cognate words); *over smalen-cumbe* 956 (14) ('narrow valley', *v.* smæl (wk.obl. *smalan*), cumb); *Smead Croft* 1700; *or* (for *-on*) *anne ston, of þanne stane* 948 (15), *on anne-, on þare stan, of þane stane* 955 (14) (*v.* stān); *on þat stanene bregge, of þare brigge* 955 (14) ('bridge made of stone', *v.* stānen, brycg); *on anne stanen wal, nord* (for *norð*) *on lang walles* 956 (14) ('wall made of stone', *v.* stānen, wall); *on anne stan tor, of þan tore* 948 (15) ('rock of stone', *v.* stān, torr); *on anne stan wal, -weal, of þan(n)e walle* 955 (14), 956 (14) ('stone wall', *v.* stān, wall); *on stanwei* 955 (14), *on stan wege, an lang weies* 956 (14), *þastur' d'ni voc' Stowey* 1489 ('stony road' or 'road paved in stone', *v.* stān, weg); *Stodelondyspath* n.d. (e15) ('the path to Studland' (par. *infra*), *v.* pæð); *an lang streame* 948 (15), *on þare stream(e), anlang streames* 955 (14) (*v.* strēam); *Swyneswell* 1381 (16) (perhaps swin² 'creek, channel', rather than swin¹ 'pig', *v.* wella, RNs. *infra*); *Taylor's Hay* 1700 (*v.* (ge)hæg); *on anne þorn(e), of þa(ne) þorn* 955 (14), 956 (14) (*v.* þorn); *the gret thorne standinge under the Banke* 1381 (16) (*v.* grēat, þorn, banke); *on þe þwers dich, of þare diche* 955 (14) (*v.* dīc; *þwers* would seem to be the OE adv. and prep. þwēores 'across' used elliptically as an adj. to mean 'lying or passing across', cf. *þwyrsmere* and *þwyrs furh* Brk 687, 689, *þwyresfura* (glossing *salebroso*) WW 520.12, and the adj. use of *cross* (in ME and ModE) and *thwart* (in ModE)); 'lands ...sometimes *Tregarters'* 1586 (from the family of Thomas *Tregarthyn* 1490, — *Tregarter* 1550); *Tyuerelles clos* 1455 (possibly an unvoiced form of the surname *Deverell, v.* clos(e)); *le Est-, le West Vyppysehyll(e)* 1525 (perhaps a voiced form of the surname *Phippes* from ME *Phip, Fip,* a pet-form of *Philip, v.* ēast, west, hyll); *Vyrellyscroce, -haye* n.d. (e15) (the surname *Verrill, v.* cros, (ge)hæg); *on anne walle, on lang walles* 955 (14) (*v.* wall); *W(h)ar(h)am(m)eswey(e)* 1357, 1382 *et freq* to 1423 ('the road to Warham' (from Kingston and Corfe), *v.* weg, cf. *Corffe way supra*); *on anne weg, of þane wige* 955 (14), *on þare wei, anlang weies* ib (*v.* weg); *þare weilaite* 948 (15) ('(by) the crossroads', *v.* weg, (ge)lǣt); *forðe an lange welles* 948 (15), *on þane-, on anne wal, an-, onlang welles* 955 (14) (*v.* well(a) 'stream'; the *wal* form could be due to influence from the Merc form wælla or to confusion with **wall** 'wall', but it is perhaps more likely to represent wēl² (WSax wǣl) 'a deep place in a stream'); *be wertrumen* 956 (14) (*v.* wyrttruma 'root, root-stock', *-en* representing either dat.sg. *-an* or dat.pl. *-um*); 'tenement called *West Acres*' 1630; *le West Barne* 1539; *the Wester tenement*

1666 (v. westerra); *le West Heye* 1525 (v. (ge)hæg); *le Westhowse* 1529 (v. hūs); *one þane westrene cumbe, þanne a dun anlang cumbes* 948 (15) ('the western valley', v. westerne, cumb); *le Wevehowse* 1539 ('building used for weaving', v. weve(n), hūs); (*Drye close alias*) *Wheat Close* 1549, 1585 (v. drȳge, hwǣte); *Whitbridge* 1545 (v. hwīt, brycg); *cultura que vocatur Vdeputte* p1483 ('pit in or near a wood', v. wudu, pytt); *on þat withi begh, of þanne wiþibedde* 955 (14), *on anne wiþig þefele* 948 (15) ('the ring of willows, the willow bed, a willow thicket', v. wīðig, bēag, bedd, þȳfel; the use of bēag with wīðig here should be compared with Wilby Sf which also means 'ring of willows' (v. DEPN, wilig, bēag); it could well be that this OE combination lies behind at least one of the other Wilbys (Wilby Nf is *Wilgeby, Willebeih* 1086 DB), as well as some of the numerous Willoughbys, which have hitherto been suspected of being cases where ON bȳ has replaced OE tūn, v. EPN 1 68, DEPN 520); *þurch þane wde* 955 (14) (v. wudu); *Este and Weste Wolgarslond* 1599 (the OE pers.n. *Wulfgār*, perhaps as a surname, with land, ēast, west, cf. Woolgarston *supra*).

Langton Matravers

The manor of Langton Matravers formed the E part of this par., and Langton Wallis or West Langton the W part. The manor of Langton Wallis also formerly included Ailwood and Westwood in Corfe C. par. *supra*, Middlebere in Arne par. *infra*, as well as lands in Ch. Knowle par., E Stoke par. and Swanage par. (Hutch[3] 1 634). Knaveswell was in Corfe C. par. *supra* in 1795 Boswell. A small part of Langton Mat. par. was transferred to Swanage par. in 1933 (Kelly).

LANGTON MATRAVERS (SY 998789)

Langeton(e) c. 1165 MontC, 1206, 1214 Cur, 1280 Ipm, 1285 FA *et freq* to 1546 Ct, — (*in*) *Pur(e)bic, -bik(e), -byk(e)* 1214 Cur, 1276, 1278 Pat, Hutch[3], 1278 (1372) *ChrP*, 1280 *Ass et freq* to p1483 *Sheen*, — *juxta Corf Castel* 1321 FF, — *iuxta Swanwich* 1392 *DCMDeed*, — *by Corft* 1399 Cl, *Langton* ((*in*) *Purbek, -bik, -byk(e))* 1321 Inq aqd *et freq* to 1575 Saxton, *Langgeton* 1332 SR, 1333 *Wim*, *Langheton* 1339 Pat, *Lanckton* 1687 Hutch[3] *Longeton(e) in Pubike* (sic) 1280 *Ass*, — *in Purbyke* p1483 *Sheen*, *Longton* 1465 Pat

Langton Averey(e in Purbyke) 1309 Hutch[3]

Langeton Walisch (*in Purbyk, -bike*) 1376 IpmR, 1376 (1393), 1376 (1396) Pat, — *Wals(s)h(e)* 1397 FF, 1416 Cl, — *Walyssh(e)*, -*ysche* 1423–1429 *Midd*, 1517, 1519 *HarlCh*, *Langton Walys(s)h(e)*, -*ysche* 1412 FA, 1454 *Ct*, 1519, 1535 *HarlCh*, — *Welssh* 1540 Hutch[3], — *Wallis* c. 1586 Tres

Lang(e)ton Maw-, *Mautravers* 1428 *Midd*, FA, 1431 ib, 1435
IpmR, 1436 *Fine*, — *Matrevers* 1497 (17), 1623 (17) *DCMDeed*,
— *Matreuers* c. 1586 Tres, — *Mutrevers* 1599 *Pitt*, — *Matreavers*
1630 (17) *DCMDeed*
Estlangton, West Langton 1550 *Midd*

'Long farm', *v.* lang¹, tūn; Hutch³ **1** 630 observes 'the village
consists of one street, near a mile in length'. Langton Wallis (no
longer marked on the maps in this par. but cf. Langton Wallis in
Arne par. *infra*) takes its name from the family of Ing(el)ram *le
Waleys* who was here in 1276 Pat, 1280 *Ass*, Ipm, 1285 FA, etc; *West
Langton* and probably *Langeton juxta Corf Castel*, — *by Corft* also
denote this manor, and *Langton Averey(e)* probably refers to the
whole or part of it, *Averey* representing OFr *Auverey, Auveré* < OG
Alverad with reference to its early possession by one of the Alvreds
of Lincoln (*v.* Hutch³ **1** 718, VCHDo **3** 55–6, and Okeford Fitzpaine
par. *infra*), cf. however Hutch³ **1** 717 where *Averey* is thought to be
a corruption of *Avenel*, a family of which name claimed advowson
of the church in 1213 (though the surname (*d'*)*Avenel* should be
read *Daneuel* (*Daneville*) according to DoNHAS **14** 110). Langton
Matravers (alternatively called *Estlangton* and probably also *Langeton
iuxta Swanwich*) takes its name from the family of John *Mautravers*
who was here in 1281 FF, 1297 Ipm, 1333 *Wim*, etc., cf. Lytchett
Matravers par. *infra*. For the affixes, *v.* ēast, west, Isle of Purbeck
supra, Corfe C. par. *supra*, Swanage par. *infra*.

ACTON (SY 990784)

Tacatone 1086 DB, *-tona* Exon, *Tachetona* 1109 Dugd, *Tac-* 1283
FF, *Take-* 1305 Cl, *Takton* 1423 *Midd*
Acton 1550 *Midd*, c. 1586 Tres, 1811 OS, (— or *Acwell*) 1774
Hutch¹

Probably 'farm where young sheep are reared', *v.* tacca, tacce,
tūn, as suggested by Ekwall in Studies² 74 and DEPN; an OE pers.n.
Tæcca or *Tacca* is less likely for the first el. (cf. Fägersten 123 who
also cites the 13th cent. Do surname Robert *Tac*). In either case the
later loss of initial *T-* is due to the wrong analysis of phrases like
'at Tacton' (cf. æt, atten in EPN and *v.* Phonol.) and to confusion
with the common p.n. *Acton* 'oak farm' from āc and tūn. The late
alternative form *Acwell* (*v.* wella; a spring is marked 6″ near Acton

Fd *infra*), and also the lost *Bitakewathe infra*, probably have the same first el. There was a mill here in 1086 DB (VCHDo 3 108).

COOMBE (SZ 006789), 1656 *DCMDeed*, *Come* 1086 DB, *Cumbe in Porebyk* 1279 Banco, *La Combe* 1305 Cl, *Comb* 1774 Hutch[1], *v.* cumb 'valley'.

DURNFORD DROVE & Ho (SY 997788), *Derneford* 1275 RH, 1281 Abbr, 1287 FF, 1288 *Ass*, 14 Mansel, 1305 Cl, 1311 FF, 1325 Hutch[3], 1356 Pat all (p), *Durn(e)ford(e)* 1327 *SR*, 1332 SR, 1333 *Wim*, 1338 Cl, 1357 Pat, 1379 *Weld*[1], p1483 *Sheen* all (p), 1572, 1721 Hutch[3], 1774 Hutch[1], *Dorneforde* 1550 *Midd*. Since all the forms before the 16th cent. found for this name are used as personal names, and since it was supposed that there was no ford here, Hutch[3] 1 631 and Fägersten 123 took this to be a transferred name, perhaps from Durnford W 363. However, Mr R. J. Saville points out that there is in fact a ford on this estate, where Durnford Drove (the main track from the former farm to its fields, *v.* drove) crosses the stream giving name to Putlake Fm *infra*; it is possible therefore that the place took its name from this ford, 'the secret or hidden ford', *v.* derne, ford. Eyton 111–12 identifies the two small lost DB manors of *Torne* with Durnford, *v.* note on lost p.ns. in Rowbarrow hundred *supra*, and cf. *La Thorne infra*. Although the names Durnford and *T(h)orne* cannot be etymologically related, *T(h)orne* may well have been an earlier name for the estate later called Durnford, a supposition supported by the probable identification of the pound at *La Thorne infra* with Court Pound *infra* (⅓ mile W of Durnford Ho; it was the pound of Langton Wallis, to which manor Durnford partly belonged (Hutch[3] 1 631)), as well as by the fact that at Durnford 'the thorn grows to its greatest height and is the only really native tree' (R.J.S.). Alternatively, even though both single-hide manors are called *Torne* in DB, the name *Torne* (and later *La Thorne*) may strictly speaking have applied only to one hide (the more westerly, as suggested by the location of Court Pound), whereas the other hide (the more easterly, perhaps bounded on the west by Durnford Drove and corresponding to the later estate of Durnford) may have had the name Durnford, perhaps even at the time of DB. For a different identification of the DB manors of *Torne*, with Thornham in Ch. Knowle par. *infra*, *v.* DBGazetteer 127.

KNAVESWELL COPSE & FM (SZ 002808), *Cnaves-* 1285 Hutch[3], *Cnaueswell* 1285 (1372) *ChrP*, *Knausewell in Purbyk* 1384 *DCMDeed*,

Knaves-, Knaueswell 1535 VE *et freq* to 1811 OS, (*farm of* —) 1734 *DCMDeed*, 'boy's or servant's spring or stream', *v.* **cnafa, wella**, named from the stream (known as The Spring) which rises just N of the farm (spring marked 6″), cf. Isle of Purbeck *supra*. The forms in *-es-* throughout show that this name was probably formed after the wk. noun *cnafa* had received analogical strong endings, *v.* -es²; in fact, as Professor Löfvenberg points out, the first el. may be an occupational surname, cf. Thuresson 128.

KNITSON (FM) (SZ 005807), *Knyghtwyneston* 1309 Hutch³, 1318 FF, *Knightwyneston* 1402 IpmR, *Knyghneston* Ed 3 *Surv*, *Knyʒteton in Purbyk* 1355 *Wim*, *Knyghteston* 1366 Hutch³, 1367 FF, 1379 *AddCh*, 1431 FA, (— *in Purbyk*) 1378 FF, *Knytteston* 1404 Cl, IpmR, *Knyghtweston* 1457 IpmR, *Knyghtston, Knyghstons Downe* 1525 *AOMB*, *Knightsen* c. 1586 Tres, *Knitson* 1811 OS, (— *Cowleaze*) 1838 *TA*, 'Cnihtwine's farm', from the OE pers.n. *Cnihtwine* and tūn, with dūn, cf. Isle of Purbeck *supra*.

LEESON HO (SZ 004787), PARK & WD, *Lesin-* 1224 Cur, *Lessenton* 1224 ib (p), *Letsinton* 1236 Cl, *Lesseton* 1243 Fees, 1288 Hutch³ (— *juxta Langeton*), *Leston* 1288 *Ass*, 1305 Cl, 1333 *Wim*, 1376 (1393) Pat, 1431 FA, 1497 (17) *DCMDeed*, *Leuston* 1332 SR (p), *Lestington* 1299 Hutch³, *Leaston* 1623 (17) *DCMDeed* (— *Fearme*), 1656 *ib*, 1712 Hutch³, *Lenston* (sic) 1774 Hutch¹, probably 'farm called after Lēofsige', from the OE pers.n. *Lēofsige* and -ingtūn, with **ferme**, cf. Lissington L (*Lessintone* 1086 DB) which Ekwall DEPN explains in this way.

WILKSWOOD FM (SY 995795)
> *Wilceswde* 1086 DB, -*wda* Exon, *Wilchesode* 1086 DB, -*oda* Exon, -*wode* 1304 Ipm, Hutch³, 1376, 1379 Pat, 1383 ib (— *in Purbyk*), 1774 Hutch¹, -*woode* 1384 Pat, -*wood or Wilkswood* 1795 Boswell, *Wilchuswode* c. 1190 *Midd* (R.J.S.), *Wylcheswod(e)* 1305 Cl, 1348 Pat ('— by Corfe Castle in *Purbyk*') *et freq* to 1423 *Midd*, -*wodde* 1535 HarlCh, *Whylcheswode* 1373 Douce
> *Wylkesworthe* 1546 *Ct*, *Wilkeswood* 1585 Hutch³
> *Wilshewode* 1550 *Midd*
> *Willis Wood* 1811 OS

The second el. is **wudu** 'wood': there were 4 furlongs of woodland here in 1086 DB, and Hutch³ **1** 638 observes 'its situation is still woody'. The first el. is probably an unrecorded OE pers.n. *Willic*, a diminutive of *Willa*. The modern form and the two 16th cent. forms with [k] may show influence from the ME pers.n. and surname *Wilk(s)* (probably < OE *Willoc*), and the other late forms from welisc (WSax wilisc) 'Welsh' and from the surname *Willis* respectively. For the affixes, *v.* Isle of Purbeck and Corfe C. par. *supra*.

There was a priory here, with a chantry or free chapel in St George's Church *infra*, referred to as *Domus Beati Leonardi de Wilchuswode* c. 1190 *Midd* (R.J.S.), 'St Leonard's chapel' 1305 Cl, *capell' de Wylcheswode, canteriam...de Whylcheswode* (Henry *atte Chapele*, chaplain, presented to —) 1373 *Douce, libera capella de Wylcheswodde* 1535 *HarlCh*, cf. 'prior of *Wylcheswode* by Corfe Castle in *Purbyk*' 1348 Pat, *prior' de Wylcheswode* 1423 *Midd*, *v.* chapel(e), atte, cf. Priory Cl *infra*. On this priory, probably founded c. 1154 by Cluniac Benedictines, *v.* R. J. Saville, *A History of the Church in Langton Matravers*, pp. 4–5, cf. VCHDo **2** 47, 98.

ACTON FD, *in campo in Takton* 1429 *Midd*, cf. *Acton Md* 1838 *TA*, from Acton *supra*. BATHING POOL, blasted out of the rock at Dancing Ledge *infra* c. 1893 (Short 20). BLACKERS HOLE, 1882 Robinson ('a huge black cave'), perhaps 'hollow at *Blackers*' ('black fundament'), *v.* blæc, ears, hol[1], but the surname *Blacker* is also possible. BLACKLANDS, 1838 *TA*, *v.* blæc, land, cf. Spyway Barn *infra*. BOWER'S ROCK (local), a rock near Green Point *infra*, no doubt from one of the local *Bower* families, cf. Mike's & Willy's Coves in Worth Mat. par. *infra*. CASTLE VIEW (local), a settlement from which Corfe castle may be seen, originally Mount Misery *infra*. CHILLMARK (WARE) (local), *Chilmark* 1571 WimCW, E of Dancing Ledge *infra*, perhaps identical in origin with Chilmark W 185, 'boundary marked with a pole or poles', *v.* cegel, mearc, with ware 'sheep walk', as elsewhere in this par., cf. Ware in Swanage par. *infra*. COLES GROUND (local), cf. *Coles Md* 1838 *TA*; a farm on land once held by the *Cole* family (R.J.S.). COOMBE COPSE & FM, cf. *Coombe howse* 1656 *DCMDeed*, from Coombe *supra*. COURT POUND, *Court Pound* (*Plot*) 1838 *TA*, cf. *curia et clausa curiæ* 1351 Hutch[3], *v.* court, pund; for a probable early reference to the pound, that of the manorial court of Langton Wallis (R.J.S.), *v. La Thorne infra*. CRACK LANE, cf. Nutcrack Lane in Arne par. *infra*, where *-crack* is from croft; however, local tradition has it that *Crack* is from creek (*v.* crike), perhaps with reference to some feature near the confluence of two

streams down to which the lane leads (R.J.S.). CUCKOO POUND, near
the par. bdy, a jocular name no doubt identical in meaning with
Cuckoo Pen in Corfe C. par. *supra*, *v.* pund. DANCING LEDGE, 1811
OS, an abandoned cliff-side quarry, perhaps so called from the action
of the waves breaking over the ledge, *v.* ledge; above it is Dancing
Ledge Ware (local), *v.* ware. FARM WD, 1838 *TA*, from Langton
Manor Fm *infra*. GREEN POINT (local), a prominent cliff fault, just
E of Dancing Ledge *supra*, over which fresh water flows from land
and on which green algae and other weeds grow (T.B.A.), *v.* grēne[1],
point. GULLY, *v.* goulet. GYPSHAYES ESTATE, *Jepshays* 1838 *TA*, from
the ME pers.n. *Jep*, a pet-form of *Geoffrey*, although Richard *Jope*
1423 *Midd* perhaps belongs here, *v.* (ge)hæg. HANGING FD (local), on
the cliff-top near foll., *v.* hangende. HEDBURY BIG COVE, BOTTOM,
& QUARRY (all local), *Headbury Bottom & Rough Grd* 1838 *TA*, on
the coast at SY 992768, from the (*H*)*eidbury* family which started the
quarry in 18th cent. (R.J.S.), *v.* cove, botm. THE HYDE (local, cf.
HYDE RD 6″), *Hyde* 1838 *TA*, probably to be identified with *la Hyde*,
la Hide 1288 *Ass* and possibly the home of Ralph *atte Hyde* 1355
Wim, — *de la Hyde* 1399 *Cl*, 'the hide of land', *v.* hīd, la, atte;
Langehyde in Purbyk 1315 *FF* (*v.* lang[1]) may belong here, cf. also
Green Hyde 1838 *TA* (*v.* grēne[1] or grēne[2], cf. *la Grene, atte Grene*
infra), *Mayne hyde fd* 1838 *ib* (*le Menehyde* 1428 *Midd*, *v.* (ge)mǣne
'held in common'), *Hide Furlong* 1695 *DCMDeed* (*v.* furlang), and
Parsonage Hyde 18 R.J.S. ('The Hyde was from mediaeval times the
farm of the priest of Langton'). LANGTON MANOR FM, cf. foll. and
Farm Wd *supra*. LANGTON WEST WD, *Langton Westwood* 1838 *TA*,
cf. 'the wood of *Langeton* in *Purbik*' 1276, 1278 *Pat*, *v.* west, wudu,
cf. Isle of Purbeck *supra*; the wood lies W of the village. LIMEKILN
BLDGS. GT & LT LINNINGS COPSE, cf. *Broad Lynings* 1656
DCMDeed, E, *Gt & Lt Lin*(*n*)*ings* 1838 *TA*, perhaps 'place(s) where
flax grows', *v.* līn, -ing[2]; near the Langton Mat.–Swanage bdy.
LITCHFIELD COPSE, 1838 *TA*, *Easter, Middle, & Wester Luttes Feild*,
Luttesfeild meadow 1656 *DCMDeed*, *Litchfield* (5 *Acres*) 1838 *TA*, the
surname *Lutt*(*e*) (from an OE pers.n. *Lutt*(*a*)), and feld, with
ēasterra, westerra; the modern form probably shows association
with Lichfield St or līc 'corpse'. MIKE'S CORNER & QUARRY (local,
near Hedbury *supra*), from *Michael* Bower as in Mike's & Willy's
Coves in Worth Mat. par. *infra*, cf. Bower's Rock *supra*. MOUNT
MISERY, now called Castle View, a hill scarred by stone quarrying
(Legg 22), also bleak and exposed (R.J.S.), cf. foll., Wt 251. MOUNT

PLEASANT, 'a greener rise' near to prec. (Legg 22), also more sheltered (R.J.S.). NEW BARN. NEW BLDGS. NINE BARROW DOWN, 1774 Hutch[1], part of the main Purbeck ridge and so named from the many tumuli, v. beorg, dūn; in fact according to Hutch[3] 1 689 there are 'in all eighteen barrows clearly distinguishable, all lying close together', and according to local tradition there were originally nineteen (R.J.S.). THE NURSERY, a wood. OAKRIDGE, *Oate errish* 1656 *DCMDeed*, 'ploughed field where oats were grown', v. āte, ersc. PIG & WHISTLE (local, SY 989767), an eroded part of the cliffs near a geological fault, perhaps so called because at 'low to half tide breakers will seem to grunt as they enter and whistle as the previous incompressible sea tries to escape' (T.B.A.), but cf. *pigs and whistles* 'fragments' (NED s.v. *pig* sb.[2] sense 1e). PRIEST'S WAY, *Prestesweye* 1305 Cl, *Preistway* 1695 *DCMDeed*, cf. *the Higher-, Lower Prestway Feild* 1656 *ib*, an ancient track doubtless used by priests passing between Worth Mat. and Swanage, both in the same ecclesiastical par. until c. 1500 (Hutch[3] 1 656), v. prēost, -es[2], weg, cf. Priests Way in Swanage par. *infra*. PURBECK STONE QUARRIES, cf. 'quarry' 1305 Cl, *claus' voc' Quare Pittes* 1550 *Midd*, *Quarry Cl* 1838 *TA*, v. quarrere, pytt. PUTLAKE FM, *Pucklake fm* 1861 Hutch[3], cf. *Pucklake Md* 1838 *TA*, 'goblin's stream', v. pūca, lacu; this 'puckish' stream (marked 6″) has often flooded the farm without warning (R.J.S.). QUEENSGROUND (local), Legg 136; it lies next to King's Ground, another recent name (R.J.S.). QUINCE HILL WD, *Quintance Hill Wd* 1838 *TA*, perhaps from a surname, but possibly an allusion to tilting at the quintaine, v. quintaine. ST GEORGE'S CHURCH (Kelly), cf. 'the church of *Langeton*' 1311 FF, *capell*'...*S'ci Georgii de Langeton* 1373 Douce, Wilkswood *supra*. SCRATCH ARSE (WARE) (local), a small cliff-top quarry near Dancing Ledge *supra* reached by sliding over a rough scree (T.B.A.), cf. Ring-Bum Gdns in Worth Mat. par. *infra*, v. ware. SEA SPRAY, a house high above the cliffs ½ mile from the sea; salt covers the windows in winter storms (R.J.S.). SERRELLS, SERRELL'S COPSE, cf. *Serrells Mdw* 1838 *TA*, from the *Serrell* family which was at Durnford Ho from 1721 (Hutch[3] 1 633). SHIT YALLERY HOLE (local), lies under Green Point *supra*, v. hol[1]; *yallery* is Do dial. for *yellow*, 'shit yellow' referring to the colour of the cliff face from the clay topsoil washed down it (R.J.S.). SMOKEY HOLE (local), a cave near Topmast Quarry *infra*, so called because it is filled with fine spray (T.B.A.), v. hol[1]. SOUTH BARN. SPYWAY BARN, 1811 OS, cf. *Spyway* 1838 *TA*, — *Fm* 1811 OS, *Spy Hill* 1774 Hutch[1]; the first el. possibly refers to the 400′ hill spur W of Spyway Barn, and the name should perhaps be compared with Spye Park W 252 (which lies high and is *(le) Spye(-)* e15), and Spy Hill YW **6** 168 (this reference is unfortunately not traceable), but cf. Spyway in Affpuddle par. *infra*; Spyway Fm is now called Blacklands *q.v. supra*. SQUARE COPSE. STEPS, from earth steps cut into the hillside, *v.* stæpe; two modern housing estates here have been named *Steppes* and *Steppeshill* (R.J.S.). TALBOT'S WD, from Thomas *Talbot*, dairyman at Wilkswood Fm *supra* in e19th cent. (R.J.S.), cf. the *Talbot* family which held Knitson *supra* from 14th cent., and the William *Talbot* who was warden of the chantry of Wilkswood in 1416 Hutch[3]. TOPMAST QUARRY (local, SY 995768), the highest of three old cliffside quarries, perhaps so called because it is at about the height of the topmast of a small schooner or other trading vessel (T.B.A.), but more likely simply 'the highest or topmost' (R.J.S.). THE WILDERNESS, on the par. bdy, *v.* wildernesse. WINDMILL BARN & KNAP, *Windmill Hill* 1882 Robinson, cf. *Windmill ground...with the Windmill that stands thereon, the Windmillhowse* 1656 DCMDeed, *Old Windmill* 1776 Map (R.J.S.), *12 Acres by Windmill, Windmill Grd* 1838 *TA, v.* windmill, grund, hūs, cnæpp; Robinson 113 takes this hill to have been the site of one of the three lodges of the forest of Purbeck, *v.* under Swanage par. *infra*. VALLEY RD, VALLEYROAD CTG. YARDS BRAKE, cf. *terra locat'...super la Yurde* 1423 Midd, *Yards* 1838 *TA*, 'brake or bracken at *Yard*' ('measure of land'), *v.* gerd, bræc[1], bracu.

FIELD-NAMES

For some fields in Langton Mat. *TA* but now in Swanage, *v.* Swanage par. *infra*. The undated forms are 1838 *TA* 123. Spellings dated 1278 (1372) are *ChrP*, 1305 Cl, 1322 Pat, 1332 SR, 1340 NI, 1423, 1429, 1550 Midd, p1483 *Sheen*, 1497 (17), 1656, 1695 DCMDeed, 1517, 1519, 1528 HarlCh, 1664 HTax, 1795 Boswell, and the rest Hutch[3].

(a) Alderbury (partly in Swanage par. *infra q.v.*); Bakers Md, Nap & South Grds (cf. John *le Bakere* 1340, *v.* cnæpp); Balston(e) (Wear) (*v.* ware; *Balston*, occurring as a local family name in 18th cent. (R.J.S.), is perhaps a p.n. in tūn or stān, but earlier forms are needed, cf. Balstone D 226 and Chestus *infra*); Barn Barton & Plot (cf. *Barneswoode* 1550, *v.* bere-ærn, -es[2], wudu); Benledge (1721, partly in Swanage par. *infra*, cf. Norledge *infra*); Besslade ((*La) Ber(e)slad* 1305, cf. *Berecroft* ib, *v.* bere, slæd, croft); Blakehill or Blacknell 1774, Blackwell or Blacknell 1795 (*v.* blæc (*blacan* wk. obl.), hyll, showing confusion with wella); Bramble Cl; Breaches Md (*v.* brēc); Bullhorne (cf. Ramshorn Lake in Corfe C. par. *supra*); Burnbake (*v.* burnbake); Captains Fd (from the quarry capstans formerly here, *v.*

capstan); Chestus (possibly to be associated with *La Northernehorchestre* (a furlong) 1305, 'grey or hoar (remains of a) fortification or earthwork', from hār², ceaster, with la, norðerne 'northern', and *Balchester* 1656 which has the same second el., perhaps with balg 'smooth' or ball 'hillock', cf. Balston(e) *supra*); Church Md; Cliff (Fd); Clothing Grd; Cockrams Md (from the *Cockram* family which was here from 17th cent., *v.* Hutch³ 1 673); The Common Fd (cf. *co'ibus campis de Est* —, *West Langton* 1550); Coombe Croft & Md (from Coombe *supra*); Coppice; Course Fds; Cowleaze (or Cut Coppice) (*v.* cut); Cradlers (cf. *Cradelersclose* 1517; the surname (occurring locally 117th cent.—R.J.S.) is from a ME *cradeler* 'one who makes cradles', a hitherto unnoticed occupational term); Cross Md; the Downe (*v.* dūn); Dry Mdw; East Fd(s) & Plain; 18 Acres; 15 Acres; 4 Acres; Furzy Close(s) & Grd, (Lt) Furzy Plot (*v.* fyrsig); Golter (*Goldcherd Croft* (probably for *Golde-*) 1497 (17), *Goldherd* 1656, *v.* gold-hord 'gold hoard', croft, identical in origin with Gaulter in Steeple par. *infra q.v.*); Grove Cowleaze (*v.* grāf(a)); Halls Cmn (from the *Hall* family, in Langton from 15th cent. (R.J.S.)); Hay brimble (probably hege 'hedge' with the Do dial. form *brimble* 'bramble' (Barnes 51), *v.* brēmel; Professor Löfvenberg compares lME *heybrere* 'hedge-briar'); Higher Fds; The Hill, Hills (cf. *La Hulle* 1305, *pastur' super montem* 1550, *Hills close* 1695, *v.* hyll); Home Cl, Fd, Md & Plot; In Hooks (*v.* inhōke); Iron Box (perhaps derogatory for hard ground; it is a small, irregularly shaped, field bordered by three larger fields); Island (perhaps from ēg-land in some figurative sense); King's Arms Inn (earlier (c. 1750) *The Mason's Arms* (R.J.S.)); Lane; (The) Linch (*v.* hlinc); Little Md; Long Cl; Long Md (— meadow 1656, *v.* lang¹, mǣd); Maslins Md; Meadow; Middle Fd (—*feild* 1656), Grd & Plot; The Moor (*the Moore* 1656, *v.* mōr); Nackers Hole (1695, no doubt 'pit or hollow used by a knacker', *v.* knacker, hol¹, cf. Gl 3 240); New Cl (1695, *v.* nīwe, clos(e)); New Ho Gdn; Next the Brook; 9 Acres; (Yonder) Norledge (*Binorthelude* 1305, *Norled(e)* 1517, 1550, *Northeled* 1519, *Norleddes* 1550, '(place) to the north of the seat or ledge', *v.* bī, norðan, hlēda, hlȳda, cf. Benledge *supra*); The Park, Parks (cf. *La Parruk* 1305, *v.* park, pearroc); Parsonage Plot (held by Rector of Studland (R.J.S.)); Plot & Cow Pens; Potatoe Plot; Priory Cl (once part of the lands of Wilkswood priory *supra*); Purbecks Fd (from a surname *Purbecke*, found locally in 18th cent., derived from the p.n., *v.* Isle of Purbeck *supra*); Quaggy Brakes ('thickets on boggy or marshy ground', *v.* quaggy, brǣc¹); Rough Grd; Rushy Plot; Savages 1861 (from the *Savage* family who were here between 1769 and 1809); 7 Acres (*Seaven acres* 1656, *v.* seofon, æcer); Sheeps Leat (*v.* scēap, slǣget); Sherwoods Fd & Wear (*v.* ware); Ship Inn; Shoemakers Shop; 6 Acres; Small Plot; Spring Md; Square Cl; Strapps (*v.* strap); Taylors Ware (cf. Henry *Taillur* 1361, *v.* ware); Threepenny Cl (with reference to a rent (R.J.S.)); 12 Acres; Two Lays (possibly from lǣs, but cf. *la lea* 1278 (1372) (p), *La Leye* 1305, *v.* la, lēah); The Ware(s) (*v.* ware); West Md(w); Wood (cf. *Wo(o)d(e) close* 1519, 1550, *v.* wudu, clos).

(b) *Asknollestone* 1423 ('farm or stone at *Asknolle*', from tūn or stān and a lost p.n. from æsc 'ash-tree' and cnoll 'hillock'); *Binetheton* 1305 ('(place) beneath the farm', *v.* beneoðan, tūn); *Broad meadow* 1656; *Broadwathe*

1656 (v. brād, cf. *Bitakewathe infra*); *Chalkottes Closys* 1528 (cf. William *Chaldecote* 1415, v. clos(e)); *Cledon* 1304 (v. clǣg, dūn); *Copped close* 1656 (v. coppod); *Croft meadow, Higher Croft* 1656 (v. croft); *Digon Haies* 1497 (17) (the pers.n. or surname *Digon*, a diminutive of *Dick*, v. (ge)hæg); *La Eldedon* 1305 (v. (e)ald, dūn, cf. Eldon in Corfe C. par. *supra* and *La Eldedoune* in Swanage par. *infra*); *Estcopse* 1550 (v. ēast, copis); *La Gore* (1305 (v. gāra); *la Grene* 1278 (1372) (p), *atte Grene* 1340 (p) (v. la, atte(n), grēne², cf. The Hyde *supra*); *Grenehaye* 1550 (v. grēne¹, (ge)hæg); *La Hethfeld* 1305, *Hethfilde(close)* 1550 (v. hǣð, feld, clos(e)); *Horse crofts* 1656; *Hunger hill* 1656 (a nickname for poor land, v. hungor, hyll); *Lambecroft* 1305 (v. lamb, croft); *La Littlecroft* 1305 (v. lȳtel); *Littledon, Northlittleton* 1305 (v. norð, lȳtel, dūn or tūn); *la lone* 1278 (1372) (p) (v. lane); *Lotericlos* 1305 (probably for *Loterisclos*, cf. William *Loter* 1322, v. clos(e)); *La Newecroft* 1305 (v. nīwe, croft); *La Newemede* 1305 (v. nīwe, mǣd); *Binorthcumbe* 1305 ('(place) to the north of the valley', v. bī, norðan, cumb); *Paynesclose* 1519 (cf. Bartholomew *Payne* 1304); *pecia terre voc' le Perche* 1550 (v. perche); *Rughull* 1423 (v. rūh, hyll); *La Rys* 1305 (v. hrīs); *Severall wathe* 1656 (v. severell 'privately owned land', cf. *Bitakewathe infra*); *Shaphaies* 1656 (v. scēap, (ge)hæg); *La Sleyacre* 1305 (v. æcer; the first el. could be slege 'slaying, slaughter', but Professor Löfvenberg suggests that it is probably an early instance of dial. *slay, sley, sleigh* 'sheep pasture', on which v. Löfvenberg SMSp **17** 93–4, Sundby SNPh **27** 105–7); *Smelecombesheved* 1305 ('head of *Smelecombe*' ('the narrow valley'), v. smæl, cumb, hēafod); *the South field* 1695 (v. sūð, feld); *Bitakewathe* 1305 (*Bi*- represents bī '(place) near'; *-take-* may be identical with the first el. of Acton *supra*; *-wathe* is probably (ge)wæd 'ford', perhaps used here in a more general sense of 'place for going, (sheep) walk' (cf. OE *wadan* 'to go, move') as suggested by the occurrence of several other early instances of *-wath(e)* in this parish (v. *Broad-, Severall- supra, Thorne-, Biwest-, Wulliewath(e)* and *Wath infra*) and by the cliff-top fields called The Wathe and *Holcombe Wath* in Swanage par. *infra q.v.*; for the development *-d* > *-th*, cf. *Wathe* Wt 202, 285); *La Thorne* 1305, *ponfald d'ni apud le Thurne* 1423 (v. þorn, þyrne, pund-fald; possibly to be associated with the two small lost DB manors of *Torne*, for which v. Durnford *supra* and note on lost p.ns. in Rowbarrow hundred *supra*, cf. foll.; the 'lord's pinfold or pound' (mentioned in a court roll for the manor of Langton Wallis) probably refers to Court Pound *supra*); *La Thornewathe* 1305 (v. þorn, cf. prec., *Bitakewathe supra*); *Three acres meadow* 1656; *La Trencheye* 1305 (v. trenche, (ge)hæg); *Wath* 1497 (17) (cf. *Bitakewathe supra*); *the west coppice* 1585; *le Westdon* 1429 (v. west, dūn); *Wester furlong* 1656 (v. westerra, furlang); *Westhaie, -hay* 1656 (v. west, (ge)hæg); *Biwestwath* 1305 (v. bī, westan or west, cf. *Bitakewathe supra*); *atte Westyate* 1322 (p) (v. atte(n), west, geat); *Whitemans haies* 1656 (v. (ge)hæg); *Wilshewode Meade* 1550 (from Wilkswood *supra*, v. mǣd); *La Wowelonde* 1305 (v. wōh, land); *La Wulliewathe* 1305 (*Wullie*- may be 'wolves' clearing' or 'wool clearing', from wulf (gen.pl. *wulfa*) or wull, and lēah, cf. *Bitakewathe supra*).

Studland

Three small tenements on the shores of Poole Harbour – Goddins, Green-land, and Phillips – were in Corfe C. par. *supra* in 1795 Boswell but are now in Studland. There have been small changes in the bdy between Studland and Swanage since 1840 *TA*.

STUDLAND (SZ 035825)

Stollant 1086 DB, *Stodlant* 1205 P
Stodland(e) 1210 P, 1213 ClR, PatR, 1235–6 Fees, 1248 *Weld*[2] *et freq* to 1514 *Ct*, *-lond(e)* 1242–3 Fees, 1255 Pap *et freq* to 1514 *Ct*, *-laund(e)* 1274 Cl, 1275 RH, 1286 Pat, 1288 *Ass*, *Stodelond(e)* 1387 Fine, 1409 *EgCh*, 1556 *PlR*, *-lande* 1543 *ib*
Stotlaund 1280, 1288 *Ass*
Stoudlond 1327 *SR*, 1332 SR, 1398 *Cecil* (— *iuxta Swanewiche, Swanewyche Stoudlond*), 1414 FF, 1543 *Ct*, *Stond-* (sic) 1339 Cl, *Stoude-* 1431 FA, *Stowde-* c. 1500 *RoyRoll*, *Stoodland* 1521 *Swan*
Stodeley (*in Purbyk*) 1385 Pat
Studlond 1512, 1546 *Ct*, *-land* 1512 *Ct*, 1575 Saxton, 1811 OS

'Tract of land where a herd of horses is kept', *v.* stōd, land, cf. Stot Fd in Corfe C. par. *supra*. The form from 1385 Pat shows confusion of the second el. with lēah, cf. Isle of Purbeck *supra*, Swanage par. *infra*.

BROWNSEA ISLAND (SZ 020880)

(*in portu de*) *Brunkes'* 1235, *Brunckes'* 1276 Cl
Brunkesey(e) 1241 Lib, 1275 Pat, 1276 Cl, 1280 *Ass*, 1302 Pat, Cl, 1303 *ib*, 1535–43 Leland, *Brumkeseye* 1318 Ch, *Bruncksee* 1576 Hutch[3], *Brun(c)ksey* c. 1586 Tres, 1597 *DROMap*
Broncheshe 1291 Tax, *Bronkesye* 1319 *MinAcct*, *Bronkesie* 1331 Douce, *Bronkeseye* 1341 (1792) *DCMDeed*, 1381 Misc, *Bronkseye* 1581 Hutch[3]
Brounkeseye 1381 (16) *Pitt*, *Brounk(e)see* 1546, 1547 *Ct*, *Brownecksey* Eliz Hutch[3]
Brymbesey Yle 1539 LP
Brow'sea, Bro'sey 1545 Hutch[3], *Brounsey alias Brunckesey* Eliz *ib*, *Brownesey* e17 Cecil, *Brownsea Island* 1811 OS, 1826 Gre
Branksey 1575 Saxton, 1695 Camd, *Branksea Island* 1773 Bayly, *Brenksey* 1695 Camd

Probably 'Brūnoc's island', from an unrecorded OE pers.n. *Brūnoc*, a derivative of *Brūn*, and ēg, as suggested in DEPN, with ile, ēg-land. Fägersten 125 follows a suggestion by Zachrisson that the first el. is an OE *brunc*, a gradation variant of an OE *brinc* which would be related to ODan brink 'brink, edge of a bank' (*v.* EPN s.v.), but preservation of the long vowel favours the pers.n.

CLAYWELL (SY 996843), 1667, 1728 Hutch³, *Cleywoll* 1332 SR (p), 'clay spring or stream', *v.* clæg, wella, from a stream flowing N into Poole Harbour and forming the Studland–Corfe C. bdy here, or from the spring marked 6" ¼ mile S, cf. *Clay Pits* 1826 Gre marked near here, and Clay Washing Beds and Newton Clay Works (both 6") ¾ mile NW, cf. Newton *infra*.

DEAN HILL (SZ 018817), cf. *Dene* 1449 FF, 1457 IpmR, *le Deane Hegge* 1546 PlR, *Dean(s)*, *Dean Md* 1840 *TA*, *v.* denu 'valley', hecg.

THE FORELAND or HANDFAST POINT (SZ 055825), *Hanfast* l16 Hutch³, *Studland castle*, — *Castell alias Hanfast Point* 1575 Saxton, c. 1586 Tres, *Handefaste, -feste Pointe* 1583 SPDom, *Handfast Point* 1861 Hutch³, *Studland Poynte* e17 Cecil, *Foreland* 1811 OS, cf. *Handfast Bay in Purbyke* c. 1500 RoyRoll. The Foreland is foreland 'cape, headland' as in N Foreland K 603. Handfast is probably 'rock stronghold', *v.* hān, fæsten, but 'high stronghold', *v.* hēah (wk.obl. *hēan*), is also possible, in either case with reference to Studland Castle *infra* or an earlier fort here, *v.* point. As a final el. OE fæsten was usually reduced in ME to -*fast*, cf. Buckfast D 293; for the development *Han-* to *Hand-*, *v.* Phonol.

GOATHORN PIER, PLANT. & POINT (SZ 015863), *Gotowre super Mare* 1286 Pat, *Gotoure* n.d. (e15) *MiltRoll*, *Gotehorn point* 1575 Saxton, *Gothorne* c. 1586 Tres, *Goattown-Paine* (sic) 1774 Hutch¹, *Goathorn(e)* 1774 ib, 1811 OS, *Goat Ord Point* 1852 Legg, probably 'bank or shore where goats were kept', *v.* gāt, ōra¹ (replaced by horn and ord), with point, but gotu, gote 'water-course, channel, stream' is also possible for the first el. For the el. ōra¹, cf. Fitzworth and Ower in Corfe C. par. *supra*, both like Goathorn on small promontories on the shore of Poole Harbour. The modern name may be due to the fact that the promontory is 'in form somewhat resembling the horn of a goat' (Hutch³ 1 675), but it has probably also been influenced by Ramshorn Lake in Corfe C. par. *supra*, cf. also Redhorn *infra*. For a fuller reference to the first form, cf. Newton *infra*.

GODDINS (lost), 1861 Hutch³, *Goddynge* 1561, 1571 ib, *Godins* c.1586 Tres, 1774 Hutch¹, *Godwins* 1633 Hutch³, 1839 *TA*, *Goddens* 1694 Hutch³, a tenement named from Thomas *Goodwin* who was granted lands here in 1545 Hutch³, situated E of Newton *infra* at about SZ 017847; like Phillips *infra* it was formerly in Corfe C. par. (1795 Boswell) but appears in Swanage *TA*.

KING'S WOOD, KINGSWOOD FM (SZ 002819) & HEATH, *Kyngeswode* 1397 Pat, *Kynswood* 1546 *Ct*, *Kingswood* (*Fm*) 1774 Hutch¹, 1826 Gre, *Kingswood Coppice & Heath* 1840 *TA*, *Kingswood wood* 1861 Hutch³, 'the king's wood', *v.* cyning, wudu, also giving its name to Kingswood Down in Corfe C. par. *supra*.

NEWTON (SZ 013849), 1575 Saxton, c. 1586 Tres, *Nyweton* 1404 Cl, 1431 FA, 'new farm or village', *v.* nīwe, tūn. An ambitious proposal in 1286 Pat 'to lay out, with sufficient streets and lanes and adequate sites for a market and church and plots for merchants and others, a new town with a harbour in a place called Gotowre super Mare, in the parish of Studland and on the King's land' refers to this place, although it was probably never more than a tiny hamlet, cf. Goathorn *supra*. In the bounds of Ower in Corfe C. par. *supra*, there is mention of *via vocat' Nywtonyswey* n.d. (e15) *MiltRoll*, 'the road to Newton', *v.* weg.

PHIL(L)IPS (lost), 1774 Hutch¹, 1861 Hutch³, *Phelpescroft* 1498 *Ct*, *Phylippes croffte* 1545, — *Crafft* 1546 both *Ct*, *Philippes* 1560, *Phelp(e)s* 1561, 1667 all Hutch³, 1839 *TA*, *Phelipes* 1571, 1586 Hutch³, *Philps* c. 1586 Tres, from the pers.n. or surname *Philip* (for the forms *Phelp*, *Philp*, *v.* Reaney 250), cf. John *Phelippes* 1487 Hutch³, and croft; this tenement, like Goddins *supra* near to which it was situated, was formerly in Corfe C. par.

SALTERNE (SZ 029836), 1454, 1489 *Ct*, (*West* —) 1543 *PlR*, *Saltorne* 1556 ib, c. 1586 Tres, cf. *Salterne Marshe* 1546 *PlR*, (*Lt*) *Salterns*, *Salterns Mdw*, *Fords Break or Salterns* 1840 *TA*, 'building(s) where salt was made or sold', *v.* salt-ærn, west, mersc; there were 32 salt-pans (*saline*) at Studland in 1086 DB, *v.* DBGeography 111–12, VCHDo **3** 22, 88, cf. Saltings in Corfe C. par. *supra* and Salterns Copse in Arne par. *infra* for other references to the salt industry in Purbeck. *Fords Break* is from the surname *Ford* (cf. John *Foord* 1664 HTax), and bræc¹.

STUDLAND CASTLE (lost), 1732 Coker, *castellum de Studlande, the Castle of Stodland* 1381 (16) Pitt, *Studland castle*, — *Castell alias Hanfast Point* 1575 Saxton, c. 1586 Tres, cf. *Castell Leyes* c. 1586 ib, *E & W Castle* (fields) 1840 *TA*, somewhat contemptuously described in 1732 Coker as 'a block-house, for the more grace called Studland Castle'; it was situated on the promontory called The Foreland or Handfast Point *supra*, *v.* castel(l), læs.

AGGLESTONE, 1811 OS, — or *Stone Barrow* 1774 Hutch[1], *Adlingston* c. 1586 Tres, *-stone or Agglestone* 1861 Hutch[3], *Aglestone* 1773 Bayly, 'a very remarkable insulated block of iron-stone... about 80 feet in circumference and nearly 20 in height' (Kelly); according to 1774 Hutch[1] 1 217 'the country people call it *The Devil's Night-Cap*; and have a romantic tradition that the Devil, out of envy, threw it from the Isle of Wight, with a design to demolish Corfe Castle; but it fell short, and dropped here' (cf. also Udal 172); Hutch[1] *loc. cit.* suggests derivation from hālig and stān, 'holy stone', and Arkell (1940) 40 suggests OE *hagolstān* 'hailstone', but the 16th-cent. spelling shows that the name probably means 'prince's stone', from æðeling and stān, cf. Adlingfleet YW 2 2, Allington par. *infra*. BALLARD CLIFF, DOWN (1811 OS, *Studland downe* c. 1586 Tres) & POINT, cf. *Ballard Hole* 1811 OS (caves marked 6″), *the Ballard Head* 1861 Hutch[3], *Bollard Head* 1882 Robinson, perhaps 'smooth or rounded headland or promontory', *v.* balg, hēafod, but the forms are too late for any certainty. An offshore rock is *Argyle Rock* 1882 Robinson (from a ship wrecked here c. 1800). BARNES' BOTTOM, *v.* botm. BENTINCK HILL, no doubt from the Rt. Hon. G. A. Frederick Cavendish Bentinck who partly restored Brownsea Castle *infra* in 1888 (Kelly), cf. Cavendish Rd, Frederick Hill, Mount Frederick and Portland Ave & Hill *infra*, all on Brownsea Island. BLACK DOWN, *Blak downe* c. 1586 Tres, *v.* blæc, dūn. BLOOD ALLEY (local), a channel in Poole Harbour (Legg 169). BRAMBLE BUSH BAY. BRAND'S BAY, FORD & POINT, cf. *claus' voc' Brondes* 1543, *Brondis* 1556 both PlR, *Brands* c. 1586 Tres, *Brand's Bay* 1661 Hutch[1], *Brands Paddock* 1840 *TA*, cf. John *Brond* 1327 SR, 1332 SR, Henry *Brand* 1525 *AOMB*; a *Quay* is marked near Brand's Point in 1811 OS. BROWNSEA CASTLE, *the castle of Brow'sea, ye castell of Bro'sey* 1545, *(the) castell(e) of Bronkse(y)* 1547, 1550, *the queen's majesty's castell of Brownecksey* 1562 all Hutch[3], *Brownsey Castell, Bromsey Castill* 1583 *SPDom*, *Bruncksey Cast'* c. 1586 Tres, *the*

Castle e17 *Cecil*, — *or fortress of Bronkesey* 1679 Hutch[3], built in 1545 (Kelly), *v.* castel(l), cf. Brownsea Island *supra*. BROWNSEA RD, a channel in Poole Harbour, *v.* road. BROWN'S LANE. CABBAGE HILL. CAMBRIDGE WD, one of several English transferred names of recent origin on Brownsea Island, cf. Lincoln Cliff, Lonsdale Rd *&* Wd, Oxford Wd, St Michael's Mount and Westminster Rd *infra*. CAROLINE CLIFF. CAVENDISH RD, cf. Bentinck Hill *supra*. CHURCH HILL, from St Mary's Church *infra*. CLOWN HILL, one of a group of four fanciful hill names on Brownsea Island taken from pantomime, cf. Columbine Hill, Harlequin Hill and Pantaloon Hill *infra*. COLUMBINE HILL, cf. prec. CURLEW CTGS. DEVIL'S DEN, on Brownsea Island, cf. Old Harry *infra*. DROVE ISLAND, 1839 *TA* (Swanage), *Grove Island* 1774 Hutch[1], 1811 OS, from grāf(a), replaced by drove, cf. Stone Island *infra*. EAST LAKE (SIDE), onc of two small pieces of water on Brownsea Island, *v.* lake, cf. West Lake (Side) *infra*. ELIZABETH HILL. FARM BLDGS, *Buildings* 1840 *TA*. FISHING BARROW, a tumulus named from a nearby ditch (Legg 108), *v.* fishing. FREDERICK HILL, cf. Bentinck Hill *supra*. GLEBELAND ESTATE. GODLINGSTON HEATH, 1811 OS, from Godlingston in Swanage par. *infra*. GOTCHABED CTGS (lost), near South Haven Point *infra* (Legg 79). GRAVEL HILL *&* POINT. GREEN DALE. GREENLAND, 1774 Hutch[1], doubtless so called because 'taken out of the wast' (1774 Hutch[1] **1** 219), *v.* grēne[1], land; this tenement, like Goddins and Phillips *supra*, was formerly in Corfe C. par. *supra*. HARLEQUIN HILL, cf. Clown Hill *supra*. HARLEY WD. HARMONY LODGE. HARRY POINT, a pointed mud-bank off Brownsea Island, perhaps the pers.n. *Harry* but cf. foll. HARRY WARREN HO, named from The Warren Wd *infra* which may earlier have been called *Harry Warren*, probably from Old Harry *infra* but possibly from a pers.n. or surname *Harry*, cf. William *Hery* 1340 NI; on the other hand the first el. should perhaps be compared with that of *le Haryleche* in Swanage par. *infra*. HILL POINT, 1811 OS. JERRY'S POINT, *Gerie Orde* c. 1586 Tres, from the ME pers.n. or surname *Geri* (*v.* Reaney 132 s.n. *Geary*), and ord, replaced by point, cf. Redhorn Quay *infra*. KING BARROW, cf. *Kings Barrow Bottom* 1840 *TA*, a tumulus, *v.* cyning, beorg, botm, cf. Kings Furlong *infra*. KNOLL HO, KNOWL HILL, *v.* cnoll. LINCOLN CLIFF, cf. Cambridge Wd *supra*. LITTLE SEA, 1811 OS, a brackish pool. THE LODGE. LONSDALE RD *&* WD, probably a transferred name from Lonsdale La, We, cf. Cambridge Wd *supra*. MANOR HO. MARYLAND, perhaps a transferred name from Maryland, U.S.A.

MEAD POINT. MIDDLE ST. MOUNT FREDERICK, cf. Bentinck Hill
supra. NELSON HILL, perhaps from Admiral Nelson, cf. Wellington
Hill *infra* also on Brownsea Island. NEWTON COPSE & HEATH (1811
OS), from Newton *supra*. NOGGETS, the name of a strip of wood on
the N slope of the main Purbeck ridge near the Studland–Corfe C.
bdy, and in fact also found as the name (*Noggetts*) of four fields in the
Corfe C. *TA* (1844) clustered around the ancient Stone Circle just
on the Corfe C. side of the bdy, cf. Rempstone in Corfe C. par.
supra. The stones in the circle are 'irregularly-shaped boulders of
hard gritstone' (RCHMDo **2** 513), and the name Noggets probably
means 'lumps (of stone)' with reference to these, from ModE *nugget*
(NED from 1852, Barnes 85 'a small knob' (of cheese)), no doubt a
derivative of SW dial. *nug* 'a lump, block', Do dial. **nog** 'a big
knob' (of cheese) (Barnes *loc. cit.*) of unknown origin, *v.* -et(t)(e).
No MAN'S LAND (local), a detached piece of cliff (Legg 167). NORTH
ST. OAK CORNER. OLD HARRY, *ye Pinakell* 116 Hutch³, *Old Harry
rock* 1765 Tayl, *the Pinnacle or Old Harry* 1774 Hutch¹, the largest
of two sea-stacks of chalk (*v.* foll.) at the tip of the Foreland or
Handfast Point *supra*, from **pinnacle** 'any natural peaked formation'
(NED sense 2), cf. The Pinnacles *infra*, and **old harry**, a familiar
name for the devil, cf. Old Nick's Grd *infra* which is nearby and
Devil's Den *supra* with their similar allusions; it probably gave name
to Harry Warren Ho *supra*. OLD HARRY'S WIFE, a sea-stack next to
prec., collapsed 1896; besides his 'wife', other rocks were known
as his 'daughter' and his 'haystack' (Robinson 155). OLD NICK'S
GRD, *Old Nicks Grd & Cliff Fd* 1840 *TA*, the name given to the
length of cliff running SW from Old Harry *q.v. supra*, from **old nick**,
a familiar name for the devil. OXFORD WD, cf. Cambridge Wd *supra*.
PANTALOON HILL, cf. Clown Hill *supra*. PARSON'S BARN, 1882
Robinson, a jocular name for the large cave once used by smugglers
below Old Nick's Grd *supra*, cf. the Do proverbial saying 'Just like
a parson's barn' (Udal 301), and cf. St Lucas Leap *infra*. PENELOPE
PARK, cf. *Park* 1840 *TA*, no doubt from *Penelope*, wife of the Rt.
Hon. G. A. F. Cavendish Bentinck, cf. Bentinck Hill *supra, v.* **park**.
THE PENS. PHEASANT HILL. THE PINNACLES, *Pinnacles* 1811 OS,
two tall pointed rocks, *v.* **pinnacle**, cf. Old Harry *supra*. PIPER'S
FOLLY, *v.* **folie**, cf. The Folley *infra*. PIPLEY BRIDGE. PORTLAND
AVE & HILL, probably from the Dukes of *Portland*, the Cavendish
Bentincks, cf. Bentinck Hill *supra*. POTTERY PIER, on Brownsea
Island, with reference to the potteries established here in 19th cent.

PUCKSTONE, 1774 Hutch[1], -*ston* 1861 Hutch[3], a 'similar curiosity' (Kelly) to the nearby Agglestone *supra*, 'goblin's stone', *v.* pūca, stān. QUAY CTGS, named from *Key* c. 1770 *DCMMap*, *v.* key. RECTORY, cf. *Rectory Gdn, Parsonage Ho & Cl* 1840 *TA*, Parson's Barn *supra*. REDEND POINT, *The Red Cliff* 1882 Robinson, a worn-down promontory, *v.* rēad, ende. RED HILL. REDHORN LAKE, 1811 OS, a channel in Poole Harbour named from foll., *v.* lacu. REDHORN QUAY, *Red Orde* c. 1586 Tres, *Redhorn* 1811 OS, 'red point', *v.* rēad, ord, a small promontory on the shores of Poole Harbour SE of Jerry's Point *supra* which had the same second el., cf. also *Coke Orde, Richeman's Orde infra*; for the substitution of -*horn*, cf. Ramshorn Lake in Corfe C. par. *supra* and Goathorn *supra*. RIALTO BRIDGE, a transferred name on Brownsea Island from the Rialto in Venice, cf. Venetia Park *infra*. ROCKET CORNER. ROSE CTG. ROUGH BRAKE, *v.* bræc[1]. SADDLE BACK, a hill, *v.* saddleback. ST ANDREW'S HILL & TERRACE, cf. *St Andrews or Brownsey Bay* 1661 Hutch[1], presumably from the former chapel and hermitage dedicated to St Andrew built on Brownsea Island by the Abbot of Cerne in the reign of Hy 2 (Kelly). Leland (1 255), writing in 1535-43, says 'ther is yet a chapelle for an heremite, it longid to Cerne Abbay'; in 1774 Hutch[1] 1 219 it is stated that 'the chapel was dedicated to St. Andrew, of which, and the hermitage, there are no remains'. ST ANNE'S HILL, one of three hills on Brownsea Island named from saints, cf. foll. and St Peter's Hill *infra*. ST GEORGE'S HILL, cf. prec. ST LUCAS LEAP, *St. Luca(')s Leap(e)* 1l6 Hutch[1], Hutch[3], used of the gap where the narrow tip of The Foreland or Handfast Point *supra* has been detached by erosion from the mainland, *v.* hlēp 'a place that can be crossed by leaping'; according to Legg 167 it takes its name from a greyhound which fell from the cliff here while coursing a hare, but perhaps the allusion is to Richard *Lucas*, rector of Studland 1536-78 (Hutch[3]), cf. the nearby Parson's Barn *supra*. ST MARK'S LODGE. ST MARY'S CHURCH (Brownsea). ST MICHAEL'S MOUNT, a transferred name from St Michael's Mount Co, cf. Cambridge Wd *supra*. ST NICHOLAS'S CHURCH, cf. 'the church of *Stodlonde*' 1255 Pap, *the Church-lands* ('lying near the church') 1861 Hutch[3]. ST PETER'S HILL, cf. St Anne's Hill *supra*. THE SANCTUARY. SAND PIT (2×), cf. *Pits* 1826 Gre. SEARLEY'S KNAP, cf. Henry *Serle* 1664 HTax (Swanage), *v.* cnæpp. SEYMER'S HILL & HO, *Seymours* c. 1770 *DCMMap*, from the surname *Seymour*, -*mer*. SHELL BAY (1″). SIGNAL (lost), 1811 OS, on Ballard Cliff at

SZ 045813. SOUTH HAVEN POINT, *Sowthe Havyn Poynte* 1539 LP, *South(h)aven Point(e)* 1575 Saxton, 1581 Hutch[3], *South Haven* 1811 OS, at the entrance to Poole Harbour opposite North Haven Point in Parkstone par. *infra*, *v.* sūð, hæfen[1], point. SOUTH SHORE LODGE. SPRING BOTTOM, *v.* spring, botm. STONE ISLAND, 1774 Hutch[1], 1811 OS, *Stony or Grove Island* 1774 Hutch[1], perhaps confused with Drove Island *supra*, *v.* stān, stānig, grāf(a). STONE ISLAND LAKE, a channel in Poole Harbour named from prec., *v.* lacu. STUDLAND BAY, 1579 Hutch[3], *-baye* 1575 Saxton, *Sandlandbaye* (sic) 1539 LP, *v.* bay[1], cf. *Blakepoole* and *Wallcote Lake infra.* STUDLAND BAY HO, cf. prec. STUDLAND FM, HEATH (*Stodelonde Hethe* 1546 *PlR*) *&* WD (l16 Hutch[3], *Stodelande Wodde* 1546 *PlR*), *v.* hǣð, wudu. SWINDALE, perhaps 'pig valley', *v.* swīn, dæl[1]. THORNY BARROW, a tumulus, *v.* pornig, beorg. TRINITY LANE *&* ST. VENETIA PARK, a transferred name on Brownsea Island from Lat *Venetia* (Venice), cf. Rialto Bridge *supra.* THE VILLA. VINERY (HILL), probably vinery 'a glass house or hot-house constructed for the cultivation of the grape vine'. THE WARREN WD, *v.* wareine, giving its name to Harry Warren House *q.v. supra.* WATER LANE (local), Legg 159. WATER POINT, 1839 *TA* (Swanage), *v.* point. WELLINGTON HILL, perhaps from the Duke of Wellington, cf. Nelson Hill *supra.* WEST LAKE (SIDE), cf. East Lake (Side) *supra.* WESTMINSTER RD, cf. Cambridge Wd *supra.* WEST WD, lies W of the village. WHITE GROUND LAKE, *White Ground* 1811 OS, a channel in Poole Harbour, with *ground* probably in the sense of 'the solid bottom or earth underlying the sea or other water' (NED s.v. sense 2), *v.* hwīt, grund, lacu, cf. Middle Ground in Arne par. *infra.* WILDERNESS, *v.* wildernesse. WILLIAM PIT. WILLOW BED. WOODHOUSE (HILL), *Wodhowse* 1543 *PlR* (p), *Woodhouse* 1744 Hutch[1], *Wood House* 1840 *TA*, 'house at a wood', *v.* wudu, hūs; Woodhouse Hill is still wooded.

FIELD-NAMES

Fields in Swanage *TA* but now in Studland are marked †. (For fields in Studland *TA* but now in Swanage, *v.* Swanage par. *infra*). The undated forms are 1840 *TA* 210 (those marked † are 1839 *TA* 214). Spellings dated 1327 are *SR*, 1332 SR, 1340 NI, n.d. (e15) *MiltRoll*, 1454 *Ct*, 1543, 1546, 1547, 1556 *PlR*, c. 1586 Tres, l16[1], Hutch[1], p1600 *DROMap*, e17 *Cecil*, 1664 HTax, c. 1770 *DCMMap*, and the rest Hutch[3].

(a) Aries Fd; Bakers Corner Flg *&* Plot; Barn and Barton; Barn Cowleaze *&* Md; Bell Hill c. 1770 (*v.* belle); Boat Cl (near Ferry Cl *infra*, *v.* bote);

Brick Works c. 1770; Broad Herne (v. hyrne); (Further) Browns Cl (cf. George *Brown* 1713); By fds (probably 'fields at a corner or bend' (here a pronounced bend in the road), v. byge[1]); Cherry hays (v. chiri, (ge)hæg); Chips Pond Cl; Cliff Fd; Common, E & W Common Down (cf. *le Comyn more* 1546, v. comun, mōr); Corbens Furzy Grd (cf. Robert *Corbyn* 1664 (Swanage), v. fyrsig); Cracker Barrow Flg (v. beorg); Cowleaze; Cross Cl; Customs Ho c. 1770; Davies Gdn; Drove; Dukes Cl & Md (cf. Robert *Duke* 1664); East Grd & Md; 8 Acres; Enclosed Heath & Lds; Ferry Cl (v. ferja, cf. Boat Cl *supra*); First, Second & Third Fd on the Hill; Fir Pound Plot (v. pund, cf. Wytch Fir Pound in Corfe C. par. *supra*); The Folley (cf. Piper's Folly *supra*); Furlong under Hedge; Further (outside) Grd; Furzey Cl, Grd, Pce & Plot (v. fyrsig); Garden Pdk; Goodes Cl; †Goulds Ho & Gdn; Granary Grd; Gravely Cl; Great Grd; the Great Pond; Heath Grd (cf. *terra regia vocata Hethfeld* n.d. (e15) (bounds described), (*le*) *Hethefylde*, -*fielde* (*hegge*) 1543, 1556, v. hǣð, feld, hecg); Hicklers End c. 1770; Home Cl & Md; Horse Cl; Lr Horse Croft; Hother Cl; Howards Cl; Kings Flg (near to King Barrow *supra*); Lamberts Well (Cl) (v. wella); Lines (*the laynes* 1556, v. leyne); Little Grd & Md; Lockets; Long Grd, Lds & Mdw; Lower Md; Madling Pit Flg (possibly the surname *Ma(u)dlin* (< *Magdalen*), v. pytt); The Mead; Meadow; Merchants Md; Middle Grd & Md; Moghays (cf. Thomas *Mogge* 1327, 1332, v. (ge)hæg); (The) Moore (v. mōr); Nappy Grd (v. cnæppig); New Cl & Plant.; New Inn 1882 Robinson; New Spring c. 1770; 9 Acres; (Further) Nor Md (possibly from ME *atten ore* '(place) at the bank', v. atte(n), ōra[1], cf. Nore Sr 227); (Gt) North Grd; Paddock; Pea Md; Peat Bog & Fd; Peat Pits c. 1770; Plot; Point Cl; Pond Fields Md (possibly from pund-fald, cf. Ponfill fd in Swanage par. *infra*); Upr Pond Pce; Preston Flg (perhaps from prēost (gen. pl. *prēosta*) and tūn); Red Rock Cl; Rough Grd & Pce; Rushy Md; Sandy Cl & Grd; Shaw Wood Gdn (v. sc(e)aga); Lr Shortlands (v. sc(e)ort, land); 6 Acres; 16 Acres & Heath; South Grd; Spere Bed (Do dial. spear 'stem of a reed', v. bedd); Square Md; Stack Yd and Hovel; Stockford ('ford marked by a stump', v. stocc, ford); Stoney Cl; Late John Talbot's Closes (cf. William *Talbott* 1664); Townsend Cmn (v. toun, ende[1]); Ullwell Hill (from Ulwell in Swanage par. *infra*); Up Hays (v. upp, (ge)hæg); Wash (on the shore of Poole Harbour, v. (ge)wæsc); Waterey or Water barrow 1861 (*Waterey barowe* l16[2], said in Hutch[3] to be situated near the shore, probably therefore 'enclosure near the water', v. wæter, (ge)hæg, with beorg); Water Mdw (cf. prec.);†West Grd; West Md; West Point c. 1770; Whit Hill (Flg) (v. hwīt).

(b) *Alum* 1578 (a wood on Brownsea Island, apparently named from 'certain mines of alum' Eliz, cf. also *coperis mynes* p1600, *the mynes* e17, v. alum, copperas, mine); *ten' voc' Barkers* 1454 (the surname *Barker*); *Blakepoole* c. 1586 (part of what is now Studland Bay *supra*, v. blæc, pōl); *Chyme Silver* 1578 (a wood on Brownsea Island, perhaps a nickname for productive land, or denoting land which provided money for church bells); *Coke Orde* c. 1586 (a promontory N of Redhorn Quay *q.v. supra*, with a first el. cocc[1] or cocc[2], but cf. Sir Edward *Coke* who held the manor of Studland e17, v. ord); *Cornerdych* n.d. (e15), *Cornediche Hedge* 1556 (v.

corner, dīc, hecg); *le est Fylde* 1543 (*v.* ēast, feld); *Hotegosmere* n.d. (e15) (in bounds of *Hethfeld supra, v.* (ge)mǣre 'boundary', cf. John *Hotego* 1327, — *Hotygo* 1332 (Arne)); *Longhay* 1547 (*v.* lang[1], (ge)hæg); *ten' voc' Lycchettis* 1454 (a surname from Lytchett Mat. or Min. par. *infra*); *la lymepytt* 1546 (*v.* lim-pytt); *a lype yeat* (*v.* hlīep-geat); *Okey ryge* 1546, *Okerige* 1547 (probably 'ridge or strip of ground at *Okey* ('oak enclosure')', *v.* āc, (ge)hæg, hrycg); *Portewey* n.d. (e15) (*v.* port-weg); *Riche-* 116[1], *Rickman's Orde* 116[2] (a promontory N of Jerry's Point *q.v. supra*, from the surname *Rich-*, *Rickman* and ord); *Ryecroft* c. 1586 (*v.* ryge, croft); *le Salte Moris* 1546 (*v.* salt, mōr); *Stoney Barowe* 116[2] (*v.* stānig, beorg, but the first part of the name could be 'stone enclosure', *v.* stān, (ge)hæg); *Wallcote Lake* c. 1586 (part of what is now Studland Bay *supra*, probably 'cottage of the Welshmen or serfs', *v.* walh (gen. pl. *wala*), cot, with lake 'pool'); *ten' voc' Wateris* 1454 (the pers.n. or surname *Wa(l)ter*); *le Weane Shord* 1546, *Wenesherde* 1547 ('a gap fit for a wagon', *v.* wægn, sceard, cf. Wainscarre Nt 69 and Wainscarth Cu 343, of identical meaning but with the ON cognate skarð as second el.); *le West Fylde* 1543 (*v.* west, feld); *Stodelande Whettefylde* 1543 (*v.* hwǣte, feld); *ten' voc' Wolriggys* 1454 (the surname *Woolridge*).

Swanage

Swanage was included in the ecclesiastical par. of Worth Mat. until c. 1500 (Hutch[3] I 656). A small part of Langton Mat. par. was transferred to Swanage in 1933 (Kelly), and there have also been small changes in the bdy between Swanage and Studland since 1839 *TA*.

SWANAGE (SZ 032788) [ˈswɔnidʒ]

 (*æt*) *Swanawic* l9 ASC (A), 12 ib (E) both s.a. 877

 Suanauuic, -vine (sic), *Suanewic* 893 (e11) Asser

 Swan-, Sonwic 1086 DB, *Swanwic, Sonwich* Exon

 Suanewiz 1186, *-wic* 1210 P (p), *-wik* 1212 Fees, *-wyk* 1268 *Ass*,   *Swanewiz, -wyz* Hy 3 Ipm, 1243 Fees, 1252 FF, 1285 FA,   *-wic, -wyc* 1228 Ch, 1264 Ipm, 1264 FineR, 1280 *Ass, -wich(e)*,   *-wych(e)* 1270 AD I, 1290 Fine, 1303 FA *et freq* to 1448 *Weld*[1],   *-wik, -wyk* 1280, 1288 *Ass*, 1305 Ipm, *-wick* 1280 *Ass, Swanne-*   *wic* 1230 Cl (p), *-wych(e)* 1428 FA, 1545 *Ct, Swandewyche*   1539 LP

 Swaneswic 1213 ClR, *-wich, -wych* 1243 Fees, 1291 Tax, *-wyk*   1280 *Ass, Swanneswych* 1350 Cl

 Swanwych(e), -wich(e) 1244 *Ass*, 1269 Pat, 1280 AD I, 1293 Cl (p)   *et freq* to 1603 *Swan, Swanwyche in Purbyke* 1479 *Mow, Swan-*   *wyke* 1409 Cl, *Svonwich* 15 *ShaftR, Swandwych(e)* 1402 Pat,   1545 *DCMDeed, Swannwiche* 1514 *Ct*

Swaynewych(e), *-wich* 1291 Tax, 1305 Cl
Sanwyche, *-wich(e)* 1525 *AOMB*, 1543, 1546 *Ct*, 1608 *Swan*,
Sawndwiche 1546 *Ct*, *Sandwich(e)*, *-wyche* 1535–43 Leland,
1547 *Ct*, 1557 *Mow* (— *alias Swanwiche*), 1566, 1590 *Swan*,
1656 *Mow* (— *otherwise Swanwich*), 1795 Boswell (— *or Swan-
nage*), 1828 *DCMDeed* (— *otherwise Swanage otherwise Sand-
wythe otherwise Swanythe otherwise Swanwyche*), *Sanewiche*
1575 Saxton, *Sandwidge alias Swannidge* 1630 (17) *DCMDeed*,
Sandwitch 1664 *GW*
Swanich or Swanwick Eliz ChancP
Swanwidge 1617 (17) *DCMDeed*, *Swanidge* 1664 HTax, *Swanage*
1811 OS

Probably 'dairy-farm of the herdsmen or peasants', *v.* swān[2]
(gen.pl. *swāna*), wīc, but swan[1] (gen.pl. *swana*) 'swan' is equally
possible for the first el., in which case the name might mean 'swannery' as suggested in DEPN, cf. Swanwick Db 189, Ha (DEPN).
The spelling *San(d)wich*, etc common from 16th cent. has no doubt
been influenced by Sandwich Kt (first el. sand 'sand') as well as by
popular etymology. There was a lodge of the forest of Purbeck 'on a
hillock near Swanwich, where there are ruins of a wind-mill' (Hutch[3]
1 463), cf. Isle of Purbeck *supra*, Windmill Knap in Langton Mat.
par. *supra*. The rectory here was called 'the rectory of *Swanwich*,
alias Worth Swanwich' 1561 Hutch[3] 1 693, cf. Worth Mat. par. *infra*
and note on ecclesiastical history *supra*.

STREET-NAMES

BATTLE MEAD, cf. BATTLEGATE (TPlan) which is *Battlemill Gate* 1839 *TA*,
according to Hardy 4 'named after a meadow a little to the north in which
a battle was fought with the Danes'; BONDFIELDS AVE, cf. *Bonfields Md*
1839 *TA*, William *de Boneuile de Withelyue* (sic, *v.* Whitecliff *infra*) 1288 *Ass*,
'tenement which was John Bonvill's' 1291 Hutch[3], and Bonvils Fm in
Worth Mat. par. *infra*; BRICKYARD LANE (TPlan), named from the Brick-
works ib; BURNHAMS LANE (TPlan), beside which is *Tom Burnham's Oak*
(local), named from a suicide's burial here (Legg 123); CAULDON AVE, cf.
Cauldon Lane 1557, *viam apud Cawdon* (sic) 1566 both *Mow*, named from
Caldron *infra*, *v.* lane; CHAPEL LANE (TPlan), probably named from the
Wesley Memorial Church ib, but cf. 'the chapel of *Swan(e)wych*, *-wich*'
1406, 1441 Pat; CHURCH HILL, cf. *Church Md* 1839 *TA*, 'the parish church
of *Swanwich*' 1459 Pat, *ecclesie de Sandwich* 1566 *Swan*; COURT RD, probably
named from the lost Court or Carrants Court Fm *infra*; DARKY LANE
(TPlan); EEL POND LANE (lost), Legg 100; ELDON TERRACE, from the Earl

of Eldon who had property in Swanage (M.H.); GANNETTS PARK, cf.
Gannetts 1839 *TA*, Edward *Gannett* 1664 HTax (Wootton G.); HERSTON
YARDS (TPlan), *-y(e)ard(e)* 1566 *Swan et freq, Hersetons Yerd* 1525 *AOMB*,
Eason Yards 1839 *TA, v.* Herston *infra*, geard or gerd; HIGH ST., cf.
Swanage St. 1861 Hutch³; HOWARD RD (TPlan), cf. *Howard Court Md* 1839
TA, Elizabeth *Howard* 1664 HTax, *v.* court; ISLE OF WIGHT RD, a cliff road
from which the Isle of Wight can be seen; LIGHTHOUSE RD, named from
the Lighthouse (6″); MANOR RD, from 'The Manor House', later a hotel
which had its name changed to 'The Victoria' in 1835 to commemorate
Princess Victoria's stay there (Hutch³ 1 657); DE MOULHAM RD, from the
family named from Moulham *infra*; THE NARROWS (local); NORTHBROOK
RD, from the lost Northbrook or Norbrook Fm *infra*; ROUND THE HEAD, the
path round the promontory of Durlston Head *infra*; SENTRY RD, cf. *Sentry*
1839 *TA*, the site of an observation post (Short 15), from eModE sentry
'a watch-tower'; STRECHE RD, cf. *Dionisia Stretche tenet apud Oulewell*
1326 *Ext*, cf. Ulwell *infra*; SUNNYDALE RD, cf. *Sunnydale (Valley)* 1882
Robinson; TOWNSEND RD, cf. *Townsend* 1861 Hutch³, *v.* toun, ende¹;
ULWELL RD, named from Ulwell *infra*; WASHPOND LANE (TPlan). Lost
street-names are *The Drong* 19 Legg, *v.* drong; *Hillane, Hyllan(e)* 1557
Mow, v. hyll, lane; *Millane* 1557 *ib, v.* myln. *Anchor Inn* is mentioned 1882
Robinson.

GODLINGSTON FM formerly MANOR HO (6″), GODLINGSTON MANOR
(1″) (SZ 015802)

> *Godlington* (als. *Golinton*) 1299 Ipm, *Godelyngton* 1381 IpmR,
> *Godelington* 1426 ib, *Godlyngton* 1546 *Ct, Godlington* 1795
> Boswell, 1825 Gre
>
> *Godelyng(e)ston* 1345, 1378 FF *et freq* to 1457 IpmR, *Godelingston*
> 1408 ib *Godlyngston* 1413 FF *et freq* to c. 1500 *RoyRoll*,
> *Godlingston* 1458 Hutch³, c. 1586 Tres
>
> *Gedelyngston* 1367 FF
>
> *Cothelynston* 1383 ImpR, *Gothelyngston* 1384 Hutch³
>
> *Golynston* 1412 FA (index *Godlynston*)
>
> *Goddleston* 1671 *Swan*

Possibly 'Godelin's farm', from the ME (OG) pers.n. *Godelin*
(Förstemann PN 660, Forssner 120) and tūn; both the masc.
(*Godelen(us)*) and the fem. (*Godelena*) forms of this pers.n. are
recorded from England (Forssner *loc. cit.*, Fägersten 126 note 3),
and either may occur here. However, in view of the consistent forms
in *-ing-, -ing(e)s-*, Dr von Feilitzen does not think the pers.n. *Godelin*
a likely first el., and suggests that a ME pers.n. **Godling* (< OE
gōd 'good' + *-ling*, cf. the OE pers.n. *Dēorling*) may be preferable.
For an early mill here, *v.* Mill Mead *infra*.

HERSTON (FM) (SZ 013787)

> *Herstune* 1086 DB, *Herestone* ib, *-tona* Exon
> *Hereston(e)* 1283 (1372) *ChrP*, 1288 *Ass*, 1333 *Wim* (p), 1348
>   *MinAcct*, 1355 *Wim*, *Herston(e)* 1288 *Ass*, 1291 Hutch³ *et passim*,
>   *Herseton* 1525 *AOMB*
> *Horston* 1423 Cl, *Hurston* 1458 Hutch³
> *Harston* 1513 *Ct*, *Hareston* c. 1586 Tres, 1575 Saxton, *Hariston*
>   1659 Hutch³
> *Herston Parva als. Hatherington* 1589 Hutch³
> *Hearston* 1656 *DCMDeed*
> *Easton* 1811 OS

'Here's farm', from an OE pers.n. *Here* and tūn. A man with this
name (spelt *Her*) held part of this manor TRE (DB). *Here* would be a
short form of names such as *Herefrið*, *Heremōd*, etc., cf. *Hering* 12
ASC (E) s.a. 603 (Redin 172), but Feilitzen 289 points out that this
base is unsatisfactory for the DB *Her*, which he considers to be
possibly from ON *Hiǫrr*. *Herston Parva als. Hatherington* apparently
distinguishes the small part of this hamlet and tithing, comprising
three fields called Verney (*q.v. infra*), which was in the manor of
Langton Wallis in Langton Mat. par. *supra*, *v.* parva; since *Hatherington* would then have roughly the same location as Verney ('fern
enclosure') it is perhaps an old name with a first el. hæddre 'heather',
possibly with -en² and tūn, 'farm overgrown with heather'. The
1811 form shows confusion with the common p.n. *Easton* from ēast
and tūn, cf. also the st.n. Herston Yards *supra*. Herston Fm is now
California Fm *q.v. infra*.

MOULHAM (local, about SZ 015800) ['mɔləm]

> *Moleham* 1086 DB, 1557 *Mow*, *Molam* 1559 ib
> *Moulham* 1291 Hutch³, 1326 Ext, 1332 SR (p) *et freq* to 1861
>   Hutch³, *Mouleham* 1299 Hutch³ (p), *Moulam* 1381 Pat (p),
>   *Moweleham* 1566 *Swan* (p), *Mowlam* 1568 Hutch³
> *Mulham* 1327 SR (p)

Probably 'Mūla's homestead or enclosure', from the OE pers.n.
Mūla and hām or hamm, but 'homestead or enclosure where there
were mules' is equally possible, with OE mūl (gen. pl. *mūla*) 'a
mule' as first el, cf. Moulton YN 286, Ch 2 207. According to Hutch³
1 669 this name 'now only survives in a parcel of ground adjoining

the south side of Godlingston farm', cf. also De Moulham Rd *supra*, Mowlem Institute and Mowlams *infra*. There was a mill here in 1086 DB (VCHDo 3 114).

NEWTON (FM & MANOR) (SZ 020790), *Nywe-*, *Niweton* 1299 Ipm, 1367, 1378 FF, 1379 *AddCh*, 1392 *DCMDeed*, 1404 IpmR, 1431 FA, *Nywton Purbyk* 1321 Ipm, *Newton* 1457 IpmR, 1560 *Mow*, (— *Fm*) 1826 Gre, cf. *Nywetoneshyde* 1333 *Wim*, *Newton Me(a)de* 1560 *Mow*, 'new farm', from nīwe, tūn, with hīd, mǣd, cf. Isle of Purbeck *supra*.

ULWELL (FM & HO) (SZ 022808), *Holewell* 1236 Fees, *Hulewlle* 1268 *Ass* (p), *Oulewell* 1291 Hutch³, 1326 *Ext*, *Ulewel* 1315 Hutch³, -*woll* 1332 SR (p), *Olewel(l)(e)* 1323 Banco, 1412 FA, 1418, a1427 Hutch³, 1442, 1449 FF, 1469 Hutch³, *Owlewill* 1457 IpmR, -*well* 1575 *Swan*, *Ulwell* c. 1500 *RoyRoll*, 1566 *Swan*, c. 1586 Tres, 1608 *Swan*, *Ulway* 1671 *DCMDeed*, 'well, spring or stream frequented by owls', from ūle, wella, the last form showing confusion with weg. There is a stream here supplied by 'a remarkably clear well or spring at the foot of the chalk hill' (Hutch³ 1 672, where the name is wrongly taken to be a corruption of *Holywell*). Cf. also *Ulwell Gap* 1882 Robinson.

WHITECLIFF FM (SZ 030807)

> *Witeclive* 1086 DB, 1216 ClR, -*cliva* 1086 Exon, *Wytecliue*, -*clyve* 1268 *Ass* (p), 1287 FF (— *juxta Swaneswych in Purbik*), 1316 FA, *Wytteclive* 1255 FF, *Wythecliue* 1288 *Ass*
> *Whyte-*, *Whiteclive*, -*clyve*, -*cliue*, -*clyue* 1251 FF, 1288 *Ass et freq* to 1340 NI, *Whyte Clyve* 1327 SR
> *Witeclyf* 1315 Hutch³
> *Whiteclife* 1339 Cl, -*clyff* c. 1500 *RoyRoll*, *White Cliffe* 1664 *GW*, *Whitecliff* 1811 OS, — *Hill* 1839 *TA*
> *Whit(t)-*, *Whytclif(f)(e)*, -*clyff* 1512–1546 Ct, c. 1586 Tres, 1664 HTax

'(Place at) the white cliff', *v.* hwīt (wk.obl. *hwītan*), clif (dat. sg. *clife*), named from the chalk cliff ⅓ mile SE. The early forms in -*clive*, etc from the OE dat. form *clife* were replaced during the 14th cent. by the forms -*clyf*, etc from the OE nom. *clif*. Whitecliff, a 16th- or 17th-cent. house, is supposed to have replaced a hunting lodge of King John (Kelly).

ALDERBURY BARN & COPSE, *Alderbury or Ail(e)sbury* 1861 Hutch³,
partly in Langton Mat. par. *supra*. ANVIL POINT, 1857 Robinson,
a promontory, so called from its fancied resemblance to an anvil
(Robinson 89), or from 'the small anvil-shaped rock just above
high water' (TGuide). THE AVIARIES (local, about SZ 033779).
BELLE VUE, *Belvere* 1839 *TA*, *Belleview* 1861 Hutch³, 'beautiful
view', *v*. bel, veeir, the second el. replaced by *view*; according to
Hutch³ it was 'formerly called Herston farm', *v*. Herston *supra*.
BUILDINGS COPSE, perhaps from a surname such as that of William
Baling 1664 HTax, but the name might also mean 'coppice near a
building' or 'coppice where building timber was cut'. CALDRON
BARN FM, *claus' voc' (le) Cauldon* 1557, 1566, 1665, *close called (the)
Cauldon* 1656, *(claus' voc' Ester) Caulden, claus' voc' le West Side
de Caulden, Cawdon* 1566, *Cawlton* 1569 all Mow, *N & S Calden*
1839 *TA*, possibly 'cold hill', from cald and dūn (confused with
denu and tūn), with ēasterra, west, sīde; alternatively, Professor
Löfvenberg suggests that the first el. may be cawel 'cabbage';
the modern form has been influenced by ModE *cauldron*, cf.
Cauldon Ave *supra*. CALIFORNIA FM (1"), *California* 1861 Hutch³,
'sometimes called Herston farm' ib, *v*. Herston *supra*, perhaps so
called from its comparative remoteness, cf. Cameron 209. CARTHION,
a house. CONNER COVE (local, about SZ 013767), a sea cave, probably
from cunner, conner 'the name of two fishes of the family *Labridæ*
or Wrasses' (NED), cf. '*Conners*. Groundfish, rife by shores with a
rocky bottom' (Barnes 57), *v*. cove. COURT FM or CARRANT'S COURT
FM, CARRANT'S COURT MANOR (all lost), 1861 Hutch³, 'the tenement
of John *Carante'* 1474 ib, *Car(r)antes Court* 1557, 1558 *Mow*,
Carrans Cort 1639 Hutch³, *Court Fm* 1839 *TA*, cf. *Carrantes Close*
1565, — *felde* 1566 both *Mow*, *Courthill* 1882 Robinson, from the
Carrant family who held this property from 1411 to 1534, cf. William
Carent 1411 Hutch³, 1438 *AddCh et freq*, *v*. court, clos(e), feld;
at about SY 026788. CURRENDON, *Coringdon* 1560 Hutch³, 1774
Hutch¹, *Coryngdon* 1571 Hutch³, *Curendon* c. 1586 Tres, 'mill
hill', or 'hill where millstones were obtained', *v*. cweorn, dūn, cf.
Coringdon in Corscombe par. *infra*. DURLSTON BAY (1774 Hutch¹,
Durleston — 1826 Gre), DAIRY & HEAD (CASTLE) (— *Head*, — *Point*
1774 Hutch¹) [ˈdɑːRlstən], 'rock with a hole in it', *v*. þȳrel, stān,
with hēafod, point; there is here, as a result of stone quarrying, a
'dark and steep tunnel cut obliquely through the solid rock'
(TGuide), but the name no doubt refers to some earlier natural coastal

feature, cf. Thurlestone D 312; for the forms in *D-* cf. Durdle Door in W Lulworth par. *infra*, Durlett W 247. FORKED DOWN END, 1811 OS, *Forket* — 1826 Gre, cf. *Forked down Bottom Cl* 1840 *TA* (Studland), *Forked Down* 1861 Hutch³, from the twin-spurred shape of the chalk ridge where it dips to form a gap, *v.* forked, dūn, ende, cf. 'the northern fork of the down' Hutch³ 1 689. FORRES SCHOOL. GIANT'S GRAVE (BOTTOM), *two low barrows known as the Giant's Grave* 1861 Hutch³, *v.* geant, botm, next to foll. (tumuli marked 6″). GIANT'S TRENCHER, a tumulus, cf. prec., *v.* trencher. GODLINGSTON HILL (*-stone Hill* 1840 *TA* (Studland)) *&* WD (1839 *TA*), from Godlingston *supra*. HALF MOON (local), a slight bay on the S coast at about SZ 016768, probably named from its shape, but perhaps denoting a cove navigable (by smugglers?) in not less than half moonlight. HOWCOMBE LEDGE (local), — *Cove & Quarry* 1882 Robinson, cf. the f.n. Holcombe *infra*. MARSH COPSE, cf. *one Marsh contayninge 2 acres* 1656 Mow, *The Marsh, Lt Marsh* 1839 *TA*, *v.* mersc. MILL CTGS, cf. 'a water mill at *Ulewel*' 1315 Hutch³, *Ulwell Mill* 1671 DCMDeed, 1861 Hutch³, *Mill Md* 1839 *TA*, *v.* myln, Ulwell *supra*, cf. foll. and Mill Md *infra*. MILL (6″), MILL POND (TPlan), *in quod' fonte iuxta molendinum in villa de Swanewyk* 1288 Ass, *the Myllpond walles* 1603 Swan, *Swanwich mill* 1861 Hutch³, cf. *unu' molend' aquatic'* 1521 Swan, *(claus' voc') Mil-, Mylhams* 1557, 1566 Mow, *claus' voc' Millandes* 1566 ib, *Mill Mdw* 1839 *TA*, *v.* myln, ponde, wall, hamm, land. MOWLEM INSTITUTE, 1882 Robinson, erected by John *Mowlem*, cf. Moulham *supra*. NORTHBROOK or NORBROOK FM (lost), 1861 Hutch³, *(claus' voc') North(e)bro(o)ke* 1557, 1566, 1656 Mow, *Ester-, Westernorthbroke* 1566 ib, *Norbrook(e)* 1774 Hutch¹, 1795 Boswell, '(place at) the northern brook', *v.* norð, brōc, with reference to the fact that it lay 'a little north of the town of Swanwich' (Hutch³ 1 659), or '(place) north of the brook', *v.* norðan, with ēasterra, westerra; the name survives only in Northbrook Rd *supra*; the brook to which the name refers is perhaps that marked on the maps just E of the road (about SZ 023801). OLDFELD SCHOOL. OLD LIMEKILN. PEVERIL POINT, *Peverell Poynt wher ys feyer landyng* 1539 LP, *Peu-, Peverel(l) Point(e)* 1575 Saxton *et freq* to 1811 OS, *Peverells Poynte* 1583 SPDom, probably from the surname *Peverell* which was common in Do (e.g. in 1332 SR), *v.* point. PIER (2 ×, one disused), cf. *a peere* 1535–43 Leland. PRIESTS WAY, *Priestway* 1839 *TA*, identical with Priest's Way in Langton Mat. par. *supra*. PROSPECT FM, 1861 Hutch³, *v.* prospect. PURBECK STONE QUARRIES,

the Quarries 1774 Hutch[1], *Stone Quarries* 1811 OS; there were 63
quarries being worked in Swanage in 1861 (Hutch[3] 1 687); they are
called *quarrs* in the articles of 'the Company of Marblers and Stone-
cutters of the Isle of Purbeck' drawn up in 1551 (Hutch[3] 1 682–3),
v. quarr(i)ere. RAGGED ROCKS (local), on coast at about SY 024768,
v. ragged 'rough'. ROUND DOWN, 1811 OS, S of Swanage, *v.*
round, dūn, cf. foll. ROUND DOWN, N of Swanage, cf. prec. SCAR
BANK HO, *v.* scar, bank(e). SOUTH BARN, S of Swanage, cf. *Barn and
Plot, Barn Grd* 1839 *TA*. STEPPING STONE (2 ×), both across small
streams. STUDLAND HILL, from Studland par. *supra.* SWANAGE BAY,
1811 OS, *San(e)wich(e) baye* 1575 Saxton, c. 1586 Tres, *v.* bay[1].
SWANAGE FM. NEW SWANAGE. TANVILLE LEDGE (local), near Peveril
Point *supra*, cf. *North Ledges* 1882 Robinson. TELEGRAPH (remains
of), *Signal* 1811 OS, on (the S) Round Down *supra*. TILLY WHIM
CAVES, *Tilly Whim* 1811 OS, the remains of an ancient stone quarry
in the face of the cliff, unworked since 1812, from the surname *Tilly*
(cf. Roger *Tilie* 1332 SR (Charlton M.), John *Tilly* 1664 HTax
(Langton Mat.)) or a p.n. *Tilly* (cf. *Tilly Mead* a1721 Robinson, and
Tillycoombe Rd in Portland par. *infra*), and whim 'windlass' (used
for lowering stone to boats), cf. Robinson 93, Db 149, Arkell (1940)
43–5; for *Tillywhim Ware* 1886 Barnes, a sheep walk above the
caves, *v.* Ware *infra.*

FIELD-NAMES

Fields now in Swanage but in Langton Mat. *TA* are marked †, and fields
now in Swanage but in Studland *TA* are marked ‡. (For a few fields in
Swanage *TA* but now in Studland, *v.* Studland f.ns. *supra*.)

The undated forms are 1839 *TA* 214 (those marked † are 1838 *TA* 123,
and those marked ‡ are 1840 *TA* 210). Spellings dated 1327 are *SR*, 1333,
1355 *Wim*, 1348 *MinAcct*, 1386, 1412, a1427, 1450, 1458, 1474, 1568[2],
1598, 1639, 1659, 1690, 1721, 1841, 1861 Hutch[3], 1448 Weld[1], 1449 FF,
1457 IpmR, 1479, 1557, 1558, 1560, 1565, 1566[2], 1569, 1570, 1656[1], 1665
Mow, 1525 *AOMB*, c. 1586 Tres, 1656[2], 1671[2] *DCMDeed*, 1664 HTax,
1774 Hutch[1], 1840 *TA* alt.app., and the rest *Swan*.

(a) Alderney (perhaps 'enclosure growing with alders', *v.* alren, (ge)hæg);
‡Ashen Grove (*v.* æscen); Benledge (partly in Langton Mat. par. *supra*
q.v.); Blacklands (*v.* blæc); Bobs Cl; Bottom Md; Bowling Alley; †Bramble
Longs (from brēmel 'blackberry bush', or a surname, cf. *tenemento...modo
in tenura Joh' Bramle* 1566[1], with lang[2]); Fd by Brewery; Brook Md (*Broke-
mede* 1560, *v.* brōc, mæd, cf. *Brook Bridge* 1791 Boswell, *Brokefurlong infra*);
Bullhouse Plot; †Cattle (perhaps 'cat hill, hill haunted by wild-cats', *v.*
cat(t), hyll, but probably simply cat(t)el 'property, livestock', cf. *Castle fodders*

4   MDT

infra); Chesters, Chesties (*Chestess* 1840, possibly analogous with Chestus in Langton Mat. par. *supra*); (The) Cliff (*le Clyff(e)* 1557, 1558, *ripas anglice the Cleiffe* 1585, *v.* clif); Close by Wood; The Common Fd (*Sanwyches Fylde* 1525, *campu' de Sandwich* 1566[1], *Swanwich(e) field* 1572, — *Feild* 1614, *Sanwich comon feilds* 1608 (*v.* comun, feld, and Swanage *supra*); (E & Upr) Cowleaze; ‡Croft; Downsay (possibly identical with *ten' Alexandri Dennet, claus voc' dennys Hey* 1566[1], — *Hay* 1584, *Denetes hay* 1603, from the pers.n. or surname *Dennet* or *Denis*, ME *Den(n)et* being a diminutive of *Den*, a pet-form of *Denis*, *v.* (ge)hæg); Eason Yards (to be identified with Herston Yards, now the name of a lane, *v.* Herston, st.ns. *supra*); 8 Acres; Eight Holes 1774, 1861 (a parcel of ground, according to Hutch[3] 1660 'a corruption of "Eight Holds", ... indicating the number of tenements or holdings into which it was anciently divided', *v.* hold); The 11 Acres; ‡Fir Hills; The 5 Acres; Flashett (*v.* flasshett, cf. Flashet in Corfe C. par. *supra*); (The) 4 Acres; Froghole (*v.* frogga, hol[1]); Front Md; ‡Gt, Lt & Upr Furze Fd (*Fursefieldes* 1603, *v.* fyrs); The Gibb (perhaps ModE *gib* 'a hump, an iron hook, etc' in some concrete or figurative sense, unless it is a short form of *gibbet* 'gallows', cf. *Gallyhey infra*); Gile's Grd (cf. the *Gill* family who had lands here c. 1586); Goosehams 1861 (-*ham* 1568[1], *v.* gōs, hamm); Graflins (near to The Grove *infra*, so possibly 'Grove furlongs', cf. The Grawlings Gl 2 xii, 173); Great Grd; Green Cl (cf. *Grenehey* a1427, *le Grenehill Hayes* 1557, *claus' voc' Greenhill* 1665, *v.* grēne[1], (ge)hæg, hyll); Greyseed; the Grove 1841 (*unam domum cum uno gardino vocat' le Grofe apud Moulham* 1412, 1448, *v.* grāf(a), cf. Graflins and Moulham *supra*); ‡N Haymead at Ulwell (*v.* hēg, Ulwell *supra*); Near the Heath (cf. *le Heeth* 1566, *v.* hǣð); Herren Grd; (The) Hill (cf. *un' claus' prati subter montem* 1566[2], *prat' iacen' subter le Hill* 1665, *v.* hyll); Hills (1659, perhaps a surname); Holcombe (1572, 1587, — *Wath* 1566[1], *muru' voc' Holcome wall* 1584, 'deep valley', *v.* hol[2], cumb, (ge)wæd (cf. *Bitakewathe* in Langton Mat. par. *supra*), wall; probably identical with Howcombe *supra*); Home Fd; Horse Grd (cf. *Horsecroft* 1521, 1566[1], — *Mead* 1568[2], *Hors(e)croftes* 1603, -*craft(e)(s)* 1612, 1671, *v.* hors, croft, mǣd); Howard Court Md (cf. Elizabeth *Howard* 1664, *v.* court); In Hooks (*v.* inhōke); Inlands (*v.* inland); In Leaze (*v.* in, lǣs); Jackalints (from Jack-a-Lent 'a figure of a man, set up in Lent to be pelted', cf. Barnes 74); Lanchard (*v.* lanchet); The Leg (*v.* leg); Little & Long Md(w); Madeow Grd; Malthouse Md; †Mead Plot; Meadow; ‡Middle Moor; Mill Md (cf. *the Mulfurlang* 1412, *le* — 1448, 'one mill and 3 a. of meadow in *Godlingston*' 1458, *v.* myln, furlang, Godlingston *supra*); Moors; †Moory Md; Mount; Mowlams (*Moulhams clos, pratum nuper in tenura Cristine Moulham* 1566[1], *meadowe called Mowlands* (sic) 1671[1], *v.* Moulham *supra*, clos(e), cf. *Moulham the More* 1412, *Moulham ys more* 1448, where *Moulham* may be the surname or the p.n., *v.* mōr); Mrs Grd ('the mistress's ground', probably dower-land or some sort of jointure); Nappy Grd (*v.* cnæppig); New Cl (1603, 1671[1], *le Neweclose* 1557, *v.* nīwe, clos(e)); New House Grd; The 9 Acres; (the) North (Common) Fd (*in campo boriali* 1333, 1521, cf. South Fd *infra*); Northleys (*v.* norð, lǣs or lēah); Orchard (Md); Oxleys (cf. *an Oxestall* 1565, *v.* oxa, lǣs, stall); ‡Parsons Md (possibly glebe-land, but cf. Henry *Persone* 1327); Partridge Md; Pea Grd; Penny-hayes (sic) ('the two *Diryheyes*' (sic) 1412, *lez Piryheyes* 1448, *Perry hayes* 1861, 'pear-tree enclosures', v. pirige, (ge)hæg); Peters Md; Plot of Heath; Pond Cl; Ponfill fd (cf. *le Pounde* 1558, *clausum voc' le Pownde, le Pound vel Pinfald'* 1560, *Punfield* 1861, — *Cove* 1882 Robinson, v. pund-fald, pund, pynd-fald; according to Arkell (1940) 46, *Punfield* is 'the amphitheatre-like recess in the cliffs at the north end of Swanage Bay' and may have been so called from its shape, cf. Pondfield in Tyneham par. *infra*, but according to Hardy 3 there was once a pond here); Racing Grd; Redsbris; Rook Md; Rough Grd & Pce; †Rualands (possibly 'rough headlands', v. rūh, hēafod-land); Selfoot (second el. perhaps fōt 'foot of a hill'); (Mrs) Serrel(l)s Freehold & Md (from a family known in Swanage since the 17th cent., cf. Thomas *Serrell* 1639); Sharps Living & Md (v. living); Shatscraft ((*claus' vocat'*) *Chedde-* 1412, 1448, *Chadecroft* 1521, *Shades Croft(e)* 1566[1], 1581, 1611, *-crafte* 1603, *Shads Crafte* 1614, cf. *1 parvum plotte prati iac'* in *Shades* 1566[1], *Shades acre* 1581, *Shadacre* 1611, *Shedsaker* 1625, *Shaddysmede* 1521, *Shades me(a)d* 1566[1], 1591, *Shoddes* — 1572, *Shad(e)* — 1585, 1592, 1603, 1671[1], *Shedes* — 1603, *Shaddes mead(e)* 1634, from a ME surname *Chedde*, *Chadde* derived from the OE pers.n. *Ceadd(a)* (Reaney 63 s.n. *Chadd*), v. croft, æcer, mǣd; some later forms show confusion with ModE *shade* 'shelter from light and heat'); ‡Shortlands (v. land); †Silken Md; (The) 6 Acres; †Small Md; Small Plot; (the) South (Common) Fd (*in campo austral'* 1333, (*Swanwiche*) *South(e)field* 1572, 1587, v. sūð, feld, cf. North Fd *supra*); South Md; Spring Cl (v. spring); Square Plot; ‡Starve Acre (a nickname for unproductive land); The 10 Acres; Three Corners; 20 Acres; Twitchens (v. twicen(e) 'the fork of a road, cross-roads'); ‡Little Ulwell Md (cf. 'the field of *Olewell*' a1427, *Ulwell Downes* 1603, v. Ulwell *supra*); ‡ Upr Moor; Verney (*Verney(s)* 1861, v. fearn, (ge)hæg, Herston *supra*); (the Common) Ware, Tenants Ware (cf. *le Clyffe voc' the Were* 1570; these fields are rough sloping pasturelands bounded on S by the cliffs; the same term (with *TA* spellings *wear, ware*) is used of similar fields in the neighbouring pars. of Corfe C. and Langton Mat. *supra*, cf. also E & W Weare in Portland par. *infra*, and the word is listed by Barnes 117 as *ware* 'a sheep walk'; a likely derivation would seem to be from OE waru[1] (which had a side-form *wære* originating in the obl. forms, v. Campbell § 589 (1), Brunner § 253 n.) 'keeping, protection, defence', perhaps with an extension of meaning to 'place where flocks are protected, where a shepherd watches over them', v. ware, clif); Washalls (v. wæscel(s) 'a washing place'); The Wathe (v. (ge)wæd, cf. Holcombe *supra*); West Coombe (v. cumb); Whistles (*Wyshels* 1560, *Easter Whissell* 1570, perhaps an OE *wiscel with some such meaning as 'marshy place', v. wisc, -el[3], ēasterra; this field, part of which is now King George's Playing Fd (TPlan), lies next to an unnamed stream at SZ 025790); ‡Lt White Hills (*Whetehulle* a1427, 'hill where wheat is grown', v. hwǣte, hyll); Wild Md (*le Wyldemeade* 1557, *Wilmead* 1665, v. wilde, mǣd); Wood; Wool Cl (v. wella); †Woolyards (1656[2], probably 'measure of land or yard near the well, spring or stream', v. wella, gerd, geard, but a compound *wull-geard 'wool yard, shearing pen' would also be possible).

(b) *claus' voc'* Bakers 1557, *Bakers Hay* 1665 (cf. William *Baker* 1557, *v.* (ge)hæg); *le Barton* 1557 (*v.* beretūn); (*marisc' voc' le*) *Black(e)more* 1557, 1656¹ (*v.* blæc, mōr); *claus' voc' le Breche(s)* 1557, 1558, 1569 (*v.* brēc); (*le*) *Brod(e)croft* 1412, 1448, 1557, 1656¹ (*v.* brād, croft); *Brod(e)-* 1572, 1603, *Broadfurlong* 1671¹ (*v.* brād, furlang); *Brodeme(a)de* 1560 (*v.* brād, mǣd); *Brokefurlong, -furlanggysmede* 1412, 1448, *Brokfourlonde* 1566¹ (*v.* brōc, furlang, mǣd); *terr' voc' Bushlers* 1603 (cf. 'the tenement of Harris *Bussheler*' 1474, *terras nuper Bushler* 1590); *Castle fodders* (a plot of meadow) 1671² (*v.* castel(l), fōdor 'food for cattle', perhaps to be associated with Cattle *supra*); *Chaunterelleslond* a1427 (cf. Edward *Chaunterell* ib, *v.* land); *Cleyhyll* 1521, *Clehill* 1603 (*v.* clæg, hyll); *le Collynges Crofte* 1557, *Thome Collens Crofte* 1560 (cf. Richard *Collins* 1664, *v.* croft); *claus' voc' Dewers* 1557 (cf. Richard *Dwyer* 1386); *the Drove in Swanwich Feild* 1614, *venellam voc' the Drove* 1634 (*v.* drove, The Common Fd *supra*); *East Hyde* 1568², *East Hide* 1598, 1721 (*v.* ēast, hīd 'hide of land', cf. Richard *atte Hide* 1348, Ralph *atte Hyde* 1355; perhaps 'east' in relation to Hyde in Langton Mat. par. *supra*); *La Eldedoune* 1333 (*v.* (e)ald, dūn, cf. Eldon in Corfe C. par. *supra*); *le Enterclose* 1565 (probably ME enterclos(e), 'a partition'); *camp' frument' anglice Errishe field* 1584, (*comm' campor' anglicie*) the *Ear(r)ishe f(f)ieldes* 1585, 1590 ('ploughed field(s)', *v.* ersc, feld); *domus mansional' voc' the fearme Howse* 1565 (*v.* farm-house); *le frythe* 1591 (*v.* fyrhðe); *Gallyhey* 1521, *Gallie Hay* 1572 ('gallows enclosure', *v.* galga, (ge)hæg, cf. the Gibb *supra*); 'the *Ger*' 1474 (possibly for *Gor*, *v.* gāra, cf. Gores *infra*); *Gomeshey* 1568¹, *-hay* 1603 (cf. *ten' Thome Gome* 1479, *v.* (ge)hæg); *Goselees* 1566¹, *-leis* 1603, *Gooselease* 1575 (*v.* gōs, lǣs); *claus' voc' Gores* 1557, 1665 (*v.* gāra, cf. 'the *Ger' supra*); *in la Grene* 1333 (p) (*v.* grēne²); *claus' voc' le Haryleche* 1557, *viam regiam apud Harrie Letche* 1570, *close called the Harry Leach* 1656¹ (perhaps 'stony stream or bog', *v.* *hærig (hær, -ig³), læc(c), lece, with later association of the first el. with the pers.n. or surname *Harry*, cf. *acr' nuper in tenura Rogeri Harris* 1558); *the Hawle House* 1570 (probably 'hall house', i.e. 'house with a hall as its principal room', *v.* hall, hūs); *Hersetons Fylde* 1525, *Herston felde,* — *mede* 1566¹, — *feild* 1614, — *meade* 1671¹, *the North Field* —, *the South Field of Herston* 1671² (*v.* feld, mǣd, Herston *supra*); *Holecrofte* 1557, 1566², *Northolcrofte, Southolcrofte* ib (*v.* hol¹ or hol², croft); *Houndecrofte* 1575 (*v.* hund (gen. pl. hunda), croft); *Howchins londe* 1566¹ (cf. John *Houchyns* 1450, *claus' pastur' nuper in tenura Johannis Howchyns de Stoodlond* 1521, *v.* land, Studland par. *supra*); *Ingrams Meade* 1634; (*le*) *Inham* 1566², 1665 (*v.* in, hamm); *Langcroft* 1521, *Lancraft* 1566¹, *Long(e) Crafte(s)* 1585, 1671¹, — *crofte(s)* 1603, 1612 (*v.* lang¹, croft); *Langlynche* 1557, 1566², *-lynge* 1565, *Long(e)lynche* 1557, *-lingh* 1665 (*v.* lang¹, hlinc); *Newe Croft* 1566¹; *claus' voc' Pardyes* 1575 (the surname *Pardy*); *Puttiershay(e)* 1557, 1656¹ (a ME toponymical surname *Puttier* 'dweller by a pit or hollow', cf. Fransson 201 s.n. *Putter, v.* (ge)hæg); *Remmestonyshyde* 1521 (probably 'the place called *Hyde* held by someone called *Remmeston', v.* hīd, cf. Robert *Rempston* 1412); *le Ryne apud Millane* 1557 (*v.* ryne, *Millane supra*); *Short(e) Me(a)de* 1566¹, 1603, 1656², *Shot Meade* 1671¹ (*v.* sc(e)ort, mǣd); *Shortes craft* 1603 (the surname *Short, v.* croft); *Sandwiche Meade* 1581 (*v.* mǣd, Swanage *supra*); *Sowtherhaye* 1558 (*v.* sūðerra, (ge)hæg); *1 claus' pastur' iuxta muros australes* 1521 ('one close of pasture next to the south walls'); (*le*) *Tad(d)meade* 1557, 1560 (*v.* tadde, mǣd); *Lewestfyld* 1449, *Le Westfeld* 1457 (*v.* west, feld); *le Whetfyld* 1521 (*v.* hwǣte 'wheat', feld); (*le*) *Whit-*, *Whytlondes*, *-land(e)(s)* 1557, 1560, 1656[1] (*v.* hwīt, land); *le Wytheber* 1412, 1448 (*v.* wiðig, bearu).

Worth Matravers

The ecclesiastical par. included Swanage par. *supra* until c. 1500 (Hutch[3] 1 656). Woodyhyde was in Corfe C. par. *supra* in 1795 Boswell.

WORTH MATRAVERS (SY 974774)

 Orde 1086 DB, *Orda*, *Urda* Exon

 Wirde 1086 DB, *Wirda* Exon, *Wrde* 1086 DB, c. 1165, c. 1170 MontC

 Wurth(e) 1220 Cur, 1236 FF, Fees (*Est-*), 1242–3 ib, 1244, 1268, 1280 *Ass*, n.d. (1372) *ChrP*, — *Fytzpayne* 1544 *DCMDeed*, *Wrth(e)* 1256, 1287 FF (— *in Porbik*), n.d. (1372) *ChrP*, *W'rth(e)* 1291 Tax

 Worth(e) 1230 Cl, 1236 FF, 1244, 1268, 1288 *Ass et freq* to 1575 Saxton, — *in Purbyk* 1375 Cl, 1384 *DCMDeed*, *Estworth* 1299 Ipm, *Worth Matrauers* 1664 HTax

 Wourth(e) 1546, 1547 *Ct*

'The enclosure', *v.* worð. Robert *Fitz-Pain* held lands here in 1212 Hutch[3], cf. 'Roger son of Pagan' 1236 FF, Robert *Fitz Payn* 1303 Hutch[3], 1360 Cl, etc. John *Mautravers* was here in 1335 Ch, 1339 Pat, cf. *ten' terr' nup' d'ni Matervers p' terr' in Wourthe* 1546 *Ct*. The forms *Estwurth*, *-worth* probably refer simply to the E part of the manor, *v.* ēast. For the affix- *in Porbik*, etc, *v.* Isle of Purbeck *supra*. The whole or part of the manor is also apparently referred to as *villa de Bitte-*, *Bytteworth* 1288 *Ass*, *Byttewrth* 14 *Weld*[2], 'Bitta's enclosure', with the OE pers.n. *Bitta* found in Bittadon D 29, Bitworthy D 82, etc. There was a mill at Worth Mat. in 1086 DB (VCHDo 3 99), cf. also *molend' de Wurth* 1244 *Ass*.

CAPLESTONE CTG (SY 979804) ['kɔplstən], *Cableston* 1431 FA, 1510, 1511, 1636, — *or Cappleston* 1861, *Cabulston* 1546 all Hutch[3], cf. *Coppleston Md* 1840 *TA*. Probably 'Cabel's farm', from a pers.n. *Cabel* and tūn. *Cabel* is perhaps a diminutive of the byname *Cabe* of obscure meaning and origin recorded once in DB (*v.* Feilitzen 213), but it could be an anglicization of Lat *caballus* 'horse' (cf. Rogerus *Caballus* 1230 cited by Reaney s.n. *Capel*); it occurs in Do as the surname of John *Cabbel* 1332 SR (Stratton), cf. Bardsley s.n. *Cabbell* who cites 13th and 14th cent. spellings for the name from Nf, O and So but wrongly associates it with the surname *Cobbold* < OE *Cūðbeald*. It is perhaps less likely that the name Caplestone contains the anglicized form of Lat *caballus* used as a common noun, recorded as lME *cabel* 'horse' from c. 1460 (MED).

CHAPMAN'S POOL (CTGS) (SY 956770)
> *on þe schort mannes pol* 948 (15) *ShaftR* (S 534 (1)), *on seortmannes pol* 955 (14) *ib* (S 573), *Shortmanpole* 1489 *Ct*
> *Shipman(')s Pool(e)* 1575 Saxton, 1579 Hutch³
> *Chapmans Pool* 1811 OS, *Chapman Poole* 1826 Gre

Possibly 'Sc(e)ortmann's pool', from an OE pers.n. *Sc(e)ortmann* and pōl¹. However, in view of the def. art. *þe* in the earliest form, Professor Löfvenberg thinks it probable that *mannes* reflects OE (ge)mǣnnes 'community', the reference being to a pool used in common, with sc(e)ort in the sense 'short in extent, small'. It may therefore be significant that Chapman's Pool, a small coastal bay, lies in two pars., since it is roughly halved by the par. boundary between Corfe C. and Worth Mat., as well as by the older boundaries in the two OE charters cited. The later forms with *shipman* 'sailor' and *chapman* 'merchant' are probably the result of popular etymology, although *Chapman* is in fact also an old local surname, cf. Robert *le Chapman de Purbyk* 1321 Orig, Thomas *Chapman* 1698 Hutch³.

EASTINGTON FM (SY 983778), *Estinton* 1209 P, n.d. (1372) *ChrP*, *Estington* 1259, 1285 FF, *Estyn(g)ton* 1285 (1372), 1306 (1372) *ChrP*, *Istone* 1291 Tax, *Eston* 1466, 1481 *Weld*¹, 1482 Hutch³, 1484 IpmR, *Eastington* c. 1586 Tres, 1811 OS, '(land) east in the village', *v.* ēast, in, tūn, though the OE adverbial form (bī) ēastan used elliptically to give a similar meaning '(land) east of the village' is also possible. The alternative forms *Istone, Eston* without medial -*in(g)*-, -*yn(g)*- may simply contain the adj. ēast and mean 'east farm', cf. Weston Fm *infra* and discussion in Gl 1 54 s.n. Eastington.

HAYCRAFT (SY 984797), *Hei-* 1466 *Weld*¹, *Hey-* 1547 Hutch³, *Haycroft* 1547 ib, c. 1586 Tres, -*crofts* 1774 Hutch¹, 1811 OS, *Haycroft ctg, Drove by Haycrofts* 1840 *TA*, 'hay enclosure(s)', *v.* hēg, croft, drove.

QUARR (SY 989797), *quarrera Petri de Clauille, Quar(r)era* (p) 1268
Ass, Quareriam 1272 (1372) *ChrP, (La) Quar(r)(e)* 1287, 1299, a1427
all Hutch[3] *et freq* to c. 1586 Tres, *(la) Quar(r)ere* 1288 *Ass*, 1366 Pat,
1401 Cl, *atte Quare* 1360 Cl, Pat both (p), *Quarry Fm* 1811 OS,
Quarr Fm 1838 *TA* (Langton Mat.), 'the quarry', *v.* quarrere; there
are traces here of ancient stone quarries now disused (Hutch[3] I 695);
for the family of *(de) Clavel* who held this place for several centuries
(e.g. *Will' de Clauyle de la Quarere* 1288 *Ass*), cf. Clavel Tower in
Kimmeridge par. *infra.* A quarry here may be referred to in *unam
accram super quareriam marmoris* c. 1190 *Midd* (R.J.S.), held by the
priory of Wilkswood in Langton Mat. *supra.*

RENSCOMBE FM (SY 965776)

    Hreminescumbe 987 (13) Finberg 613 (S 1217)
    Romescumbe 1086 DB, *-cumba* Exon
    Rembescumb 1212 Fees, *Remp(e)scombe* 1459 *Weld*[1], 1545 *Ct*
    Remescumb 1275 Pat, 1280 *Ass*, *-combe* 1316 FA, 1552 *Bodl*,
        Remmescumb 1276 Cl, *-comb(e)* 1327 *SR et freq* to 1552 Hutch[3],
        Remys- 1512 *Ct, Remscombe* 1539 *ib*, c. 1586 Tres
    Ramescome, Rammescumb 1288 *Ass*
    Rennscumbe 1291 Tax, *Renscombe* 1811 OS
    Rymescombe 1512 *Ct*
    Rentscomb 1861 Hutch[3]

'Raven's valley', *v.* hremn, cumb, or 'Hremn's valley' from an
OE pers.n. *Hremn,* cf. *Remeswelle infra* which was probably near
Renscombe. The DB spelling in *-o-* is probably due to orthographic
confusion of *o* and *e.* Part of the cliff SSW of Renscombe Fm is
known locally as Renscombe Cliff, cf. foll.

ST ALBAN'S or ST ALDHELM'S HEAD (SY 962752), 1811 OS, *the
foreland of Seynt Aldem'* c. 1500 *RoyRoll*, *S(ainct) Aldelmes-,
-us Point* 1535–43 Leland, *Seint Aldamys* 1539 LP, *St Adeym* 1565
SPDom, St. Albans Head 1826 Gre, 1840 *TA, St. Aldhelm's head,
now vulgarly called St. Alban's head* 1861 Hutch[3], cf. *Cliff of St.
Albans and Renscombe* 1840 *TA,* the promontory on which St
Aldhelm's Chapel stands, *v.* foll., foreland, point, hēafod, Renscombe
supra. The cliff top behind St Aldhelm's Head is known locally as
St Aldhelm's Plain.

St Aldhelm's Chapel (SY 961755), *capelle regis de Sancto Audelmo* 1252 Cl, *capella Sancti Aldelim* (sic) *extra Corf* 1259 ib, *capella/-um Sancti Aldelini* (sic) 1291 Tax, 1381 (16) *Pitt, the chappell of St Aldeline* (sic) 1381 (16) *ib, Capella Sancti Aldelmi* 1428 FA, *S(c)t Aldams Chapell* 1575 Saxton, c. 1586 Tres, *Sainct Aldomes Chaple* c. 1586 ib, *St. Aldhelm's chapel* 1861 Hutch³, a small, square Norman chapel, also referred to as 'the chapel of Renscombe' 1558 Hutch³ (*v.* Renscombe *supra*), dedicated to St Aldhelm, first bishop of Sherborne 705–9 (*v.* VCHDo **2** 1 ff), *v.* chapel(e), cf. prec.

Seacombe Bottom (SY 981773), Cliff & Quarry (all 6"), Seacombe Gallery (local), *Secombe, Secombesmede* 1306 (1372) *ChrP, Seacomb(e) quarry* 1786, 1861 Hutch³, — *Cliff* 1811 OS, — *Bottom & Fd* 1840 *TA*, 'valley opening on to the sea', *v.* sǣ, cumb, with mǣd, botm, cf. Seacombe Ch **4** 329; gallery is a mining term meaning 'an underground passage, a level or drift' (NED s.v. sense 7).

Weston Fm (SY 969773), *Westeton* 1281 Misc, *Westyngton* 1304 (1372) *ChrP, Weston* 1490 *Ct*, 1535, 1560 Hutch³, 1811 OS, (*Worth alias*) *Weston-Worth* 1545–75 Hutch³, cf. *Weston Eweleaze, Weston Ho & Ridge, Under Weston* 1840 *TA*, '(land) west in/of the village' or 'west farm', *v.* west, westan, in, tūn, par. name *supra*, Bonvils Fm *infra*, cf. Eastington Fm *supra*.

Woodyhyde Ctgs & Fm (SY 974804) ['udiaid], *Wodewehide* 1311 FF, 1431 FA, (*La*) *Wodewehyde* 1422 Hutch³, p1483 *Sheen, Wydow*- 1557, *Widdo*- 1609, *Widdow hide* 1701 all Hutch³, *Woodehid(e)* 1566 Swan, c. 1586 Tres, *Woodheide* 1568 Hutch³, *-hyde Lane* 1603 Swan, *-hide* 1721 Hutch³, *Woddie*-, *Woddy Hide* 1591, 1603 Swan, *Woodie*- 1639 Hutch³, *Woody Hide* 1774 Hutch¹, — *Lane* 1840 *TA*, 'widow's hide of land', *v.* wuduwe, hīd, with lane, probably named from Hawise de Baschelville, the widow of Hugh Fitz Grip, who in 1086 DB held 116 hides in Do, including 3 virgates in Worth Mat. (VCHDo **3** 46, 109); it would then be distinguished from the two manors held here in 1086 DB by Roger Arundel (op. cit. 99).

Abbascombe (local, SY 979771), *Abbotts Coombe* 1840 *TA*, cf. Edward *Abbott* 1664 HTax, *v.* cumb. Black Man's Stile (local, near Seacombe Bottom *supra*), from a Lascar seaman who got ashore but was found dead here after the wreck alluded to in Halswell *infra* (T.B.A.). Bonvils Fm, *Bonfield's fields fm or Weston fm* 1754 Hutch³, *Weston*,

Weston-Worth, alias Bonvils or Bondfields fields 1774 Hutch[1], *Bodmans Fd* (sic) 1840 *TA*, *Bodminsfield* (*qu. Bonviles field*) 1861 Hutch[3], from Henry *Bonvyll* 1546 *Ct*, *v.* Weston Fm *supra*, cf. Bondfields Ave in Swanage par. *supra*. BUTTERY CORNER (local), a quarry shelf at St Alban's Head *supra*, perhaps buttery 'place for storing liquor', with reference to smuggling. COMPACT FM, *Downshays Barn* 1811 OS, *v.* Downshay Fm *infra*. THE COTTAGE. CRAB HOLE (local), a cave below West Man *infra*, *v.* crabba, hol[1]. CULVERWELL (lost, SY 975794), 1811 OS, cf. *Culverwell Down & Md* 1840 *TA*, 'well, spring or stream frequented by doves', *v.* culfre, wella; a spring is marked 6″; *Coluerlyde* 1306 (1372) *ChrP* has the same first el. with hlȳde 'noisy stream' or hlid[1] 'slope', cf. *Seelid infra*. DOWNSHAY FM & WD, *Dunshay* c. 1586 Tres, *Duncehay* 1646 SC, *Downhays* 1811 OS, *Downshay Fd & Wd* 1840 *TA*, probably 'Dun's enclosure', cf. William *Dun* 1327 *SR*, *-Don* 1332 *SR*, *v.* (ge)hæg, but the first el. is possibly dūn 'hill', cf. (*Home & Lt*) *Down* 1840 *TA*, a group of fields adjacent to Downshay Wd, and *v.* Compact Fm *supra*. EMMETTS HILL, *Emmit* — 1811 OS, *Emmett Hill* 1840 *TA*, *Emmet's Hill* 1861 Hutch[3], 'ant hill', *v.* æmette, hyll, cf. Ampthill Bd 67, C 78, Do dial. *emmet-but*, or *emmet-hill* (Barnes 62); it is a large barrow situated on the cliff (tumulus marked 6″), so perhaps the name was jocular. FLOWER MDW. GALLOWS GORE CTGS, where several tracks meet to cross the Kingston–Langton Mat. road, *v.* galga, gāra; here three Swanage men who had fought for the Duke of Monmouth during the rebellion of 1685 were hanged, drawn and quartered by the soldiers of Jas 2 (Swanage TGuide). HALSWELL BARS, CLIFF & ROCK (all local, about SY 980763) ['ɔzwel], *Halsewell quarry* 1861 Hutch[3], from the East Indiaman 'Halsewell' wrecked below the cliffs here in 1786 (Hutch[3] 1 704), *v.* barre, cf. Black Man's Stile *supra*. HARMAN'S COPSE & CROSS (RDS), *Armons Cross* 1840 *TA*, the surname *Harman*, *v.* cross(-roads). HILL BOTTOM, *The* — 1844 *TA* (Corfe C.), *Bottom* 1811 OS, (*the hamlet of* —) 1861 Hutch[3], *v.* hyll, botm; the valley below North Hill and West Hill *infra*. INSTOW, perhaps as Professor Löfvenberg suggests, from in 'inner' and stōw in some special sense, e.g. 'place where animals were herded', cf. EPN 2 159–160. LOOKOUT & ROCKET POST, cf. *Signal* 1811 OS, all on St Alban's or St Aldhelm's Head *supra*. EAST & WEST MAN, 1811 OS, two rounded coastal hills over 300′ separated by Winspit Bottom *infra*, cf. also *Bodmans Man* 1840 *TA* for which *v.* Bonvils Fm *supra*; their shape might suggest PrWelsh **mamm** 'breast, breast-like hill' (cf. OE *mamme* 'teat'), but Professor Jackson suggests comparison with the use of man in the Lake District to mean 'cairn or pile of stones on the top of a hill', *v.* NED s.v. *man* sb.[16], PNWe **2** 13. MANOR HO (remains of). MIKE's & WILLY'S COVES (local, near Seacombe Bottom *supra*), from *Michael* and *William* Bower who were quarrymen at the end of the last century (T.B.A.), *v.* cove, cf. Bower's Rock in Langton Mat. par. *supra*. NECKLACE (local, SY 981771), *Nicholesdon* 1306 (1372) *ChrP*, *Old & New Nicholas Down* 1840 *TA*, perhaps 'the hill of St Nicholas', to whom the church is dedicated, *v.* St Nicholas's Church *infra*, dūn, but a pers.n. or surname *Nichol* is a possible alternative for the first el.; *Nic(h)ol* was the usual vernacular form of Lat *Nicolaus*. NORTH HILL, 1840 *TA*, N of Renscombe Fm *supra*. PIER BOTTOM (local), a gully in the cliffs S of Emmetts Hill *supra*, *v.* botm. PRIMROSE HILL, 1811 OS. RING-BUM GDNS (local), part of the shore at St Alban's Head, perhaps from the vb. wring 'to hurt, squeeze, etc' and bum 'buttocks', cf. Scratch Arse in Langton Mat. par. *supra* and Molly's Gdn in Corfe C. par. *supra*. ROOKERY. ST NICHOLAS'S CHURCH, cf. 'the church of *Worthe*' 1321 FF, *ecclesie de Worth* p1483 *Sheen*, cf. Church Fd *infra* and Necklace *supra*. SHEEPFOLD. SQUARE & COMPASS (P.H.), the insignia of the local quarrying industry. SUNNYDOWN SCHOOL. (LR & TOP) SUTTON (local), (*Bodmans*) *Sutton* 1840 *TA*, *Suddon* 1306 (1372) *ChrP*, 'south hill', *v.* sū ð, dūn; for *Bodmans*, *v.* Bonvils Fm *supra*; S of the village at SY 972755. TURNPIKE CTGS (local), at Gallows Gore *supra* (Legg 26). WATCH ROCK (local), a coastal feature near Seacombe Bottom *supra*, perhaps 'rock where watch was kept', *v.* watch. WEST HILL, 1840 *TA*, W of Renscombe Fm *supra*, cf. Westhill Fm in Corfe C. par. *supra*. WINSPIT (BOTTOM) (6″), WINSPIT EAST END (local), *Winspit quarry* 1786, 1861 Hutch[3], *Winspit* 1811 OS, perhaps 'stone pit with a winch', *v.* wince, pytt; Arkell (1940) 44, (1941) 33, suggests derivation from spitu 'a spit of land' and dial. *whin* 'hard rock' (only NCy according to EDD and NED, though noted by Arkell as in use in Sx in 19th cent.), but Professor Löfvenberg points out that if the second el. is in fact spitu, the first may rather be wind[1] 'wind' or winn[1] 'pasture'. WORTH FM & QUARRIES.

FIELD-NAMES

The undated forms are 1840 *TA* 265. Spellings dated 1244 are *Ass*, 1272 (1372), 1306 (1372), 1340 (1372) *ChrP*, 14 *Weld*[2], 1340 NI, 1472, 1474, 1477, 1478, 1481 *Weld*[1], 1490, 1545, 1547 *Ct*, 1550 *Midd*, 1664 HTax, 1690 *Foster*, 1844 *TAMap* (Corfe C.), and the rest Hutch[3].

(a) Bad Croft (cf. *Bordecroft* 1306 (1372), which is probably from **bord** 'board, plank' or the ME surname *Borde* (*v.* Reaney s.n. *Board*), with **croft**, but cf. **bord-land**); Barns Cl (cf. George *Barnes* 1664); Barton Md (*v.* **barton**); Broad Mdw; (Bodmans) Canaan (a transferred Biblical name, probably a nickname for productive land, 'land flowing with milk and honey'; for Bodmans, *v.* Bonvils Fm *supra*); Church fd (near to St Nicholas's Church *supra*); the Cliff; Conygarth (*v.* **coning-erth** 'rabbit-warren'); Copse; Cowleaze (freq); E & W Croft; Dinney (perhaps 'enclosure in a valley', cf. *la Dene* 1306 (1372), *v.* **denu**, (ge)hæg); Drove; Dry Md; East Md; East of the house; 8 Acres; Gt Eweleaze; 4 Acres; 4 and 20 Acres; Goile (*Guile* 1844, *v.* **goyle**); Great Md; Grove Md; Haycrofts 5, 7 & 2 Acres, Haycrofts Furzy Grd & Little Md (from Haycraft *supra*); Heiffields (*v.* **hēg**); Herring Hill; Higher Md; Home Fd; Horn Cl (probably from its shape, *v.* **horn**); Horse Croft; Little Md; Long Cl & Md; Meadow; Mead West of the House; Middle Fd & Plains (*v.* **plain**); (Lt) Midlakes ('(land) between streams', *v.* **mid**, **lacu**); Miles's Md; Milking Barton (*v.* **milking**, **barton**); Mount; New Cl; Newfoundland (if a transferred name, perhaps denoting prosperity rather than remoteness since this field has stone quarries in it and is near the village; but possibly from **new-found**, **land**); North East Fd (cf. *Northfeld* 1306 (1372), 1340 (1372), *v.* **norð**, **feld**); North Grd, Hill & Rd; Nunbarrow East & West (*Nonnebergh* 1306 (1372), 'nun's hill', *v.* **nunne** (gen. sg. *nunnan*), **beorg**; however, since there is no evidence of any land here having been possessed by a nunnery – on the contrary Nunbarrow is in Eastington which was held by Christchurch Priory –, the OE pers.n. *Nunna* is also a possible first el.); Orchard; Park Mdw (cf. *parcum...* *de Wrthe* 14, *v.* **park**); Lt Peaked Cl (*v.* **peked**); Peaks Cl (cf. *Pyke's land* 1609, John *Pyk* 1340); Pheasant Copse; Phicks Md (the surname *Fick*); Pig Acres; Plot; Quarry Fd (cf. Quarr *supra*); Rickbarton; Rough Grd; Rushy Md; Serrells Md (from the *Serrell* family who were here in 1721); Sheepsleight (*v.* **slæget**); Sheepwash (*v.* **wæsce**); 6 Acres; South East Fd; South Fd (*in Southfeld byestbrok, in Suthfeld biwestebrouk* 1306 (1372), *Southfeld* 1490, *v.* **sūð**, **feld**, **bī**, **ēastan**, **westan**, **brōc** ('to the east and west of the brook')); South Md; 10 & 3 Acres; Vicarage Acre; Warren; West Bottom & Cl; Withy Bed (Md); Worth Cowleaze, Fd (*co'ibus campis de Wourth* 1550, *Worth Feilds* 1690), Hill & Md.

(b) *cotag' voc' Avereys* 1490 (the pers.n. or surname *Averey*); *bernardesdon* 1306 (1372) ('Bernard's hill', from the ME (OG) pers.n. *Bernard*, perhaps as a surname, and **dūn**); *biriacre* 1306 (1372) ('plot of arable at the fortified place', *v.* **burh** (gen.sg. or dat.sg. *byrig*), **æcer**); *Bynehilakyr* 1490 (*v.* **bēan**, **hyll**, **æcer**); 'land called *Dolling's*' 1609 (cf. Henry, John *Dollyng(e)* 1547, 1561); *Eston mede* 1472–1481 (*v.* Eastington *supra*, **mæd**); *Forde* 14 (*v.* **ford**);

Fremancroft 1306 (1372) (*v.* frēo-mann (gen. pl. -*manna*), croft); *Estmest-*, *Middel-*, *Westmesthide* 1306 (1372) (*v.* ēastmest, middel, westmest, hīd); *Nether-*, *Ouerknapp* 1306 (1372) (*v.* neoðerra, uferra, cnæpp); *longeforlong* 1306 (1372) (*v.* lang[1], furlang); *louecotesforlong* 1306 (1372) ('furlong at *Louecote*', from furlang and a lost p.n. from the OE pers.n. *Lufa* and cot 'cottage', though OE lufu 'love' or an OE luf- 'slope' (*v.* Sandred 246) are also possible for the first el.); *Maidenwelleforlong* 1306 (1372) ('furlong at *Maidenwelle*', from furlang and a lost p.n. from mægden 'maiden' and wella 'well, spring, stream'); *le Middelstyȝele* 1272 (1372) (*v.* middel, stigel); *ad novam viam* 1272 (1372); *North(er(e)) forlong, in cultura boriali* 1306 (1372) (*v.* norð, norðerra, furlang); *Northwode* 1244 (p), 1304 (1372), — *in Purbik, in campo binorthwode* 1272 (1372) ('north wood' or '(place) north of the wood', *v.* norð, bī, norðan, wudu, and Isle of Purbeck *supra*); *Popesgore* 1306 (1372) (the surname *Pope* and gāra); *Remeswelle* 1306 (1372) (*v.* hremn, wella, but the first el. could be an OE pers.n. *Hremn*, cf. Renscombe *supra*); *Rouclos* 1472–1481 (*v.* rūh, clos(e)); *Secroft* 1306 (1372) (*v.* sǣ, croft); *Seelid* 1306 (1372) (*v.* sǣ, hlȳde or hlid[1], cf. *Coluerlyde* s.n. Culverwell *supra*); *Shorteforlong* 1306 (1372) (*v.* sc(e)ort); *Smalhulle* 1306 (1372) (*v.* smæl, hyll); (*Southe*) *buttes* 1306 (1372) (*v.* butte); *Southforlong* 1306 (1372); *la Twyneldehegge* 1272 (1372) (perhaps 'the hedge at *Twynelde*' ('the double slope'), *v.* twinn, helde, hecg); *Westercomp* 1306 (1372) (*v.* westerra, camp[1]); *Woderys(e)* a1427, 1454, *Wodrise* 1478 (*v.* wudu, hrīs); *Worthe Woodde* 1545 (*v.* wudu).

II. HASLER HUNDRED

Hasler hundred consists of the W part of the Isle of Purbeck *q.v. supra*. Blashenwell and Encombe in Corfe C. par. (dealt with under Rowbarrow hundred *supra*) were included in Hasler hundred in 1327 *SR*, 1332 SR, 1664 HTax and 1795 Boswell, likewise Langton Wallis in Langton Mat. par. (also dealt with under Rowbarrow hundred *supra*) in 1327 *SR* and 1332 SR, and West Holme in East Stoke par. (dealt with under Winfrith hundred *infra*) in 1664 HTax and 1795 Boswell. The parts of Arne added from the out-parishes of Wareham were not in Hasler hundred (see note under Arne par. *infra*). The hundred was annexed to the manor of Steeple in the early 14th cent. (Ipm IV 313, V 330). For a reconstruction of it as it was in c. 1086 GeldR, *v.* VCHDo 3 142–3.

HASLER HUNDRED

Haselore hundret c. 1086 GeldR, (*hund*' *de*) *Haselor(e)* 1198, 1199 P, 1212 Fees, 1244, 1268 *Ass et freq* to 1546 Ct, *Hassellor(e)* 1265 Misc, 1412 FA, *Aselore* 1268, 1280 *Ass*, 1285 FA, *Hasellore* 1288 *Ass et freq* to 1509 BrEll, *Haselehore* 1316 FA, *Hasyllore* 1548 Pat, *Hasilor* 1795 Boswell

(*hund*' *de*) *Haselovere* 1210–12 RBE, *Haseluor* 1279 Ch

(*hund' de*) *Heselore* 1244, 1280 *Ass*
(*hund' de*) *Haleslore, Haleslour* (sic) 1280 *Ass*

'Hazel slope', from hæsel and ōra (the two forms in -*overe* and -*uor* showing confusion or alternation with ōfer[1] 'bank' or ofer[2] 'hill', cf. Haselor Wa 211). The hundred takes its name from Hasler in Steeple par. *infra*, a small coppice ½ mile NW of Steeple church on the steep S slopes of the Purbeck Hills, described in Hutch[3] 1 550 as 'two or three grounds called Hasler. In one of them is a barrow, overgrown with hazlewood, from the plenty of which hereabout the hundred takes its name. Here the hundred court was formerly kept, but at present in a cottage called the West Mill, near Corfe; though still in the hundred' (*v.* West Mill in Corfe C. par. *supra*).

LOST OR UNIDENTIFIED PLACE-NAMES IN HASLER HUNDRED

Colpyttes 1546 *Ct* ('pits where coal was dug or charcoal was burnt', *v.* col[1], pytt); *Hamel-* 1303, 1346, *Hameleton* 1428 FA (the first el. is hamol 'crooked, scarred', perhaps originally with dūn 'hill' rather than tūn 'farm', cf. Hambledon Hill in Ch. Okeford par. *infra*; in 1303 this place appears under Hasler Hd, but in 1346 and 1428 under Rowbarrow Hd although in association with Kimmeridge *infra*; Hutch[3] 1 555 thought the name *Hamel(e)-ton* a mistake for 'the hamlet of Kimmeridge'); *de la Hegg* 1268 *Ass* (p) (*v.* hecg); *loco qui vocat' le Heuede* 1280 *Ass* (*v.* hēafod); *de La Marche* 1280 *ib* (p) (*v.* marche 'boundary'); *atte Milne* 1288 *Ass* (p) (*v.* atte, myln); *tres virgatas Uphull, terre de Up hull in purbich* n.d. (1372) *ChrP* ('(land) upon the hill', *v.* upp, hyll, cf. Isle of Purbeck *supra*; possibly near Kimmeridge par. *infra*, but cf. Uphill in Coombe K. par. *infra*); *Wallesbrigg* 1346 Hutch[3] 1 555 (perhaps 'bridge by or with a wall', *v.* wall, brycg, but the first el. could be the same word used as a surname; possibly near Kimmeridge par. *infra*).

Arne

Arne was until the last century a chapelry of Wareham Holy T. parish (Hutch[3] 1 98–9). Since 1894 Arne has included the whole of the former out-parish of Wareham Holy T. (Middlebere, Redcliff, Stoborough, etc) and part of Wareham Lady St M. (Worgret, etc) (Kelly, cf. Wareham par. *infra*). Middlebere was formerly included in the manor of Langton Wallis (Hutch[3] 1 634, *v.* note under Langton Mat. par. *supra*). Worgret was included in Barrow hundred in 1288 *Ass*, 1332 SR, 1664 HTax, 1795 Boswell.

ARNE (SY 973881)

Arn(e) 1268 *Ass* (p), 1316 FA, 1319 *MinAcct*, 1327 *SR*, 1332 SR, 1388 Pat, 15 *ShaftR* (— *in Purbik*), 1512 *Ct et freq*, *Arnee* 1646 SC

Harn(e) Ed 1 Hutch[3], 1285 FA, 1288 *Ass*

Arun 1445 Hutch[3]

Aren 16 *Pitt*, 1575 Saxton, e17 Cecil (— *in purbeck*)

Erne 1647 SC, *Earne* 1700 Hutch[3]

Probably 'the house or building', *v.* ærn (so DEPN), although this name would then be an apparently unique example of the simplex use of this el. But if the *H-* in three of the early forms is organic, the dat.pl. *harum* of hær 'rock, heap of stones, tumulus' would be possible, in allusion to Arne Hill *infra* (167') on which two tumuli are marked (6"), cf. Harome YN 70, Herne Bd 137. For the addition *in Purbeck*, cf. Isle of Purbeck *supra*.

EARL'S MEAD (lost), 1554, 1861 Hutch[3], *prati voc' Eorlesmed* 1393 *MinAcct*, *Earles meade* 1620 *DCMDeed*, *Earls(-)Mead* 1774 Hutch[1], 1843 *TA* (Wareham Holy T.), 'the earl's meadow', *v.* eorl, mæd, situated 'on the west side of Wareham Causeway' (Hutch[1] 1 25, cf. South Causeway *infra*) and possibly named either from the Earl of Leicester who held the manor of Wareham in 1272, or from the Earl of Gloucester who held it in 1316 (Hutch[3] 1 81).

HAYMORE (lost, about SY 965885), 1571 Hutch[3] (— *Marsh*), 1774 Hutch[1], 1861 Hutch[3], 'the moor called *Hymore extra Wareham*' 1280 ib, (*pastur' voc'*) *Hymore in Purbyk(e)* 1456 *Weld*[1], 1461 *Rent*, 1463 *Weld*[1], *Hey-* 1464, 1469 *ib*, *Hygh-*, *Highmore in Purbike*, *-byke* 1474 *MinAcct*, 1475 *Weld*[1], 'marshy ground where hay was made', *v.* hēg (WSax (hī(e)g), mōr, with mersc, cf. Isle of Purbeck *supra*, Wareham par. *infra*.

MIDDLEBERE FM (SY 968864), E MIDDLEBERE BARN, S MIDDLEBERE, *Middlebere* 1291 Hutch[3], 1826 Gre, *Middel-*, *Myddelber(e)* 1376 (1393) Pat *et freq* to 1498 *Ct* (with addition *in Purbike*, *-byke* 1459, 1470 *Lane*), *-beare* 1468 IpmR, *Midlebere* 1550 Midd, *-bury* c. 1586 Tres, *East —*, *West Middleburgh* 1774 Hutch[1], *-borough* 1795 Boswell, 'middle (woodland) pasture or wood', *v.* middel, bǣr[2] or bearu, cf. Isle of Purbeck *supra*; perhaps 'middle' in relation to Arne and Corfe C. par. *supra*; *West* probably refers to Middlebere Fm. For the confusion of the second el. in later forms with burh (dat.sg. *byrig*) 'fortification', cf. Haselbury B. par. *infra*. Middlebere was formerly part of the manor of Langton Wallis, cf. Langton Mat. par. *supra* and Langton Wallis *infra*. There were salt-pits here at least as early as the 12th cent., *v.* Salterns Copse *infra*.

REDCLIFF FM (SY 932866), REDCLIFFE CTGS, *Radeclive* 1256 Cl, *Redclyffe* 1545 Ct, 1586 DCMDeed, 1624 *DCMDeed* (— *Farme*), *-cliff(e)* 1554 Hutch[3], 1811 OS, *(the) Farme of Redclyf(fe)* 1585 Pitt, *Red Cliff* 1826 Gre, '(at) the red cliff', *v.* rēad (wk. obl. *rēadan*), clif (dat. sg. *clife*), so called 'from the red cliff on the banks of the river [the Frome] near which it stands' (Hutch[1] 1 26).

RIDGE (FM) (SY 937865), *Rygge* 1431 FA, *Rydge* 1632 Pitt, *Ridge* 1795 Boswell, 'the ridge', *v.* hrycg.

SLEPE (FM) (SY 964859) [slip], *Slepe* 1244 Ass, 1428 Midd, 1575 Saxton, *Sleape* 1584 DCMDeed, *Slape* 1811 OS, *Sleppe* 1244 Ass, *Slep(p)* 1632 Pitt, 'a slippery muddy place', *v.* slæp, cf. Slepe in Lytchett Min. par. *infra* and Slape in Netherbury par. *infra*; this is low-lying ground near Poole Harbour. According to Hutch[3] 1 463 there was once a hunting lodge here, cf. Hartland Moor *infra*, Isle of Purbeck *supra*. For a description of the bounds between Slepe and Stoborough *infra*, and between Slepe and *Midder Curcy infra*, in 1632, *v.* Pitt f. 61.

STOBOROUGH (SY 924862)

Stanberge 1086 DB, 1284 Cl, *-be(r)gh* 1293 Ipm
Stabergh 1253 Drew, 1280 Ass, 14 Wim, 1319 MinAcct, *-berge* p1483 Sheen
Stoburgh(e) 1315, 1412 FF, 1477 DCMDeed (— *iuxta Warham*), 1483 MinAcct, 1495 Ipm, *-bargh* 1431 FA, *-bor(r)o(u)gh(e)* 1512, 1546 Ct, 1585, 1632 Pitt, 1664 HTax (*Borough of —*), *-broghe* 1513 Ct, *-browe* 1545 ib, *-burrough* 1624 DCMDeed, *-borrow* 1707 Eg, *Stoughborough* 1515 Ct, *Stowboro(we)* 1535 Ct, 1575 Saxton, c. 1586 Tres, *-borough* 1773 Bayly, *Stouborowe* 1539 Ct, *Stoveberowe* c. 1628 Strode

'Stony hill or barrow', *v.* stān, beorg, cf. Warham par. *infra*. For the loss of ME *-n-* before a labial consonant, cf. W Stafford par. *infra*; for the replacement of the second el. by burh 'fortification', cf. Charborough in Morden par. *infra*. There was a mill here in 1086

DB (VCHDo **3** 87), cf. the mention of a water mill here or in Worgret *infra* in 1409 Hutch³ 1 415.

WORGRET (SY 907869) ['wəːgət]

   Vergroh 1086 DB, Exon

   Weregrote, Wiregrote 1086 DB

   Wergerod(e) 1202 FF, 1244, 1288 *Ass*, *-rede* 1288 *ib* (p), *Wergh(e)-rode* 1227 FF, 1244, 1268 *Ass*, *Wereghrode* 1266 FF, *Werwerode* 1288 *Ass*, *Wer(e)grede* 1331 Pat, 1393 Fine

   Wirgorod 1244 *Ass* (p), *Wirgrode* 1285 FA, *-rede* 1327 *SR*, 1370 *DCMDeed*, 1474 *Weld¹*, 1483 *MinAcct*, *Wyrwode* 1280 *Ass*, *Wirerode* 1288 *ib*, *Wyr(e)gherode* 1288 *ib*, 1544 *DCMDeed*, *-rede*, *Wyrhgherode* 1288 *Ass*, *Wyrede* 1314 Pat, *Wyrg(e)red(e)* 1316 FA, 1326, 1327 *Ass* (— *iuxta Warham*) *et freq* to 1457 *Weld¹*, *Wirgerede* 1337 DorR, *Wyreherode* 1544 *DCMDeed*

   Worcherod 1244 *Ass* (p)

   Wurg-, Worgrode 1311 Ipm

   Wyrthgrede 1381 *DCMDeed*

   Wygrete 1412 FA, *Wygrett* 1533 AD V

   Wolgrett 1572 *Comm*, *Wooll gret* 1697 *DCMCt*

   Worgret 1575 Saxton, 1773 Bayly, *-rett* 1795 Boswell, *Wurgrett* 1545 *DCMDeed*, *Wo(o)rgreate* 1584 *ib*

   Wargat c. 1586 Tres

'The gallows', *v.* **wearg-rōd**, as first proposed by Ekwall in Studies¹ 91, cf. Wareham par. *infra*; Ekwall *loc. cit.* suggested that the hard *-g-* may have arisen from early misdivision of the compound as *wear-grōd*. Worgret is one mile W of Wareham on the road to Dorchester. There was a mill here in 1086 DB (VCHDo **3** 76, 95), cf. Stoborough *supra*.

ARNE BAY, 1774 Hutch¹, called *Hope Bay* 1844 *TAMap, v.* **bay¹**; *Hope* is probably hōp² 'a hoop', referring to its almost circular shape, rather than hop¹ 'enclosed plot in marshland'. ARNE DAIRY HO, FM, HEATH (1778–88 *DROSurv*), HILL & Ho. BALLS LAKE, a small channel in Poole Harbour, possibly named from some onshore feature, *v.* **ball** 'rounded hill', but cf. Sam *Ball* (Wareham) 1650 DCMDeed, *v.* **lacu** 'water-course'.BANK GATE CTGS. BARTLETT'S FIRS, cf. Thomas *Bartlett* 1765 Hutch³. BEGGAR'S LANE. BIG WD. BOG LANE, cf. *Bog* 1843 *TA* (Wareham Holy T.), *v.* **bog**. BOWER POINT, *Bowerpoint* 1811 OS, probably būr¹ 'cottage', *v.* **point**, but perhaps the surname *Bower*.

BROAD LOOE, — *Loo* 1811 OS, a small channel in Poole Harbour; the term *loo(e)*, also used in the names of two similar channels, Shag Looe and Wood Bar Looe in Wareham par. *infra*, is probably the Corn word lo 'inlet of water, pool' found in the Corn r.n. Looe (RN 258–9), cf. EPN s.v. luh. BROAD MARSH. BROOKS'S ISLAND (lost), 1778–88 *DROSurv*, 1845 *TA*, *Brixes Isle* 1811 OS, cf. *Brookes Gdn*, *Brookes's Salt Plot* 1778–88 *DROSurv*, 1845 *TA*, the surname *Brook(e)(s)*, cf. John *Broke* 1477 DCMDeed, sometimes confused with the surname *Brix*, cf. John *Brix* 1340 NI (E Stoke) and Brixeys Lane in Wareham par. *infra*, v. ēg-land, salt[2]; the island, once c. 150 yards SW of Gigger's Island in Wareham par. *infra*, has now disappeared. CHURCHILL'S CTG (lost), W of the village (Legg 79). CLUMP (lost), 1826 Gre, at SY 966885, v. clump. COOMBE, 1826 Gre, *Combe* 1811 OS, cf. *Coomb Hill* 1750 DROCt, *Goom Hill*, *Coombe Coppice & Moor*, *North Coombe* 1778–88 *DROSurv*, 1845 *TA*, *Middle & South Coombe* 1845 *ib.*, v. cumb 'valley'. CREECH (lost), 1826 Gre, at SY 920853 but perhaps due to a misreading of Creech Heath (in Ch. Knowle par. *infra*) on 1811 OS. EASTMORE (lost), 1861 Hutch[3], *Estmore* 1291 (16) *Pitt*, *-moore*, *-moure* 1545–1629 *DCMDeed*, *Higher East Moor* 1679 DCMDeed, 'eastern marshy ground', v. ēast, mōr; situated 'west of Stowborough, lying against the R. Frome' (Hutch[3] 1 100); perhaps *east* in relation to Worgret *supra*. FROXEN COPSE, — *Coppice & Cl* 1845 *TA*, — *Heath* 1778–88 *DROSurv*, 1845 *TA*, *Frogston(e)* 1750, 1777 *DROCt*, *Froxon* 1778–88 *DROSurv*, 'stone or rock where frogs are found', v. frogga, stān. GALLOWS HILL & PLANT., where the Corfe C.-Wareham road crosses the Arne–Corfe C. par. bdy, v. galga, hyll. GOLD POINT, *Aren pointe* 1575 Saxton, *Arnpoynt* c. 1586 Tres, *Arne or Cold Point* 1774 Hutch[1], *Gold Point* 1778–88 *DROSurv*, 1811 OS, — *or Goer Point* 1845 *TA*, at first 'the promontory near Arne (*supra*)', v. point, then 'cold promontory', v. cald, later replaced by or confused with gold. Gold Point faces NE on to Poole Harbour. GOLD POINT HEATH, from prec. GRANGE RD, *the road to Grange* 1774 Hutch[1], to Creech Grange in Steeple par. *infra*. GRIP HEATH, v. gryppe 'ditch, drain'. HALFWAY HO (P.H.), roughly half-way between Wareham and Corfe C.; a building on the same site (or some other feature in the immediate vicinity) is called *Hixon(s) Head* 1811 OS, 1826 Gre, probably from the surname *Hickson* with hēafod 'hill-top' (there is a hill here). HARTLAND MOOR, cf. *Harttesknolle* 1545 Ct, *Hartnole Hill* 1632 *Pitt*, 'hart's hill-top or hillock',

v. heorot, cnoll, with hyll; Hartland Moor lies ½ mile SW of Slepe
supra where there was once a hunting lodge, cf. Isle of Purbeck
supra. HIGH TOR, *v.* torr 'a rock, rocky outcrop', cf. Turford *infra*;
there is a hill here with earthworks (6"). HOLME LANE, to E Holme
par. *infra*. HYDE'S QUAY, *Hydes* — 1811 OS, from the *Hyde* family
which dug clay nearby and shipped it from here in 17th–18th cent.
(Legg 43), cf. *atte Hyde de Wyrgrede infra*. IVY CTGS. KING'S ARMS
(P.H.). KING'S BARROW (a tumulus, marked 6"), giving its name to
KING BARROW, THE KING'S BARROW; *King-Barrow* 1774 Hutch[1],
Kings Barrow 1811 OS, cf. *Kings Barrow Grd* 1843 *TA*, 'the king's
barrow', *v.* cyning, beorg, due to its associations, legendary or otherwise, cf. the account of its excavation in 1767 in Hutch[3] 1 100 where
the opinion is cited that 'it is highly probable that it belonged to some
petty prince or chieftain of the Saxons or Danes'. LANGTON WALLIS
(HEATH), names reminiscent of the fact that Middlebere *supra* was
formerly part of the manor of Langton Wallis, a name now lost apart
from this transferred instance, *v.* Langton Mat. par. *supra*. THE
LOOK OUT, a house on the Wareham–Corfe C. road. LUDCROFT
(lost), 1774 Hutch[1], 1861 Hutch[3], *North* —, *the Souther Ludcrofte*
1624 *DCMDeed*, perhaps the ME surname *Lude* (common in Do
in 1332 SR), *v.* croft, norð, sūðerra; it is described by Hutch[3] 1
101 as 'a farm in Stowborough tithing, on the east'. MAIN CHANNEL,
1811 OS, *Great Channell* 17 *DROMap*, the largest channel in Poole
Harbour, cf. Middle Channel *infra*; alternatively known as *the
Swatchway* 1882 Robinson, *v.* swatchway. MELANCHOLY LANE,
perhaps jocularly so called because it leads nowhere; it is marked
but not named on 1811 OS. MIDDLEBERE HEATH (*-beere-* 1811 OS),
LAKE (*-beere Channel* 1811 OS, a channel in Poole Harbour) &
QUAY (on Poole Harbour, now disused), cf. *Middleburgh Bay* 1661
Hutch[1], all from Middlebere *supra*. MIDDLE CHANNEL, *Little Chan-
nel(l)* 17 *DROMap*, 1811 OS, in Poole Harbour, cf. Main Channel
supra. MIDDLE GRD, 1811 OS, a mudbank between two channels in
Poole Harbour, cf. White Ground Lake in Studland par. *supra*.
THE MOORS, *v.* mōr. NEW INN (P.H.). NEW LINE FM (local), from a
railway line used for transporting clay in 19th cent. (Legg 46).
NUTCRACK LANE, cf. *N & S Nutcroft, Nutcroft Leg* 1843 *TA*
(Wareham Holy T.), *v.* hnutu, croft, leg, cf. *Notcrofte* Gl 4 140.
PATCHINS POINT, *Pagins* — 1778–88 *DROSurv*, 1845 *TA*, *Patchins
or Pagans* — 1861 Hutch[3], the surname *Patchin*, *v.* point. RIDGE
WHARF, on R. Frome, from Ridge *supra*. RODWELL, possibly

hrēod 'reed' or rōd[2] 'a cross', with wella, cf. Springfield *infra* which
is 300 yds N. RUSSEL QUAY, 1811 OS, — *key* 1774 Hutch[1], *Russel
Point* 1609 ib, cf. *crofta q' Petrus Russel tenuit* 1319 *MinAcct*, *v.*
key, point. ST EDWARD'S CTG, so called because it is 'said to be built
upon the foundations of the cottage to which the body of Edward the
Martyr was taken and hidden in a well in the garden' (Swanage
TGuide), *v.* St Edward's Bridge in Corfe C. par. *supra.* ST
NICHOLAS'S CHURCH, 'the chapel of *Arne*' 1388 Pat, *Arnee Chappell*
1646 SC, formerly 'a chapel of ease to the church of Holy Trinity
in Wareham' (Hutch[3] 1 99). SALTERNS COPSE, cf. *Kitsaltorn*
1749, *Saltorns* 1762, (*Kitt*) *Saltern* 1777 all *DROCt*, *Hither,
Middle & Yonder Saltern* 1819 DCMDeed, (*Kid*) *Salton* 1778–88
DROSurv, (*Dry Grd or*) *Hither Salton, Kid, Middle & Yonder
Salton* 1845 *TA*, 'building(s) where salt was made or sold', *v.*
salt-ærn; *Kit(t)*, *Kid* may represent the pers.n. or surname *Kit(t)*,
with loss of possessive -*s* due to metanalysis of *Kit's Saltorn*. There
were salt-pans here at an early date: *salinis...ad manerium...de
Langetona adiacentibus* a1165 MontC ('salt-pans adjacent to the
manor of Langton (Wallis)', *v.* Middlebere *supra*), *salinis...in
Purbeke* c. 1170 ib (cf. Isle of Purbeck *supra*), 'the salt-pits of
Middelbere' 1376 (1393) Pat, and *domus voc' Salthouse* 1423 *Midd*
(*v.* salt[1], hūs), all refer to salt making in this area, cf. also the reference
in 15 *ShaftR* (ff. 60v–61) to a hide of land in Arne devoted entirely
to the production of salt, over twenty tenants of the Abbey of St
Edward at Shaftesbury holding one or more salt-pans each; there
are numerous saltings marked in this area (6″); for other references
to the salt industry in Purbeck, *v.* Saltings in Corfe C. par. *supra*,
Salterne in Studland par. *supra*, and VCHDo 2 327, 3 22–3. SHIPSTAL
POINT, *Shepstall* c. 1586 Tres, *Shipstol Point* 1774 Hutch[1], *Shipstal*
1811 OS, cf. *Sheepstall Bay* 1661 Hutch[1], 'a sheepfold', *v.* scēap,
stall, with point. SLEPE COPSE, HEATH (*Sleap* — 1778–88 *DROSurv*,
1845 *TA*, *Slape* — 1811 OS), MOOR (*Sleap* — 1778–88 *DROSurv*,
1845 *TA*) & PLANT., from Slepe *supra*. SOLDIERS RD (local), Legg
154. SOUTH CAUSEWAY, *the Causewaye leadinge betweene Wareham...
and Stoborough* 1620 DCMDeed, *South Causey* 1707 Eg, *Wareham
Causeway* 1774 Hutch[1], cf. *Causeway by Cobs Leg* 1843 *TA* (Wareham
Holy T.), *v.* caucie, Cobs Leg *infra*, cf. *Midder Curcy infra*; it is
described in Hutch[1] 1 22 as 'a causeway raised on stone, 800 paces
long'; 'south' in relation to Wareham par. *infra.* SOUTH LAKE, a
channel in Poole Harbour, *v.* lacu. SPRINGFIELD, *v.* spring, cf.

Rodwell *supra*. STOBOROUGH CROFT, GREEN, HEATH (1811 OS) &
WITHY BED, from Stoborough *supra*. SUNNYSIDE, a house. THREE
BARROWS, three tumuli marked 6″, *v.* beorg. TURFORD, *Torford* 1811
OS, probably 'ford at the rock', *v.* torr, ford, cf. High Tor *supra*;
Turford is on the shores of Wareham Channel (the estuary of R.
Frome) in Wareham par. *infra*, and this was perhaps a place where
the river could at one time be crossed, but there is also a small stream
or inlet marked 6″ to which the name might refer. TURNER'S COVE,
1811 OS, *Turners* 1707 *Eg*, cf. Martha *Turner* 1789 Hutch[3], *v.* cove.
WEST LANE, 'west' with reference to the Corfe C.–Wareham road.
WEST SPRING LAKE, a channel in Poole Harbour, *v.* spring, lacu.
WITHY BED, 1843 *TA* (Wareham Lady St M.). WORGRET FM,
HEATH (1811 OS), HEATH FM & HILL, from Worgret *supra*.

FIELD-NAMES

Fields now in Arne but in Wareham Holy T. *TA* are marked †, and fields
now in Arne but in Wareham Lady St M. *TA* are marked ‡. The undated
forms are 1845 *TA* 8 (those marked † are 1843 *TA* 239 and those marked
‡ are 1843 *TA* 240). Spellings dated 1305, 1389, 1428, 16, 1518, 1584,
1627, 1633, 1654 are Hutch[3], 1326 *Ass*, 1327 *SR*, 1332 SR, 1340 NI,
n.d. (1372) *ChrP*, 1379 Weld[1], n.d. (15) *ShaftR*, 1422, 1423 *Midd*, 1477,
1565, 1624 *DCMDeed*, 1483 *MinAcct*, p1483 *Sheen*, 1547[2], 1545 *Ct*, 1572
Comm, 1579 Hutch[1], 1632 *Pitt*, 1664 HTax, 1737, 1738, 1740, 1747, 1748,
1749, 1750, 1753, 1755 *DROCt*, 1778–88 *DROSurv*, 1849 *DRO*, and the
rest DCMDeed.

(a) The Acres (1778–88); Arne Md (1778–88); Arne Moor (1778–88,
— *Moure* 1545, *v.* mōr); Bakers Salt Plot (1778–88, cf. Thomas *Baker*
1532, 1664, *v.* salt[2]); †Barkers md; †Barn Cl; Hr & Lr Barn Cl (1778–88);
† Hr & Lr beetles md (*Bydellismede iuxta Stoburgh* 1477, *Bidell'mede* 1483,
'the beadle's meadow', *v.* bydel, mǣd, though it is possible the first
el. is used as a surname); Bitters Gall (Salt Plot) (1778–88, 'wet spot
frequented by the bittern', *v.* butur, galla, cf. Isle of Purbeck *supra*); †Hr,
Middle & Lr Bland (perhaps analogous with Bland YW **6** 264, for which
Ekwall DEPN suggests OE gebland 'commotion, storm', hence 'windy
place'); ‡Bonds 7 acres (cf. 'tenement... late of Terricus *Bonde*' 1389, and
Bonds Cl in Wareham par. *infra*); †Brick kiln Cl; Bridle Marsh (1778–88,
'watery land fit for a horse to cross', *v.* brigdels, mersc); †‡Broad Cl, Broad
Cl (1778–88); †Broad greens (the surname *Green*, or grēne[2] 'grassy spot');
Broom Cl (1778–88); †Browns fd; †Burds gdn (cf. *Bush-head Gdn* in Wareham par. *infra*); †(Lt) Burnham (*prat' voc' Bernesham* 1422, *the Aldrene-
burnames* 1565, *Burn(e)ham Lake*, — *Meade* 1624, 'Beorn's enclosure',
from the OE pers.n. *Beorn* and hamm, with alren, lacu, mǣd); †Bushrods
inclosure (from the Do surname *Bushrod*); †Calves Pdk; †Canal withey
bed (*v.* canel); †Castle cl (*v.* castel(l); the significance of the term in this

name is not apparent); †Cherry hays (v. chiri, (ge)hæg); †Clay ho; †Cliff (cl) (cf. *Clifton Barrow* 1632, v. clif, tūn, beorg); †Hr, Lr & Middle cobs leg (cf. Nicholas *Cobb* 1664 (Wareham), v. leg); Common (1778–88), †The Common; ‡Conegre Mdw (v. coninger); Coppice Closes (1778–88); Coreans Blind Lane (1778–88), Hill (1778–88, *Gorrings* — 1747) & New Cl (1778–88) (cf. *Late Corens* 1802 (B.K.), *Coreans Tenement* 1807 (ib), perhaps to be associated with *Garinges* n.d. (1372) (f. 127v) which is possibly an old folk-name in -ingas, either 'the people of (a man called) *Gāra*' or 'dwellers at the gāra or triangular piece of land', cf. Goring O 51, v. blind); Cosloe (1778–88, *Costlows* 1819, perhaps 'mound(s) where a trial was held', v. cost[1], hlāw, cf. Coarselow Db 25); †Cothey plot (v. cot, (ge)hæg); †Late Cribbs md (cf. Nicholas *Crubbe* 1305, Hugh *Crybbe* 1585); ‡Croft; †Crumplers md; Cull (Cl) (1778–88), Brookes Cull (ib, perhaps from OE (WSax) cwylla 'spring, well'; for *Brookes*, v. Brooks's Island *supra* and cf. Downlands *infra*); Dock Cl (1778–88, v. docce); Downlands (*Downslands* 1740), Brookes Downland (1778–88, v. dūn, land, cf. Brookes Cull *supra*); †Duckhouse md & plot; †Durhams cl (cf. Edmond *Derham* 1664 (Morden)); East Acres (1778–88) & Cl (ib); ‡Lt & Upr east fd; †8 acres; Elm Tree Coppice & Moor (1778–88); †Enclosure; 5 Acres (1778–88), †(East) 5 acres, 5 Acres against town; ‡Fooks Hill Grd (cf. Henry *Fouke* 1434, John *Fooke* 1664); †4 acres; †Lr 14 acres; Furzey Grd (1778–88), Vineyard (ib) & Weat Cl (ib, v. vinȝerd, hwæte 'wheat' or wēt); †Furzey Grds; Fustle Gate Moor (*Furze Hill Gate* 1737, *Fustle* 1778–88, v. fyrs, hyll); Gattles Fds (1749, 1778–88, perhaps a p.n. 'goat hill', v. gāt, hyll, or the like, or a surname derived from such a p.n.); †Gildings moor (the surname *Gilding*, or a reduced form of the surname of Hugh *Guldewyn* 1332); Go Croft (1778–88, *Goocroft* 1749, perhaps 'cuckoo enclosure', v. goke, croft, cf. Cuckoo Pen in Corfe C. par. *supra*, but the first el. may be a surname derived from the same word, cf. Gooks Ho in Corfe C. par. *supra*); Dripping Pan Goddus, Hr & Middle Goddus (*Goddest* 1737, *Goddis* 1746, *Goddess* 1748, *Goddus* 1778–88, 1819 (*Lower* —), perhaps 'good sheep-fold', v. gōd[2], eowestre; 'dripping pan' is a complimentary nickname for productive land, v. Cameron 209, but it could also refer to shape); †Gold moor (golde 'marsh marigold' or gold 'gold', cf. Gold Point *supra*); †Gooddens fd (cf. Stephen *God(e)wyn(e)* 1305, 1327, 1332, Robert *Gooden* 1664; for the development in the surname, cf. Goddins in Studland par. *supra*); ‡Great fd; †Great grd; Great Grd (1778–88); ‡Green Cl; Green Cl (1778–88, v. grēne[1]); Greenfield or Stoney Cl (1778–88, *Green Fd* 1747); Greens Fd (1778–88) & Moor (ib, cf. Simon *Grene* 1546); Inner, Outer & Yonder Ground Above Moor (1778–88); †Hr, Lr & Middle half acre; Ham (v. hamm); Hatchets Cl (1778–88) & Md (ib); Hay Croft (1778–88, v. hēg); †Heady md (perhaps ME hefding 'headland of a common field, etc', cf. Heady Fds YW 2 284); Heath Hill (1750); Hern (*Horn* 1778–88, v. hyrne 'angle, nook', horn 'projecting nook of land, bend', cf. Three Horn Cross *infra*); †Home barn cl, Home Cl (Plot), Home Md & Plot; ‡Home Grd; †Horse Cl (lag) (v. lagge); Horse Grd (1778–88); Inner & Outer Jackhams (1778–88, 'small water-meadows', v. jack, hamm; by the Frome estuary); †Jenkins' grd; ‡Jiggers Ham (cf. Lawrence *Grigger* (probably for

Gigger) 1664, *v.* hamm, cf. Gigger's Island in Wareham par. *infra*); †Kitcats
cl (perhaps 'close where the game of tip-cat was played', or an allusion to
the 18th-cent. Whig club in London, *v.* kit-cat, cf. NED s.v.); Kite Moor
(1778–88, *v.* cȳta); ‡Knotmoor (*v.* cnotta); Gt & Lt Lachover (1778–88,
probably 'swampy river-bank or slope', *v.* læcc, ōfer[1] or ofer[2]); Langleys
Island (1778–88, cf. Samuel *Langley* 1664 (Wareham)); †Lawn (cf. *the
Wester Lawnes* 1624, *v.* launde, westerra); Limekiln Cl (1778–88); Little
Grd (1778–88); †Little Moor; †Long Cl; Long Cl (1778–88); †Longlands
(*v.* land); †Long md (*Longe Meade* 1624, *v.* lang[1], mǣd); ‡Hr & Lr Long
Md; †Loops Cl, Loops Salt Grd (1778–88, cf. George *Loop(e)* (of *Slepe*)
1633, 1654, 1664); †Lynch Common & Lane (Cl) (*v.* hlinc); †Marsh,
†The salt marsh (cf. *mariscus* 1326, *v.* mersc); Mead Cl (1778–88), Meadow
(*Mead* ib, *v.* mǣd); Merry Fd (1778–88, an area of swamp and scrub remote
from village, so probably myrge 'pleasant' used ironically, cf. Merry Fd in
Corfe C. par. *supra*, but Do dial. *merry* 'the wild cherry' (Barnes 81) is
perhaps also possible); †Middlebere Cmn (from Middlebere *supra*); Middle
Fd Vineyard (1778–88, *Vineyard* 1748, *v.* vinȝerd); †Middle Grds & Md;
‡Mil(l)ditch Md (*Myldyche* 1545 *DCMDeed*, with reference to Wareham
Mill in Wareham par. *infra*, *v.* dīc); †‡Moor; ‡Motts grd; Nether Cl
(1778–88); ‡New Cl, Gt & Hthr New Closes (1778–88); †New en-,
inclosure; ‡New Gdn; †‡New Md; †New Pce; †9 acres; North Cl (1778–
88), Grd (ib) & Plot (ib); (Lt) Norton Plot (Norden — 1819, perhaps
from norð, denu); †Old Md; †Ord Cl (cf. 'two grounds called *Orde*',
Orde Point 16, *v.* ord, point); Park (1740, *v.* park); †Parmiters (moor)
(cf. Mathew *Parmonter*, *-munter* 1340, *-menter* 1350, John *Parmiter* 1658);
Peak (*Pook* 1778–88, *v.* pēac 'something pointed', the earlier form perhaps
influenced by Pook *infra*; it is at the tip of Gold Point *supra*); †Pit flg (*Pitt
furlonge* 1624, *v.* pytt, furlang); Pitts Fd, Plot, Salt Grd & Salt Plot (all
1778–88, cf. *Pitts Tenement* 1664, from the *Pitt* family who were lords of the
manor from 16th cent.); Place (1778–88, perhaps an altered form of plæsc
'pool'); ‡Hr & Lr Plot; (Inner & Outer) Pook (1778–88), Pook Marsh
(ib; *Pook* is perhaps a back-formation from *Pook Marsh* 'watery land where
goblins are found', *v.* pūca, mersc, cf. Peak *supra* and foll.); Pooks Cl
(1778–88, 'goblin's close', cf. prec.); †Popals Md (cf. William *Paple* 1546,
— *Pople* 1552); †Priory gdn & md (*the Priory Meade alias Home Meade*
1624, perhaps belonging to St Mary's Priory in Wareham par. *infra*, or
to Holme Priory in E Holme par. *infra*); Ridge Md (1778–88), Gt & Lt
Ridge Moor (1738, *v.* hrycg); Rogers Croft (1778–88) & Fd (1747); ‡Rough
Leaze (*v.* lǣs); †‡Rough Pasture; †Rough Pce; Round Cl (1778–88); Rushy
Marsh (1778–88); Rye Cl (1778–88); Salt Grd (1778–88, *v.* salt[2]); †Sconce
(*Sconse Meadowes* 1624, *v.* skonce 'small earthwork, shelter (from the elements)', cf. YW 4 168, Wt 130); †Scots cl; ‡Sedge Grd (*v.* secg[1]); †‡7
Acres; Sharps Croft (1778–88); ‡6 Acres; Gt & Lt Somershire (1778–88,
Lt Somersetshire 1819, perhaps 'share of land used only in summer', *v.*
sumor, scearu, or 'Somer's share of land' from the ME surname *Somer*
common in Do (e.g. 1332 SR), if one may assume the second el. has been
confused with or replaced by scīr 'district' which has led in turn to the
substitution *Somerset-* for the first el.); South Cl (1749); South Gates

(1778–88); South Grd (1778–88); South Hay (1778–88, — *Hayes* 1753, *v.* (ge)hæg); Spear Grass Beds (1778–88, *v.* spear-grass); Stall Croft (1778–88), West Stall Plot (ib, *v.* stall); †Stepping Stones (cf. foll.); ‡Steps Pond Grd (perhaps 'pond with or near steps or stepping-stones', *v.* stæpe, ponde, cf. prec., but a surname *Step(s)* derived from some other p.n. is possible); Stone (1778–88, *v.* stān); Stoney Cl (1778–88); Stoneylands (ib, *v.* stānig); †late Tanyard (*v.* tanyard); †Tarrants (Cl) (the surname *Tarrant* from one of the Do places of that name); †Three Cornered Cl; Three Horn Cross (*Tree Horn Croft* 1755, *Three Horn Close* 1778–88, probably 'three-cornered enclosure', *v.* horn, cf. Hern *supra*; *-cross* may represent *-crofts*); †Inside, Middle & Outside Tidemoor (cf. *pasture overflowen in wynter with the tyde* 1585 *Pitt*; 'marshland covered by the flood-tide', *v.* tide, mōr, cf. Tide Moors in E Holme par. *infra*); Tophill Plot (1778–88, perhaps 'plot at the top of the hill', *v.* topp, cf. foll.); ‡Tops Hill ground (perhaps the surname *Top(p)*, but cf. prec.); Trenchards Cl (1778–88, cf. John *Trenchard* 1518); †2 Acres; ‡Venoms Mdw (perhaps 'meadow at *Venom*' from a lost p.n. *Venom* 'marshy enclosure', *v.* fenn, hamm, but a surname from such a p.n. is also possible); Hill Vieland (1778–88, cf. Hugh *Vye* 1547[2]); ‡Vittleford (perhaps 'Fitela's ford', from the OE pers.n. *Fitela* with voicing of initial *F-*, cf. Fittleton W 330, Fittleworth Sx 126, and ford; but the first el. could be the OFr pers.n. *Vitel* or a surname formed from it, cf. also Radulfus *Vitulus* p1483 (Wareham) from Lat *vitulus* 'calf'); Well Cl (& Gdn) (1778–88), †Well Cl (*v.* wella); †Welsteads Cl (cf. William *Wellsteed* 1707 *Eg*); †West Cl; (Gt & Lt) West Cl (1755), West Cl and Cote (1778–88, *v.* cot); ‡ (Lt & Hr) West Fd; †Westhill; Whitelake Md (1778–88, *v.* hwit, lacu, cf. *Whitepill Lake uppon the west side of Rydge* 1632, *v.* pyll, Ridge *supra*; the whiteness is perhaps that of salt deposits, cf. Salterns Copse *supra*, and foll.); White Moor (1778–88, cf. prec.); ‡late Whites (cf. John *White* 1507); †Windmill; Withy Moor (*v.* wiðig); Wreath Cl (1778–88, *Wreath or Weather Close* 1849, cf. Do dial. *wreath* 'a rod used in hurdle-making' (EDD s.v. *wreath* sb.[1] sense 3), 'a withe to keep hurdles and stakes together' (NED s.v. *wreath* sense 9), or 'underwood, brushwood' (EDD loc. cit. sense 5); the alternative first el. may be a poor spelling for *withe* (OE wiððe) or represent OE weðer 'a wether').

(b) *the Crosse Lake* 1632 ('stream flowing across', *v.* cross, lacu); *Fluxfurd Bridge* 1632 (cf. *regia via apud Flokesbrigge* 1423; the first el. is either the word flōc 'fluke, flounder' (perhaps appropriate if the bridge or ford lay near the tidal estuary of R. Frome), *v.* -es[2], or the surname derived from this word, cf. Richard *Flouk* 1332 (Sturminster M.), with brycg, ford; the spelling of the 17th-cent. form has perhaps been influenced by ModE *flux* 'the flowing in of the tide' (NED s.v. sense 4)); *terram le Hargg'e* p1483 (the form would seem to be corrupt); *Hornymore* 1545 (first el. possibly eModE *horny* 'hard or horn-like in texture, having horn-shaped projections', cf. horn, *v.* mōr); *atte Hyde de Wyrgrede* (p) 1379 (*v.* atte, hīd, Worgret *supra*, cf. Hyde's Quay *supra*); *Kype-Cross* 16 (perhaps cȳpe 'osier-basket (esp. for catching fish)', with cros); *atte Lake* (p) 1332 (*v.* atte, lacu); *the Lamp Light Close* 1572, 'Lamp Light Close(s)' 1579, 1627 (for maintaining a lamp in St Mary's Church in Wareham par. *infra*); *Little Crosse* 1632 (*v.* lȳtel, cros); *Longford* 1632 (*v.* lang¹, ford); *Midder Curcy* 1632 (probably for *Middel* —, *v.* middel, caucie, cf. South Causeway *supra*); *furlong' vocat' Surecrofte* 1428 ('sour or damp enclosure', *v.* sūr, croft, or 'enclosure where sorrel grows', *v.* sūre, unless this name is to be associated with *Seman Scoria...crofta* n.d. (15) (f. 61)); *Washingpole Hill* 1632 (*v.* washing, pōl¹, hyll; the combination with *Hill* might suggest that the pool was a sheep-wash); *Weaneford* 1632 (perhaps 'ford suitable for wagons', *v.* wægn (wæn), ford); *in campo de Wyrgrede juxta Wareham* 1428 (*v.* Worgret *supra*).

East Holme

EAST HOLME (SY 898860)

   Holne 1086 DB (2×), c. 1107 (14) *AddCh*, 1107–22, 1159, a1165 MontC, 1221 Cur *et freq* to 1431 FA, — *in Purbyk* 1374 Cl, *Holna* 1086 Exon, Hy 1 (14) *AddCh*, c. 1106 BM I, c. 1107 (14) *AddCh*, c. 1121 MontC, Steph (14) *AddCh*, a1165 MontC, 1214 Cur, 1290 Cl, *Holen* c. 1172, *Holn* 1189–99 MontC, 1285 FA

   Hulmo (prior de) 1206 P

   Houme, Hounne 1214 Cur, *Holm* 1218 FF, 1306 Pat, *Holme* 1280 Ass, 1337 Cl, 1512 *Ct*, 1535 Hutch³, 1546 *Ct*, *Holum* 1287 (1313) Ch, 1409 Cl

   Estholn(e) 1288 *Ass*, 1426 FF, Mansel, 1427, 1463 *Weld¹*, c. 1500 RoyRoll, *-holm(e)* 1288 *Ass*, 1512 *Ct*, 1535 *Hutch³*, 1575 Saxton, *Esteholme* 1545 Hutch³, *East Holme* c. 1586 Tres

'(At) the holly tree', *v.* holegn, -e²; for the change *n* > *m* cf. Holme YW **2** 269, ModE *holm-oak* and dial. *holm* (Barnes 73); *East* in relation to West Holme in East Stoke par. *infra* where some of the early forms may strictly belong, *v.* ēast. For the former Cluniac priory here, *v.* Holme Priory *infra*.

HOLME MOUNT (SY 906844), c. 16 Hutch³, 1774 Hutch¹, *the west syde of Holemount* 1546 *Ct*, 'the hill at Holme', *v.* mont. It reaches 210' and is described by Hutch³ **1** 555 as 'a little hill...on which is an imperfect fortification'; two tumuli are marked 6″. One of the customs of Corfe Castle (c. 16) was that 'the ffree barons and inheritours of Corffe...ought to drive their cattayle to Holme Mount in the West Walke, on Whitsonday yearly, there to depasture that daye and three dayes followinge' (Hutch³ **1** 498), *v. the West Walke infra*.

HOLME PRIORY (SY 899859), on the site of a Cluniac priory, a cell of the priory of Montacute (So), founded about the middle of the 12th cent. (a1165 MontC, *v.* VCHDo **2** 80 ff), usually referred to as *prioria*, but cf. *Cella de Holme* 1535 Hutch[3], *Holme a celle to Montegue* 1535–43 Leland. In fact the priory of Montacute had lands here as early as c. 1107 (14) *AddCh*, cf. also *Sancte Marie de Holna* Steph (14) *AddCh*.

WOODBURY COPPICE (SY 897852), — *Hill* 1841 *TA, Wodebury* 1323 *MinAcct*, 'fortified place at the wood', *v.* wudu, burh (dat.sg. *byrig*); there is apparently no evidence for an ancient site here, cf. Woodbury in Bere R. par. *infra.*

BAGSHOT, perhaps from bagga and scēat, cf. Bagshot Sr 153, EPN **1** 17 and Bagshot W 354 which has a different origin. BATTLE PLAIN, 1861 Hutch[3], the site of a battle during the Civil War (Short 99), *v.* bataille. DOREY'S CTG & FM. HOLME FM, HEATH & LANE (PLANT.). JOB'S PLAIN, 1841 *TA*, cf. Henry *Jobbe* 1340 NI (Kimmeridge). LYCH GATE, *v.* lich-gate. MONKS' POND, described in Hutch[3] **1** 554 as 'an old fish-pond, traditionally known by the name of "the Monks' Pond"'. It is near Holme Priory *supra* and is probably the 'fish-pond' mentioned in an inquisition of 1281 (VCHDo **2** 80). NEW BARN (CTGS). ST JOHN'S CHURCH, built in 1866 (Kelly). SQUIRREL CTG (local), Legg 117. THREE LORDS' BARROW, 1843 *TAMap*, a tumulus (marked 6″) where the bounds of four pars. – E Holme, Arne, Ch. Knowle and Steeple – now meet, but no doubt at one time a bound of three manors. WITHY BED, cf. *New Willow Bed* 1841 *TA, v.* wiðig.

FIELD-NAMES

The undated forms are 1841 *TA* 110. Spellings dated 1391, 16, 1545 are Hutch[3], 1393 Fine, 1463, 1640 *Weld*[1], 1664 HTax.

(*a*) Barrow Cl (*v.* beorg); Brick Kiln Cl; Bushy Plot; (Hr) Butts green & 5 Acres (*v.* butt[2] or butte, grēne[2]); (Button's) Cowleaze; Creech (a piece of water meadow on R. Frome (once) belonging to the manor of East Creech in Ch. Knowle par. *infra,* referred to as 'three perches of meadow on the south side of the river Frome' Ed **1** Hutch[3], 'an acre of meadow in Holme Mead, near the river Frome' 1391 ib, cf. Povington, Worgrett, and *Holme Mead infra*); Dovers Md (cf. Thomas *Dover* 1664); Dragling Acre; (Hr) 5 Acres; 4 Acres; Gt Fourty Acres; Front Mdw; Gally's Water Mdw (the surname *Gally,* or galga 'gallows'); Hr & Lr Hams, (Hr) Ham(s) Cl (*v.* hamm); Holme Ho; Kite Hills (*v.* cȳta); Little Cmn & Plot; Hr & Lr

Madmoors (probably 'marshland used as meadow', *v*. mǣd, mōr, cf. Madgrove in Ch. Knowle par. *infra*; for the development to *Mad-*, cf. Madden Gl 3 34); New Cl & Coppice; Overlake ('stream near a bank or slope', *v*. ōfer[1], ofer[2], lacu, or 'higher stream', *v*. uferra); Gt & Lt Peak (*v*. pēac); Plantation; Plats (*v*. plat[2]); Potters Fd; Povington (a piece of water meadow on R. Frome, no doubt once belonging to the manor of Povington in Tyneham par. *infra*, cf. Creech *supra*); Rabbit Holes; Rum Pits (perhaps rūm[2] 'spacious, wide', unless this is an allusion to the smuggling of *rum* (the spirit)); 7 Acres; Small pce by the River; 10 Acres; Tide Moors (*v*. tide, mōr, cf. Tidemoor in Arne par. *supra*; the field lies next to R. Frome; according to Hutch[1] 1 23 'even at present [i.e. 1774], on great spring tides, the tide flows up to *Holm Bridge*' (one mile further up river in E Stoke par. *infra*)); 12 Acres; Water Mdw; Way Cl (*v*. weg); Weld's Acre & 3 Acres; Well Cl (*v*. wella); White's Island; Worgrett (a piece of water meadow on R. Frome (once) belonging to the manor of Worgret in Arne par. *supra*, referred to as 'an acre of meadow in *Holnemede*' 1393, cf. Creech and Povington *supra*, *Holme Mead infra*).

(*b*) 'close...called *le courte*' 1545 (*v*. court); 'Holme Mead' 1391, *Holnemede* 1393, 1463, *Eastholme Mead* 1640 (*v*. mǣd, cf. Creech *supra* and West Holme Md in E Stoke par. *infra*); *the Weste Walke* c. 16 (*v*. west, walk 'sheep-walk', cf. Holme Mount *supra*).

Kimmeridge

Swalland was in Corfe Castle par. *supra* in 1795 Boswell.

KIMMERIDGE (SY 917798)

    Cameric 1086 DB, Exon

    Cuneliz 1086 DB

    Kimerich 1212 Fees, 1244 *Ass* (p), 1323 *Ct*, 1344 (14) Cerne, *Kimerik* 1244 *Ass* (p), *Kymeriz* 1268 *ib* (p), *Kymery(c)z* 1268 *ib* (p), *Kymerich(e)*, *-rych(e)* 1280 *ib* (p), 1288 *ib*, 1291 Tax, 1303, 1316 FA, 1327 *SR*, 1332 SR, 1344 (14) Cerne, 1346, 1428, 1431 FA, 1464 *Weld*[1], — *in Purbyk(e)*, *-bik* 1376 *Ass*, Pat, 1384 *DCMDeed*, 1411 *Weld*[1], — *Magna* 1405, 1414 Mansel, *West* — 1470 Hutch[3], *Kymerigh* 1303 FA, *Kymershe* 1373 IpmR, *Kymerycche* 1428 FA, *Kymeryg(g)e* 1489 *Ct*, 1553 Mansel (*Greatt* —), 1554 ib (*Grete* —), *-rige* 1526 Hutch[3], *-rege* ib, 1535 *Ct*, *-ridge* 1545 *ib*, *-rydge* 1546 *ib*, *Kymbrige* 1512 *ib*, *Kimbridge* 1575 Saxton, c. 1586 Tres, *Great Kimridge* 1630 Hutch[3], *Great Kimmeridge* 1795 Boswell

    Kemeriz 1224 Cur, 14 Mansel (p), *-rich* 1230 P (p), 1288 *Ass*, *-rice* 1244 *ib* (p), *-rych* 1280 *ib* (p), *Kemerydge in Purbeyke* 1563 *Mansel*

Cumerig(g), *-rygg(e)* 1285 FA, *Cumerich* 1303 FA, n.d. (1372)
ChrP, *-rych* 1340 NI, *-righ* 1303 FA
Kynerich 1288 *Ass*

Probably 'convenient or splendid strip of land, stream, or narrow road', *v*. cȳme, ric, as suggested in DEPN s.n. and EPN **1** 123; of the possible meanings 'convenient road' would perhaps well describe the track which runs from Smedmore Hill down through Kimmeridge to the coast at Kimmeridge Bay (*q.v. infra*), for this seems to afford the only easy access to the sea for two miles in either direction. A possible alternative first el. would be the OE pers.n. *Cȳma* derived from the adj. *cȳme* and suggested by DEPN as the first el. of Kimpton Ha and Hrt. The second el. has been influenced or replaced by OE hrycg 'ridge', as with other names derived from ric, cf. Mouldridge Db 352, Lindridge ib 507. *Great* (*v*. grēat, magna) and *west* (*v*. west) in relation to Little (or East) Kimmeridge *infra*, cf. also Isle of Purbeck *supra*. A possibly analogous name to Kimmeridge is *Boteridge* (*Botterage*) the old name for Kimmeridge Bay *q.v. infra*; the second el. could of course here be hrycg, but on the other hand it could be ric as in Kimmeridge, with bāt 'boat', bōt 'remedy, privilege', or the OE pers.n. *Bōta*; the fact that in DB Kimmeridge consists of two holdings, *Cameric* with 5 hides and *Cuneliz* with 1½ hides (VCHDo **3** 77, 95), could reflect an ancient division of the ric into two parts, each with its distinctive name (Hutch³ **1** 563 however takes the smaller holding to be that represented later by Little Kimmeridge and *Chaldecots infra*).

CHALDECOTS (lost, about SY 932784), 1765 Tayl, 1861 Hutch³, *Chelde-* 1244 *Ass* (p), *Kalde-* 1285 FF, 1285 (1372) *ChrP*, *Chalde-* 1285 FA (p) *et freq* to 1774 Hutch¹, *Ghalde-* (sic) 1285 FA (p), *Chaelde-* n.d. (1372) *ChrP*, *Chalcote* 1482 Hutch³ (p), 1484 IpmR (p), *Chaldecot* 1545 Hutch³ (p), *Chald(e)cott(e)* 1732 Coker, 1795 Boswell, *Chaldicot* (*Fm*) p1795 *Mansel*; *Chalcotts Kymerige*, *Chalcotes Kymerege* 1526 Hutch³, *Chalcotes* 1482 ib, 1484 IpmR, *Chal(l)d-cottes land(e)* 1590 *Mansel*, originally 'cold cottage', *v*. cald (WSax ceald), cot, from its high, exposed situation ½ mile from the coast; the family of (*de*) *Chelde-*, *Chaldecote*, etc which took its name from this place remained here for many centuries, hence the later possessive, manorial name *Chaldecots*.

LITTLE KIMMERIDGE (SY 925781), 1795 Boswell, *Parva Kymerych* 1316 FF, *Little Kemerych* 1374 Cl, thereafter with spellings as for par. name *supra* and *Lytel(l)*-, *Littel-* 1405 Mansel *et freq* to 1518 ib, *Lit(t)le-* 1563 *Mansel et passim*, *Est-* 1417, 1421 FF, 1472 *Weld*[1], 1484 IpmR, *Little or East-Kimeridge* 1774 Hutch[1], 'little' and 'east' in relation to Kimmeridge *supra*, *v*. lȳtel, ēast.

SMEDMORE HO (SY 925788), *Metmore* 1086 DB, *Smethemor(e)* 1242 Ch, 1288 Ass (p), *Smedemor(e)* 1244 *ib* (p), 1268 *ib* (p) *et freq* to 1426 FF, *-mour* 1340 NI (p), *Smedeme more* (sic) n.d. (1372) *ChrP*, *Smedmor(e)* m13 *Weld*[1] (p) *et freq* to c. 1586 Tres, *-mour* 1387 Cl (p), *Smed(e)mor(e) in Purbyk*, *-bik* 1393 Hutch[3], 1427 *Weld*[1], *Smeadmore* 1701 Hutch[3], 'smooth or level moor', *v*. smēðe[1], mōr; the estate was formerly held by the family who took their name from this place, hence *Smedmors Kymerege* 1526 Hutch[3].

CLAVEL TOWER, a 19th-cent. folly, cf. foll. CLAVELL'S HARD, *Clavels-* c. 1825 Map, from some member of the *Clavel(l)* family, here from an early date (cf. John *Clavyle de Smedmore* 1423 *Midd*, *v*. Smedmore *supra*), perhaps in particular from Sir William *Clavel* who unsuccessfully tried to establish an alum industry here in the early 17th cent. (Hutch[3] 1 556), cf. foll., *v*. hard 'firm beach or foreshore, jetty'. CUDDLE, a high part of the cliffs, perhaps something like 'Cuda's hill', from the OE pers.n. *Cuda* and hyll, although Arkell (1941) 36 points out that this is where the alum works was situated (cf. prec.) and suggests the Co mining term caudle 'a thick muddy fluid', cf. Legg 57. D PLANT., so called from its shape. DOWN (lost, SY 925778), 1826 Gre, cf. *Gt & Long Down Close* p1795 *Mansel*, *v*. dūn. GAULTER GAP, a low part of the shore at Kimmeridge Bay *infra* named from Gaulter Ctgs in Steeple par. *infra*, *v*. gappe. GRANGE PLANT., *v*. grange. GREY LEDGE, one of the Kimmeridge Ledges *infra*. HARRY'S WOOD. HEN CLIFF, 1811 OS, — or *Kimmeridge Head* c. 1825 Map, perhaps 'stone cliff', *v*. hān, clif, cf. Hencliff Gl 3 79, but alternatively the first el. may be hēah (wk.obl. *hēan*) 'high' or henn 'hen'. KIMMERIDGE BAY, 1826 Gre, *Kimeridge—* 1774 Hutch[1], earlier *Boteridge poole* 1575 Saxton, c. 1586 Tres, *Botterage* 1579 Hutch[3], discussed under Kimmeridge *supra*, *v*. bay[1], pōl[1]; Hutch[3] 1 555 reports that there was formerly 'a large quay or cobb' here. KIMMERIDGE COASTGUARD STATION, *the Coast Guard station*, *the Preventive station* 1861 Hutch[3]. KIMMERIDGE DAIRY. KIMMERIDGE FM, *Kimeridge* — p1795 *Mansel*. KIMMERIDGE LEDGES, — *Ledge* c. 1825 Map, a two-mile stretch of shoreline rock shelves of Kimmeridge Clay, three of which are called Grey Ledge *supra*, Yellow Ledge *infra*, and High Ledge in Corfe C. par. *supra*, *v.* **ledge**. LIAS ROCKS (local), on the shore below Clavell's Hard *supra*, *v.* lias. MAPLE LEDGE, a shoreline shelf of rock, *v.* **mapel**, cf. Kimmeridge Ledges *supra*. METHERHILLS, *Mether Hill* 1861 Hutch³, probably 'middle hill', *v.* **middel, hyll**, cf. Metherall D 175, 427, but mǣðere 'a mower' is also a possible first el. NEWMEAD PLANT., cf. *New Mdw* p1795 *Mansel*. THE ROOKERY. ROPE LAKE HEAD, *Rope Lake* 1861 Hutch³, perhaps 'stream or water-course near a rope of land', *v.* **rāp, lacu**, with **hēafod**, cf. Rope Ch 3 68; however, Arkell (1941) 37 suggests that the name may refer to a rope or rope ladder suspended here for climbing the cliff. SWALLAND FM, p1795 *Mansel, Swalland(e)* 1545 Hutch³, Eliz ChancP, 17 *Pitt*, 1811 OS, *Swallonde* 1590 *Mansel, Swolland* 17 *Pitt*, probably to be associated with John-, Robert *Swanlond* 1376 Pat, 'land of the herdsman, -men or peasant(s)', *v.* **swān, land**, cf. *Swallondes goyle, Swallandes goile* 1590 *Mansel*, 'ravine at Swalland', or 'belonging to someone called *Swalland*', *v.* **goyle**. WITHY BED, *Withe Bed* (sic) p1795 *Mansel*. YELLOW LEDGE, one of the Kimmeridge Ledges *supra*.

FIELD-NAMES

The undated forms are p1795 *Mansel* (map T 12/71). Spellings dated 1323 are *Ct*, 1332 SR, 1340 NI, 1558 Hutch³, 1563, 1590 *Mansel*.

(*a*) Barley Croft; Chiteswood; Church Cl; Cliff Md; Coopers Md; Cow Lea(ze); Cunnigar (*v.* coninger); (Lr) Ewe Lea(ze); The Farm Mdw; The 4 Acres; Furlongs Cl; Great Mdw; High Lds; Home Grds; (Lt) Kimmeridge Hill; Knappy Grds (*v.* cnæppig); Lawn (*v.* launde); Little & Long Mdw; Orchard; Paddock; Park Mdw (cf. 'a drove on the west part of the close called the Park at Smedmore' 1558, *le Parke apud Smedmore* 1563, *v.* drove, park, Smedmore *supra*); Petty Cl (*v.* pety); Rushey Grd; 6 Acres; Smedmore Cow Leaze & Cliff Grd, Smedmore Home Grds & Hill (from Smedmore *supra*); South Fd; Stonehip Mdw (from Stonehips in Steeple par. *infra*); Swalland Md (from Swalland *supra*); Tenanten Fd (probably 'the tenants' field', with the Do dial. pl. ending *-en* for *-s* (Barnes 16), *v.* -ena); West Fd.

(*b*) atte *Celer* (p) 1323, 1340 (*v.* atte, celer); atte *Mulle* (p) 1332 (*v.* ˷nyln); *West Craft* 1590 (*v.* croft).

Church Knowle

CHURCH KNOWLE (SY 941819)

> *Cnolle* (2 ×), *Chenolle, Glole* 1086 DB, *Canolla* Exon
>
> *Cnoll(e)* 1181–2 P, 1202 Cur (p) *et freq* to 1340 NI with variant spellings *Cnol* 1204 ClR, *Cnnolle* 1291 Tax, *Cnolla* 14 Mansel

(p); *Knoll(e)* 1202 Cur (p) *et freq* to c. 1586 Tres, — *in Purbeck* 1544 *DCMDeed*; *Knowle* 1621 Mansel

Churic(h)cnoll(a) 14 Mansel, *Churechecnolle* m14 *Mansel et freq* with variant spellings *Church(e)-* from 1346 Mansel, *Cherche-* m14 ib, *Chirche-* m14 *Mansel* (p), *-cnoll(e)* from 14 *Mansel*, *-knoll(e)* 14 *ib et freq* to 1576 Saxton, *-Knole* 1604 *Mansel*, *-knowle* 1658 *ib*

'Hill top', *v.* cnoll, cf. Knowle Hill *infra*, with the later addition 'Church' perhaps to distinguish it from Bucknowle *infra*, *v.* cirice, cf. Isle of Purbeck *supra*. There was a priest here (at *Glole*) in 1086 DB (VCHDo 3 89), and the church is mentioned in 1237 Pat, 1261 Ipm, 1263 Cl, *v.* St Peter's Church *infra*. For the DB spellings, cf. Knowlton in Woodlands par. *infra* and *v.* ANInfl 49, 122, 137. A different identification of DB *Glole*, with Lutton Gwyle in Steeple par. *infra*, is proposed by DBGazetteer 122; *Glole* follows *Stiple* in the DB text, but the identification is formally unlikely.

BARNSTON CROSS RDS & FM (SY 931816), *Bernestun* l13 Hutch[3], *-ton(e)* 1288 *Ass*, 1328 FF, 1332 SR (p) *et freq* to l14 *Mansel*, *Bernyston in Purbeck* 1553 Mansel, *Barneston* 1375 ib *et freq* to 1563 *Mansel*, — *in Purbik* 1427 *Weld*[1], *Barnyston* 1401, 1554 Hutch[3], *Barnston* c. 1586 Tres *et passim*, — *Fm* 1844 *TA*, *Barnson* 1826 Gre, 'Beorn's farm', from the OE pers.n. *Beorn* and tūn, cf. Isle of Purbeck *supra*. *Be(o)rn* is named as the tenant TRE of this manor, then called *Cnolle, Canolla* (forms included under Church Knowle *supra*), in 1086 DB (VCHDo 3 96), cf. also *Beorn faber* n.d. (15) *ShaftR* (f. 62). Barnston Cross Rds are where the road N to Wareham, called 'the King's highway leading towards Wareham' l13 Hutch[3] (possibly also referred to in *la Port(e)wey(e)* 14 Mansel, 'road leading to a market town', *v.* port-weg), crosses the E–W road from Church Knowle to Steeple, called *via...versus Berneston* m14 *Mansel*, this being the 'white way' which gave its name to Whiteway Fm *infra*. Barnston farm house ('remains of Manor House' 6″) dates from Ed 3.

BRADLE BARN & FM (SY 931806) ['breidl], *Bradelege* 1086 DB, *-le* c. 1170 MontC, 1285 FA *et freq* to 1374 Cl (— *in Purbyk*), 1399 FF, *(apud) Bradeliga(m)* Hy 3 Hutch[3], p1483 *Sheen, Bradelegh(e)* 1242–3 Fees, 1346 FA, *-ley(e)* 1285 FA, 14 Mansel, *-lea* ib (p), *-lee* 1303 FA, *Bradel(l)* c. 1326 Hutch[3], 1384 *DCMDeed et freq* to 1580 *Mansel, Bradlee* p1483 *Sheen, -ley* c. 1586 Tres, *Bardell*

1563 *Mansel, Bradle* 1575 Saxton *et passim, Braddle Fm* p1795 *Mansel, East Bradle Fm, West Bradle Barn, Bradle Hr Barn* 1844 *TA*, 'broad wood or clearing', *v.* brād, lēah. There was woodland here one furlong in length and half a furlong in width in 1086 DB (VCHDo 3 100). There is mention of an 'oratory' (*oratorium*) here c. 1326 Hutch[3], p1483 *Sheen,* cf. *Prestysmede infra,* and of the 'highway to *Bradele*' 14 Mansel.

(WEST) BUCKNOWLE HO (SY 949814) ['bʌknəl, 'bʌgnəl], 1844 *TA, Bubecnolle* 1285 FA (p), *Bubbeknolle* 1306 Banco, 1318 Ass, 1452, 1454 FF, *Bobe-* 1327 *SR* (p), *Bove-* 1400 Hutch[3], 1420 FF, *Bou-* 1412, *Boueknoll(e)* 1431 FA, *Bucknoll* 1584, — *als. Bubbeknoll* 1594 Hutch[3], *Bucknowl(e)* 1795 Boswell, 1811 OS, 'Bubba's hill top', no doubt with reference to *Bucknowle Hill* 1844 *TA,* from the OE pers.n. *Bubba* and cnoll, cf. Church Knowle *supra,* Melbury Bubb *infra,* and Bucknole D 628 which has the same origin.

COCKNOWLE (SY 933820), 1826 Gre, *Kokemille* (probably for *-nulle*), *Kokenhule Lake* 14 Mansel, *Cocknowl* 1811 OS, *Gt & Lt Cocknoll* (*Fd*) 1844 *TA.* The 14th-cent. forms are unreliable and no etymology can be safely proposed, but the OE pers.n. **Cocca* or a wk. ME gen.pl. in *-en(e)* of cocc 'woodcock' (*v.* -ena) are possible for the first el., with either hyll 'hill' (suggested by the first 14th-cent. form) or hygel 'hillock' or hylu 'hollow' (both possible to explain the second 14th-cent. form), cf. the f.n. *Cokenhull* in W Knighton par. *infra;* the modern name has been adjusted by analogy with Church Knowle and Bucknowle *supra. Kokenhule Lake* doubtless refers to the stream running S from Cocknowle into the Corfe River, *v.* lacu.

EAST CREECH (SY 927826)

> *Crist* 1086 DB
> *Criz* 1086 DB (2 ×), Exon, 1181–2 P, *Crihz* 1212 Fees
> *Cric* 1086 DB, *Crich(e), Crych(e)* 1224 Cur, 1280 Ch, 1285 FA, 1291 Tax *et freq* to 1545 Ct, *Erlescrich* 1301 Pat, *Est(e)crich(e)*, *-crych(e)* 1337 Hutch[3] *et freq* to 1546 Ct, *-krych* 1346 Mansel, *Crihc* 1264 Ipm, *Chryicht* 1275 RH, *Cryk* 1285 FA
> *Crech(e)* 1204 ClR, 1244 FF, *Este-* 14 Mansel, *Es-, Eastcreche* 1563 *Mansel,* E Crech c. 1586 Tres, *East Cretche* 1586 Hutch[3]
> *Cr(o)ugh* 1303 FA, *Cruch* 1303 Hutch[3]

'The mound, hill or barrow', from PrWelsh *crūg, v. Jackson
310, referring to Creech Barrow *infra* which gave its name to a tract
of land which 'is about 3¼ miles long, and extends from the boundary
of the parish of Corfe Castle on the east, to that of Tyneham on the
west' (Hutch³ 1 598), cf. Creech Grange and West Creech (where
some of the early forms cited above may strictly belong) in Steeple
par. *infra*; for an analogous tract of land with a name of identical
origin, cf. The Croach Ch 3 36. *Erlescrich* may allude to the Count
of Mortain who held the part called *Crist* in 1086 DB (VCHDo 3
87), v. eorl. *East* in relation to Creech Grange and West Creech, v.
ēast. The remains of a Roman villa were discovered ½ mile WNW
(SY 935827) about 1889.

EAST ORCHARD (SY 945808), WEST ORCHARD (FM), *Horcerd* 1086 DB,
Exon, (*Le, La*) *Orchard(e)* 1291 Cl, 1347 IpmR *et freq* to c. 1586
Tres, — *in Purbike, -byk* 1382, 1384 Hutch³, *Horchard* 1299 Banco,
Est Orchard 1399 Mansel, (— *in Purbyk*) 1440 FF, *Est Orcherd*
1544 DCMDeed, *East Orchard* 1658 Mansel, — *Fm* 1844 *TA*,
Westorchard in Purbyk 1398 Cecil, *West Orchard* 1399 Mansel *et
passim*, — *Down*, —*Fm* 1844 *TA*, 'a garden, an orchard', v. orceard,
ēast, west, dūn; there was an orchard (*virgultum*) here in 1086 DB
(VCHDo 3 109). Cf. Orchard Hill Fm *infra*, Isle of Purbeck *supra*.

WHITEWAY FM (SY 924813), 1844 *TA*, *Wyteweye* 1284 Banco
(*Est-*), 1285 FA (p), 14 Mansel, *-wcyhe* (sic) 1291 Tax, *-waye* 14
Mansel, *Whyte-* 1290 Pat, 1329 Hutch³, *Whiteweye* 1329 Pat,
Purbyke Whytwey, Whytwey (*iuxta Bradlee*) *in Por-, Purbyke,*
(*Est*)*whyt(e)wey, Estwytewea* p1483 Sheen, *-wytway* 1544 Hutch³,
E. Whitwaye c. 1586 Tres, *East Whiteway* 1795 Boswell, cf. *Whiteway
Hill* 1844 *TA*, 'white way', v. hwīt, weg, taking its name from 'the
conspicuous white way or road leading over the chalk hill. This road
is very ancient, as is evident from the great depth of the banks on
each side' (Hutch³ 1 589), cf. Barnston Cross Rds *supra*. *East* to
distinguish it from Whiteway (earlier *West Whiteway*) in Tyneham
par. *infra*, and cf. Isle of Purbeck and Bradle *supra*. In p1483 Sheen,
besides the forms cited above, Whiteway is once (f. 43) represented
by the curious form *Hyntwey*, apparently an error or nonce formation
influenced by the name of the grantor Mary *de Hynneton* (= Hinton
Martell or Parva par. *infra*), but cf. hynt 'a road'.

BARE CROSS, where another track crosses the E–W 'ridgeway' (cf.
Ridgeway Hill *infra*), perhaps 'exposed cross or crossroads', v. bær¹

(cf. NED s.v. *bare* adj. sense 3 'open to view'), cros or cros(s). BLACKHILLS PLANT., *v.* blæc, hyll, or a surname. BLUE POOL, a flooded clay pit so called from its colour. CHALDECOT'S WD, from the family of (*de*) *Chelde-, Chaldecote* who held lands in East Creech *supra* from the late 13th cent. and who probably came from Chaldecots in Kimmeridge par. *supra*, cf. William *de Cheldecote*, Hugh (*de*) *Chaldecote* l13 Hutch³, 14 Mansel, etc. CHURCH FM (local). CLAY PIT (2×), *Clay Pits* 1844 *TA*. COTNESS (WD), *Cotnes* (*Copse & Md*) 1844 *TA*, possibly 'projecting piece of high land with a cottage or cottages', *v.* cot, næss, cf. Cotness YE 250. CREECH BARROW, 1774 Hutch¹, 1811 OS, *Crechbarrow* 1610 Speed, cf. *magnum montem* 14 Mansel, a 'remarkable conical hill...resembling in form a volcanic mountain in miniature' (Hutch³ 1 606), 637' high and giving its name to East Creech *q.v. supra*, Creech Bottom, etc. *infra*, *v.* beorg 'hill, tumulus' (a tumulus is marked 6"); in 1774 (Hutch¹ 1 206) the ruins were still visible on its summit of 'the principal lodge of the isle and forest of Purbeck', referred to as *Crechbar(r)ow Lodge* 1575 Saxton, c. 1586 Tres, *The Lodge* 1610 Speed, *v.* loge, cf. Isle of Purbeck *supra*. CREECH BOTTOM (1844 *TA*), HEATH (1811 OS) & WOOD, from prec., *v.* botm, hæð. EAST CREECH FM, *Creech Fm* 1844 *TA*, from East Creech *supra*. DODSON'S FM. FURLONG'S COPPICE, *v.* furlang, or a surname. FURZEBROOK, 1811 OS, *v.* fyrs, brōc. FURZEBROOK HO (cf. — *Fm* 1844 *TA*) & RD, from prec. GERALD'S PLANT. GRANGE RD, to Creech Grange in Steeple par. *infra*. THE GWYLE, *Guile* 1844 *TA*, *v.* goyle. HIGHER DOWN (lost), 1811 OS (about SY 935796), cf. *The Down* p1795 Mansel, *Lower Down* 1844 *TA*, *v.* dūn. HOP YARD, *Hop Yard Copse* 1844 *TA*, *v.* hoppe, geard. HORSEGROUND COPPICE, cf. (*Lt*) *Horse Grd* 1844 *TA*, *v.* hors; but *Horse* may be the possessive form of a surname, cf. John *Hore* p1483 Sheen. ICEN BARROW, perhaps īsern 'iron' in some literal or figurative sense, *v.* beorg (a tumulus is marked 6"), cf. Icen Way in Dorchester par. *infra*. JOHN'S PLANT. KILLWOOD (COPPICES), *Kilnwood* (*Copse*) 1844 *TA*, *v.* cyln, wudu, cf. Old Limekiln *infra*. KNOWLE FM, from foll. or Church Knowle *supra*. KNOWLE HILL, *Knowl* — 1811 OS, cf. *Knowle Hill Down* 1844 *TA*, *v.* cnoll, Church Knowle *supra*; the name is used of a high stretch of the Purbeck chalk ridge separating the two halves of the par. KNOWLE LODGE, from prec. or Church Knowle *supra*. LILLYHAYS COPPICE, cf. Lilley Brook Gl 2 97, Lilly Wood Ess 396. OLD LIMEKILN (SY 946823), cf. Killwood only ½ mile NW but the other side of Knowle Hill, and *Lime Kiln* 1811 OS

(SY 935803). MADGROVE, *Mad Grove Copse* 1844 *TA*, probably
'grove by or with a meadow', *v.* mǣd, grāf(a), cf. Madmoors in E
Holme par. *supra*, but the first el. could be the adj. mad 'foolish'
giving the name a meaning like 'grove planted as a foolhardy venture'
or 'grove gone wild'. NEWFOUNDLAND, p1795 *Mansel*, probably so
called from its remoteness (it is near the S extremity of the par.).
NEW HO. NEW INN, 1844 *TA*. NORA'S PLANT. NURSERY, 1844 *TA*.
ORCHARD HILL FM, *Orchard Hill or Orchard Common* 1604 *Mansel*,
1682 *DCMDeed, Orchard Hill (Barn)* 1844 *TA*, from (East & West)
Orchard *supra*. POLAR WD, cf. William *Pollard*, — *Pallard* p1483
Sheen. PUDDLE MILL (FM), *Pudlemill* c. 1586 Tres, *mills called
Puddle Mills* 1621 *Mansel, Puddle Mill* 1667 Eton, 1811 OS, cf.
Robert *de Molendino* 14, John *atte Mulle* 1346 Mansel, *Mill Cowleaze
& Hams* 1844 *TA, v.* puddel 'muddy pool', myln, hamm; the mill
is situated on the stream called Corfe River 6" (earlier *Wych*), cf.
Paddle Dock in Corfe C. par. *supra*. RACHEL'S PLANT. RANDALLTOWN,
probably the pers.n. or surname *Randall* in a late formation with
-*town* (*v.* tūn). RICHARD'S FM, cf. John *Ricard* 1332 SR. RIDGEWAY
HILL, from the ancient 'ridgeway' which runs E–W along the ridge
of the Purbeck Hills, *v.* hrycg, weg, cf. Bare Cross *supra*. ST PETER'S
CHURCH, 'church of St. Peter at *Churchnolle*' 1327 Hutch[3], a 13th-
cent. building, cf. Church Knowle *supra*. SHOTTS LANE (local), cf.
the f.n. Great Mdw *infra*, Adam *le-, -de Schot* p1483 *Sheen*, Thomas
Shott of *Stepyll* c. 1500 *RoyRoll* (*v.* Steeple par. *infra*). SNUGG'S FM
(local). STONEHILL DOWN, part of the high chalk ridge of the Purbeck
Hills, *v.* stān. THORNHAM, *v.* þorn, hamm; the two small manors
of *Torne* 1086 DB are identified with this place by DBGazetteer 127,
but cf. Durnford in Langton Mat. par. *supra*. WADHILL COPPICE,
(*Copse in*) *Row Waddle* 1844 *TA*, 'hill where woad grew', *v.* wād,
hyll, or 'clearing where woad grew' with the second el. lēah develop-
ing as in Bradle *supra, v.* rūh, cf. Woodhill Coppice *infra*. WHITEWAY
WITHY BED, *Withy Bed* 1844 *TA*, from Whiteway *supra*. WOODHILL
COPPICE, *Woodle* 1844 *TA*, cf. *Woodedols* 1580 *Mansel* which may
also belong here, possibly the same name as Wadhill Coppice *supra*
(only 300 yds. distant), cf. the development of Woodhill W 267
which contains wād, but the first el. may be wudu 'wood'. WOOLLAND
GROVE, *Woolens Grove Copse & Mdw* 1844 *TA, Wooland* 1842
Tennent, probably 'land near the spring or stream', *v.* wella, land;
it lies alongside a stream and a spring is also marked 6". (YELLOW)
WITHY BED, *Withy Bed* 1844 *TA*.

FIELD-NAMES

The undated forms are 1844 *TA* 62. Spellings dated 1242–3 are Fees, 1268, 1280 *Ass*, l13, c. 1326, 1483, 1511, 1558, 1636 Hutch³, 14 Mansel, 1323, 1379 *MinAcct*, 1384, 1682 *DCMDeed*, p1483 *Sheen*, 1664 HTax, 1704, 1770, 1784, 1842 Tennent, and the rest *Mansel*.

(a) (Lr) Aldermoor (v. alor); Allans (cf. *Allondes hedge* 1580, probably the surname *Allan, Allon*, the earlier form having excrescent -*d*, but possibly a p.n. in land); Arable; Barnston Hill (from Barnston *supra*); Berwell (perhaps from beorg, wella); Beshard (or Crate), Beshard Green & Md (*Besha* 1842, perhaps from sceard 'gap', with bēos 'bent grass' or bēo 'bee', cf. Crate *infra*); Lr & Middle Bottom; Bradle Down & Heath, West Bradle East & West Fds (from Bradle *supra*); Brickyard; Broad Fd & Md; Browns Cmn (from the *Browne* family who were here in the 17th cent., v. Hutch³ I 583); Brushets ('places overgrown with brushwood, thickets', v. brushet, Do dial *brushet* 'brushwood, scrub' (Barnes 52) from ME *brusche* 'brushwood' and the suffix -*et*(*t*)(*e*)); Calves house Md, Calve's Plot; Cats Hole (— *Knowle* 1842, v. catt, hol¹, cnoll); (Hr & Lr) Champions (probably a surname, but possibly ModE champaign (< OFr *champagne*) 'open, level country', often spelt *champion* in 16th and 17th cent.); Chickens Cl (from cīcen or a surname); Common Cl (*the* — p1795) & Grd; Conygre (v. coninger); Coombe (Grd & Mdw) (v. cumb); Copper Md (cf. Copper Bridge Md in Corfe C. par. *supra*); Copse; Corner Fd; Cowleaze (freq, *Kent's Cowlease* 1770); Cowman's Cl 1842; Cow Pasture p1795; Crabb Cl (v. crabbe 'crab apple'); Crate (Md) (v. croft); Creech Copse, Cowleaze & Hill (from Creech Barrow or East Creech *supra*); Cross Cl (v. cros); Cross Lanes Cowleaze (v. cross); Cuckoo Grd; Dry Cl and Cothy Plot (*Dry or Coath Plot* 1842, v. cothe, cothy); Dyett's Cmn (cf. *Diet's Tenements* p1795); East Mdw (cf. *the Easter Meade* 1604, — *Meadow* 1682, v. ēasterra, mæd); Egg Cl (apparently ModE egg, although the significance of the name is uncertain); (The) 8 Acres (Mdw); The 18 Acres; 11 Acres; Ferlands (perhaps 'strips of land at a distance', v. feor, land, but possibly from furlang); Fir Clump; Firs (v. firr, but perhaps fyrs 'furze'); (The) 5 Acres; Foul Fd 1842; (Lr) 4 Acres (Under Barrow) (the reference is to Creech Barrow *supra*, v. under); French Grass Ground (p1795, v. french grass); Frogley (v. frogga, lēah); Frying Pan (so called from its shape); Furze Hill; Furzy Grd; Galleys (perhaps galga 'gallows', or a surname); Garden (cf. *Gardinum* 1242–3); Gilders Cowleaze; Golds Mdw p1795 (cf. Edward *Golde* p1483); Grange Heath (from Creech Grange in Steeple par. *infra*); Great Md; Great Mdw (-*or Shotts Meade* 1842, cf. Shotts Lane *supra*); Green Cl & Down; Green Specks (Professor Löfvenberg suggests that the second el. may be eModE *speck* 'small piece of ground' (NED sb.¹ sense 2c)); (Rough Brake in) the Grove (v. bræc¹, grāf(a)); Hams (v. hamm); Hatchards Plot (cf. William *Hatchard* 1704); Heath; Hr & Lr Heymoors; Hill Grd; Holehays ('hollow enclosures, or enclosures lying in a hollow', v. hol¹, hol², (ge)hæg); Home Cl (*the* — 1658); Home Md(w); Homes Barrow (— *barrowe* 1580, the surname *Home*, v. beorg); Horse Cl (— *or Freddies*

1842, cf. Horseground *supra*); Inhooks Md (*v.* inhōke); Jacobs Plot p1795;
Joe's Grd; King(')s Acre; Knowle Fd (*in campo de Cnolle* m14, from Church
Knowle or Knowle Hill *supra*); Great Knowle (near Bucknowle *supra, v.*
cnoll); (Little) Knowles (cf. prec.); Lanty (thought by Tennent 8, 53 to be a
local 'corruption' of *lanchard, v.* lanchet); Little Fd; Long Md(w); (Marl
Pit in) Marl Hill (cf. *quodam marlerio de Cnolle* 1268, *v.* marle); Mead(ow);
Mizmaze (*v.* mizmaze); Moorhayes (*v.* mōr¹, (ge)hæg); Nappy Cowleaze &
Grd (*v.* cnæppig); New Cl & Grd; Newmans (— *Jack-me-lads* 1842, cf.
Robert (*le*) *New*(*e*)*man* (*de Wareham*) p1483); (The) 9 Acres; Nordon Wd
('north hill', *v.* norð. dūn); North Mdw; Oakey Cl (*the Easter or Oakey
Close* 1658, perhaps 'oak enclosure', *v.* āc, (ge)hæg, ēasterra); Oat Md;
(Old) Orchard, Orchard Bridge Cowleaze, Orchard Copse (Cowleaze),
Orchard Plot (cf. East & West Orchard, Orchard Hill Fm *supra*); Pasture
Pce; Peak (*v.* pēac); Peas Plot & Flgs (*v.* pise); Lr & Upr Pines; Pitmans;
(Field by) Plantation (& Furze); Plot; Pond (Cl); Pot Belly and Hollow
Belly (a humorous name, no doubt referring to undulating ground); Potato
Grd; Gt & Lt Red Barrow (*la Redberghe* 14, 'red hill or tumulus', *v.* rēad,
beorg); Road Coppice, Roadway (*v.* rād-weg); Roomes Mdw p1795; Rough
(freq, *v.* rough, cf. Row *infra*); Rough Bank(s), Grd & Plot; Row (freq,
alternating with Rough *supra, v.* row); Rowbarrow (*Rubergh* 1379, *v.*
rūh, beorg); Rumseys (Cmn); Rush Cl; Rushy Md; Sally Hole 1842 (*v.*
salig); Sedg ups (*v.* secg¹, hop¹); (E) 7 Acres; Sew's Grd; Shiplands (Copse
& Md) (*v.* scēap, land); Shop Close (Md) (*v.* sc(e)oppa 'shed', but possibly
scēap 'sheep', cf. Shop Hayes in Corfe C. par. *supra*); (Middle & Outside)
6 Acres (*v.* outside); 16 Acres; East Slide Banks (perhaps to be associated
with *La Sleede infra*, with some such later development as in Snipe End
Wt 255 (< snæp), but Professor Löfvenberg suggests that *Slide* is eModE
slide 'a landslip' (1664 NED), cf. West Slide Banks in Steeple par. *infra*);
South Fd; South Md ((*the*) *South Meade* 1604, 1682, *v.* sūð, mǣd); Splotts
1784 (*v.* splott); Stokes Hayes (from (ge)hæg and the surname *Stoke*, cf.
John *de* (*E*)*stok*(*e*) 14, Alice *de Estoke*, William *Stokys* p1483, probably from
one of the Do Stokes, but possibly from a lost p.n. in this par., *v.* stoc);
Strips (*v.* strip); Sulfoot (possibly to be associated with *on scyleford* 948 (15)
ShaftR (S 534 (1)), *of Scylenford*(*e*) 956 (14) *ib* (S 632), *Shulford* 1381 (16)
Pitt, a bdy point in the Corfe Castle charters; the first el. is perhaps an adj.
*scylen (< WSax *scielen), an -*en* derivative with *i*-mutation of OE
sc(*e*)*alu* 'shale, shell, husk, etc', cf. *stān-scilig* 'shaly, stony' (BT), with ford,
hence 'stony ford'); East & West 10 Acres, 10 Acres Mdw; Terra Nova;
The 13 Acres; (The) 3 Acres; Tubb's Mdw (cf. Thomas *Tubb* 1664); 12
Acres; (Lt) 2 Acres; Vineyards (*v.* vinȝerd); Way Cl (*v.* weg); Well Cl (cf.
'messuage near *le Well*' 14, *v.* wella); West Md(w); Weston Cowleaze
(*Weston's* — 1842); Wet Cl; White Md (*v.* hwīt); Wild Md (*v.* wilde);
Witch Hams 1842, Whitch Mdw (cf. *acr' prati apud le Wych* 1323, the r.n.
Wych, the old name for the Corfe River, cf. Wych Channel & Lake in RNs.
infra, v. hamm); Withy Lakes (*v.* wīðig, lacu); Wood; Worth (*v.* worð).

(*b*) *the barly furlonge* 1580 (*v.* bærlic, furlang); 'Barter's tenement' 1636;
Bennets Hayes 1658 (*v.* (ge)hæg); *Burne Downe* 1580 (probably 'hill cleared
by burning', *v.* bryne, dūn); *Cle*(*a*)*ngerwel*(*l*) 1558, 1563 ('the well, spring

or stream at *Cle(a)nger'* ('the clayey wooded slope'), *v.* clæg, hangra, wella); *Cothayes* 1658 (*v.* cot, (ge)hæg); *Cutteham* m14, *Kotteforlange* l14 ('the enclosure and furlong at the water-channel', *v.* cut, hamm, furlang); *the farme close* 1580 (*v.* ferme); *terre voc' gamoldeschewole* l14 (perhaps 'Gamall's scarecrow', from the ON pers.n. *Gamall* (or a surname derived from it), and scīewels (*v.* NED s.v. *shewel*; forms without final -*s* appear as early as 1285)); *Harvest Bower* 1580 ('temporary hut used in the autumn or when gathering the corn', *v.* hærfest, būr[1]); 'crofts called *Hoes'* l13 (probably 'heels of land', *v.* hōh (nom.pl. *hōas, hōs*)); *Atterhurn de Cnolle* 1280 (p), *de la Hurn(e) ib,* 14 (p) (*v.* atter, hyrne, cf. Church Knowle *supra*); *langlond* p1483 (*v.* lang[1], land); 'Meak's Plot' 1483; *Out Mead(e) and/or Wooll peeces* 1604, 1658 (*v.* ūt(e), mæd, wella, pece); 'Plott's house' 1511; (*prato voc'*) *Prestysmede* c. 1326, p1483 (*v.* prēost, mæd; given to the chaplain of the oratory at Bradle *supra*, cf. *terram persone* l14); *Prustushouse* 1384 (*v.* prēost, hūs); *Ryalls* 1621 ('hills or nooks where rye is grown', *v.* ryge, hyll, halh, or a surname); (*La*) *Shortelonde* m14, l14 (*v.* sc(e)ort, land); *La Sleede* l14 (*v.* slæd, cf. East Slide Banks *supra*); *Swier yeate* 1580 (perhaps from Swyre in Corfe C. par. *supra*, *v.* geat 'opening, gap, gate'); *the West Close* 1604, 1682; 'West field of *Church Cnolle'* 14; *La Wodediche* l14 (*v.* wudu, dīc).

Steeple

Creech Grange in this par. was formerly in Bindon Liberty (Hutch[3] 1 349), *v.* note under Winfrith Hundred *infra*. Blackmanston and Lutton in this par. were formerly parcels of the manor of Povington in Tyneham par. *infra* (Hutch[3] 1 607).

STEEPLE (SY 912809)

 Stiple 1086 DB, 1464 Pat, *Stypele* 1285 FA, *Stipille in Purbyke* 1439 AD VI, *Stipull* 1464 Weld[1], *Styple* 1554 *Mansel*
 Stuple, Stupel(l)(e) 1204 ClR, 1212 Fees, 1268 *Ass* (p), 1275 RH *et freq* to 1509 BrEll, *Stuple in Purbik* 1399 AddCh, *Stupull* 1428 FA, 1512 AD IV
 Stepel, Steple 1222 Pat, 1262 Ipm, 1263 Cl, 1278 QW *et freq* to c. 1586 Tres, *Stepul(l)(e)* 1348 *MinAcct*, 1384 *DCMDeed*, 1385 Cl, *Stepyll in Purbyke* c. 1500 *RoyRoll*, *Steeple* 1614 *Mansel*, *Steepple* 1640 *DCMDeed*

'Steep place', *v.* stēpel (WSax stīepel, stȳpel), named from 'its situation under a steep hill' (Hutch[3] 1 596), cf. Steepleton Iwerne and Winterborne Steepleton pars. *infra*, Isle of Purbeck *supra*. The spellings in -*ille*, -*ull(e)* may suggest that the name was popularly interpreted as 'steep hill' from stēap and hyll.

BLACKMANSTON FM (SY 915808), *Blachemanestone* 1086 DB (2×),
Blac-, *Blakmanton* 1288 *Ass*, *Blakemeston* 1376 *ib*, Pat, 1444 (p),
1446, *Blakmyston* 1443 (p), *Blak(e)monston* 1451, *Blak(e)manston*
1457 all *Weld*[1], 1458 FF, (— *in Purbyke*) 1473 *Weld*[1], *Blackmonston*
c. 1586 Tres, *Blackmanston* 1614 *Mansel*, *Blackmaston* p1795 *ib*,
'Blæcmann's farm', from the OE pers.n. *Blæcmann* and tūn, cf.
Isle of Purbeck *supra*, *Beklond infra*.

CREECH GRANGE (SY 912823), 1640 *DCMDeed*, *grangia apud Crich*,
grangia de Stepel 1319 *MinAcct*, *Criche grange*, *Chryche Grange*
1535 VE, *manerium sive grangiam de Crich* 1540 Hutch[3], *ye Grange*
1575 Saxton, *the Graunge* c. 1586 Tres, *v.* grange; it formerly belonged to Bindon Abbey (in Wool par. *infra*) (*v.* Hutch[3] I 598); for
Creech, *v.* foll. and East Creech in Ch. Knowle par. *supra*.

WEST CREECH (SY 895825), 1795 Boswell, *Crich(e)* 1319 *MinAcct*
et freq to 1509 *BrEll*, *West(e) Crych(e)* 1324 (17) *Pitt*, 1459 Pat,
-criche 1452 *Weld*[1], 1512 *Ct*, *West Creche* 1575 Saxton, *W. Cruche*
c. 1586 Tres, from Creech Barrow in Ch. Knowle par. *supra*; *West*
in relation to prec. and East Creech in Ch. Knowle par. *supra* (where
some early forms which may strictly belong to West Creech are cited),
v. west.

GAULTER CTGS (SY 908792) ['goultə], *claus' voc' Goldehorde* 1451
Weld[1], *Goulthred* 1614, *Goulthead* p1795 *Mansel*, *Goulthard* 1842
TA, 'gold hoard, treasury', *v.* gold-hord, cf. *Gaulter Gap* in Kimmeridge par. *supra*; the f.n. *Golter* in Langton Mat. par. *supra* has the
same origin.

HURPSTON (SY 924806), *Herpere* 1086 DB, *Harpera* Exon, *la Harpine*
1109 Dugd (II.70), *Herperston* 1340 NI (p), *Harpeston* 1376 *Ass*,
Pat, *Harpstone* 1795 Boswell, 1861 Hutch[3] (— *or Harpston*), *Harpson*
1811 OS, a difficult name. The DB and Exon spellings would seem
to mean 'the harper', *v.* hearpere, and *la Harpine* is a Fr translation
of this, *v.* harpin; Hurpston is on the Corfe River and the term
was perhaps used figuratively to mean 'the murmuring brook', cf.
Harper's Brook Nth 2 and Harperwell YW 2 80 where the same usage
is possible. In the 1340 form this name (later reduced to *Harp(e)-*) is
combined with tūn 'farm' or stān 'stone'; the latter seems most likely
in view of the existence of a large stone (Stone 6″, Harp Stone 1″)

some 300 yards W of Hurpston, described by Hutch³ 1 609 as
'a remarkable stone placed at right angles to its natural bed, and
rising 9 ft. above the ground', cf. Roger *atte Stone* 1327 *SR*;
according to local tradition, this stone is so called because when the
wind is in the right quarter the grooves on its surface cause a singing
noise not unlike that of a harp (R.J.T.). For another interpretation of
this name, as an OE **hearpere* meaning 'river occasionally dried up'
or 'barren place' from a Gmc **herp-*, **harp-*, etc, *v.* Tengstrand MN
99–100. There was a mill here in 1086 DB (VCHDo 3 108).

HYDE CTG (SY 918807) & WD, *Longa Hyda* 1244 *Ass* (p), 1285 FA,
La Langehide 1288 Misc, 1399 *AddCh*, *-hyde* 1288 *Ass*, *Langehyde
in Purbyk* 1315 FF, *Longhide* 1494, 1623, *Longe Hyde* 1649 all
Hutch³, *de la Hyde* 1315 ib (p), *Hyde* 1544 *DCMDeed et passim*,
— *Wood(s)* p1795 *Mansel*, 1842 *TA*, *Hide* 1861 Hutch³, 'long hide
of land', *v.* lang¹, hīd; 'so named from its form. It is a long strip of
land' (Hutch³ 1 608).

LUTTON (SY 901809), 1325 Hutch³, 1375 Pat *et passim*, *Lutton'*
1280 *Ass*, 1376 *ib*, 1451 *Weld*¹, *Lutteton'* 1288 *Ass*, *Luton* 1376 Pat,
perhaps 'Lutta's farm' from the OE pers.n. **Lutta* which lies
behind OE *Lutting* (Redin 174), cf. Litteridge Gl 1 119, and tūn.

ALDER BED, *Gt* & *Lt* — p1795 *Mansel*, *v.* alor, bedd. ALDER MOOR,
Aldermoor Copse 1842 *TA*, *v.* mōr. ASH COPPICE, cf. *Ash Mdw* 1842
ib. BEACH COPPICE, p1795 *Mansel*, *Beech Copse* 1842 *TA*, *v.* bēce².
THE BELT, a narrow wood, *v.* belt. BLACKMANSTON WITHY BED,
Gt Willow Bed p1795 *Mansel*, *Withy Bed* 1842 *TA*, from Blackmanston *supra*. BOTTOM COPPICE, — *Copse* 1842 *ib*, *v.* botm. BREACH
PLANT., (*Fross'*) *Breech* 1842 *ib*, 'land broken up for cultivation (and
frequented by frogs)', *v.* frosc, brēc. BRIDEWELL (PLANTATIONS),
Brid- 1811 OS, *Bridewell* 1826 Gre, possibly 'well, spring or stream
frequented by brides (for fertility rites?)', *v.* brȳd, wella, but
alternatively the first el. might be an OE brȳd 'surging' or brȳde
'surging stream' suggested for this type of name by Löfvenberg
26–7, cf. Bridewell W 150, Bridwell D 537, Bridewell(s) Gl 3 xi,
4 107; it lies ¼ mile W of a small stream (an affluent of R. Frome)
rising ½ mile SE. BROADMOOR FM, 1842 *TA*, *v.* brād, mōr. CARROT
BANK, now a coppice but perhaps 'slope where carrots were grown',
v. carotte, banke. CLAUD'S FIRS. CLAY PITS. WEST CREECH FM (1842
TA) & HILL (1842 *ib*), from West Creech *supra*. D PLANT., so called

from its shape. DAIRY CTGS, cf. *Dairy Hill Copse*, (*Rough in*) *Dairy
Hills* 1842 *TA*. DEVIL'S STAIRCASE, a steep stretch in a lane between
Kimmeridge Down *infra* and a ford (marked 6″) on the Corfe River,
v. dēofol. DODGY CL, perhaps the ModE derogatory term dodgy
'evasive, tricky, etc'. DRINKING BARROW, a tumulus named from a
nearby ditch (Legg 107), *v*. drinking. THE FLATS, ledges of flat rock
in Kimmeridge Bay (*v*. Kimmeridge par. *supra*), *v*. flat. GOUGH'S
SHOOT, *Calfshoot* (*Plant*.) 1842 *TA*, 'steep slope used by calves',
v. calf, scēot[3], cf. Do dial. *shoot* 'a steep hill, or the road down it'
(Barnes 98) and Shoot Md *infra*. GRANGE ARCH, also known as
Bond's Folly, built *c*. 1740 by Denis *Bond* of Creech Grange, *v*.
folie. GRANGE GATE (1811 OS), HEATH (1811 ib) & HILL (1842
TA), cf. *Grange Fm & Wd* 1842 *ib*, all from Creech Grange *supra*.
GREAT PLANT. & WD. GREY'S COPPICE. HASLER, 1774 Hutch[1],
Haizlors (*Copse*) 1842 *TA*, *Hasilor Grds* 1861 Hutch[3], the former
meeting place of Hasler Hundred *q.v*. *supra*. HOLLOW DITCH. HORSE
COPPICE, p1795 *Mansel*, — *Copse* 1842 *TA*. HURPSTON COPPICE,
Hurpson Copse 1842 *ib*, from Hurpston *supra*. HURST MILL, 1811
OS, *Hurst's Mill* 1861 Hutch[3], 'derives its name from a Henry
Hurst who had a mill here in 1636' Hutch[3] **1** 598, but this surname
may in turn come from a p.n. in the locality, *v*. hyrst. IVO'S PLANT.
KEEPER'S LODGE. KENNETH'S PLANT. KIMMERIDGE COPPICE (*Kimeridge* — p1795 *Mansel*) & DOWN (lost, 1826 Gre at SY 913800),
from Kimmeridge par. *supra*. KING'S STANDING, a plantation,
probably 'royal hunting stand', *v*. cyning, standing, cf. Isle of Purbeck *supra* for other references to hunting in this area; however, the
surname *King* is also a possible first el., cf. John *Kyng* of *Blakemeston* 1376 Pat (*v*. Blackmanston *supra*) and *Kings Path Cowleaze*
1842 *TA*. LITTLE WD. LOUISA'S FIRS. LOWER GROUNDS, *Lower
Ground* (*Plant*.) 1842 *TA*, cf. *Higher Ground* 1842 *ib*. LUTTON
GWYLE (*Guile* 1842 *ib*) & WITHY BED (*Withey* — 1842 *ib*), from
Lutton *supra*, *v*. goyle; DBGazetteer 122 identifies *Glole* 1086 DB
with Lutton Gwyle, but this form probably belongs under Church
Knowle par. *supra*. MARE POND, *v*. mere[2]. NATHAN'S COPPICE,
— *Copse* 1842 *TA*. NATTYS, a small wood. NEW HALL, cf. Whitehall
infra. NIGEL'S PLANT. NORTH HILLS PLANT., (*Brake in-, Firs
Waste in*) *North Hill* 1842 *TA*, *v*. bræc[1]. OAK CTGS. OLD BOND ST.,
a humorous allusion to the London street built by Sir Thomas Bond
who was probably related to the Bond family which has been at
Creech Grange since 1686 (Hutch[3] **1** 598, 605). ORCHARD CTGS,

cf. *the Orchard* 1384 *DCMDeed*, 1842 *TA*, *v.* orceard. POLE COPPICE,
— *Copse* 1842 *TA*, perhaps 'coppice where poles are got', *v.* pāl.
POMFREY'S PLANT., *Cumfries* (sic) (*Cowleaze*) 1842 *TA*, cf. John
Pumfray 1664 Hutch³. RAYMOND'S FIRS. ROOKERY (CTGS), (*The*)
Rookery 1842 *TA*. ST JOHN'S CHURCH, built in 1746 from the ruins
of Holme Priory in E Holme par. *supra*. ST MICHAEL'S CHURCH, cf.
ecclesiam de Stepel 1280 *Ass*, 'parish church of St Michael of *Stypele,
alias Stypulle*, and *Cryche*' 1485 Hutch³, 'the church of *St Mychell
in Steple*' l16 ib, *v.* Steeple, West Creech *supra*. SHEPHERD'S CTG,
cf. William *de Lutton* als. William *Baillif* of *Lutton* als. William
Shiphyrd of *Lutton* 1375 Pat, cf. Lutton *supra*. SMEDMORE HILL,
from Smedmore in Kimmeridge par. *supra*. STEEPLE LEAZE FM &
WD, *Steeple Lease* 1774 Hutch¹, *-Leaze* 1795 Boswell, (— *Copse,
—Fm*) 1842 *TA*, *v.* lǣs. HR & LR STONEHIPS, *Lr Stonehip, Stonehip
Coppice, Stonehips Md* p1795 *Mansel*, — *Copse* 1842 *TA*, 'heap(s) of
stone(s)', *v.* stān, hēap (cf. Do dial. *hipe* (Barnes 72)). TAYLOR'S
CTG. THORNHILL'S COPPICE, cf. *Thornhill* 1842 *TA*, *v.* þorn, hyll.
WASHING LEDGE, a pointed shelf of rock in Kimmeridge Bay (*v.*
Kimmeridge par. *supra*), perhaps so called with reference to its use
for washing or to the movement of the tide, *v.* washing, ledge.
WHITEHALL, *v.* hwīt, hall, cf. New Hall *supra*. HR, LR & N WITHY
BED, *Withey Beds* 1842 *TA*.

FIELD-NAMES

The undated forms are 1842 *TA* 195. Spellings dated 1280 are *Ass*, 1319,
1323¹, 1379 *MinAcct*, 1323² *Ct*, 1325, 1566, 17 Hutch³, 1340 NI, 1382
Fine, 1384 *DCMDeed*, 1451 *Weld*¹, 1614, p1795 *Mansel*, 1664 HTax.

(a) Back Fd & Mdw (*v.* back); Baddy Cl; Bare Lds (Copse); Barn
Copse, Grd & Md; Barton Grd (*v.* barton); Blackmanston Copse &
Cowleaze (*The Cow Leaze* p1795, from Blackmanston *supra*); Blacksmith's
shop; Blinds Plot (the surname *Blind* and plot, but perhaps from blind
'hidden' and splott, cf. Splots *infra*); Bradle Down (from Bradle in Ch.
Knowle par. *supra*); Bramble Plot; Break neck (cf. Brickneck in Corfe C.
par. *supra*); Brickiln Cl (*The Brick Kiln* — p1795); Brimley (cf. *Brambly
Coppice* p1795, 'bramble clearing', *v.* brēmel, lēah); Calves Cl, Grd & Plot,
Calveshouse, Calves House Copse (*v.* calf, hūs); Chick Md (*v.* chick);
Churchill (from St John's Church *supra*, *v.* hyll); Clay Hills; Cliff Md (cf.
pastur'...*super la Clyf* 1319, *le Clif* 1323¹, *v.* clif); (The) Copse; Course
Fd (probably ModE course 'the practice of hunting (hares) with hounds');
Court Md (cf. *Court Close* 17, *v.* court); Cowleaze (freq), Cowleaze Copse;
The Down (*la Done* 1319, *le Doune* 1323¹, cf. *the North Downe Close, the
South Downe* 1614, *v.* dūn); Lr Dredger; Drong Md (*v.* drong); N & S

Drove, Droveway (*v.* drove, weg); Dry Grd; (Long) 8 Acres; 11 Acres;
(Upr) Eweleaze; Ferry's Grd; The 15 Acres; Fir Clump & Plant.; (Field
under) Firs; (The) 5 Acres; 5 Yards (*v.* gerd); (The) 4 Acres; Furzy Grd;
The Gardener's Md; Gilhams Md; Gravel Pit; Great Md(w); Green
Down; Ground before the door; Ground behind Copse; The Ground;
Grove Plot; Harris' (cf. 'tenement late in the tenure of George *Harris*' 17);
Heath (Grd) (cf. (*le*) *Heth*(*e*)*feld* 1323[1], 1379, 1382, *v.* hǣð, feld); Hill Md;
Home Md; The Homestal p1795 (*v.* hām-stall); Horse Cl & Grd; Hunger
Hill (a nickname for poor land, *v.* hungor, hyll); Hurpson Lane & Md(w)
(from Hurpston *supra*); Hyde Copse, Cowleaze & Md (from Hyde *supra*);
Jacks Hays (Head) (*v.* (ge)hæg, hēafod); Jenkin's Home Md; Lake Md (*v.*
lacu); Lanes (cf. Robert *in le Lane* 1340, *v.* lane); The Leg (*v.* leg); Lime
Kiln Coppice p1795; Little Grd, Md(w) & Plot; Long Cl, Copse, Leaze,
Md & Slip (*v.* lǣs, slip(p)e); Lucke's Grd; Luton Barn Yd (cf. 'the grange
of *Lutton*' 1325), Lut(t)on Eweleaze (from Lutton *supra*, cf. *campo apud*
Lutton 1280); Thomas Man's Grd; Hr & Lr Mead, The Mead, Meadow
(cf. *Mead Close* 1614, *v.* mǣd); Middle Fd; Middle Md Copse; Nappy
Gdn (*v.* cnæppig); New Cmn; Newfoundland (cf. Newfoundland in Ch.
Knowle par. *supra*); New Grd; 9 Acres; North Fd (1614); Oak Copse; Old
Rd; Over Lake (probably '(land) above or across the stream', *v.* ofer[3], lacu);
Paceys Plot; Paine's Coppice p1795; Park (*v.* park); Pasture & Firs;
Pasture Pce; The Plot; Pond Fd; Potato Grd; Pisseck's Coppice, Pissetts
Md p1795, Prissett's (probably the surname *Prissick*); Quar Cl (Row) (*v.*
quarrere, rāw); Quirt Md; Rick Yd (Plot); Rilands (*v.* ryge, land); Rodway
Fd p1795, Roadway (*v.* rād, weg); Rogers Md; Rough Bank & Brake (*v.*
bræc[1]); Rough Cl, Grd & Pce; Round Copse & Mdw; Rye Grds (*v.*
ryge); Sandpit Fd p1795, Sandpit Md; Sedgy Grd (*v.* secgig); 7 Acres;
Sharnoll's (perhaps a surname from a lost p.n. *Sharnoll* 'the dirty well,
spring or stream', *v.* scearn, wella, cf. Sharnal K 120, but cf. Charnel in
Tyneham par. *infra*); Sheep Rd; W Sheep Sleight (*v.* slæget); Shoot Md
(*v.* scēot[3], cf. Gough's Shoot *supra*); Short Lds; 6 & 16 Acres; W Slide
Banks (*v.* E Slide Banks in Ch. Knowle par. *supra*); Small Md & Wd;
Splots (*v.* splott); Outside Strap (*v.* outside, strap); Straw Cl (*v.* strēaw);
(The) 10 Acres; (The) 3 Acres; 3 Cornered Pce; 3 Yards (*v.* gerd); (Lt)
Trout Grd(s), Trout Mdw ('fields (near streams) where trout are caught', *v.*
truht); Turnip Grd; Turnpike Md (*v.* turnpike); (The) 2 Acres; Wash
Pond Md (*v.* wæsce); Water Mdw; Way Cl (*v.* weg); Welcome (probably
'valley with a well, spring or stream', *v.* wella, cumb, but perhaps a nickname
for a pleasant field); West Copse, Fd & Md; White Fd (*v.* hwīt); Whiteway
Hill (cf. Whiteway in Tyneham par. *infra*); Wild Md (*v.* wilde); Wills(')
Ho & Md (cf. Edith *Wills* 1566); Woar (possibly from ōra[1] 'bank', with
prosthetic *w*- before *o*, or a rounded form of ware 'sheep walk'); Woodbury
Hill Cowleaze (*v.* wudu, beorg or burh (dat. sg. *byrig*), cf. Woodbury in
E Holme par. *supra*).

(*b*) atte Bere (p) 1323[2] (*v.* atte, bǣr[2] or bearu); *firma de* (*Blakemonston*
voc' *le*) *Beklond, pastur' de Beeklond* 1451, *Beakes Land*, — *Mead* 1614
('land and meadow belonging to Bec', with reference to the fact that Blackmanston *supra* was formerly parcel of the manor of Povington in Tyneham

par. *infra* and as such belonged to the Abbey of Bec-Hellouin in Normandy
(Hutch³ 1 608, 621), cf. Milborne S. par. *infra*, v. land, mæd); *turbar' voc'*
Depdelf 1379 ('(turf-pit called) deep pit', v. dēop, (ge)delf, cf. *Hobbyngmor,*
Paddecdelf infra); *Ebbemor* 1323² (the first el. could be ebba 'ebb, low tide'
with reference to a tidal affluent of R. Frome, with mōr); *Grange Mills*
1664 (from Creech Grange *supra*, v. myln); *Hobbyngmor* 1379 (possibly
'hobgoblin's moor', from an unrecorded *hobben, *hobbin, a diminutive
of hob(be) which is a pet form of *Robin*, cf. Reaney s.n. Hobbins 166, and
mōr, but a first el. hobbing 'place characterized by tussocks', from hobb(e)
'tussock, hummock' and -ing¹ or -ing², is a more likely alternative, cf.
Hobmoor Wa 34; the 1379 reference is to the 'turf-pit called *Depdelf*' here,
v. *supra*); *Langeland* 1384 (v. lang¹, land); *plac' in qua...molend' situat' voc'*
Mulleham 1379 (v. myln, hamm); *turb' vocat' Paddecdelf* 1379 (v. padduc
'frog', (ge)delf, cf. *Depdelf supra*); *Southfield* 1614; *Stony Close*, — *Mead*
1614 (v. stānig).

Tyneham

Blackmanston and Lutton in Steeple par. *supra* were formerly parcels of the
manor of Povington in this par. (Hutch³ 1 607).

TYNEHAM (SY 882804) ['tainəm]

Tigeham 1086 DB (2×), 1185 P (p), *Tiham* 1194 ib, 1244 *Ass*
(p), *Tigenham* 14 Mansel (p)

Tingeham 1086 DB (2×), *Estingham* 1288 *Ass*, Est-, *Westangham*
(sic) 1288 *Ass*, *Westingham* 1550 DCMDeed

Tyn(h)am 1244 *Ass* (p), 1280 ib (p), Ch, 1285 FA (p), 1291 Tax,
1316 FA *et freq* to 1464 Weld¹, *Es(t)-, Wes(t)tyn(h)am* 1280 *Ass*,
1285 FA *et freq* to 1545 Ct, *Es(t)tin(h)am* 1285 FA, 1288 *Ass*,
Churchetinam, Cherestinam 1285 FA, *Westinham* 1288 *Ass*,
Wesynham (sic) 1332 SR, *Westnam als. Westinham* 1555 DCM-
Deed

Thenham (sic) 1280 *Ass*, Est-, *Westthynham* 1306 FF

Teynham 1328 Banco, *Weste(y)n(e)ham* 1523 DCMDeed, 1537
Hutch³

Tyneham 1445 (16) DCMDeed, *West* — 1445 (16) *ib*, 1546 *Ct*,
1774 Hutch¹, *Est* — 1546 *Ct*, *East Tyneham* 1774 Hutch¹, *South*
Tyn(e)ham 1638 Hutch³, 1774 Hutch¹, *Great* —, *Little Tyneham*
1774 ib

Probably 'goat's enclosure' from tige (gen.sg. *tigan*) and hamm,
as suggested in DEPN and EPN, but formally a possible alternative
for the second el. would be hām 'homestead'. The early spellings in

-ing(e)ham are perhaps due to association with place-names containing OE -ingahām. *Great* and *South* Tyneham are (or were) alternative names for *East* Tyneham, and *Little* Tyneham is (or was) an alternative name for *West* Tyneham, v. ēast, west; the 13th-cent. forms *Churche-, Cherestinam* must refer to the church (now St Mary's Church *infra*) in (West) Tyneham, v. cirice.

BALTINGTON (SY 876804)

 Boltington, Bultington 1280 *Ass* both (p)
 Baltington(e), -yng- 1284 Banco, c. 1300 *Milne*, 14 Mansel, 1327
  SR (p) *et freq* to 1614 *AddCh, Baltintone* c. 1300 *Milne*,
  Baltyntone 14 Mansel, *Baltingthone* 14 ib, Ed I Hutch[3]
 Baltingeton 1287 FF
 Baldyngton 1329 Orig, Pat
 Balkington 1648 *AddCh* (*the Farme of* —), 1795 Boswell, 1811 OS

 Probably from an OE pers.n. and -ingtūn 'farm called after'. The spellings from *Ass* may well be corrupt, but *Balt-, Bald-* in the majority of early spellings may suggest some such pers.n. as **B(e)aldðrȳð* (v. DEPN s.n. Balterley St), *B(e)aldhere, B(e)aldhūn* or *B(e)aldheard* (for OE *d* to *t* before *h*, v. Ekwall in SNPh 1 97 ff, Waltham Sx 77, Brk 112, cf. also *Balt, -balt* for OE *Beald, -beald* in 1086 DB (Feilitzen 98, 193, 207)).

 CHAPEL CL (SY 895806), 1861 Hutch[3], the site of the former chapel of St Margaret at (North) Egliston *infra*, referred to as *capella Scē Margar' de Eglyneston, capella Beate Margar' de Eglemenesdon* 1288 *Ass*, 'the chapel of St. Margaret, *Eglineston*' 1290 Pat, cf. 'Eggliston in the parish of St Margaret in the Isle of Purbeck' 1523 Hutch[3].

 N & S EGLISTON (SY 894807, 899798) ['eglstən], *Egelineston* 1202 *Ass*, 1285 FA, 1288 *Ass*, *Egelmeston* (sic) 1280 *Ass*, *Egg(e)leneston* 1285 FA, *Eglyn(e)s-, Eglineston* 1288 *Ass*, 1290 Pat, 1327 *SR*, 1380 *Mansel, Eglemenesdon* (sic) 1288 *Ass*, *Eglyng(e)ston* 1332 SR, 1377 *Ass*, *Eghelinstona, Eg(e)leynstun, -ton* p1483 *Sheen, Eg(g)lis-, -lyston* 1325 Hutch[3], 1427 *Weld*[1], 1445 Mansel (*— in Purbyk*), 1523 Hutch[3], 1545 *Ct, Eg(g)leston(e)* 1376 Pat, *Ass et freq* to 1774 Hutch[1] (*North* —, *South* —), *Egulston* 1528 Hutch[3], *Eccleston* 1587 DCMDeed, *Eagleston* 1646 SC, probably 'Eggelin's farm', from the OG pers.n. *Eggelin* and tūn (confused with dūn 'hill' in one 13th-cent. form). Dr von Feilitzen points out that this pers.n. is attested by OHG

Eckilin (Förstemann PN 29), and occurs as *Eggelinus* in 14th-cent.
German sources and as *Egelinus* in England (*Mauricius Egelini* 1222
Domesday of St Paul's 30–2, cf. Reaney s.n. *Eglin*). This is a post-
Conquest p.n., for in 1202 *Ass* (roll 1171) a third of this manor was
recovered by *Agatha qui fuit uxor Engelini* (sic, m. 10, cf. the OG
pers.n. *Engelin* (Forssner 73), note the variant spelling *Egelin* in
the same roll (m. 11)). 'The grange of *Egliston*' is mentioned in
1325 Hutch³, and for the former chapel of St Margaret here, *v.*
Chapel Cl *supra*.

POVINGTON (SY 883821) [ˈpɔviŋtən]

>   *Povintone* 1086 DB, *Povincton* 1205 Hutch³, *Povin(g)-, Pouin-,*
>   *-yn(g)ton* 1212 Fees, 1244 *Douce*, 1258 Cl, 1285 FA, 1288 *Ass,*
>   1327 *SR et passim, Povi-* 1222 Cur, *Pouyton, Bouyngton* (sic)
>   1288 *Ass, Poryngton* (sic) 1291 Tax, *Poventon* 1434 Hutch³
>   *Puninton* (sic for *Puu-*) 1223 FF
>   *Peuynton, Pyuynton* 1280 *Ass, Peiuynton* 1316 FA

Probably 'farm called after Pēof(a)', from the OE pers.n. *Pēof(a)*
found as *Peuf(a)* in LVD (Searle 388, Redin 34), and -ingtūn.
The 13th-cent. form in *B-* probably shows confusion with Bovington
in Wool par. *infra*. There was a mill here, claimed for the king's use,
in 1086 DB (VCHDo **3** 90), cf. *atte Mulle infra*. For the 'priory' here,
probably only a grange, *v.* VCHDo **2** 118–19 and the f.n. Monks
Bottom *infra*.

WHITEWAY (SY 874821) (FM, HILL, & PLANT.), *Whitewey* 1327 *SR*
(p), *boscu' de Whitewaye, the wood of Wytewaye* 1381 (16) *Pitt,*
Whitway 1451 *Weld¹, West Whitwey, a wood called Whitwaye* c. 1586
Tres, 'Byle's tenement alias West Whiteway farm' 1685 Hutch³,
West Whiteway, Whiteway Dairy 1811 OS, *Whiteway Hill, Plant. &*
Wd 1841 *TA*, 'white way', *v.* hwīt, wēg, taking its name from 'a
conspicuous white road or way leading over the chalk hill from
Lulworth to Tyneham' (Hutch³ **1** 624); *West* to distinguish it from
Whiteway (earlier *East Whiteway*) in Ch. Knowle par. *supra*;
'Byle's tenement' from John *Bile* 1615 Hutch³.

WORBARROW (SY 871797) (BAY & TOUT), *Wyrebarowe* 1462 Pat,
a Cryke in purbyke called Wyrbarow c. 1500 RoyRoll, *Worthbar(r)ow*
bay(e) 1575 Saxton, c. 1586 Tres, 1861 Hutch³, *Wor-* 1579 Hutch³,
1774 Hutch¹, 1811 OS, *Worebarrow (Bay)* 1795 Boswell, *Mor-*

barrowe (sic for *Wor-*) 1658 *AddCh*, *Warbarrow Bay* 1773 Bayly,
— *Tout* 1841 *TA*; the second el. is beorg 'hill', possibly with reference to what is now Worbarrow Tout (*v.* tōt(e) 'look-out hill')
described in Hutch³ 1 619 as 'a little rocky conical hill...almost
environed by the sea, being joined to the continent by a neck of
land', *v.* bay¹, crike 'a creek'. The forms are too late for any certainty
about the first el., but it is possibly OE weard 'watch' (as in Warborough O 138, cf. DEPN; for the *Wyr-*, *Wor-* spellings from OE
wear-, cf. Worgret in Arne par. *supra*) or its mutated variant *wierde
of similar meaning (*v.* Woodsford par. *infra*), cf. Wor Barrow in
Wimborne St G. par. *infra* which is probably analogous: the form
from 1462 Pat occurs in a commission 'to set the accustomed watches
at a place called *Wyrebarowe* by *Pole* [i.e. Poole par. *infra*], for the
safety of the town and the adjacent country'. The spellings in
Worth- probably show association of the first el. with worð 'enclosure'. The early loss of *-d-* may be partly due to influence from OE
waru¹ 'defence, guard', cf. Warborough O 138 which has no *-d-*
spellings later than 13th cent. and which Ekwall (DEPN s.n.) in fact
interprets as containing waru¹ rather than weard. Worbarrow Tout is
also known as *Worbarrow Knob* (Short 45), 1882 Robinson, *v.*
knob. Caves here are called *Wer Coves* c. 1825 Map.

ALMS GROVE (GATE), *Ames Grove* (*Wd*) 1841 *TA*, from a surname
with grāf(a), geat; this gate, like Maiden's Grave Gate *infra*, is at a
point where the road running along the top of the Purbeck ridge
meets the Tyneham–Steeple bdy, cf. also Lawford Sheard Gate *infra*.
BLACK CTG. BOWER'S COPPICE, from a family here in 19th cent.
(Legg 109). BRANDY BAY, probably so called with reference to
smuggling, cf. Arkell (1941) 36 who notes that 'there is a sequestered
way up the cliff where kegs could be conveniently brought up'.
BROAD BENCH, 1811 OS, a coastal shelf of rock, *v.* benc. THE CAT,
probably an inn. CHARNEL, on the coast, perhaps ModE charnel
'cemetery, charnel house', but cf. Sharnoll's in Steeple par. *supra*.
COASTGUARD STATION, *Watch Room* (*Coast Guard*) 1841 *TA*. EARL'S
KITCHEN, part of Povington Heath *infra*, probably alluding to the
Earl of Hertford to whom the manor of Povington was granted in
1582 (Hutch³ 1 623), *v.* cycene. EGLESTON DOWN (lost), 1826 Gre,
from Egliston *supra*. EGLISTON GWYLE, cf. prec., *v.* goyle. FAREWELL'S
CTG. FIVE BARROW HILL, FIVE BARROWS, *The 5 barrowes* c. 1586
Tres, '*Five barrows*', *a line of barrows running north and south* 1861

Hutch[3], *v.* beorg; Legg 108 notes that there are in fact 6 barrows here. GAD CLIFF, 1811 OS, *Gadcliffe* 1841 *TA*, a stretch of high coastal cliffs; the first el. is perhaps ModE **gad** (< ON *gaddr* 'spike, nail') in one of its many senses (e.g. 'spike, goad, rod, stake, etc') with reference to an actual 'gad' or used figuratively; this word is used in Purbeck for a 'wedge to cleave stone', and Arkell (1941) 35 notes that 'when seen from the east at a distance Gad Cliff has a strikingly wedge-shaped silhouette'. GARDENER'S CTG, cf. John *Jardyn* 1327 *SR*, 1332 SR (from OFr *jardin* 'a garden'). GOLD DOWN, 1811 OS, possibly from **gold** 'gold' in some connection now obscure, or **golde** '(marsh) marigold'. HOBARROW BAY, probably 'hill or tumulus on a spur of land', *v.* hōh, beorg. LAWFORD SHEARD GATE, at a point where the track running along the Purbeck ridge was crossed by one from Tyneham where the ford may have been; the first el. may be **hlāw** 'hill, tumulus', *v.* ford, sceard 'cleft, gap', cf. Alms Grove Gate *supra*. LIMEKILN PLANT., 1841 *TA*, cf. *Hr & Lr Limekiln(s)* 1841 *ib.* LONG COPSE. LONG EBB, a narrow ledge of shore-line rocks pointing to sea, probably 'place where the tide ebbs a long way', *v.* **ebba**. MAIDEN'S GRAVE GATE, cf. Alms Grove Gate *supra*; a nearby oak is known as 'the Coffin Tree', both names probably alluding to a suicide's burial (Legg 122). PONDFIELD, a small round cove probably so called from its shape. *v.* pund-fald 'a pinfold, a pound', as suggested by Arkell (1940) 46, cf. Robert *de la Pondfalde*, — *de la Puntfeld* 1288 *Ass* and Ponfill Fd in Swanage par. *supra*. POOL POND, apparently tautological, *v.* pōl[1], ponde. POVINGTON BARROW (tumulus marked 6″), FM (— *Farme* 1664 HTax), HEATH (1811 OS, — *heathe* c. 1586 Tres), HILL (1841 *TA*) & WD (1841 *ib*), all from Povington *supra*. QUARRY (marked 6″, ½ mile NE of Baltington *supra*), cf. *petrar' de Querrer' de Baltyngton* 1457 *Weld*[1], *v.* quarrere. REMPSTONE GATE, cf. *Rainstone Fd* 1841 *TA*, where the road from Whiteway *supra* crosses the par. bdy (which is also the bdy of the Isle of Purbeck) to E Lulworth par. *infra*; the name may refer to a former stone circle recorded by Warne in e19 and assumed by Legg 109 to have been here, cf. Rempstone in Corfe C. par. *supra*. ROOK GROVE, *Rook Grove* (*Wood*) 1841 *TA*, *v.* hrōc, grāf(a). ST MARY'S CHURCH, cf. 'the church of *Teynham*' 1328 Banco, and the 13th-cent. church alluded to in the forms cited under Tyneham *supra*. STICKLAND'S CTG, the surname *Stickland* from Winterborne Stickland par. *infra*. THORN BARROW, tumulus marked 6″, *v.* þorn, beorg. TYNEHAM CAP, 1861 Hutch[3], 'on the summit of the south hill' ib, perhaps the word cæppe 'cap' used figuratively (cf. similar uses of hæt(t) 'hat' and hōd 'hood'), or an altered form of copp 'hill-top, summit', cf. Golden Cap in Stanton St G. par. *infra.* TYNEHAM FM (*Tineham* 1811 OS), GREAT WD (*Tyneham Wd* 1841 *TA*), GWYLE (*the goyle* 1648 *AddCh, Guiwle* 1841 *TA, v.* goyle) & HO (1826 Gre, *Tineham Hal* 1811 OS, *v.* hall).

FIELD-NAMES

The undated forms are 1841 *TA* 234. Spellings dated 1327 are *SR*, 1332 SR, 1337, 1615, 1685, 1736, 1861 Hutch[3], 1340 NI, c. 1500 *RoyRoll*, 1648 *AddCh*, 1774 Hutch[1].

(a) Bagington Hill (cf. Baginton Wa 155); Balstons Plot; Barnet Pce (v. bærnet(t)); Barn Md & Pce; Belt; Botany Cowleaze & Withey Bed (from Botany Fm in E Lulworth par. *infra*); Bottom Md; Broad Md; Buffins; Buttal Grd (butt[2] or butte, probably with hyll); Hr & Lr Butts (v. butte, cf. prec.); Calves House Fd & Grd; Christophers (— tenement 1861, from Thomas *Christopher* 1736; earlier called *Cockram's* from John *Cockram* who bought it in 1615 (Hutch[3] 1 624)); Church Fd & Flg; Cliff, Outercliffe (cf. *the Clevys* c. 1500, v. ūterra, clif); Common; Coombe Bottom (v. cumb, botm); Coppice Grd & Walk; Cowleaze (freq); Drove; East Hill; Egglestone Fd, Great Md & Little Md (from Egliston *supra*); 8, 18 & 11 Acres; (E & W) Eweleaze; 15, 4 & 14 Acres; French Grass Grd (v. french grass); E & W Furlong, Furlong Withey Bed; Furzy Plot (Coppice) (cf. *plott of Fursie grounde newly inclosed* 1648, v. fyrsig); Garden Plant.; Glebe Md; Great Md(w); Green Cl; Hedgerow; Hill; Holefield (cf. *Holmede* 1545 DCMDeed, v. hol[2]) and Avenue; Home Cl, Md(w) & Plot; (Green) Horse Cl (Coppice), Lr Horse Coppice, Horsehouse Grd, Horse Plot; Hungry Hill (a nickname for poor land); Land; Legg (v. leg); Lenthills (perhaps 'hills associated with the season of Lent', cf. Gl 4 201 for similar names, but probably a surname from some such place as Lenthill D 465); Littlehay (v. (ge)hæg); Long Cl & Md; Lower Grd & Md; (Hr & Lr) Meadow; Monks Bottom (an allusion to the former possession of the manor of Povington *supra* by the Abbey of Bec-Hellouin, cf. *Beklond* in Steeple par. *supra,* v. munuc, botm); Hr & Lr Moor; Moreys Plot; Mount Md; New Grd & Pce; 9 & 19 Acres; North Hill; Orchard; Paddock; Further, Hr, Lr & Middle Piece; (N & W) Plantation; Pollard's Md & Plot; (Further) Pond Cl; Poulden's Plot; Pound; Povington Mdw (from Povington *supra*); Rick Yd; Rough; Round Grd; 17 Acres; Sheepleaze (v. læs); 6 & 16 Acres; Small Md; (Hr) 10 Acres (on the Hill); 20 & 2 Acres; Way Grd; Well Plot; West Fd; West Hill; West Md(w) (Plant.); (Hr, Long & Lr) With(e)y Bed; Wolcomb 1774 (v. wella, cumb); Wood (Walk).

(b) *de la Bere* 1327 (p) (v. bearu or bǣr[2]); *atte forde* 1327, 1332 both (p) (v. atte, ford); *atte Hide* 1327 (p) (v. hīd); *atte Mulle* 1337 (p), 1340 (p) (v. myln); *Parishe's tenement* 1685 (from Christian *Paris* 1615).

III. WINFRITH HUNDRED

Winfrith hundred is an amalgamation of the two GeldR hundreds of *Winfrode* and *Celberge*. In c. 1086 GeldR *Winfrode* hundred contained Chaldon H., Coombe K., E & W Lulworth, E Stoke (part), Winfrith N. and Wool, whilst *Celberge* contained Moreton, Owermoigne, Poxwell, Warmwell, Watercombe and Woodsford as well as Ringstead (in Osmington, now in Culliford Tree hundred) and (probably) Broadmayne (now in St George hundred) and Little Mayne (in W Knighton, now in Culliford Tree hundred), *v.* Eyton 115f, 119f, 141f, Anderson 120, VCHDo 3 143–4. The amalgamation of the two hundreds had taken place by 1285 FA (ii.9), by which date Broadmayne and Little Mayne were excluded; Ringstead was still in this hundred in 1795 Boswell. Chaldon H., W Lulworth and Wool are now in Bindon liberty (*v. infra*); in 1332 SR it comprised only Wool, but in 1795 Boswell it also contained Bexington (in Puncknowle), Chaldon H., Creech Grange (in Steeple), Mill St. (in Fordington), Longcutts (in Winfrith N.), W Lulworth, East Pulham (in Pulham), and Westworth (in Edmondsham); Hutch³ 1 349 adds Chamberlayne's Mill (in Bere R.), The Priory (in Dorchester), and Wareham. Owermoigne was in Winfrith hundred in 1332 SR but is a liberty in 1664 HTax and 1795 Boswell (*v.* Owermoigne par. *infra* for references to Owermoigne liberty). Wareham was a borough in 1332 SR and remains such in 1664 HTax and 1795 Boswell (with its three pars. of Holy Trinity, Lady St Mary and St Martin); it has been included in this hundred for topographical convenience. West Holme in East Stoke par. is a tithing in Hasler hundred.

WINFRITH HUNDRED, *Winfrode hundret* c. 1086 GeldR, *hundredum de Win-*, *Wyn(e)frod(e)* 1130 PR, 1195 P, 1204 Cur, 1212 Fees *et freq* to 1288 *Ass*, *Windfrodhundredum* 1178 P, *Winfrodhundr'* 1189 ib, 1196 ChancR, *hundredum de Wilfro(r)d* 1194, 1195 P, and spellings as for Winfrith Newburgh par. *infra*, 'Foreign Hundred of *Winfrod*' 1265 Misc, 'the manor of *Wynford* with the inhundred (*hundredo intrinseco*) and the foreign hundred' 1269 Ch. Named from Winfrith Newburgh par. *infra* which was the *caput* of the hundred and to which it was annexed (Anderson 120–1).

CELBERGE HUNDRED (lost), *Celberge hundret* c. 1086 GeldR, thought by Anderson 120 to survive in Chilbury Plant. in Owermoigne par. *infra* which would in fact be fairly centrally placed within this old hundred. Anderson *loc. cit.* thinks the meaning may be 'chalk hill' from **calc** (WSax **cealc**) and **beorg** (topographically suitable), but formally the first el. could equally well be **ceole** 'throat, channel' or **cegel** (WSax **ci(e)gel**) 'pole, post'.

BINDON LIBERTY, *Lib' Abbatis de Bynedon* 1280 *Ass*, *Libertas de Bynedon(e)* 1327 *SR*, 1332 SR, *hd of Bynedon* 1337, 1354 Pat, *Bindon Libertye* 1664 HTax, *Liberty of Bindon* 1682 *Weld*[1], named from Bindon in Wool par. *infra*.

Chaldon Herring

This par. is in Bindon liberty (*v.* note under Winfrith hundred *supra*).

CHALDON HERRING or EAST CHALDON (SY 792833) [ˈtʃɔːldən]

Celvedune 1086 DB, *Cealvaduna* Exon, *Calvedone* DB, Exon, *-dona* Exon

Chauue-, *Chauvedon* 1199 CartAnt, 1242–3 Fees, 1244, 1268 *Ass* (p), 1285 FA (p), *Chaunedon* (sic) 1214 FineR, 1227 FF, *Chauudone Haregang* (sic) 1288 *Ass*

Cauvedon 1215 Cur

Chanedon (sic) 1218 FF, *Chandon* (sic) 1227 ib, 1258 ib (— *Hareng*), 1291 Tax (— *Haryngg*), *Chavedon Hareng* 1235–6 Fees, *Chaue-*, *Chavedun* 1268 *Ass* (p), 1269 Ch (p), *-don* 1443 *Weld*[1], *Chauedon-*, *Chaudun Harang* 1288 *Ass*, *Chaudon Haryngg* 1428 FA

Chalve-, *Chaluedon(e)* 1224 ClR, 1234 (13) *HarlCh*, 1234 (1279) Ch, 1243 FF (— *Hareng*), 1244 *Ass* (p), 1268 *ib* (— *Harang*), 1269 Misc (*Est-*) *et freq* to 1489 *Ct* with the additions *-Harang* (to 1340 NI), *-Heryng* (from 1332 Cl) and *Est-*; *Chaveldon Harang* 1288 *Ass*, *Chalnedon* (sic) *Haryng* 1291 Tax, *Chaluedoun* 1399 Cl, *Chalfuedon* 1414 *Weld*[1], *Chaulvedon* 1499 *Ct*

Calvedon Harang 1297 Cl, Pat, *Caluedon* 1445 *Weld*[1]

Chalvesdon Heryng 1428 FA

Chaldon 1501 Pat, (*Est* —) 1535 VE, 1574 *Russ* (— *Hearynge*), 1575 Saxton (*Est* —), 1594 *Ilch* (*East* —), 1652 *Weld*[1] (— *Hearinge*), *the mannor and Fearme of Chaldon Hearing* 1587 *Russ*, *Chalden alias Chaldon Hearing* 1595 *ib*, *East Chauldon* 1640 *Weld*[1]

'Hill where calves were pastured', *v.* calf (WSax gen.pl. *cealfa*), dūn, cf. Chaldon Sr 42; for the hill itself, *v.* High Chaldon *infra*. The family of *Harang* were here from the time of Hy 2 (Hutch[3] 1 340, 2 521), cf. also Thomas *Hareng* 1199 CartAnt, Terricus *Harang* 1203 Cur, Phillip *Hareng* 1227 FF; the same family gave its name to Winterborne Herringstone par., Herrison in Charminster par., and

Langton Herring par. (all *infra*). *East* in relation to West Chaldon or Chaldon Boys *infra* where some of the early forms without affix may strictly belong, *v.* ēast. For the AN vocalisation of preconsonantal *l* in *Chauvedon*, etc., *v.* ANInfl 146 ff, Feilitzen 78.

WEST CHALDON or CHALDON BOYS (SY 778828)

West Chalve-, Chaluedon 1269 Misc, 1280 Ch, 1404, 1459 *Weld*[1], 16 *Winch, Westchaldon* 1454, 1459 *Weld*[1], 1535 VE, 1640 *Weld*[1], 1811 OS

Chau(e)don Boys 1270 FF, 1285 FA, 1299 Ipm, *Chalve-, Chaluedon(e) Boys* 1280 Ch, 1288 *Ass et freq* to 1428 FA, *Chalnedon* (sic) *Boys* 1291 Tax, *Chandone-, Chandeneboys* (sic) 1291 Tax, *Chalwedonboys* 1293 FF, *Chalveldon* (sic) *Boys* 1344 Pat, *Chaudeneboys* 1428 FA, *ChalderBoys* (sic) 1531 *Weld*[1]

West in relation to Chaldon Herring *supra*, *v.* west; *Boys* from the family of *de Bosco* or *Boys*, cf. Robert — 1269 Misc, Hugh *de Bosco* 1280 Ch. There was at one time a church here, referred to as 'the church of *Chaluedone Boys*' 1294 FF, *ecclesie de Westchaluedon* 1404 *Weld*[1], cf. Hutch[3] 1 344, *v.* St Nicholas's Church *infra*.

WEST FOSSIL DAIRY & FM (SY 792851, 795852)

Foresteshull 1227 FF (p), *Forsteshull* 1254 ib, 1280 Ch, *-hill* 1288 *Ass, Forstehull* 1280 Ch

Forteshull 1227 FF, 1280 Ch, *Fortishull* 1288 *Ass*

Forshull(e) 1244 *Ass* (p), 1275 RH, 1279 FF, 1300 Ipm *et freq* to 1484 *MinAcct* with the addition *West-* in 1404, 1475 *Weld*[1], *Westforeshull* 1319 Pat, *Forshill* 1329 ib, 1437 *Weld*[1] *et freq* to 1469 *MinAcct* with the addition *West-* in 1443 *Weld*[1], 1461 *Rent, Forsshull* 1408, 1413 *Weld*[1], *West Forsehill* 1535 VE

Furshyll 1435 *Weld*[1]

Fosthell 1589 Comm, *Fossell* 1705 *Weld*[1], *Lr & Middle Fossill* 1811 OS, *Foss(hi)ll Fm* 1865 *Weld*[1]

Probably 'hill called *Forst*' ('the ridge'), *v.* forst (gen.sg. *-es*), hyll, cf. Forest Hill O 171, Furzehill W 245, Frosthills Wt 283, as first suggested by Tengstrand MN 100–1; alternatively, as Professor Löfvenberg points out, the first el. may be an OE pers.n. *Forst*, originally a byname, *v.* Tengvik 376, Reaney 126. The hill itself is called *Fossill Hill* in 1841 *TA*. *West* in relation to East Fossil in Winfrith N. par. *infra*, *v.* west; some of the early forms cited above may strictly belong there. In 1811 OS West Fossil Dairy is called *Lower Fossill*, West Fossil Farm is *Middle Fossill*.

THE GRANGE (SY 791831), GRANGE DAIRY, (*le*) *Grange* 1464, 1638 *Weld*[1], *Farme and Graunge of Easte Chaldon* 1583 CoRO, (*East*) *Chaldon Grange* 1640, 1703, *Chaldon Grange Farme* 1682 all *Weld*[1], *v.* grange; like Creech Grange in Steeple par. *supra* it probably formerly belonged to Bindon Abbey. Some of the above spellings may refer to *Grange Farm* 1774 Hutch[1], 1861 Hutch[3], situated 'almost opposite East Chaldon, about half a mile to the north' (Hutch[3] 1 343); and *grang'...apud Forsshull* 1408 *Weld*[1] may also belong here, *v.* West Fossil *supra*. Grange Dairy seems to be referred to as *Hr Chaldon* 1811 OS.

ST NICHOLAS'S CHURCH (SY 790831), on the site of an earlier church or churches referred to as *æcclesiam de Calvedone* 1086 DB, Exon, *ecclesie de Chaluedon Herig* (sic) 1343 Ilch, 'church of *Chaldon*' 1501 Pat, *ecclesie de Chaldon* 1535 VE. In 1861 Hutch[3] its dedication was unknown, but it has since received the dedication of the lost church of West Chaldon *supra*, which according to Hutch[3] 1 344 was dedicated to St Nicholas.

TADNOLL DAIRY & MILL (SY 792869), *Tadenhole* 1281 Banco, *Tadenoll* 1394, *Taten(h)al(l)(e)s-, -hallis-, -myll, -mill* 1455–1490, *Tad(d)ynolle(s)myll* 1463–1473 all *Weld*[1], *Tahenhallysmyll* (sic) 1498, *Tatenolysmylle* 1499 Ct, *molendin' granifer' apud Tadnoll* 1562, *Tadwell* (sic) 1587 Russ, *Tadnoll Mill* 1663, 1682 *Weld*[1], *Tadknowle Mill* 1663 *Weld*[1]. There can be no certainty about either the first or second el. of this name. The meaning may be 'toad infested nook or hollow' from tadde, tāde (gen.sg. -*an*, gen.pl. -*ena*) and halh or hol[1], either of which would be suitable topographically (the place is marshy and low-lying, in a bend of a river, and in the corner of the par.), cf. Frognal(l) K 279, 527. But some of the forms could be seen to contain OE hnoll 'top of the head' (perhaps originally used, in a transferred sense, of Tadnoll Barrow in Owermoigne par. *infra*, a tumulus 600 yds N of Tadnoll Mill on the Owermoigne–Moreton bdy, cf. PNGl 1 10), and there may in fact be two different names here with the same first el. (heall 'hall' and wella 'well' have also influenced the forms). An alternative first el. (perhaps more likely than tadde, tāde if the second el. is hnoll) is an OE pers.n. *Tāda* (suggested for e.g. Tadlow Ca 66) or the OE pers.n. *Tāta* (cf.

Tattenhall Ch **4** 97). Forms like *Tatenhallesmyll* could contain a surname *Tatenhall* taken from the place, but it is more likely they mean 'mill belonging to *Tatenhall*', etc., *v.* myln; for earlier references to a mill in Chaldon Herring (though not necessarily this one), *v.* Mill Stream *infra*.

BAT'S HEAD, a small coastal promontory, perhaps so called because frequented by bats, *v.* bat, hēafod, but *Bat* may be a surname (cf. Henry *(le) Bat* 1327 *SR*, 1332 SR (Wool)), cf. foll. BAT'S HOLE, 1865 *Weld*[1], a coastal feature near prec., *v.* hol[1]. BEAUFORT FM, from the Duke of Beaufort who held the manor of Chaldon Herring at the end of the 18th cent. (Hutch[3] 1 342). BUSH BARROW, 1865 *Weld*[1], a tree-covered tumulus marked 6″. BUTTER ROCK, an offshore rock. THE CALF, the smaller of two offshore rocks, cf. The Cow *infra*, The Blind Cow and The Bull in W Lulworth par. *infra*, Cow & Calf Rocks YW **4** 214. CHALDON DOWN (1811 OS) (BLDGS), cf. *(New) Down* 1865 *Weld*[1], *v.* dūn. EAST & WEST CHALDON FMS (lost, 1865 *ib*). HIGH CHALDON, 1865 *ib*, the hill which gave name to Chaldon Herring *supra*. (OLD) CHALK PIT, cf. *Chalk Pit (Grd)* 1865 *ib*, Chalk Pit Fd in Owermoigne par. *infra*. CHAPEL (Site of), 'formerly a small chapel, the remains of which have been converted into a dwellinghouse' Hutch[3] 1 343. CHIDEOCK FM, probably a surname from Chideock par. *infra*, cf. John *Chidiock* 1369 Hutch[3] (witness in a Winfrith N. charter); it is less likely to be an identical but independent p.n. CLAYLAND COPPICE, *v.* clæg, land. COASTGUARD STATION, cf. *Signal Ho* 1811 OS. THE COW, the larger of two offshore rocks, cf. The Calf *supra*. CROSS (remains of), cf. *Erlewinescroff* (probably for *-cross*) 1227 FF, 'Erlewin's cross', from the OHG pers.n. *Erlewin* and cros. (OLD) DOWN BARN, from Chaldon Down *supra*. FIVE MARYS, *Five Mary Barrows* 1774 Hutch[1], *Five Mary's Grd* 1865 *Weld*[1], *Five Meers* 1765 Taylor, 1811 OS, a line of tumuli lying along an old track on the crest of a 300′ ridge, perhaps an old bdy between West Fossil *supra* and Chaldon Herring, and so possibly containing (ge)mære 'boundary' as suggested in Hutch[1] 1 124. FORD'S BARN. GOSTELOWES FM, from Richard *Gostelowe* who 'built a seat here in 1728, which is now converted to a farm-house' Hutch[3] 1 342. GREAT COPPICE. HILL BARN. THE HUT DAIRY. LORD'S BARROW, *Lords* — 1811 OS, a tumulus where the road from W Chaldon *supra* to Galton in Owermoigne par. *infra* crosses the par. bdy. THE MANOR HO (1″), *Chaldon Manor house* 1652 *Weld*[1].

MIDDLE BOTTOM, near West Bottom *infra*, *v.* botm. NEWMAN'S
COPPICE & CTG, cf. William *Niweman* 1392 *Ct*, John *Nywman* 16
Winch. NORTHGROUND DAIRY, *Northgrounds* 1638 *Weld*[1], *North Grd*
1811 OS. ROUND POUND 1811 OS, a small earthwork of unknown
date, perhaps at one time used as a pound for cattle, *v.* pund.
ST NICHOLAS'S FM, from St Nicholas's Church *supra*. SAILOR'S
RETURN (P.H.). SANDY DROVE, cf. *Droveway* 1865 *Weld*[1], *v.* drove.
SWYRE HEAD, 1811 OS, a worn-down coastal promontory, *v.* swēora
(late WS swīra) 'neck of land', cf. Swyre Head in Corfe C. par. *supra*.
VICARAGE FM, cf. *land in the Common Fd called Vicarage Land* 1785
SalisT, *Vicarage Gdn & Lawn* 1865 *Weld*[1]. WARDSTONE BARROW,
1811 OS, a tumulus on a high part (over 500') of Chaldon Down
supra overlooking the coast, probably 'stone or rock from which
watch was kept', *v.* weard, stān; the original cremation was covered
by a flat stone (RCHMDo 2 441). THE WARREN, WARREN HO, cf.
West Cliff Warren 1865 *Weld*[1], *v.* wareine. WEST BOTTOM, cf. Middle
Bottom *supra*.

FIELD-NAMES

The undated forms are 1865 *Weld*[1] (E64). Spellings dated 1227 are FF,
1279, 1280[2] Ch, 1280[1] *Ass*, 1327 *SR*, 1340 NI, 1375 Cl, 1392, 1393, 1498
Ct, 1484 *MinAcct*, 16 *Winch*, 1562, 1587 *Russ*, 1664 HTax, p1795 *Mansel*,
1841 *TA* 46, and the rest *Weld*[1].

(a) Bags Bottom (cf. Richard *Bagge* 1392, *v.* botm); Bank; Barn Pce;
Batch Bottom (*v.* batch); Bottom (Md); Brick & Broad Cl; Chaldon Fd
(1682, *in campo de Chalvedon* 1393); Old Clay Pit; (E & W) Cliffs; Clover
Cl, Old Clover Grd; Gt, Middle & Lt Common; Cooks Bottom (cf. Editha
Coukes 1392); Coppice 1841; (Picked) Cow Leaze (*v.* picked); Coyatts
(perhaps from cū and geat, but possibly a surname from Coryates in
Portisham par. *infra*); East Fd 1841 (— *feild* 1652); Easy Go (probably a
name for land easy to plough); 11 Acre(s) (Cmn); Ewe Leaze (Pce); Farm
Md; 15, 5, 40, (The) 4 & 14 Acres; Foxholes (*v.* fox-hol); Front Md; E &
Lr Furlong; Furzey Plot (*v.* fyrsig); Gorse Fd (*v.* gorst); Grange Md (from
The Grange *supra*); Great Md (*ye Greate Meade* 1652, *v.* grēat); Green Hill
Grd, Greenhills (Md); Hr & Under Hill; Hoare (perhaps from an OE
*Hāre or *Hāra 'the grey one' used of a hill, cf. Horn Down Brk 480,
Harwell ib 521–2, and possibly to be associated with the form *Horeduneslan*
1227, 'lane to or near the hill called *Hore*, or the grey hill', *v.* hār[2], dūn,
lane); Home Cl, Flg & Md; Horse Cl Cow Leaze & Md (*Ye Horse closes*
1652); Horse Md & Plot; Lillington's Md (cf. *Joh' Lylyngton...domum*
1562, *Geo' Lillingtons house*, Edward *Lillington* 1664); Limbury's Cl,
Cowleaze & Pdk 1841 (the surname *Limbury*, from Lymburgh's Fm in
Marnhull par. *infra* or Limbury Fm in Netherbury par. *infra*); Lime Kiln
(Grd & Pce); Lobs Pound & Shed (*Lobbs Pound* p1795); Long Grd &

Md; Lower Fd; Mile Stone Grd; Mill Stream (cf. *molendinum...in Chaluedon Harang* 1280[1], *one water grist mill* 1652, Tadnoll Mill *supra*, *v.* grist-mill; there was a mill at Chaldon Herring in 1086 DB (VCHDo 3 67)); Newfoundland; New Cl; New Md (*Newemede* 1279, *v.* nīwe, mǣd); New Pce; 9 Acre Md; Oat Cl; Old Lane; Paddock; Parish Rd; Parsonage Cowleaze, Down, Fd & Pdk 1841; Pennings (possibly from Sir Thomas *Poynings* to whom this manor was granted in 1542 Hutch[3] 1 340, 343, cf. Mount Poynings in W Lulworth par. *infra*); Peters Pool; Plough Hill Down; Pump Holes (perhaps alluding to a well, cf. *pump-pit* EDD); (Gt & Lt) Rough Croft; Rough Grd & Md; 7 Acre Cmn; Shots (cf. Mary *Shott* 1664 (Steeple)); 6 & 16 Acres; Stumbledown (perhaps a nickname for a rough, steeply sloping field); Taps (cf. Tapps Pdk in Coombe K. par. *infra*); 10 Acres; 3 Acre Md; Trents Cl & Grd (cf. John *Trente* 1498); E & W 12 Acres; Venton (perhaps from fenn and tūn); Waddon (*v.* wād, dūn); Water Mdw; West Fd 1841 (*common feild called Westfeild* 1652); Wet Corner Md; Wheat Cl; Whetstone (*v.* hwet-stān); White's Md (cf. John *Whyte* 1340, 1498, *orreum Ricardi Whyte* 1562); Whittle (*Whethull* 1227, West Whittle 1841, cf. Richard *Whethull* 1392, *v.* hwǣte, hyll); Withey Bed (cf. *le Witheber* 1462, *v.* wīðig, bearu).

(*b*) *close called Ye Backside* 1652 (*v.* backside); *La Bie* 1227 (*v.* byge[1] 'corner, angle, bend of a river'); *Bremehull* 1227 (*v.* brēme[1] or brēme[2], hyll); *Brimecherche* 1227 (the first el. is perhaps identical with that in prec.; the second el. may be PrWelsh crūg 'hill, barrow' rather than OE ciric 'church'); *Buckesclose* 1587 (cf. John *Bucke* 1498); *Cumba, Cumbe* 1227 (*v.* cumb); *Eltecumbe* 1227 (perhaps from an OE pers.n. *Elta* (*v.* Nth 70), or elfitu, and cumb); *Estmede* 1562 (*v.* ēast, mǣd); *close called forsell's* 1587, *Fostle Close* 1652, *forsehyll Come* 1562, *camp' de Forshull* 1394, *Forshilsfyld* 1457 (*v.* clos(e), cumb, feld, and (West) Fossil *supra*); *Ye Greate Downe* 1652 (*v.* grēat, dūn); *Hangelond* 1227 (*v.* hangol, land); *Hydiestansilie* 1227 (perhaps from stān-scilig 'stony (ground)', cf. the f.n. *Stonschulye* in Portland par. *infra*; *Hydie-* is obscure); *Homerclose* 1587 (probably for *Home-*); *Ye Little Meade* 1652; *commonfeild called the Middle feild* 1652; *Mogham* 1457 (perhaps the surname *Mogg*, *v.* hamm); *the moore* 1587, *Ye Moores* 1652 (*v.* mōr[1]); *Newclose* 1652; *Northdowne* 1635 (*v.* norð, dūn); *Parkyns Close* 1587; *Pilecroft* 1459 (probably 'small enclosure made with stakes', *v.* pīl, croft, but it is possible the name should be associated with William *Pylye* who held lands in Chaldon H. 1280[2]); *Pittescumbe* 1227 ('valley with a pit in it', *v.* pytt, cumb, but cf. William *Pytte* (also called *Pyt(te)-, Putman*) 1440); *tenement' voc' Pudelthynk* 1456, *-thyng, -thing(e)* 1457–1481, 1484, *Pudelsthyng* 1464 (from Robert *de Pydele* 1280[2], *v.* þing 'property'); *Purdeysleyghton* 1404 (cf. Robert *Purdeu* 1280[2], John *Purdey* 1327, *v.* lēac-tūn); *La Radehull* 1294 Banco (*v.* rēad, hyll); *Reyes Croft* 1293 Banco (the surname *Rey*, *v.* croft); *Riecnap* 1227 (*v.* ryge, cnæpp); *Roughey* 1404 (*v.* rūh, (ge)hæg); *Ruchedich* 1227 (*v.* dīc; Professor Löfvenberg points out that if *c* in *Ruche-* is a scribal error for *t*, the first el. may be rȳ(h)ð 'rough ground'); *Tadnall Mead* 1652 (from Tadnall *supra*); *William Toopes Ground, — New Close corner* 1682 (cf. Bernard *Toope* 1652); *Uplangelond* 1227 (*v.* upp 'higher up', lang[1], land, but cf. ModE *uplong* prep.

'up along' (NED 1762), adj. 'extending upwards' (ib 1875)); *atte Wode* (p) 1434 (v. atte, wudu); *Wolhey* (v. wella, (ge)hæg); *La Wurthe* 1227, *close called Werth* 1587, *Word Mead* 1652 (v. worð, mǣd).

Coombe Keynes

Wool par. *infra* was a parochial chapelry belonging to Coombe Keynes in 1795 Boswell.

COOMBE KEYNES (SY 843842)

    Cume 1086 DB (2 ×), Exon
    Cumba, Cumb(e) 1166 RBE (p), (— *Willelmi de Cahaignes*) 1199 P, 1210–2 RBE (p), 1212 Fees, 1236 ib *et freq* to 1288 *Ass, Cumbe (Chaynes)* 1276–84 Ipm, *Cumbe Kayn(n)es,* — *Kaymes,* — *Keynes* 1288 *Ass*, 1303 FA, 1306 Pat, 1308 FF
    Comb(e), Comba 1280, 1288 *Ass*, 1291 Tax *et freq* to 1434 *Weld*[1], *Comb(e) Kaynes* 1299 Cl *et freq* with variants *Kaynis, Caynes, Keynes, Kayne, Kaynys, Canes, Kynes, Kayns, Keynys, Kayes, Kaynas, Keynez, Keayn, Caines*
    Coumb(e) Caynes, — *Kaynes,* — *Keynes,* — *Kaynys* 1302 AD III *et freq* to 1443 *Weld*[1], *Coumbe* 1361 Pat, *Coume* 1408 *Weld*[1]

'(At the) valley', v. cumb. The manor was held by William *de Cahaignes* in 1199 (P), and continued in the possession of this family until at least the 14th cent. (1235 Hutch[3], 1282 Cl, 1285, 1303, 1306 FA, 1308 *Weld*[1], 1386 Fine, etc.), cf. Tarrant Keynston par. *infra*, and Southcombe and *Kaynysmede infra* in this par. There is mention of a barton (*bertona*) and a grange (*grang'*) here in 1445 *Weld*[1], and of a chace (*chaceam*) in 1450 *ib*.

CHURCH COPPICE (SY 841842), cf. *Churcheforlong, -furlong* 1438 *Weld*[1], *-furlang(e)* 1443 *ib*, *Chirchefurlong* 1446 Rent, *Church Close or Church furlong* 1686 *Weld*[1], *Church Md* 1839 *TA*, from Holy Rood Church *infra*, v. cirice, furlang, clos(e).

COOMBE WOOD (SY 833844), *bosco de Combekaynes,* — *Keynes* 1434, 1470 *Weld*[1], *boscus voc' Iveley al' dict' Combewod* 1446 Rent, (*bosco voc'*) *Combewod(e)* 1447 *Weld*[1] *et freq* to 1504 *ib*, *-wodde* 1460 *ib*, *bosco apud Combe* 1464 *ib*, *Co(o)mb(e) Wood(s)* 1640–1686 *Weld*[1] *et passim*, 'the wood at Coombe', v. wudu, Coombe Keynes *supra*; cf. John *At(t)(e) Wode* 1432–1438 *Weld*[1], v. atte. The alternative name *Iveley* is *Eve-, Eueley* 1447, 1448 *Weld*[1], perhaps 'woodland glade where ivy grows', v. īfig, lēah, although alternatively, as Professor Löfvenberg points out, the first el. may be the OE pers.n. *Ifa, Iofa, Eofa* (Redin 99, 92). In 1086 DB there was 'woodland 6 furlongs long and as much in width' in the larger of the two manors of *Cume* (VCHDo 3 73).

HOLY ROOD CHURCH (SY 843841), rebuilt in 1860 (Kelly), but earlier references to a church here are *ecclesiam de Cumbe* 1280 *Ass*, 'the church of *Coumbe*' 1361 Pat, *ecclesie parochialis de Combe* 1434 *Weld*[1], *the Church of Comb-Keines* 1774 Hutch[1], cf. Church Coppice *supra*.

KICK HILL COPPICE (SY 848845), *Kykehull(e)* 1428, 1429 *Weld*[1], -*hill* 1446 Rent, 1452 (— *in Combekaynes*), 1455, -*hyll* 1451 (*campo voc*' —), 1471 (*via harnesial*' *voc*' —), *Kikehulle* 1431, *le Kegehyll* 1433 all *Weld*[1], *Kickhill Coppice & Plot*, (Lr) *Kickhill* 1839 *TA*, probably 'look-out hill', from the verbal stem, or from a substantival derivative, of ME kiken 'to watch, peep' (NED s.n. *keek* from c. 1386, now only in N dial.), and hyll, cf. tōt-hyll the first part of which is related to OE *tōtian* 'to peep'; an identical name may be Kite Hill Wt 43, which is *Keke hylle* Ed 4. The hill has an elevation of only 200′ but would command a view N and E. The Scand. pers.n. *Kíkr*, **Kíki* (Fellows Jensen 171) is probably out of the question here, but cf. Henry *Kyk* 1332 SR (Lt Bredy).

KIMBERT'S END (SY 848842), *Kymput* 1422 (*regia via apud* —), 1428, -*puttes* 1449, 1450 (*clauso voc*' —), -*pyt* 1450, -*pytlond* 1452, *Kimpitt(e)s Close* 1686, 1705, *Kymeput(t)* 1425–1433, -*pyt(t)(e)* 1434 (*aquam currentem de quodam fonte voc*' —), 1435–1445, *Kyneput* 1435, *Kemepyt* 1436, 1502, *Kyempyt* 1445 (*cursum aque in venella apud* —), -*pit(lond)* 1446 all *Weld*[1], *Kyympit(teslond)* 1446 Rent, 'Cȳma's pit', from the OE pers.n. *Cȳma* (cf. Kimpton Hrt 15, Kimbland D 69), and pytt (cf. Coombe Chalk Pit *infra*), with land, clos(e), ende, probably here in the sense 'end of a village'; the road (*regia via, venella*) referred to is probably that between Coombe K. and E Lulworth; there is a stream marked (6″) 450 yds ENE and a spring 300 yds NW (cf. *aquam, fonte*).

OAKLEY WD (SY 835842), *Ocle* 1443 *Weld*[1], *Okeley* 1445 *ib* (*fald*' *apud* —), 1446 Rent (*boscus voc*' —), -*ly(e)* 1638 *Weld*[1], 117 *ib*

(— *Coppice*), *Ockely Wood* 1640 *ib*, *Oakley* 1641 Hutch[3], *Oakeley grounds* 1686 *Weld*[1], *Oak(e)ly* 1705 *ib*, 1774 Hutch[1], cf. *Oakley Bottom, Down, Hill & Rough Pce* 1839 *TA*, 'oak glade or clearing', *v.* āc, lēah, with wudu, copis.

RODFORD WITHY BED (SY 875845), probably *Rodeford* 1408 *Weld*[1] (p), 1416 *ib*, *Rodford* 1446 *Rent*, c. 1628 *Strode* (*place called* —), 'reedy ford', *v.* hrēod, ford; on Luckford Lake (*v.* RNs.) but there is no ford marked here now.

ROW DOWN COPPICE (SY 828839), 1839 *TA*, *Rowedon* 1408, (*le*) *Row(e)dovne, -down(e), -doun(e)* 1434 (*montem vocat'* —), 1435, 1442 (*boscus voc'* —) all *Weld*[1] *et freq* to 1839 *TA*, *1 furlong voc' Rodoun* 1446 *Rent*, (*le*) *Roudoun* 1457, 1464 *Weld*[1], *Roughdown(e)* 1638 *ib*, 1641, 1861 Hutch[3], 'rough hill', *v.* rūh (wk.obl. *rūgan*), dūn, cf. *Roudon* in E Lulworth par. *infra*.

SOUTHCOMBE (lost), 1403 IpmR, 1412 FA, 1416 Cl, 1422 *Midd*, *Weld*[1] *et freq* to 1861 Hutch[3], *-comb* 1403 IpmR, *-Combe* 1478 *Weld*[1], 1582 Hutch[3] (— *alias Combe*), *Southecombe* 1438, 1442 *Weld*[1], *Suthcumb* 1287 Ipm, *-combe* 1435–1445 *Weld*[1], *Sutcombe* 117 *ib*, cf. *Southcombe(s)lane* 1433, 1434 *ib*, *Southcombesclose* 1435 *ib*, *Suthcombelond* 1446 *Rent*, *Southcombepitte* 1450 *Weld*[1], possibly 'south valley', *v.* sūð, cumb, with lane, clos(e), land, pytt, but the name may mean 'the south part of Coombe (Keynes)' in view of the 1582 form (— *alias Combe*) and the description of it in Hutch[1] 1 127 as 'anciently a manor, or a moiety of the manor of Comb-Keines, and called Paynel's manor. It was given by William Keines to John, son of Fulke Paynel [in the time of Ed 1]'.

TRENDLECOMBE (lost, about SY 835841), 1635 *Weld*[1], 1686 *ib*, 1861 Hutch[3], *-comb* 1641 *ib*, 1774 Hutch[1], *Trendel-* 1463 *Weld*[1], 1705 *ib*, *Trendellcombe* 1638 *ib*, possibly 'circular valley', *v.* trendel, cumb, although in view of the nearby *Trendyley* 1446 *Rent*, *Trenley* 1839 *TA*, Trendlecombe could be 'valley near *Trendyley*' ('circular clearing'), *v.* lēah, cf. Trenley Gl 2 220; Hutch[3] 1 348 describes Trendlecombe as 'now joined with Oakley' (*q.v. supra*) and as 'lying half a mile W of Combe' (i.e. Coombe K. *supra*).

UPHILL (lost), 1795 Boswell, *Vppe-*, *Uppehull(e)* 1268 *Ass* (p), 1278 QW (p), *-hill* 1285 Banco, 1449 Hutch[3], 1456 IpmR, *Hupehill*

1275 RH (p), *Uphull(e)* 1292 Hutch[3], 1379 IpmR, 1380 Misc, 'lands called *Opehill* or *Uphill*' 1323 Hutch[3], *Up Hill* 1861 ib, '(land) higher up or upon the hill', *v.* upp, uppan, hyll.

VICARAGE COPPICE (SY 853848), 1839 *TA*, situated near *Vicarage Hill* 1839 *TA*, on the par. bdy almost a mile from the Vicarage *infra*; it is possibly identical with *Vycaryhegge* 1446 *Rent*, *le Vicaryshegge* 1448 *Weld*[1], *Vicarshege* 1451 *ib* 'the vicar's hedge', from vicarie, vicare, hecg, cf. also *Vicaryesyate* 1444 *Weld*[1], *le Vykersyate* 1446 *ib*, *le Vykerslane* 1446 *Rent*, *v.* geat, lane; a surname *Vicar(y)*, cf. e.g. Walter *Vicar* 1332 SR (Powerstock), Nicholas *Vicory* 1332 ib (Owermoigne), is perhaps a less likely first el. in view of the use of the def.art. le.

WALGROVE (lost), 1431 *Weld*[1] (*bosc' voc'* —), 1446 *Rent*, 1448 *Weld*[1], 1629 *DCMDeed* (*the Towne of* —), 1861 Hutch[3], — *Wood, ground called Walgroue* 1686 *Weld*[1], *Walegroues Wood* 1640 ib, *Wallgroue* 117 ib (— *Coppice*),1705 ib, *-grove* 1795 Boswell, *Wall Grove* 1839 *TA*, *v.* grāf(a) 'grove, copse', wudu, copis; it is not possible to determine the first el., which could be walh 'Welshman, serf', wall 'wall', or walu 'ridge'; Hutch[3] 1 348 describes Walgrove as 'a little ground half a mile N of Combe' (i.e. Coombe K. *supra*).

WEST WOOD (SY 834848), WESTWOOD COPPICE, *Westwod(e)* 1283 Cl, 1288 *Ass* (p), 1320 FF (— *juxta Cumberkaynes*) *et freq* to 1504 *Weld*[1] (*bosco vocat'* —), *Westwodhegge* 1446 *Rent*, *Westewode* 1531 *Weld*[1], *Westwood* 1635 *ib*, — *Farme* 1703 *ib*, *the farm of Westwoods* 1641 Hutch[3], *Westwoods Barn & Yd* 1839 *TA*, 'west wood', *v.* west, wudu, with hecg; it lies NW of Coombe K., cf. North Wood *infra*.

ASHY DROVE, *v.* drove; Ashy is perhaps 'ash-tree enclosure', *v.* æsc, (ge)hæg, as in *Ashey Closs* 117 *Weld*[1], *v.* clos(e), but cf. *Ashly Close* 1686 *ib*, which seems to contain lēah, and *Hr & Lr Ash Close, Ash Lane Plant.* 1839 *TA*; the latter may contain lane, but cf. *A(y)ssh(e)-, Aisshel(e)yn(e)(s)croft(e)* 1445–1451 *Weld*[1], 1446 *Rent*, 'enclosure at *Assheleyne*' ('arable strip near an ash-tree'), *v.* æsc, leyne, croft. BELLEVUE PLANT. BRAMBLE COPPICE, cf. *Bremelclose* 1531 *Weld*[1], *Brembly Close* 1705 *ib*, *Bramble Close* (*Coppice*) 1839 *TA*, *v.* brēmel, -ig[3]. CLARE TOWERS, a gateway to Lulworth Park in E Lulworth par. *infra*, perhaps named from *Clare* Weld, died 1691 (M.H.). COOMBE BEACON (172'), cf. *Bekonbarry* 1446 *Rent*, *v.*

(ge)bēacon, beorg 'hill, mound'; several tumuli are marked near here (6″). COOMBE CHALK PIT, *Coombe Green & Chalk Pit*, *Chalk Pit* (*Cl & Fd*) 1839 *TA*, cf. *le pytte* 1433 *Weld*[1], *unam magnam quarreram* 1440 *ib*, *querrer' de Combekaynes* 1462 *ib*, v. pytt. COOMBE HEATH, *Combe* — 1663 *Weld*[1], cf. (*le*) *Hethfild* 1445 *Weld*[1], 1446 *Rent*, *-feld* 1484 *Weld*[1], *Hethehill* 1484 *ib*, *Heath Hill* 1686 *ib*, v. hǣ̆ð, feld, hyll. COOMBE LOTS, v. hlot. DARK HILL PLANT., near foll., cf. Dark Hill Gl 3 229. DARK HOLE, v. deorc, hol[1]. DUCKPOND PLANT. EAST FM, E of the village, cf. West Fm *infra*. EWEYARDS COPPICE, *Ewe yd Coppice* 1839 *TA*, cf. (*The*) *Eweleaze* 1839 *ib*. THE FORT, a building. KENNEL FM, KENNEL HILL PLANT., KENNEL RINGS & WD, probably from kenel 'a kennel', but cf. Thomas *Kennell* 1682 *Weld*[1]; Rings perhaps refers to an earthwork, cf. The Rings in Corfe C. par. *supra* and Rings Hill in E Lulworth par. *infra*, but there is nothing marked (6″). THE LAKE, a pool on the par. bdy in Luckford Lake, v. lake, cf. foll.; an earlier name for it might be *le Mere* 1423 *Weld*[1] et *freq* to 1443 *ib*, *la Mere* 1429 *ib*, v. mere[1] 'a pool', and *Jolyfmer ad finem ville de Combe* 1446 *Rent* may also belong here, perhaps 'pleasant pool', v. jolif, but cf. *Marg' Jollyffe* 1618 *Weld*[1] (Wool). LAKE HILL PLANT., named from prec., cf. *Meyrhill* 1446 *Rent*, v. mere[1], hyll. LIMEKILN CTGS, *Lymekylls* 1638 *Weld*[1], *-Kills* e18 *ib*, *Limekill* 117 *ib*, *Lymekillnes* 1686 *ib*, *Lime-Kiln* (a farm) 1774 *Hutch*[1], cf. *Lyme Kill grounds* 1647 SC, v. līm-cyln. NEWTOWN (HILL), *Newton* 1795 Boswell, 1811 OS, v. nīwe, tūn. NORTH LODGES, *Lodge* 1826 Gre, *The north lodge* 1839 *TA*; they stand at the N entrance to Lulworth Park. NORTH WD, 1839 *TA*; it lies N of West Wd *supra*. OLD HILL (lost), 1703 *Weld*[1], 1861 *Hutch*[3], *Oldhill* 1638, 1686 *Weld*[1], *Old Hill* (*Coppice*) 1839 *TA*, v. ald, hyll; *Hutch*[3] 1 348 describes it as a farm 'half a mile N of Combe' (i.e. Coombe K. *supra*). SWEET HILL (lost), 1861 *Hutch*[3], *Sweetehills* 1638, e18 *Weld*[1], *close called Sweethills* 1686 *ib*, 1839 *TA*, 'pleasant hill(s)', v. swēte, hyll; *Hutch*[3] 1 348 describes it as a farm 'half a mile N of Combe' (i.e. Coombe K. *supra*). VARY CLUMP & COPPICE, cf. *Vary Hill* 1839 *TA*, perhaps 'bull or pig enclosure' from fearr or fearh and (ge)hæg, cf. Fairyhall Ess 422. VICARAGE, 'the vicarage-house' 1650 *Hutch*[3], cf. Vicarage Coppice *supra*. WAREHAM FOREST (1″), from Wareham par. *infra*, cf. Wareham Gates & Lodge in E Lulworth par. *infra*. WEST FM, W of the village, cf. East Fm *supra*.

FIELD-NAMES

The undated forms are 1839 *TA* 64. Spellings dated 1280[1] are Ch, 1280[2], 1292, 1299, 1541, 1561, 1584, 1641, 1861 Hutch[3], 1319 FF, 1327 *SR*, 1332 SR, 1340 NI, 1346 FA, 1375 Cl, 1392, 1393, 1438[2] *Ct*, 1446[1], Eliz *Rent*, 1477 *MinAcct*, 1629 *DCMDeed*, 1664 HTax, and the rest *Weld*[1].

(a) Barn(s) Cl; Bellhuse Down (from Belhuish in W Lulworth par. *infra*); Boveways ('above the way(s)', *v.* bufan, weg); Broad Grd; Broom Hill Coppice (*Bromehull* 1444, *-hill* 1445, (*le Nether*) *Brom(e)hill, bosc' voc' Bromehill* 1446[1], *Bromehylle* 1450, *bosc' de Bromell* 1505, *Bromehill(s) Wood* 1640, l17, *Broomehill Coppice* l17, *v.* brōm, hyll, neoðerra); Bushrods Hthr & Yonder Plant., Bushrods 3, 4, 5, 7 & 9 Acres (perhaps 'bushy clearing', *v.* busc, rod[1], cf. (*terre apud*) *le Bussh(e)* 1450, 1452); Clay Shard (*v.* clǽg, sceard); Hthr & Yonder Cl; Coombe Fd (from Coombe K. *supra*); (Hr) Coppice; Cowleaze; Crate (Barn & Yd) (*le Crofte* 1435, *v.* croft); 18, 11 & 15 Acres; the Fishpond; 14 Acres; Furlands (Coppice) (*v.* furlang, cf. *Furlang' tendent' super Milwey* 1444, *furlong' butt' super Whithill* 1445, cf. *Milwey, Whithill infra*); Furzy Hill (Coppice) (*Furs(e)hull(e)* 1433, 1444, *-hyll, -hill* 1434, 1446[1], 1453, *Firs-, Fyrshill, -hyll* 1443, 1446[1], *Forshill* 1447, *v.* fyrs, hyll); Gt & Green Lot (*v.* hlot); Halls Cl; Hard Labor (an uncomplimentary nickname); Hiffords Lot (*Hyford* 1447, 'hay ford', *v.* hēg, ford, with hlot, cf. Hyford in Winfrith N. par. *infra*); Hr & Lr High Acres (*Heyacr* 1436, *les Heyacres* 1446[1], *Highakers* l17, *High Acres* 1686, *v.* æcer; the first el. could be hēah 'high' or hēg 'hay'); Home Croft & Md(w); Joyce's mdw; Long Cl (Coppice) (*Langclose* 1531, *Long Closes* 1686, *v.* lang[1], clos(e)); Long md (*Langmede* 1447, *v.* lang[1], mæd); Madams md; Maggot Hill; 9 Acres; the Park, Park Plant. (*the Parke of Combe Keynes* 1686, *v.* park, cf. Coombe K. *supra*); Parsons Lot & Md (*v.* hlot); Phillis Grove (*v.* grāf(a)); Plot; The Pound (cf. *punfald'* 1450, *v.* pund, pund-fald); Sheep Slight (*v.* slæget); 16 Acres; Sourdocks (Coppice & Plant.) (*v.* sour dock 'common sorrel'); South Plot; Stony Grd; Tapps Pdk (cf. Thomas *Tapp* 1584); 10, 13, 25, 21 & 27 Acres; Well Plot (cf. John *Welle* 1439, — *atte Well* 1442, 1479, — *At(te)well* 1448, 1450, *v.* wella, atte, cf. Willis 10 acres *infra*); Whites lot (cf. *pratum nuper Henr' Whyte* 1484, *v.* hlot); Willis(') 10 acres (cf. *claus' voc' Harewilcroft* 1436, *Harriwellys crofte* 1439, *Herrywyllys-, -willes-, -willys-, -williscroft* 1446[1], 1446[2], 1447, 1451, *Harrywillescroft* 1452, possibly 'enclosure belonging to Harry Well(s)', *v.* croft, cf. Well Plot *supra*, but the first part of the name could be a p.n. from hærig 'stony' and wella (WSax wiella)); Withy Bed (cf. *le Wythyys* 1433, *With'ber'* 1452, *v.* wiðig, bearu).

(b) *Bakersclous, -croft* 1446[1] (cf. *Bakerland* in Wool par. *infra*, *v.* clos(e), croft, both freq in this par.); *Baldewynsclos, Baldynglond* 1446[1] (the OG pers.n. *Baldwin, v.* land, as freq in this par.; for *Baldyng* as a development of *Baldwin, v.* Reaney s.n. *Balding*); *Barleg* 1446[1], 1450, 1451, *Barrelegge* 1447 (perhaps 'bare leg of land', *v.* bær, leg); *Barrycroft* 1436, 1446[1] (*v.* beorg); (*le*) *Blak(e)heg(g)e* 1447–1504 (*v.* blæc, hecg); *Bobehey* 1446[1], *Burbey Close* 1686 (perhaps from the OE pers.n. *Bob(b)a* and (ge)hæg);

(*bosc' apud*) *Boyslane* 1446², 1453, 1492, -*land* 1446¹ (cf. Rose *de Boys* 1327, v. lane, cf. W Chaldon in Chaldon H. par. *supra*; *Boyswale* 1438 may contain the same surname, perhaps with walu 'ridge', swalg 'pit' or wēl² (WSax wǣl) 'deep pool'); *Bord(e)lond* 1445, 1446¹, 1447 (v. bord-land 'land held by a bordar'; at the larger of the two DB manors of *Cume* there were 9 bordars, at the smaller only one, v. VCHDo 3 73, 96); *Brend(e)wall* 1446²– 1451 (cf. John *Brende* 1446²–1484, — *Brynde* 1446¹, Hugh *Breynde* 1479, v. wall); *Brodeacre* 1446¹ (v. brād, æcer); *le Buttys* 1444, *les Buttes* 1446¹, *lez buttes* 1447 (v. butte); *Combe Calenge* 1436, *Callynche* 1438, *loco voc' le Calenge in le Hethfild* 1446¹ (v. calenge '(land in) dispute', cf. Coombe Heath *supra*); *claus' voc' (le) Caneryhule* 1492, -*hylle* 1494, *via apud Caneryhele* 1493, *Canary Land(e)s* 1635, 1638, *Canere Grounds* l17, *Canary* e18 (the first part of the name may be a ME formation from can(n)e 'cane, hollow stem of a reed, etc.' and the suffix -erie, -erye, with some such meaning as 'reed-bed' or 'place where reeds were used for artifacts'; the second el. -*hule*, etc. is from either hygel or hylu, cf. le Hyle *infra*); *Carteres-, -yscroft(e)* 1433, *Carterescroftescherde* 1450 (cf. William *carectarius* 1327, *terr' Roberti Carter* 1392, v. sceard); *Cokes close* 1501 (cf. John *Coke de Wolle* 1446¹, cf. Wool par. *supra* and foll.); *Robbyncokkesclos* 1446¹ ('Robin Cokk's close', cf. prec. and Reaney s.n. *Cock*); *the common of Combe Keynes* 1686; *Combemede* 1434, 1479, (— *iuxta Bynedon*) 1435, *Combekaynesmede* 1446¹ (v. mæd, cf. Coombe K. *supra* and Bindon in Wool par. *infra*); *Cote Closes* 1663, *Cottclose* 1686, 1705 (v. cot); *Courteclose* 1531 (v. court); *Crokewell'hey* 1435, *Croukkulhay* 1446¹, *Crokelhey* 1492 ('enclosure at *Crokewell*' ('well or stream provided with a pot or where pots were found', v. crocc, wella, (ge)hæg); *le Cros* 1451 (v. cros); *La Dene* 1306 FF, *le Dene* 1425 *et freq* to 1455, *le deane* 1531, *Dean* 1541 (v. denu); *le Doune* 1463 (v. dūn); *le Dreve* 1446¹, *le Dreue* 1502 (v. drǣf, cf. The Drove in Winfrith N. par. *infra*); *Emmote(s)hey* 1443, 1445, *Emmottyshey* 1447 (the fem. pers.n. *Emmot*, a pet form of *Emma*, and (ge)hæg); *Fillollesgrove* 1446¹ (cf. *terram Johannis Filloll in Walgrove* 1448, v. grāf(a), cf. Walgrove *supra*); *boscus voc' Foxley* 1446¹, *Foxleys* 1448 (v. fox, lēah); *tenement' voc' Fryescote* 1442 (cf. Ralph *le Frye* 1280¹ (Wool), v. cot); *Gil-, Gylettis londe* 1443, *Gylet(t)ys-* 1444, *Gillottys-* 1446¹, -*es-* 1446², *Gilletteslond* 1447 (the pers.n. *Gillet, -ot*, a diminutive of *Giles* or *Gill*); *unam gutter apud...le Goter* 1450 (v. gotere); *viam voc' Greneway ducent' versus Westwod* 1446¹, *Greneway* 1453 (v. grēne¹, weg, cf. West Wood *supra*); *Gunnetesclose* 1422 (the fem. pers.n. *Gunnot*, a diminutive of *Gunne*, cf. John *Gunne ib*); *Hakeney londes* 1438², *Hakenaylond* 1438, (*terr' vacu' voc'*) *Hak(e)ne-* 1445, 1493, *Hak(e)n(e)ylond* 1446¹ *et freq* to 1493 (v. hakeney 'horse kept for riding or hiring out', but cf. John *Hakeney* 1299 (Winfrith N.)); *atte Hale* 1346 (p) (v. atte, halh (dat.sg. *hale*), cf. *le Hyle infra*); *le Headacre* 1446¹ (v. hēafod, æcer); *le Heedlond* 1446¹ (v. hēafod-land); *Hegges-* 1442, *Hegge-* 1443, 1446¹, 1450, *Hegthorn(e)* 1448, 1450 (v. hecg, þorn); *le —, la Hyle* 1423 *et freq* to 1433, *le Hill* 1450, *le Hile* 1451 (probably from the WSax dat.sg. form *hēale* of halh 'a nook, a corner of land', but hygel 'a hillock' or hylu 'a hollow' are also possible, cf. *Caneryhule* and *atte Hale supra*); *Holm(e)bussh* 1440, 1450 (v. holegn, busc); (*le*) *Holtecombe* 1435–1445, 1446¹, *Holtecombpittes, le Over holtecombe* 1446¹,

Holtecombehed, Holtecombesete 1446[2] ('wooded valley', *v.* holt, cumb, with pytt, uferra, hēafod); *Humleclos* 1491 (perhaps from humele 'the hop plant'); *Kaynys-* 1444, *Káynesmede* 1445 *et freq* to 1531, *Keynes-* 1638, *Caines Mead(e)* 1l7, *Caynes* 1682 (the surname *Keynes*, cf. Caines' Md in Winfrith N. par. *infra,* Coombe Keynes *supra, v.* mǣd); *le Knollake* 1446[1] (*v.* cnoll, lacu, cf. John *atte Knolle* 1327, *v.* atte); *the Lamplight Close...in the Towne of Walgrove* 1629 (no doubt given to provide a lamp for the church, *v.* lampe, cf. Walgrove *supra*); *Langebarghysthorne* 1433, *Langberys-, Langbarrythorn* 1446[1] ('thorn-tree at *Langebargh*' ('long hill or barrow'), *v.* lang[1], beorg, þorn); *Langehaye* 1436 (*v.* (ge)hæg); *le Langehegie* 1439, (*le*) *Lang(e)heg(g)e* 1443–1450, *le Longhegge* 1446[1], 1447 (*v.* hecg); *Lang(e)ley(e)* 1443 *et freq* to 1484, *Langlegh* 1444, *Lang(e)ley(s)hed(e)* 1443–1453, *-hedlond* 1448, *Herwardi(s)lang(e)le* 1443, *Hervord Langley* 1446[2], *Hereford'langley* 1448 ('long clearing', *v.* lang[1], lēah, with hēafod(-land), cf. Henry *Hereward* 1327, 1332); *Langlond* 1453 (*v.* lang[1], land); *Laurenceclos* 1446[1] (cf. John *Lauerans* 1393, Edward *Laurence* 1561); *terr' voc' le lede* 1434 (*v.* lǣd 'water-course'); *le Lenche* 1446[1], 1447 (*v.* hlenc 'hill-side'); *furlong' voc' Lexdon* 1446[1] (*v.* dūn; the first el. may be the OE pers.n. *Leaxa* proposed for Lexden Ess 376); *le Littulacre* 1446[1] (*v.* lȳtel, æcer); *le Litell-* 1434, *le Lytel(l)downe, -doune* 1434 *et freq* to 1450, *Littuldoun* 1446[1] (*v.* dūn); *le Lytellwode* 1437 (*v.* wudu); *Lombley* 1446[1] (*v.* lamb, lēah); *terre apud Lusarne* 1445 ('louse-infested, or insignificant, building', *v.* lūs, ærn, cf. Luscott D 33); *Malyncroft* 1446[1] (cf. John *Malyn* 1393); (*le*) *Marlyngpit(t)* 1446[1] (*v.* marling, pytt); *Maryonhey* 1446[1] (the pers.n. or surname *Maryon* and (ge)hæg); *Maundevyleclos* 1446[1] (the surname *Mandeville*); *Menacris* 1443, *Meenacres* 1445, 1446[1] (*v.* (ge)mǣne, æcer); *Middlecrofte* 1435 (*v.* middel); *Milsherd* 1453 (*v.* myln, sceard); *Milwey* 1444, *le Mylwaye* 1446[1] (*v.* myln, weg); *close called Moynes* 1686 (cf. John *le Moyne* 1280[2], *claus' Johannis Moigne* 1440); (*le*) *Mok(ke)lehey* 1443 *et freq* to 1451 (*v.* micel, (ge)hæg); *Newbrake* 1686 (*v.* nīwe, bræc[1]); *le Neueclose* 1433, *Newclose* 1531 (*v.* nīwe); *la Nyw-* 1423, *le Nuwe-* 1425–1431, *Neu-, Newelond* 1446[1], 1450, *Newland* 1686, (*le*) *Nuwes-* 1435–1438, *Newes-* 1446[2], 1447, *Neus-, Nueslond* 1531, *Newes* 1686 (the first el. would seem to be the surname *New,* common in Do as (*le*) *Niwe* in 1332, *v.* land); (*le*) *Northfild* 1445, 1446[1], 1448 (*v.* norð, feld); *Oblands* Eliz, 1641 (perhaps hob 'hobgoblin' or hobb(e) 'tussock' and land); *claus' voc' Oyearde* 1531, *Oyards* 1686, 1705 (perhaps 'crooked enclosure', *v.* wōh, geard); *le Nether-, le Overorchard* 1446[1] (*v.* neoðerra, uferra, orceard); (*le Nether-, le Over*) *Otecroft* 1446[1] (*v.* āte); *alt' via voc' Perysmer* 1494 (cf. *pratum nuper Ricardi Pyrys* 1469, somewhere in this hundred; from the surname *Perry, Pirie* (from pirige 'pear-tree'), with mere[1] 'pool' or (ge)mǣre 'boundary'); (*le*) *Portway* 1445, 1446[1], 1453, *Portwayfurlong* 1446[2] (*v.* port-weg, furlang); *le Rygore* 1444, *Ryegoors* 1445, *les Rygors* 1446[1], *Rygorys* 1447 (*v.* ryge, gāra); *Row Close* 1686 (*v.* rūh); *Ruysshehey* 1450 (*v.* risc, (ge)hæg); *Salterne* 1449 MinAcct, *Salternebrugge iuxta lanciam de Purbyke* 1446[1] (*v.* salt-ærn, brycg; the bridge must have crossed Luckford Lake (*v.* RNs.) which forms the bdy of the Isle of Purbeck *supra*); *claus' apud le Sappys* 1425 (perhaps from sæppe 'a fir-tree', but cf. *Sopps infra*); *lez Seuen Acres* 1446[1] (*v.* seofon, æcer); *Shaphay* 1448 (*v.* scēap, (ge)hæg); *S(c)hap-*,

Shappehull 1442, 1443, *Shaphill* 1446[1], 1453, *Shaphillyspit* 1446[1] (*v.* scēap, hyll, pytt); *Shipe-*, *Shypelond* 1432–1438, *Ship-*, *Shyplond* 1433 *et freq* to 1453, *alta via voc' Schyplonyswey* 1505 (*v.* scēap (WSax scīep), land, weg); *Shortewode* 1531 (*v.* sc(e)ort, wudu); *Shovill* 1460 (*v.* scofl 'a shovel', perhaps used of a valley resembling the hollow blade of a shovel, cf. foll.); *Shoylclos* 1446[1] (cf. John —, Richard *Shoyl* 1332 (Langton Long B.), but the first el. may be identical with prec.); *le Slade* 1444, 1446[1], 1450 (*v.* slæd); (*le*) *Smeth(e)feld* 1435–1444, *Smeth(e)fild* 1445, 1446[1], *Smyth'fild* 1453 (probably 'smooth field', *v.* smēðe[1], feld, but the first el. could be smið (gen. pl. smiða, smeoða) 'a smith' or smiððe, smeðe 'a smithy'); *Smokacre* 1436, 1446[1] (*v.* smoca, æcer); *Snellyng(g)ys-*, *Snellyng(g)espyt*, *-pit* 1444 *et freq* to 1450 (cf. Richard *Snelling* 1664 (Chaldon H.), *v.* pytt); *Somerwelle* 1433–1435 (*v.* sumor, wella, but cf. William *Somer* 1327, 1332); *close called Sopps* 1686 (cf. Adam *Sop* 1319 (Wool), but possibly identical with *le Sappys supra*, cf. also *Soppley* 1477 which may however not belong here, *v.* lēah); *South Close* 1686, 1705; (*le*) *South'fild* 1446[1], 1448 (*v.* feld); *le Southfurlong* 1446[1] (*v.* furlang); (*claus' in*) (*le*) *S(o)uth(')strete* 1435–1452 (*v.* sūð, strǣt); *Spaldewynclos* 1452 (cf. Emma *Spillewin* 1292); *le Spryng* 1447 (*v.* spring); *Stertlake* 1446[1] (*v.* steort, lacu); *le Stile* 1448, 1451 (*v.* stigel); *le Stonybarry* 1446[1] (*v.* stānig, beorg); *Taylepyt(te)* 1444, *Tailpit*, *-pyt* 1446[1], 1453 (*v.* tægl, pytt); *Terryeshull* 1433 (cf. Maud *Terryes* 1375 (Winfrith N.), *v.* hyll); *le Tounemenfeld* 1425 *et freq* to 1433 (*v.* tūnmann, feld); *Turkynsclos(e)* 1435, 1436, 1446[1], *-knoll* 1448, *-lond(e)* 1436, 1444 (a ME surname *Turkyn*, probably a diminutive of *Turk* from ON *Þorkell*, cf. Reaney s.n. *Turk*, *v.* cnoll); *Twynnynglane* 1446[1] (perhaps 'lane that divides (two pieces of ground)', *v.* twinnyng, lane); *Twyn(e)wode* 1439, *Twynwod* 1445 *et freq* to 1452, *-woddes* 1446 ('(land) between the woods', *v.* betwēonan, wudu); *Warynsclose* 1435 (the pers.n. or surname *Warin*); *Warmery-* 1447, *Warmer-hill* 1451, 1453 (*v.* hyll; the first part of the name is obscure); *Waterhill* 1443, *-hull ib*, 1444, *le Waturhill* 1446[1] (*v.* wæter, hyll); *le Waturslade* 1446[1] (*v.* slæd); *Westfild* 1445, 1446[1] (*v.* west, feld); *Westhey* 1446[1] (*v.* (ge)hæg); *le Whitediche* 1446[1] (*v.* hwīt, dīc); *le Whitefurlong* 1446[1] (*v.* hwīt, furlang); *Whytehull* 1444, (*le*) *Whit(e)hill* 1445, 1446[1], 1447 (*v.* hwīt, hyll); *Wodefurlong* 1428 (*v.* wudu, furlang); *Wodelond* 1435 (*v.* land); *altam viam duc' versus Wolle*, *Wolleway* 1446[1], *Wolway* 1453 ('road to Wool', *v.* Wool par. *infra*, weg).

East Lulworth

EAST LULWORTH (SY 860820) [ˈlʌlwəːþ, ˈlʌləþ, ˈlɔlwəːþ, ˈlɑuwəːþ]

Lulvorde 1086 DB (2 ×), *-wrda* Exon, *Loloworde* 1086 DB (2 ×) *Lolewurda* 1184, 1185 P, *-wrdhe* 1212 Fees, *-worth* 1303 FA (*Est* —), *Lollewurda* 1186, 1187 P, *-worth(e)* 1234 Pat, 1244 *Ass* (p), (*Est-*) 1268 *ib et freq* to 1439 *Weld*[1] (*Est-*), *-wurth* 1279 Cl, *Est(e)lollewrth* 1288 *Ass*, 1291 Tax, *Hyst-*, *Histlollewrth* 1291 Tax, 1428 FA, *Lolleworth als. Lollesworth* 1320 Ipm

Lulewurda 1187 P, *-wrth(e)* 13 *Weld*[1], 1269 Ch (p), *-worth* Ed 4
Rent (*Est-*), *Lullewurd(a)* 1194 P, 1251 Cl (p), *-wurdi* 1196
ChancR, *-worth(e)* 1199 CartAnt, 1230 ChancR, 1232 Cl, Pat,
1234 (1279) Ch, 1244 *Ass* (p) *et freq* to 1531 *Weld*[1] (*Este-*)
with *Est-* from 1285 FA, *-wurth* 1230 P, 1234 (13) *HarlCh*,
1235–6 Fees, 1244 *Ass* (p), FF, 1280 Ch, *-wurdh* 1230 P,
-wrth 1234 (13) *HarlCh*, 1280 *Ass*, 1290 Ch, (*Est*)*lulworth*
1430 Ct *et freq* to 1575 Saxton, *Lullworth* 1498 Ct, *Estlully-
worth* 1504 Pat
Lolesworhe 1197 FF, *-worth* 1242–3 Fees, *Lollesworth* 1268 *Ass*
(p), 1288 *ib* (*Est-*), 1294 Pat, 1319 Ipm, 1320 Cl
Lulleswrða 1202 P, *-wrde* 1203 ib (p), *-wrðe* 1203 P, 1204, 1205
ib both (p), *-worth* 1275 Cl (p), 1284 *Ass*, 1288 *ib* (*Est-*), 1301
Ipm (p), *-wrth* 1280 *Ass* (p)
Lilleswurth 1244 *Ass* (p), *Estlillesworth* 1288 *ib*, (*Est*) *Lilleworth*
1535–43 Leland
Est Loollworth 1582 *DCMDeed*

'Lulla's enclosure', from the OE pers.n. *Lulla* and worð; the early
forms in *-s-* show interchange with the strong form of the pers.n.
found in Lolworth C 180, and the isolated form *-wurdi* (1196)
shows interchange of the second el. with worðig. *East* to distinguish
it from West Lulworth par. *infra* where some of the above forms
without affix may strictly belong, *v.* ēast.

ARISH MELL (SY 855803), — *Gap* 1861 Hutch[3], *Arsmyll* 1454 *Ct*,
Arestmiss (sic) (a bay) 1579 Hutch[3], *Arish Mill* 1634, 1790 ib, 1811
OS, *Arishmell Beach, Cliff & Rd* 1841 *TA*; the first el. is ears
'fundament, buttock', no doubt with reference to some topographical
feature (Arish Mell is on the coast at a gap in the chalk cliffs), with
myln; the first el. has been influenced by SCy dial. *arrish* 'stubble
field' (*v.* ersc); for earlier speculation about the meaning of 'this
beautiful name', *v.* Arkell (1941) 34. There is no mill here now, but
it is possibly that referred to as 'the mill of *Lulleworth*' 1234 (1279),
1279 Ch, and it certainly gave name to *Mill Down* 1841 *TA* (*Muldon*
1417 *Weld*[1], *Mildon(nesfete)* (probably for *-fote*) 1438 *Ct, Mil-,
Myldon* 1461, Ed 4 *Rent*, 1484, 1663 *Weld*[1], *-down* 1664 *ib, v.* dūn,
fōt, used of the chalk down W of Arish Mell), and the nearby *Mulborn
Close* 1841 *TA* ('mill stream', marked on *TAMap, v.* burna), cf. also
Walter (*le*) *Muleward* 1327 *SR*, 1332 SR (< OE myle(n)weard
'miller').

MDT

BOAT KNOLL (SY 866813), 1774 Hutch[1], *Knoll* 1328, 1358 Hutch[3], *Knowle* 1795 Boswell, *Boyt Knowl* 1770 RCHM, cf. *Knolegroue* 1640 *Weld*[1], *Knowle grove* 1686 *ib*, 'the hillock', *v.* cnoll, with grāf(a); the first el. is probably a surname, cf. *Welthen Boyt* 1664 HTax (Langton H.); the place, described by Hutch[1] 1 141 as 'once a manor and hamlet, now only two grounds of 56 acres', was probably the home of Henry —, Roger *atte Knolle* 1327 *SR*, Lucy —, William *atte Knolle* 1332 SR, *v.* atte; there is a tumulus marked here (6").

FLOWER'S BARROW (SY 864805), *Flouresberi* 1381 Misc, *-bery* 1473 *MinAcct*, *-bury* 1462, 1464 *Weld*[1], 1475, 1476 *MinAcct*, *Flowresburye*, *Flour(e)bury(e)* 1381 (16) *Pitt*, *Flowrysburye*, *Flowersbery*, *Flower- borrow hill* c. 1586 Tres, *Flowers Barrow* 1774 Hutch[1], — *or Rings Hill* 1861 Hutch[3]. The second el. is burh (dat.sg. *byrig*) 'pre-English earthwork', with reference to the hill-fort here (RCHM **2** 489); there has been later replacement by beorg 'hill, barrow'; for Rings Hill *v. infra*. The first el. could be flōr 'a floor', as in Floore Nth 82 and Flower Fm Sr 318 where it possibly refers to Roman tesselated pavements, *v.* -es[2]; on the other hand it could be the surname *Flour* of some medieval owner, cf. Reaney s.n. *Flower*.

GATEMERSTON (SY 844813), 1280, 1288 *Ass*, 1303, 1346, 1428 FA, 1774 Hutch[1], *Gatemar(e)ston* 1236 FF, 1286 Ipm, 1313 FF, *-tun* 1253 Ipm, *Gat(e)mor(e)ston(e)* lHy 3 *CottCh*, 1449 *Weld*[1] (p), *Gatemers(s)hton* 1343–5 Ipm, *Yatemerston* 1361 IpmR, *Gat(e)meston* 1393 *Weld*[1] (*camp' de* —) *et freq* to 1795 Boswell, *Gat(e)myston* 1402 *Weld*[1], 1431 FA, *Gatmerston* 1502 Ipm, *Gadmeston* 1531 *Weld*[1], *E & W Gadmanstone* 1841 *TA*. The first part of the name may be a p.n. (from gāt (gen.pl. *gāta*) 'goat' and (ge)mǣre 'boundary', mere[1] 'pool', or mōr 'moor'), or a surname from such a p.n., cf. the entry in lHy 3 *CottCh* (xxv. 34): *Ego Ricardus de Gatemore dedi...Domino Rogero filio Pagani militi...omnia que habui... in villa de Gatemorestone*, *v.* tūn. The name is now only used of two fields; the earlier hamlet may have been destroyed by fire (Hutch[3] 1 377).

HAMPSTEDE (lost), *Hamsted(e)* 13 *Weld*[1] (*bosco de* —), 1279 Ch ('wood of —'), 1280 *Ass* (*boscum qui vocat'* —), *Hampsted(e)* 1234 (1279) Ch ('wood of —'), 1262 *ib*, 1435 *Weld*[1], 'homestead', *v.* hām-stede, Sandred 88, 285. It is possible that the first part of *Hamper's Hill* 1841 *TA* contains this lost name, in which case the site of the hām-stede must have been just S of the village at SY 860816.

BALL COPPICE, *Ball* 1841 *TA*, 1861 Hutch[3] (*a small barrow on* —),
v. ball 'rounded hill'. THE BELT, *v.* belt. BINDON PLANT., from Lt
Bindon in W Lulworth par. *infra.* BLACK BARROW, 1826 Gre, — *Firs
& Rd* 1841 *TA*, *Blakebury* 1413 *Weld*[1], probably 'dark-coloured hill',
v. blæc (wk.obl. *blacan*), beorg (showing confusion with *byrig*,
dat.sg. of burh); although marked as a tumulus (6″), it is in fact a
natural mound (RCHM **2** 445). BOTANY FM, PLANT. (1841 *TA*) &
WD, cf. *Botany Withey Bed* 1841 *ib*, a transferred name from Botany
Bay in Australia, cf. Gl **4** 200, etc. BOWLING GREEN WD. BROOM'S
PLANT., *lo Grete* , *lo Lytelbrowme* 1530 *Weld*[1], *Grete-*, *Lytlebrome*
1531, 1538 *ib*, E & W Brooms' 1841 *TA*, cf. *Bromdyche* 1440 *Ct*,
Ed **4** *Rent*, *Bromediche* 1461 *ib*, *v.* brōm '(place characterized by)
broom', grēat, lȳtel, dīc. CLAY PIT PLANT. COCKPIT HEAD, a high
part of the cliff, perhaps identical with *Copcourt Poynt* c. 1586 Tres,
1774 Hutch[1], in which case Cockpit shows metathesis of medial
[pk] to [kp] and subsequent rationalization, *v.* cockpit, hēafod,
point; *Copcourt* could be 'large house at a hill-top', *v.* copp, court,
but cf. Cop Court O 102. COVER HOLE, a sea cave, *v.* hol[1], cf. *cover-
hole* 'a hole provided with a lid or cover' (1669 NED); the bluff above
the cave is called *Culver* by Short 45. COW CORNER, a coastal feature,
perhaps named from a rock, cf. The Calf and The Cow in Chaldon
H. par. *supra*, and The Bull and The Blind Cow in W Lulworth par.
infra. CUCKOO POUND, cf. Cuckoo Pen in Corfe C. par. *supra.*
DAIRY HO (lost, SY 852831), 1811 OS. EADY PIT, *Needy Pit Grd* 1841
TA, *v.* pytt. FERNY BARROWS, 1861 Hutch[3], cf. *Vernehyll* 1530
Weld[1], *v.* fearn, hyll; two tumuli are marked (6″). GORE HOLMES,
1841 *TA*, cf. *le Gore* 1461 *Rent*, 1462 *Ct*, Ed **4** *Rent*, *v.* gāra 'triangular plot of ground'; the second el. is Do dial. *holm* 'holly', *v.*
holegn. GRAVEL PIT. HALCOMBE VALE, *Hawkcombe or Hoccombe
bottom* 1861 Hutch[3], *v.* cumb, vale, botm; the first el. is perhaps
hafoc 'hawk'. HOME FM. LAKE PLANT., from The Lake in Coombe
K. par. *supra.* LODGE WD, from Park Lodge *infra* or from North
Lodges in Coombe K. *supra*, cf. *Lodgcloss* 1640 *Weld*[1], *Lodge Close*
1686 *ib*, — *Plot* 1841 *TA*, *v.* loge, clos(e). LULWORTH CASTLE, 1841
TA, *Castle* 1811 OS, cf. *The Castle farme* 1703 *Weld*[1], *Castle Gdn*
1841 *TA*, *v.* castel(l); it was begun c. 1608 (RCHM **2** 146) and
replaced 'the goodly maner place of the Newborowes, lordes of
Est Lilleworth' (1535–43 Leland **1** 253). LULWORTH HEATH, 1686

Weld[1], *Lullworth Heath* 1663 *ib*, cf. *Heth(e)feld Dernepath* 1288
Ass, *la Hethfeld* 1415 *Weld*[1], *via Regia...versus Bruer'* 1461 *Ct, the
North Heath* 1663 *Weld*[1], *Little* —, *Littel Heath Lane* 1663, 1664
ib, the Heath gate 1861 Hutch[3], *v.* hǣð, feld, derne 'secret, hidden',
pæð 'path'. LULWORTH PARK, 1811 OS, 'park of East Lullworth'
1641 Hutch[3], *the Parke (of East Lulworth)* 1663, 1686 *Weld*[1], *the
Park* 1841 *TA*, cf. *the Parkegate* 1686 *Weld*[1], *Hr Park, Park Fm &
Plant.* 1841 *TA, v.* park, geat; in c. 1586 Tres it is simply *Lulworth
Wood*, cf. also *warenna d'ni apud Lull'* 1455 *Weld*[1]. MAIDEN PLANT., *v.*
mægden; archaeological finds near here suggest Roman occupation
(RCHM 2 602). MANOR YD. MONASTERY FM, 1841 *TA*, so called
because it was originally built in 1795 as a monastery for some
refugee Trappist monks (Hutch[3] 1 385). MONASTERY LANE, *Road to
Monastery Fm* 1841 *TA*, cf. prec. MOUNT PLEASANT, 1811 OS, a
complimentary nickname. NEW BARN, 1841 *TA*. NEW BARN PLANT.,
1841 *TA*, named from *New Barn* 1811 OS. OLD MARL PLANT., *Old-
marle* 1440 *Ct, close called Old Marle* 1686 *Weld*[1], *Lt & Old Male Plant.*
1841 *TA, v.* ald, marle. PARK LODGE, one of the lodges to Lulworth
Park *supra*, cf. *The East Lodges* 1841 *TA*, Lodge Wd *supra*. PARK WD,
Parke — 1640, 1682 *Weld*[1], near Lulworth Park *supra*. PIGEON CLUMP.
POUND, *The* — 1841 *TA*, cf. *ponfald'* 1413, 1440 *Weld*[1], *v.* pund,
pund-fald. RINGS HILL, 1841 *TA*, so named from the hill-fort called
Flower's Barrow *supra*, cf. The Rings in Corfe C. par. *supra*. ST
ANDREW'S CHURCH, *the paroch chirch* 1535–43 Leland, dates from l15
(RCHM 2 144), but earlier references to a church here include
ecclesia de Estlolleworth 1326 *Ass*, 'the church of *Est Lolleworth'*
1361 Pat, whilst the reference to the church once situated at St
Andrew's Fm in W Lulworth par. *infra* as *Sayntandre Westchurch
juxta Estlolleworth* 1353 FF may suggest that the 'east' church (i.e.
probably that of E Lulworth itself), was already at this date dedicated
to St Andrew; cf. also *cot' prope simitorium* 1461 *Ct, Church furlong*
1640, 1686 *Weld*[1], *v.* cirice, furlang. SEA VALE FM, *the sea-farm* 1861
Hutch[3], cf. *Secumbe* 1279 Ch, *v.* sǣ, cumb. SEVEN ACRE WITHY BED,
Withey Bed by 7 Acres 1841 *TA*. VICARAGE, *aule Rectorie* 1462 *Ct, the
viccaridge house* 1664 HTax, cf. *Parsonage Md & 3 Acres, Parson's
Md, Rough Lot & 2 Acres* 1841 *TA*. VINEYARD COPPICE, cf. *Hr & Lr
Vineyard* 1841 *ib v.* vinȝerd. WAREHAM GATES & LODGE, cf. *The
Wareham Rd* 1841 *ib*, named from Wareham par. *infra*, cf. Wareham
Forest in Coombe K. par. *supra*. WATER BARROWS, two tumuli are
marked 6″, the largest having a deep ditch water-filled in winter

(Legg 107), cf. Waterey barrow in Studland par. *supra*. WELD ARMS
(P.H.) (Kelly), *The* — 1841 *TA*, from the *Weld* family. WITHY
BEDS, (*Gore Holmes*) *Withey Bed* 1841 *ib*, cf. Gore Holmes *supra*.

FIELD-NAMES

The undated forms are 1841 *TA* 132. Spellings dated 1197 are FF, 1234
(1279), 1279 Ch, 1327 *SR*, 1332 SR, 1340 NI, 1392, 1429, 1430, 1431, 1432,
1436, 1438, 1439, 1454, 1461[2], 1462, 1464, 1498 *Ct*, 1461[1], Ed 4 *Rent*, 1473,
1475, 1476 *MinAcct*, 1481, 1503, 1597, 1662, 1665, 1703 Hutch[3], 1664[1]
HTax, 1774 Hutch[1], and the rest *Weld*[1].

(*a*) Aaron's Lot (*v.* hlot, as freq in this par.); Barber(')s Md & Plot;
Barrow Hayes ((*le*) *Barryhey*(*e*)*s* 1461[1], Ed 4, 1473, *Barriheis* 1475, 1476
(*v.* beorg, (ge)hæg); Broad Cl; Burngate Lane (from Burngate in W Lulworth
par. *infra*); Canary Md (-Close 1703, 1774, cf. *Caneryhule* in Coombe K.
par. *supra*; according to Hutch[1] 1 140 there was here 'by tradition...
anciently a chapel'); Chalkpit Grd; Cherry Lot (cf. Charles *Cherry* 1662);
Cockram's (Cowleaze & Mdw) (cf. Bartholomew *Cockram* 1665); Common
Hill; Conygar Fd, Nursery & Wd (*Conynger Hill* 1529, 1531, *Coneger hill*
1640, *Conigeere Hill* 1686, *v.* coninger, hyll, cf. *Conynglond* 1461[1], Ed 4,
Connyng 1462[2], *Conesmede* 1530, *Cowney Meade* 1640, 1686, *prat' apud*
Conynges 1531, *v.* coning, coni, land, mæd); The Coombe Rd (to Coombe
K. par. *supra*); Cowleaze (Pond Pce); Cox's Mdw & Rough Pce, Cox's
2, 3, 4 & 7 Acres (cf. John *Cokkes* 1429); Dippo Withey Bed (perhaps a
surname, cf. Walter *Dypon* 1332 (Holt)); Dogs Cl; Down Pce (cf. *le Dowene*
1438, *v.* dūn); Drove; The Drying Grd; East Fd (*Estfeld* 1430, *le Estfild*
1454, *camp' oriental'* 1461[1], *v.* ēast, feld); New Englands (probably inland
'land near a residence', but perhaps a transferred name from New England,
U.S.A., cf. also John *Engelond* 1392 (Winfrith hundred)); Eweleaze; The
Fir Pound (*v.* pund); The Fishpond; 4 Acres; Lt Furzy Md (cf. *Furseclose*
1531, *v.* fyrs); (Lt) Garland's Coppice, Garland's (Mdw) (cf. Thomas
Garland 1664[1] (Wool, Owermoigne)); Gun Grd; Home Fd & Pdk; Icehouse
Pce (*v.* ice-house); Limekiln Pce; Little Md; New London Plant. (probably
a fanciful name); Long Cl (1686); Long Grd; Longlawns (cf. *Langelondeswey*
1439, *v.* lang[1], land, weg); Long Plant.; The (Rough) Lots; The Meadow;
Miller(')s Lot & Md; The Monk's Burying Grd (cf. Monastery Fm *supra*);
New Md; Hr & Lr Newnham's (*Nywenam* 1414, 1436, *New(e)n(h)am* 1414
et freq to 1686, *Newneham*(*s*) 1474, 1530, cf. *Newemanesyate* (sic) 1436,
Newnamyate 1487, *le more vocat' Gildon' Newnam*, *Newnamps yate* 1530, 'new
enclosure', *v.* niwe (wk.obl. *nīwan*), hamm, with geat 'gate'; for *Gildon'*,
cf. *ten' nuper Rogeri Gildene* 1432); 9 Acres; (The) Orchard; Peaked Md
(*v.* peked); Jacob Penney's Lot (cf. William *Penny* 1664[1], cf. foll.); Piney
Mdw (perhaps the same surname as prec., but cf. *foss' apud Pyne...via*
regia adiacens 1464, which would seem to be pīn 'pine-tree', and *croft' voc'*
Penyalhey 1461[1], Ed 4, the final el. of which is probably (ge)hæg); Plantation; The Plot; Pond Cl; Ramstone's Lot (cf. David *Rempston* 1597
(Winfrith N.)); Roberts' Lr & Middle Lot; Rough Pce; Round Plant.;

Sandpit Gdn & Plot; Sea Barn (Pce); 7 Acres; Seymour's Lr & Middle Lot, Seymour's Md(w) (cf. widow *Seymer* 1664[1]); Shag's (Lt) Mdw (perhaps a surname, though it is tempting to connect it with *parcell' terre de vasto domini apud Shorthagge* 1454, *v.* sc(e)ort 'short', hagga 'haw' (for 'hawthorn'?)); Sheeplands, Sheepland's Fd (*Shiplondes* 1438, *v.* scēap (WSax scīep), land); 6 & 16 Acres; Stoney Combe's (*Stonycomb* 1473, *v.* stānig, cumb); Tabby Cat Pce; Hr & Lr 10 Acres; (Peaked) 3 Acres (*v.* peked); Tower Pce; Town's Lot; 12 & 2 Acres; Water Mdw, Water Mead Rd.

(b) *le Backside* 1603, *the* — 1686 (*v.* backside); Barnclos Ed 4, *Bernehey* 1461[1] (*v.* bere-ærn, clos(e), (ge)hæg); *close called the Barton* 1686 (*v.* beretūn); *Bekkesgrove* 1482 (cf. widow *Beck* 1664, *v.* grāf(a)); *claus' voc' Bisshop(p)s* 1461[1], Ed 4, *Bishopps gate* 1664[2] (the surname *Bishop*, *v.* geat); *Bismereslane* 1432 (cf. John *Busemer* 1332, 1340, *v.* lane); *Blakelondes* 1438 (*v.* blæc, land); *le Breche* 1454 (*v.* brēc); *Bremly Closs* 1640, *Brembly Close* 1686 (*v.* brēmel, -ig[3]); *Bumshill* 1640, 1686 (perhaps 'hill shaped like buttocks', *v.* bom, hyll, but the same word used as a surname is also possible, cf. Richard *le Bum* 1327, — *le Bom* 1332 (Phillyholme in Hawkchurch)); *Canonbern* 1432 ('the canon's barn', *v.* canoun, bere-ærn); *Cattes-* 1461[2], *Cutteslane* 1530 (the surname *Catt* or *Cutt*, *v.* lane); *Cock(e)nell* 1530, 1640, 1686, *Cuckenelles* 1531 (perhaps 'Cocca's hill', from the OE pers.n. *Cocca* and hyll, but cf. Cocknowle in Ch. Knowle par. *supra*); *Cort Closs Mead* 1640, *Court Close Mead* 1686 (*v.* court); *Cow Closs* 1640, — *Close* 1686 (*v.* cū); *Cremers(mede)* 1530, 1531, *Crewers Meade* (sic) 1640, 1686 (cf. William *Crymer* 1461[2]); *atte Cr(o)uch(e)* 1327, 1332, 1340 all (p) (*v.* atte, crūc[3] 'cross'); *close called Deverells Pittes* 1686 (the surname *Deverell*, *v.* pytt); *Eight akers* 1640, — *acres* 1686; *El(l)stub(b)s* 1640, 1686 (*v.* elle(r)n, stubb); *Foreweye* 1410–1414 (perhaps '(land) in front of the road', *v.* fore, weg, unless it is an alteration of fær-weg 'cartway'); *tenement' nuper Frounceys* 1431, *Fraunseishay* 1432, *claus' nuper Frounceys* 1436, *Frounceyslondes* 1438 (cf. John *Franceys* 1429, *v.* (ge)hæg, land); *Frekeslond* 1461[1], Ed 4, *tenement' nuper Johannis Freyk, toft' mes' voc' Frekes* 1462 (*v.* land); *Gatstrippe* 1438 (probably 'strip of ground on which goats are kept', *v.* gāt, strip, cf. strīp); *Gryneclosse* 1530, *Greneclose* 1531 (*v.* grēne[1]); *via' pedestr' et equestr' in Halgereslane* 1430, *Algare lane* 1462, *Algarslane* 1488, 1530 (the surname *Algar*); *Hanful(les)hill* 1438 (probably a surname (from OE *handfull* 'a handful'?), *v.* hyll); *Haukynsthyng* 1461[1], Ed 4 (the surname *Hawkin(s)*, *v.* þing); *Lullworth Higher Gate* 1663 (*v.* geat); *Houpereslane* 1417 (cf. John *Houpere* 1430); *Knoylez mede* 1531 (cf. Thomas *Knoyle* 1481, *v.* mæd); *Lane clo(u)se* 1530–1538 (*v.* lane, clos(e)); *Law-* 1530, *Lowmede* 1531 (*v.* hlāw, mæd); *lez lekebeddys, -beddes* 1459, *claus' voc' Likebed(d)* 1473–1476 ('bed(s) of leeks or garlic', *v.* lēac, bedd); *furlang' voc' le Mase* 1438, *Maze* 1664[2] (*v.* mase 'a maze'); *Merly* — 1640, *Meerely furlong* 1686 (*v.* mere[1] 'pool' or mere[2] 'mare' or (ge)mǣre 'boundary', lēah); *Newclose* 1603, 1686; *Newdiche* 1530 (*v.* dīc); *Peercloss* 1640, *Peere close* 1686 (*v.* peru 'pear', but cf. John *Peres* 1454); *Aleynpresteslond* 1461, Ed 4 ('Alan Prest's, or Alan the priest's, land', *v.* prēost, land, cf. foll.); *Prestespitt* 1413 ('priest's pit', *v.* prēost, pytt, but cf. prec.); *Prestleghlondes* 1438 ('lands at *Prestlegh*' ('priest's clearing'), *v.* prēost, lēah, land, cf. prec.);

regiam viam...voc' Pupel-, Pipeltoneslane 1392 (cf. Richard *Pypelton ib, v.* lane); *camp' vocat' le Quarre* 1413 (*v.* quarrere); *Red(e)goldeshey* 1461[1], 1463, Ed 4 (*v.* (ge)hæg; the first part of the name may be the surname *Tredegold*, cf. Richard *Tredegold* 1435 (Coombe K.), the forms in *R-* showing loss of *T-* due to metanalysis of *at Tr-*); *Rydeputte* 1438 ('red pit', *v.* rēad, pytt); *Ryelondes* 1438 (*v.* ryge, land); (*via reg' voc'*) *Row-, Roudoun(e)lane* 1456– 1467, *port' de Roudoun* 1459, *claus' voc' Roudon* 1473–1476, *bosc' in Rowgh- downe* 1530, *Rowdowne* 1640, 1686 ('rough hill', *v.* rūh (wk.obl. *rūgan*), dūn, with lane, cf. Row Down Coppice in Coombe K. par. *supra*); *Scottes* 1417 (cf. Avice *Scot* 1327, *ten' nuper Roberti Scot* 1438); *Sefurlange* 1438 (*v.* sǣ, furlang); *Shortlond(es)* 1430, 1473 (*v.* sc(e)ort, land); *Short(e)wode* 1410, 1455, *-wood* 1640, 1686 (*v.* wudu); (*le*) *Somerlese* 1530 (*v.* sumor, lǣs); *le Southfild* 1461[1], 1462[2], Ed 4 (*v.* sūð, feld); *Stodfalda* 1234 (1279) (*v.* stōd-fald 'stud-fold'); *Topps Perocke* 1635 (cf. *cot'* —, *pratum nuper Johannis Tuppe* 1454[2], 1489, — *Toupe* 1477, somewhere in this hundred, *v.* pearroc); *close at Under downe* 1686 (*v.* under, dūn); *Vigeylondes* 1438, *claus' voc' Vygowes* 1461[2], *terre voc' Vigeys* 1461[1], *Vigoishey* 1473–1476 (probably a surname, though an obscure one, with land, (ge)hæg); *Well Closs* 1640, — *Close* 1686 (*v.* wella, clos(e)); *Westclose* 1603, 1686; *Westfeld* 1431, *camp' occid'* 1461[1] (*v.* feld); *Wigwells* 1640, *Wittwells* 1686 (possibly a surname); *Wlfeuecume* 1197 ('Wulfgifu's valley', from the OE fem. pers.n. *Wulfgifu* and cumb); *Wovelylondes* 1462 ('lands at *Wovely*' (possibly 'wolves' wood'), *v.* wulf (gen.pl. *wulfa*), lēah, land, but there may be a connection with prec.); *le Yegrasse* 1529 (*v.* eegrass 'aftermath').

West Lulworth

This par. is in Bindon liberty (*v.* note under Winfrith hundred *supra*). It was formerly a chapelry in Winfrith N. par. Belhuish Fm and St Andrew's Fm were until 1888 detached parts of E Stoke par.

WEST LULWORTH (SY 825807)

> *Westlullewrth* 1258 FF, *-worth(e)* 1268 *Ass*, 1279 *Ch et freq* to
> 1442 *Weld*[1], *man' et Hundr' de* — 1397 (1792) *DCMDeed*
> *Westlolleworth* 1268, 1288 *Ass*, 1344 Ipm, 1388 Fine, Cl
> *West Lel(l)isworth, West Lilles Worth* 1288 *Ass*
> *Westlullesworth* 1290 FF
> *Westlulworth* 1442 *Weld*[1], 1575 Saxton *et passim*
> *West Lilleworth* 1535–43 Leland

v. west, cf. East Lulworth par. *supra* where early forms for the name are to be found.

BELHUISH FM (SY 829830)

> *Behylde Hywysche,* — *Hiwich* 1303 FA, *Becholehywysh* [sic] 1304
> Banco

Belhywyssh 1331 *Weld*[1], *-hewisch* 1406 AD I, *-hwys(s)h* 1436, 1443
Weld[1], *-hewys(s)h(e)*, *-hewissh(e)* 1444 *ib*, 1449 *MinAcct*, 1456
Weld[1], 1457 *MinAcct* (*firma de* —), 1462 *ib*, 1464 *Weld*[1],
-huysshe 1481, 1490 *ib*, *-huish* c. 1628 *Strode*, 1638 *Weld*[1],
1686 *ib* (— *Farme*) *et passim*.
Belehiwich 1346 FA, *-huyssh* 1428 ib, *-huwys(s)h*, *-huwissh* 1438–
1442 *Weld*[1], *-huywyssh* 1443 *ib*
Boyelehuysshe 1399 Cl
Beylehuwyssh 1402 *Weld*[1]
Beelhewyssh 1447 *Weld*[1]
Bel(l)huse farme l17, 1703 *Weld*[1], *Bellehuse* 1843 *TA* (E Stoke)

Fägersten is probably right in taking the first part of this name to be
the OE fem. pers.n. *Bēaghild* (for which *v.* Sx 563, Zachrisson ETT
74), with hīwisc 'household, measure of land that would support a
family'. The same woman probably gave her name to 'the spring of
Beyeliswll' 1279 Ch, *Belewylwater* 1391 *Weld*[1], '(the water of)
Bēaghild's spring or stream', *v.* wella, wæter. The pers.n. *Bēaghild*
probably occurs also as the surname of Geoffrey *Beilde* 1332 SR (Up
Cerne), John *Belde* 1327 *SR*, — *Beilde* 1332 SR (Ch. Okeford).

LITTLE BINDON (SY 831798), 1589 Hutch[3], 1774 Hutch[1], *Binedon*,
'the place of *Bynedon*, where the abbey was first begun' 1234 (1279)
Ch, 'the place of *Old Bynedon*...where the abbey was first built'
1279 ib, *Haldebynedon* 1335 DoNHAS **55** 15, *Byndoun* 1399 Cl,
Lit(t)le Byn-, *Bindon* 1535 VE, Eliz *Rent*, 1586 *Weld*[1] (*mannor of*—),
1686 *ib* (*the Lodge and Warren called* —), *parva Byndon* 1578 (17)
Pitt, cf. *Bindon Warren* 1703 *Weld*[1], '(place) within the hill', from
binnan and dūn, with reference to BINDON HILL, 1811 OS, with loge
and wareine. This was the site of the original foundation of Bindon
Abbey c. 1150 before it was transferred to Wool in 1172 (Hutch[3]
1 350, VCHDo **2** 82, RCHM **2** 151); *Old-* and *Little-* therefore
distinguish it from Bindon Abbey & Fm in Wool par. *infra* where
earlier spellings for the name are to be found, *v.* ald, lȳtel. Little
Bindon itself was erected in the 13th cent., the E part forming a
chapel (RCHM **2** 151) which was 'converted into a warren-house'
(Hutch[1] **1** 163).

BURNGATE (FM) (SY 835817)
   'the grange of *Brumzete*' 1233 Hutch[3]
   'the grange of *Bruniethe*' 1234 (1279) Ch, *Brunnegate* 1262 ib,

'grange of *Brunegat(e)*' 1279 ib, *-yate* 1285 FA, 1288 *Ass*, *Brunyate* 1280 Ch

Bronyethe 1280 *Ass*, *Bronegate* 1291 Tax, *Brounzate* 1346 FF, *Bronyate* 1436 *Weld*[1]

Bromyeth 1280 *Ass*, *-yate* 1331 Pat

Burn(e)yate 1462 *Ct*, 1481 *Weld*[1], *-gate* 1535 VE, Eliz *Rent* (*the mancion howse called* —), 1586 *Weld*[1] (*mannor of* —), 1664 HTax (— *Farme*), 1703 *Weld*[1]

Probably 'brown gate', v. brūn[1], geat, as suggested by Fägersten 141. It was no doubt a grange of Bindon Abbey (in Wool par. *infra*) which possessed two virgates of land in (West) Lulworth from 1172 (VCHDo **2** 82) and tithes in Burngate in 1535 VE (VCHDo **2** 86); *Grange* 1473 *MinAcct*, 1490 *Weld*[1], probably also belongs here, v. grange. It is situated on the Wool–W Lulworth road where it crosses the old bdy of St Andrews Fm *infra*, once a detached part of E Stoke par.

HAMBURY HO & TOUT (SY 816803), — *Down* 1843 *TA*, *Hanbrey Downe* Eliz *Rent*, *Hanbury* 1597 Hutch[3], 1664 HTax (— *Farme*), *-brow* 1705 *Weld*[1], *Hamborough* 1589 Hutch[3], 1640, 1686 *Weld*[1], *-brough* 1646 SC, *Hambury-taut, or toote* 1790 Hutch[3], *Holcombe, or Hamburgh* (a farm) 1795 Boswell, possibly 'high hill or barrow', v. hēah (wk.obl. *hēan*), beorg, with reference either to Hambury Tout itself (a high rounded hill above the cliff rising to 454', v. tōt(e) 'a look-out'), or to the tumulus on its summit (RCHM **2** 446), v. also dūn; the second el. has of course been replaced by burh (dat.sg. *byrig*). *Holcombe*, the alternative name for the farm, is *Holcomb* 1541 Hutch[3] ('grange and farm of —'), 1597 ib, 'hollow valley', v. hol[2], cumb, which aptly describes the valley in which the present Hambury Ho is situated, cf. Holcombe in Alton P. par. *infra*.

ST ANDREW'S FM (SY 836810), 1811 OS, *St. Andrew* 1284 Cl, *Sanctum Andream* (acc.) 1303 FA, *Seynt* —, *Seint* —, *Saynte Andrew(e)(s)* 1412 ib *et freq* to 1530 *Weld*[1], *Lul(l)(e)-*, *Lolleworth(e) St. Andrew* 1302 FF, 1430 Fine, 1433 Cl, 1502 Ipm, 1861 Hutch[3], *Seint Andreueschurche juxta Brounzate* 1346 FF, *Sayntandre West-church juxta Estlolleworth* 1353 ib, *Seynt Andrewes church* 1388 Fine, Cl ('manor of —'), *St. Andrew church by Byndoun* 1399 Cl, *St Andrew(s) Farme* c. 1628 Strode, 1703 *Weld*[1], so called from 'a church which stood there dedicated to St Andrew, all traces of which have long disappeared' (Hutch³ 1 421, site marked 6"), v. cirice, cf. Burngate, E Lulworth par., Lt Bindon all *supra*; *West* is in relation to E Lulworth par. *supra*, perhaps more specifically in relation to St Andrew's Church there *q.v.*, v. west. The form *Stokes St Andrew* 1293 Ipm may also belong here, v. E Stoke par. *infra* of which this was a detached part.

BACON BLUFF (local) & HOLE, coastal features, so called from 'the streaky appearance' of the cliffs here (Arkell, DoNHAS **66** 163), v. bluff, hol¹. BALL STONE, an offshore rock, v. ball. BELHUISH COPPICE, *Bellehuse* — 1843 *TA* (E Stoke), from Belhuish Fm *supra*. BLACK ROCK, an offshore rock. BLACK ROCKS, cliffs in Lulworth Cove *infra*, cf. prec. THE BLIND COW, an offshore rock, cf. The Bull *infra* and Cow Corner in E Lulworth par. *supra*. BRITTWELL HO, v. wella. THE BULL, an offshore rock near The Blind Cow *supra*. (LT) BURN-GATE WD, *Burn(e)gate Wood* 1640, 1663 *Weld¹*, cf. *Burngate Coppice* 117 *ib*, from Burngate *supra*, v. wudu, copis. CHRISTMAS ROCK (local), an offshore rock (Short 64). CHURCH ROCK, an offshore rock, called *Bellow's* (= Belhuish *supra*?) *Church* by Short 64. COASTGUARD STATION, referred to as *Nelson Fort* by Hutchings 85, cf. Look-out *infra*. DAGGERS GATE, *Daggers* 1843 *TA*, the surname *Dagger*, v. geat; on the bdy between W Lulworth and Winfrith N. DUNGY BEACH & HEAD, perhaps dyncge 'manured land', cf. Dunge W 146; referred to as *Dungeon Crags & Head* by Short 64. DURDLE DOOR, 1861 Hutch³, *Dirdale Door* 1811 OS, *Duddledoor* c. 1825 Map, *Durdle or Dudde Door* 1826 Gre, an arched rock projecting into the sea; the first part of the name may be either from OE *(ge)þyr(e)lod* 'pierced', pa.part. of the vb. *þyr(e)lian* 'to pierce', or from an OE adj. **þyr(e)lede* 'having a hole', derived from the sb. pȳrel 'hole', perhaps with hyll 'hill', v. dor, duru, cf. Durdle Pier in Portland par. *infra* and Durlston in Swanage par. *supra*. DYKE, iron age earthworks on Bindon Hill *supra* (RCHM **2** 489), referred to as 'the dike of Julius Cæsar' in 1279 Ch. EAST BOTTOM, E of the village, v. botm. EAST OVER, *Eastover Grd* 1843 *TA*, on the E side of Lulworth Cove *infra*, v. ōfer¹ 'bank, sea-shore'. EAST POINT, the E promontory enclosing Lulworth Cove *infra*, cf. West Point *infra*. FOSSIL FOREST, a coastal feature (v. Chatwin 35, plate VI B). OLD GRAVEL PIT. THE HAMMER (local), an offshore rock (Short 65). HOLY TRINITY CHURCH (Kelly), rebuilt 1870 to replace 'the chapel of West Lull-worth dedicated to the Holy Trinity' (Hutch³ 1 442); according to

RCHM 2 151 'the old church of the Holy Trinity stood 350 yards to the east' (marked 6"), cf. *Church fd* 1843 *TA*. LITTLE BEACH, a coastal feature. LOOK-OUT (2 ×), on the cliff top and no doubt used by coastguards, cf. Coastguard Station *supra*. LULWORTH COMMON, 1811 OS. LULWORTH COVE, 1774 Hutch[1], cf. *the Creke of Lulworthe* 1539 LP, *the Haven* Eliz *Rent, Lulworth hauen* 1575 Saxton, — *Bay* 1773 Bayly, *the Cove Inn* 1882 Robinson, *v.* cove, crike, hæfen[1], bay[1]. LULWORTH FM. MACKEREL ROCK, an offshore rock perhaps named from the fish, but cf. '*Makerel* virgate' 1279 Ch, Thomas *Makerel* 1327 *SR*, 1332 SR (E Lulworth). THE MAN O' WAR, an offshore rock so named from its resemblance to an e19 warship, cf. foll. MAN O' WAR COVE, from prec. MARM TOUT (local), a promontory near Durdle Door *supra* (Short 64), *v.* tōt(e). MOUNT POYNINGS, 1774 Hutch[1], *Mountpoynynges* 1575 Saxton, even in 1774 only the site of the house of this name built by Thomas, Lord *Poynings*, probably between 1541–6 (Coker 44, Hutch[3] 1 441), *v.* mont; the forms *Penens gate* 1682 *Weld*[1], *Pennens* 1843 *TA* probably also belong here, *v.* geat, cf. the f.ns. Pennings in Chaldon H. par. *supra* and in Osmington par. *infra*. MUPE BAY, LEDGE & ROCKS, *Mewup hill* 1753 Collins, *Muop's Bay* 1774 Hutch[1], 1861 Hutch[3], *Mupe Cove* c. 1825 Map, *Mupe Grd* 1843 *TA*, perhaps 'small bay frequented by sea-gulls', *v.* mǣw, hōp[2]; two of the rocks here are called *Arish* (*v.* ears, cf. Arish Mell in E Lulworth par. *supra*) and *Wreckneck* (Short 45). NEWLANDS FM & WARREN, *v.* nīwe, land, wareine. NORMAN ROCK. OLD QUARR (local), a disused quarry near Stair Hole *infra* (Short 64), *v.* quarrere. OSWALD CTG, cf. St Oswald's Bay *infra*. PINION ROCK, an offshore rock, perhaps so called from its resemblance to a *pinion* 'bird's wing, etc.' POTTER'S HOLE, a coastal feature, *v.* hol[1]. RED HOLE, a coastal feature, *v.* DoNHAS 94 23. ST OSWALD'S BAY, cf. Oswald Ctg *supra*. SCRATCHY BOTTOM, a flinty, seaward facing, valley, *v.* botm. SEA HORSE (local), an offshore rock (Short 64). SMUGGLERS' CAVE, a cave in the cliffs below one of the Look-outs *supra*. STAIR HOLE, 1882 Robinson, *Starhole* 1279 Ch, possibly 'steeply sided hole', *v.* stǣger[2], hol[1], which would admirably describe this feature (Chatwin 95, plate VIA), though the 13th cent. form suggests rather stær 'a starling'; above Stair Hole is STAIR HEAD (Short 64), *v.* hēafod. WEST DOWN FM, *West Down* 1843 *TA*, NW of the village, cf. *West Lulworth Downe* 1650 WeyM. WEST POINT, opposite East Point *supra*. WHITE NOSE HILL (lost), 1811 OS, a headland at SY 824798, cf. White Nothe in Owermoigne par. *infra*.

FIELD-NAMES

Fields in E Stoke *TA* but now in W Lulworth are marked †. The undated forms are 1843 *TA* 248 (those marked † are 1843 *TA* 201). Spellings dated 1234 (13) are *HarlCh*, 1234 (1279), 1262, 1279, 1280 Ch, 1244 FF, 1280² *Ass*, 1284 Cl, 1484 *MinAcct*, 1498 *Ct*, Eliz *Rent*, 1645 Hutch³, 1650 WeyM, 1664² HTax, and the rest *Weld*¹.

(*a*) Barnes Plot; Blackland(s) (*Blacklands yeate or gate* 1650, — *gate* 1682, *v.* blæc, land, geat); The Bottom (*v.* botm); Lr, N & S Breach (cf. *Breach Corner* 1682, *v.* brēc, corner); Broad Cl; †Bulls Batch (cf. 'the croft of Hugh *le Bole*' 1284, *v.* batch); Butchers Plot; †Calves Cl; Cliffe Fd (*v.* clif); Cribbs Plot & Barn; †Crookhorn (near Winkhorn *infra*, second el. perhaps horn 'horn-shaped piece of land'); †Down; Down Barn & Yd, East Arable Down (*the downe* 1664¹, *v.* dūn); †East Md; 18 Acres; Ellis Croft (cf. *toft*'... *quondam Johannis Eylys* 1484, *cot' nuper Johannis Elys* 1498); Eweleaze; Fookes Plot; 4 & 14 Acres; Hasty's Plot; Home Fd; The Jolly Sailor P.H.; Knapwell Fd (cf. *Knapway gate* 1682, *v.* cnæpp); Knights Md; Longwells Fd (probably 'the field at Longwell ('long stream')', *v.* lang¹, wella); Middle Fd (1686 *the* —), *The Middell Feild* 1664¹); †Middle Md; Mill Plot (cf. *the water myll* Eliz, *the grist Mill att West Lulworth* 1686, *v.* myln, grist-mill; on this mill *v.* Hutch¹ 1 163, Hutch³ 1 441; an earlier reference to 'the mill of *Lulleworth*' 1234 (1279), 1279 may also belong here, but cf. Arish Mell in E Lulworth par. *supra*); Moreys Plot; Pape Hill (possibly the surname *Pape*); Pennys Plot (perhaps with reference to a penny rent, *v.* pening); †Pitts (cf. *pratum nuper Johannis Pytte* 1469, somewhere in this hundred); Red Hill; Rickbarton (Plot); Sandpit Fd; Shop Fd & Mdw (sc(e)oppa 'shed' or scēap 'sheep'); Snaghill (Corner) (*land called Snaghill* 1705, possibly snag 'tree-stump' or 'sloe', cf. Snag Fm in Corfe C. par. *supra*); South Fd; †South Grd; †Spring Grd (*v.* spring); Symers Plot (cf. Thomasin *Seymore* 1664², Roger *Seamer* 1686); †20 & 29 Acres; 22 Acres; Well House Md; West Fd (*the Westfeild* 1664¹); †West Md; Williams Md (cf. Henry *Williams* 1475 (Winfrith N.)); Willis Plot (cf. *terr' Johannis Willys* 1451); Windway Grd ('winding path', *v.* (ge)wind, weg); †Winkhorn (cf. Crookhorn *supra*; the first el. is perhaps Do dial wink 'a winch', cf. wince).

(*b*) *the Barley Feild* 1664¹ (*v.* bærlic); *Belhuse gate*, — *Lane end* 1682 (from Belhuish *supra*, *v.* geat, lane, ende); *Brembelcumb(e)* 1234 (1279), 1234 (13), 1280 (1706), *Bremelcumb* 1280² (*v.* brēmel 'bramble', cumb); *Brenham* 1262; *the Brewinge howse standing upon the Haven with the water myll* Eliz, *le Brewhowse* 1638 (*v.* brew(ing)house, cf. Lulworth Cove and Mill Plot *supra*); *the East Field* 1686; *Furzeymire pit* 1650; *Hemerhill foote* 1650 (*v.* fōt); *Homeclose* (*apud Seynt Andrewes*) 1530, 1531 (cf. St. Andrew's Fm *supra*); *curs' aque subter le Horspoyll*, (*via regia apud*) *Horspou(y)(l)lake* 1440 ('pond or pool used by horses', *v.* hors, pōl¹, with lacu 'stream'); *Hurst Meade* 1686 (*v.* hyrst); *la Park' de Brunegate* 1402, 'the park' 1645 (*v.* park, Burngate *supra*); *close called the parrock* 1686 (*v.* pearroc); *le sente* 1498 (*v.* senget 'place cleared by burning'); *de la Stane* (p) 1244, 1280 (*v.* stān); *le Stubble feild* 1638 (*v.* stubbil); *Townesend* 1664¹ (*v.* toun, -es², ende); *the Wheate Feild* 1663.

Moreton

MORETON (SY 805894)

Mortune 1086 DB (2×), *-ton(e)* 1194, 1195 P, 1201 FF, 1235–6
Fees, 1254 Pat *et freq* to 1607 *Feth*, *-ten* 1575 Saxton
Moreton 1195 P, 1306 FF, 1502 Pat, 1607 Feth *et passim*
Murton 1318 FF
Mourton(e) 1332 SR, 1340 NI, 1346 FA *et freq* to 1462 Pat,
Mowreton 1414 *Weld*[1]

'Marshland farm', *v.* mōr, tūn.

HURST (SY 792901), *Herste* 1251 Drew, *(H)urste* c. 1300 *Milne* (p),
Hurst(e) 1318 FF, 1402 IpmR, 1404 *Weld*[1] *et passim*, 'copse or
wooded hill', *v.* hyrst; Hurst probably represents the smaller of the
two units described as *Mortune* in DB; for an early mill here, *v.*
Mill Cl *infra*.

THE BROAD, a wide part of R. Frome, *v.* broad. BROOMHILL BRIDGE,
1838 *TA*, *Brumel Bridge* 1791 Boswell, cf. *pontes apud Bromhillesmylle*
1437 *Weld*[1], from Broomhill in Winfrith N. par. *infra*, built 1769
(RCHM **2** 175) over the tributary of R. Frome earlier called *Maynewater*, *v.* Main Water Cl *infra*; cf. (land) *Atte Brigge* c. 1300 *Milne*,
Northbridge, *-brydge* 1607, 1618 *Feth*, *the Stoninge brydge* 1625 *ib*,
some of which may refer to earlier bridges here or at Hurst *supra*, *v.*
atte, brycg, norð, stānen 'stony, made of stone', cf. Hurst Bridges
infra. DAIRY WALK, to Moreton Dairy *infra*. DICK O' TH' BANKS
PLANT., from Dick o' th' Banks in Owermoigne par. *infra*. FIR HILL,
cf. *Fir Hall Plant.* 1838 *TA*, *v.* firr. FRAMPTON ARMS (P.H.), from
the *Frampton* family who have held this manor since 1376 (Hutch[3]
1 394). (OLD) GRAVEL PIT(S), cf. *Plant. West of Gravel Pit* 1838 *TA*.
HEDERA CTG, from Lat *hedera* 'ivy'. HURST BRIDGES, 1838 *TA*
(Affpuddle), built 1834 (RCHM **2** 175) over R. Frome, but cf. *Hurst
bridge* 1592, 1607 *Feth*, 1791 Boswell, *Hurst Ford* 1773 Bayly, from
Hurst *supra*, *v.* brycg, ford, cf. Broomhill Bridge *supra*. HURST
COPSE, LT HURST COPPICE, HURST FM (1811 OS, — *Farm Ho* 1838
TA, cf. *Hurst Ho Plant.* 1838 *ib*) & HEATH, from Hurst *supra*. MILL,
there was a mill here in 1086 DB (VCHDo **3** 87), cf. *Overmulwey*
c. 1300 *Milne*, 'higher mill way', *v.* uferra, myln, weg, and cf. Mill
Cl *infra*. MORETON DAIRY, *Dairy Ho* 1811 OS, cf. Dairy Walk *supra*;
it is described in RCHM **2** 178 as 'Broom Pound, formerly Moreton
Dairy', cf. Broom Pound *infra*. MORETON FM. MORETON HEATH,

1811 OS, *in bruera* 1525 *AOMB*, *the heathe* 1618 *Feth*, *the comin
hearth* (sic) 1661 *ib*, *v.* comun, hǣð. MORETON HO, 1838 *TA* (—
Lawn), *The Mansion House* 1774 Hutch[1], built in 1744 to replace a
manor house built in 1580 (Hutch[3] 1 400). NEW MORETON (lost),
1811 OS, a planned development of l18 or e19, ¾ mile WNW of the
village at SY 793897. MORETON PARK, *the Parke* 1636 *Feth*, *v.* park,
cf. Cantor & Wilson 6 180–1. NEW ENTRANCE, cf. *New Gate* 1838
TA, leading into prec. OBELISK, 1811 OS, erected 1785 in memory of
James Frampton, cf. Frampton Arms *supra*. OLD KNOWLE, 1811 OS,
The Old Knowle Barrow 1838 *TA*, *Old Knowl Hill* 1839 *TAMap*,
v. cnoll 'hillock', cf. *Knol, Byesteknoldich* ('(place) to the east of
Knoldich', *v.* bī, ēastan, dīc 'ditch'), *bytweneknol* ('(place) between the
hillocks', *v.* betwēonan) all c. 1300 *Milne*, and *camp'...vocat'
Southeknoll* 1469 *Weld*[1] (*v.* sūð); Old Knowle is a natural hillock
on which there are three barrows (RCHM 2 446). RAGGED FIRS,
a plantation, *v.* ragged. RED BRIDGE. ST NICHOLAS's CHURCH, rebuilt
1776 on the site of a medieval church. WEST GATE, 1838 *TA*
(— *Plant.*), on the W bdy of Moreton par. WEST LODGE, cf. *The New
Lodge, New Lodge Plant., Lodge Fd* 1838 *TA*, at the entrance to
Moreton Park *supra*. WEST WD, 1838 *TA*, cf. *West Wd Corner &
Fd ib*, SW of the village.

FIELD-NAMES

The undated forms are 1838 *TA* 153. Spellings dated 1280 are Ch, c. 1300
Milne, 1332 SR, 1392 *Ct*, 1525 *AOMB*, 1607, 1609, 1612, 1618, 1625, 1626,
1636, 1667, 1668, 1673, 1676 *Feth*, 1664 HTax, and the rest *Weld*[1].

(*a*) Allens Old Mill Ham (*v.* myln, hamm; for the mill in question, *v.*
Mill Cl *infra*); Barley Ham (*Barlyche-* 1453, *Barlicheham* 1453 (*cursu'
aque apud* —), 1455, *v.* bærlic, hamm); Bates Cl (Plant.); Baylands (Plant.)
(sic) (perhaps to be connected with *Braylond* c. 1300, *v.* land, cf. Braytown in
Winfrith N. par. *infra*); Bridge Md (near Hurst Bridges *supra*); Broad Cl;
Broom Pound (Coppice) (near to Broomhill in Winfrith N. par. *infra*, *v.*
brōm, pund, cf. Moreton Dairy *supra*); Colts Park (colt 'a colt', or the
surname Colt, with park); Cooks 2 Acres (cf. John *Cox* 1664); Copse Cl;
Corn Fd (*the Corne feild* 1636, 1668 (*a bridge over the loer part of the Lake
in* —), *v.* corn[1] 'corn, grain', lacu 'stream', cf. *Cornebarrowe* 1612, which
may however contain corn[2] 'a crane', *v.* beorg); Cow Leaze, First & Second
Cow Lot, Cow Pasture (cf. *Cowse Close* 1525, *v.* cū); Drove (cf. *le Drove end*
1625, *v.* drove, ende); 8 Acres; Ewe Leaze; 5 Acres; French Fds Ham
(*v.* frensche 'French', perhaps for french grass or french wheat, and hamm);
Furzy Grd; Garden Cl; (Lt) Hay Marsh (*v.* hēg, mersc, cf. (land) *atte
Heyweldich* c. 1300, *v.* wella, dīc); Hill Cl Plant. (cf. *Huppe Hulle* c. 1300,

'(land) higher up or upon the hill', *v.* upp, uppan, hyll, cf. Uphill in Coombe
K. par. *supra*); Hilliers Md; Close at Hurst Green (from Hurst *supra*, *v.*
grēne[2]); Hurst Mds (— *meade* 1636, cf. prec.); Upp Hurst (*Huppe hurste*
c. 1300, *Uphurst (corner)* 1618, 1636, '(land) upon *Hurst*', or 'the higher part
of *Hurst*', *v.* upp, uppan, cf. prec.); Island (*v.* ēg-land); Little Cl & Md;
Long Fd & Mdw; Lot Cl, (Gt) Lot Fd (*v.* hlot); (Lr) Main Water Cl
(*Maynewater (Close)* 1612, 1618, cf. (*cursus aque apud/de/vocat'*) (*le*)
Mayn(e)water 1449 *et freq* to 1525, possibly named from Broadmayne par.
infra, since *Maynewater* is the small tributary of R. Frome, forming the bdy
between Moreton and Winfrith N., which rises near Broadmayne, *v.* wæter;
however the first el. could be main[1] 'demesne', cf. also *Maynefurlonge*
c. 1300); Marlpits; Marsh (Cl, Md & Plant.), Broad (Moreton) Marsh, Lt
New Marsh (*þe merche* c. 1300, *le Marshe* 1618, *Marshe close* 1612, *v.*
mersc); Matford Md ('ford used at mowing time', *v.* mǣð, ford, or
'maidens' ford', *v.* mægð[1]; for a discussion of this common p.n., *v.* Gl
2 207); Mill Cl (from *Hurstmill* 1636, cf. Hurst and Allens Old Mill Ham
supra); Moor Cl (*Mower close* 1612, *the moore clooses* 1673, *le Moore* 1676, *v.*
mōr); Moreton Common Fd (cf. *in campo de Morton* 1392, 1394); Moulins
Ditch; New Barn & Yd; New Barrow; New Cl & Grd; Nursery; (Lt)
Paddock (*v.* pearroc); Upr Pine Mdw (*v.* pīn); Plot; Poor Altmt; Rough
Pasture; 7 Acres (Md); 17 and 18 Acres; Sheep Walk; 6 Acres; W Snelling
Grd & Md (from Snelling in T. Puddle par. *infra*); South East & South
West Corner; Spring Coppice; Stoney Crofts; (E & W) 10 Acres, 10 Acres
Plant.; Three Corner Pce; Wall Moor (Md) (*Wallimore* 1618, perhaps 'moor
of the Welshman or serfs', *v.* walh (gen.pl. *wala*), mōr, cf. Walmore Gl 3
204); The New Water Mdw; West Cl (Coppice); West Mdw (*West(e)mede*
1280, c. 1300, 1404 (*prat' iuxta Hurste voc'* —), (*le*) *Westmeade* 1609, 1618,
v. west, mǣd, cf. Hurst *supra*); West Orchd; Withey Bed (*Wythibed* c.
1300, *v.* wīðig, bedd); Wood (cf. *Wdelak* c. 1300, *v.* wudu, lacu 'stream');
Woolgaries Moor (cf. Oakers Wd in Affpuddle par. *infra*).

(b) *le West Barton* 1607 (*v.* beretūn); (land) *atte Beckeberwʒe, atte berwe*
c. 1300 ('at the (Becca's) barrow or hill', from the OE pers.n. *Becca* and
beorg, *v.* atte); *via in Bowelleslan'* 1414 (the surname *Bowell*, with lane);
the/le Cawsewey 1607, 1618, *le Causeway* 1626, *the Carsway* 1673 (*v.* caucie);
campum orientale c. 1300 ('the east field'); *Flexlond(e)* c. 1300 (*v.* fleax
'flax', land); *le ham* 1609 (*v.* hamm); *Huppe Haukeshulle* c. 1300 ('hawk's
hill', *v.* hafoc, hyll, or 'Hafoc's hill', from an OE pers.n. *Hafoc*, with
upp(an) 'upper, upon'); *Hetlond* c. 1300 (probably, as Professor Löfvenberg
suggests, from hǣð 'heath', with land); *Hurstehamm* c. 1300 (*v.* hamm,
cf. Hurst *supra*); (land) *atte Lake, Byestelak, Bovelake, forlake* c. 1300 ('land
at the stream, to the east of the stream, above the stream, and in front of the
stream', *v.* atte, lacu, bī, ēastan, bufan, fore); *Langford Weare* 1636 (*v.*
lang[1], ford, wer); (land) *atte lynche* c. 1300 (*v.* atte, hlinc); (land) *Atte
mere* c. 1300 ('at the pool', *v.* atte, mere[1], or 'at the boundary', *v.* (ge)mǣre);
the Meedle Way 1667 (probably 'the middle way', *v.* middel, weg); *Middelserde* c. 1300 (probably 'middle gap', *v.* middel, sceard, cf. *Wyserde infra*);
Myddlelake 1618 (*v.* middel, lacu); *the North Street* 1667 (*v.* norð, strǣt);
le Owte lett 1618 (*v.* utlete 'outlet, channel', cf. *le Outelete* in Winfrith N.

par. *infra*); *the piled weare* 1636 ('the weir made with stakes', *v.* pīl, -ed³, wer); *Prestesclos* 1440 (cf. William *Prest* 1444, *mesuagio Galfridi Prest* 1464, *v.* clos(e)); *Rodelake* c. 1300 ('reedy stream', *v.* hrēod, lacu); (land) *Atte sonddidich* c. 1300 ('at the sandy ditch', *v.* atte, sandig, dīc); *campum Haustrale* c. 1300 ('the south field'); *Stoklond* c. 1300 (*v.* stocc 'tree-trunk, log', land); *Huppe Tanglond* c. 1300 (*v.* tang 'tong, forceps', land, with upp(an) 'upper, upon'); (*Byeste þe*) *þotre hamme* c. 1300 (possibly '(land to the east of) the outer enclosure', *v.* bī, ēastan, þe, ūterra, hamm, but *þotre* could also be a poor form for *þrote*, cf. foll.); *la Throte* 1391, (*cursum aque apud*) *Throtemede* (*in austral' parte ripe de Frome*) 1393, 1414 (*v.* þrote 'throat, narrow passage', mǣd, cf. prec.); *Tope* c. 1300 (*v.* topp 'hill-top'); *Vatelode, -lomd* (sic), *Vaytelond* c. 1300 (Professor Löfvenberg suggests that the first el. is possibly fat 'rich, fertile', probably with land although the first form could be from (ge)lād 'river crossing'); *campum occidentale* c. 1300 ('west field'); *Wilkins Hamme* 1636 (the pers.n. or surname *Wilkin*, with hamm); (land) *Atte Wyserde* c. 1300 (the second el. is perhaps sceard 'gap', cf. *Middelserde supra*, *v.* atte); *Wothehurn, -lond* c. 1300 (the first el. may be an old r.n. *Woth* found elsewhere in Do as an earlier name for R. Brit (*v.* RNs.), although it may be used here as a surname (cf. *de Woth* 1332 referring to Wooth Grange in Netherbury par. which takes its name from the river), with hyrne 'angle, nook', land); (land) *Atte Yatdich* c. 1300 (*v.* atte, geat, dīc).

Owermoigne

Now a separate liberty (as in 1664 HTax, 1795 Boswell), but in the hundred of *Celberge* in c. 1086 GeldR, and in Winfrith hundred in 1327 *SR*, 1332 SR (*v.* note under Winfrith hundred *supra*). Holworth, since 1880 in this par., was formerly a detached part of Milton A. (Hutch³ **4** 398).

OWERMOIGNE (SY 768853) ['ɔːrmɔin]

    Ogre 1086 DB, 1244 *Ass*, 1267 Pat, *Oghre* 1244 *Ass*

    Ogres 1210–2 RBE, 1244 *Ass*, Fees, 1268 *Ass*, 1269 Ch *et freq* to 1348 Pat, *Gres*, *Ogris* 1275 RH, *Ogeres* 1288 *Ass*

    Oweres 1212 Fees, *Oares* 1285 FA, 1314 Hutch³ (— *Moigne*)

    Hore 1212 Fees, *Ore* 1288 *Ass* (p), 1320 FF, 1327 *SR*, 1332 Cl, 1394 Pat, 1408 ib, 1430 ib (— *Moyne*, *Ogres or Owre Moygne*), 1453 *Weld*¹

    Our(e) 1219 Fees, 1313 Pat, 1314 Ipm (— *Moyngne*), FF (— *Moigne*) *et freq* to 1459 *Weld*¹, *Overe* 1350 Ipm, *Ovre Moigne* 1375 IpmR, *Owre* 1431 FA, 1460 *Weld*¹, 1486 Ipm (— *Moygne*), 1575 Saxton, 1811 OS (— *Moyne*), *Liberty of Ower Moigne* 1664 HTax

    Egres 1291 Tax, 1428 FA

    Ocrise 1389 Pat

This is a difficult name and at present no satisfactory explanation can be offered. Ekwall DEPN thinks it is probably ofer[2] 'slope, ridge': this is topographically suitable as the place lies at the N foot of a steep E–W ridge, but it is unlikely on phonetic grounds in view of the dominant -g- spellings among the early forms, although clearly the name has been associated with ofer[2] (or with ōfer[1] 'river-bank') at an early date. The alternation of early forms with and without -s (perhaps a nom.pl. ending) is also noteworthy.

The manor was held by the family of *Moigne* (< OFr *moine* 'monk') from the beginning of the 13th cent. (Radulfus *Monachus* 1210–2 RBE, 1212 Fees, William *le Moyne* 1244 *Ass*, Fees, etc.), cf. Shipton Moyne Gl 1 108 which according to Hutch[3] 1 455 was held by the same family. The first proper reference to Owermoigne liberty is 1664 HTax, but cf. *Lib' Willelmi le Moygne* 1280 *Ass* mentioned in connection with Owermoigne.

BLACKWATER FORD (SY 786869), 1811 OS, *cursus aque apud/voc' Blak(e)-, Blacwater* 1449–1459 *Weld*[1], 'dark-coloured stream', *v.* blæc (wk.obl. *blacan*), wæter, with ford; this was doubtless another name for the stream that joins R. Frome near Broomhill Bridge in Moreton par. *supra*, cf. Main Water Cl ib.

CHILBURY PLANT. (SY 765852), cf. *Barn* —, *Batch* —, *Higher* — & *Parsons Chilbury* 1840 *TA*, thought by Anderson 120 to represent a survival of the name of the old GeldR hundred of *Celberge* (*q.v.* under Winfrith hundred *supra*), *v.* batch 'hillock'.

GALTON (SY 777852) [ˈgɔːltən]

  Gaveltone 1086 DB, *Gawelton(e)* 1269 Ch, 1288 *Ass* (— *iuxta Ogeres*), 1305 FF (*Est-, West-*), *Gauelton* 1280 *Ass*, (*Este-*) 1288 *ib*, 1305 Ipm
  Galtone 1086 DB, 1269 Ch, -*don* 1212 Fees, -*ton* 1268 *Ass*, 1271 Ch, 1361 Cl, 1457 *Weld*[1], 1795 Boswell
  Gauton 1235–6 Fees
  Gaulton 1244 *Ass* (p), 1269 Ch (p), 1275 RH, 1285 FA, 1288 *Ass* (*Est(e)-, Weste-*), 1319 Pat (p) (*Est-*) *et freq* to 1498 *Ct*, *Gauleton* 1244 *Ass*, *Gawlton* 1392 *Ct*, *Gauulton* 1421 *Weld*[1], *Gawleton* 1440 Cl
  Ga(u)lwelton 1303 FA, *Galmelton* 1399 Cl, *Gaulveton* 1498 *Ct* *Caulton* 1389 Cl

'Farm subject to tax or rent', v. gafol[2], tūn, with ēast, west, cf. Owermoigne *supra*; the reference to rent should perhaps be connected with the fact that the smaller of the two DB manors of Galton was held by four free men TRE who are probably identical with the four men holding it for a rent of 12s. 4d. in 1086 (VCHDo **3** 34, 114). In any case, as Dr von Feilitzen points out, Ekwall's alternative suggestion for the first el. in DEPN, OE gagel 'gale, bog-myrtle', is not possible in view of the DB form *Gaveltone*. The 13th-cent. form in *-don* shows confusion of the second el. with dūn 'hill'. There was a mill here in 1086 DB (VCHDo **3** 111).

HOLWORTH (SY 767834) ['hɔləd, 'houlwə:þ], (*at*) *Holewertþe* 843 for 934 (eME) ASCharters, (*apud*) *Holewourthe* 843 for 934 (17) BCS 739, *Holverde* 1086 DB, *-verda* Exon, *Holewrth* 1204 FF (p), 1288 *Ass*, *-wurðe* 1212 P, *-wrdhe* 1212 Fees, *-worth(e)* 1280 Ch (p) *et freq* to 1450 *Weld*[1], *-wroth*, *-wych* (probably for *-wrth*) 1291 Tax, *-wurth* 1317 *MiltC*, *Holworth* 1275 RH, 1774 Hutch[1], *Holworthye* 1541 (17), 1574 (17) *Pitt*, *Helwarde* 1575 Saxton, *Halworth* 1578 (17) *Pitt*, *Helwarden* 1610 Speed, c. 1825 Map, 'enclosure in a hollow', v. hol[1], worð; some of the early forms seem to contain the OE variant weorð; for the late *-worthye* and *-warden* forms, v. worðig and worðign. For the deserted medieval village here, v. RCHMDo **2** 35.

SOUTH DOWN FM (SY 758821), 1840 *TA*, *Suddon* 1327 *SR* (p), 1332 *SR* (p), 1412 FA, 1478 IpmR, 1486 Ipm, *Sudden* 1340 NI (p), 1645 Hutch[3] ('farm of —'), 1795 Boswell, *Syddon* 1375 IpmR, *Sutton* 1648 SC, *Sooden Farme* 1664 HTax, 'south hill or down', v. sūð, dūn; it lies about two miles S of Owermoigne on the S slope of a hill ridge; Hutch[3] **1** 459 has a heading *Sudden* but notes that 'it is now... always called South Down Farm'.

BALLAST CTG & KNAP, *Ballast* 1840 *TA*, perhaps ModE ballast, with cnæpp 'hill-top'. BARTLETT'S COPPICE, 1840 *TA*. BASCOMBE BARN, cf. John *Bascombe* 1664 HTax (Wool), Thomas *Bascombe* 1827 SCat (occupying *Ower Moigne Fm*). THE BEAR, an offshore rock. BOWLEY'S PLANT. BRIMSTONE BOTTOM (BARN), from brimstone (lit. 'burning stone', v. bryne, stān), botm, cf. Brimstones Gl **3** 202; it is near Burning Cliff *infra*. BROWNJOHN'S PLANT. BUBBLE SPRING. BURNING CLIFF, so called from the spontaneous ignition of the bituminous shale here in 1826, giving rise to a fire that lasted for four years (Chatwin 26), cf. Brimstone Bottom *supra*. CASTLE LANE, 1861

Hutch[3], probably with reference to Court Ho *infra*, or to the nearby earthwork (6″), *v.* castel(1). CHURCH, rebuilt 1883 (Kelly); an earlier church in Owermoigne is referred to in 1320 FF, 1332, 1343 Cl, 1348 Pat. COLMAN'S FM, cf. John *Coleman* 1327 *SR* (Warmwell). COURT HO, *Moignes Court* 1861 Hutch[3], cf. Hr & Lr Court Fd 1840 *TA*, *v.* court, cf. Owermoigne *supra*; for this l13 moated house, *v.* RCHM **2** 184, Taylor 107. COWHERD'S KNAP, *v.* cnæpp. DICK O' TH' BANKS, — *of the* — 1811 OS, probably '(the place) of Dick o' th' Bank(s)', i.e. of Richard Bank(s); the surname type with *o' th'* (equivalent to *atte, de la*, etc.) is common in NCy in ME. EAST FM, 1840 *TA*, E of the village, cf. West Fm *infra*. FIR PLANT. GALLOWS HILL, *v.* galga, hyll; there is mention of a gallows associated with the manors of Winfrith N. and Owermoigne in 1275 Hutch[3] **1** 455. GALTON FM, 1840 *TA*, cf. Galton *supra*. GALTON HEATH, GALTON-HEATH CTGS, *Galton Heath* 1811 OS, cf. *centum acras Bruere in Gawelton iuxta Ogeres* 1288 *Ass*, *v.* hǣ ð, cf. Galton, Owermoigne *supra*. GRAVEL PIT PLANT., near Gravel Pits (6″). HAM COPPICE, *v.* hamm. HEATHFIELD CTG. HIGHER BARN. HOLLY CTG. HOLWORTH DAIRY, FM & HO, from Holworth *supra*, cf. 'the farm of *Holworth, alias Chaldecote Holworth*' 1636 Hutch[3], named from Francis *Chaldecote* ib. SOUTH HOLWORTH BARN & CTGS, *South Holworth* 1774 Hutch[1], cf. *East & North Holworth* 1774 ib, from Holworth *supra*. HORSE PLOT PLANT., cf. *Horse Grds* 1840 *TA*. KING ROCK, a coastal feature. KITCHELL'S COPPICE, Hr & Lr Kitchets (sic) 1840 *TA*. THE LAKE, LAKE PLANT., *v.* lake. LILLINGTON'S FM, cf. Henry *Lillington* 1664 HTax (Ringstead in Osmington). LONG MEAD COPPICE, *Long Md* 1840 *TA*. MOIGNE COMBE (a house), — WD, *v.* cumb, cf. Owermoigne *supra*. MOIGNS DOWN (BARN), *Moygnes Downe* 1618 *Mansel*, 'farm of *Moygnes Down*' 1645 Hutch[3], *Moynes Down* (*Fm*) 1774 Hutch[1], *Moignes Down Fm & Md* 1840 *TA*, *v.* dūn, cf. Owermoigne *supra*. MOUNT SKIPPET, 1811 OS; on the common but unexplained minor p.n. (*Mount*) *Skippet*, — *Skippitts*, etc., v. M. Gelling, NQ **18** (1971) 190 and Brk 49, cf. Lr & Hr Skippet in Bradford P. par. *infra*. MOWLAM'S BARROW (Kelly), 1811 OS, *Mawlands* — 1826 Gre, the surname *Mowlam* from Moulham in Swanage par. *supra*, *v.* beorg. MYRTLE CTG. NEW GATE CTGS, on the road to Dorchester. ORCHARD COPPICE & FM. OWERMOIGNE DOWN BARN, *Over Down* 1840 *TA*, cf. John *atte Doune* (parson of Owermoigne) 1389 Pat, *v.* dūn, atte. OWERMOIGNE HEATH (FM), *Owre Heath* 1811 OS. OVERMOIGNE (sic) MILL, *Owre Mill* 1811 OS, cf.

Milcroftes 1452, 1459 *Weld*[1], *Mill Cl & Fm* 1840 *TA*, v. **myln**, **croft**; there was a mill in Owermoigne in 1086 DB (VCHDo **3** 97). OWER WD, 1840 *TA*, cf. prec. RINGSTEAD BAY, 1773 Bayly, from Ringstead in Osmington par. *infra*. SIX ACRE COPPICE, cf. *Six Acres* 1840 *TA*. SKIPPET PLANT., from Mount Skippet *supra*. SOUTH LODGE, S of Moigne Combe *supra*, cf. West Lodge *infra*. SPLIT ROCK, a coastal feature. SUMMER CTGS. TADNOLL BARROW, 1811 OS, *Tad-knowl Barrow* 1839 *TAMap*, from Tadnoll in Chaldon H. par. *supra*, v. **beorg**. TAVERN FM. TINKER'S BARROW (PLANT.), the surname *Tinker*, or 'where tinkers gathered', v. **beorg**, cf. Tinker's Copse in Corfe C. par. *supra*. WEST BARN. WEST FM, 1840 *TA*, W of the village, cf. East Fm *supra*. WEST LODGE, W of Moigne Combe *supra*, cf. South Lodge *supra*. WHITE NOTHE or WHITE NOSE, *the White North* (sic) 1649 WeyM, *White Nore* 1811 OS, *White cliff or White nore Point* c. 1825 Map, a coastal promontory, for which the forms probably represent genuine alternative names; *Nothe* is to be compared with The Nothe (also a promontory) in Weymouth par. *infra*, v. **hnoþ** 'knoll, hill'; *Nose* is **nose** 'promontory, headland'; and *Nore* is probably **ord** 'point' or **ōra**[1] 'bank, shore', with *N-* from the met-analysis of an OE *hwītan orde, -ōran*, v. **hwīt** (wk. obl. *hwītan*) 'white', here referring to chalk cliffs. WITHY BED.

FIELD-NAMES

The undated forms are 1840 *TA* 162. Spellings dated 1269 are Ch, 1317 *MiltC*, 1327 *SR*, 1332 SR, 1340 NI, 1675 Hutch[3], 1774 *DCMMap*, 1827 SCat, and the rest *Weld*[1].

(a) Badgers Hole; Barn Cl; Brick Fd(s); Butts Cl (v. **butt**[1], **butt**[2], **butte**); Chalkpit Fd 1774 (from Chalk Pit in Chaldon H. par. *supra*; this was one of the common fields of Galton *supra*, cf. *campu' de Gaulton* 1459); Cliff Pce (cf. John (*atte*) *Clyue* 1327, 1332, v. **atte**, **clif**); Close; Clover Ld; Common Green; Conegar (v. **coninger**); Coppice Cl; Corner Cl; Gt & Lt Cowleaze, Fir Cow Leazes; Hr & Lr Dewberries (cf. *dew-berry* 'a species of blackberry'); Drove (v. **drove**); East Fd (1774; both Galton and Owermoigne had a common field of this name, cf. *camp' de Ore* 1453); Ewe Leaze; Fatlands ('fertile strips of land', v. **fat**, **land**); 5 & 4 Acres; Galton Cmn & Down (cf. Galton *supra*); Goulds (cf. John *Gould* 1675); Granary Pce; Great Living, Md & Pce (v. **living**); Haycroft (Coppice & Drove) (v. **hēg**, **croft**); Higher Md; Home Cl; Kings Pound (cf. *Kyngesgore* 1269, probably the surname *King*, v. **gāra**, **pund**); Kit Lane Cl (perhaps **cyte** 'cottage', or the pers.n. *Kit*); Liston Hill (*Linston* — 1827); Little Coppice & Md; Long Cl; Middle Fd (1774); Murren Plot (perhaps **murrain** 'infectious disease of cattle'); New Enclosure; 9 Acres; East & West North Hill; Old

Enclosures; (Ower) Cmn; Ower North; Park Md (*v.* park); Peaked Md
(*v.* peked); Pitclose; Plantation; Pollards Pit (cf. William *Pollard* 1327
(Poxwell)); Pond Cl; Reach (*v.* rǣc); Resolution (for other nicknames of
this abstract type, *v.* the f.ns. of Halstock par. *infra*); Rick Yd; Rostley Md
('wood or glade where rafters or beams were got', *v.* hrōst, lēah, cf. Rossley
Gl 1 169); Round Btm & Md; 17 Acres; Slitmoor (perhaps 'muddy marshland', *v.* slēte (WSax slīete), mōr); South Lds; Spring Mds (*v.* spring); Street
Md; Towns End Fd 1774 (*v.* toun, ende); Trip Cl (Do dial. trip 'a culvert
over a ditch or small watercourse'); 12 Acres; Water Mdw; West Fd (1774).

(*b*) *vie que ducit versus Bernardestone* 1317 (the ME (OG) pers.n. *Bernard*,
with tūn 'farm'); *pratum domini Binutheton* 1317 ('beneath the village', *v.*
beneoðan, tūn, cf. John *Boueton* 1332, 'above the village', *v.* bufan);
Brodemede 1317 (*v.* brād, mǣd); *Depecrundale* 1317 ('deep chalk-pit or
quarry', *v.* dēop, crundel, cf. *lapid' in querrer' de Oure,* — *Owre* 1459, 1472,
1481, cf. Owermoigne *supra*); *Estmede de Gaulton* 1452 (*v.* ēast, mǣd,
Galton *supra*); *regia via apud la Fosse* 1392 (*v.* foss 'a ditch'); *Frykonesmede*
1317 (probably a surname from ME *frik(e)* 'brisk' (cf. Robert *Fryk'* 1332
(Nthr Compton)) and *-un* suffix, with mǣd); *in the Heye* 1332 (p) (*v.* (ge)-
hæg); *atte Hulle* 1340 (p) (*v.* atte, hyll); *atte Pyle* 1332 (p) (*v.* atte, pīl
'stake, post, pile'); *punfaldum domini* 1317; *I rete* ('fishery') *voc' le Spurt*
1459, 1460 (probably from spyrte 'wicker-basket, eel-basket', as suggested
by Professor Löfvenberg, rather than from spyrt 'a spirt of water');
Stotingmede 1317 (possibly for *Stocing-, v.* stoccing 'a clearing of stumps',
mǣd, but cf. Stottingway in Upwey par. *infra*).

Poxwell

POXWELL (SY 742841)

> *Poceswylle* (2 ×) 987 (13) Finberg 613 (S 1217)
> *Pocheswelle* 1086 DB, *-wella* Exon
> *Pokeswel(l)(e)* 1188 P (p), 1202 ib (p), 1203 Cur (p), 1244 *Ass*,
>   1285 FA, 1288 *Ass*, 1291 Tax *et freq* to 1575 Saxton, *-wll(e)*
>   1212 Fees, 1271 Ch (p), *-hull* (sic) 1280 *Ass*, *-woll* 1311 *Weld*[1]
>   (p), *-wull* 1340 NI
> *Pokewell* 1203 Cur (p)
> *Pockeswell* 1273 Cl, *-woll* 1332 SR, *Pokkeswell* 1450 *Weld*[1]
> *Pekeswell(e)* 1288 *Ass*
> *Pokeleswell* 1288 *Ass*
> *Pakeswell* 1344 (14) Cerne, 1428 FA
> *Pok'* 1389, 1398, 1412 *Weld*[1], *Pokes* 1392 *Ct*, *Pock'* 1408 *Weld*[1]
> *Pokyswell(e)* 1392, 1393 *Ct*, *Pocuswelle* 1393 *AD*
> *Poxwell* 1535 VE, 1575 Hutch[1] (— *Hungerford*), 1811 OS, *Poxewell*
>   1664 HTax

The second el. is probably swelle or (ge)swell 'swelling' used topographically in the sense 'steeply rising ground', as suggested by Ekwall Studies[2] 152–3, cf. Swell Gl 1 226; Poxwell lies in a gap in a long ridge (cf. *Pokeswelle(s)yate infra*), but as pointed out by Arkell (1941) 39, the Warmwell–Osmington road which now follows this N–S gap formerly turned W up the steep ridge here direct to Osmington, and this steep ascent may well have been the 'swell' alluded to. The first el. could then be an OE pers.n. *Poca* (cf. Pockley YN 72), or an OE *poc(c)e 'a frog' related to MLG, MDu *pogge* and suggested by Ekwall DEPN for Polebrook Nth (*Poche*-DB, *Pokebroc* 12 *et passim*), cf. also the surname *Poche* found in this par.: William *Pothe* (probably for *Poche*) 1332 SR, — *Poche* 1340 NI. On the other hand Fägersten's suggestion that Poxwell is 'Poc's spring', from an OE strong pers.n. *Poc* (cf. OE *pocc* 'small-pox') and well(a) (WSax wyll(a)), remains a possibility; a spring is marked (6″) just S of the village. The same first el. possibly enters into the nearby Pixon Barn in Osmington par. *infra*. The affix -*Hungerford* in the form from 1575 suggests some connection with the *Hungerford* family which held lands elsewhere in Do (Hutch[3] 4 175), but no reference to it here has been noted.

JOHN BEER'S CTG. HR & OLD DOWN BARN, cf. *le Hyedoun* 1452 *Weld*[1], *pastur' apud Heydoun* 1462 *ib*, *The Down or Furze Grd*, *Barn Pce* 1840 *TA*, *v.* hēah 'high' or hēg (WSax hī(e)g) 'hay', dūn. THE PLANTATIONS, cf. *East*, *New & Road Plant.* 1840 *TA*. POXWELL BIG WD. POXWELL DROVE, cf. *Drift Way Barn & Yd* 1840 *TA*, *v.* drove, drift. POXWELL FM (formerly MANOR HO), *the mansion-house* 1774 Hutch[1]. POXWELL GROVE. POXWELL LODGE. OLD QUARRIES, *querrer' de Pokeswell* 1457–1459 *Weld*[1], *Pokeswell quarries* 1774 Hutch[1], cf. *E & W Quar* 1840 *TA*, *v.* quarrere. ST JOHN THE BAPTIST'S CHURCH, erected 1868 to replace an older church then pulled down, cf. *ecclesiam de Pokeshull* 1280 *Ass*, 'the church of *Pokeswell*' 1348 Pat.

FIELD-NAMES

The undated forms are 1840 *TA* 175. Spellings dated 1332 are SR, 1433 Hutch[3], 1664 HTax, and the rest *Weld*[1].

(a) Acre; Bridles Acre & Cowleaze (cf. William *Brytle* 1433); Butt Mdw (*v.* butt[1], butt[2], or butte); Coppice; (E & W) Cowleaze; Dairy Yd; East Fd; 4 Acres; Great Fd; Hedge Row (Plant.); Hewsh (Cl) (*v.* hīwisc); Highsun

Corner; Hither Pce; Hoopers Ctg (cf. John *Hopere* 1332 (Owermoigne));
Horse Pond; Lambing Yd; Long Mdw; Mead; Middle Fd; New Grd;
New Md; (Lr) Orchard; Ornamental Grd; Parsonage Coppice; Paynes
Md; Peakston; Rams Grd; 7 Acres; Stoney Fd; 24 Acres; Voscombe Md
(perhaps 'fox valley', *v.* fox, cumb, cf. Foscombe Gl 3 153); Vyes Md (cf.
Henry *Vye* 1664); Waryhall Btm *&* Hill (the first el. may be wearg 'a felon',
with hall or halh); West Fd; Withy Bed; Woods Cl (Drove); Woolfreys
Md; Gt Yew Leaze (*v.* eowu, lǣs).

   (b) (*curs' aque apud*) *Haselet* 1414 (*v.* hæslett 'a hazel copse'); (*reg' via
apud*) *Pokeswelle(s)yate* 1412 (*v.* geat 'gate, opening', possibly with reference
to the gap in which the village is situated, *v.* Poxwell *supra*); *via voc' Steny-
brygge* 1413, *pons voc' Stenebrigge* 1460, *vie regie iuxta Stenbrygge, -brigge*
1478 (*v.* stǣnig 'stony, made of stone', brycg 'bridge, causeway').

East Stoke

West Holme in this par. is a tithing in Hasler hundred *supra*. Rushton and
Bestwall were in Worgret tithing in 1795 Boswell, and the W part of
Stoborough tithing was in this par. at the same date (*v.* Arne par. *supra*).
In 1888 various detached parts of E Stoke were transferred to other pars.,
Belhuish Fm and St Andrew's Fm to W Lulworth par. *supra*, Bestwall and
Swineham to Wareham St M. par. *infra*.

EAST STOKE (SY 870865)

   ?*Stoches* 1086 DB (f. 79b)
   Stokes 1166 RBE (p), 1244 *Ass*, 1291 Tax, 1293 Ipm, 1358 Pat
      (p), *Estokes* 1316 FA (p)
   Stok(e) 1284 Cl, 1285 FA, 1288 *Ass*, 1303 FA *et freq* to 1498 Ct,
      '— by *Bynedon* (*Abbots*)' 1380 Misc, 1382 Pat, — *iuxta Bynedon*
      p1483 Sheen, — *alias East Stoke iuxta Bindon* c. 1628 *Strode*,
      Estok(e) 1316 FA (p), 1335 Cl (p), 1346 FF (— *juxta Bynedon*),
      1403 Pat ('— by *Byndon*'), 1412 FA, 1422 *Weld*[1] (— *iuxta
      Bynedon*)
   Stokke 1412 FA
   East Stoake 1664 HTax

'Outlying farm buildings, a secondary settlement', *v.* stoc (nom. pl.
stocu, new ME pl. *stokes*). *East* perhaps in relation to Bindon (Abbey)
in Wool par. *infra*, cf. the form *Bindonestok* 13 EPN **2** 154 (source
untraced) which may refer to East Stoke rather than to Bindon
Abbey as suggested *loc. cit.*; however the isolated form *Westok* 1359
Strode, if it is not an error for *Estok*, suggests that there was earlier
a 'West Stoke' too, *v.* ēast, west. The bounds of the manor of E

Stoke are given in c. 1628 *Strode* M4. For the identification of the
Count of Mortain's DB manor of *Stoches* with E Stoke, *v.* Hutch³
1 410, Eyton 142, Fägersten 144, DBGazetteer 120; VCHDo 3 87,
142 identifies it with Stock Gaylard in Lydlinch par. *infra.*

BINNEGAR (SY 878871) [ˈbinəgə], 1545, 1585 Hutch³ (*East* —), 1811
OS, *Beningere* 1299 Banco, *Bennegere* 1316 FA, *Benegar* 1318,
Beneger 1409 both FF, 1355 *Wim*, *Est benynger* 1432, *Est benigar*
1450 both Hutch³, *Benyngar* 1463, 1477 *Weld*¹, *Benygar* 1476, 1482
ib, *Beniger* c. 1628 *Strode*, *Benigare*, *Bynnegare* 1638 *Weld*¹, *Binegar*
1826 Gre. Fägersten 144 suggests comparing this name with Binegar
So which is probably 'slope where beans grow', from bēan and
hangra (cf. DEPN for an alternative first el.), and Dr von Feilitzen
finds this etymology acceptable for Binnegar. However, Professor
Löfvenberg notes that none of the ME forms clearly point to hangra
as second el., and suggests that the first el. may be the OE pers.n.
Beonna (Redin 61), the second el. gāra 'triangular plot of land'.

HETHFELTON (SY 852883) [ˈhefəltən]
   Elfatune, Hafeltone (2 ×) 1086 DB, *Ælfatune* Exon
   Hechfelton (probably for *Heth-*) 1199 CartAnt, *-tun* 1227 FF,
      Hethfelton 1280 Ch, 1315, 1331, 1344 all Pat, 1355 IpmR, 1571
      Hutch³ ('manor and grange of —'), 1811 OS
   Hethfelderton 1227 FF
   Ethfeld 1234 (13) *HarlCh*, 1234 (1279) Ch
   Hetfelton 1280 Ch, *-feldyngton* 1291 Tax
   Hethfeldton 1280 (1706) *Weld*¹, *Hetherfelton* 1344 Inq aqd,
      Hethefel(d)ton 1535 VE, *Ethfilton* 1541 Hutch³, *Heathfelton*
      (*als. Heathelton*) 1625 DoIpm, *Heathfieldton* 1765 Tayl
   Hethelton Mead(ow) 1638, 1682 *Weld*¹
   Heckelton 117 *Weld*¹
   Hefleton, Heffelton ham 1703 *Weld*¹

'Farm at *Hethfeld*' ('open land overgrown with heather'), as
suggested by Fägersten 145 and Ekwall DEPN, *v.* hǣð, feld, tūn,
with mǣd and hamm. It is suggested in Hutch³ 1 417 that the name
may mean 'Æðelflǣd's farm', from the woman called *Ædelflete* (OE
Æðelflǣd) who held TRE the largest of the three DB manors of
Hethfelton (VCHDo 3 95), but as Dr von Feilitzen notes, nothing
in the run of forms points to this pers.n. There was at one time a

grange of Bindon Abbey here (Hutch[3] 1 370, 417, cf. 1234 (13) *HarlCh* 58/H/45 in which *terram de Ethfeld* is granted to the abbey).

WEST HOLME (SY 887858), c. 1586 Tres, *Westholn(e)* 1288 *Ass* (*molendino de* —), 1404, 1412 *ib*, 1417 FF, 1449 Mansel, *Westholm(e)* 1288 *Ass* (*molendino de* —), 1316 FF, 1380 Misc, 1614 *Mansel*, *v.* west, cf. East Holme par. *supra*, where earlier forms are to be found; the mill here is also mentioned in 1411 Hutch[3] (1 419) and 1412 *Ass*.

LUCKFORD COPPICE (SY 877858), *Luggeford* 1381 Misc, *Lug(g)eford* 1381 (16) *Pitt*, *Ludgeford* c. 1586 Tres, *Luckford* 1774 Hutch[1], 1843 *TA* (— *Fd & Wd*), 1861 Hutch[3], possibly 'Lugga's ford', from an OE pers.n. *Lugga* (suggested for Lugworthy D 180, cf. the Do surnames Robert *Lug*(') 1327 *SR*, 1332 SR (Haselbury B.), William *Lugg*' 1332 SR (Gillingham)), and ford. However the first el. could alternatively be a Brit r.n. identical with R. Lugg (Radnor, Sa, He) and Luke Brook (He) which are derived from Brit **Leuc(ouiā)* (Jackson 309, 556–7, cf. Ekwall RN 268–9); Luckford would then mean 'ford over R. *Lugg*', *Lugg* being an earlier name for the stream now called Luckford Lake (*v.* RNs.) which flows N into R. Frome and forms the W bdy of the Isle of Purbeck *supra*; the ford itself (*Luggeford*) is a point on this same Purbeck bdy, and is no doubt to be identified with the ford marked 6″ where Luckford Lake is crossed by the East Stoke–West Holme road just W of Luckford Coppice.

RUSHTON (SY 878866)

> *Ristone* (4×) 1086 DB, *Ristona* Exon, *Riston* 1218 FF, *Ryston* 1251 ib, 1280 Ch, 1316 FA, *Risseton* 1299 Ipm, *Rysston* 1303 FA
>
> *Ruston* 1304 Ipm ('—by *Frome*'), 1305 Cl ('—near *Forme*' (sic)), 1318 FF, *Russton* 1355 *Wim*
>
> *Ris(s)h(e)-*, *Rys(s)h(e)ton* 1313 FF, 1330 Ch ('—by *Warham*'), 1331 Pat (p), 1332 Misc, 1435 *Midd*
>
> *Rus(s)h(e)ton* 1318 FF, 1344 Cl, 1392 *DCMDeed* (— *iuxta Bynedon*) 1412, 1431 FA, 1435, 1550 *Midd*, 1638 *Weld*[1], Hr & Lr Rushton 1861 Hutch[3]
>
> *Ruyssheton* 1463–1476 *Weld*[1], 1477 *MinAcct*, 1478 *Weld*[1]

'Farm or enclosure where rushes grew', from risc, rysc, and tūn, cf. R. Frome in RNs., Wareham par. and Bindon in Wool par. *infra*; there was a mill here in 1086 DB (VCHDo 3 95).

STOKEFORD (SY 867874), STOKEFORD FM, STOCKFORD CTG, *Stokford(e)* 1244 *Ass* (p), 1280 *ib* (p), 1318 FF, 1463 *Weld*[1], *Stokeford* 1355 *Wim*, *Stokkeford* 1445 Hutch[3], *Stock(e)ford(e)* 1535 VE, c. 1628 *Strode*, 1638, 1682 *Weld*[1], *Stoke ford* c. 1628 *Strode*, 'the ford near to Stoke', *v*. E Stoke *supra*, ford; the ford was no doubt across R. Frome just S of the farm where there is now a bridge.

WOOL BRIDGE (SY 844872), WOOLBRIDGE FM formerly WOOLBRIDGE
> *Wullebrigg* 1244 *Ass* (p), *Wllebrygg* 1291 Tax, *Wulbryge* 1535 VE
> 'bridge of *Welles*' 1279 Ch, *Wele(s)brigg* 1283 Banco, 1303 FA, *Wellebrigge* 1318 Ch, 1343 IpmR, -*brugge* 1353 Pat, *Wellesbrigg* 1346 FA
> *Wolbrigg* 1288 *Ass* (*tabernam in ville de* —), -*brygge* 1428 FA, -*bridge* 1578 *AD*, *Wolleberg* 1316 FA, *Wol(l)ebrigg(e)* 1343 Misc, 1344 (14) Cerne, *Wollesbrigg* 1344 (14) ib, *Wolle bridge* 1535-43 Leland, *Wool(l) Bridge* Eliz Rent, 1794 *DCMDeed* (*chapel of* —), 1811 OS, *Woolbridge* 1582 Hutch[3] ('grange of —'), c. 1628 *Strode*

'The bridge near Wool', *v*. Wool par. *infra*, brycg; this is an important crossing of R. Frome. In 1774 Hutch[1] **1** 156 the present bridge (probably 16th-cent.) is described as 'a large bridge of stone of five arches' and the farm as 'now converted into a farmhouse... formerly a neat and elegant building of brick', cf. RCHMDo **2** 275, 406. The grange here possibly belonged to Bindon Abbey; a chapel is marked on the 6″ map. The 14th-cent. spelling -*berge* shows metathesis of *r*.

BAKER'S WELL (VALLEY), cf. Reginald *Pistor* 1327 *SR* (Wareham), Thomas *Baker of Arne* 1650 Hutch[3]. BARKUS COPPICE, *Barkis* 1843 *TA*. BATTERY BANK, an ancient dyke on Stokeford Heath *infra*, *v*. battery, bank(e), cf. The Rings in Corfe C. par. *supra*. BINNEGAR COPPICE, FM (1″), HALL (1811 OS), LANE, MILL (*Hungerhill Mill* 1826 Gre) & PLAIN, all named from Binnegar *supra*, cf. S Hungerhill *infra*. BIRCH WD. BLACK BARROW (lost), 1811 OS, *v*. blæc, beorg; it refers to the tumulus marked (1″ and 6″) at SY 867856. BLACK DOG INN, cf. Dog Plant. *infra*. BUNKER'S HILL COPPICE, *Bunkers Hill* 1843 *TA*, probably an allusion to the American battle of Bunker Hill in 1775. CALF CLOSE COPPICE, *Calves close(s)* c. 1628 *Strode*, 1635, 1682 *Weld*[1], *Two Calfe Closes* l17 ib, *Calves Close (Coppice)* 1843 *TA*,

cf. *Calves Plot* 1843 *ib.* CARRIAGE DRIVE, leading to Hethfelton *supra.*
CHICKS HILL (FM), *Chicks Hill* 1843 *TA*, cf. *Chicks Cl & Mdw*
1843 *ib*, cf. Hugh *Chyk*, — *Chik* 1305, Richard *Chike* 1312 both
Hutch[3]. COWLEAZE KNAP, *Cowleaze* 1843 *TA*, *v.* cnæpp. DEVIL'S
BRIDGE, across Holy Stream *infra*, *v.* dēofol. DOG PLANT., from Black
Dog Inn *supra*, cf. *Dog Grd* 1843 *TA*. DOVER'S PLANT., cf. *Dovers*
Mdw 1843 *TA*, Thomas *Dover* 1664 HTax (Stoborough in Arne).
FARM COPPICE & HEATH, probably from Binnegar Fm *supra* or
Trigon Fm in Wareham par. *infra*. FORD HEATH, from Ford in
Wareham par. *infra*. FOX POUND, *Fox preserve* 1843 *TA*, *v.* fox,
pund, cf. The Preserve *infra*. FRENCH GRASS COPPICE, *French Grass*
1843 *TA*, *v.* french grass. GRANT'S CTG & PLOT. GREAT PLANT.
HETHFELTON FM & HOLLOW, cf. *Hethfelton Wd* 1826 Gre, from
Hethfelton *supra*, *v.* hol[1]. HETHYPIECE BUNGALOW, *Heathy pce* 1843
TA. HIGHWOOD (HEATH), *Highwoods* (a close) c. 1628 *Strode*,
Highwood c. 1628 *ib*, 1811 OS, *v.* hēah, wudu, cf. Highwood Wd in
Wool par. *infra*. HILL CTGS. HOLLY WD, perhaps holegn 'holly', but
Holy Stream *infra* flows through this wood to meet R. Frome so the
first el. may be hālig 'holy'. HOLME BRIDGE, HOLMEBRIDGE (CMN),
(*pratum apud*) *Holmebrygge* 1530 *Weld*[1], *-brydge* 1531 *ib*, *Holm(e)*
Bridge 1535–43 Leland, c. 1628 *Strode*, 1811 OS, 'the bridge near
Holme', *v.* brycg, E Holme par. and W Holme both *supra*; the
bridge, which crosses R. Frome and was described in 1535–43
Leland as having four arches, has given its name to the hamlet of
Holmebridge. WEST HOLME HEATH, *Holme Heath* 1811 OS, cf. W
Holme *supra*. WEST HOLME HO & LODGE, cf. prec. HOLY STREAM,
a small tributary of R. Frome, probably named from foll. HOLY WELL,
near prec., *v.* hālig, wella, cf. Holly Wd *supra*. SOUTH HUNGERHILL
(lost, SY 884883), 1774 Hutch[1], 1861 Hutch[3], *South Hungerill* c. 1628
Strode, described in 1861 Hutch[3] as 'a farm on the south side of the
river Piddle, almost opposite North Hungerhill or Trigon', *v.* sūð,
Trigon Hill in Wareham par. *infra*. JUBILEE PLANT. LADIES' LOOKOUT,
cf. *Lady's Mdw* 1843 *TA*. LAUREL BOTTOM. LODGE, cf. *Lodge Cl*
1843 *TA*. LONG BOTTOM. LONG COPPICE, 1843 *TA*. LONG THORNS,
Longthorns 1811 OS, *v.* þorn. LYTCHET BRIDGE & LANE, *place called*
Letches Bridge, round the Litch 1682 *Weld*[1], from læcc, lecc, 'stream,
bog', with brycg, lane; the modern form of the name has been
influenced by Lytchett Mat. & Min. pars. *infra*. MANOR FM.
NEWFOUNDLAND, a wood, perhaps so-called from its remoteness.
THE NURSERY, cf. *Hr Nursery Wd* 1843 *TA*. OLD PARSONAGE, *the*

Parsonage house c. 1628 *Strode, Parsonage* 1826 Gre, cf. *the Parsons Coppice* c. 1628 *Strode, Parsons Copse Grd, Parsonage Md* 1843 *TA*. PAYARDS PLANT., *Payards* 1843 *TA*, probably a surname. THE PRESERVE, cf. Fox Pound *supra*. PUDDLE COPPICE, 1843 *TA, v.* puddel 'pond'. RUSHTON CMN, 1843 *TA,* — *Comon* 1621 (17) *Strode,* cf. *Rushton heath* 1621 (17) *ib, v.* common, hǣ ð, Rushton *supra*. ST MARY'S CHURCH (2×); the old church, now in ruins, was taken down in 1848 (Hutch³ 1 422); it is referred to as 'the church of *Estoke by Byndon*' 1403 Pat, *ecclesia de Stoke iuxta Bynedon* p1483 Sheen, *Ruin* 1811 OS, and gave name to *Churchelane* 1474 Weld¹ and *Church close* c. 1628 *Strode,* 1843 *TA, v.* lane, clos(e). The new church was built 1828 (Kelly). SHEPHERD'S PLANT. SOUTH HEATH, S of Farm Heath *supra*. SODDON (lost, SY 893853), 1811 OS, *Sodom Grd* 1843 *TA,* perhaps to be identified with *pastur' apud Suddon* 1323 *Min-Acct,* 'south hill', *v.* sū ð, dūn, but cf. Sodern in Charminster par. *infra*. SPRATLEY WD, 1843 *TA,* perhaps 'wood where poles or spears were got', *v.* sprēot, lēah. SPRUCE ROAD, a plantation, *v.* spruce. STOKE CMN, 1811 OS, cf. *Hr Common* 1843 *TA*. STOKE HEATH. STOKE MILL, *molend' de Stokes* 1244 *Ass, Stoke farme (and Mill)* 1621 (17) *Strode,* cf. *Mulham* 1284 Cl, *Mill Cl* 1843 *TA, v.* myln, hamm; if the identification of the DB manor of *Stoches* with E Stoke *supra* is correct, there was also a mill here in 1086 (VCHDo 3 87). STOKE-FORD CMN & HEATH, cf. *Stockford Fd & Moor* 1843 *TA,* from Stokeford *supra*. TOUT HILL, *v.* tōt-hyll 'look-out hill'. TWENTY ACRE COPPICE, cf. *20 acres* 1843 *TA*. WEST FIELD WD, *campo occidental'* 1359 *Strode, West Fd* 1843 *TA*. WITHY BED, cf. *The Over* —, *ye Nether Withiber* c. 1628 *Strode, the lower withy-beere* 1628 Hutch³, *v.* wīðig, bearu. WOOLBRIDGE HEATH, from Woolbridge *supra*.

FIELD-NAMES

For some fields in E Stoke *TA* but now in other pars., *v.* W Lulworth par. *supra* and Wareham St M. par. *infra*. The undated forms are 1843 *TA* 201. Spellings dated 1280 are Ch, 1284 Cl, 1359, 1621 (17), c. 1628 *Strode,* 1393 *Ct,* 1446 *Rent,* c. 1586 Tres, 1622 Hutch³, 1664 HTax, and the rest *Weld¹*.

(a) All Rush (perhaps alor 'alder' or hall 'large house', with risc 'rush-bed'); Ashley Cl (*v.* æsc, lēah); Back Moor (*v.* back, mōr); Barn Cl; Barrow Cl (possibly to be associated with *la Bergh, la Berwe* 1280, *v.* beorg 'hill, barrow'); Batters Cl (cf. John *Battere* 1393); Bellehuse Md (*Bellhuis* — 1635, *Belhuish Mead(e)* 1638, 117, *Bellhuse Mead* 1703, from Belhuish in

W Lulworth par. *supra*, formerly a detached part of E Stoke par., *v.* mæd);
The Bogs (*v.* bog); Breach (*terre voc' le Breche* 1463, *v.* brēc); Briar's Fd &
Md; Brick Cl (cf. foll.); Brick Kiln (Acre, Cmn & Moor); Broad Lds
(*Broadlands* 1621 (17)); Broad Md (4 Acres); Broom Cl & pce (*Nether* —,
Over Broome close c. 1628, *v.* brōm, clos(e), neoðerra, uferra); Bull Grd &
Mdw (*Bull close*, — *ground*, — *mead* c. 1628, *v.* bula); Butts (*v.* butt¹ or
butte); Candles Moor; Carthouse Grd; Chapel Hill; Coppice Cl & Lane,
Hr Coppice (cf. *the* (*Lower*) *Coppice* c. 1628, *v.* copis); Crabb Mdw (*Grabbe-
med* 1284, *Crabbemede* 1414, *Crabb Mead* c. 1628, cf. *ij pont'* . . . *reperat' int'*
Crawmede (probably for *Crabb-*) *et Stoke* 1414, *Crabbebrygge* 1391, *Crab
bridge* 1621 (17), *Crab's Bridge* 1791 Boswell, *v.* crabbe 'crab-apple', mæd,
brycg, cf. E Stoke *supra*); Deweys Moor (cf. William *Dewy* 1664 (Wareham));
Doreys Md; Drove; Dunnings; East Fd & Grd; 8 & 18 Acres; 11 Acres
(Cowleaze); Eweleaze; Fishers Barn & Plot (cf. Anthony *Fisher* 1664);
5 Acres; Fooks Md (cf. John *Fooke* 1664 (Wareham)); 4 Acres (Md);
14 Acres; Gosloe (cf. Cosloe in Arne par. *supra*); Goulds Ham (cf. William
Golde c. 1586, *Goolds house* c. 1628, *v.* hamm); Gravel Pit Pce; Great Grd
(Copse); Greenwood, Lt Greenwoods; Gunville (probably the surname,
cf. Tarrant Gunville par. *infra*); Hatchet Copse (perhaps hæcc-geat 'hatch-
gate', but cf. *ten' nuper Johannis Haket* 1463); Hayters Acre (cf. Edmund
Hayter 1664 (Wareham)); Hedge Row; West Holme Md (*Westholnemede*
1463, *Westholme Mead* 1640, *v.* mæd, W Holme *supra*); Home Cl & Coppice; Horse Cl & Moor; (Wood in) Hundred House (*v.* hundred, though the
significance of the term here is not apparent; *house* may represent *hows*,
pl. of *how* from hōh 'heel of land'); Hurst (*v.* hyrst); Island (*v.* ēg-land);
Kilkenney (a transferred name from Kilkenny, Eire, cf. Gl 1 27); Lane;
Land; The Lawn (*v.* launde); The Leg, Leg Mdw (*v.* leg); Furzy, Gt & Lr
Line's, Gt Line's Copse, Lines 10 Acres (probably 'arable strips', *v.* leyne,
but the surname *Line* is possible); Linnis (perhaps identical with prec.);
Little Md(w); Loaches; Long Grd; Lower Md; Malm Pit(ts) (*v.* malm
'sand, soft stone', pytt, cf. W 445); Michelmoor (*Mochel-*, *Michelmore*
1463, *Mitchel(l)moore*, *Mitchilmoore* (*Mead*) 1621 (17), *Michel(l)mo(o)re*
1638, 1640, 'great marsh', *v.* micel, mycel, mōr); Middle Fd & Grd;
Milestone fd (*v.* mīl-stān); The Moor, Gt & Lt Moor (*v.* mōr); The Mount
(& Shed); (Gt & Lt) New Grd; Newlands; 9 Acres (Md); Peaklands (*v.*
pēac); Peat Moor (*v.* pete); Pierce's Mdw (cf. William *Pearce* 1664); Pond
Cl; Pound Cl (*v.* pund); Princes Plot; Pylands Acre (*v.* pēo or pie²); Rick
Barton Plot; Road pce; Rough (*v.* rough); Row (*v.* row); The Running
Acre (*v.* running); Rushton Md (1621 (17), — *Meade* 1686, 'meadow of
Ruston' 1318 FF, *v.* mæd, Rushton *supra*); Rushy Moor & Pce; Saw Pit
(*v.* saw-pit); 7 Acres (Md); 17 Acres; Shots Mdw (cf. Mary *Shott* 1664);
6 Acres (Md); 16 Acres; Slip (*v.* slip(p)e); Sloetree Cl (*v.* slāh-trēow);
Spicers Cl & Plot (cf. William *Spicer* 1455 (Winfrith N.)); Stall Cl (*v.*
stall); Stoke Mdw (*Stokemede* 1408, cf. *Estmed(e)* 1284, 1463, *the East Mead*
1621 (17), (*Stoke*) *East mead* c. 1628, *v.* E Stoke *supra*, mæd, ēast); Swan
P.H.; Taplins; 10 & 13 Acres; Thistly Cl; Thoroughfare (*v.* thurghfare);
Three Cornered pce; Tillage Cl (*v.* tillage); Timber Hill; Toddy's Acre
(probably a familiar diminutive of the surname *Tod(d)* from ME *tod(de)*

'fox'); Tumble Down (perhaps a nickname for a rough field, cf. Brickneck in Corfe C. par. *supra*); Turnpike Rd; 12 Acres (Md); West Coppice; Whitegate Md; Witts Md(w); Wood Cl, Hr Wood Grd.

(b) *Cadburys land* 1621 (17); 'Crocker's tenement' 1622; *Dell close* c. 1628 (v. dell); *ham' prati...voc' Dertfordesham* 1463 (v. hamm, probably with a surname from Dartford K); *Eylewyneshey* 1284 (the OE pers.n. *Æðelwine*, or a surname from it, with (ge)hæg); *Estforlange* 1284 (v. ēast, furlang); *Gesefield* (sic) 1284 (v. gōs (nom.pl. gēs), feld); *pastura que vocat' la Gyyng'* 1359 (this form is difficult; it may belong with *La Wysine infra*); *ham' prati...voc' Grangeham* 1463 (v. grange, hamm); *Haverland Field* 1621 (17) (v. hæfera, land); *de la Hyde* 1284 (p) (v. hīd); *de la Hirne* 1284, *atte Hurne* 1405 (both p) (v. hyrne, atte); *La Lac, La Lake* 1299 Banco (v. lacu); *ham' prati...voc' Leuerham* 1463 (v. lǣfer, hamm); *ham' prati...voc' Litulham* 1463 (v. lȳtel, hamm); *the Lords woods* c. 1628; *ham' prati...voc' Medelake* 1463 (v. mǣd, lacu); *ye Middle Wood* c. 1628; *New close* c. 1628; *next the River* 1621 (17); *Pynehey* 1359 (perhaps 'enclosure with a fence held together by pegs', v. pinn, (ge)hæg, cf. Pinhay D 637); *Prestl(e)y* 1621 (17) (v. prēost, lēah); *ham' prati voc' Ryngham* (v. hring, hamm); *Sheepland(s) (Field)* 1621 (17) (v. scēap, land); *Three close* c. 1628 (possibly for *Tree —*, v. trēow); *La Wysine* ('an acre of land in the upper *cultura* extending over —'), *Wychingesham* ('meadow of —') 1284, *pratum voc' Wyngñsham* 1359, *Wiggen ham* c. 1628 (the forms, though somewhat inconsistent, should probably be taken together, and it is possible that *la Gyyng' supra* (if this is for *la Wyyng'*) and *quemdam riuolum voc' Veysyngmore usque lanc' de Stoke* 1446 (in the bounds of *le Hethfild* in Coombe K. par. *supra*) also belong here; possibly 'the wych-elm place', from wice with an -ing[2] suffix, later compounded with hamm and mōr); *ham' prati...voc' Wortham* 1463 (v. hamm; first el. wyrt 'plant, vegetable' or worð 'enclosure').

Wareham Lady St Mary & St Martin

In 1894 the pars. within the borough (Holy Trinity Within, Lady St Mary Within and St Martin's Within) were combined to form the one civil par. of Lady St Mary. In the same year the out-parish of Holy Trinity and parts of Lady St Mary (S of R. Piddle or Trent) were added to Arne, and parts of St Martin and Lady St Mary (N of R. Piddle or Trent) were added to Morden. Wareham is a borough by prescription; the borough bdys were extended in 1931 to include parts of the pars. of Arne and Wareham St Martin.

WAREHAM (SY 924873) ['wɛːəʀəm, 'wɛːrəm, 'wɔrəm]

(æt, into, from, fram, to, on) *Werham* l9 ASC (A) s.a. 784, 876 and 877, m11 ib (C) s.a. 982, 12 ib (E) s.a. 877, *Werham* 893 (e11) Asser, 979–1066 *Coins*, c. 1025 (1562) BurgHid, e12 FW, 12 SD, 1348 Pat, 1405 Cl, *Wer(ha), Wer(h)e(i), Werhn, Wre, Weri* 1066–1087 *Coins*, *Wereham* 1535–43 Leland (*æt, to*) *Wærham* c. 930 DEPN, 12 ASC (E) s.a. 784, 876, 979, 980, 1113

(*on, æt*) *Werhamme* 11 ASC (D) s.a. 979, 980

(*at, æt*) *Warham* e12 ASC (F) s.a. 979, 980, *Warham* 1086 DB
(8 ×), Exon (3 ×), 1148 (1408) Pat, 1194 P *et passim* to 1431 Cl,
Wara, Warh Hy 1 *Coins, War(r)am* 1152–8 MontC, 1244 *Ass et
freq* to 1442 Pat, *Waham* Hy 2 CartAnt (p), *Warrhā* 1214 ClR,
Wharam 1340 NI, *Wareham* 1476 Cl *et passim*
Weyrham 1280 *Ass*

'Homestead by a weir', *v.* wer, wær, hām, cf. Warham He, Nf
(DEPN). Kökeritz 128 thought hamm 'river meadow' a preferable
second el. on account of the town's situation on low-lying land
between R. Piddle and R. Frome, but the overwhelming majority
of the early forms favour hām (*v.* Tengstrand MN 101, where the
spellings for the first el. are also discussed). For the weir and fishery
here, *v.* The Fishery *infra*. Wareham is called *Burgus de Warham*
1288 *Ass, the Burrough of Wareham* 1640 *DCMDeed*, cf. *Warhamhdr'*
1168 P, *Warham maner et hundred* 1425 Ipm which refer to the
hundred of the borough itself (Anderson 124).

WAREHAM PARISHES, CHURCHES
AND CHAPELS

(*v.* Hutch³ 1 97 ff)

ALL HALLOWS CHAPEL (lost), 'the chapel of Allhallows' 1627 Hutch³,
Chappell called Alhallowes 1629 *DCMDeed, All Hallows Chapple* 1747 *Ryder,
formerly Allhallows' Chapel* 1774 Map, situated on the corner of North St.
and Cow St., cf. *Alhalon Well infra.* THE PRIORY, *Lib' Prioris de* — 1280
Ass, prioratum de Warham 1288 *ib*, 'prior and monks (convent) of St
Mary('s), *War(e)ham*' 1290, 1329 Pat, *prior de Warham* 1291 Tax, '(alien)
priory of *Warham*' 1348, 1376 Pat, *domus de Warham* 1355 Hutch³, *Priory*
1774 Map, cf. *the Pryorye Close infra*; for this priory, which was founded e12
as a cell to the abbey of Lyre, as well as for the earlier Anglo-Saxon monas-
tery (where Edward the Martyr's body was temporarily housed, cf. St
Edward's Bridge in Corfe C. par. *supra*), *v.* VCHDo 2 121–2. ST JOHN'S
CHAPEL (lost), *capellam Sancti Johannis Baptiste* p1483 *Sheen, peece of
ground where sometimes stood the Church of St John* 1629 *DCMDeed, formerly
St Iohn's Church* 1774 Map, cf. St John's Hill *infra.* ST MARTIN, *parochia
Sancti Martini* 1340 NI (— *de Wharam*), 1350–1615 *DCMDeed* (— *iuxta
Wareham*), 'the church of St Martin, *Wareham*' 1348–1388 Pat, *ecclesia
Sancti Martini* 1428 FA, (*capelle Omnium Sanctorum que nunc dicitur*)
capella Sancti Martini (*de Wareham*) p1483 *Sheen, the Parish(e) of St*

Martens, -in(s) 1593–1640 DCMDeed, Marten's parish 1623 Hutch[3], St Martins (Church) 1707 Eg, c. 1753 DROMap, cf. Martin's Lane infra; the church in Wareham belonging to the abbey of Horton in 1086 DB is thought probably to be St Martin's by VCHDo 3, 26, 40. ST MARY, Ecclesia beate Marie (Prioris de Warham) 1291 Tax, 1428 FA, p1483 Sheen, 1547 DCMDeed, parochia beate Maria (virginis) (in Wareham) 14 Marten, 1584 DCMDeed, parochia Sanctæ Mariæ de Wharam 1340 NI, Ecclesia beate Marie virgine de Warham 1445 DCMDeed, cimiterium Sancte Marie p1483 Sheen, our(e)-, Owre Lady —, Ladie(s) Church(e) 16 Pitt, 1545 DCMDeed, 1577 AD V, 1620 DCMDeed, parische of our lady 1545 ib, ecclesia parochialis beate Marie de Wareham 1560 ib, our lady parishe 1584 ib, (the) Church Yard(e) (of our Ladies church) 1620 ib, 1747 Ryder, 1774 Map, (Lady) St Marys Church c. 1753 DROMap, 1774 Map, cf. Church Lane & St., Church Green infra; the prior of Wareham was the rector of St Mary's church, v. The Priory supra; the church in Wareham with one hide of land held by the Abbey of St Wandrille in 1086 DB (VCHDo 3 82) may belong here (Eyton 129–130, RCHMDo 2 304). ST MICHAEL (lost), par(r)ochia Beati|Sancti Michaelis (de War(h)am) l13 Wim, 14 Marten, 1340 NI, 1428 Hutch[3], 1510, 1584 DCMDeed, 'church of St Michael, Warham' 1339–1376 Pat, Ecclesia Sancti Michaelis 1428 FA, grounde of...Saynt Michaelles 1548 DCMDeed, the parish of St Michaell 1629 ib, St Micha(e)l(l)s (Church) 1707 Eg, c. 1753 DROMap, formerly St Michael's Church 1774 Map, cf. St Michaels Lane infra. ST NICHOLAS (lost), parochia Sancti Nicholi de Warham 1356 DCMDeed, capella Sancti Nicholi p1483 Sheen. ST PETER (lost), 'church of St Peter, (Warham)' 1348–1392 Pat, parochia Sancti Petri (in Wareham) 1419, 1547, 1584 DCMDeed, Ecclesia Sancti Petri 1428 FA, St Peters 1550 DCMDeed, 1707 Eg, c. 1753 DROMap, peteres peryshe 1561 DCMDeed, the parish of St Peter 1629 ib, Town Hall formerly St Peter's Church 1774 Map; according to Hutch[1] 1 32 the church was rebuilt as a town-hall in 1768. HOLY TRINITY, Ecclesia Sancti, -e Trinitatis (de War(e)ham) 1291 Tax, 1399 AddCh, 1428 FA, p1483 Sheen, 1510 DCMDeed, 'church of Holy Trinity, Warham' 1294, 1387 Pat, parochia Sancte, -ae Trinitatis de W(h)ar(h)am 14 Wim, 1340 NI, 1584 DCMDeed, capellam Sancte Trinitatis p1483 Sheen, Trenitie parish 16 Pitt, parys(s)(c)h(e) of the blessyd Tr(e)ynyt(i)e 1545, 1548 DCMDeed, the Trynyt(y)e (church) 1565, 1584 DCMDeed, Trinity parish 17 Pitt, — Church c. 1753 DROMap, 1774 Map, the parish of St Trinity 1629 DCMDeed, cf. Trinity Lane infra; this church is to be identified with 'the chapel of St Andrew' and 'the chapel of the Holy Trinity' held by Sherborne Abbey in 1145 and 1163 respectively (Hutch[3] 1 101, VCHDo 2 65). Unidentified is capelle de Warham 1329 Rawl, cf. capellano de Warham 1244 Ass.

WAREHAM STREETS AND BUILDINGS

ABBOTTS QUAY (TGuide), from the Abbot of Sherborne who was patron of the church of Holy Trinity supra, v. Quay infra. BELL'S ORCHD (LANE), cf. Bells Lane, Bells Orchard Close 1747 Ryder, Bells garden 1707 Eg, Symond

Bell 1623 Hutch³. BRIXEYS LANE, 1774 Hutch¹, cf. John *Brixey* 1747 *Ryder*, Brixes Isle in Arne par. *supra*; this lane is called Nundico in TGuide, *v. infra*. CARRION LANE (lost), 1747 *Ryder*, probably eModE carrion 'garbage, etc.'; there is a mention of a refuse heap near St Mary's in 1582 WeyR, cf. this clause in the constitutions of the borough 1623: 'And that no carrion or noysome thing be put or laid in or about the town to the greevance of the people, it is ordered, that all such carrion, filth, or noysome thing, shall be burned in some convenient place' (Hutch³ 1 126). CHURCH LANE & ST., *the heigh Waye to Owr lady churche* 1545 *DCMDeed, Owr-, Our Lady(e)* —, *Ladie Stre(a)te* 1548, 1552 *ib*, 1580, 1582 AD V, (*Lady St Marys or*) *Church Lane* 1747 *Ryder*, c. 1753 DROMap, named from St Mary's Church *supra*. CONNIGER LANE, 1774 Map, *Conegar* — 1747 *Ryder*, cf. *Cuniger Close* c. 1628 *Strode*, 'a meadow called *Conygeare* beyond the E walls, near the river' 1774 Hutch¹, *v.* coninger 'rabbit-warren'. COW LANE, *Cow Street(e)* 1679 *DCMDeed*, 1774 Map, perhaps a drove for cattle, or where they were sold, *v.* cū. DOLLINS LANE (lost), 1774 Map, *Dollings* — 1747 *Ryder, Bollins Lane* (sic) c. 1753 DROMap, cf. John *Dol(l)ing* 1621 (17) *Strode* (E Stoke), 1664 HTax. EAST ST., 1747 *Ryder, vico orientali* 1445 *DCMDeed, in orientali vico...versus Bestwall* 1547 *DCMDeed, the Est(e) Stret(e)* 1545, 1561 *ib*, *thest streatte* 1550 *ib*, *v.* ēast, cf. Bestwall *infra*. EAST WALLS, *by the easte walles* 1584 *DCMDeed, Garden next East Walls* 1747 *Ryder, v.* Town Walls *infra*. HATTERS (6″), SHATTER'S HILL (TGuide), cf. Walter *Hatter* 1434 *DCMDeed*, Lawrence *Shatter* 1664 HTax. THE HIGH STREET (lost), 1623 Hutch³, *Wareham Heigh strete* 1545 *DCMDeed, the high streate* 1548 *ib, the (other) Heyghe Strete* 1561 *ib, v.* hēah; no doubt a collective term for the whole line of East St.–West St. or North St.–South St., cf. High East St. in Dorchester par. *infra*. HOWARD'S LANE, 1774 Map, *Haywards als. Black Lane* 1747 *Ryder, Black Lane or Haywards Lane* c. 1753 DROMap, *Hayward's or Dugdales Lane* 1763 Williams, possibly the surname *Hayward*, but more probably an allusion to the officer called the hayward whose duties are described in the 'constitutions' of the borough 1623 as 'keeping the kine and horses about the comens and comonable ground' (Hutch³ 1 126–7), cf. William *Dugdale* 1770 Williams, *v.* blæc 'dark'. KING EDWARDS CRESCENT, perhaps in allusion to King Edward the Martyr, *v.* The Priory *supra*. MARKET PLACE (lost), c. 1753 DROMap, *forum (de Warham)* 1268 *Ass*, p1483 *Sheen, the markettplace* 1548, 1629 *DCMDeed*, cf. *the Pigg markett ib*, Cattle Market 6″, St John's Hill *infra, v.* market; on the market in Wareham, *v.* Hutch³ 1 94. MARTIN'S LANE, 1774 Map, *Bonnet(t)s (Lane) or St Martins Lane* 1747 *Ryder*, c. 1753 DROMap, *Bernards' Lane* 1762 Williams, probably named from St Martin's Church *supra* at the back of which it runs, but cf. *Harry M'tens lane* 1545 *DCMDeed; Bonnet(t)* and *Bernard* are surnames, cf. Stephen *Bonnett* 1770 Williams. MILL LANE, 1747 *Ryder, Myllane, Millane* 1461 *DCMDeed, North Mill Lane* 1658 DCMDeed, leading to Mill Ho (earlier *North Mill*) *infra, v.* myln. MORETON'S LANE, *Groupe Street, Groop Lane, Lane from East Street to North Walls* 1747 *Ryder, Mortons Lane or Groop Lane* c. 1753 DROMap, *Mortons Lane* 1774 Map, cf. Richard *Morton* 1545 Hutch³; the earlier name may be from OE grōp(e) 'a ditch, a drain' or from OE grāpian 'to grope', the latter commonly used of a dark and disreputable alley, cf. YE 289, O 40. NEW ST., 1747 *Ryder*, also called *Hobb's Lane* from John *Hobbs* 1770 Williams. NORTH ST., c. 1753 DROMap, *the north streete* 1584 *DCMDeed*, *the heigh waye from Wareham...to the... northe bridge* 1586 *ib*, v. norð, cf. North Bridge *infra*. NORTH WALLS, 1747 *Ryder*, *the North Walles* 1628 *DCMDeed*, *the heigh waye...from the north bridge...to the west walles* 1586 *ib*, v. Town Walls *infra*, cf. North Bridge *infra*. POUND LANE, 1747 *Ryder*, v. pund; the pound is at the W end of the lane. QUAY, c. 1753 DROMap, *the key* (*of Warham*) 1548 *DCMDeed*, 1623 Hutch³, 1747 *Ryder*, *le Key in Warham* 1548 *DCMDeed*, *Hayters Quay* 1770 Williams, v. kay, cf. Abbotts Quay *supra*, George *Hayter* 1702 Williams; on the history of the quay, and for regulations governing its maintenance and use in 1623, v. Hutch³ 1 93-4, 126; on the history of Wareham as a port, v. Hutch³ 1 93 and VCHDo 2 177 ff. ROPER'S LANE, 1545, 1548 *DCMDeed* (*the* —), *Roopers Lane* 1673 DCMDeed, 'lane where the ropemaker(s) lived', v. ropere. ST MICHAEL'S LANE (lost), 1747 *Ryder*, *venelle que ducit versus ecclesiam Sancti Michaelis* 1428 Hutch³, *St Michals Lane* c. 1753 DROMap, *a lane called Marcombs or St Michael's* 1774 Hutch¹, named from St Michael's Church *supra*; *Marcombs* is probably from the surname *Markham*. SHATTER'S HILL, v. Hatters *supra*. SOUTH ST., c. 1753 DROMap, *in austral' vico* 1560 *DCMDeed*. STRECHE RD (TGuide), cf. Walter *Stretch* 1297 FF, John *Stre(e)che* 1389 Hutch³. TANNERS LANE, c. 1753 DROMap, 'lane where the tanner(s) lived', v. tannere, cf. Walter (*le*) *Tannere* 1327 SR, 1340 NI. TINKER'S LANE, 1733 DCMDeed, *Tinckars Lane* 1584 *DCMDeed*, *Tinckers Lane* 1673 DCMDeed, 'lane where the tinker(s) lived', v. tynkere; called *Pinchers Lane* (perhaps an error) 1762 Williams. TOWN WALLS, *ex opposito magni muri* 1l3 *Wim*, *muros de Warham* 1445 *DCMDeed*, *prope muros occidentales* 1510 *ib*, (*the*) *west wall(e)s* 1545 *ib et freq* to 1747 *Ryder*, *the town(e) walles* 1545-1550 *DCMDeed*, *the walles of Warham* 1586 *ib*, *Shortwalls* 1747 *Ryder*, v. wall, cf. East Walls and North Walls *supra*; the walls, the remains of 10th cent. ramparts, still enclose the town on W, N and E, v. Hutch³ 1 94-5, RCHMDo 2 303-4. TRINITY LANE, 1658 DCMDeed, *Trinite lane* 1510 *DCMDeed*, *Trynyt(i)e lane* 1517, 1548 *ib*, named from Holy Trinity Church *supra*; it follows the line of the bailey of the 12th cent. castle, v. Castle Cl *infra*. WEST ST., c. 1753 DROMap, — *Streete* 1707 *Eg*. WYATT'S LANE, c. 1753 DROMap, *Wyats* — 1747 *Ryder*, 1767 Williams (— *or Black Lane*), cf. John *Wiatt* 1664 HTax, Howard's Lane *supra*.

Lost street-names include *blyndlane end* 1602 *Feth* (v. blind, lane, ende, probably in Keysworth *infra*); *Cheakinlane* 1551 *DCMDeed*; *Clover Square* 1747 *Ryder* (v. clāfre); *in australi parte Magne Crucis* 1517 *DCMDeed*, *by the broken Crosse* 1545 *ib*, *houses near the Cross* 1747 *Ryder* (v. cros); *Folly Lane* 1855 Williams (near a 'folly', also called *Mount Pleasant* (ib)); *parua venella* 1547 *DCMDeed* ('little lane'); *a lyttle lane...callyd lommes londe* 1548 *DCMDeed*, *lomes lane* 1552 *ib*, cf. *lommeslotte* (meadow) 1548 *ib* (probably the surname *Lo(o)m*; lane shows confusion with land, v. hlot); *Turnpike-gate* 1824 Pigot (with reference to one of the three turnpike roads leading W, N and S out of Wareham on 1774 Map).

Buildings include ALMSHOUSES, *in domo pauperum de* —, *domui elemosine de Warham* 1418 Hutch³, *domui elemosinarii* 1547 *DCMDeed*, *(the) Alm(e)s-hows(s)e, -hous(s)e (of Warham)* 1545–1671 *ib*, 1774 Map, Hutch¹, cf. *le Almes garden* 1517 *DCMDeed*, *terr' pertin' domui elemosinarii* 1547 *ib*, *the Allmeshousselonde* 1548 *ib*, *a garden belonging to the Almeshousse* 1551 *ib*, *the Almes Land* 1707 *Eg* (*v.* ælmesse, hūs, gardin, land; the almshouse was rebuilt in 1741 and again in 1908 (Kelly)); *Cart House* c. 1753 DROMap; *Dairy House* 1747 *Ryder*; *Dissenter's* (sic) *Meeting House* 1774 Map; *The Free-School* 1774 Hutch¹; *the parsonage of Saint Martens,* — *Saynt Martyns* 1545, 1548 *DCMDeed* (*v.* St Martins Church *supra*); *toftum rectorie ecclesie Sancti Michaelis* 1428 Hutch¹, *Parsonage of St Michael* 1624 *Pitt* (*v.* St Michael's Church *supra*); *ye parsonage of ye trynytie* 1551 *DCMDeed*, *Parsonage House* 1747 *Ryder*, 1774 Map (*v.* Holy Trinity Church *supra*); *the New Porch, the Porch upon the Key* 1707 *Eg* (*v.* porch, cf. Quay *supra*); *domus Sancti Leonardi de Warham* 1288 *Ass*; *School House* 1747 *Ryder*; *le Storehouse* 1572 *Comm*, *a toft called the Storehouse* 1627 Hutch³; *Town Hall formerly St Peter's Church* 1774 Map (*v.* St Peter's Church *supra*).

Inns include *the Anchor* 1707 *Eg*; *(the) Angel(l) (Inn)* 1707 *Eg*, 1842 *TA*; *Antelope* 1824 Pigot; *Bear Inn* 1747 *Ryder*; *Black Bear* 1824 Pigot; *Brick-layer's Arms* 1824 Pigot; *Bull head Inn* 1747 *Ryder*, *a house then known by the sign of the Bull-Head* 1762 Hutch³; *Country House* 1824 Pigot; *Duke of Wellington* 1824 Pigot; *Duke of York* 1824 Pigot; *Fox & Lamb* 1826 Gre, — *Inn* 1842 *TA* (at SY 944915); *Golden Lyon Inn* 1747 *Ryder*; *Hit or Miss* 1824 Pigot; *Horse & Groom* 1824 Pigot; *Kings Arms (Inn)* 1747 *Ryder*, 1824 Pigot; *Lord Nelson* 1824 Pigot; *New Inn* 1824 Pigot; *(the) Red Lyon (Inn)* 1707 *Eg*, 1747 *Ryder*, *the Red Lion* 1861 Hutch³; *Rising Sun* 1824 Pigot; *Rose & Crown (Inn)* 1747 *Ryder*, 1824 Pigot; *the Salmon Inn* 1770 Williams; *the Swan* 1707 *Eg*; *Three Tuns* 1824 Pigot; *White Hart* 1824 Pigot; *Windmill Inn* 1747 *Ryder*.

BESTWALL FM ESTATE, N & S BESTWALL FM (SY 927875), N BESTWALL HO (SY 931882)

Beastewelle 1086 DB, *Bestewelle, Estwelle* 1280 *Ass*, *Bestwell* 1284 Cl

Bustewalle 1293 Ipm

Biestewalle 1293 Ipm, *Byestewall(e)* 1310 FF (— *juxta Warham*), 1316 FA, 1399 Cl, *Brestewalle* (for *Bieste-*) *juxta Warham* 1315 FF, *Biestewalles* 1412 FA, *Beestewalle by Wareham* 1440 Cl

Byestwall 1412 FF, p1483 (— *iuxta Wareham*), 1627 Hutch³ ('the mansion-house of the farm of —'), *Beestwall* 1431 FA, *Biestwall* 1495 Ipm, *Byeastwall* 1613 Hutch¹, 1690 Hutch³ (*Lower* —)

Biwestwalles (sic) 1412 FA

ecclesia de Byestawell p1483 *Sheen*

Bestwall 1547, 1552 *DCMDeed et passim*, *Bestwall Farme* c. 1628 Strode, *North* —, *South Bestwall, Lower Bestwall* (or *Twynham*)

1774 Hutch[1], *Bestwall or Twyneham* 1795 Boswell, *Bestall Farms* 1826 Gre, *Upper or Bond's Bestwall* 1861 Hutch[3]

'(Place) to the east of the wall', *v.* bī, ēastan, wall, describing its situation just outside the east walls of Wareham, cf. East Walls, Town Walls *supra*. *Twyn(e)ham* would mean '(place) between the rivers (Piddle or Trent, and Frome)', *v.* betwēonan, ēa (dat. pl. ēam), cf. Twineham Sx 279, Twinham Ha (DEPN), but it is possible that *Twyn(e)ham* is an error for *Swyn(e)ham*, *v.* Swineham *infra*. *Upper or Bond's Bestwall* is another name for South Bestwall, cf. Denis *Bond* 1653 Hutch[3].

BUSH-HEAD GDN (lost, about SY 925877), c. 1753 DROMap, *loco vocat' Beresherd* 1445 DCMDeed, *unu' croft' in Warham voc' Birdesierd* 1456, 1457 Weld[1], *1 croft iuxta Warham vocat' Birdeseyrd* 1461 *Rent*, *Butsherd* 1545 DCMDeed, *Butshot(t) Ground* 1545, 1547 *ib, uno gardino apud busharde* 1584 *ib*. The second el. is gerd 'measure of land' or geard 'enclosure'. The first el. is probably a pers.n. or surname; it may be tempting to connect it with the *Burde* who held Rushton (3 miles W of Wareham in E Stoke par. *supra*) TRE (VCHDo **3** 95), and whose name Feilitzen 211 thinks may be from OFr *Burdel*, a derivative of Lat *burdo* 'mule', cf. also the surnames Robert *Berde* 1332 SR, Edward —, John *Burd* 1664 HTax (all Wareham), though other origins are possible for these (*v.* Reaney s.n. *Beard, Burd*). A somewhat similar name to this one is Bridzor W 197 (*Bredesherd* 1207, *Brudesherd* 1208, etc.).

CAREY (FM) (SY 904881, 897884) ['kɛːri], *Kerre, Keire* 1220 Cur, *Carry* 1318, 1409 FF, *Karree* 1355 *Wim*, *Karry* 1431 FA, *Carye Farm* 1611 Hutch[3], *North Cary or Cold Harbour* 1774 Hutch[1], 1861 Hutch[3], *South Cary* 1774 Hutch[1], 1861 Hutch[3] (*— or Cary Mills*), cf. *Cary Mill* 1811 OS. It is tempting to suppose that this is perhaps a Brit r.n. identical with R. Carey D 3 and R. Cary So (*v.* Ekwall RN 70f, Jackson 612–3), which may then have been an earlier name for (the lower course of) R. Piddle or Trent on the N bank of which Carey and Carey Fm stand, cf. Keysworth Fm *infra*. However, as Professor Löfvenberg points out, the double *r* in the ME forms tells against this derivation. There was a grist-mill and a tucking-mill here in 1611 Hutch[3], and a paper-mill in 1774 Hutch[1]. For Cold Harbour, *v. infra*.

CASTLE CLOSE (SY 922873), c. 1753 DROMap, *pastur' infra castr'*
ville de Warham 1393 *MinAcct*, *Castell close* 1548 *DCMDeed*, *Castle
Hill* 1582 Hutch³ (*close called —*), 1595, 1610 ib, 1774 Hutch¹, the
site of the former 12th cent. castle which is referred to as *cast' de
Warham* 1369 *MinAcct* and which was no doubt the home of
Geoffrey *de Castello* 1280 Ch and William *de Castro* 1319 *MinAcct*,
cf. also *Castle Close Lane* 1716 DCMDeed, *v.* castel(l), clos(e), hyll,
King's Works **1** 40, **2** 852, RCHMDo **2** 324–5. Trinity Lane *supra*
follows the line of the castle bailey. *Castellum Warham* 1086 DB
and various 12th cent. references to 'the castle of Wareham' belong
under Corfe Castle *q.v.* in Corfe C. par. *supra*, cf. King's Works **1** 27,
2 852; in *castellum quod dicitur Werham* 893 (e11) Asser, 12 SD (both
s.a. 876), the reference is certainly to Wareham, but ASC s.a. 876 has
simply (*into*) *Werham*, and *castellum* here must refer to the Anglo-
Saxon burh (Asser's use of *castellum* showing that Wareham had
been fortified by 893, possibly already by 876).

THE FISHERY (SY 922871), on R. Frome, referred to as 'Elizabeth
de Burgo's free fishery at Wareham' 1327 Pat, *Salmon Fishery* 1774
Map, cf. *de piscaria per totam aquam Frome* p1483 *Sheen*; it is often
alluded to in conjunction with the fishery to the N of the town on R.
Piddle or Trent, as in *totam piscarinam duorum cursuum aquar' vocat'
North and South river, et quod' stagn' vocat' a Weare fixat' sup' le
South ryver* 1542 Hutch³, 'the fishery in the North and South
Rivers' 1595 ib; for other references to the fisheries at Wareham, *v.*
VCHDo **2** 320.

E & W HOLTON (SY 963914, 953908), HOLTON FM (SY 961913),
Holtone 1086 DB, *Holton* 1211 Cur (p), 1318 FF, 1332 SR (p), 1412,
1431 FA *et passim*, *Westholton* 1593 *Feth*, *DCMDeed*, 1602 *ib et freq*,
East Holton Farme 1663 *DCMDeed*, 'farm in or near a hollow', or
'farm in or near a wood', *v.* hol¹, holt, tūn, with ēast, west; the
bounds of 'the comon of heathe' at Holton are given in 1597 *Feth*.

KEYSWORTH FM (SY 939891), *Kaerswurth* 1227 FF, *Karesworthe,
Keresworth iuxta Warham* 1309 *Ass*, *Kisworthe* 1469 IpmR, *Kes-
worth(e)* 1575 Saxton, c. 1586 Tres, 1591 *Feth*, 1795 Boswell,
Cays(e)-, Kays(e)worth(e) 1589–1593 *Feth*, *Keys(e)-, Keisworth(e)*
1592–1612 *ib*, 1618 *CH*, 1811 OS, (— *alias Caysworth*) 1640
DCMDeed, possibly 'enclosure by the river *Carey*', or 'enclosure
belonging to Carey', *v.* worð, Carey (Fm) *supra*; Keysworth Fm

stands on the N bank of R. Piddle or Trent some two miles downstream from Carey (Fm). However, as Professor Löfvenberg points
out, the earliest forms suggest OE cærse, cerse 'cress' as first el.,
with later loss of r possibly due to dissimilation, cf. DEPN s.n.
Kesgrave Sf; 'cress enclosure' is therefore a more likely interpretation. The form *Kaerswurth* 1227 is tentatively identified with
Charisworth in Charlton M. par. *infra* by Fägersten 111; for the
present identification of *Kaerswurth* (said to be a member of *Acford*,
i.e. Shillingstone par. *infra*), cf. the tithing in Cranborne hundred
listed as *Shillingston cum Keysworth* in Hutch[3] 3 369, and the various
members of the family of *Skilling* or *Skyllyng* involved in writs
concerning Keysworth in 1309 *Ass*.

NORTHPORT (SY 920881), *Northeport iuxta Warham* 1370 *DCMDeed*,
Northport (iuxta Warham) 1381 *ib*, 1398 *Cecil*, 1422 *Midd*, 1545
DCMDeed, *North-Port* 1774 Hutch[1], probably '(place) to the north
of the town', *v.* bī, norðan, port[2], although there are no traces of bī
in the forms, cf. Westport Ho, *Portmanmore infra*; in 1774 Hutch[1]
it is described as 'a small farm just without the walls of Wareham'.

PORTMANMORE (lost), 1291 (16) *Pitt*, 1469 FF, *Portmannemour* 1319
MinAcct, *Portman moure* 1545 *DCMDeed*, 'marshy ground belonging
to the townsmen', *v.* port-mann (gen.pl. -*manna*), mōr, cf. *Port-
mannis medewe* 1510, 1517 *DCMDeed*, 'townsman's meadow', *v.*
mǣd, perhaps identical with *Port(e)lond(e) meado(w)e* 1548–1551
DCMDeed, *Portlandmede* 1561 *ib*, *Portland Mead(ow)* 1689 DCM-
Deed, 1707 *Eg*, *Portham meade infra parochiam Sancti Michaelis in
Wareham* 1584 *DCMDeed*, *Portham commonly (called) Portland
(Meadow)* 1774 Hutch[1], *v.* port[2] 'town', land, hamm, cf. Northport
supra, Westport *infra*; in 1774 Hutch[1], *Portham* is described as part
of 'a large common for cattle, belonging to the townsmen'.

WESTPORT HO (SY 921871), *Bywesteport* 1264 Ipm, *Westeport(e)*
1274 FF, 1316 FA, 1327 *Ass*, — *iuxta Warham* 1336, 1370 *DCMDeed*,
Westport(e) 1276 Cl, (— *iuxta Warham*) 1288 *Ass*, FF, 1381
DCMDeed et passim, *Wesport* 1367 (1372) *ChrP*, 'land in the Westport' 1393 Fine, *the housse of the sayd Westporte* 1548 *DCMDeed*,
cf. *Westport(e)moore, a waye callid the drove that enteryth thorough
the sayd Westportegrounde* 1548 *ib*, probably '(place) to the west of
the town', *v.* bī, westan, port[2], with hūs, mōr, drove, grund; formally,
Hutch[1] 1 30 could be right in supposing that 'it takes its name from

its situation near the West gate or port of Wareham', *v.* port³, cf. *portam occidentalem de Warham* n.d. (1372) *ChrP, mes'...iuxta portam occidentalem ville de Wareham* p1483 *Sheen,* but the el. port³ is rare in p.ns. and would certainly be less appropriate for the analogous Northport *supra* which lies ¼ mile N of the town wall, cf. also *Portmanmore supra.*

ASHCROFT, *v.* æsc, croft. N BESTWALL WITHY BED (*Withey Bed* 1843 *TA* (E Stoke)) & WD, from N Bestwall *supra.* BIRCH PLANT. & WD (1842 *TA*). BLACK HEATH, BLACKHEATH CTG. BLACK HILL, 1811 OS. BLOODY BANK, 1774 Hutch¹, a stretch of the town wall, 'so called from the execution there of Mr. Baxter, Mr. Holman, and several others, who fell a sacrifice to their attachment to the Duke of Monmouth, in the year 1684; they were tried and condemned at Dorchester assizes, and ordered to be executed at Wareham by the infamous Judge Jefferies' (Hutch³ 1 94), but cf. DoNHAS **66** 68. BOWLING GREEN, 1747 *Ryder,* cf. 'a little square work...now called the Bowling-Green, having formerly been applied to that use, but seems designed for some military purpose' (Hutch¹ 1 23), cf. RCHMDo **2** 326. BRICK KILN PLANT., cf. *Brick Kiln Pond and Grd* 1842 *TA,* from Old Kiln *infra.* BROOMHILL COPPICE, *Bromehill* 1593 *Feth, DCMDeed,* 1612 *Feth, -hilles* 1615 *DCMDeed, the Weste —, the east Broome Hill* 1602 *ib, Broomehill(s)* 1612 *Feth,* 1627 *DCMDeed, Broom Hill 11 Acres, Broomhill Mdw, Broom Hills* 1842 *TA, v.* brōm, hyll, cf. *Bromie Moore* 1593 *Feth, Browne* (sic) *more* 1597 *ib, Brome more* 1612 *ib, v.* brōmig, mōr. (E) BROWN DOWN PLANT., 1842 *TA, E, Middle* & *W Brown Down, Brown Down Coppice* 1842 *ib, v.* brūn¹, dūn. BUCK'S COVE (ISLAND), cf. William *Bucke* 1437 DCMDeed, *v.* cove. CAMP CTG, cf. *Camp Grd* 1842 *TA,* perhaps an ancient site, *v.* camp² 'encampment'. CAREY HEATH, *Cary* — 1811 OS, from Carey *supra.* CARRIAGE PLOT, near Sandford Ho *infra.* CHRISTMAS CLOSE (1″), 1707 *Eg,* 1843 *TA,* cf. *Christmas Land, parte of Christmas, viz. the greate house* 1707 *Eg,* cf. Robert *Crissmasse* 1532 DCMDeed. CHURCH GREEN (TGuide), 1747 *Ryder,* cf. *Owr lady Ch(o)urche ground(e)* 1545, 1548 *DCMDeed, a garden belonging to the chourche of our lady* 1551 *ib, ten' ecclesie parochialis beate Marie de Wareham* 1560 *ib,* cf. St Mary's Church *supra.* CLEAN HOLLOW PLANT., 1842 *TA, v.* clǣne. COLD HARBOUR, 1811 OS, *North Cary or Cold Harbour* 1795 Boswell, 'shelter from the cold', or 'cold shelter', *v.* cald, here-beorg, cf. Carey *supra;* it is situated on the Bere R.–

Wareham road. COLD HARBOUR HEATH, from prec. THE COVERT, *v.* covert. COWLEAZE COPPICE, cf. *Cowleaze* 1842 *TA*. THE DECOY (*Decoy* 1811 OS, *Decoy Pond* 1846 *TA* (Morden)), DECOY HEATH & Ho (both 1811 OS), OLD DECOY POND (1846 *TA* (Morden)), from decoy 'pool with netted approaches for the capture of wildfowl'. DIGBY'S CTG, 1842 *TA*. DOUBLE BOW, a plantation, so named from its shape. DRIVE PLANT., *v.* drive. DUCK POND. EIGHT-HATCH PLANT., *v.* hæc(c) 'hatch-gate, wicket', though the reference here could perhaps be to sluices or floodgates on R. Piddle or Trent. FANCY'S ROW, cf. *Field by Fancys, Fancy's Drove* 1842 *TA*, perhaps a surname from ME *fantasie, fantsy* 'apparition; whim; desire, etc.', *v.* rāw, drove. FERNCROFT FM, *Vernicroft* 1774 Hutch[1], *v.* fearnig, croft. FISH POND. FORD PLANTATIONS, from *Ford* 1811 OS, on R. Piddle or Trent where the par. boundaries of E Stoke, Bere R. and Wareham St M. meet, *v.* ford, cf. *Ford fd* 1842 *TA*, Ford Heath in E Stoke par. *supra*. FURZE BRAKE, 1842 *TA*, *v.* fyrs, bræc[1]. GARDEN WD. GIGGER'S ISLAND, *Giggers island* 1774 Hutch[1], — *Isle* 1811 OS, an island in Poole Harbour named from the local *Gigger* family (John *Gigger* 1584 Hutch[3], etc.), cf. *Giggars* 1707 *Eg, the house late Gigger's* 1774 Hutch[1], Jiggers Ham in Arne par. *supra*. GLEBE HO (TGuide). GOLD COURT (lost), 1545 *DCMDeed* (*Tenement called* —), 1774 Hutch[1], *Gould Court* c. 1753 DROMap, *v.* court; the first el. is probably a surname, cf. *terr' ad caput pontis de Froma in parte occidentali ubi Osmundus aurifaber mansit, Edwardo Golde de Warham de...mes'... inter ecclesiam Sancte Trinitatis...et ripam que vocatur Wroune, Rob' Gold de Warham* p1483 *Sheen*, cf. South Bridge *infra*, Holy Trinity Church *supra*, R. Frome in RNs. *infra*; in Hutch[1] I 21 it is described as follows: 'On the South side of the key was a large old house...called Gold-Court. It seems to have been the habitation of a family of note who owned it. One *Robert Golde* of Wareham frequently occurs, t. E.III in old deeds. But tradition says it had its name from gold, etc. being coined here, when the mint existed.' For the Anglo-Saxon mint at Wareham, *v.* ASCoins 145. GORE FDS (*Gore Fd* 1846 *TA* (Morden)) & HEATH (1811 OS, — *heathe* 1597 *Feth*), *v.* gāra 'gore of land', here describing the large triangular area bounded by the Wareham–Morden road, the N bdy of Wareham St M. par., and the old bdy of Morden par. (as in 1846 *TA*). GRAVEL PIT, cf. *le gravell pytt* 1602 *Feth*, *v.* gravele, pytt. GUNNING'S CORNER. THE HASSOCKS, *v.* hassuc. HAZEL COPPICE, 1842 *TA*. HEATH CTG(s), named from some of the extensive heathland in this par., cf. *le heathe* 1584 *DCMDeed*, *Southe heathe* 1589, 1597 *Feth*, *the comon of heathe* 1597 *ib*, (*N & S*) *Heath, Inclosed Heath, Heath in plantation, Heath Land* (*E of the Hill*), *Heath pasture* 1842 *TA, v.* hǣð. HILL VIEW. HOLLY COPPICE, cf. *Holme Bush Close* 1627 *DCMDeed, v.* holegn, busc. HOLTON CLUMP, HEATH (1811 OS), HEATH CTG, MERE (*Shore Lake* 1811 OS) & POINT, from E & W Holton *supra, v.* mere[1], scor(a), lake. HOMEMEADOW COPPICE, *Home Md* 1842 *TA*, cf. *the Home acre* 1602 *DCMDeed, Home Cl*, (*E & W*) *Home fd* 1842 *TA, v.* home. JUNIPER, 1846 *TA* (Morden), a plantation, *v.* juniper. KEEPER'S LODGE. KEYSWORTH POINT, 1811 OS, from Keysworth *supra*. KING'S BRIDGE, *Kyngesbridge* 1593 *DCMDeed, Kingbridge* 1597 *Feth, Clay bridge otherwise called Kingesbridge* 1628 *DCMDeed, v.* cyning, clǣg, brycg, cf. *terr' Regine* 1547 *DCMDeed, a* (*greate*) *garden of the kinges Ma'tes* 1548, 1551 *ib*, *Kings Plot* 1842 *TA* (perhaps a surname); the bridge carries the Wareham–Poole road across Sherford River and was no doubt used in the transport of clay from the pits around Wareham to Poole. KING'S BRIDGE COPPICE, *King —* 1842 *TA*, from prec. LAUREL CTG. LODGE PLANT., 1842 *TA*, from Wareham Lodge in Bere R. par. *infra*. LODGE WD, from South Lodge *infra*. LONGMEADOW COPPICES, *Long Mdw* 1842 *TA*. LOWER POND, cf. Higher Pond in Morden par. *infra*. MIDDLE BRIDGE, COPPICE & COPSE. MILL HO, *molendini aquatic' voc' North Mill iuxta Warham* 1451 *Weld*[1], *the northe myllys* 1525 *Pars*, 'two water-mills, called North Mills, and a marsh' 1545 Hutch[3], (*the*) *North Mill*(*s*) 1613 Hutch[3], 1774 Map, 1795 Boswell, *Mill and Mdw* 1842 *TA*, cf. *Mill Crofts, Mill Ham Pasture* 1842 *ib, Mill Moor* 1846 *TA* (Morden), *v.* norð, myln, hamm; the mills were situated just outside the N wall of Wareham on R. Piddle or Trent; *John atte Mulle* 1370 *DCMDeed, molendinum Prioris de Warham* 1392 *ib*, and *molendino de Wareham* p1483 *Sheen* may also belong here, but cf. Wareham Mill *infra, v.* atte. MORDEN HEATH (1826 Gre), from Morden par. *infra*. NARROW PLANT., 1842 *TA*. NEW MEADOW COPPICE, *New Mdw* 1842 *TA*. NORTH BRIDGE, *pontem de Pedle* p1483 *Sheen*, (*the*) *Nort*(*t*)*he Brygge* 1520–1 *Pars, a great bridge of vi. archis over Trent ryver, alias Pyddildour* 1535–43 Leland, *the northe bridge* 1584–1628 *DCMDeed*, 1774 Hutch[1], *v.* norð, brycg, R. Piddle or Trent in RNs. *infra*, cf. South Bridge *infra*. NORTH CAUSEWAY, *causeway between the North bridge and North port* 1774 Hutch[1], *v.* caucie, cf. North Bridge and Northport *supra*, South Causeway in Arne par. *supra*. NORTH CHANNEL, 1811 OS, in Poole Harbour.

NORTH LODGE, cf. South Lodge *infra*. NORTHMOOR FM, *v.* mōr.
NORTHPORT HEATH, from Northport *supra*. NUNDICO, occurs twice
6″, once as the name of a long strip of low-lying heathland 1½ miles
N of Wareham and W of the Wareham–Morden road (*Nundice* 1846
TA (Morden)), and once as a name for the quarter of the town of
Wareham near the W wall (though in TGuide it is given to Brixeys
Lane *supra* which is in this quarter); the name is obscure, unless it is
intended to represent the Lat phrase *non dico* (1st pers.sg. pres. indic.
of *dicere*) 'I do not say', or *non dic* (2nd pers.sg. imperative) 'do not
say', perhaps used as a frivolous or waggish name either for an
otherwise nameless place, or for a place with improper associations,
cf. *Groop Lane*, an earlier name for Moreton's Lane *supra* which
crosses Brixeys Lane. (OLD) NURSERY, cf. *Lr & New Nursery* 1842
TA. OAK GROVE, 1842 *ib*, cf. *Oakwood* 1842 *ib*. OLD KILN, *Old Kiln,
Pits, Bldgs and Rough Grd* 1842 *TA*, *v.* Brick Kiln Plant. *supra*.
OLD RAM, bdy stones where the par. bdys of Bere R. and Wareham
St M. meet the old bdy of Morden (as in 1846 *TA*), perhaps so called
from their fancied resemblance to a ram, *v.* ramm. OLD RAM PLANT.,
1842 *TA*, from prec. OVAL PLANT., 1842 *ib*, so called from its shape.
GT OVENS HILL, cf. *the Hollowaye called Ovens* 1597 *Feth*, perhaps a
surname, cf. William *atte Ouene* 1332 SR (Woodlands), denoting one
who lived at an oven or furnace, *v.* ofen; for *Hollowaye* 'hollow way',
v. hol², weg. PART SQUARE PLANT., 1842 *TA*, cf. *Heath land Square
Plant.* 1842 *ib*, so called from its shape; 'Part' is no doubt elliptical for
'part of'. POND PLANT., 1842 *ib*, from Fish Pond *supra*. RIVER HO
(TGuide), near R. Piddle or Trent. ROCK LEA JETTY & WD, cf.
Rockley Coppice, Fd & Moor 1842 *TA*, from Rock Lea Point in
Hamworthy par. *infra*. ROUNDABOUT, 1842 *TA*, a plantation, named
from its shape, cf. Wa 336. RUSHY BOTTOM, 1811 OS, *Bushy —* 1826
Gre, *v.* botm. ST JOHN'S HILL (TGuide), *St Joanes Hill* 1623 Hutch³,
St Iohns Hill 1774 Map, *a waste piece of ground called St John's or
Jones's Hill or the Saw Pits* 1774 Hutch¹, cf. *Saw Pitt(s) Green* 1747
Ryder, c. 1753 DROMap, *Sawpits* 1824 Pigot, named from the lost
St John's Chapel *supra*, cf. *peece of ground where sometimes stood the
Church of St John* 1629 DCMDeed, *v.* hyll, saw-pit, grēne²; in the
'constitutions' of the borough 1623 it is stated that on market day
'the swine that are to be sold shall be brought to St Joanes Hill'
(Hutch³ **1** 125). ST MARTIN'S HILL, in Wareham St Martin par.
SANDFORD (BRIDGE, FM, HO & RD), *Sanford Ditche* 1606 *Feth*,
-*Bridge* 1791 Boswell, *Sampford Mill* 1671 Drax, *Sandford (Bridge)*

1811 OS, *Sandford Moor & Plot* 1842 *TA*, 'sandy ford', *v.* sand,
ford, dīc; the ford was where Sandford Rd (*the waye from Wareham
to Southe Lytchett* 1597 *Feth*) crossed a now unnamed tributary
(perhaps *Sanford Ditche*) of R. Piddle or Trent. OLD SAND PIT.
SEVEN BARROWS, 1811 OS, tumuli beside the Bere R.–Wareham road.
SHAG LOOE, *Shaggloo* 1811 OS, a channel in Poole Harbour, named
from *Shagrock* 1609, 1626 Hutch[1], perhaps from shag 'cormorant',
with rokke, lo, cf. Wood Bar Looe *infra* and Broad Looe in Arne par.
supra. SHEPHERD'S PLANT., 1842 *TA*, cf. *Shepperds Gdn* 1842 *ib.*
SMITH'S KILNS, cf. *Smyths* 1707 *Eg*, *House late Smiths* 1747 *Ryder*,
Andrew *Smith* 1664 HTax. SOUTH BRIDGE, 1774 Hutch[1], *Pontem de
Wareham, Warrhame Bridge* 1381 (16) *Pitt*, 'the bridge of *Wareham*'
1383 Pat, *pontis de Froma* p1483 *Sheen, a fair bridge of vj. archis upon
Fraw or Frome River* 1535–43 Leland, (*one landinge place callyd*)
Warham Bridge 1565 *SPDom*, c. 1586 Tres, *the South bridge* 1584
DCMDeed, Wareham Bridge 1774 Hutch[1], *v.* sūð, brycg, cf. R.
Frome in RNs. *infra*, North Bridge *supra.* The present bridge was
built in 1927. SOUTH LODGE, cf. North Lodge *supra.* SWINEHAM,
1675 Hutch[3] (*South* —), 1811 OS, *Swynham, a close of pasture* 1650
Hutch[1], *Swinesham* 1715 Hutch[3], cf. *Swineham Home Fd, Swineham
N & S Cowleaze, Swineham River Bank, Swinehams 8 Acres* 1843
TA (E Stoke), probably 'water-meadow where swine were kept', *v.*
swīn[1], hamm, cf. Swineham Gl **2** 67, but its situation between the
mouths of R. Frome and R. Piddle or Trent where they flow into
Poole Harbour makes swin[2] 'creek, channel' a possible first el., cf.
also Bestwall *supra.* SWINEHAM POINT, from prec. TABLE PLANT.,
1842 *TA*, near to *Table ld* 1842 *ib*, perhaps ModE table in some
literal or topographical sense. TANTINOBY FM. TRIANGLE PLANT.,
1842 *TA*, cf. *Triangular pce & Plant.* 1842 *ib*, so named from their
shape. (N) TRIGON FM, TRIGON HO, TRIGON HILL (1842 *TA*, *Gt.
Trigdon* 1811 OS), (LT) TRIGON HILL PLANT. (1842 *TA*), cf. *E & W
Trigon Grd, Heath Land Little Trigon Hill, Trigon tree plant.,
Trigon Vales* 1842 *TA*, probably from trigon 'a triangle' (1600 NED),
describing the shape of the hill or the farm, although 1811 OS has
interpreted it as a compound with dūn 'hill'; an earlier name for
Trigon Hill (and/or Fm) was *North Hungerhill* 1774 Hutch[1], 1861
Hutch[3] (— *or Trigon, — now called Trigon Hill*), *Hungerhull* 1318
Ch, *Hunigerhill* 1464 *Weld*[1], *Hungerhill* 1483 *MinAcct*, 1484 IpmR,
Hungerill c. 1628 *Strode*, cf. *Hungerhill Heath* 1811 OS, a con-
temptuous name for poor land, *v.* hungor, hyll; 'north' to dis-

tinguish it from S Hungerhill in E Stoke par. *supra*. WAREHAM CHANNEL, 1811 OS, — *Channell* 17 *DROMap*, in Poole Harbour, *v.* channel. WAREHAM COMMON, *Warham common* 1551 *DCMDeed*, *The Common* 1612 *Feth*, 1795 Boswell, cf. *the northe comon* 1597 *Feth*, *a large common for cattle* 1774 Hutch[1], (*The Inner*) *Common* 1842 *TA*, *v.* common. WAREHAM MILL, 1824 Pigot, probably identical with *the West myll* 1550 *DCMDeed*, *two water mills called West Mills* 1636 DCMDeed, *Westmills* 1774 Hutch[1], *West Mill* 1861 Hutch[3], *v.* west, myln, cf. *Mill gdn & Homestead* 1843 *TA*, Millditch Md in Arne par. *supra*, and Mill Ho *supra*. WEST FD COPPICE, cf. *le Westfeild Shard* 1589 *Feth*, *Westfeild yate* 1592 *ib*, *le Westfilde* 1593 *ib*, *West Fd* 1842 *TA*, *v.* west, feld, sceard 'gap', geat 'gap, gate'; 'west' in relation to Keysworth Fm *supra*. WEST WD, 1842 *TA*, 'west' in relation to Birch Wd *supra*. WITHY BED, cf. *Willow Bed* 1842 *TA*, *Withey Bed* 1843 *TA* (E Stoke), *Withy Bed* 1846 *TA* (Morden). HR & LR WOOD. WOOD BAR LOOE, *Woodbarloo* 1811 OS, a channel in Poole Harbour, perhaps one 'obstructed by a wooden bar', *v.* barre, lo, cf. Shag Looe *supra*. WOODBINE CTG. YOUNG'S FM, cf. John *Young* 1606 Hutch[3].

FIELD-NAMES

For some fields in Wareham Lady St M. *TA* but now in Arne, and for all fields in Wareham Holy T. *TA*, *v.* Arne par. *supra*. Fields in Morden *TA* but now in Wareham are marked †, and fields in E Stoke *TA* but now in Wareham are marked ‡. The undated forms are 1842 *TA* 241 (Wareham St M.) or 1843 *TA* 240 (Wareham Lady St M.) (but those marked † are 1846 *TA* 152 and those marked ‡ are 1843 *TA* 201). Spellings dated 1280 are Ch, 1280[2] *Ass*, 1284 Cl, 1288 FF, 1291 (16), 17[2] *Pitt*, c. 1295, 1477, 1510, 1547, 1561, 1562, 1631, 1650, 1688, 1689, 1698, 1722, 1733, 1748 DCMDeed, 1319, 1393 *MinAcct*, 1327 *SR*, 1332 SR, 1340 NI, 1340[2] Pat, n.d. (1372) *ChrP*, 1383, 1388, 1555 Hutch[3], 1457 *Weld*[1], p1483 *Sheen*, c. 1500 *RoyRoll*, 1582 AD, 1589, 1590, 1591, 1592, 1593[1], 1597, 1602[2], 1606, 1611, 1612 *Feth*, 1590[2] *Hen*[2], 17 *Rent*, 1664 HTax, 1707 *Eg*, 1747 *Ryder*, c. 1753 DROMap, 1774 Hutch[1], 1854 alt. app. (*TA* 241), and the rest *DCMDeed*.

(a) Alder Bed; Aldown (*Alldown* 1854); Andrews Ham (*v.* hamm); Appletree plot; Arable fd. ‡Ash Grove (cf. Richard *de Fraxino* 1284); †Backside Fd (cf. *uno parcella terr' vocat' a backesyde* 1584); Bailiffs House (cf. Ralph *Baillif* 1340, William Coxe, *bailiff* 1547); Barn Cl (Plant.), Barn Grd, ‡Barn Pce; †Barn(s) Plot (cf. Thomas *Barnes* 1664); Barrack fd; (Plant. in) Barrow Hill (*Barrow Hill* (*close, -Moores*) 1627, *v.* beorg); Belt (*v.* belt); ‡Bestwall Mdw & River Bank (from Bestwall *supra*); Bog (Ld), Boggy fd, †The Bog (*v.* bog); Bonds Cl (cf. Terence *Bonde* c. 1295); Breach

(1593[1], *v.* brēc); †Brick Kiln Plot; Broad Md; Brooks (cf. John *Broke* 1477);
Broom Cl; Browns Ctg, Plot & Plant.; †Bugbys Beaches (*v.* bēce[2]); ‡Bushy
Md; Calves Plot; Chafins 1774 (cf. William *Chaffyng* 1332 (Holt)); Chalk
Pits; Clay Pits; Clump (*v.* clump); Coneygar (*v.* coninger); Coppice and
River Walk (cf. *Copice Close* 1593[1], *v.* copis); ‡Cottage fd; Cottage Gdn &
Dairy Plot; ‡Cowleaze (Moor); Cox's Coppice, Mdw & Plot (cf. Hugh
Cok 1332, William *Coxe* 1547); Currant Corner (cf. William *Courant*
1561, *v.* corner); Days Moor; Dorys Cl; Drove Grd (cf. *a Waye callid the
drove* 1548, *v.* drove); ‡Drove Wd (cf. prec.); East Fd (cf. *le Estfield* 1593[1]);
East Mdw (cf. *le Estmeade* 1593[1], *Eastmeade* (*bridge*) 1611, 1612); ‡East
River Bank; East Wd; 8 Acres; ‡Lr 18 Acres; 11 Acres; Emberleys Md &
Plot (cf. Stephen *Em(b)erly* 1631, 1650); Entrance Plant. (*v.* entrance);
Farm fd; †Fenwicks 10 Acres; Ferney Cl (*v.* fearnig); (Lr) Firs, Middle
Firs (Plant.) (*v.* firr); 5 Acres; ‡The Ford Cl (*v.* ford); 4 Acres (*Fower* —
1602[1]); 14 Acres (Plant.) (*Fowerteene acres* 1627); Furze (Pasture), Furzey
Pce (cf. *the furses* 1602[2], *v.* fyrs); ‡Gilliams Leaze (cf. John *Gillam* 1664
(Wool), *v.* lǣs); †Gradys Fd; Gravel Hill Grd; Great Moor; Hanging Grd
& Moor (possibly from hangende 'steep, sloping', but perhaps places where
criminals were hanged); †Harveys (cf. Julian *Harvey* 1664); †(Lt) Hatchings
(Coppice), Hatchings 12 Acres (perhaps an -ing[2] derivative of hæcce
'fence'); Lr & Upr Heartsease (*v.* heartsease 'tranquility', also a name for
the wild pansy); †Hedge Row; Higher Fd; †Higher Pce; Hill Pce; †Hill
Cl; W Holton (Great) Md (from W Holton *supra*); ‡The Horse Island;
(‡Hr & Lr) Horsemoor; Hospital plot (cf. *Spytle* 1590, *claus' voc' Spittle*
1593[1], *Spittill Corner* 1597, *v.* spitel 'hospital, religious house', corner;
perhaps to be associated with the 16th cent. hospital in Wareham noted in
VCHDo **2** 107, or with the lands held in Wareham by the Knights Hospital-
lers noted in VCHDo **2** 92); †Hovel pce; 120 acres Plant.; Upr & Lr
Hutchins, †Hutchings Md (*Howchines* (*Keye*), *Westhowchen, claus' de Rowgh
grounde voc' Westhutchines, claus' voc' Esthutchines, Esterhutchens* 1593[1],
Moory grounde called Hutchines Key 1593[2], *Easter Hutchens* 1606, cf. Joan
Howchyns 1510, *v.* key, west, ēast, ēasterra); Island; West Ivy Bush;
Keysworth Drove & Heath (from Keysworth *supra*); †(Lt) Knappy Pce
(*v.* cnæppig); †Land; ‡The Lawn (*v.* launde); †Lenningtons 4 Acres &
Md; ‡Limekiln Fd; †Little Fd; Little Md (*Litle Meade* 1545 DCMDeed);
Little Plot; ‡Lodge Cl; Long Cl; †Long Fd; Long Grd; Long Lds; Long
Lawns (*v.* land or launde); Lovelace's (Coppice); †Lower Acre Plot;
†Lower Fd; ‡(Hr) Lower Md; Lower Plot; †Marsh's Heath; Mead pce,
(The) Meadow (cf. *the meade* 1707); Middle Cl, Fd & pce; Miles's Md;
†Mitchells Rough Pce (cf. Richard *Myhell* 1457); E & W Moor; Mud
Moor; Nethouse (Md) (*v.* neethowse); Nevilles Drove (cf. Edward *Neville*
1555); New Cl & Grd; New England (probably a nickname for a remote
field); (‡Lr) 9 Acres; North East & North West fd; Oat Fd (cf. *Oate close*
1602[1], *v.* āte); The One Acre; The Orchard; Organ Coppice & Md (from
Organ in Lytchett Min. par. *infra*); Pain(e)s Cl 1747, c. 1753 (cf. William
Payne 1383); (Lt) Paddock (cf. *lez Parrockes* 1593[1], *v.* pearroc); Park Cl
(*Parke Close* 1593[1], 1627, *v.* park); Parsons Moor (cf. *the parsons meddoo
of the Trynyte, pratum apertinent' parsone exclesie Trinitatis* 1565, *v.* persone,

mǣd, cf. Holy Trinity Church *supra*); ‡Patch Croft (*v.* patche 'small plot
of land', but cf. *Poschescrofte* in Winfrith N. par. *infra*); Peaked Cl & Plot,
†Peaked Grd (*v.* peked); Peak fd (*v.* pīc); †Peat Moor (*v.* pete); Phippards
Grd (cf. William *Phippard* 1747); Pickards (Mdw); Pinhorns pce; Plain
fd (probably plain 'flat meadow'); Pleasure Grd; Plot; Pond Grd; Pooles
Ctg; Ram Corner (*v.* ramm); ‡Red Cliff Mdw (from Redcliff in Arne par.
supra); Rickbarton; ‡Rodgers Moor; Rough Grd & Pce; †Rough Plot;
Row Pce (*v.* rūh (wk. obl. rūgan) 'rough'); Rye fd (*v.* ryge); Gt & Lt Salt
Marsh (*v.* salt[2], mersc); (The) 7 Acres (*Seaven acres* 1602[1]); ‡17 Acres;
†Shoulder of Mutton (so called from its shape); Shrubs (*v.* scrubb); Sidelong
Plot (*v.* sidelong); (The) 6 Acres; 16 Acres; 60 Acres plant.; Slade Cl (1627,
v. slæd); Slip (*v.* slip(p)e); Small Plot; ‡South Mdw; Spear Bed (*v.* spear,
bedd); Square fd; Strap (*v.* strap); ‡Strip (*v.* strip); ‡13 Acres; (Hr & Rough)
3 Acres; Three Cornered Plot; Tongue (*v.* tunge); Plant. against Turnpike;
12 Acres (1280 ('meadow called —')); (Second) 20 Acres; †2 Acres; Vale
(*v.* vale); Wadding (Place) (perhaps wād 'woad' with -ing[1] or -ing[2]); (New)
Water Mdw; Way Cl (*v.* weg); Well Cl (1627, *v.* wella); Well Plot; West
Md (*le Westmeade* 1593[1], *v.* west, mǣd); ‡West Mdw; West Plant.; N & S
White grd (*v.* hwīt); East of Wood, Little Wd; Woolfrys Rough Pce (cf.
Thomas *Wolfreis* 1562).

(*b*) *Acres claus'* 1589, *claus' voc' Akers* 1593[1] (the surname *Acres*);
Alhalon Well 1545, *Allhollan well* 1582 (from All Hallows Chapel *supra*, *v.*
hālga (gen. pl. hālgena), wella); *Baycroftes* 1597 (perhaps beg 'berry' with
croft); '3 acres in the tillage called *le Bye* near the high way' 1288 (*v.* byge[1]
'river-bend', probably with reference to a bend in R. Frome); *Buishops more*
1628 (*v.* biscop, mōr, but cf. William *Bisshopp* 1707); *Boveknollcroft* p1483
(held by Robert *Boveknoll ib*, 'above the hillock', *v.* bufan, cnoll, croft, but
the surname may derive from Bucknowle in Ch. Knowle par. *supra*);
Brandishayes 17 (the surname Brand, *v.* (ge)hæg); *Broad(e)sharde iuxta Mar'*
1593[1], 1593[2], 1602[1], *Broadsheard in Holton* 1631 (*v.* brād, sceard, cf. Holton
supra); *Broode Yate close* 1597 (*v.* brād, geat); *Brocmore* 1589 (*v.* brōc
'stream' or brocc 'badger', with mōr); *Bucklondes Close* 1560 (perhaps
'close at *Bucklond*', *v.* bucc 'buck', land); *Bucknams Close* 1552, 1620,
Buckmans Close 1584 (perhaps 'close at *Bucknam*' ('he-goat's enclosure'),
v. bucca, hamm, influenced by the surname *Buckman*); *a garden lying at
Bull Stake* 1707 ('stake used for bull-baiting', *v.* bula, staca, cf. Bulstake
Bridge O 35); *de la bure* (p) n.d. (1372) (*v.* būr[1]); *tenement called Bythewoods*
1748 (cf. John *Bythywood* 1664, — *Bythewood* 1707); *the Corne feild* 1591
(*v.* corn[1]); (*la-, le-, the*) *Corner(e) Gardyne, -den* 1510[2], 1517, 1552 (*v.*
corner, gardin); *londes late apperteyninge to the late fraternitye of corpus xp̄i*
1550, *2 gardens still known by the name of Corpus Christi* 1774 (cf. 'in the
town was anciently a fraternity, gild, or chantry, called Corpus Christi'
1774 Hutch[1] 1 21); *uno gardino in paroch' Sancti Petri in Wareham voc' le
Crooked garden* 1584 (*v.* croked, gardin); (*burgag' voc'*) *Denneworthe, -worthi*
n.d. (1372) (perhaps 'Denna's enclosure', from an OE pers.n. *Denna* (cf.
Denny Hill Gl 3 202) and worð, worðig); *Dye House Close* 1747 (*v.* dey-hus
'dairy'); *Fromondesmulle* 1336 (cf. John *fromund* n.d. (1372), *Joh' Fremond
de Wareham*...*ten' iuxta capellam Sancte Trinitatis* p1483, *v.* myln, cf.

Holy Trinity Church *supra*); *atte Gate* (p) 1393 (*v.* atte, geat); *Gillingham's* 1707; *the Goodman* 1597 (in the bounds of 'the comon of heathe' at Holton *supra*, perhaps elliptical or some special use of the word goodman 'head of a household, etc.'); *cultura que vocat' la Goore* 1336 (near Westport *supra*, *v.* gāra, cf. Gore Fds *supra*); *the Grove close* 1602¹ (*v.* grāf(a)); *le gullyes* 1589 (*v.* gully); *atte Halle* (p) 1327, 1332, 1340² (*v.* atte, hall); *North Hawes* 1722, *West Hawes* 1733 (*v.* haga¹); *Hollys garden* 1584, *Holleses* 1707 (the surname *Holly(s)*); *Holwell lake* 1589, *Hollowelake* 1602² ('stream called *Holwell*' ('hollow stream'), *v.* hol², wella, lacu); *place called Hoopers Crosse* 1597 (cf. *mess' quod' Will' le Oupere tenet* 1319, Peter *le hopere* p1483, *v.* cros); *claus' voc' ye urne crofte* (*v.* hyrne, croft, cf. Robert *Atterhurn de Cnolle* 1280², *v.* atter; *Cnolle* is probably Ch. Knowle par. *supra*); *Judas garden*...*given to the mainteynance of a light called Judas light* 1629 (*v.* gardin); *Keysworth Slyte* 1590² (from Keysworth *supra*, *v.* slæget); *pratum quod vocat' Langemede apud Westeport quot iacet iuxta Ripam de Frome* 1336 (*v.* lang¹, mæd, cf. Longmeadow Coppices and Westport *supra*, R. Frome in RNs. *infra*); *Loveridge's* 1707; *Marple hedge* 1589 (perhaps mapel 'maple-tree', with hecg); *Martins howse* 17², *Martin's Pitch* 1707 (*v.* pitch 'place where a stall is set up, etc.'); *Matravers Meade* 1698; *Mead(e)lake(s)* 1589, 1592, 1602², *Meadelake close* 1593¹ (*v.* mæd, lacu); *Newberryes Lands, Newburryes* 1707 (cf. Mr *Newboroughe* 1547); *Oakelys* 1707 (cf. John *Okeley* c. 1500); *Picked close* 1597 (*v.* picked); *Play Skinn Lae* (sic) 1627; *Prestescroft* 1319, p1483 (*v.* prēost, croft, cf. *terr' Rector' Martini* 1547²); *the Pryory(e) Close* 1548, 1552, *le Priorie Close* 1552, *the Priory grownde, Priory Howse, — House* 1620 (from The Priory *supra*); *Ropers londe* 1550 (*v.* land); *Ruyschenam, -an* 1545, *lyt(t)le Ruyssh(e)nam* 1548 ('rushy enclosure', *v.* riscen, hamm, with lȳtel); (*prato de) Sacmore* 1291 (16), c. 1295², *Sack(e)mour(e)* 1545, *meddoo yn Sakemouer* 1565 (perhaps 'marshy ground disputed about in a lawsuit', *v.* sacu, mōr); *Shamelys* 1419 (*v.* sc(e)amol); *claus' voc' Sharpeford* 1593¹ (*v.* scearp 'sharp, steep', ford); *messuage called Shergalls* 1688; *Smedmore's* 1707; *Southmore* 1612 (*v.* sūð, mōr); *Standerwoddes garden* 1561², *-woodes-* 1584 (probably a surname from a p.n. meaning 'stony wood', *v.* stæner, wudu); *Stanfordbridge* 1597 ('bridge at *Stanford*' ('stony ford'), *v.* stān, ford, brycg); *Stoclonde* 1319 (probably from stocc and land, cf. foll.); *Stockele* 1477² (probably 'tree-stump clearing', *v.* stocc, lēah, cf. prec.); *Strande Close* 1593¹, *Strond Close* 1606 (*v.* strand); *Sudden Hill* 1597 (probably 'south hill', *v.* sūð, dūn); *the towne gardyns* 1548 (*v.* toun, gardin); *Westhayes* 1593¹ (*v.* west, (ge)hæg); *White's Tenement* 1689; *Wyccheworthe* 1319 (probably 'enclosure by the wych-elm(s)', *v.* wice, worð); *Wynedsweare lake, -waye* 1611 (cf. Stephen *Wynard* 1388, *v.* wer, lacu, weg); *Wolland* 1597 (probably from well(a) (WSax wyll(a)) and land).

Warmwell

Watercombe par. *infra* was formerly in this par. (Hutch³ 1 339).

WARMWELL (SY 753859 ['wɔ:məl]

Warm(e)welle, Warmemoille 1086 DB, *Warmewella* Exon

Werm(e)well(e) 1152–58 MontC, 1205 FF, 1209 P (p), 1210 ib (p), Cur, 1214, 1215 ib, 1217 FF, 1236 ib (p), 1244 *Ass et freq* to 1353 *Midd* (p), 1518 *Ampthill, -wull(e)* c. 1165 MontC, 1242–3 Fees, *-wel* 1244 *Ass* (p), *-vill* 1271 Ch, *-wl* 1291 Tax, *-wolle* 1293 *Ilch* (p), e14 *Wim* (p), 1303 FA, m14 Hutch[3]

Warm(e)well(e) 1166 RBE (p), 1203, 1204 (p), 1210, 1212, 1214 Cur, 1244 *Ass* (p) *et passim, -wule* 1201 FF (p), *-wulla* Hy 1 *AddCh, -woll* 1311 *Weld*[1] (p), 1346 FA (p), *-wull* 1340 NI, *-wel* 1389 *Weld*[1], *-wyll* 1405 *ib, -will* 1437 FF

Weremew(e)ll(e) 13 *Weld*[1] (p), 1244 *Ass* (p)

Wermell 1244 *Ass* (p), 1288 *ib*

Wearmwlle Hy 3 (14) Cerne (p)

Warwell 1412 *Weld*[1]

Warmell 1440, 1471 *Weld*[1], 1510 *Ampthill*, 1682 *Weld*[1], *Warmull* 1575 *Saxton*

Wermeswyll 1498 *Ampthill*

'Warm spring', *v.* **wearm** (wk. obl. *wearman*), **well(a)** (WSax **will(a), wyll(a)**); a spring is marked (6″) ¼ mile N of the village.

BEECH FM & PLANT., *v.* **bēce**[2]. BLACK HILL (CLUMP), *Black Hill (Fd), Blackhill Heath* 1843 *TA* (W Knighton), *v.* **blæc, hyll**. BRICK HILL (COPPICE), near Works (6″). (OLD) CHALK PIT, cf. *Chalk Pit Furlong (at the Pit)* 1841 *TA, la Pytte in Churchefurlong* 1466 *Weld*[1], *v.* **pytt, furlang,** cf. Checkforlands *infra* and foll. CHURCH (Holy Trinity), cf. *ecclesiam de Wermewell* c. 1165 MontC, *ecclesia de Warmewulla* Hy 1 (14) *AddCh, ecclesiam Sancte Marie de Warmewell* Steph (14) *ib, Churchelane* 1440 *Weld*[1], *Churcheforlong* 1393 *ib, -furlong* 1466 *ib, v.* **cirice, lane, furlang**. EVENINGS FORD, perhaps the surname *Evening, v.* **ford**, but this name is possibly connected with Empool in W Knighton par. *infra q.v.* FOXHOLES WD, *v.* **fox-hol**. THE GLEN, *v.* **glen**. GRAVEL PITS. HOPE WD, cf. *cursus aque apud le Hop* 1466 *Weld*[1], *Hope Md* 1841 *TA, v.* **hop**[1] 'small enclosed valley'. KEEPER'S LODGE. LASTRIDGE WITHY BED & WD, cf. *Lastridge Plant. & Copse* 1841 *TA*, perhaps from **hrycg** 'ridge' with the OE pers.n. **Lǣsta* postulated by Ekwall DEPN for Lastingham YN, or, as Professor Löfvenberg suggests, possibly from **hrycg** and **lǣs** 'pasture', with intrusive *t* between *s* and *r*. MOREY'S ORCHD, cf. *unu'*

Toftu' cot' cum j Withebar nuper in tenur' Dauid Moris 1450 *Weld*[1],
Moreys Md 1841 *TA*, *v.* wīðig, bearu, cf. Willow Bed *infra*. NORTH
HEATH (1841 *TA*), — FM, N of Warmwell Heath *infra*. OUTER
HEATH, *v.* ūterra. PATS CASTLE CTGS & PLANT., *v.* castel(l); perhaps
a jocular name, at least no archaeological remains have been noted
here. THE PLANTATION, cf. *Plantation* (& *Coppice*) 1841 *TA*.
PLOUGHMAN'S COPPICE, *Plowmans* 1841 *TA*. POLE COPPICE, *v.* pāl
'pole' or pōl[1] 'pool'. RYECLOSE, probably from ME *atter ie* '(place)
at the stream', *v.* atter, ēa (dat. sg. *īe*); it lies on the S bank of the
now nameless stream on which Warmwell Mill *infra* is situated.
SAND PIT. STROUD'S MOOR WITHY BED, *Strouds Moor* 1841 *TA*, cf.
Stroud's Bridges 1791 Boswell, *John Strode* (*de Watercombe*) 1599
Whil, Hutch[3]. TYNEHAMS WITHY BED, cf. Walter *Tyn(h)am* John
Hutch[3], 1332 SR. VYSE BARN, cf. *At Vyes stonen still* 1841 *TA*,
Henry *Vye* 1664 HTax; *stonen still* perhaps means 'enclosure made
of stone', *v.* stānen, stell (WSax stiell), cf. *Still'place infra*. WARMWELL
CROSS (lost), 1863 Hutch[3], a cross-roads, *v.* cross. WARMWELL DOWN
BARN, *Warm(ew)ellesdoun* 1453–1462 *Weld*[1], *Warm(ew)eldoun* 1465,
1466 *ib*, cf. *the Sheepe Downe* 1618 *Mansel, Down, Further Down
Fivelands,* (*Yonder*) *Down Grd* 1841 *TA*, *v.* dūn. WARMWELL DROVE,
cf. *Droves Md* 1841 *TA*, *v.* drove. WARMWELL HEATH, 1811 OS,
Warmewell Heath 1639 *Mansel*, cf. *Heath* (*Plot*), E *Heath* 1841 *TA*.
WARMWELL HO, *the mansion house* 1861 Hutch[3]. WARMWELL MILL,
1811 OS, cf. *Mill Md* 1841 *TA*; there were two mills in Warmwell in
1086 DB (VCHDo **3** 89, 108), and mills are mentioned here in 1320
FF, Hutch[3], 1323 ib, cf. also John — 1327 *SR*, 1332 SR, Henry
atte Mulle 1332 ib, *v.* atte, myln. WARMWELL NEW LODGE.
WARMWELL WD.

FIELD-NAMES

The undated forms are 1841 *TA* 242. Spellings dated Ed 3, 1333, 1335,
1657 are Hutch[3], 1327 *SR*, 1332 SR, 1604, 1618, 1639 *Mansel*, 1664 HTax,
and the rest *Weld*[1].

(*a*) Banch Drove (perhaps for *Bench* —, *v.* benc, drove); Upr & Lr
Batts; Berrys; two meadows called Bounds (cf. Cuthbert *Bound* 1657);
Calves Cl; Checkforlands (probably identical with *Chalkefurlong* 1466, *v.*
calc, furlang, cf. (Old) Chalk Pit *supra*); Hr & Lr Cooks (cf. *lez Cokkes*
1458, *v.* cocc[1], but perhaps a surname, cf. Robert *Koc* 1327); Coppice;
Counters Md; Cowleaze; East Fd (*la Estfeld* 1466, *v.* ēast, feld); Farm
Gdn & Hedge; Fineham (Coppice) (perhaps 'wood-pecker's enclosure', *v.*
fina, hamm); Footlands (Coppice) (*v.* fōt, land); Forehill (*v.* fore, hyll);
14 Acres; Furzey Cl; Golehays (*claus' voc' Goldheys* 1454, from gold or golde,

and (ge)hæg, but cf. Robert —, William *Galey(e)* 1332; there are medieval settlement remains here (RCHMDo 2 329)); Goose Hams (*v.* gōs, hamm); Grants House (cf. John *Graunt* 1664); Great Fd & Barn; Great Plant. & Coppice; The Green (*pastur' voc' le Grene* 1458, *v.* grēne²); (the Green in) Green Hill (*v.* grēne¹); (Eastern & Western) Home Cmn; Horse Cl (cf. *Horswell* 1438, 1466, *v.* hors, wella); Kennel & Cl; Kneels Knap (*v.* cnæpp); Long Lemmons (cf. William *Lumman* 1664 (Woodsford)); Lime Kiln Cl; Hr, Lr & Middle Md; Middle Fd (*la Myddelfeld* 1466, *v.* middel, feld); Mount (Coppice) (*v.* mont); Mynty Cl (perhaps analogous with Minety Gl 1 77, from minte 'mint' and ēg 'water-meadow'); (Lt) New Cl (*New Close* 1639, cf. Purselands *infra*); New Md; Overleach (probably '(land) across the stream or bog', *v.* ofer³, lece); Oxmead; Pease Cl (*v.* pise); Pigs Closes; Pitty Cl; Pound Gdn, Hr & Lr Ponds (*v.* ponde); Pound Lane & Waste (*v.* pund, cf. *ponfald* 1438); Poxwell Gate & Hedge (from Poxwell par. *supra*); Rough Purslands, Purslands Md (*Purselands Meadowe, Purse-lands alias the New Closes* 1639; the first el. is probably a surname, cf. Thomas *Purse* 1664 (Winfrith N.), *v.* land, mæd, cf. New Cl *supra*); Rack Cl (*v.* rakke, near Tucking Mill Md *infra*); Salisbury Md, Salisbury's Plant. & Copse; Samways Cl (the surname *Samways*); 6 Acres; Small Coppice; Stanleys (cf. John *Standly* 1664); Tallwers (probably a form of the surname *Taillefer, Telfer*); 10 Acre; Thornhills; Three Cornered Plot; Tucking Mill Md (cf. Rack Cl *supra*); 24 acres; Watercombe Eweleaze (from Watercombe par. *infra*); Westburys (probably a surname); (At the Crook in the Hedge) West Fd (*la Westfeld* 1466, *v.* west, feld, crok 'bend'); (Lt) West Md; Westwood Coppice; White Hill; Willow Bed (cf. Morey's Orchd *supra*); Lt Wood Cl, Wood Cl Coppice; Wooddons Btm (the first part of the name may be 'woad hill', *v.* wād, dūn, cf. *Waddon* 1408 (somewhere in this hundred), with botm).

(*b*) *Alysaunderfurlong* 1466 (the usual ME form of the pers.n. or surname *Alexander*, *v.* furlang); *Bordelond* 1466 (*v.* bord-land 'land held by a bordar'; at the three DB manors of Warmwell there were in all 15 bordars, *v.* VCHDo 3 87, 89, 108)); *Bromeknoll* 1466 (*v.* brōm, cnoll); *Cadieshey* 1441 (cf. Richard *atte Well* als. *Cady* 1464 (Winfrith N., *v.* atte, wella), William *Cady* 1664 (Owermoigne), *v.* (ge)hæg); *fossat' apud Croketaysshe* 1466 (*v.* croked, æsc); 'the cross in the vill of *Warmewelle*' 1333; *Doukelane* 1442, 1466, *Dukkeslane* 1449, *Duclane* 1450 (cf. *terre...nuper Johannis Doke* 1438, *1 rod' ...nuper Johannis Dooke* 1441, *v.* lane); *le Estcombe* (*apud Warmewellesdoun*) 1453 (*v.* ēast, cumb, cf. Warmwell Down Barn *supra*); *Grayfurlangeshede* 1441 (*v.* grǣg¹ 'grey' or grǣg² 'badger', furlang, hēafod 'headland (in a common field)'); *Hatterslond* 1466 (cf. *ten' cum pratum nuper Johannis Hatter* 1438, *v.* land); *la Heth'feld* 1465 (*v.* hǣð, feld, cf. Warmwell Heath *supra*); *venella voc' Hethenstrete* 1438 (*v.* hǣðen 'heathen', strǣt; the first el. may suggest a road thought to have been used by the pagan English or by Danish marauders (cf. here-pæð), but probably has the meaning 'heathy, growing with heather', cf. Haven Street Wt 32, 281); *La Hide* 1275 Banco, *La Hyda* Ed 3 (*v.* hīd 'hide of land'; this is taken by Hutch³ 1 433 to refer to Watercombe par. *infra*, which was assessed for 1 hide in 1086 DB, *v.* VCHDo 3 70); *the higher Feilde* 1618; *le Knoll* 1458 (*v.* cnoll); *Lang(e)stret(e)* Ed 3,

1393 (*regia via voc'* —), 1438–1442, *Longstrete* 1438–1457 (*v.* lang[1], strǣt, probably with reference to the Poxwell-Affpuddle road); *Lydzard* 1335 (perhaps 'yard with a gate', *v.* hlid[2], geard); *claus' voc' Lynyng(g)eslond* 1450, 1454 (the first part of the name may be from līn 'flax' with an -ing[2] suffix, *v.* land); *ten'...voc' Lukasplace* 1462 (the pers.n. or surname *Lucas* (*Luke*), *v.* place); *Mayne Close* 1604 (from Fryer Mayne in W Knighton par. *infra*); *Oldemede* 1465 (*v.* ald, mǣd); *claus' voc' le Parke* 1450, 1458, *S(o)uth-*, *Northparke* 1454, 1460 (*v.* park); *Radewell* 1412 (*v.* hrēod 'reed' or rēad 'red', wella); *Sand Knol* 1335 (*v.* sand, cnoll); *Sharpesclose, Sharpsherd* 1466 (cf. John —, William *Sharpe ib*, *v.* clos(e), sceard); *Shortelond* 1335 (*v.* sc(e)ort, land); *ten' voc' Still'place* 1462 (cf. *terr'-*, *mes' nuper Roberti Still(e)* 1451, 1463, *v.* place, cf. Vyse Barn *supra*); *la Sourelond* 1466 (the first el. may be sūr 'sour, damp' or sūre 'sorrel', but cf. *claus'...nuper in tenur' Hen' Surr'* 1450, *v.* land); *Tarentclose* 1465 (a surname from one of the Do Tarrants, *v.* clos(e)); *Thirtye acres* 1618; *Threaris* (for *-acris*) 1408, *Threacresdyche* 1440, *Threacrendiche* 1454 (*v.* þrēo, æcer, dīc; *-acren-* is an analogical S wk.gen.pl., *v.* -ena, Phonol.); *Tobledescorner* 1457, 1458 (perhaps a form of the surname *Theobald*, *v.* corner); *Turnebulshey* 1450 (the surname *Turnbull*, *v.* (ge)hæg); *campis de Warmwell* 1412, *campo de Warmewell* 1438, *Warmewelfeld* 1471 (*v.* feld).

Watercombe

This par. was formerly part of Warmwell par. *supra* (Hutch[3] 1 339).

WATERCOMBE (SY 757848)

    Watrecome 1086 DB, *-coma* Exon, *-cumbe* 1299 Cl (p)
    Watercumb(e) Hy 1 (14) *AddCh*, c. 1165 MontC, 1204 Cur (p), FF, 1242–3 Fees, 1244 *Ass*, 1269 Ch, 1275 Cl, 1280 *Ass* (p), 1285 FA (p), *-cumba* Hy 1 (14) *AddCh*, *-combe ib*, 1263 Ipm, 1327 *SR* (p), 1332 SR (p), 1368 Fine *et passim*, *-coumbe* 1264 (e15) *MiltRoll*, 1340 NI (p), *-come* 1280 FF, 1337 *Ass*, *-cum* 1288 *ib*, *-cumme* 1323 Pat (p)

'Wet valley', *v.* wæter, cumb. There is mention of ½ mill here in 1086 DB (VCHDo 3 70), at which date Watercombe was assessed for one hide, cf. *La Hyda* in Warmwell par. *supra*.

BUGS' LANE, probably the surname *Bug(g)*, but cf. Walter *Bukke* 1332 SR (Owermoigne). BLACKLAND'S CLOSE, *v.* blæc, land. CHALK PIT. GILLARD'S COPPICE. GRAVEL PIT. SKIPPET HEATH, from Mount Skippet in Owermoigne par. *supra*. WATERCOMBE FM, — *Farme* 1639 *Mansel*, *mesuage of Watercombe* 1604 *ib*. WATERCOMBE HEATH (CTG).

FIELD-NAMES

The undated forms are 1840 *TA* 175 (Poxwell). Spellings dated 1438, 1457 are *Weld*[1], the rest are Hutch[3].

(*a*) Watercombe North & Middle, Watercombe Md.

(*b*) *Morforlang* 1335 (*v.* mōr, furlang); '(tenement called) Pokeswells —, Poxewell's lands' 1599 (from the family of Robert *Pokeswell* 1430); 'the field of Watercombe' 1335, *campo de Watercombe* 1438, *Watercombefild* 1457 (*v.* feld).

Winfrith Newburgh

West Lulworth par. *supra* was formerly a chapelry in this par. (Hutch[3] 1 339). Longcutts in this par. is in Bindon liberty.

WINFRITH NEWBURGH (SY 805844)

    Winfrode 1086 DB, Exon, *-froda* Exon, *Win-*, *Wynfrod(e)* 13 *Weld*[1] (— *Newburgh*, — *Neuburg*), 1210–2 RBE, 1212 Fees, 1213, 1214 Cur, 1236 FF *et passim* to 1288 *Ass*, — *Neuburgh* 1289 *Weld*[1], 1297 Pat, *Wyne-*, *Winefrod(e)* 1227 FF, 1308 Pat, *Winfroud* 1250 Fees

    Win-, *Wynfrot* 1195, 1210 P, 1246 Ipm (— *als. Winfrod*), 1268 *Ass*, 1288 *ib* (— *Neuborgh*), 1703 *Weld*[1] (— *als. Newborough*)

    Wyn-, *Winford(e)* 1210–2 RBE, 1212 Fees, 1267 (1269) Ch, 1268 *Ass*, 1271 Pat, 1275 RH, 1446 *Rent*, *Wine-*, *Wyneford* 1250 Fees, 1280 *Ass*, 1437 *Weld*[1] (— *Neuburgh*)

    Winfret, *Winifrat* 1216 ClR, *Wynfrete* 1575 Saxton

    Wimfrost 1228 Cl

    Wymfrod(e) 1244 Fees, *Ass*, 1268 *ib*, 1276 Pat, 1279 Ch, 1280 *Ass*, Ch, 1288 *Ass*, 1297 Pat (— *Neuburgh*)

    Wynnfred 1244 *Ass*, *Wyn-*, *Winfred(e)* 1273 Cl, 1278 QW, 1280 *Ass*, 1282 Cl, 1288 *Ass* (— *Neuburgh*, — *Neuburth*, — *Nouborthe*, — *Neesburgh*), 1291 Tax, 1311 Cl (— *Neuborgh*), 1311 *Weld*[1] (— *Neburg*), 1318 Ch, 1319 FF (*-neburgh*) *et freq* to 1447 Cl with the affix *Ne(u)b(o)urgh*; *Wynifrede* 1278 QW, *Wynfrede and Neburgh* 1388 Cl, *Wynefred(e)* 1288 *Ass* (— (*et*) *Neuburgh*), 1291 Pat, 1436 *Weld*[1], *Wynfreud* 1294 (1313) Ch

    Wim-, *Wymfred(e)* 1244 *Ass*, 1260 Cl, 1279 FF, Pat, 1280 *Ass* (— *iuxta Benedon*), 1288 *ib* (— *Neuburg(h)*), 1315 Pat (*Neuburgh-*), 1332 SR

    Wind(e)ford 1250 Fees (p)

Wylefrod 1250 Fees (p)
Wynfro 1268 *Ass*
Wemfrod 1279 Ch
Wunfrot 1289 Cl
Win-, Wynfrid Neuburgh 1309 *Wim*, 1313 Pat
Wynfryth 1399 Pat (— *als. Wynflyth*), 1535 *DCMDeed* (—
    Nowbro), *Wynffrythe* 1554 *Ampthill, Winfrith Newborough* 1705
    Weld[1]
Wynfreth 1412 FA, 1431 ib (— *Neuburgh*), 1436 *Weld*[1], 1440 *ib*
    (— *Neburgh*), 1450 *ib*, 1461 *Rent*, 1498 *Ct, Wyynfreth* 1444
    Weld[1]
Woneford Neuburgh 1435 *Weld*[1]

Originally a stream name from PrWelsh wïnn[3] 'white, bright' and
PrWelsh frud 'stream', identical in origin with Winford So (DEPN)
and Wynford Eagle par. *infra, v.* Ekwall RN 462–3, Jackson 555–6.
The r.n. Win is a back-formation from the p.n. The family of *de
Neuburgh, de Nouo burgo* (from *le Neubourg* in Normandy (Eure))
was here from the time of Hy 1 (Fees 89), and is mentioned in 1195
P, 13 *Weld*[1], 1210 P, 1228 Cl, 1250 Fees *et freq* to 1332 SR. *Benedon*
is Bindon in Wool par. *infra.* The bounds of the manor of Winfrith
Newburgh are given in 1682 *Weld*[1] (M78).

BROOMHILL FM (SY 809880)

Bremehull 1227 FF
Bromeshulle 1244 *Ass* (p)
Bromhill 1244 *Ass*, 1436 *Weld*[1] (p), 1440 *ib*, -*hull(e)* 1280 *Ass* (p),
    1288 *ib* (p), 1289 *Weld*[1], 1327 SR (p), 1332 SR (p), 1330 FF,
    1353 Pat, 1390 *Weld*[1], 1392 *Ct* (p), 1416 *Weld*[1], (land) *atte
    bromulle* c. 1300 *Milne, Bromphull* 1390, 1391 *Weld*[1], *Bromehull*
    1414 *ib, Bromyll* 1453, 1466 *ib, Bromehill, -hyll* 1464, 1478 *ib*,
    1587 *Russ*, 1795 *Boswell, Broomhill* 1773 Bayly
Bromhul(le)-, -hullesmull(e) 1404, 1421 *Weld*[1], (molend' aquatic'
    voc') *Bromhil(les)myll(e)* 1437, 1440 *ib, Bromyl(le)s-, Bromel(ly)s-,
    Bromyl(l)ysmyll(e)* 1450–1489 *ib*, 1461 *Rent*, 1468, 1484 *MinAcct*,
    1498, 1499 *Ct, Bromyll' myll* 1477 *MinAcct, Bromehill Mill*
    1640, 1703 *Weld*[1], 1811 OS, *Brommill Mill* 1664 *Weld*[1],
    Broomehill Mill(s) 1682 *ib*

'Broom-covered hill', *v.* brōm, hyll, with myln 'mill', atte 'at
the'. The earliest form, if it is not an error for *Brome-*, contains a

derivative brēme[1] 'broom, bramble' or brēme[2] 'broom grove'; the gen.sg. form *Bromes-* may also suggest a collective sense for the el. brōm.

The farm (formerly the mill) stands where the Winfrith Newburgh–Moreton road crosses a tributary of R. Frome, cf. Broomhill Bridge in Moreton par. *supra*. This road is probably that referred to as *regia via apud Bromphull* 1390 *Weld*[1], *via' harnes' apud Bromhilmylle* 1440 *ib*, *via regia voc' Bromylleswey* 1478 *ib*, v. weg, cf. (*arabil'/pastur'*) *Bi-*, *Bywest(e)bromhull(e)wey* 1392, 1393 *Weld*[1], 1393 *Ct*, '(land) to the west of', v. bī, westan. There was earlier a fishery here, cf. *piscarie aque d'ni de Frome de dicto molendino* 1484 *MinAcct*, and the reference to the repair of *lez Werez et le flodeyatez* here in 1466 *Weld*[1]; *fossat' apud Bromhill-*, *Bromyll Outgutche* 1452 *Weld*[1] may refer to a sluice or a mill race, *outgutche* being perhaps related to gote 'channel', gyte 'pouring forth', etc., but cf. ModE *outgush* 'strong outflow' (1839 NED).

EAST & WEST BURTON (SY 833869, 820859), BURTON DAIRY & FM, *Burton(e)* 1210–2 RBE, 1244 FF (p), 1256 *ib*, 1262 Ch, 1280 *Ass* (*Est-*), 1280 Ch (*Est-*, *West-*), 1288 *Ass*, 1293 Cl (*Est-*), 1315 Pat (*Little-*), 1332 SR *et passim* with affixes *E(a)st-*, *West(e)-*; *Estburton iuxta Wynfred Neesburgh* 1288 *Ass*, *Bureton* 1212 Fees, *Borton* 1271 Ch, (*West-*) 1280 *Ass*, 1288 *ib* (p), 1333 Misc (*Est-*), (*West-*) 1390 *Weld*[1], 1392 *Ct* (*Est-*), 1392 *Weld*[1] (*Est-*, *West-*), 1394 *ib* (*Est-*), 1416 *ib*, *Buriton*, (*Est)buryton* 1285 FA, *Bourton* 1392 *Ct* (*Est-*), 1392 *Weld*[1] (*Est-*, *West-*), 1393 *Ct* (*West-*), 1393 *Weld*[1] (*Litel-*), 1416 *ib*, 1531 *ib* (*West-*), *Burton Mill(s)* 1641 Hutch[3], 1682 *Weld*[1], *West Burton Farme* 1682, 1703 *ib*, 'fortified farmstead' or 'farmstead near a fortification', from burh-tūn, with ēast, west, lȳtel, myln; there is no archaeological evidence for a fortification here; 'little' may have referred to West Burton. The bounds of East Burton are given in 1682 *Weld*[1] (M78 p. 31). For the deserted medieval village of West Burton, v. RCHMDo **2** 380. There was a mill at *Burton* in 1256 FF, cf. also *East Burton Mill* 1589 *Comm*.

EAST FOSSIL DAIRY & FM (SY 799853, 806849), *Estforshull(e)* 1398, 1414 *Weld*[1], *East Foreshill* 1442 Hutch[3], *Estforshill* 1456 IpmR, 1541 *Russ*, *Estforcyll* 1535 *DCMDeed*, *-ell* 1535 *ib*, 1587 *Russ*, *East Forcell* 1652 *Weld*[1], *-sell* 1682 *ib*, *Higher Fossill* 1811 OS, 'east' and 'higher' in relation to West Fossil *q.v.* in Chaldon H. par. *supra*, v. ēast.

EAST KNIGHTON (SY 812856), KNIGHTON FM, *Knyt(t)eton* 1244
FF (?), 1250 Drew, 1280 Ch, 1288 *Ass*, 1421 *Weld*[1], *Kni(h)tteton*
1254, 1279 FF, *Kniste-, Knysteton* 1268 *Ass*, 1285 FA, *Kny(ʒ)gh(t)-
(t)(e)ton(e)* 1294 (1313) Ch, 1329 Pat *et freq* to 1498 *Ct*, '*Knyghteton
by Bynedon*' 1313 Pat, *Knighton juxta Bynedon* 1313 Inq aqd,
Knyʒtteton 1332 SR (p), *Knyt(t)h(e)ton* 1405, 1421 *Weld*[1], *Knyicthton*
1408 *ib*, *Knythtteton* 1421 *ib*, *Knygt(h)on* 1445, 1457 *ib*, *Knynghton*
1498 *Ct*, *Knighton* 1664 *Weld*[1], *East* —, *West Knighton* 1774 Hutch[1],
'farm of the youths or retainers', or 'farm of the knights, farm held
by knight service' if the name is of post-Conquest origin, from cniht
(gen.pl. *cnihta*) and tūn, with ēast, west, cf. Bindon in Wool par.
infra; West Knighton is no longer on the maps.

MARLEY BOTTOM, POND, WOOD (SY 810830), & WOOD BARN, (*sub-
bosc' apud*) *Muryle* 1390, 1402 *Weld*[1], (*sub*)*bosc' apud Mir-, Myrlegh*
1440 *ib*, (*bosc' d'ni apud/voc'*) *Miri-, Myryley* 1451–1457 *ib*, (*bosc'
d'ni voc*' —, *bosc' fraxin' de* —) *Meri-, Meryley* 1456, 1457 *ib*, 1461
Rent, 1462 *Weld*[1], 1469, 1473 *MinAcct*, 1475–1487 *Weld*[1], (*bosc' frax'
de* —, *subbosc' apud* —, *bosc' d'ni voc'*) *Myre-, Mireley* 1456–1466
Weld[1], 1469 *MinAcct*, 1475 *Weld*[1], *bosc' d'ni voc' Moryley* 1468
MinAcct, *bosc' d'ni voc Merley* 1474 *Weld*[1], *Myrley* 1484 *MinAcct*,
Morely coppice 1641 Hutch[3], (*the Coppice Wood called*) *Merly Wood*
l17, 1682 *Weld*[1], *Marl(e)y Wood* l17 *ib*, 1811 OS, *Marley Wood*
(*Bottom & Down*) 1843 *TA*, *Murley Wood* 1826 Gre, 'pleasant wood
or clearing', or 'wood or clearing where merry-making took place',
from myrge, lēah, with wudu, botm, dūn.

BAILEY'S DROVE, cf. *Baillywille Furlong* 1461 *Rent*, *v*. baillie 'bailiff'
(possibly occurring as a surname here), drove, wella, furlang. THE
BEECHES. BLACKNOLL (HILL), *Blacknoll* 1811 OS, cf. *Blacknowle
poor house* 1843 *TA*, 'dark-coloured hillock', *v*. blæc, cnoll. BRAY-
TOWN, *Brayston* 1451 *Weld*[1], the surname *Bray* with tūn, cf. the f.n.
Baylands in Moreton par. *supra*. BURTON CHURCH (— *Chapel & Yd*
1843 *TA*), CROSS, HEATH (cf. *Burton Common* 1843 *TA*) & PIT
(*Ye Chalkpitt* 1621 *Weld*[1], *Burton Chalkpit* 1843 *TA*, cf. *Chalkepitt
Field* 1682 *Weld*[1], *Chalk pit piece* 1843 *TA*), all named from East &
West Burton *supra*, cf. Chalk Pit Lane *infra*. THE CEDARS. CHALK PIT
LANE, leading to Burton Pit *supra*. CLAYPITS LANE, cf. *Clay Pits Lot*
1843 *TA*. COALHILL DROVE, *I furlong terre voc' Coulhill* 1461 *Rent*,
Colehill l17 *Weld*[1], 'hill where charcoal was burnt', or 'cool hill',
from col[1] or cōl[2], hyll, cf. Colehill par. *infra*. COLTSCLOSE CORNER,

1811 OS, *Colt(')s Close* 1843 *TA*, from colt 'a colt', or the surname *Colt*, cf. the f.n. Colts Park in Moreton par. *supra*. THE DROVE, 1682 *Weld*[1], *ye Droue* 1705 *ib*, cf. *Droveyate* 1663 *ib*, *Drove end* 1682 *ib*, *v*. drove 'road on which cattle are driven', geat, ende, cf. foll.; the forms *regia via voc' le Drevewey* 1392 *Ct*, *viam voc' la Dreue* 1416 *Weld*[1] may also belong here; they contain the related dræf with a similar meaning to drove, cf. *le Dreve* in Coombe K. par. *supra*. DROVE HILL, from prec. EASTWARD, near the E bdy of the par. at 300', perhaps to be associated with *le Eastewood* 1588 *Comm*. THE FOLLY, *The Folly Piece* 1843 *TA*, *v*. folie. FOSSIL COPPICE, 1843 *TA*, from East Fossil *supra*. GATMORE FM, *Catemore* 1389 *Weld*[1] (*aque voc'* —), *Gatemour* 1414 *ib*, *Gatmor(e)* 1461 *Rent* (*1 furlong iuxta* —), 1477 *Weld*[1], *Lit(t)le Gat(t)mor(e)* 1663, 1664 *ib*, *Gate Moor* 1843 *TA*, 'marshy ground where goats were kept', *v*. gāt (gen.pl. *gāta*), mōr, with lȳtel. GIDDY GREEN, probably a nickname of contempt, from gydig 'mad, foolish', grēne[2], but the surname *Giddy* is possible, cf. also John *Gydyion* 1375 Cl. GRANT'S BARN, — & *Yd* 1843 *TA*, cf. *Grants (Mdw)*, *Grant's Lot* 1843 *ib*, William *Graunt* 1664 HTax. HYFORD CTG, *Hi-*, *Hyford(e)* 1398, 1457 *Weld*[1], 1682 *ib* (— *Bridge*), *Hiefordesdoun* 1461 *Rent*, *Highford* 1587 *Russ*, *Hiyerd meadow* 1664 *Weld*[1], *Highford Ham & Mead*, *Rough by Highford Gate* 1843 *TA*, 'hay ford, ford used chiefly at hay-making time', from hēg (WSax hī(e)g) and ford, with brycg, dūn, mæd, hamm, and geat; the ford was across R. Frome. KINGS BARTON FM, cf. *Kyngesmede* 1244 *Ass*, *Kyngmede* 1391 *Weld*[1] *et freq* to 1469 *MinAcct*, *Knygmede* (sic) 1471 *Weld*[1], *Kings' Mdw*, *King's Barn & Yd* 1843 *TA*, *v*. beretūn, mæd, bere-ærn; *King(s)* could be the surname *King* (cf. *ten' nuper Walteri Kyng* 1464 *Weld*[1], somewhere in this hundred), but it should be noted that in 1086 DB Winfrith Newburgh was a royal manor (VCHDo **3** 65–6), *v*. cyning. KNIGHTON HEATH, cf. *camp' de Knyghton* 1394 *Weld*[1], *Knighton Common* 1811 OS, from East Knighton *supra*. KNIGHTON LANE, cf. prec. LONGCUTTS FM, (*maner of*) *Langcott(e)s* 1516 Hutch[3], 1535 *DCMDeed*, *-cotes* 1774 Hutch[1], *Longcotts* 1795 Boswell, 'long cottages', from lang[1] and cot (new ME nom. pl. *cotes*). THE MOORS, cf. John *de la More* 1288 *Ass*, John *in la more* 1327 *SR*, John *in Themore* 1332 SR, John *atte Moure* 1391 *Weld*[1], (*le*) *Mour(e)dych*, *-diche* 1403, 1416 *ib*, *le More* 1457 *ib*, *ye Moor*, *Moor Close Meadow*, *Moorland Feild* 1621 *ib*, *Moore Close (Field)*, *the Moore Meadow* 1682 *ib*, *the More* 1705 *ib*, *Lr & Middle Moor*, *Moory Cl*, *Moory Lane Pce* 1843 *TA*, *v*. mōr 'marshy ground', atte, dīc. NEWBURGH FM, cf. *Newborough Field* 1682 *Weld*[1], the surname *Newburgh*, cf. Winfrith Newburgh *supra*. PHEASANTRY. PORTWAY, 1811 OS, *v.* port-weg 'way to a market-town', with reference to the Owermoigne–Wool road which is part of the way from Dorchester to Wareham. POUNT'S BARN, cf. *Pounce Ground* 1843 *TA*; perhaps the surname *Pound*, cf. Robert *Pounde* 1498 *Ct*. PRIORSLAWN DAIRY, *Pryers Land* 1663, 1682 *Weld*[1], *Priars Lande*, *Priars Longe* (probably for *Londe*) gate 1664 *ib*, *Gt & Lt Priors Land*, *Priors Land Md* 1843 *TA*, cf. *Priors Mdw*, *Priors Furze Pce*, *Priors Large Pce*, *Little Priors* p1795 *Mansel*, 'prior's land', from prior, land; the allusion is to the priory of Hermitage (*v.* Hermitage par. *infra*), cf. *tenent' Prior' de Ermytage in Knyghton* 1469 *MinAcct*, *Prior' de (H)ermitage pro terr' in Knyghton* 1498 *Ct*, *v.* East Knighton *supra*. RANDALLS FM, cf. Richard *Randall* 1664 HTax (W Lulworth), now called SLEIGHT BLDGS (1"), cf. 'a ground called *Sleight*' 1641 Hutch[3], *the Sheep Slaite* 117 *Weld*[1], *Slight* (*West gate*) 1682 *ib*, *Slight*, *Slaight* 1843 *TA*, from slæget 'sheep pasture'. RECTORY FM, cf. (*Winfrith*) *Glebe*, *Parsonage Cl* 1843 *TA*, St Christopher's Church *infra*. RED LION INN, 1843 *TA*. RISING SUN (P.H.). RUSHPOND. ST CHRISTOPHER'S CHURCH, cf. *æcclesiam de Winfrode* 1086 DB, Exon, *ecclesiam de Wimfred* 1244 *Ass*, *ecclesiam Sancti Petri in villa de Winfrod* 1268 *ib*, *ecclesie paroch' de Winfrith* 1535 VE, *le Church howse* 1638 *Weld*[1], *the Churchway* 1664 *ib*, cf. Rectory Fm *supra*. SAND PITS, cf. *Sandhills Pce* 1843 *TA*. SCHOOL LANE. SEVEN STARS (P.H.). SHIP INN. SLEIGHT BLDGS (1"), *v.* Randalls Fm *supra*. STONY POST CTGS, *Stoney Post* 1843 *TA*, 'post or pillar made of stone', *v.* stānig, post. VINE'S DOWN BLDGS, cf. Margaret *Vyne* 1682 *Weld*[1]. WATER BARN, cf. Robert *atte Water* 1375 Cl, *Waterlake* 1416 *Weld*[1] (*via vocat'* —), 1682 *ib* (land in), 1705 *ib*, *v.* wæter 'stream', atte, lacu 'stream'; Water Barn is on the bank of R. Frome; there is no connection with foll., where some of the early forms cited above may belong. WATER LANE, some two miles from prec., so called because it runs alongside the stream which gave Winfrith Newburgh *supra* its name. WHITCOMBE HILL (1811 OS) & VALE (FM), *v.* hwīt, cumb, vale. WINFRITH DOWN BLDGS, *la/le Doun(e)* 1416, 1488 *Weld*[1], *Wonefordesdowene* 1438 *ib*, *Wonefordon*, *Wynfreth' dowene* 1440 *ib*, *le Comyndoun* 1451 *ib*, *Winfrith Down(e)* 1663, 1682 *ib*, 1843 *TA*, *the downe of Winfreth* 1682 *Weld*[1], (*Middle*) *Down* 1843 *TA*, *v.* dūn, comun. WINFRITH DROVE, FIELDS FM (cf. — *Field* 1843 *TA*, *the common fieldes of Winfrithe and Wolle* 1578 *AD*), HEATH (1843 *TA*, *the Heath* p1795 *Mansel*, cf.

Winfrith Common 1682 *Weld*[1], *Great Common* 1843 *TA*), Hill (1811
OS) & Ho (*The Great House at Winfrith* p1795 *Mansel*, cf. *Winfrith
Farm(e)* 1682 *Weld*[1], p1795 *Mansel, Winfrot farme* 1703 *Weld*[1]), all
from Winfrith Newburgh *supra*, cf. Wool par. *infra*. Withy Bed,
Withey Bed 1843 *TA*, cf. *la Wy(t)hebere* 1413, 1438 *Weld*[1], *le Withebar*
1450 *MinAcct, Withi-, Witheber* 1461 *Rent, claus' voc' le Wethyber*
1464 *Weld*[1], *le Westside le Wythe-, Wethi-, W(h)itheber* 1464, 1466
ib, 1468, 1469 *MinAcct*, 1472 *Weld*[1] (-*q' est lancera de Chaluedon*),
1475, 1481 *ib*, *v*. wiðig, bedd, bearu, west, sīde, cf. Chaldon H.
par. *supra*.

FIELD-NAMES

The undated forms are 1843 *TA* 248. Spellings dated 1195, 1281, 1330,
1340[2], 1392[2], 1516, 1524, 1609, 1614, 1626, 1641, 1768 are Hutch[3], 1227 FF,
1244, 1280, 1288 *Ass*, 1279 Ch, 1327 *SR*, 1332 SR, 1340 NI, 1375 Cl,
1392[1], 1393[2], 1498, 1499 *Ct*, 1446, 1461 *Rent*, 1450, 1459, 1469, 1470, 1474[2],
1484 *MinAcct*, 1541, 1587 *Russ*, 1589 *Comm*, 1607 *Feth*, 1650 WeyM, 1664
HTax, p1795 *Mansel*, and the rest *Weld*[1].

(*a*) Arable pce; Arnages Plot (cf. Robert *Arneys* 1332); Barn Cl & pce,
Piece above the Barns (cf. *Barn Fd* p1795); Battricks Lot (cf. Mary *Battrick*
1682, *v*. hlot, as freq in this par.); Billets Ho & Ld p1795 (a form of the
surname *Bellett*); Blackbury, Blackberry fds (*Blakeborgh* 1393, *Blakebarry
in le Westfild* 1451, 'black hill or barrow', *v*. blæc (wk. obl. *blacan*), beorg,
cf. *Westfild infra*); Broad Cl; Brook Lawn; Broomhill Ld, Long Mdw by
Broomhill (cf. *prato apud Bromphull* 1391, *medo at Bromehill* 1587, *v*. mǣd,
Broomhill Fm *supra*); Burnt Plot; Burton Grd (*v*. E & W Burton *supra*);
Burts Knapp (cf. William *Burt* 1682, *v*. cnæpp); Butchers Cl; Butts (*v*.
butt[2], or butte); Caines' Md (cf. *Kaynysmede* in Coombe Keynes par. *supra*);
The Chalk pit, Chalkpit fd; Close; Coakes' Ctg & Cl (cf. Robert *Cok* 1327,
terr' Edith Couk' 1394); Cott Hayes (*v*. cot, (ge)hæg); Common pce;
Coopers Cl; The Copse p1795; Cowleaze (freq, cf. *Hr, Middle & Lr Cow
Leaze* p1795); The Cow Yd p1795; Crockers Hay (*v*. (ge)hæg, as freq in
this par.); Cross Cl (*v*. cros); Crown Cl (cf. foll.); The Crown Inn; Dames(')
Lot (*v*. hlot); Draytons Md; Dry Plot; Duck Plot; Dudgemoor (*Duddesmore*
1461, *Dudmoors* p1795, 'Dudd's marshy ground', from the OE pers.n.
Dudd and mōr); East Md; 18 Acres; Fern Croft p1795 (*v*. fearn, croft,
freq in this par.); Filton(')s Lot (cf. John *Felton* 1768); 5 Acres (cf. *Knighton
Five acres* 1682, *v*. E Knighton *supra*); (Little) Ford Ham (cf. *le Forddoun*
1461, *Foord Downe* l17, *v*. ford, hamm, dūn); Fore Grd (*v*. fore); Fossil
Cmn & fd (*campo de Est Forshill* 1541, *The Fossill South Fd* p1795, cf.
Forshillhege 1461, *Forsell Letch, — Meadow* 1682, *Fossills Cow Lea* p1795,
all from E Fossil *supra*, *v*. hecg, lecc 'stream, bog', cū, lǣs); 4 Acres;
Furmedge's Lot (cf. Joane *Furmage* 1682 (Wool)); Galton's Ham (cf. John
Galton 1609 (E Lulworth), *v*. hamm); Garden pce; Great Barrow (*Grate-
bergh* 1227, *Westgretbarry* 1451, *terre voc' Est-, Westgretebary* 1461, 'great

hill or barrow', from grēat (wk. obl. *grēatan*) and beorg, with ēast, west); Great Cl (cf. *Winfreth Farme greate Close* 1682); Great Fd & Lot; Green Road Pce; Greystone Bottom (*Gryestonesforlong* 1392[1], *1 furlong' terre iuxta le Greyston* 1461, '(furlong at) the grey stone', *v.* græg[1], stān, furlang, botm); Guttershare Fd (perhaps 'share of land near a watercourse', *v.* gotere, sc(e)aru, cf. Water Gutter Fd *infra*); Hancock(')s Bottom (cf. William *Hancock* 1498); The Hanging (*v.* hanging); Hedgerow; Higher Pce; Home Barrow p1795 (*v.* home, beorg); Home Cl & Grd; Home Pce p1795; Hoods Living & Lot (cf. Thomas *Hudde* 1498, Henry *Hodde* 1516, *v.* living); Hyde Md, Hydes Grd (cf. John *atte Huyde* 1392[1], 1392[3], *v.* hīd 'hide of land', atte); Island; Little Md; Long Cl (1470[2], *Langclos* 1470, *v.* lang[1], clos(e)); Long Grd & Md (cf. John *Langmede* 1489, *v.* lang[1], mǣd); Martin Hill (cf. *Martynes-*, *Martinesmede* 1393, Gilbert *Martin* 1392[2]); Mead Gate Cl (cf. *Wynford Mede* 1446, *Winfrith Meade*, — *Meadow* 1682, (*the*) *Meade close* 1589, 117, *v.* mǣd, cf. Winfrith Newburgh *supra*, *Medeweye infra*, and foll.); Meadow (cf. prec.); Milk Hills (*Milkehill* 1589, 'hill pastures yielding good milk', *v.* meoluc); Mill Cl (*Mill Close pasture* 1621, *the Mill Close* 117, cf. *terr' voc' Toukyngmylfurlang* 1450, *molend' aquatic' nuper Johannis Cator* 1457, *firma molendini aquatici d'ni* (*vocat' Gristmyll*) 1469, 1470, *Mildowns or Mildons barrow* 1650, *Mill Down* p1795, *v.* myln, clos(e), tucking-mill, grist-mill, dūn, beorg; there was probably a mill in Winfrith Newburgh in 1086 DB, *v.* VCHDo 3 65–6); The New Cl p1795; Ninehams(' Down) (perhaps from ME *atten innome* '(place) at the enclosed ground', *v.* atten, innōm, with dūn, cf. Ninehams Sr 312, but a surname of this origin is equally possible); Norris' Living, Lot & Pdk (*v.* living); Northbrook Fd, Ham & Plot ((*land in*) *Northbrooke* 1682, 1705 (*v.* norð, brōc, hamm); (Home) North Fd (*le Northfild* 1461); North Md (— *Mead(e)* 1682); Oat Hill (Down) (*Oatehill* 117); Old House Grd; Paddock (*v.* pearroc); Pain(e)s (Cl & Pdk) (*Paynes Close* 1682, cf. Richard *Payn* 1340, *terr' Walteri Payn* 1451, *pratum-*, *cot' nuper Johannis Payn(e)* 1455, 1498); Parker's Ctg p1795; The Peak (*v.* pēac); Pitmans Orchd (cf. Edward *Pittman* 1626); The Plots; Pluddy Marsh (*meadow in Plodding Marsh* 1682, from pludde 'pool, puddle', perhaps with -ing[2], and mersc, cf. Ploddy Gl 3 xiii, 179); Propriation Mdw (from propriation 'the action of making one's own'); Purn Croft (*Purnel(le)croft* 1392[3], 1412, 1478, *Purnill(le)-*, *Purnyl(le)crof(f)t-(t)e(s)* 1412, 1413, 1461, *Purnellescroft* 1474, *Purnecrof(f)t(e)* 1413 *et freq* to 1652, *Purnecraft end* 1682 (the fem. pers.n. *Pernel*, *Purnel*, a contracted form of *Petronilla*, with croft; the name should probably be connected with the ½ virgate of land in Chaldon Herring granted to Bindon Abbey by *Purnelle de Bosco* in 1280 Hutch[3] 1 351); Quarry Barrow p1795; Rill Coombe (Down) (probably to be identified with *Rewl(e)-* 1449, 1452, *Rewelcomb(e)* 1478; cumb 'valley' may have been added to an earlier name *Rew(e)l(e)* from a misdivision of ME *atter ewelle* '(place) at the spring', *v.* atter, ǣwell (for the OE (wk.) fem. form *welle*, *v.* EPN 2 250); the unexplained Rewlea D 465 (*Reyle-* 1330, *Rewlacomb* 1583) may be analogous, though here the first spelling would seem to suggest derivation from rǣge 'roe, female roe-deer'); Ryelands (*Ry(e)-*, *Rielond* 1392[1], 1405 *et freq* to 1471, *Rigge-*, *Rieg-* 1487, *Rieghlond* 1488, *Ry-*, *Rilands* 1663, 1664[2], *Ryland's Fd* p1795, v. ryge, land); Scotts Knapp (*Scottesknapp* 1451, cf. Richard *Scot* 1332, v. cnæpp); 7 Acres (*close called 7 acres* l17); Shilling Plot (possibly in allusion to rent, v. scilling); 6 Acres (*le Sexacres* 1461, v. sex); The Sloop Inn; Smoakhams p1795 (probably 'enclosures held by the payment of "smoke-money"', v. smoca, hamm, cf. *Smokacre* in Coombe K. par. *supra*); South Md (1682, 1705); Spear Bed (v. spear, bedd); Stanleys Green; Stoney Course Lots p1795; Strawberry (Cl & Mdw) (perhaps from strēaw 'straw' and beorg 'hill or barrow'); Strip (v. strip); Tewkesbury's (Lots, Md, & Hither Pce) (cf. Henry *Tewxberry* 1664 (E Lulworth)); 13 acres; Three Cornered Md & Pce; Toms Cl (p1795, cf. David *Tomes* 1664 (W Lulworth)); 24 & 22 Acres; Wain Yard (possibly to be identified with *claus' voc' Est-, Westwynard, Wynarde Furlong* 1461, *Est-, Westwynerd-, -wynard-(es)-, -winardesclos(e)* 1462 *et freq* to 1484, *Winner Close* l17, v. wīn-geard 'a vineyard', with ēast, west, furlang, clos(e); the form *Wain-* then shows association with wægn 'wagon', cf. *Weynyate* 1392[1], somewhere in this hundred, 'gate or gap fit for a wagon', v. geat); Warnbury's (*Wambury-, burough Field* 1682, possibly 'mound or barrow resembling a wen or tumour', v. wenn, beorg, cf. Wamborough So, etc. (EPN 2 254), with feld); Water Gutter Fd (v. wæter, gotere, cf. Guttershare Fd *supra*); Water Mdw; Weir Grd (v. wer); West Cl; Wheatcroft (*claus' voc' W*(h)*atecroft* 1413, (*le*) *Whetcroft* 1440, 1464, *W*(h)*atcroft* 1456, 1461, *the Wheate Croft* l17, v. hwǣte 'wheat', croft); Wheatlands (Corner & Plant.) (*Whitland(es) Feild, — Field* 1621, 1682, v. hwīt 'white', land); (Gt) White Hill, Whitehill (bottom) (*le Whitehill* 1451, *Whitehill, -hell Field* 1682, v. hwīt, hyll); Winfrith St. p1795; Wood Hill; Woods; Yearlands (possibly 'strips used for ploughing', v. ere-[3], land, cf. Yarlands in Chickerell par. *infra*).

(b) (*bysouth*)*akerdych* 1391, *Aker-* 1392[1], 1393, *Acredych* 1404 ('(land to the south of) acre ditch', v. bī, sūðan, æcer, dīc); *venellam voc' Aysshely-lane* 1477 ('(lane at or to) the ash wood or clearing', v. æsc, lēah, lane, cf. Edward *atte Nassh* 1416 ('at the ash', v. atte(n)), William *Ayssheley* 1486, and Ashy Drove in Coombe K. par. *supra*); *2 roods called Backery* l17; *prat' voc' Battedeham* 1391 (v. hamm); *the Beacon poices* l17 (v. (ge)bēacon); *terre supra Benygerd, 1 furlong voc' Benygerdlond* 1461 (v. land); '*Berwe* or *la Bergh*' 1281 (v. beorg); *prati voc' Byn(e)ham* 1435, 1462, *Westbynham* 1442, *Bynehamsmede* 1446 ('bean enclosure', v, bēan, hamm, with west, mǣd); *Blakelondis-, Blakelondeswey, -way* 1393, 1498 (v. blæc, land, weg); *the blinde lane* 1664[2] (v. blind, lane); *Bolehaies* 1589 (v. bula, (ge)hæg); *Boles closes* 1641 (cf. Walter *Bole* 1340, *land of Thomas Boule* 1404, *terr' nuper in tenur' Johannis Boule* 1451); *Borislad(e)* 1682, 1705 (perhaps 'boar's valley', v. bār, slæd, but the first el. may be a surname (Reaney 37)); *Bradewey* 1461, *Broadwayes Crofte* 1682, *Broadway Cross* l17 (v. brād, weg, croft, cros); (*1 furlong voc'*) *le Breche* 1461, 1477 (v. brēc); *Bremly-, Bromli-forlong* 1393, *Bromyl-* 1452, *Bremy-, le Bremylfurlong* 1461 (probably 'brambly furlong', from brēmel, -ig[3], and furlang, influenced by brōm 'broom', cf. *Bromylcroft infra*); *Bringoales* 1682; *ten' voc' Brittons* 1458 (cf. *terr' nuper Thom' Britton* 1451); *le Broadwoode* 1588 *Comm*; *Bromyl-, Bromehilcroft* 1464, *Bromyllesfild* 1489, *Bromylsgrove* 1461 (probably 'enclosure, field, and grove belonging to Broomhill *supra*', v. croft, feld, grāf(a), but cf. *terr' Willelmi Bromyll* 1451, *ten' quondam Johannis Bromyll* 1484, where the surname is derived from that p.n.); *Burdens Corner* 1663 (cf. Percival *Burden ib*, *v.* corner); *Burton Fields*, — *Meade* 1682, *West Burton Meadow* l17, *B(o)urton Mo(o)re* 1531, 1635, l17, *Burton Courtmoor als. Moor-Court* l17 (all from E & W Burton *supra*, *v.* feld, mǣd, mōr, court); *le Bury* 1460 (*v.* burh); *via regia subtus Calfhey* 1450², (*claus' voc'*) (*le*) *Calfhey* 1461 (*v.* calf, (ge)hæg, cf. *Chalhay yswey infra*); *regia via iuxta Carpuntersdore* 1389 (cf. Michael *Carpunter ib*, *v.* duru or dor 'door, gate, gap'); *dom' voc' Carthous* 1474² (*v.* cart-house); *Chaldon Meade* 1682 (from Chaldon H. par. *supra*, *v.* mǣd); *Chalhay yswey* 1499 ('the road to *Chalhay*', perhaps identical with *Calfhey supra* with *Chal-* from WSax cealf, *v.* weg); *Charlecroft* 1393 *et freq* to 1478, *-crot* 1463, *Charel-* 1440, *Charlcroft* 1451 ('peasants' enclosure', *v.* ceorl (gen.pl. *ceorla*), croft); *Charncroft* 1393 (perhaps scearn 'muck'); *Chatecroft* 1413; *Clanis* 1589, *Claene* (*corner*) 1664² (a surname, with corner); (*via regia voc'*) *Cleystrete* 1441–1487, *via regia apud Estend de Claystrete* 1450², *Claystret* 1471 (*v.* clǣg, strǣt, ēast, ende); *Cnolle* 1244 (p), *atte Knolle* 1389 (p), *Boueknoll* 1402 (p) ('(at the, above the) hillock', *v.* atte, bufan, cnoll); (*ten' voc'*) *Cod(d)es-, Coddysplace* 1392¹, 1392³, 1393², *God(d)esplace* 1392³, 1393 (cf. William *Cod* 1332 (Chaldon H.), 1375, *v.* place); (*via voc'*) *Col(l)e(s)lane* 1412, 1413, *Colls Corner* 1682, *Coles Closes* l17 (cf. Richard *Colles* 1414, Robert *Coll(ys)* 1498, *v.* lane, corner, clos(e)); *regia via in* —, *regia via apud la Combe* 1389, 1390 (*v.* cumb); *lez copies* 1456 (*v.* copis); *the Courte Close* 1589 (*v.* court); *Croddehay* 1393 (*v.* (ge)hæg; the first el. may be ME *crud(de), crod(de)* 'curd'); *Crooked Close* 1589, (*place called*) *Crooked Stile* 1682 (*v.* croked, stigel); *atte Crouche* (p) 1390, 1392¹ ('at the cross', *v.* atte, crūc³); *Crowehay* 1392¹ (*v.* crāwe 'crow', (ge)hæg); *le Culver clos, Culver lond* 1461 (*v.* culfre 'dove', clos(e), land); *Dammons gate*, — *Howse* 1664² (cf. John *Dammon* 1664 (Broadmayne); (*haie domini*) *Biwestedurnefordesyat* 1393, 1394 ('to the west of Durneford's gate', *v.* bī, westan, geat, cf. William- 1390, John *Durneford* 1402); *toft' voc' Dynyasclos* 1391, *claus' voc' Denyashey* 1461 (probably a form of the pers.n. or surname *Denis*, cf. Walter *Denyas* 1332 (M. Crichel), *v.* clos(e), (ge)hæg); (*le*) *Estfild, -fyld* 1449, 1457, 1460, *la Estfeld* 1477, *the East Field* 1682 (*v.* ēast, feld, cf. *le Westfild infra*); (*la*) *Fennyford(e)* 1393, *Fernyford* 1461 ('muddy or ferny ford', *v.* fennig, fearnig, ford); *Fiftyneakres* 1398 (*v.* fīftēne, æcer); *prat' apud la Fyschous* 1391 (*v.* fisc, hūs); *Flourlond* 1404 (cf. the analogous Flower Lds in Charminster par. *infra*); *cursus aque apud Frelondsherd* 1453 ('gap at *Frelond*' ('land free from service or charge'), *v.* frēo, land, sceard, cf. Freeland Sx 162); *le Furslade* 1450, *le Forsslade* 1461 (*v.* fyrs, slæd); *the Furzie close* l17 (*v.* fyrsig); *Gannersplace* 1393 (no doubt a surname but the form is doubtful, *v.* place); *Garliham* 1461 (perhaps gār-lēac 'garlic', hamm, cf. *lez lekebeddys* in E Lulworth par. *supra*); *terre voc' Gildonleyn* 1461 (cf. Henry *le Gilden* 1340², *v.* leyne 'arable strip', cf. Newnham's in E Lulworth par. *supra*); *regia via voc' Goldmoreslane* 1389 (cf. *terr' Edward Goldemor* 1392¹, *v.* lane); *regia via apud le|la Gore* 1414, 1416 (*v.* gāra); *regia via apud Grenedeche* 1414 (*v.* grēne¹, dīc); *le Grenewey* 1450² (*v.* grēne¹, weg); *ten voc' Harries* 1458 (cf. *cot'|pratum nuper (in tenur')* *Agnet' Harry(e)s*, — *Harries* 1454, 1469, 1484); *Harn(e)hull* 1394, 1414, *bysoutheharnhulle* 1404 ('(to the south of) the rocky hill', *v.* hæren, hyll, bī, sūðan, though hār² (wk. obl. *hāran*) 'grey' or hara (gen.sg. *haran*) 'a hare' would also be possible first els., cf. Harnhill Gl 1 75, Harn Hill Gl 3 114); *Hart-* 1438, *Hertcom(be)* 1451, 1461 ('stag valley', *v.* heorot, cumb); *Hearth Bay* 1682 (in bounds of E Burton *supra* near R. Frome, so probably bay² 'a dam'; first el. perhaps ModE hearth 'fireplace of a smith's forge, etc.'); *le Hethfild* 1461, 1469 (*v.* hǣð, feld); *ten' voc' Hymburys* 1458 (cf. *ten' nuper-, terr' Radulphi Hymbury* 1451, 1454); *le Hope* 1463 (*v.* hop¹ 'small enclosed valley'); (*la*) *Hulle* 1390, 1412 (cf. John *de la Hulle* 1288, *v.* hyll); *ten' voc' Hurdys* 1458 (cf. *ten' nuper Johannis Hurd* 1457); *la Hurste* 1393 (*v.* hyrst); *Islyaker* 1391 (*v.* æcer); *via voc' Keymerslane* 1412, *Kymershegge* 1482 (cf. Beatrice *K(e)ymer(e)s* 1412, 1413, Thomas *Kymer* 1487, *v.* lane, hecg); *una ham voc' Kotterynpoul* 1391 (perhaps 'cottagers' pool', *v.* cotere, pōl, if *-yn-* represents a ME wk.pl. -ene, *v.* -ena); (*unu' cotag' voc'*) (*la*) *Knappyde-, Knappidehall(e)* 1391, 1392³, 1393, 1393², (*le*) *Knappedhall(e)* 1450, 1459, 1461 (*v.* hall; the first part of the name probably means 'provided with an ornament', from ME *knap(pe)* '? an embossed ornament on or under a roof' (c. 1475 (c. 1400) MED) and -ede; *knapped* 'broken' in the phrase *knapped flints* is not recorded before 1861 NED, though the vb. *knap*¹ from which this word is derived is recorded from c. 1470); *Ladiclos* 1461 ('close dedicated to the Virgin Mary', *v.* hlǣfdige, clos(e)); *atte Lake* (p) 1389 (*v.* atte, lacu); *Lanmede* 1391, 1455, *Landmede* 1394, *Westlanmede* 1438 (from mǣd and land, the latter perhaps in the sense 'estate, boundary', cf. Brk 782, *Londmede* Gl 4 148); *Langlynche* 1451 (*v.* lang¹, hlinc); *Lascombe* 117 (first el. perhaps lǣssa 'smaller', *v.* cumb); *prat' voc' Laufulham* 1459 (perhaps 'lawfully held enclosure', from ME laghful 'lawful' and hamm, but a surname is possible, cf. William —, Richard *Langh'f(o)ul* (probably for *Laugh-*) 1332 (Canford M.)); *Est-, Westlidwort* 1461; *Loksherde* 1438 (cf. *cotag'/prat' nuper* (*in tenur*) *Willelmi Lukkes, — Lokeys* 1460, 1464, 1469, *v.* sceard 'gate, gap'); *curs' aque apud Lorteborn* 1412 ('dirty stream', *v.* lort(e), burna); *Loueacre* 1414 (from lufu 'love' and æcer, perhaps in allusion to a courting place); *Maynards Furres* 117 (*v.* fyrs); *le Marle* 1438, *Marling-, Marlyngcroft* 1393, *Marlyngput* 1389, *-pit* 1461, *Marlepytfurlong* 1450 (*v.* marle 'marl', marling, croft, pytt, furlang); *Bi-, Bywestemed(e)wey(e)* 1398, *the old Meade Way, the Thornebush in the westside of Meadway* 1682, 'meadow path', *v.* mǣd, weg; *Bi-, Byweste-* is '(land) to the west of —', *v.* bī, westan); *Merkynhill* 1451 (*v.* hyll, cf. merkin 'the female pudendum' 1656 NED); *Met(e)lond* 1390 (Professor Löfvenberg suggests that the first el. may possibly be identical with that in OE *metecorn* 'allowance of corn to dependants'); *Middle Field* 1682; *Modeldych* 1390, 1393, *-dich* 1393, *Moduldich* 1451, *Muddeldiche* 1459, *-dyche* 1498 (perhaps '(ditch at) mud hill', from mudde, mode and hyll, with dīc); *Nadderham* 1391 ('enclosure frequented by adders', *v.* nǣddre, hamm); *Netelgurner* 1486 ('granary surrounded by nettles', *v.* netel(e), gerner, if *-gurner* is for *-garner* or *-gerner*); *lez Nyneacres* 1461 (*v.* nigon, æcer); *North Close* 1682, 117; *Odammesclos* 1393 (the surname *Odam*, *v.* clos(e)); *terre apud le Toppe de Ordhill* 1461 (perhaps 'point(ed) hill', *v.* ord, hyll, with topp); (*loc' voc'*) *le Outelet(e) iuxta Estburton* 1456 *et freq* to

1484, *Outlett* 1682 (*v.* utlete 'outlet, channel', cf. *le Owte lett* in Moreton par. *supra*, E Burton *supra*); *le Parke Coppy* 1588 *Comm* (*v.* park, copis); *meadow called Pileham* 1682 (*v.* pīl 'pile, stake', hamm); (*fossat' apud*) *Pleystret(e)* 1413–1442, *Playstret(e)* 1472, 1475 (*v.* plega 'play, sport, games', strǣt, cf. *Pleystrete* in Preston par. *infra*); *Poschescrofte* 1404, *Potchecroft* 1452, *Pac(c)hecroftys*- 1445, *Patchecroftlane* 1457, *Po(t)checroft(es)lane* 1450[2], 1452, 1478, 1490, *Pochecrafte ys lane* 1498, *Poschislane* 1393, *Powchy lane* 1607 (cf. William *Posh* 1330, — *Poissh* 1332, John *Possch* 1375, *v.* croft, lane, cf. Patch Croft in Wareham par. *supra*); *Presburgh* 1440 (perhaps 'priest's manor house', *v.* prēost, burh); *Puckysbarry, Puckysway* 1451 ('goblin's hill or barrow, and path', *v.* pūca, beorg, weg); *punfald'* 1413– 1484 (*v.* pund-fald 'pound'); *Purbecke gate* 1682 (perhaps 'gate on road leading towards Purbeck', *v.* Isle of Purbeck *supra*, geat); (*la More voc'*) (*la*) *Redde* 1475 (perhaps a circumlocution (and then ellipsis) for 'the red moor', *v.* rēad, mōr, but possibly hrēod 'reed, reed-bed'); *le Rigge* 1461 (*v.* hrycg 'ridge'); *curs' aque apud Rodlake* 1414 (*v.* hrēod 'reed', lacu); *Round Doles* 1682 (*v.* round, dāl); *le Rowbargh* 1475, *Roucroft* 1442 (*v.* rūh (wk. obl. rūgan), beorg, croft); *Sallarsacre* 1451 (probably a form of the surname *Sellar*, *v.* æcer); *close called Shadbury* 1589, *Shabury Corner* 1682 (perhaps from scēad or sc(e)adu and burh (dat. sg. *byrig*), with corner); *Scherfeld* 1404 (*v.* scīr[2] 'bright', feld); *curs' aque apud Shyteport* 1412, *reg' via in Shitportstrete* 1452 ('dirty market', or 'dirty gateway', from scite 'dung' and port[2] or port[3], with strǣt); *Shitten Stile* 1682 (from shitten 'filthy', and stigel); *ten' voc' Slyves* 1463, 1477 (cf. *ten' nuper Agn' Slyue* 1416); *le S(o)uth-do(u)n* 1449, 1455 (*v.* sūð, dūn); *le Southfild* 1451, 1461 (*v.* feld); *Soutlude* 1408 (*v.* sūð; the second el. may be hlȳda 'ledge' or hlȳde 'noisy stream'); *curs' aque apud Spitele*, — *Spitile* 1398, — *la Spytell* 1414, (*la*) *Sputel(e)*, *la Sputule* 1414, 1416 (*v.* spitel 'hospital, religious house'); *Stakeford* 1457 ('ford marked by stakes', *v.* staca, ford); *Stanesmede* 1455, *-more* 1461 (cf. Peter *del Estane* 1195, Robert *de la stane* 13, 'at the stone or rock', *v.* stān, mǣd, mōr); *Stepps* 1663 (associated with a watercourse, *v.* stæpe 'step, stepping-stone'); *cursum aque apud le Sterte* 1404 (*v.* steort 'tail of land', cf. *Stertlake* in Coombe K. par. *supra*); *the Stonebridge* 1663 (cf. *Stenyngbridge* 1531, *v.* stān 'stone', stǣnen 'made of stone', brycg); *Stuntecnoll* 1279, *Stincknoll(e)* (*Moore*) 1663, 1664[2], *Stinkenole* — 1663, *Stinknell Moore* 1664[2] ('Stunta's hillock', from the OE pers.n. *Stunta* and cnoll, but the first el. could be stunt 'steep', cf. Stuntney Ca 220–1, with mōr); *via regia iuxta le Swell* 1438 (*v.* swelle 'rising ground', but cf. foll.); *Swilyate* 1454 (from swille 'sloppy mess' and geat 'gate', perhaps here 'flood-gate', cf. Swilgate Gl 1 12 and prec.); *Teneakyrs* 1486 (*v.* tēn, æcer); *Twelfacres* 1451, *Mr. Clavells twelve acres* 1682 (*v.* twelf); *1 acr' Undertheholes* 1392[1] ('below the hollows or holes', *v.* under, hol[1]); *warenn'* 1280 (*v.* wareine); *atte Walle* (p) 1392[1] (*v.* atte, wall); *le Westfild* 1451, *West Field* 1682 (*v.* west, feld); *1 quarta acr' iac' bywesteton* 1391 ('to the west of the farm or village', *v.* bī, westan, tūn); *Whit(e)field* 1682 (*v.* hwīt, feld); *Whitefurlong* 1451 (*v.* hwīt, furlang); *viam apud Whitsshey* 1394 (cf. William *White* 1393[2], *pastur' Johannis White* 1463, *v.* (ge)hæg); *prat' voc' Wilde-, Wyldeham* 1391, *aque et piscar'...apud Wildemede* 1393, 1457 ('wild or desolate enclosure and meadow', *v.* wilde, hamm, mǽd); *Winfreth Weare* 1682 (*v.* wer 'weir', cf. Winfrith Newburgh *supra*); (*prat' voc'*) *Withi-, Wythi-, Wythy(h)am* 1393, 1394, *Witheham* 1461 (*v.* wiðig 'willow', hamm); (*le*) *Wodcombe* 1451, 1461 (*v.* wudu, cumb); *de la Wodecote* 1280 (p) (*v.* wudu, cot); *Wod-* 1451, *Wode-* 1478, *Woodfurlong* 117 (*v.* wudu, furlang).

Woodsford

WOODSFORD (SY 763906), EAST & WEST WOODSFORD, WOODSFORD STRANGWAYS (site of)

> *Werdesford* 1086 DB, 1194 P (p), 1210–2 RBE, 1212 Fees, 1213 Cur (p), 1268 *Ass* (p), 1268 FF (*Est-*), 1280 *Ass*, 1285 FA (*Est-, West* —), (*Est* —) 1303 FA, 1335 Pat, 1336 FF, Cl (— *Bellet*), 1361 *Ilch* (— *Belet*), 1440 IpmR (*Est-*), 1444 *Weld*[1], 1445 FF (— *Bolet*), 1457 IpmR (— *Bolet*), -*fort* 1086 Exon, *Werdeford* 1196 ChancR (p), 1197 P (p), 1241 Ch, 1268 *Ass* (p) *et passim* to 1353 Pat (— *Belet*, — *Abbot's*), 1388 Cl (— *Belet*), *Est Werdford* 1303 FA
>
> *Wardesford* 1086 DB, 1323 Pat, 1428 FA, *Wardeford* 1221 Sarum, 1275 RH
>
> *Wirdes-, Wyrdesford(e)* Hy 3 (14) Cerne (p), Ed 1 *AD*, 1280 *Ass* (-*belet*), 1282 Orig (— *Belet*), 1291 Tax, 1298 *AD*, 1306 Abbr, 1317 Pat (— *Belet*), 1318 FF, Ch, 1320 ib, 1332 SR, 1335 Pat, 1340 ib (*Est* —) *et freq* to 1498 *Ct* with the additions *Est-* or -*Belet, Westwyrdesford* 1408 *Weld*[1], 1431 FA, *Wyrde-, Wirdeford(e)* 1244 *Ass* (p), 1327 *SR*, 1412 FA, 1467 *Weld*[1], -*fforde* 1535 VE, *Wyrte-* 1270 (1372) *ChrP, Wyrdus-* 1389 *Weld*[1], 1392 *Ct, Wyrdys-* 1417 *Ilch, Wirdisford* 1428 FA
>
> *Weyrdeford* 1268 *Ass*
>
> *Wodesforde Belet* 1280 *Ass, Woddes-* 1544 *Ilch, Woodford* 1575 Saxton, *Woodsford* 1682 *Weld*[1], 1741 Hutch[3] (— *Strangways*), *East Woodford, West Woodford or Woodford Strangeways* 1774 Hutch[1]
>
> *E(a)stwordesford* 1337 DorR, 1428 FA, *Wordesford Bolet* 1458 *AD Vrideford* 1344 (14) Cerne

Probably 'Wīgheard's ford', from the OE pers.n. *Wīgheard* and **ford**, as suggested by Ekwall (DEPN); a N–S road crosses R. Frome here (now by a bridge, but there are still two fords marked 6″ further downstream). A possible alternative for the first el., postulated by Kökeritz PN Wt 67, is an OE (WSax) **wierde** 'beacon', an *i*-mutated variant of OE *wearda* or *wearde* 'beacon' which are cognate with OE weard 'watch' and correspond to ON *varði*, *varða* 'beacon, cairn', cf. Goth *wardja* 'watcher' (for *wearda*, *wearde*, cf. also Löfvenberg 219, Ekwall DEPN s.n. Wardington); early forms without genitival -*s* are quite frequent, but the more numerous forms with -*s* would have to be explained as analogical; for a much later beacon here, *v.* Woodsford Castle *infra*. The parcel later called East Woodsford belonged to Cerne Abbey in 1086 DB (VCHDo 3 76), hence -*Abbot's*, *v.* abbod, ēast; that later called West Woodsford belonged to William *Belet* in 1086 DB (VCHDo 3 113) (remaining in the possession of this family until the time of Ed 2), and came to the *Strangways* family in the 18th cent. (Hutch[3] 1 449), hence the affixes -*Bel(l)et*, -*Bolet*, -*Strang(e)ways*, *v.* west. There was a mill at West Woodsford in 1086 DB (VCHDo 3 113).

(OLD) GRAVEL PIT(s). HIGHER BARN. ST JOHN THE BAPTIST'S CHURCH, cf. 'church of *Werdeford*' 1297 Pat. STURT'S WEIR, on R. Frome, cf. Humphrey *Sturt* to whom the farm of East Woodsford belonged a1774 (Hutch[1] 1 167), *v.* wer. WOODSFORD CASTLE (remains of), — CASTLE FM, *Woddeford Castelle, the Castle of Woodesford* 1535–43 Leland, *Wodesforde Castell, Castrum de Wodsforde* 1579 *Wal*, *Woodsford Castle* 1811 OS, cf. *Castelclose* 1544 *Ilch*, *v.* castel(l); the castle was originally built in 1350 (Kelly); in 1861 Hutch[3] 1 450–2 parts of the castle are referred to as *the King's Room, the Queen's Room, the Guard Chamber, North & South Hall*, and *the Light or Beacon Tower* (supposed to have housed 'a light or beacon to guide passengers through the ford'). WOODSFORD DAIRY, *Dairy House* 1811 OS, 1840 *TA*. WOODSFORD FM formerly MANOR HO. WOODSFORD HEATH, 1811 OS, *The heath* 1840 *TA*, cf. *Little & New heath close, Great & Large heath Fd, Higher, Long & Middle heath Ground* 1840 *ib*, *v.* hæð. HIGHER WOODSFORD, 1811 OS, cf. *Lower Woodsford* 1840 *TA*.

FIELD-NAMES

The undated forms are 1840 *TA* 262. Spellings dated 1332 are SR, 1333, 1335 Hutch[3], 1340 NI, 1423 DorR, 1664 HTax, and 1732 Coker.
(a) Brake Fd (*v.* bræc[1]); Broad Cl; Bushy ham (*v.* hamm); Chalky Fd; Home Cowleaze & Barton, Middle & West Cowleaze; Driftway (*v.* drift, weg); East Fd; 18 Acres; (East & West) Eweleaze; Ferney Fd; 5, 40, & 14 Acres; Fry Md (cf. John *Frye* 1423); Great Md; Gregorys Md; Grove Grd; Gunhill (1732, *v.* gun; Coker quotes a tradition of 'the neighbour inhabi-

tants' to the effect that this is 'where they sawe the ordnance planted' when Woodsford Castle *supra* 'was beseiged and beaten down with ordnance', *v*. also Hutch³ 1 453); Hancocks Md; Heathy Cl; Horse Cl & Ham (*v*. hamm, as freq in this par.); The Knap, Knap Cl (*v*. cnæpp); Long ham; Longbridge ham; The Mead (cf. *Woodsford Mead* 1688 PlR); Moor or 17 Acres; East, Gt & Lt Moor; New Grd; Parsons ham (*v*. persone, but possibly a surname, cf. William *Person(es)* 1332, 1340); The Peak (*v*. pēac); The piece; Rick Yd; Rushy Grd & Plot; Ryals (cf. John *Ryall* 1664); Rye Fd; Six Acre Md; 16, 10, 3, 12, 28 & 22 Acres, East & West 20 Acres; Way Grd; Withy Bed, Withys; Wood Md.

Wool

Wool is in Bindon liberty (*v*. note under Winfrith hundred *supra*); it was a parochial chapelry belonging to Coombe Keynes in 1795 Boswell.

WOOL (SY 846866)

> ?*æt Wyllon* 1002–12 ASWrits, *Wille* 1086 DB (2×)
>
> *Welle* 1086 DB (2×), *Well(e)* Hy 3 Ipm, 1244 *Ass*, 1l3 *Ilch* (p), 1268 *Ass*, 1275 RH, 1276 Pat *et freq* to 1344 ib
>
> *Welles* 1166, 1210–2 RBE both (p), 1212, 1219 Fees, 1244, 1268 *Ass*, 1271, 1279 Ch
>
> *Woll(e)* 1249 FF, 1280 *Ass*, 1285 FA, 1331 Cl, 1333 Pat, 1355 Ipm, 1361 Pat (-*by Byneton*), 1377 *Ass*, 1403, 1425, 1438, 1638, 1663 all *Weld*[1]
>
> *Wull* 1251 Cl (p), 1268 *Ass*, 1568 *Ct*
>
> *Wool(l)* 1575 Saxton, 1578 *AD*, 1682 *Weld*[1]

'(At) the springs', from wella, -(e) (WSax wiella, -(e)), cf. Bindon Abbey *infra*. The form *æt Wyllon* (for other possible identifications of it, *v*. ASWrits 484) represents dat. pl. -um; forms in -*e* represent wk. nom. pl. -an or dat. pl. -um; forms in -*es* represent str. nom. pl. -as. Three springs are marked (6″) S of the village, cf. Spring St., Springfield Ctg, Well Head Cl all *infra*, and Hutch³ 1 348 where the name Wool is said to derive 'from the springs that abound there', in particular 'from a beautiful stream of water, which rises or wells up in a body, at the head of a small meadow...on the south side'. According to Hutch³ *op. cit.* 'Wool and Woolbridge are indifferently used, but among the poor it generally goes by the latter name', *v*. Wool Bridge in E Stoke par. *supra*.

STREET-NAMES: SPRING ST., cf. Springfield Ctg *infra*. Names of streets and buildings in Bovington Camp *infra* largely allude to scenes of fighting in the

First World War, e.g. BAPAUME RD, CAMBRAI HO, COLOGNE RD, MENIN RD, MESSINES RD & SQ, RHINE RD, ST OMER HO, ST QUENTIN HO, SOMME RD, YPRES SQ.

BINDON ABBEY (SY 855867), — FM (854866)

> *Binadon* 1154–9 CartAnt (*domui de* —, *Ecclesie Sancte Marie de* —), 1199, 1200 ib, 1204 LibR, John *AddCh, -d[ona]?* 1191–7 France, *Binnadun* John *AddCh*
>
> *Binedon(e)* 1199 CartAnt, 1200 ib (*ecclesie sancte Marie de* —), 1208 ChancR, 1210 CartAnt, 1212 Fees, 1214, 1215 Cur, 1218 FF, 1219 Pap, 1230 ChancR, Cl *et freq* to 1291 Tax (*Abbas de* —), *-dun(e)* 1230 P, 1251 Pat, *Bynedon(e)* 1210–2 RBE, 1211 ChancR, 1218 FF, 1226–8 Fees (*Abbas de* —), 1232 Cl *et freq* to 1431 FA, 1280 *Ass* (*Lib' Abbatis de* —, *vill' de* —), 1330 Pat ('— Abbey'), 1335 DoNHAS 55 15 (— *Abbas*), 1382 Pat (— *Abbots*), *-dun* 1268 *Ass*, *-ton* 1275 RH, 1361 Pat, *-doun* 1396, 1402, 1422 all Cl, *Bynydon* 1333 ib (p)
>
> *Binnedon* 1199 P, 1204 LibR, 1215 ClR, *-den* 1208 ib, *-dun(e)* Hy 3 (14) Cerne, 1227 FF, 1251 Pat, *Bynnedun* 1229 ib, *-don* 1288 *Ass* (*Abb' de* —)
>
> *Binnendon* 1200–14 P, *Bynnen-* 1208 ChancR, *Bynnyn-* 1320 Pat, *Binningdon* 1331 Cl
>
> *Binendon* 1201, 1205 ChancR, 1209 Libr, 1238 Cl, *Binin(n)-* 1214 ClR, 1219 Fees, *Biningden* 1310 Cl, *Bynen-, -in-, -yndon* 1237, 1259 ib *et freq* to 1344 Pat, *Bynig-* 1259 Cl, 1268 *Ass*, *Byning-* 1288 ib, *Bynyngdon* 1335, 1347 Cl, *-ton* 1360 ib
>
> *Benedon* 1280 *Ass*, 1325, 1329, 1362 all Pat, *Beny-* 1288 *Ass*, 1361 Cl, *Benendon* 1298 ib
>
> *Buen-, Bylyn-, Bydendon* 1280 *Ass*
>
> *Byn-, Bindon(e)* 1288 *Ass* (*Abb' de* —, *quoddam vinar' in vill' de* —), 1291 Tax, 1296 Fine, 1316 FA, 1331, 1333 Pat, 1385 Cl *et freq* to 1535 VE (*Monasterium Beate Marie de* —), 1638 *Weld*[1] (— *Rectoria*), 1682 ib (— *Rectory*), *-doun* 1399, 1400, 1406 all Cl, *Great Bindon* 1774 Hutch[1]

'(Place) within the hill', *v.* binnan, dūn, with reference to the original site of this Cistercian abbey at Little Bindon near Bindon Hill in W Lulworth par. *supra*; it was founded there c. 1150 and transferred to its present site in 1172 (Hutch[3] 1 350, VCHDo 2 82, RCHM 2 151). *Great Bindon* refers to Bindon Fm and is so named to distinguish it from Little Bindon *loc. cit.* Forms in *-den* and *-ton*

show confusion of the second el. with **denu** and **tūn**. For a form
Bindonestok 13, *v.* East Stoke par. *supra.* The abbey Lodge (6″) is
probably referred to in *le Gatehowse* 1638 *Weld*[1], cf. *a plott of ground
by the Gatehouse* 1682 *ib, v.* **geat, hūs, plot.** For Bindon liberty *v.*
Winfrith Hundred *supra.*

BOVINGTON (SY 828886), — FM (827883), *Bovintone* 1086 DB,
Bovin-, -ynton 1236 Fees, 1254 *Salis,* 1280 Ch, 1315, 1331, 1335 all
Pat, *Bou-, Bovyngton* 1288 *Ass,* 1312 Ipm, 1330 Pat, 1403 *Weld*[1],
Bonyngton (sic) 1291 Tax, *Bouygton* 1393 *Weld*[1], *Bovyndon* 1327–
1343 Cl, -*den* 1328, 1329 ib, *Bovehampton* 1475 *Weld*[1], 1478 *ib* (p),
Bovingdon, -ton 1535 VE, *Bovington Farme* 1682, 1703 *Weld*[1], 'farm
called after Bōfa', from the OE pers.n. *Bōfa* (Redin 85), and
-**ingtūn.** Forms in -*don* and -*den* show confusion of the final el.
with **dūn** and **denu**; forms in -*hampton* show confusion with **hām-tūn.**
There is mention of a 'church of St Andrew' here in 1330 Pat.

WOODSTREET FM (SY 856857)

> *Windestorte* 1086 DB, -*steort* 1225 FF
>
> *Wdestert* 1199 CartAnt (*terram de* —), *Wudestort* 1234 (13)
> HarlCh (*terram de* —), *Wodestort* 1234 (1279) Ch, -*stert(e)* 1280
> ib, 1285 FA, 1319 FF, 1331 Pat, *ten' apud Wodestertesleyen*
> 1423 *Weld*[1], *Woodsterte* 1535 VE, *Wodester* 1280 (1706) *Weld*[1]
>
> *Wodestret(e)* 1279 Ch, 1280 (1706) *Weld*[1], 1291 Tax, 1304 Orig,
> *Woodstreet* 1568 Hutch[3], 1582 ib ('grange of —'), 1703 *Weld*[1]
> (— *Farme*), 1811 OS, -*streat* 1774 Hutch[1], -*strett* 1774 ib,
> 1861 Hutch[3], *Woodstrete als. Woodstert* 1588 *Comm*
>
> (*Firme de*) *Woodsteed, Woodsteed Firma* 1638 *Weld*[1], *Woodsted
> Farme* 117 *ib*

If the DB and 1225 spellings were to be relied upon, this would
be 'windy tongue of land', or 'tongue of land near a winding path or
stream', from wind[1] or (ge)wind[2] and **steort**, with **leyne** 'arable strip';
the farm is situated on a narrow strip of cultivated land between areas
of woodland and at the head of a small stream which flows through
this strip to R. Frome. However, all the other spellings show that
the first el. was at an early date taken to be **wudu** 'wood', and it is
possible that the two spellings in *Winde-* are errors for *Wiude-* or
Wuide- where **wudu** may show influence from its early OE variant
widu, cf. Woodbury Hill in Bere R. par. *infra* for a similar eME form.
The second el. has undergone metathesis of *r*, which would make it

indistinguishable from ME *strete* < OE strǣt 'street', and the forms
in -*ste(e)d* show confusion with **stede** 'place'. The grange here probably belonged to Bindon Abbey *supra*. For a possible allusion to the
early medieval ownership of Woodstreet, *v.* the f.n. *Bakerland infra.*

ANDOVER CTGS, perhaps named from Andover Ha. BARN COPPICE,
Barne Copice 1640 *Weld*[1]. BETTY'S GRAVE, at the point where the
boundaries of Wool, E Stoke and Bere R. meet. BINDON MILL,
1703 *Weld*[1], *le Tucking Myll* 1635, 1638 *ib, the 2 Tucking Mills at
Bindon* 1682 *ib, Tucking Mill Hamms, -homes* 1682, 117 *ib, v.* **tucking-
mill, hamm,** Bindon Abbey *&* Fm *supra,* cf. Stony Weir, *Racke
Close infra*; other references to mills here or elsewhere in Wool are
'the mill of *Welle*' 1280 Ch, *the grist Mills, the Millers plott* 1682
Weld[1], *Mill lands, Plot below the Mill* 1839 *TA, v.* **grist-mill, plot.**
BINDON VILLA. BLINDMAN'S WD. BOVINGTON CAMP (1″), an army
camp; for names of buildings and streets here, *v.* Wool street-
names *supra.* BOVINGTON HEATH (1839 *TA*) *&* LANE, named from
Bovington *supra.* COLE WD, 1640, 1682, 117 all *Weld*[1], 1839 *TA,
Colewode* 1452 *Midd, v.* **wudu;** the first el. is uncertain, but it is
possibly col[1] 'coal, charcoal' in allusion to a wood where charcoal
was burnt, cf. foll. COLLIER'S BARN, COLLIERS LANE, the surname
Collier from ME *coliere* 'a maker or seller of charcoal', cf. prec.
CORNERWAY, cf. *the Corner Feilds* 1663 *Weld*[1]. CRANES MOOR, *Crane
Moor* 1839 *TA, v.* **cran, mōr;** it is near R. Frome; **corn**[2], a metathesized form of **cran,** may occur in the surname of Elizabeth *Corne*
1682 *Weld*[1]. DORSET WD, *Dorchester Coppey* 1588 *Comm,* — *Wood*
1640 *Weld*[1], (— *Coppice*) 117 *ib, Dorster Wood* 1839 *TA,* cf. *Dorchester Close* 1638 *Weld*[1], probably named from Dorchester par.
infra although a surname is possible, *v.* **copis.** EIGHT ACRE COPPICE,
Eight acres (Coppice), Davis Eight Acres 1839 *TA,* cf. John *Davey*
1498 *Ct.* FAIR FD, cf. *The Fair House* 1839 *TA, v.* **feire** 'fair, market';
the allusion is probably to the annual 'fair for cattle' or to 'another
termed the Dog-fair' when 'the boys of the village consider them-
selves at liberty to whip and drive away any dogs that they find at
large in the streets' (Hutch[3] 1 349). FROME CTG, near R. Frome, *v.*
RNs. *infra.* FURZY COPPICE, cf. *Pond plot Furzy Hill* 1839 *TA.*
HAREMERE WD, *Haremere* 1433, 1434, 1435 all *Weld*[1], *Haremare
Copice* 1640, 117 *ib, Hare Meare Coppice* 117 *ib, Hare Mare* (*Trees &
Wood*) 1839 *TA*; this wood is situated on the bdy between Wool
and Coombe K., so the second el. is likely to be (ge)mǣre 'boundary'

rather than mere[1] 'pool'; the first el. could be hær 'rock' or hæren 'rocky', hār[2] (wk. obl. *hāran*) 'grey' (perhaps with the meaning 'old'), or hara (gen. sg. *haran*) 'a hare', cf. *Harn(e)hull* in Winfrith N. par. *supra*. HIGHER WD, above Bovington *supra*. HIGHWOOD WD, *High Wood* 1839 *TA*, from Highwood in E Stoke par. *supra*. HOLY ROOD CHURCH, cf. *ecclesie de Wolle* 1403 *Weld*[1], *the Chapel of Wool* 1774 *Hutch*[1], *Chapel Fd, Church Close* 1839 *TA*. KNAP COPPICE, *v.* cnæpp. LAYS COPPICE, cf. *The Lays* 1839 *TA*, probably ModE dial. *lea, ley, lay* 'pasture-land, grass-land', an elliptical use of the adj. *lea, ley, lay* from OE lǣge 'fallow'. HR & LR LONG BOTTOM, cf. *Great Bottom (nine Acres), Little Bottom* 1839 *TA*, *v.* botm. LONG COPPICE. MONCTON BUSHES, *Monkton Bushes* 1839 *TA*, cf. *Munckton gate* c. 1628 *Strode*, 'farm belonging to the monks', *v.* munuc, tūn; the reference is no doubt to the monks of Bindon Abbey *supra*. NEW BLDGS. OLD DROVE, cf. *place called Drove* 1682 *Weld*[1], *(The) Drove, Wool Drove* 1839 *TA*, *v.* drove, Wool *supra*. PEPPERCLOSE TREES, *Pepper Close (Coppice & Trees)* 1839 *ib*, probably pepper with reference to soil characteristics, tinkers, peppercorn rent, or the crop itself, but the surname *Pepper* is also possible, cf. John *Piperwhit de Wolle* 1377 *Ass* ('pepper-white'). GT & LT PERRY COPPICE, *Great & Little Perry, Perry Wood, Little Perry Coppice* 1839 *TA*, cf. *Perry Legg Corner* 1682 *Weld*[1], *v.* pirige 'a pear-tree', leg. PIONEER RD, leading to Bovington Camp *supra*. PUG PIT, 1839 *TA*, 'goblin-haunted pit', *v.* pūca, pytt; for this name, cf. Gl 4 163 and the sur-name of William *Poukepitte* 1447 *DCMCt* (Osmington); the el. pūca also occurs as the surname of John *Puke* 1280 *Ch* who held land in Bovington *supra*. QUARR HILL (PLANT.), *Quar Plant.* 1839 *TA*, *v.* quarrere 'a quarry'. SEAFORTH CTG. SPRINGFIELD CTG, *v.* spring 'well-spring', cf. Spring St., Wool *supra*. STONY WEIR, — *Mead* 1843 *TA* (E Stoke), cf. *molendinum et piscaria de le Weare* 1635 *Weld*[1] which probably refers to this weir on R. Frome and to Bindon Mill *supra*, *v.* stānig 'made of stone', wer; for the fishery at Bindon *v.* Hutch[3] I 349; a similar weir further upstream is described as *the Stone Weare round against Bovington* 1682 *Weld*[1], cf. Bovington *supra*. WATER WHEEL, on a branch of R. Frome. WOODMAN'S CROSS, cf. Edward-, Benjamin *Woodman* 1664 HTax, *v.* cross 'cross-roads'. WOOL FM & HEATH (1811 OS, *Wooll Heath* 1682 *Weld*[1], *v.* hǣð; the bounds of Wool Heath are given in 1682 *Weld*[1] (M78 p. 46)).

FIELD-NAMES

The undated forms are 1839 *TA* 64. Spellings dated 1234 (1279), 1279, 1280 are Ch, 1268 *Ass*, 1327 *SR*, 1330 Pat, 1332 SR, 1393, 1568 *Ct*, 1449 *MinAcct*, 1535 VE, 1578 *AD*, c. 1586 Tres, 1589, 1641, 1861 Hutch³, 1589² *Comm*, c. 1628 *Strode*, 1658 *DCMDeed*, 1664 HTax, and the rest *Weld*¹.

(*a*) Alder Moor & Hedgerow; Allens Gdn (cf. Robert *Alayn* 1327); Barngate Md (from Burngate in W Lulworth par. *supra*); Bear Hams ((*prat' voc'*) *Beereham*(*s*) 1635, 1638, *the two Bearehames* l17, *Bearehams meadow* 1682, perhaps 'bare enclosure(s)', from bær¹ and hamm, but bær² 'pasture' or bearu 'wood' are also possible first els.); Bell Drong 1861 (a road above the church, according to Hutch³ 1 354 so called because of a tradition that the bells of Bindon Abbey were stolen and hidden near it, *v.* belle, drong); Bindon Lane (cf. *one Rush Plott at the head of Bindon Lane, place called Bindon gate* 1682, *v.* Bindon *supra*); Bindon Md (cf. 'the ham (*hammum*) of meadow which lies on the north of *Binedon* abbey' 1280, *v.* Bindon *supra*); The Black Bear Inn; Blandfords Bottom & Grd (cf. John *Blandford* 1664); Bourings Plot; Bovington Higher & Lower Wd (*v.* Bovington *supra*); Breach Cl, Breach Six Acres, Breaches Ham (cf. *le Brache* 1618, *Breach Field, place called Breach Barrs* 1682, *v.* brēc, barre 'a barrier'); (Little) Brick Kiln Cl; Broadfield; (Lr) Close; Cockrow (*Cockrode* (*Wood*) c. 1628, 1640, *Cock Ro*(*a*)*de* (*Wood*) l17, *v.* cocc-rodu 'cock-shoot'); Coles Barrow 1861 ('a large barrow in Wool Heath', *v.* beorg, cf. foll.); Coles Cl (cf. Eustace *Cole* 1332); Common Pce (cf. *Wooll Common* etc. *infra*); Conygar (Heath) (*v.* coninger); Cowleaze; Dairy Hills; Dry Md; Eweleaze; 5 acres; Flags Plot (cf. John *Flagg* 1682); The folly Cl (*v.* folie); Foxbury Plant. ('fox's earth', *v.* fox, burg); The Gravel Pit; The Ham(s) (*v.* hamm, as freq in this par.); Hill Cl; Home Plot (cf. *lez Home Closes* 1618, *v.* home); Horse Cl (*Hosseclasse* (sic) 1502, *Horseclose* 1531, 1635, *Two Hors Closes* l17, *v.* hors, clos(e)); Hurst Md (*v.* hyrst); Jeans Plot; Knowle Cl (*v.* cnoll); Land; Long Cl & Grd; Lucas Cl (cf. William *Lucras* (sic) 1682); The moor (cf. *la Mormede* 1280, *v.* mōr, mǣd); New Md; 9 Acres; Gt Onyx, Onyx Cl & 7 Acres (*atte Hundynoke* 1444 (p), *Howndinoke* 1535, *Hunnocks Close* 1635, *Honings Wood* 1640, 3 *closes called Hownocks, Homeinge Coppice* l17, *place called Hunnicks Stile, Honox Close next to Honox Lane* 1682, *Hunnox* (*Lane*) 1699 (18), 1703, 'the oak-tree frequented by dogs', *v.* hund, āc, with atte 'at the', stigel; -*yn*-, -*in*- in the earliest forms represents a ME wk.pl. -*ene*, *v.* -ena); The Orchard (cf. *le old Orchard* 1635, *v.* ald, orceard); Oxleaze (Little Wd) (*Oxeley Coppey* 1588 Comm, *Oxleas Wood* 1640, *Oxles Wood, Oxeleyes* l17, *v.* oxa, lēah or lǣs, copis); Pearces Plot; Pigeon House Cl; Pit; Pond Cl; The Pound (*v.* pund); Random (reading uncertain) Barn; Red Grd; Rick Barton Wd; Rookery; (Little) Rough Grd; The Sand Pit; Saxeys Ham (a surname, occurring three times in 1332 SR as *Sexi*, and as *Sexey* 1664 (Bere R.), from the ON pers.n. *Saxi*); Shepherd's plot; 6 Acres; Smiths Plot (cf. John *Smith* 1664); Snells Plot; Snooks Moor (cf. William *Snowk* 1393); 10 & 12 Acres; 20 Acres Md; The Warren (*v.* wareine); Water Cl, Little Water Md; Well Head Cl (cf. *the Wellhead*

194 DORSET

Ditches 1618, *(place called) Wellheadmoore* 1663, 1682, *v.* well-head 'source of a stream, spring', dīc, mōr, cf. Wool *supra*); West Fd; Wood Cl; (Middle) Woodpine (perhaps wudu-binde 'wood-bine'); Woodrows plot & Barn (cf. John *Woderove* 1327); Woodstreet Drove (*v.* drove, Woodstreet *supra*); Young Creech 1861 (*le Yonger Coppey* 1588 *Comm, Yongcreech Wood* 1640, *Yonkridge Coppice* l17, *v.* copis, possibly a Brit name from PrWelsh *crūg 'a hill', but earlier forms are needed; *Yo(u)n-* may represent gen.pl. *eowena* of OE eowu 'a ewe', cf. Youngcombe D 289).

(*b*) the *Arbor garden* 1682 (*v.* erber 'a garden', gardin); 'a meadow called *Bakerland*' 1589, *Bakerham (Meade, -Meadow)* 1638, l17, 1682, 1703 (cf. John *Baker* 1682, *v.* land, hamm, mæd, cf. *Bakersclous, -croft* in Coombe K. par. *supra*; some of these names may be older than the spellings suggest; in any case it should be noted that three virgates of land in Woodstreet *supra* were held in 1086 DB by Osmund *pistor* 'the baker' (VCHDo 3 114), and that Robert *de Welle(s)* held two hides of land in Wool in 1211 by the service of being the King's baker, likewise William *de Welle* 40 shillings rent in 1272 (Hutch³ 1 349)); *the Barley Frith* 1663 (apparently bærlic 'barley' and fyrhðe 'wood'); *place called Barton gate, Barton Meade* 1682 (*v.* beretūn); *Belbens meadow* 1682 (the surname *Belbin, -yn* found three times in 1664 HTax); *Byndon Wood* c. 1586, *Bindon Wood(s)* c. 1628, 1640, l17, *Bindon Woode ground* 1682 (from Bindon Abbey & Fm *supra*); *Bovington ditch* 1682 (*v.* dīc, Bovington *supra*); *Curcheford* 1268 (perhaps 'ford near a church', *v.* cirice, ford); *the East Field* 1682; *place called Gooseham* 1682 (*v.* gōs, hamm); *place called Hangmans Thorne, Langmans Thorne between Wooll Field and Burton Fields* 1682 (ModE hangman or the surname *Langman, v.* þorn, cf. Wool, E & W Burton in Winfrith N. par. *supra*); *Hasell Wood* 1640, l17, *Haslewood Coppice* l17 (*v.* hæsel); *Hymercombe* 1484 (*v.* cumb; the first el. may be hymele 'a hop plant', cf. *Le Hopyard infra*); *Holcombe* 1488 ('hollow valley', *v.* hol², cumb); *Le (old) Hopyard* 1635, 1638, *the old —, the new hopyard* l17, *v.* hoppe 'hop plant', geard, cf. *Hymercombe supra*); *le Hundredakyrs* 1484, *-acres* 1488 (*v.* hundred, æcer); *Iland Mo(o)re* 1638, l17 (*v.* ēg-land or ēa-land 'island', mōr); *Inne Court* 1682 (*v.* inn, court); *Westlarkebury* 1484 (probably 'lark hill', from lāwerce and beorg, a common name, with west); *Liver close adjacen' le Tucking Myll, Liverclose Mead* 1635, *Le(a)verclose (Mead)* 1638, *Liver Close* 1682 (*v.* lǣfer 'rush, reed', clos(e), mæd, cf. Bindon Mill *supra*); *Two Middle Closes* l17; *the Middle Field* 1682; *(place called) Newbridge* 1682; *the North River* 1682 (*v.* rivere, with reference to the banks of) R. Frome or one of its branches or tributaries); 'the park' (at Bindon) 1641 (*v.* park); *(the) Pear(e)-, Peeretree Close* 1635, 1682, l17 (*v.* peru, trēow); *one Racke Close* 1682 (*v.* rakke, cf. Bindon Mill *supra*); *Ruddestan* 1330; *Rush ground* 1703; *Seaven acres* 1682; *Sowthe Bere Coppie* 1588 *Comm, Southbery* (a coppice) 1641 (*v.* sūð, bearu, copis); 'wood of *Stocwud* without the abbey of *Bynedon*' 1234 (1279), *Stot-*1279, *Stocwode* 1280, *bosc' de Stokewod* 1449 (perhaps 'wood belonging to Stoke' with reference to E Stoke par. *supra*, *v.* wudu, cf. Bindon Abbey *supra*); *the Summer Feild* 1663 (*v.* sumor); *Well house* 1682 (*v.* wella, hūs, cf. Well Head Cl *supra*); *Wetheber Copice* 1640, *Withibery Coppice* l17 (*v.* wiðig, bearu, copis); *the Commons* 1618, *Wooll Common* 1682, *the common* *fieldes* 1578, *Wooll greene* 1682, *prat' de Wull* 1568, *Wo(o)ll Mead(e)* 1589[2], 1638, 1682, *the Common Mead* 1696 (18) (cf. Wool *supra*; the bounds of Wool Common, Wool Mead, and the common fields are given in 1682 *Weld*[1] M78 p. 46); *place called Woollem Crosse* 1682 (perhaps 'cross or cross-roads at *Woollem*' ('Wool hamm'), *v.* cros, cross).

IV. CULLIFORD TREE HUNDRED

This hundred was larger in c. 1086 GeldR than it is now (Anderson 118–19, VCHDo **3** 146–7), and parts that were included then have been included again here for topographical convenience, viz. Bincombe (now in Frampton liberty *infra*), the whole of Winterborne Came (part now in Frampton liberty), Portland (now a separate liberty, *v. infra*), Preston (now in Sutton Poyntz liberty, *v. infra*), Wyke Regis and Elwell in Upwey par. (now a separate liberty, *v. infra*), and Weymouth and Melcombe Regis (once separate boroughs, now united). Ashton in Winterborne St Martin par. was also a tithing in this hundred, *v.* St George hundred *infra*. Ringstead in Osmington par. and Frome Billet in West Stafford par. were tithings in Winfrith hundred and St George hundred respectively. Besides Preston and Sutton Poyntz itself (in Preston par.), the liberty of Sutton Poyntz contained Putton and East Chickerell in Chickerell par., and Stockwood par. (included in Yetminster hundred). Wabyhouse liberty consisted of part of Upwey par.

CULLIFORD TREE HUNDRED

  Cuferdestroue hundret c. 1086 GeldR

  hundredo de Cuiluertestrie 1195 P, *Culuertestriehundredo* 1196 ChancR

  Culverdestre 1228 (1352) Pat, *Culuerdestre(ue), Queluerdestre* 1244 Ass, *Cul-, Coluredestre, Culuestdetre, Cufferestre* 1268 *ib*, *Cul-, Kuluerdestre* 1280 *ib*

  Keuerdestre 1265 Misc

  Cylwardestre 1278 QW

  Kelfardestr' 1280 *Ass*

  Culfordestre 1275 RH, 1285 FA, 1389 Ipm, 1409 Cl, 1412 FA, *Kulfordestorre* 1399 Ipm

  Culvardes-, Culuardestre 1285 FA, 1288 *Ass*, 1308 Ipm, 1346 FA, 1352 *Ilch, Culfardestre* 1288 Ass, 1311 Cl, 1327 *SR*, 1332 SR

  Calwardestre 1288 *Ass*

  Kuvesdestre [Kynewardestru] 1303 FA

  Coly-, Colifordestre 1428, 1431 FA *et freq* to 1481 *MinAcct*, *Culifardestre* 1435 Fine, *Cullifordestrete* (sic) 1447 *DCM*, *Colyfford' Hundredum* 1502 Eton, *Colyffordystry, -tree* 1530 *Weld*[1], *Colyffordtre* 1539 LP

Named from the barrow called Culliford Tree in Whitcombe par. *infra* which was the meeting place of the hundred (Hutch³ 2 484). The final el. is trēow 'a tree'. The first part of the name is difficult. Feilitzen (215 note 4) suggests a pers.n. **Cylferð < *Cytelferð*, an anglicized form of ON **Ketilfrøðr*, ODan **Ketilfrith*. Alternatively Anderson (xi note 1) suggests that the first el. is an OE **cylfweard* 'mace-keeper' (used as a term for one who presided over the sessions of the hundred court), or (*op. cit.* 119) a pers.n. from the same word **cylfe* (corresponding to ON *kylfa* 'a club, the prow of a ship' and probably occurring as a p.n. el. with the meaning 'hill' in Kilve and Kilton So, *v.* EPN s.v. **cylfe*, DEPN s.n. Kilve) with -*weard* or -*heard*.

PORTLAND LIBERTY, 1795 Boswell, *Insula de Portlond* 1332 SR, *Liberty of Portland* 1664 HTax, cf. *Hundred' de Portlond(e)*, -*la(u)nd(e) et Wyk(e)* 1280, 1288 *Ass, v.* Wyke Regis & Elwell liberty, Portland par. *infra.*

SUTTON POYNTZ LIBERTY, — *Pointz* — 1795 Boswell, *Liberty of Sutton Points* 1664 HTax, cf. *Lib' Hug' Poynz* 1280 *Ass, v.* Sutton Poyntz in Preston par. *infra.*

WABYHOUSE LIBERTY, 1795 Boswell, *Liberty of Wayby House* 1664 HTax, *Liberty of Upwey alias Waybaiouse* 1863 Hutch³, *v.* Upwey par. *infra.*

WYKE REGIS & ELWELL LIBERTY, 1795 Boswell, *Wyke et Helewoll* 1332 SR, *Liberty of Weeke Regis and Elwell* 1664 HTax, *v.* Wyke Regis par. and Elwell in Upwey par. *infra,* cf. Portland liberty *supra.*

LOST OR UNIDENTIFIED PLACE-NAMES IN CULLIFORD TREE HUNDRED: *apud Barryhill in via regia* 1457 *Ct* (first el. perhaps beorg 'barrow', *v.* hyll); *Corrington* 1664 *Weld*¹ (perhaps from cweorn 'quern, hand-mill' and tūn, cf. Coringdon in Corscombe par. *infra,* but possibly a name in -ingtūn with an OE pers.n. *Cor(r)a,* cf. Corringham Li (DEPN)); *le Gore* 1460 *Ct* (*v.* gāra); *via regia vocat' Lytelgroue* 1457 *Ct* (*v.* lȳtel, grāf(a)); *Norbrooke* 1682 *Weld*¹ (probably '(place) to the north of the brook', *v.* norðan, brōc, cf. Westbrook in Upwey par. *infra*); *Weymede* 1460 *Ct* ('meadow by R. Wey', *v.* mǣd, RNs. *infra*).

Bincombe

Bincombe is in Frampton liberty, *v.* note under Culliford Tree hundred *supra.* In 1933 parts of Bincombe were added to the borough of Weymouth, and parts of the pars. of Broadwey, Preston and Upwey were added to Bincombe, for civil purposes (Kelly).

BINCOMBE (SY 686846)

   Beuncumbe 987 (13) Finberg 613 (S 1217)

   Beincome 1086 DB

   Biemcomme 1129 CartAnt, *Biemecomma* 1157 France, *Biencomme* 1157 ib, 1190 (1332) Ch, 1375 Pat, *-coma, -combe* 1174–82 France, *-comb* 1321 Winch (p), *Byencombe* 1398, 1405 Pat

   Bincumbe 1244 *Ass* (p), *Byncomb(e)* 1327 *SR*, 1332 SR *et passim* to 1459 *Weld*[1], *Binckombe* 1664 HTax, *Bincomb* 1670 Sheridan

   Bencumbe 1252 Ch, 1288 *Ass, -combe* 1326, 1387 Pat, 1393 *AD, Benecumbe* 1288 *Ass,* 1376 IpmR, *-comb(e)* 1375 Pat, 1376 Misc, *Benscumbe* 1291 Tax

Probably 'valley where beans are grown', from **bēan** and **cumb** (DEPN), cf. the f.n. *Piscombe infra.* Kökeritz 125 suggested that the first el. might be *bēona,* gen.pl. of **bēo** 'bee', but this looks extremely unlikely in view of the absence of early forms with medial *-e-* (apart from *Biemecomma* 1157), and since in any case **bēo** seems to form compounds only in the stem-form.

BINCOMBE BARN, DOWN (1811 OS, cf. *Down* 1838 *TA*), DAIRY, FM (LOWER —), HILL (1838 *TA*) & MARSH DAIRY (cf. *la Mersh* 1441 *HarlRoll, The Marsh* 1838 *TA*), all from Bincombe *supra, v.* **mersc.** EAST FM, cf. *The North Farm* and *The West Farm* 1837 *TAMap.* HILL BARN, from Bincombe Hill *supra.* HOLY TRINITY CHURCH, cf. 'the church of *Byncombe*' 1348, 1360 Pat, *Rectoriam (de Byncombe)* 1440, 1441 *HarlRoll,* and the f.n. *Cherchull infra;* a church here is mentioned in 1174–1182 France. RIDGEWAY HILL, 1680 *Sheridan, Ridgway hill* 1774 Hutch[1], named from the Roman road between Dorchester and Weymouth, *v.* Ridgeway in Upwey par. *infra.* ROW BARROW (lost), 1811 OS, a tumulus marked 6", *v.* **rūh** (wk. obl. *rūgan*), **beorg,** cf. Rowbarrow Hundred *supra.*

FIELD-NAMES

The undated forms are 1838 *TA* 18. Spellings dated 1129 are CartAnt, 1190 (1332) Ch, 1327 *SR*, 1332 SR, 1376 Misc, 1459 *Weld*[1], 1664 HTax, 1674, 1675 *Sheridan*, and the rest *HarlRoll*.

(*a*) Baker's Plot (cf. Richard *Baker*, granted manor of Bincombe in 1560 Hutch[3] 2 278); Broad Md (or Butts) (cf. 'the meadow called *le Brad*...' 1376, *pratum vocat' Brodemede* 1441, *v.* brād, mǣd, cf. foll.); Butts Md (*v.* butt[2] or butte, cf. prec.); Clan (cf. *Clandon* 1376, 1441, *Clandenescorde* 1376, *Clanden* 1439, *Northclandon* 1441, 1442, *Clandonys(fete)* 1446, 1447, from clǣne 'clean, clear of weeds' and dūn 'hill', with norð and fōt 'foot of a hill', cf. the identical (but apparently separate) Clandon in the adjacent par. of Winterborne St M.; the forms of the second el. show confusion with denu 'valley'; -(*s*)*corde* is perhaps an error; the modern f.n. Clan would seem to be the result of back formation); Clapcot's House Cl, Clappcott's Ctg, Orchd, Plot & South Cl (cf. Clapcotts in Winterborne Her. par. *infra*); The Common; Cooper's Orchd & Plot; Fook's Plot; Gravel Altmt; Home Cl; House's Plot; Huish Btm (*v.* hīwisc); Lane Cl; (Great) Linch (*v.* hlinc 'ridge', cf. Smallinch *infra*); Middle Fd; New Grd; Pearce's Plot (cf. William *Pirys* 1443); Piscombe (cf. *Puscumbeswey, Purscombesweye* 1376, 'valley where peas are grown', *v.* pise, cumb, with weg); The Pound (*v.* pund); Quarry Pce & Lime Kiln (cf. *querrer de Byncombe* 1459); The Royal Oak Inn & Bowling Alley at Ridgway (*v.* Ridgeway in Upwey par. *infra*); Smallinch ('narrow ridge', from smæl, hlinc, cf. (Great) Linch *supra*); Snaverland (*Snawefurlong* 1376, 'furlong where the snow lies long', *v.* snāw, furlang); (Tibbs') South Closes (cf. 'the south pasture' 1376); South Fd (Altmt) ('the south field' 1376); Wallis's Plot; West Fd ('the west field' 1376); West Md.

(*b*) *Ærnelai* 1129, *Arnelai* 1190 (1332), *Ernlee* 1376 ('wood or clearing frequented by eagles', from earn (gen.pl. *earna*), and lēah); *Alphillicomme* 1129, 1190 (1332) ('Ælfhild's valley', from the OE fem. pers.n. *Ælfhild* and cumb; the medial -*i*- may represent an OE gen.sg. inflection -*e*); *Bigleye* 1443 (perhaps 'bees' nest clearing' from bīc and lēah); *Bovetheton* 1327 (p) ('above the village', *v.* bufan, tūn); (*viam Regiam in*) (*La*) *Brodelane* 1440, 1447, *Brodelanesende* 1441 (*v.* brād, lane, ende); *le Caucey-, la Causey-, calcetu' inter Rectoriam* (*de Byncombe*) *et ten' Johannis Palet* 1439, 1440, 1441 (*v.* caucie 'raised way in marshy land'); *Cherchull, Churchull* 1376, *Churchehill* 1441 (*v.* cirice, hyll, cf. Holy Trinity Church *supra*); *la Co*(*u*)*mb, le Coumbe Hethfeld* 1376 (*v.* cumb, hǣð, feld); *campo voc' la Cornefelde* 1440, -*fylde* 1446 (*v.* corn[1] 'corn, grain', feld); 'the east field' 1376; *lez Eweforlong* 1376 (*v.* eowu, furlang); *Framptewey* 1376 (perhaps 'road to Frampton', *v.* weg; Frampton par. is some 8 miles distant but Bincombe was a member of Frampton liberty); *Fulewyll* 1376 ('dirty well, spring or stream', *v.* fūl (wk. obl. *fūlan*), wella (WSax wiella)); *Furlongishede* 1446 (*v.* furlang, -es[2], hēafod 'headland'); *Greweforlong* 1376 (perhaps an error for *Crowe*- or *Crewe*- from OE crāwe, crǣwe 'crow'); 'the lord's *heymede*' 1376 (*v.* hēg 'hay', mǣd); *Hethfeld* 1376 (*v.* hǣð, feld, cf. *le Coumb Hethfeld supra*); *Holecomb* 1376 (*v.* hol[2] (wk. obl. *holan*), cumb); *la Knoll* 1443 (*v.* cnoll);

Lyde- 1445, 1446, *Lidelonde* 1447 (the first el. could be hlēda, hlȳda 'bench, ledge' or hlȳde 'noisy stream', *v.* land); *Litel-* 1442, 1446, *Lytellane* 1445 (*v.* lȳtel, lane); *foss' vocat' Mededíche* 1441 (*v.* mǣd, dīc); *semitem apud Merestike* 1443 ('boundary stick or post', *v.* (ge)mǣre, sticca); *Myddelhull* 1376 (*v.* middel, hyll); 'the north field' 1376; 'the *Portweye*', *la Portwey*(*e*) 1376, *Portewey* 1446 (*v.* port-weg 'road leading to a market town', probably with reference to the Dorchester–Weymouth road, cf. Ridgeway Hill *supra*); *Pothull* 1376 (pot(t) 'a pot' or potte 'a deep hole, a pit', with hyll, cf. Pothill Sx 187); *la Rewe* 1376 (*v.* rǣw 'row of trees, hedgerow'); *Snooks-* 1674, *Snooke Lane* 1675 (the surname *Snook*, cf. Snooks Moor in Wool par. *supra*); *le Sondylonde* 1444 (*v.* sandig, land); *Soure* 1443 (perhaps the adj. sūr 'sour, damp' used elliptically for 'sour land', but sūre 'sorrel' is also possible, cf. Sewer D 308 and the lost f.n. *le Soure* in Preston par. *infra*); *Spurehey* 1446, 1447, *Spurhay* 1447 (*v.* (ge)hæg; Professor Löfvenberg suggests that the first el. is probably OE *spura*, a side-form of spora, 'a spur (of land)', *v.* Luick § 78 and Anm. 2); *atte Strete* 1327 (p) (*v.* atte 'at the', strǣt, perhaps with reference to the Dorchester–Weymouth Roman road, cf. *co'i strata ville* (*de Byncombe*) 1442, 1447); *Suttewey*(*e*) 1376, 1443 (*v.* weg; the first el. may be an OE pers.n. *Sutta* suggested for Sutcombe D 168, Sotwell Brk 529); *Waleland* 1376 (possibly 'land of the Welshmen or serfs', *v.* walh (gen.pl. *wala*), land); 'the *Waterfury*' 1376 (probably 'furrow or trench near the water', from wæter and furh (WSax dat. sg. *fyrh*); Professor Löfvenberg notes that the ME form *-fury* probably reflects an OE side-form **fyr(i)g* in the dat., cf. Campbell § 628); 'the winter field' 1376.

Broadwey

In 1933 part of Broadwey was transferred to the borough of Weymouth and the remainder transferred to Bincombe for civil purposes (Kelly).

BROADWEY (SY 667835)

?Wai(*a*) 1086 DB, Exon, *Veia* 1142 France, *Waie* 1166 RBE (p), 1210 P, 1227 FF, *Waya* 1236 Fees, *Waye* 1269 Misc

Brode Way 1243 Fees, *-way*(*e*), *-waie* 1280 *Ass et freq* to 1483 *Weld*[1], *-wey*(*e*), *-weie* 1269 Misc *et freq* to 1487 *Weld*[1] (*curs' aque in-*), *Brode Wey* 1428 FA, *Bordwey* 1326 Midd, *Brodway* 1664 HTax

Bradeweye 1249 FF, 1291 Tax, 1371 Pat, *-way*(*e*) 1280, 1288 *Ass*, 1428 FA, *Bradwey* 1575 Saxton

Waye Nichole 1318 FF, *Waye Nich'* 1340 NI, *Wey St Nicholas* 1437, 1442 Hutch[3]

One of several places named from R. Wey (*v.* RNs. *infra*), the others being Creketway, Rowaldsway, Southway, Wayhoughton all probably in this par., Radway (probably) in Preston par., Causeway

in Radipole par., Upwey par. and Stottingway in Upwey par., and
Weymouth par. all *infra*. The affix *Broad-* refers to 'the river's
expanding itself at this place to a greater breadth' according to Hutch[1]
1 419, but it is perhaps more likely that it refers to the size of the
village or manor, *v*. brād 'broad, large'. *Nichole*, etc., is from the
dedication of the church, *v*. St Nicholas's Church *infra*. There were
no less than eight DB manors called *Wai(a)* and although it is almost
certain that at least one of these represents what later became
Broadwey, it is not possible to identify them individually in spite of
the attempt to do so by Eyton 121–2, cf. DBGeography 74 ff,
VCHDo **3** 147 fn. 67, DBGazetteer 117.

CREKETWAY (lost), 1774 Hutch[1], 1863 Hutch[3], *Kriketesweie* 1371
AD I, *Crikettesway* 1412 FA, *Crykettesweye* 1420 FF, *Kre(c)ketway(e)*
1549, 1601 Hutch[3], *Cricketway(e)* 1549, 1649 ib, a manor on R. Wey
(*v*. RNs. *infra*, cf. Broadwey *supra*), named from the family of
(*de*) *Cru(c)ket*, *Cri(c)ket* from Cricket So which had lands in Broadwey
from 1269 (Hutch[3] **2** 485–7) and which is mentioned here in 1303
FA, 1315 Cl, 1327 *SR*, etc.; it probably lay in the E part of the par.
(Hutch[3] **2** 487); the same family no doubt possessed the 'lower
water-mill called *Criketesmull* in *Weye Ruwant*' 1392 AD I, *v*. **myln**,
cf. Rowaldsway and *Orchardesmull infra*.

NOTTINGTON (FM) (SY 662826), *Nouington* (probably for *Notting-*)
1199 CartAnt, *Notinton* 1212 Fees, *Notington* 1234 (13) HarlCh, 1234
(1279) Ch, 1487 Weld[1], *Notrington* (sic) 1279 Ch, *Nottingeton* 1280
(1706) Weld[1], *Not(t)yngton* 1388 FF *et freq* to 1483 Weld[1], *Estnottyng-
ton* 1525 Hutch[3], (*West*) *Nottington* 1594 DCMDeed, *Nettington*
1811 OS, 'farm called after Hnott(a)', from the OE pers.n. *Hnott(a)*
(cf. hnott 'bare, bald') and -ingtūn, with ēast, west; the strong form
of the pers.n. is found in Natsley D 58 and Natsworthy D 528, the
weak form is possible in *Hnottan forð* BCS 1217 and *Hnottan
mæræ* BCS 491 (cf. Brk 780).

ROWALDSWAY (lost), *Wayernaud* (for -*eruaud*) 1249 FF, *Waye
Rewald* 1285 FA, *Rowaldeswey(e)* 1299 Ipm, 1299 (e15) *MiltRoll*,
1436 FF, *Way(e) Rouald* 1299 Ipm, 1299 (e15) *MiltRoll*, *Ronwaldes-
weye* (for *Rou-*) 1303 FF, *Waye Rywaud* 1313 Ipm, *Way Ryward*
1314 Hutch[3], *Wayernwaut* (for -*eruwaut*) 1316 FF, *Wayruwart* 1316
Hutch[3], *Waye Rowand* (for -*aud*) 1370 AD I, *Weye Rowaud* 1384 Cl,
— *Roel* 1384 AD I, — *Ruwant* (for -*aut*) 1392 ib I, II. — *Briawnt*

(sic) 1395 ib I, *Wey —, Way Rewal(l)d als. Caux-, Cawx-, Cawsewey*
1512–1525 *Pars*, a manor on R. Wey (*v.* RNs. *infra*, cf. Broadwey
supra), probably named from a certain *Rualet de Waie* mentioned in
1166 RBE (p. 218) as suggested in Hutch³ **2** 486. The 16th cent. *alias*
forms suggest that it was near Causeway in Radipole par. *infra*.
For an early mill here, *v. Orchardesmull infra*.

SOUTHWAY (lost), *Sutwaye* 1285 FA, *Suthwei* c. 1296 Hutch³, *-waye*
1303 FA, *South Wey* 1464 DCMCt, *South(e)wey* 1465 *Weld*¹, 1481 *Ct*,
1486 *Weld*¹, a manor on R. Wey (*v.* RNs. *infra*, cf. Broadwey *supra*),
v. sūð 'south'; presumably situated south of Broadwey.

WAYHOUGHTON (lost), *Wayehogheton*, (*pontem in*) *villa de Wayhouton*,
Wayhoute all 1288 *Ass*, either another unidentified manor on R. Wey
(*v.* RNs, *infra*, cf. Broadwey *supra*), or an alternative name for one
of the other manors named from the river; the affix *Hogheton*, etc. is
probably a post-Conquest formation similar to that in Winterborne
Houghton par. *infra* and meaning 'Hugh's manor', *v.* tūn; this may
in fact be one of the three manors called *Waia* held by Hugh fitz Grip
and his wife in 1086 DB (VCHDo **3** 69, 103); on the other hand the
Hugh in question could be the Hugh *de Waie* mentioned as having
interests in both *Waie* and *Winterborn* in 1210 Hutch³ **2** 486. For the
bridge (*pontem*) here, cf. the f.n. Bridge Mdw *infra*.

BROADWEY FM & HO. COFFIN PLANT., perhaps the surname *Coffin*
(common in 1664 HTax). FORD, cf. Nicholas *Atteford* 1327 *SR*,
-atte forde 1332 SR, John-, Nicholas *atte Ford(e)* 1340 NI, *v.* atte,
ford. JONES'S HOLE, *Jone's Hole* 1841 *TA*, the pers.n. *John* or *Joan*
with hol¹ 'hole, hollow'; a spring is marked 6″. LITTLEMOOR (RD),
prat' voc' Lytil- 1431 *Weld*¹, *Litulmore* 1445 Rent, *Little Moor* 1841
TA, cf. *pastur' voc' le More iuxta molendinum* 1445 *Rent*, *Moor Mead*
1841 *TA*, *v.* lȳtel, mōr, cf. Mill *infra*. THE LOOK-OUT, a small 200′
hill but commanding good views S, *v.* look-out. LORTON CTGS, FM
& HO, possibly 'dirty farm' from lort(e) and tūn. MILL, cf. *firma
molend' aquatic'* 1445 Rent, 1483 *Weld*¹ which could refer to an earlier
mill here (in Broadwey village itself), or to a mill elsewhere in the par.,
cf. also *Mill Mdw* 1841 *TA*, *Criketesmull* discussed under Creketway
supra, Nottington Mill and *Orchardesmull infra*; there is also mention
of a mill in Broadwey in 1316 Hutch³ **2** 485, and some of the eleven
mills mentioned in 1086 DB as belonging to the eight manors called
Wai(a) must also have been in Broadwey. NEW COPPICE, 1841 *TA*.

NEW INN. NOTTINGTON MILL, cf. Nottington, Mill *supra*. NOTTING-
TON SPA, an e19 bath house enclosing a 'medicinal spring' with 'a
strong fetid sulphureous smell, not much unlike gunpowder newly
enflamed, and a flavour resembling boiled eggs, sometimes rotten
eggs' (Hutch[1] 1 420), now 'fallen into disuse' (Kelly), *v.* spa.
OLD MANOR HO. RECTORY, cf. 'rectory of St Michael Broadway'
1330 Hutch[3], 'rectory of St Michael the Archangel *Brodeway*' 1470
ib, cf. foll. ST NICHOLAS'S CHURCH (Kelly), cf. 'church of *Brodewey*'
1286 Banco, 1378 Pat; according to Hutch[1] 1 420 'it was dedicated to
St Michael before 1402, afterwards to St Nicholas', but cf. Rectory
supra and the 14th cent. addition *Nich(ole)* for Broadwey *supra*.
THORNHILL FM, *pastura in Thornhulle* 1431 *Weld*[1], *terre voc' Thorne-
hill* 1445 *Rent*, *Thornhill* 1774 Hutch[1], *v.* þorn, hyll, cf. Icen Dairy
in Upwey par. *infra*. TWO MILE COPPICE, situated two miles from the
centre of Weymouth, though this may not be the explanation of the
name. WATER WHEEL, on R. Wey. WATERY LANE, alongside R.
Wey. WEYSIDE, near R. Wey.

FIELD-NAMES

The undated forms are 1841 *TA* 28. Spellings dated 1326, Ed 3, 1332[2] are
Midd, 1327 *SR*, 1332[1] SR, 1384 Cl, 1392 AD II, 1431, 1465, 1486, 1682
Weld[1], 1445 *Rent*, 1457, 1481 *Ct*, 1464 *DCMCt*, 1543, 1624 Hutch[3], 1651
DCMDeed, 1664 HTax, 1689 *Seymer*, and the rest DCMDeed.

(*a*) Acre & half; Atkin's Cl; Baylis' Plot (cf. Richard *Baley* 1543 (Upwey));
Bazil (*Barseele gate* 1653, *Bassels* 1687, possibly to be identified with
Barkeshulle 1431, *-hill* 1445, which may mean 'hill with a birch-tree', from
beorc and hyll, although the first el. could perhaps be a reduced form of
bark-house 'a tannery'); Boot Acre; Bridge Mdw; Broadlands; Brown's
Hill; Coppice Cl; (Gt & Old) Cowleaze; (Lt) Crock Hole (probably 'hollow
where potsherds were found', *v.* crocc, hol[1]; for Roman remains in this par.,
v. Hutch[3] 2 490, RCHMDo 2 616); Drove (*v.* drove); 18 Acres Md; Ewe
Leaze; First Cmn; 5 & 4 Acres; Furzy Grd (cf. *le Furs iac' inter le Redlond
et Brodewey* 1445, *v.* fyrs, cf. Redlands in Radipole par. *infra* and Broadwey
supra); Gravel lands (*Gravillands, Gravellands* 1689, *v.* gravele); Great
Coppice & Md (*the Great Meadow* 1687); Green Hill; Grove (Grd) (*v.*
grāf(a), cf. *terre voc' Forgrove* 1445 which is probably '(land) in front of the
grove', *v.* fore); Gundries (cf. John *Gundry* 1664); Halter Path Md; Home
Fd or Nap (*v.* cnæpp); Home Md; The Houses Hills; Keeve Md (from cȳf
'vessel, tub', cf. Do dial. *keeve* or *kive* 'a large tub used for the wort to work
in when brewing' (Barnes 76)); Lime Kiln Ewe Leaze; Lincoln's; Long
Acre & Mdw; Marsh Mdw (cf. (*Mocketts*) *Marsh* 1689, William *Mockett ib*,
v. mersc); Moon's Leaze (*Mo(o)neslease* 1622, *-leazue* 1657, *Mohun's lease
Gate* 1651, *Mowneslease* 1682, the surname *Moon*, ME *Mo(h)un*, with læs

'pasture'); Mustard Pound (perhaps '(old) pound used for growing mustard', *v.* **mustard, pund,** cf. Pound Cl *infra*); Nag's Head; New Mdw; Nine Yards (*v.* **gerd** 'measure of land'); North Mdw; Parish Md ('the parish meadow' 1624, cf. *la comune pasture* Ed 3 (Fr)); Peter's Md; Pitlands (*Putlond* 1445, *v.* **pytt, land**); Plashett (*Plasshet-* 1431, *Plasshotmede* 1445, from plaschiet 'marshy pool' or plaissiet 'enclosure made with wattles', and **mæd**); Pound Cl (*Pount—* 1651, cf. Mustard Pound *supra*); Puddle Hole (*v.* **puddel** 'a pond or pit full of water', **hol**[1] 'hole, hollow'); Puxy Gdn & Md (perhaps 'goblin-haunted stream' from pūca (ME *puke*) and **ēa**, probably originally the name of the stream now called Pucksey Brook, *v.* RNs. *infra*); Rack Md (*v.* **rakke**); Road Cmn; Round Acre; Rush Md; Sheep Plot; Sheep's Bridge; Shortlands (cf. Upwey par. st.ns. *infra*); North 16 Acres; Snook's Hill (cf. *Snooks Lane* in Bincombe par. *supra*); South Hill & Mdw; Spring (*v.* **spring**); Stall Cl (*v.* **stall**); Summer Cl (*v.* **sumor**); 10 & 3 Acres; Three Corner Md; Tucker's Hill (cf. Henry (*le*) *Touker*(*e*) 1327, 1332[1]); Little 2 Acres; Water Mdw; Wear Md (*Little W*(*e*)*are Meade* 1666, 1689, from **ware** 'a sheepwalk' or **wer** 'a weir'); West Bottom (*v.* **botm**); White Roughit (partly in Preston par. *infra q.v.*); Willow Beds & Water, Willow Plot; Winshind.

(b) *Backelane Close* 1651 (*v.* **back**); *Batrick Close* 1689 (a surname); 'a cottage on the waste of Broadwey called *Behind Town*' 1677; *Byn*(*e*)*lond* 1431, 1445 (*v.* **bēan** 'bean', **land**); 14 *acr' Bitwenelynche* 1326, *iij acr' apud Twynlynche* 1445 ('(land) between ridges', *v.* **betwēonan, hlinc**); (*prat' de*) *Brad*(*e*)*mor*(*e*) 1332[2], 1431, 1445 (*v.* **brād, mōr** 'marshy ground'); (*bosc' voc'*) *Chal*(*ke*)*croft* 1445 (*v.* **calc, croft**); *Cleyfurlong* 1445 (*v.* **clæg, furlang**); *terris in p' Glopton'* 1457, *terr' nuper Cloptons in South*(*e*)*wey* 1464, 1465, 1481, 1486 (the surname *Clopton* from one of the numerous p.ns. called Clap-, Clopton in other counties, cf. also Clapton in Broadwindsor par. *infra*, Southway *supra*); *Colecombe* 1326 (perhaps 'cool valley', *v.* **cōl**[2], **cumb**); *Comon Close* 1689; *terre voc' le Croft* 1445 (*v.* **croft**); *La Don* 1326, *terre voc' le Doun* 1445 (*v.* **dūn,** cf. *Middeldon, Nordon, Suddon, Westdon infra*); *Dryftclos* 1445 (perhaps ME drift 'drove, herd, flock' (c. 1450 NED), or an early example of the same word with the meaning 'road on which cattle are driven' (1686 NED), with clos(e)); *Dunnes Lane* 1674 (the surname *Dunn*); *pastur' in la ferne* 1332[2] (analogous with Verne in Portland par. *infra*, or a collective use of fearn 'fern', cf. Brk 290); *Fontlond* 1445 (possibly **funta** 'spring', with land; however the form should perhaps be *Fout-* from fōt 'foot (of a hill), etc'); *Glouersclos* 1445 (the surname *Glover, v.* clos(e)); *di' acr' voc' le Gore, prat' in les Goryhammes* 1445 (*v.* **gāra** 'triangular plot of land', **hamm**); *Little Grave* 1689 (*v.* **græf**); *hevedlond* 1326, *le Hedlond* 1445 (*v.* **hēafod-land**); *Hoddersacr', -clos* 1445 (the surname *Hodder, v.* **æcer,** clos(e)); *Inslade* 1445 ('inner valley', *v.* **in, slæd**); *Langelond* 1326 (*v.* **lang**[1], **land**); *Leteneheie, -heye* 1326, *le Lentonheys* 1445 ('enclosure used in Spring or Lent', from lencten and (ge)hæg, cf. Lentney So); *Makerelmede* 1445 (probably the surname *Ma*(*c*)*kerel*(*l*), *v.* **mæd**); *Middel-* 1326, *Midduldon* 1445 (*v.* **middel, dūn,** cf. *La Don supra*); *Mowry Close* 1651 (*v.* **mōrig**); *le Netherfurlong* 1445 (*v.* **neoðerra, furlang**); *terre voc' Nevbury* 1445 (perhaps 'hill newly brought under cultivation', from nīwe and beorg, but the second el. could be burh 'manor house' in which case nīwe would mean 'newly

built'); *terre voc' Nordon* 1445 ('north hill', *v.* norð, dūn, cf. *La Don supra*);
(*claus' voc'-, terre iuxta*) *North(h)all(e)* Ed 3, 1445 (from norð with hall 'hall'
or halh 'a corner of land'); *le Okehey* 1445 (*v.* āc, (ge)hæg); *Okelond* Ed 3
(*v.* āc, land); 'a close called the *Orchard'* 1384 (*v.* orceard, cf. foll.);
Orchardesmull 1392 (probably named from prec., *v.* myln, cf. Mill *supra*; it
was situated in Rowaldsway *supra*); *Padefurlang* 1326 (*v.* pad(d)e 'toad',
furlang); *Perkins Place* 1635; *Poleacr'* 1445 (from pāl 'stake, pole' or pōl[1] 'a
pool', with æcer); *atte Purye* 1332 (p) (*v.* atte 'at the', pirige 'pear-tree');
Ryelond 1445 (*v.* ryge, land); *prat' voc' le Ryver* 1445 (from ME rivere,
probably here in the sense 'banks of a stream frequented for hawking');
Style Hayes 1689 (*v.* stigel, (ge)hæg); *Suddon* 1445 ('south hill', *v.* sūð,
dūn, cf. *La Don supra*); *la Suthfelde cum Suthelak'* 1326, *Southfeild* 1651 (*v.*
sūð, feld, lacu 'stream'); *Bysuthflete* 1295 Banco (*v.* bī, sūðan, flēot); *the
Swan* (inn) 1683; *Westdon* 1431 (*v.* west, dūn, cf. *La Don supra*); *Westfeld* 1431,
le Westfild 1445 (*v.* west, feld); *v acr' in le Worthe* 1445 (*v.* worð 'enclosure').

Chickerell

Putton and East Chickerell were in the liberty of Sutton Poyntz, *v.* note
under Culliford Tree hundred *supra*. In 1933 parts of Chickerell were
transferred to the borough of Weymouth, and parts of the pars. of Radipole,
Upwey and Wyke Regis were added to Chickerell, for civil purposes (Kelly).

CHICKERELL (SY 644806), EAST CHICKERELL (SY 656807)

Cicherelle 1086 DB

Chik-, Chykerel(l) 1227 FF, 1236 Fees (*West-*), 1243 ib (*West-*),
1280 *Ass*, 1285 FA (*Est-, West-*), 1288 *Ass*, 1291 Tax, 1302 FF,
1303 FA (*Es(t)-, West-*) *et passim* with frequent additions *Est-,
West(e)-* to 1481 *Weld*[1], *Westchickerelle* 1386 Cl, (*West*) *Chickerell*
1682 *Weld*[1]

Westchiceres 1268 *Ass*

Chikerl' 1288 *Ass*

Checherell 1288 *Ass*

Chekerell 1375 IpmR (*East-*), 15 *Midd* (*Es-*), 1461 *Ct*, 1529
Weld[1], 1575 Saxton (*Est-, West-*), (*East*) *Check(e)rill* 1664 HTax

Schekerel 1393 *AD*

Chickerill W. 1795 *Boswell*

This name is obscure. It has been compared with Buckerell D 610
(*Bucherel* 1165, *Bokerel* c. 1200, *Bukerell* 1221), Chackrell D 548
(*Chakerell* 13), Cheverell W 238 (*Chevrel* 1086, *Cheverel(le)* 1166,
Chiverell 1175), and R. Petteril Cu 23, RN 323 (cf. DEPN) (*Peterel,
Petrell* 1268, *Peyterel* 1285), but none of these names have been
satisfactorily explained, cf. also the f.n. Chickerell (*Chiterell,
Chyterell* 1439, *Chitterell* 1615) in W Stafford par. *infra.*

PUTTON (SY 651801)

Podinton(e) 1237 FF, 1285 FA, *Podi-*, *Podyton* 1288 *Ass*, 1293, 1312 Ipm, 1315 Cl *et freq* to 1415 ib, *Poding-*, *Podyngton* 1293 Ipm, 1306 FF, 1332 SR, 1333 Fine *et freq* to 1499 Ipm, *Podynton* 1333 Ipm, 1339 Fine, Cl (p), 1340 ib, *Podyngton alias Putton* 1558 Hutch³

Pudinton 1282 Banco, *Pudington* 1288 *Ass*, *-yngton* 1327 *SR*, *Puddington* 1408 IpmR, *Pudy'ton* 14 *Midd*, *Pudicot* [*Pudynton*] 1303 FA

Pydynton 1360 Fine

Putton 15 *Digby*, 1430 FF, 1465 *Weld*¹ *et passim*

Puttynge 1497 Ipm

'Farm called after Puda', from the OE pers.n. *Puda* (Redin 107, cf. Pudford Wo 65) and -ingtūn. The alternative form *-cot* in 1303 is from cot 'cottage'; for interchange of cot and tūn, cf. Luffincott D 152, Waddlestone D 188. In the late form *Puttynge, -ing* is probably only analogical resulting from weakening of *-ton* to [tən].

ALEXANDRA INN. BRACKLANDS, changed from *Blacklands* 1839 *TA*, *v.* blæc, land. CERNE VILLA, probably named from Cerne A. par. *infra*. CHARLESTOWN. CHICKERELL MOOR, 1839 *TA*, *the Moore* 1700 *Mont*, *v.* mōr. CROOK HILL, 1811 OS, 1839 *TA* (Chickerell), *Crooks Hill* 1839 *TA* (Fleet), cf. (*South*) *Crook*, *Crook Plot* 1839 *TA* (Chickerell), *Crooks Close* 1839 *TA* (Fleet), a Brit p.n. from *crūg 'a hill, a mound' with explanatory hyll; the small hill in question is partly in Fleet par. *infra*. THE ELMS. EWELEAZE SPINNEYS, cf. *Eweleaze* 1839 *TA*. FAIRFIELD HO. FURZEDOWN FM, *Furzedown* 1811 OS, *Furze Down*, (*Lower*) *Fuzze Down* 1839 *TA*, cf. *Furzeland* 1811 OS, *v.* fyrs, dūn, land. GREAVES FM. OLD LIMEKILNS, cf. *Lime Kiln Fd* 1839 *TA*. LUGGER INN, cf. *Luggers Close* 1839 *TA* which apparently contains the surname *Lugger*. MANOR FM. MARQUIS FM, named from Marquis of Granby P.H. MONTEVIDEO, a house. MORN LODGE. PUTTON LANE. ST MARY'S CHURCH, cf. *ecclesie de Schekerel* 1393 *AD*, 'the church of Chikerell' 1404 Pat. TIDMOOR POINT, *Tidemoor Point* 1811 OS, (*Great*) *Tedmore*, *Tedmore Close* 1839 *TA*, 'marshy ground reached by the flood-tide', *v.* tide, mōr, with point 'promontory', cf. the f.ns. Tidemoor in Arne par. and Tide Moors in E Holme par. both *supra*. VICTORIA INN. YARLANDS, *Yarland* 1811 OS (placed ½ mile further W than modern name), *Yearlings* 1839 *TA*, possibly 'strips used for ploughing', from ere-[3] and land, cf. the f.n. Yearlands in Winfrith N. par. *supra*.

FIELD-NAMES

The undated forms are 1839 *TA* 57. Spellings dated 1227 are FF, 1303, 1346 FA, 1332 SR, 1340 NI, 1588, 1651 Hutch[3], 1664 HTax, 1703 *Mont*, 1799 *DCMDeed*.

(*a*) Babep(?); Banell Cl (cf. Francis *Bunnell* 1664 (Upwey)); (Top) Bank (*v.* bank(e); Top- is perhaps elliptical for 'top of the—', *v.* topp 'hill-top'); (the) Barl(e)y feild 1703; Barn Stays (perhaps ModE stay 'a prop, support', cf. the nearby Plovers Stays *infra*); Barrow Cl & Leaze (*v.* beorg); Batch (*v.* batch 'hillock'); Bindleaze (perhaps from binde 'a climbing plant' and lǽs); Blacklands (*v.* blæc, land); Broad Md; Bustles Pce (cf. Nicholas *Bussel* 1332); Buxy Cl (perhaps to be associated with Sampson *de la Boxe* 1227, Henry *de Boxe* 1303, 1346, *v.* box 'box-tree'; *Buxy* may be 'box-tree enclosure', or 'Box's enclosure', if the second el. is (ge)hæg); Calves Cl; Carrot(s) Cl; Carter Md (cf. Robert *le Cartere* 1340); Chickerell Cmn 1799 (cf. *in communi pastura* 14); Church Yd; Cistern Fd; (Old) Cowleaze; Croft Cl; Cucumber Plot; Cut Queens; Darkland (Cl & Md), Darklane Md (perhaps from deorc 'dark' and land or lane, but *Darts Lane* 1700 may belong here, in which case the first el. may be a surname); Dorothy Cl; Dove Cott (*v.* dovecot); Droveway to Tedmore (*v.* drove, weg, cf. Tidmoor Point *supra*); Dukes Cl (perhaps with reference to the Duke of Bolton or the Duke of Cleveland who once held this manor, *v.* Hutch[3] 2 493); Dungeon (*v.* dungeon); 8, 5, 4 & 14 Acres; Fur Cl; Furze—, Furzy Grd, Furz(e)y—, Fuzze Bed; Gaz(e)ing (Fd) (probably to be associated with *Gasson Furlong* 1799, from gærs-tūn 'paddock', but possibly from gærsing 'grazing, pasture'); Gravel Lds; Green Lane; Grove; Hanging Cl (from hangende 'steep, sloping' or hanging 'a steep slope'); Hannams Cl & Md (cf. James *Hannam* 1588); Headlands; Hollands Cl; Home Cl & Md; Homestead Barn; Horse Leaze; 100 Acres; Hurstlands (*v.* hyrst); Lake Cl; Lane Cl; Little Mdw; Long Cl & Md; Gt, Hr, Lt & Middle Marsh (*v.* mersc); Mays Cl; Meatwherelands (this form is possibly corrupt; it is adjacent to Wheat Farland *infra*); Midfield Flg 1799; Moor(s) Cl, Moor Fd & Grd (cf. *Mower Bridge* 1791 Boswell, *v.* mōr); New Cl, Grd, Inclosure & Md; 9 Acres; Nore Grd, Hill & Md (from a misdivision of ME atten ore '(place) at the bank or edge', *v.* atte(n), ōra[1]); North Grd & Md; Orchard; Paddock; Park; Pear Tree Grd; Pickett's Cl; Plovers Stays (perhaps plover (the bird); for the obscure second el. cf. Barn Stays *supra*); Pond Cl; Poor Ho & Gdn; Preamble Hill; Purple Md; Putton Fd, Mdw, Plain & Wall (from Putton *supra*); Quarry Cl; Rectory Lawn; Ridge (*v.* hrycg); Road Cl; Rough Cl; Rowlands ('rough strips of land', *v.* rūh (wk. obl. rūgan), land); Rushmead 1799; Short; 6 Acres; Slade Flg 1799 (*v.* slæd); Small Md; Spa Well (*v.* spa, wella); Sprats Hill; Stable Md; Stalls (Orchd) (*v.* stall); Strap (*v.* strap); Thorns Cl; Three Corner Cl & Fd; Top of Hill; Town Md; Townsend (*v.*

toun, ende); Tullins Pce; Tumble Down (cf. an identical f.n. in E Stoke par. *supra*); 2 Acres; West Md; Wheat Farland ('wheat furlong', from **hwǣte** and **furlang**, cf. Meatwherelands *supra*); Willow Bed (Cl), Willow Cl; Woodcocks Walk (from **woodcock** (the bird) or the surname *Woodcock*, *v.* **walke**).

(b) *Gormere* 1293 Ipm (*v.* **gāra, mere**[1] or **(ge)mǣre**).

West Knighton

WEST KNIGHTON (SY 732876)

 Chenistetone 1086 DB

 Cnititon 1208 Cur, *Cniht(t)eton* 1214 ib (p), *Knighton* 1222 ib, *Knicteton* 1226 Pat, *Knichton* 1236 Fees, *Kny(g)ht(et)on(e)* 1288 *Ass*, 1294 Pat (— *Mayne*), 1327 *SR*, 1340 NI, 1346 FA, 1348 Cl ('— near *Mayne*') *et freq* to 1481 *Weld*[1], *Knyȝthton* 1270 (1372) *ChrP, Knyth(e)ton* 1270 (1372) *ib*, 1332 SR, 1369 Pat, 1396 Fine ('— by Dorchester'), *Knittetone* 1285 FA, *Knython* 1300 Ipm, '*Knyghtone by Dorchestre*' 1369 Cl, *Westknyghton* 1452 *Weld*[1] (p), *Knyghton iuxta Dorchestre* 1466 *ib*

 Knigteston 1288 *Ass*

 Kyngtetonemayne 1297 Pat, *Kyngton* 1303 FA

'The farm of the thegns or retainers of a high personage', from **cniht** (gen.pl. *cnihta*) and **tūn**; this manor was held TRE by two *taini* or thegns (VCHDo **3** 95). Hutch[3] **2** 498 cannot be correct in supposing that West Knighton 'received its name from the Knights Templars or Hospitallers who had a preceptory and lands in this parish' since they were not here until the 13th cent., cf. Fryer Mayne *infra*. For the AN spelling *Cheniste-* in DB, *v.* Zachrisson IPN 104, 113. For the affixes, *v.* Fryer Mayne and Dorchester par. *infra*; the comparatively late addition *West-* must be to distinguish it from East Knighton in Winfrith N. par. *supra*, *v.* **west**. The 1303 form shows confusion of the first el. with **cyning** 'king'. There were two mills here in 1086 DB (VCHDo **3** 95).

HR & LR LEWELL FM (SY 732876, 742897) ['lu:əl], *Lewelle* 1086 DB, *Liwelle* ib, 1201 FF, *Liwella* 1194, 1195 P both (p), *Lywolle* 1285 FA, *Leywell* 1454 *Weld*[1], *Lewell Farm or Stafford otherwise East Stafford* 1669 Hutch[3], *Lewell or East Stafford* 1774 Hutch[1], 1863 Hutch[3], *Lewel* 1811 OS, probably 'well or spring with a shelter', from **hlēo(w)** and **wella** (cf. Brindiwell D 414 which is probably 'well with a wooden covering'); in view of the early *i-* forms, as Professor

Löfvenberg notes, the first el. is likely to be WSax hlīeg, hlīg, or hlīewe rather than hlēo(w). Several springs are marked 6″. For East Stafford, which formed a joint tithing with Lewell in 1795 Boswell, *v. infra.*

FRYER MAYNE (remains of MANOR HO) (SY 738865), FRYER MAYNE FM (733862), *Mayne Hospital(l)'* 1244 *Ass*, 1464 *AD*, *Mayne* 1275 RH, 1278 QW, 1290 Ch, 1327 *SR*, 1332 SR, *Meyne Hospital'* 1280 *Ass*, *Mayne* —, *Maine Ospitalis* 1285 FA, *Mayne Hospitell* 1447 *HarlRoll*, *Frarenemayne* 1337 DorR, *Frerynemayne* 1394 *Weld*[1], *Freremayn(e)* 1449 Pat *et freq* to 1533 Hutch[3] ('the mansion of —'), *Freer Mayne* 1516 ib ('maner place of —'), 1564 ib, *Frier Mayne* 1601 ib ('the site and manor house of —'), *Fryer Mayne alias Freer Mayne* 1714 ib ('mansion house and farm of —'). For Mayne, *v.* Broadmayne par. *infra* and cf. foll.; the affixes -(*H*)*ospital(is*), -*Hospitell* and *Frarene-*, *Frer(yn)e-*, etc. allude to the preceptory and lands of the Knights Hospitallers here from the 13th cent. (VCHDo **2** 90–2), *v.* frere, -ena (the *-ene-*, *-yne-* spellings represent a ME wk. gen.pl. *-ene*). A chapel here (site marked 6″) is mentioned in 1516 Hutch[3], 1533 ib. There was a water mill here in 1338 Hutch[3], cf. *Mill Mead* 1843 *TA*, *v.* myln, mǣd.

LITTLE MAYNE FM (SY 723871), 1785 *SalisT*, *Maine* 1086 DB (f. 80a), 1201 Cur, *Parva Maene* 1202 FF, *Parua Mene* 1288 *Ass*, *Mayne Syrard*, — *Sirard* 1285 FA, *Lyttlemayne* 1306 FF, *Lytele Mayne* 1309 ib, *Lytelmayn(e)* 1347 Ipm, 1436 *Weld*[1] *et freq* to 1486 *ib* with variant spellings *Lytell-*, *Litul-*, *Litel-*, *Lytul-*, *Litil-*. 'Little' to distinguish it from Broadmayne par. *infra* q.v., *v.* lȳtel; -*Syrard*, -*Sirard* from the family of that name who held this manor from at least as early as the beginning of the 13th cent. up to 1436 (Adam *Shirard*, — *Syrad* 1201 Cur, FF, Robert *Sirard*, Henry *Syrard* 1285 FA, etc., *v.* Hutch[3] **1** 431, **2** 503); the DB tenant-in-chief of *Maine* was Hugh, first earl of Chester (VCHDo **3** 88) and it is noted by Tait (IPN 130) that the family of *S(h)irard* which was here was descended from the *S(c)irard* who was a Cheshire tenant of the same earl. A former chapel here dedicated to St Stephen (Hutch[3] **2** 503) is mentioned in 1306 FF, 1437 *Weld*[1], 1454 *DCMDeed*.

RADESLOW (lost), 1380 Misc, 1412 *Weld*[1], *Radesle* 1244 *Ass* (p), 1412 FA, *Radesloe* 1268 FF, 1269 Ch, *Redeslo* 1275 RH, 1278 QW, *Radeslo* 1280 *Ass*, 1312 Ipm, 1315 Cl, 1331, 1339 FF, 1344 Pat,

Radeslowe 1379 IpmR, *Radesslow* 1412 *Weld*[1], 'red slough' from rēad (wk. obl. *rēadan*) and slōh, cf. Rassler Bk 189, Ratsloe D 443; the forms (*via de*) *Slow(es)lane* 1412 *Weld*[1] and *venella vocat'* *Rotteslowlane* 1473 *ib* probably also refer to this place, although the first could contain a surname, cf. Alice *Sloo* 1318 *MiltC* (Osmington), William *Slo(o)* 1413 *Weld*[1] (Winfrith hundred), *v.* lane; the place was already described as *Radeslowe vacua placea* in 1379 IpmR and as 'an empty place called *Radeslow*' in 1380 Misc; Fägersten 155 suggests that it was somewhere near Fryer Mayne *supra.*

EAST STAFFORD (lost), 1569 Hutch[3], 1664 HTax, 1669 Hutch[3] (*Lewell Farm or Stafford otherwise* —), 1774 Hutch[1] (*Lewell or* —), 1795 Boswell, 1863 Hutch[3] (*Lewell or* —), *Estaford* 1303 FA, 1327 *SR*, *Eststaford* 1332 SR, *Staff' Hosp(italis)* 1201 P, 1288 *Ass*, *Stafford Hospitalariorum* 1202 P, *Stafford (H)ospitalis* 1280 *Ass*, 1285 FA, so called to distinguish it from West Stafford par. *infra q.v.*, *v.* ēast; -*Hospitalis* etc. because like Fryer Mayne *supra* it was held by the Knights Hospitallers. It was probably one of the two DB holdings called *Sta(n)ford* although both these forms have been included under West Stafford par. *infra.* In 1327 *SR* and 1332 SR it formed a joint tithing with Fryer Mayne, and in 1795 Boswell a joint tithing with Lewell *supra.* In 1516 and 1601 Hutch[3] there is mention of 'the farm and war(r)en of conyes (conies) called Stafford (alias East Stafford)', in 1569 ib of 'the fishery and waters of East Stafford', and in 1601 ib of swans maintained here. For a mill here, *v.* Lewell Mill *infra.*

BLACK HILL CTGS, from Black Hill in Warmwell par. *supra.* BOTTOM HEATH BARN, cf. *Barn Heath* 1843 *TA*, *v.* botm, hǣð. BRAKE CTG, cf. (*Little*) *Brake* 1843 *ib*, *v.* bræc[1] 'brake, brushwood'. (OLD) CHALK PIT, cf. *the Chalk Pit, Chalk Pit Furlong* 1785 *EnclA*, *Pit Close*, *Quarry pit field* 1843 *TA*, (Old) Gravel Pit(s) *infra*, *v.* pytt. CHURCH (St Peter's), cf. 'church of *Knythton*' 1369 Pat. COMMON PLANT., cf. *The Home Common* 1785 *EnclA*. EMPOOL BOTTOM & HEATH, — *Water* 1785 *ib*, — *Heath & Mdw* 1843 *TA*; on 1844 *TAMap*, *Empool* is the name given to the stream flowing in Empool Bottom and it perhaps means 'the even or smooth pool or stream' from emn (an assimilated form of *efen*) and pōl[1]; it is possible that Evenings Ford in Warmwell par. *supra*, situated ½ mile downstream from where the stream called *Empool* is joined by another from Broadmayne, is connected with this name; the same stream may have been called

Evening, 'the even or smooth one' from efen and -ing[2], as an alternative to *Empool* but with similar meaning. FRYER MAYNE DAIRY & WD, from Fryer Mayne *supra*. (OLD) GRAVEL PIT(S), cf. (Old) Chalk Pit *supra*. HERON GROVE, *Herring Grove* 1843 *TA*, cf. Thomas *Heryng* 1327 *SR* (W Stafford), Winterborne Herringston *infra*, v. grāf(a). HIGHGATE LANE, cf. Highgate Mx 123. HUCK BARROW, perhaps from hōc 'hook, angle, corner' with beorg; it is situated where the par. boundaries of W Knighton, Woodsford and Warmwell meet. HUISH BARN, v. hīwisc 'a household, a measure of land that would support a family'. WEST KNIGHTON FM, cf. 'the mannor and capital messuage or farme, knowen by the name of the great farme' 1570 Hutch[3]. KNIGHTON HEATH BARN & WD, cf. *The Heath* 1785 *EnclA*, *Knighton Heath* 1811 OS, Bottom Heath Barn *supra*. LEWELL LODGE, 1863 Hutch[3], *Lewel* — 1811 OS, from Lewell Fm *supra*. LEWELL PITS. LEWELL MILL, *Lewel Mill* 1811 OS, probably identical with 'a mylne called East Stafford mylne' 1512 Hutch[3], *molendin' de Est Stafforde*, *Est Stafforde Mill* 1552 (1674) *Mansel*, 'the watermill called East Stafford Mill' 1669 Hutch[3], cf. *Mill Close* 1785 *EnclA*, *Mill Gdn*, *Mdw & Plot*, *Tucking Mill Md* 1843 *TA*, v. myln, Lewell Fm and East Stafford *supra*. There was a mill at the smaller of the two manors called *Sta(n)ford* in 1086 DB (VCHDo 3 84). LOSCOMBE BARN, N & S LOSCOMBE PLANT., cf. *viam regiam vocat' Louscombe* 1530 *Weld*[1], *Loscombe Close & Common* 1785 *EnclA*, 'valley with a pigsty', from hlōse and cumb, which is probably the usual meaning of this common Do name; the road referred to in 1530 is no doubt the Broadmayne–Dorchester road, cf. *Dorchester New Rd, Dorchester Path Corner & Furlong* 1785 *EnclA*. MAYERS POND (PLANT. & WD), *Mayers Pond Plant.* 1843 *TA*, cf. William *Mayer* 1664 HTax. NEW INN. OLD KILN. SALT HILL PLANT., v. salt[1], hyll, perhaps in allusion to a place where salt was made or stored. TENANTREES, *Tenantries* 1843 *TA*, probably ModE tenantry 'land let out to tenants'. YEWLEAZE BARN, *Ewe Leaze* (*piece*), E & W Great Eweleaze (*drove way*) 1843 *TA*, v. eowu, lǣs.

FIELD-NAMES

The undated forms are 1843 *TA* 120. Spellings dated 1201, 1268 are FF, 1552 (1674) *Mansel*, 1561 Hutch[3], 1664[1] HTax, 1785 *EnclA*, and the rest *Weld*[1].

(a) Bounds Cl 1785; Bushey & Gt Breach 1785 (v. brēc); Bussells Cl (cf. the f.n. Bustles Pce in Chickerell par. *supra*); Chipp's Corner 1785; Close;

Coppice; (Old) Cowleaze; Crofts 1785; Demons Cl; Dry Mdw; Dungeon Cl 1785 (*v.* dungeon); 8 & 18 Acres; Fig Mdw (perhaps the surname *Fig(g)*); Froome's Cl 1785; Great Mdw; Gregoles (cf. *terre in Griggegore* 1437, of which the first el. is either a pers.n. or surname *Grigg* (a short-form of *Gregory*), or ME grigg(e) 'a diminutive person, a dwarf', with gāra 'gore of land'); Grey Stone Bottom 1785; Whitecombe Halter Path Gate & Rd 1785 (*v.* Whitcombe par. *infra*); Hilly Grd & Mdw; Home Cl; Home Plot 1785; Howlets Cl 1785; Knighton St. 1785; Leagers (Plant.); Lewell Flatt, Lane & Plain, South Lowell Plain (from Lewell Fm *supra*, *v.* flat, plain); Long Cl (1785) & Fd; Luckhams pond plant.; (Little) Marsh (*v.* mersc); Little Mayne Down (1785 *SalisT*) & Mdw (from Little Mayne *supra*); Mead Cl 1785; Meadow; Moor; New Cl 1785; Parish Plot 1785; Parsonage higher Grd (— *Orchard & Plot* 1785); Peake Md (*v.* pēac); Pines; Pond Cl 1785 (cf. *Cramborne ponde infra*); Pounds Cl (cf. Leonard *Pount* 1664[1], but pund 'a cattle pound' is possible, cf. *Dunfald* (sic, possibly for *Pun-*) 1201, *ponfald* 1437, *v.* pund-fald); Roadway Grd; 7 and 4 Acres; Sheds Cl (cf. *Farm called ...Shades Hole* 1779 *EnclA*); Sheepland 1785; Stride Md 1785; 6 and 3 Acres; 10 Acres; 13 Acres; Three corner pce & Plot; 21 Acres; 24 Acres or Brake (cf. Brake Ctg *supra*); Vallens Cl (Mdw) 1785; Well Cl (cf. *aquam de fonte infra manerium* 1458, *v.* wella).

(b) *le Brodeclos* 1437 (*v.* brād, clos(e)); *Cocken Hill* 1560, *Cokenhull* 1561 (*v.* hyll; for the first el. cf. Cocknowle in Ch. Knowle par. *supra*); *Cramborne ponde* 1664[2] ('stream frequented by cranes or herons', *v.* cran, burna, with ponde, cf. Pond Cl *supra*, Cranborne par. *infra*); *de la Dene* (p) 1268 (*v.* denu); *Gilleclos* 1441 (probably the ME pers.n. *Gille*, a pet-form of *Gillian*, with clos(e)); *le Langhay* (*v.* lang[1], (ge)hæg); *Palmede* 1552 (1674) (*v.* mǣd; the first el. is perhaps pāl 'pole, stake'); *the Southewest felde* 1552 (1674) (*v.* feld).

Osmington

Ringstead was a tithing in Winfrith hundred, *v.* note under Winfrith hundred *supra*.

OSMINGTON (SY 725830)

    (*at*) *Osmyntone* 843 for 934 (eME) ASCharters, (*apud*) *Osmingtone* 843 for 934 (17) BCS 739

    Osmentone 1086 DB, *-tona* Exon, *-ton* 1393 *AD*

    Osmin-, Osmynton(e) 13 *Salkeld* (p), 1212 Fees, 1244 *Ass* (p), 1280 *ib*, 1285 FA, 1288 *Ass*, 1311, 1336, 1341 all Pat

    Oselington 1212 P

    Os(e)munton 1288 *Ass*, *Osmonton* 1451 *Weld*[1], *Osmanton* 1575 Saxton

    Osseminton 1288 *Ass*

    Osmyng-, -ington(e) 1291 Tax, 1293 Cl, 1318 *MiltC*, 1320 FF, 1324 Pat (p) *et passim*

    Osemyngton 1339 Cl, 1387 Pat, 1543 *Weld*[1]

Osmyg-, *Osmigton* 1392, 1393 *Weld*[1] (p)
Esmyngton 1428 FA

Probably 'farm called after Ōsmund', from the OE pers.n. *Ōsmund*
and *-ingtūn*; the two OE charter forms are of course from late
copies. As pointed out by Fägersten 155, Hutch[3] **2** 505 cannot be
correct in supposing that 'the vill seems to derive its name from
Osmund, its patron saint, and most ancient diocesan, the first Bishop
of Salisbury', since St Osmund died in 1099; instead it seems likely
that the church at Osmington was dedicated to St Osmund because
the p.n. was supposed to contain the bishop's name, *v.* St Osmund's
Church *infra*, cf. Pancrasweek D 156, Winterborne Farringdon in
Winterborne Came par. *infra*.

RINGSTEAD (SY 750816)

Ringestede 1086 DB (4×), 1244 *Ass* (p), 1293 Cl (p) (*Up-*),
1299 Ipm, 1475 *Ampthill*, *Ryngested(e)* 1280 *Ass*, 1288 *ib* (p),
1361 Cl, 1389 *Weld*[1] *et freq* to 1576 *Ampthill*, *Est Ryngested*
1504 *ib*, *Rynggested* 1288 *Ass* (p)

Ringhesteta, *-stede* 1086 Exon, *Rynghestede* 1498 *Ct*

Ring-, *Ryngsted(e)* 1227 FF, 1262 ib, 1264 Ipm, 1276 FF, 1285
FA (p), 1291 Pap *et passim* with additions *Est(e)-* from 1285
FA to 1554 *Ampthill*, *Eyst-* 1408 *ib*, *East-* 1774 Hutch[1], *West-*
from 1285 FA to 1774 Hutch[1], *Up-* 1303, 1346 FA, *Uppe-*
1428 ib, *Middle-* 1774 Hutch[1]

Rigstede 1275 RH, *Regge-* 1278 QW, *Rygestede* 1392 *Ct*

Ryngstod 1280 *Ass*

Ryngustede 1392 *Ct*

Rynstede 1421, 1440 *Weld*[1]

Rengstede 1452 *Weld*[1]

Estring-, *-ryngsteed* 16 *Ampthill*, *Ringsteed* 1634 *ib*, 1663, 1682
Weld[1], *Rinksteed* 1663 *ib*

Ryngston (sic) 1575 Saxton, *Ring-* 1610 Speed

Ringstead East, Middle & West 1795 Boswell

Probably from an OE **hring-stede* 'place or site with, or in, a
ring', with reference to a stone circle, to a circular enclosure, or to
some other circular feature not now apparent, *v.* Sandred 103, 285
who discusses this name and five other occurrences of the compound
in England and refers to Scandinavian parallels. However Ekwall

DEPN may be correct in thinking that the first el. is hringe fem. 'ring', used here in the specialized sense 'salt-pan' (Ringstead is on the coast); the forms with medial -e- (*Ringestede* etc.) might then be accounted for, although these could equally well be from a gen.pl. *hringa* of hring masc. Ringstead was formerly a parish and a village (the site of which is marked 6"); in 1774 Hutch[1] 1 430 it is said that 'the manors are extinct and the vills depopulated'. But the three farms of East, Middle, and West Ringstead still formed a joint tithing in Winfrith hundred in 1795 Boswell, *v.* ēast, middel, west; *Up(pe)-ringe-, -ryngsted(e)* was perhaps an alternative name for East Ringstead (Hutch[3] 2 506) or for Upton *infra* (RCHMDo 2 179), *v.* upp 'higher up'. There was ½ mill in one of the DB manors called *Ringestede* (VCHDo 3 101), and a water-mill in Ringstead is mentioned in 1227 FF. Remains of a Church (mentioned in 1227 FF and 1291 Pap) are marked 6".

UPTON (SY 742830), 1361 Cl (p), 15 *MinAcct* (— *iuxta Ringstede*), 1811 OS, *Vpton* 1447 *DCMCt*, 1455 *Weld*[1], *vppertowne* 1664 *ib*, *Spraggs Upton* 1774 Hutch[1], *Ringstead Upton* 1795 Boswell, *Upton Ringstead* 1826 Gre, 'higher farm', or 'higher part of the village', *v.* upp, tūn, perhaps the part of Osmington referred to as *superior villa* in 1318 *MiltC* and probably so called in contrast to Netherton Fm *infra*; in the 1664 form the first el. has been replaced by ModE upper; for affix *Ringstead, v.* prec., for *Spraggs*, cf. East Fm Dairy *infra*. Upton itself now lies in a valley, but the name must originally have referred to the higher ground to the S between Upton and Upton Ho *infra*, cf. also East Fm Dairy *infra*.

BLACK HEAD (LEDGES), *Black Head* 1840 *TA*, a coastal feature, probably that referred to as *The Blake Roke* 1539 LP, *v.* blæc, hēafod, ledge, rokke. BOAT COVE (lost, about SY 730818), 1811 OS, *Boat Cliff* 1826 Gre, *v.* bāt, cove, clif. BRAN LEDGE & POINT, coastal features probably named from (*West*) *Brandown* 1840 *TA* which is *Auorbrandon* 1318 *MiltC*, probably 'broom hill' from brōm and dūn, *v.* ledge, point; *Auor-* is probably, as Professor Löfvenberg points out, the ME prep. *afore* 'in front of', cf. Do dial. *avore* (Barnes 47). THE CABIN. OLD CHALK PIT, cf. *calcetu*' 1447 *DCMCt*. CHARITY FM, probably with reference to lands which were part of some charitable endowment, cf. Wa 334. COOMBE BOTTOM, cf. *via (Regia) vocat' Combewey* 1408, 1440 *Weld*[1], *Great & Little Coomb(e)*

1840 *TA*, *v.* cumb, botm, weg. DAIRY. EAST FM, E of Osmington, cf. West Fm *infra*. EAST FM DAIRY, from prec., called *Spraggs Fm* 1811 OS, the surname *Spragg*, cf. Upton *supra*. THE ELMS. EWE-LEAZE BARN, cf. *Ewe Leaze Bottom* 1840 *TA*. FIR COPPICE, *Fir Plant*. 1840 *TA*. FRENCHMAN'S LEDGE, a coastal feature, cf. *2 acr' ten' Frensh'* 1304 *Winch*, Thomas *le Freynsch* 1318 *MiltC*, William *Frenshman, mulleward* 1447 *DCMCt*, *v.* ledge. THE GLEN, *v.* glen. GOGGIN'S BARROW, *v.* beorg; a tumulus is marked 6″, but cf. RCHMDo **2** 447. GROVE FM, *Grove* 1840 *TA*, *v.* grāf(a). HALL'S FM. HANNAH'S LEDGE, a coastal feature, *v.* ledge. ICEHOUSE. MANOR HO. NETHERTON FM, 'lower farm', or 'lower part of the village', *v.* neoðerra, tūn, perhaps originally a name for the part of Osmington referred to as *inferior villa* in 1318 *MiltC*, and probably so called in contrast to Upton *supra*. OSMINGTON HILL, HO (1857 Hutch³) *&* LODGE. OSMINGTON MILLS, — *Mill* 1811 OS, cf. *Mulaker, Nich' le Wayte...tenet...ij molend' et terre* 1318 *MiltC*, *Mill Cove* c. 1825 Map, *Mills Lane Mead* 1840 *TA*, *v.* myln, æcer; there was a mill at Osmington in 1086 DB, *v.* VCHDo **3** 78. PERRY LEDGE, a coastal feature, perhaps the surname *Perry* from pirige 'a pear-tree', *v.* ledge. PHOENIX. PICNIC INN. PIT HO, near a quarry, *v.* pytt, cf. William *Poukepitte* 1447 *DCMCt*, 'goblin's pit', *v.* pūca. PIXON BARN, *Poxton* 1840 *TA*, situated on the Osmington–Poxwell bdy where the old road between the two villages crosses it, so the first el. is possibly the same as that in Poxwell par. *supra*, with tūn or stān. PLOUGH INN. POOL LEDGE, a coastal feature, *v.* pōl¹, ledge. POXWELL BOTTOM DAIRY, from Poxwell par. *supra*, *v.* botm. PRESTON RD, to Preston par. *infra*. OLD QUARRIES, cf. *querrer' de Osmyngton* 1459 *Weld¹*, *Quar Gates, Under Quars* 1840 *TA*, *v.* quarrere, geat, under. REDCLIFF POINT, *Radcliff Pt.* c. 1825 Map, *Ham Cliff* 1773 Bayly, 1811 OS, a coastal promontory, *v.* rēad, clif, point; *Ham* may be from hamm in the sense 'promontory' or from the wk. obl. form *hēan* of hēah 'high'. RINGSTEAD DAIRY, BARN *&* LEDGE (c. 1825 Map), from Ringstead *supra*, *v.* ledge. SANDY BARROW, 1840 *TA*; a tumulus is marked 6″. SHORT LAKE, SHORTLAKE DRIVE *&* HO, *v.* sc(e)ort, lacu; a small stream is marked 6″. SPRING BOTTOM (HILL), *Springbottom* 1811 OS, *Spring Bottom Yew Leaze* 1840 *TA*, *v.* spring, botm, eowu, lǣs; springs are marked 6″. ST OSMUND'S CHURCH, cf. *ecclesie parach' de Osmenton* 1393 *AD*, *v.* par. name *supra*. UPTON FM *&* HO, *Vpton Farme house* 1664 HTax, cf. Upton *supra*. WATERFALL. WEST FM, W of Osmington, cf. East Fm *supra*. WHITE HORSE

(HILL, 1840 *TA*), 'a large representation of King George III on his charger...formed by removing the turf from the white chalk' (Hutch³ **2** 505).

FIELD-NAMES

The undated forms are 1840 *TA* 161. Spellings dated 1304 are *Winch*, 1318 *MiltC*, 1327 *SR*, 1332 SR, 1447 *DCMCt*, 1465 *Weld*¹, e17 Hutch¹, and 1863 Hutch³.

(*a*) Banky Md; Barn Pce; Barton Pce; (Plot) Beach (*bece*¹ 'stream, valley' or *bēce*² 'beech-tree'); Becken—, Becon Md, Beckon Coppice, Large Becken (probably (ge)bēacon 'signal, beacon'); Bramble Flg (*Bremeliuorlang*, *Bremylyforlang* 1318, *v*. brēmel, -ig³, furlang); E & W Bullens, Bullen's Md; Bye Md (probably byge¹ 'a corner, the bend of a river'); E, N & S Cle(a)ves (*Clives* 1318, *v*. clif (nom. pl. *clifu, cliofu, cleofu*), cf. foll.); Cliff (cf. *Cliffurlang, (By)clifmede* 1318, *v*. clif, furlang, bī '(place) near', mǣd, cf. prec.); Coast Guard Gdn & Houses; (W) Common; Common Land Wall Cl; Common Plot; Copering Pine (cf. John *Coperone* 1332 (Preston)); Coppice; Court Fm (cf. *Bovecurt* 1318, '(place) above the large house', *v*. bufan, court); Cow Leaze (freq); Crooked Walls (*v*. croked, wall); Dodwell Down (possibly from the OE pers.n. *Dodda*, or ME dodde, and wella, with dūn); (The) Down, Nether Down Md (*la Doune, Lange-, Shortedoune, Yndone* 1318, *v*. dūn, with lang¹, sc(e)ort, in 'inner'); Drift Way (*v*. drift); East Croft & Plant.; 8 Acres (*Eghteaker* 1318, *v*. eahta, æcer); 18 Acres; Fore Hill(s) & Lds (*v*. fore); Fose Hill (Plain) (cf. the f.n. Foss Hill in Preston par. *infra*); 4 & 14 Acres; Great Mdw; Hanging Grd & Md (*v*. hangende); Hill Pce; Hitt's Fm 1863 (cf. Edward *Hitt* e17); Holes (*v*. hol¹); Home Fm & Md(w); Homestead; Horse Cl; Land's Barn; Langford Lawn (perhaps to be connected with *Langeforurde* 1318, which may mean 'long projecting piece of ploughed land' from lang¹ and fore-erð, *v*. land or launde); Large Mdw; Limekiln Fd & Grd; Little Fd & Md; Long Cl (Copse); E & W Long Lay (*v*. lay 'pasture-land'); Long Md; Mashings; Hr & Lr Mead (cf. *Medeaker, Medfurlang* 1318, *v*. mǣd, æcer, furlang); Mear's Md (cf. John *le meer* 1318, *ten' Johannis Meire, venella nuper Thome Meere* 1447, *v*. Hutch³ **2** 505); Mico's Fm 1863 (belonged to Mico's charity in Weymouth, *v*. Hutch³ **2** 508); Moor; New Fm; New Grd; Newman Thorn; New Plant.; 9 Acres; North Hill & Md; E & W Oat Hill (*v*. āte); Gt & Home Orchard; Ornamental Grd; Ox Leaze Md; Park (*Park*' 1318, cf. Walter *de Parco* 1318, — *atte Parke* 1327, *v*. park, atte(n)); Hr & Lr Pennings (probably from Sir John *Poynings* to whom the manor of E Ringstead was granted in 1541 Hutch³ **2** 506, cf. Mount Poynings in W Lulworth par. *supra*); Plough Fd; Puzzard Orchd (possibly an unvoiced form of buzzard (the bird), perhaps as a surname); Rick Yd; (Under & Upr) Ridlinch (*v*. hlinc; first el. (ge)ryd(d) 'cleared' or rēad 'red'); Road Cl; Rose Cl; Rough Grd; Rowland's Flg (cf. *Rowland* Huish who purchased part of the manor of E Ringstead in 1591 Hutch³ **2** 506); Sandy Nap (*v*. cnæpp); 16 Acres; South Hill; Swosfield's Md; 10 Acres; Thorney Break (*v*. bræc¹); 3 Acres; Three Corner Grd & Pce; 20 Acres (*Twentiakres* 1318, *v*. twēntig, æcer);

Two Crosses; Under Ground; Upper Fd; Vincilo; West Croft; Weymouth Cl; White Walls (cf. *Walaker* 1318, *v.* wall, æcer); Wild Mdw (*Wyldemede* 1318, *v.* wilde, mǣd); With(e)y Bed & Berry (*v.* wiðig, bedd, bearu); Yew Leaze (freq, *v.* eowu, lǣs).

(*b*) Nether-, *Suthbinaker* 1318 (*v.* neoðerra, sūð, bēan, æcer (as freq in this par.)); *Blakelond* 1318 (*v.* blæc, land (as freq in this par.)); terre...*voc' Bonnesplace* 1447 (cf. Robert *Beone* 1318, — *Bone* 1327, 1332, *v.* place); *Bovehyle* 1318 (*v.* bufan '(place) above', cf. *le Hyle* in Coombe K. par. *supra*); la *Breche* 1318 (*v.* brēc); atte *Brigge* 1318, 1327, *atte brygge* 1332 all (p) (*v.* atte, brycg); Nether-, *Overbrokaker* 1318 (*v.* neoðerra, uferra, brōc); terre...*placeam*...*voc' Cinttelane* 1318 (read as *Contelane* by Hutch[3] 2 506, possibly from ME c(o)unte 'the female private parts'); *Croklynch* 1318 (probably 'ridge or bank where potsherds were found', *v.* crocc, hlinc); *Cruchaker* 1318 (perhaps crūc[3] 'a cross'); *Bydolfinesheye* 1318 (cf. John *Dolfyn* 1318, *v.* bī '(place) by', (ge)hæg); *Dorlynch* 1318 (*v.* hlinc; first el. dor or duru 'door, gate', or dora 'humble-bee'); *camp' oriental'* 1318); *Byeuelakedich* 1318 (perhaps eowu 'a ewe', with bī '(place) by', lacu, dīc); *Florlond* 1318 (cf. the analogous Flower Lands in Charminster par. *infra*); atte *Floudcherde* (or *-therde*) (a f.n.) 1318 (*v.* atte '(place) at the', flōd 'flood, tide', perhaps with sceard 'cleft, gap'); La *Gore* 1318 (*v.* gāra); *Hayward-mede* 1318 (*v.* hayward, mǣd); *Heuedaker* 1318 (*v.* hēafod); ten' atte *Lane*, ten' *in La Lane* 1304 (cf. Walter atte *Lane*, —*Attarlane* 1318, *v.* atte, lane); *Langaker* 1318 (*v.* lang[1]); *Langhegge* 1447 (*v.* hecg); (Over-, *Up*)lang(e)lond 1318 (*v.* uferra, upp); *sup' lhouse* 1318 (probably '(land) above the pig-sty', *v.* hlōse); *medius camp'* 1318; *Bynortheslade* 1318 ('(place) to the north of the valley', *v.* bī, norðan, slæd, cf. *Sladaker infra*); *Overlonde* 1318 (*v.* ōfer[1] or ofer[2]); *Paiesesaker*, *Paiseshole* 1318 (cf. Adam *Pays* 1318, *v.* æcer, hol[1]); *Papelynch* 1318 (perhaps papol 'a pebble', hlinc); atte *Punfolde* 1318 (p), *Ponfald* 1327 (p), *Ponfold* 1332 (p) (*v.* atte, pund-fald); *Rowedon*, Under *Roudone* 1318 ('rough hill', *v.* rūh (wk. obl. rūgan), dūn, with under); *Rylond* 1318 (*v.* ryge); *Sedden* 1321 (first el. obscure, second el. perhaps denu 'valley'); *Shortlond* 1318 (*v.* sc(e)ort); *Sladaker* 1318 (cf. *Bynortheslade supra*); atte *Sperke* 1332 (p) (cf. Richard *Sparc* 1332, *v.* atte, spearca 'brushwood'); *Stubacre* 1318 (*v.* stubb); *Swykaker* 1318 (*v.* swice 'a trap'); atte *Toneshende* 1318 (p) (*v.* atte, toun, ende); *Uppehulle* 1318 (*v.* upp, hyll); *Virnhulle* 1318 (*v.* fearn, hyll); *Waram* 1318 (perhaps a transferred name from Wareham par. *supra*; the *Warham* family were lords of the manor of Osmington in the 17th cent., Hutch[3] 2 505); *In the Wassch*, *Wassh'me* 1318 (probably near the coast at Ringstead, *v.* (ge)wæsc 'shore flooded at high tide', possibly with hamm); *camp' occident'* 1318; *Westynbrugge* 1447 (*v.* brycg; *Westyn-* may be from westerne 'western' or from bi westan '(place) to the west of', *v.* westan); *Whitaker* 1318 (*v.* hwīt, æcer); Nuther-, Over *Wedylond* 1318 (*v.* wēod 'a weed, grass', -ig[3], neoðerra, uferra); *Wudeforlang* 1318 (*v.* wudu, furlang); atte *Wulle* 1318 (p) (*v.* atte, wella (WSax wylla)); *Northymstal*, *Suthymstal* 1318 (Dr K. I. Sandred suggests for this an OE hemm-stall 'site of a hemm' ('hem, border', possibly 'enclosure'), cf. NoB 55 (1967) 81; Professor Löfvenberg suggests the first el. of *-ymstal* may be OE impa, impe 'sapling', cf. OE trēowsteall 'grove, plantation'; *v.* norð, sūð).

Portland

Portland is a liberty in itself, *v.* note under Culliford Tree hundred *supra*.

(ISLE OF) PORTLAND (SY 690720)

(*on*) *Port* lg ASC (A) s.a. 837, 12 ib (E) s.a. 837

On Portlande 862 (14) BCS 535, *Portland(e)* 978 × 984 (14) *Add* (S 938) (*insulam de* —), m11 ASC (C) s.a. 982, 1053–66 (12) ASWrits, 12 ASC (E) s.a. 1052, 12 SD, 1205 Pap, 1212 Fees *et passim*, *-laund(e)* 1100–7 (l13) WinchCath, 1244 *Ass* (p) *et freq* to 1290 Fine, *-lond(e)* c. 1127 (l13) WinchCath, 1268 *Ass et freq* to 1460 *Weld*[1], *Porthlond* 1249 Acct

Porland(a) 1086 DB, Exon, 1156 PR, 1194 CurR, 1236 Cl *et freq* to 1275 RH, *-laund* 1235 Cl (p) *et freq* to 1267 Pat, *-lond* 1296 Ipm

Portelaund(e) 1270, 1283 Cl, 1284 (1285) Ch, 1297 Cl, *-lond* 1305–1461 Pat, 1340 Cl, *-land* 1319–1371 Pat

'The harbour', *v.* port[1], no doubt with reference to Portland Harbour *infra*, with the later addition of land 'land, tract of land, estate'; Fägersten 165 suggests that the whole name should probably be understood as 'land forming (or giving protection to) a harbour'. The loss of interconsonantal *t* in *Porland(a)*, etc., and the *-laund(e)* spellings, show AN influence, *v.* Feilitzen 95, ANInfl 153 ff.

PORTLAND STREETS & BUILDINGS

AVALANCHE RD, named from the 'Avalanche', a ship lost with all hands off the island in 1877. CLEMENT'S LANE, cf. Nicholas *Clement* 1323 *Ct.* EASTON LANE & SQ, both 1892 Map, from Easton *infra*. GROVE RD, named from Grove *infra*, cf. 1861 Hutch[3] 2 822: 'Close by the prison is a street of houses sometimes called Clifton, but now usually known as Grove Road', *v.* clif, tūn. HIGH ST. (2 ×), cf. Wakeham St. *infra*. MALLAMS, earlier a f.n., *Mallan(d)es*, *Mallam(e)s*, *Mallenes* 1608 *LRMB*, the second el. of which is probably land '(strip of) land'; the first el. may be malu 'a gravel ridge' or māl[1] 'rent', cf. Mollands Ess 126. REFORNE ST., cf. Reforne *infra*. STRAITS, probably eModE strait 'a narrow lane' (NED sense B7), but cf. the f.n. Straights in Preston par. *infra*. TILLYCOOMBE RD, named from *Tillie Combe*, *mead called Tillyecome* 1608 *LRMB*, *Tilley Coombe* 1839 *TA*; the first part of the name may be an old p.n. from tigel 'tile' and lēah '(clearing in) a wood', cf. Tiley in Minterne M. par. *infra*, with cumb 'valley', but cf. Tilly Whim Caves in Swanage par. *supra*. VERNE RD, cf. *Vearn Street Road* 1783 Bettey[1], *Verne Street* (*Common*) 1839 *TA*, named from Verne Yeates *infra*. WAKEHAM ST., named from Wakeham *infra*, probably identical with *the high streate* and the *one streat of houses in the isle* mentioned in 1535–43 Leland 1 252, cf. High St. *supra*. WIDE ST., 1839 *TA, Widestreet(e)* 1650 *ParlSurv, v.* wid. ZIGZAG RD. Lost st.ns. are *Calcott's Rd* 1892 Map; *Churchknapps Streete* 1650 *ParlSurv, Nap Street* 1839 *TA* (cf. *(close called) Church Knappe* 1582 WeyR, 1608 *LRMB*, named from the old church at Church Hope Cove *infra, v.* cnæpp 'hill-top').

Churches include *St Georges Church* 1811 OS, *Avalanche Church* (cf. Avalanche Rd *supra), Church of St Andrew & Our Lady, St John's Church, St Peter's Church* all 1892 Map, cf. Church Hope Cove *infra*. Other buildings include *Ayles House* 1747 Bettey[1]; *Bellevue House* 1892 Map; *Churchouse* 1608 *LRMB* (from the old church at Church Hope Cove *infra); The Convict Prison* 1861 Hutch[3] (now a Borstal); *Drill Hall* 1892 Map (also 6″); *Jubilee Hall* 1892 Map; *Methodist Chapel* (several) 1892 Map (one formerly known as *Conjurers Lodge* because founded by believers in witchcraft, another as *Ranters' Chapel, v.* Bettey[1] 82, 84); *Parish house* 1792 Bettey[1], *Poor House* c. 1825 Map (*v.* Bettey[1] 64 ff); *The personage* 1535–43 Leland, *The Vicar's House* 1861 Hutch[3] (then in ruins, *v.* ib 2 830); *Parsonage* 1892 Map (at Chesil *infra); Portland Rectory* 1892 Map (= RECTORY 6″); *Schoolhouse* 1792 Bettey[1] (later known as *Maister's School* from the schoolmaster Henry Pearce nicknamed *Master Harry, v.* Bettey[1] 94); *the Verne (Citadel)* 1861 Hutch[3] (*v.* Verne Yeates *infra); Vicarage* 1892 Map (at Grove *infra).* Inns on 1892 Map are: *Clifton Hotel* (cf. Grove Rd *supra), Devonshire Inn, Eight Kings Inn, George Inn, Grove Inn* (also 6″), *Mermaid Inn, New Hotel, Portland Arms Hotel, Prince Alfred Inn, Royal Breakwater Hotel, Royal Exchange Inn, Royal Hotel, Victoria Hotel* and *Volunteer Inn*.

CHESIL (6″, 1″), CHISWELL (Kelly) (SY 684735), *Chesill* 1608 *LRMB, Chessell* 1783 Bettey[1], *Chissell or Chiswell* 1795 Boswell, *Cheselton* 1575 Saxton, *village of Chisleton, Chessellton* 1650 *ParlSurv, Chisell Tonne* 1710 Map, named from foll., *v.* tūn 'farm or village'.

CHESIL BEACH, — *Bank* 1811 OS, *the Chisil, bank of Chisil, Chisille bank* 1535–43 Leland, *The Beach of Pebbles* 1710 Map, *The Beach or Chesil, called also Steepstone Beach* 1774 Hutch[1], from cisel 'shingle', with bece[1], bank(e), stēap 'steep', stān, cf. prec.; this ridge of pebbles extends for some 16 miles between Portland and Burton Bradstock.

CHURCH HOPE (OPE 1″) COVE (SY 697710), c. 1825 Map, *Churchhope* 1710 ib, named from the church of St Andrew abandoned in the 18th cent. and now a ruin (remains marked 6″), *v.* cirice, with Do dial. ope 'an opening in the cliffs down to the water's edge' (Barnes, *v.* NED s.v. *ope* sb. sense 2b, and cf. Clay Hope, Longstone Ope, and the f.ns. Thirtoop and *Langnope* all *infra),* and cove 'small bay'. The church itself is 'church of *Portlaund*' 1172 (l13) WinchCath,

ecclesiam Sancti Andr' de Portlaund 1268 *Ass*, The *paroche chirch*
1535–43 Leland, *Portland church* 1575 Saxton, *Old Church* 1773
Bayly, and is also mentioned in 1263–1380 Pat; it gives name to *one*
parcell of stonie ground called Churchlane 1608 *LRMB*, v. lane or
land, to *Church Point Wear* 1839 *TA*, v. point, ware and to *Church-*
knapps Streete and *Churchouse supra*.

EASTON (SY 692718), 1608 *LRMB*, 1650 *ParlSurv* (*village of* —),
Eston 1323 *Ct*, *East Town* 1774 Hutch[1], *Eastown* 1795 Boswell,
'east farm or village', v. ēast, tūn, cf. Weston *infra*.

FORTUNESWELL (SY 686735), 1795 Boswell, *Fortunes Well* 1608
LRMB, probably 'lucky well or spring', or 'well or spring in which
fortunes could be told', from ModE fortune and wella, cf. Fritwell
O 211 and Elwell in Upwey par. *infra* for names of similar meaning;
in 1608 *LRMB* it was described as 'a place to pen in cattle'.

GROVE (SY 699725), 1608 *LRMB* (*above* —, *pasture called* —),
1839 *TA* (*above* —, *Little* —), *la Groue* 1321–1324 *MinAcct* (*pastura*
in —, *prati de* —), 1324 *Ct* (*terre in* —), *le Groue* 1323 *MinAcct*, cf.
Grove Corner, *Highe Grove Crofte* 1608 *LRMB*, *Grove Point* c. 1825
Map, v. grāf(a) 'a grove, a copse', with corner, croft, point.

REFORNE (Kelly, about SY 688720), 1756 Hutch[3], 1839 *TA* (-*close*),
1892 Map, *Riffhorne* 1608 *LRMB*, *Raytown* (sic) 1795 Boswell; the
second el. is possibly horn 'projecting piece of land, or headland';
the first el. may be eModE riff 'a rift, a chink' (from 1602 NED), a
variant of *rift* 'a cleft, a fissure'. Alternatively, as pointed out by
Professor Löfvenberg, the first el. could be ModE *reef* 'a narrow
ridge or chain of rocks, shingle, or sand, lying at or near the surface
of the water', the earliest form of which is *riff(e)* (1584 NED s.v.
reef sb.[2] sense 1, cf. especially the quotation from 1742 ib which
refers to Portland as being joined to the mainland by 'a prodigious
Riff of Beach', i.e. Chesil Beach *supra*); however the situation of
Reforne in the centre of the island near to Easton, only c. ½ mile
from the W coast but some 1½ miles from Chesil Beach, makes
reference to this particular feature unlikely.

SOUTHWELL (SY 688701), 1608 *LRMB*, 1650 *ParlSurv* (*village of*—),
1861 Hutch[3] (— *or Southville*), -*welle*, -*wool* 1608 *LRMB*, 'south
well, spring or stream', v. sūð, wella; it is in the S of the island.

VERNE YEATES (SY 689729), *pastura super Ferne* 1321 *MinAcct*, *Vearn* 1783 Bettey[1], *close called Ferneyate, close at Fearne yates, Verne yates* 1608 *LRMB, Vern Gate* 1839 *TA, Yeates* 1892 Map, cf. *Fern Hill* c. 1825 Map, *Vern Cl & Cmn* 1839 *TA, the Verne Hill* 1861 Hutch[3], probably from fergen 'mountain, wooded hill', cf. Fern Down in Hampreston par. *infra* and the lost p.n. *la ferne* in Broadwey par. *supra*, with geat 'gate, gap', hyll; this is the highest part of the island (about 400' at Verne Yeates, rising to nearly 500' at *the Verne Hill*); the 'gates' may refer to gaps or passes on the main north–south route between Fortuneswell and Easton, or to actual gates (two are marked on the roads near here on 1710 Map), cf. Roger *atte yate* 1332 SR, *Atyates, Yateland, (Nether) Yates* (all closes) 1608 *LRMB, Yeats Croft* 1839 *TA*, some of which may belong here, *v.* atte 'at the', land, croft. Cf. also *Vern Signal* 1811 OS, *the Verne (Citadel)* (a defensive work) 1861 Hutch[3] (now H.M. Prison 1″).

WAKEHAM (Kelly, about SY 696715), 1774 Hutch[1], *Wacombe* 1608 *LRMB*, 1650 *ParlSurv, village of Wacum* 1650 *ib, Weakham* 1710 Map, *Wykeham* c. 1825 Map, *Wakem* 1828 Bettey[1], perhaps from wacu 'a watch, a wake' and cumb 'valley'.

WESTON (SY 686712), 1324 *Ct*, 1346 Pat (p), 1608 *LRMB*, 1650 *ParlSurv (village of —), -tone* 1324 *Ct*, 1582 WeyR, *Weston towne, Wesson* 1608 *LRMB, West Town* 1774 Hutch[1], *Westown* 1795 Boswell, 'west farm or village', *v.* west, tūn, cf. Easton *supra*.

ADMIRALTY QUARRIES (lost), 1892 Map. ALMA CTGS, — *Terrace* 1892 Map, probably from the battle of Alma in the Crimean War, cf. foll. BALACLAVA BAY, *Balaclava* 1892 Map, from the port near Sebastopol made famous during the Crimean War, cf. prec. BILL OF PORTLAND, 1649 WeyM (*the —*), 1811 OS, *The Beell* 1710 Map, *Portland Bill* 1773 Bayly, *Beale Point (vulgarly called the Bill)* 1774 Hutch[1], cf. *Beale Rock* 1892 Map, *v.* bile 'bill, beak', used here of the tapering southern promontory of the island, cf. Selsey Bill Sx 84, with point; the same feature is called *The point of the race* in 1575 Saxton, cf. *The Rasce of Portland, wyche ys in lengythe v mylles* 1539 LP, *a very perilous surf, generally known by the name of the Race of Portland* 1861 Hutch[3], *v.* race 'a rush of water'; for the various lighthouses on the Bill, *v.* Hutch[1] 1 586, Hutch[3] 2 823, RCHM 2 253, and cf. *Hr & Lr Light Ho* 1839 *TA*. BILL QUARRIES, from prec. BLACKNOR,

Black Nore 1892 Map, a rounded coastal promontory, probably 'black bank or shore', from blæc (wk. ob. *blacan*) and ōra[1], cf. God Nore and Portland Nore *infra*. BLOW HOLE, a coastal feature, no doubt a perforated cave into which the sea is blown, *v.* hol[1], cf. Cave Hole, White Hole *infra*. BOAT HAUL (lost, SY 681686), 1811 OS, — *Hole* 1826 Gre, a coastal feature, a place where boats could be hauled up, or a cave, *v.* hol[1]. BOTTOM COOMBE QUARRIES, *Bottom Coombe* 1839 *TA*, cf. *Above Coombe* 1839 *ib*, *v.* botm, cumb, above, cf. Coombefield Quarries *infra*. BOWERS QUARRIES, probably the surname *Bower*, but cf. Wallsend Cove *infra*. BRESTON QUARRIES, *Bradeston* 1324 *Ct*, *Soothe and Nootherne Breston* 1582 WeyR, *Eastmost* —, *Souther Breston*, (*Easter-*, *Souther*) *Bresson*, *Briston field* 1608 *LRMB*, (*South of*) *Breston* 1839 *TA*; if the 14th cent. form belongs here this is from brād (wk. obl. *brādan*) 'broad' and stān 'stone', possibly used in the sense 'stone quarry', cf. Longstone Ope Quarries *infra*, with sūð, norðerne, ēastmest, ēasterra and sūðerra; the development to *e* in the first el. is paralleled in Breadstone Gl 2 214 which has *e*-spellings from 1561 (cf. also Bledington Gl 1 213), *v.* also the f.n. Castles *infra* for a 14th cent. *Brede-* spelling possibly from brād. BROADCROFT QUARRIES, *Broadcroft(e)* 1608 *LRMB*, 1839 *TA*, *v.* brād, croft. BUTTS QUARRIES, cf. (*Short*) *Butts* 1839 *ib*, *v.* butte 'short strip', but possibly a surname, cf. William *Butts* 1792 Bettey[1]. CASTLETOWN, 1892 Map, a modern name from Portland Castle *supra*. CAVE HOLE, 1774 Hutch[1], 1861 Hutch[3], *Keeve's Hole* 1861 ib, *Caves Hole* 1892 Map, described in Hutch[1] as 'a cavern...in the shape of a dome perforated at the top' through which the sea is forced during a storm, *v.* cave, hol[1], cf. Blow Hole *supra*. CHALKLANDS QUARRIES, *Chalklands* 1839 *TA*, *v.* calc, land. CHESIL COVE, *Chesil or Chiswell Bay* 1892 Map, from Chesil (Beach) *supra*, *v.* cove. CLAY HOPE (OPE 1"), 1892 Map, on the coast, *v.* clǣg, ope, cf. Church Hope Cove *supra*. COOMBEFIELD QUARRIES, *Co(o)mbe-*, *Coumb(e)feild*, *-field* 1608 *LRMB*, *Coombe Fd* 1839 *TA*, named from (*meade called*) *Co(o)mbe*, *Coumbe* 1608 *LRMB*, cf. 2 closes called *Coombes* 1608 *ib*, *Coombs Lake* 1839 *TA*, from cumb 'valley', with feld, lacu 'stream', cf. Bottom Coombe Quarries *supra*. COTTONFIELDS QUARRIES; the first part of the name (*Cotton-*) may represent an old p.n. from OE (*æt*) *cotum* '(place) at the cottages', *v.* cot. COVE CTGS, from Chesil Cove *supra*, cf. *Cove house & Well* 1839 *TA*. CROWN FM; for demesne lands in Portland belonging to the Crown, *v.* Hutch[3] 2 816. CULVER WELL, *Culverwell*, *-will* 1608

LRMB, *v.* culfre, wella. DUNCECROFT QUARRIES, *Dunscrofte(s)* 1608
ib, *Dunce Croft, Dun(er) Croft* 1839 *TA*, the surname *Dun(s)*, *v.*
croft. DURDLE PIER (1″), 1892 Map, *New Key or Dirtle pier* 1773
Bayly, *Dirdale Pier* 1811 OS, cf. *Durdle Wear* 1839 *TA*, perhaps
identical in origin with Durdle Door in W Lulworth par. *supra*,
or a name transferred from there; *wear* is ware 'a sheep walk', as
freq in this par. EASTON LANE, cf. Easton *supra*. FANCY BEACH, from
the surname *Fancy* (W.H.P.C.) and beach (used in Portland of
'topsoil dug out in opening new quarries' (B.K.)). FOLLY PIER,
1811 OS, *New or* — ('deemed a bad one as to the Sea as well as the
Roads to it') 1800 Bettey[1], *v.* folie, cf. King's Pier *infra*. FRANCE
QUARRIES, *pasture called Fraunce* 1608 *LRMB, France* 1839 *TA*, cf.
French Crofte 1608 *LRMB*, possibly a transferred name, or denoting
land owned by a Frenchman, *v.* croft. FRESHWATER BAY (1892 Map)
& QUARRIES, probably in allusion to a spring or stream, cf. Freshwater Steps in Corfe C. par. *supra*. GOD NORE, 1811 OS, perhaps
'good shore', from gōd (wk. obl. *gōdan*) and ōra, or 'Gōda's shore'
from the OE pers.n. *Gōda*; however the name may be a late formation on the analogy of names such as Blacknor *supra*, cf. Portland
Nore *infra*. GROVE CLIFF (1892 Map) & INN, from Grove *supra*.
HR HEADLANDS QUARRY, *Headlands* 1839 *TA*, *v.* hēafod-land; some
of the old open fields divided into strips are still shown on the 6″ map
(1938 ed.). INDEPENDENT QUARRIES. INMOSTHAY QUARRIES, *Inmost
Haye* 1582 WeyR, *Inmost Haie, Inmust(e) Haie, -haye* 1608 *LRMB*,
'enclosure furthest in(land)', *v.* inmost, (ge)hæg. KING BARROW
QUARRIES, *Kingbarrowe, -barry, -borrowe, Kingeberrie* 1608 *LRMB*,
(Under) Kingbarrow 1839 *TA*, *v.* cyning, beorg 'hill, barrow', cf.
King Barrow in Arne par. *supra*. KING's PIER (HOLLOW), *The Crane
& Pier* 1710 Map, *Kings Key* 1773 Bayly, *the King's Pier* 1774
Hutch[1], used in shipping stone from *the King's Quarries* 1774 ib
owned by the Crown; for other piers on the N and E coast of Portland
used in the stone trade, cf. *Chine* — 1800 Bettey[1], *Chene Pier* 1892
Map (N of Freshwater Bay, cf. *(rockie ground called) Chine* 1608
LRMB, *v.* cinu), *Underbank Pier* 1800 Bettey[1] (cf. f.ns.), *New Pier*
c. 1825 Map (just N of King's Pier), Durdle Pier and Folly Pier
supra, Pier *infra*, and *v.* Hutch[3] 2 826. LAND MARK, an obelisk on Bill
of Portland *supra*. LIMEKILN CAVE, 1892 Map, named from *Old
Lime Kiln* 1892 ib, cf. *(above) Lyme Crofte* 1608 *LRMB, Above Lime
Croft* 1839 *TA*, *v.* līm, croft. LLOYD'S CTG. LONG ACRE QUARRIES,
Long(e) Acre 1608 *LRMB*, 1839 *TA*, *v.* lang[1], æcer. LONGSTONE OPE

QUARRIES, *Long Stone ope* 1839 *ib*, from lang[1] and stān, perhaps in the sense 'stone quarry', cf. Breston Quarries *supra* which are nearby, with ope 'opening in the cliffs', cf. Church Hope Cove *supra*. LOOK OUT, 1892 Map. THE MERE, 1892 Map, (*The*) *Mare* 1710 Map, 1811 OS, *v.* mere[1] 'a (sea) pool'. MUTTON COVE, 1892 Map, *Flews Mutton Cove* 1839 *TA*, cf. *Lur Flews Wear ib*, John *Flew(e)* 1608 *LRMB*, *v.* cove, ware; *Mutton* may be an allusion to smuggling, *Lur* is probably a pet-form of *Laurence*; cf. the f.n. Thirtoop *infra*. NICODEMUS KNOB, 1892 Map, a column of rock left after quarrying, used as a navigation mark, *v.* knob. OLD HILL. PARK QUARRIES, *Park* 1839 *TA*, *v.* park. PENNS BATH & WEARE (— *Wear* 1839 *TA*), named from the *Penn* family, cf. foll., *v.* bæð 'bathing-place', ware. PENNSYLVANIA CASTLE, *Pen-* 1826 Gre, built in 1800 by John *Penn*, governor of Portland and grandson of William *Penn*, founder of Pennsylvania, cf. John *Penne* 1397 *MinAcct* and prec. PERRYFIELD, cf. *la Pury* 1418 DorR, *Perrie, Perrye, Perrishard* 1608 *LRMB*, *Hr & Lr Perry* 1839 *TA*, *v.* pirige, pyrige 'pear-tree', sceard 'gap'. PIER (at Castletown), *Wooden Pier* 1892 Map. PORTLAND BREAKWATER, *The Breakwater* 1861 Hutch[3], enclosing Portland Harbour *infra*; two defensive works on the break-water were called *the Inner Pier Head Battery* and *the Breakwater Fort* 1861 Hutch[3]. PORTLAND CASTLE, *The castell* 16 *RoyMap*, *the new castel in Portland* 1535–43 Leland, *Portland Bulwark* 1540 LP, *Port(e)land(e) Castell* 1575 Saxton, 1583 *SPDom*, *The Castle* 1710 Map, *The New Castle* 1774 Hutch[1], built by Hy 8 to defend the harbour, cf. Rufus Castle *infra*; *the kepe* is mentioned in 1585–6 RCHM, and *the moate* and *an ould trencher without the wall of the castle* in 1623 ib. PORTLAND HARBOUR, cf. 'the Road of Portland', 'Portland Roads' 1588 Hutch[3], *Portland Road* 1710 Map, *v.* road 'sheltered water where ships may ride'. PORTLAND NORE (lost, SY 697742), 1811 OS, 1892 Map, perhaps a late name on the analogy of Blacknor *supra*, cf. God Nore *supra*, but possibly a genuine mis-division of *Portlan(d) ore*, *v.* ōra[1] 'shore, bank'. PORTLAND TRAMWAY, *Freemans Incline* 1892 Map, used for carrying stone. PRIORY, *ground called Priorie, Pryorie* 1608 *LRMB*, *v.* priory; perhaps to be associated with the priory of St Swithun's, Winchester (the Old Minster) which held Portland from the time of Edward the Confessor until 13th cent. (VCHDo **3** 30). PULPIT ROCK (local), so called from its shape. QUARRY HEAD (lost, SY 702727), 1811 OS, cf. *Quarry Land* 1839 *TA*, from the stone quarries on Portland which are *querrer' de Portlond* 1460 *Weld*[1], *The Quarries* 1710 Map, cf. *pasture called the Quarrs*

1608 *LRMB*, *v.* quarrere, hēafod. RUFUS CASTLE (ruins of), *Old castle* 1710 Map, *Rufus's Castle* 1811 OS, probably a 15th cent. rebuilding of a 12th cent. castle (RCHM **2** 252), but 'supposed to have been built by William Rufus' (Hutch³ **2** 811), although Bettey[1] 16 suggests an allusion to Robert, Earl of Gloucester, who was also known as Rufus or the Red Earl and who is said to have taken it in 1142. It is also 'vulgarly called Bow and Arrow Castle' on account of its being 'full of small loop-holes' (Hutch³ **2** 816), and is mentioned by Leland (**1** 252) as 'a castelet or pile not far from [the] streate', cf. Portland Castle *supra*. SAND HOLES, 1892 Map, a coastal feature, *v.* hol[1]. SAW MILL TAVERN, from *Stone Saw Mills* 1892 Map. SHAMBLES (lost), c. 1825 Map, *The Shambles called by Hollingshed the Shingles* 1774 Hutch[1], a sandbank 3 miles SE of Portland, *v.* shingel[2] 'shingle', sc(e)amol 'shelf (of sand)'. SHEAT QUARRIES, *close called Shete* 1608 *LRMB*, *Sheat* 1839 *TA*, *v.* scēat or scīete 'corner of land'. SHEPHERDS' DINNER QUARRY, cf. Robert *le Shepherde* 1323 *Ct.* E, N *&* S SHIP CHANNEL, approaches to Portland Harbour *supra*. SILKLAKE QUARRIES, *Silk(e)lake* 1608 *LRMB*, *Silk Lake* 1839 *TA*, cf. *Silk Lane* 1839 *ib*, probably from sēoluc 'gully, drain' with lacu 'stream', but cf. Adam *Se(y)lk(e)* 1323 *Ct*, 1332 SR. SMALL-MOUTH SAND, from Small Mouth in Wyke R. par. *infra*. SOUTHWELL LANDSLIP, 1892 Map, a cliff fall, cf. Southwell *supra*. STONE INN. SUCKTHUMB QUARRY, *Sutcombe* 1608 *LRMB*, *Suckthumb* 1839 *TA*, 'south valley', *v.* sūð, cumb; the amusing modern rationalization has resulted from metathesis of *tc* to *ct*, while a further rationalization is apparent in *Suckthumb or Suckton Quarry* RCHMDo **2** 450. SWEET HILL, 1839 *ib*, *v.* swēte. TAR ROCKS, probably from torr 'rock', but perhaps 'rocks the colour of tar'; close to Blacknor *supra*. TOPHILL or UPHILL (both local), used of the higher part of the island, cf. *pasture called Hill*, *Upon the Hill* 1608 *LRMB*, Underhill *infra*, *v.* hyll. TOUT QUARRIES, (land) *in* —, *up(p)on Toute, Towtefield* 1608 *LRMB*, *(South)Tout, North Tout Wear* 1839 *TA*, *v.* tōt(e) 'a look-out (hill)', ware. TRADE QUARRIES, (land) *in Trade, Tradefeild, -furlonge* 1608 *LRMB*, *Trade* 1839 *TA*, *v.* trade 'path, way'. UNDERHILL (local), *Under the Hill* 1608 *LRMB*, used of the Chesil and Fortuneswell district below Verne Yeates *supra*, cf. Tophill *supra*. VICTORIA BLDGS *&* GDNS, cf. *Victoria Hotel* 1892 Map. WALLSEND COVE, (land) *at (the) Walls End* 1608 *LRMB*, *Walls End (Cove)* 1839 *TA*, cf. (land) *at Wall Bower* 1608 *LRMB*, *v.* wall, ende[1], būr[1] 'cottage', cf. Bowers Quarries *supra*; the 'wall' is a field wall (W.H.P.C.). WAKEHAM QUARRIES, from Wakeham *supra*. WAYCROFT QUARRIES, *Way Croft Quarrys* 1783 Bettey[1], *Under Way Crofts* 1839 *TA*, cf. *Wayhaie* 1608 *LRMB*, *Ways Close* 1839 *TA*, *v.* weg, croft, (ge)hæg, but some of these forms may contain a surname from Upwey par. etc., cf. Robert *Mulet de Weye* 1323 *Ct*, Robert *Way* 1792 Bettey[1]. E & W WEARE, *rockie ground in Eastware, stonie ground in* —, *close called Westw(e)are, Westweare Mead*, cf. *wast ground in* —, *rockie ground in Southw(e)are* 1608 *LRMB*, *Greens Ware* 1788 Bettey[1], *North Wear, Wear Close* 1839 *TA*, *v.* ware 'a sheep walk', discussed under Ware in Swanage par. *supra*; it is possible that the form *Oare* 1608 *LRMB* belongs here too (with rounding and lengthening of *a* and loss of *W*-), cf. the f.ns. *Wath, Wade infra*, but alternatively *Oare* may be from ōra[1] 'bank'. Hutch[3] 2 822 describes the 'weirs' in Portland as 'uneven slopes of grass land formed by successive land-slips', and Bettey[1] 53 notes their use as 'dumping places for rubble' from stone quarrying. WEST BAY, *The* — 1710 Map, *v.* bay[1]. WEST CLIFF, 1892 Map, — *Common* 1839 *TA*, cf. *les cliffes* 1607 Hutch[3], *past' under the Cliff* 1608 *LRMB*, *v.* clif. WESTON QUARRIES, from Weston *supra*. WHITE HOLE, a coastal feature, *v.* hol[1]. WIDE STREET QUARRIES, *v.* Wide St. *supra*. WINDMILL (disused), cf. (land) *by the Windemill* 1608 *LRMB*, *between Mills* 1839 *TA*, *v.* windmill; two windmills (both surviving as ruins) are marked on 1626 Map, and these and a water-mill are mentioned in 1774 Hutch[1] 1 582. WITHIES CROFT QUARRIES, *la Wytherscroft* 1418 DorR, *Withies* —, *Withers Crofte* 1608 *LRMB*, *Withys* —, *Widows Croft* 1839 *TA*, *v.* wiðig 'willow', croft.

FIELD-NAMES

The undated forms in (*a*) are 1839 *TA* 173; the undated forms in (*b*) are 1608 *LRMB*. Spellings dated 1288 are *Ass*, 1323[1], 1324 *Ct*, 1332 SR, 1385, 1790, 1861 Hutch[3], 1582 WeyR, 1608 *LRMB*, 1650 *ParlSurv*, 1664 HTax, 1710 Map, 1783, 1788, 1791, 1792, 1812, 1845 Bettey[1], and the rest *MinAcct*.

(*a*) Agnes(') Croft; Andrews(') Wear (cf. Thomas *Andrewes* 1664, *v.* ware (as freq in this par.)); Back Lane Stile (*Backlinge Stile* 1608, *v.* stigel); ('bove-, West) Barland(s) ((*up(p)on*) *Barr(e)land* 1608, *v.* barre 'bar, barrier', land (as freq in this par.)); Barley Croft (1582, 1650, -*crofte* 1608, *v.* bærlic, croft (as freq in this par.)); (Upr) Barrow Hill (freq), Burrow Hill (*Barrowe*—, *Barry(e)* —, *Barrie* —, *Barrhill, Barrell* 1608, *v.* beorg 'barrow, hill', hyll, cf. *Barrowes* 1608); Bay(s)croft (*Baye Crofte* 1608, *v.* bay[1] or bay[2]); Beans; Binhays (*Bynheye* 1323, *Byn-, Benhaies* 1608, *v.* bēan 'bean', (ge)hæg (as freq in this par.)); Blindmare (cf. *Blinde End* 1608, *v.* blind 'dark, hidden', with (ge)mǣre 'boundary' and ende[1]); ('Bove) Bollands ((*above*) *Bollandes, Bollondes* 1608, cf. Ralph *Bolle* 1323[1]); Bombs Lane (cf. (land) *above Bumbes* 1608, possibly from bum 'buttocks', either as a topographical term or as a surname, cf. Bumble *infra*); Bottom Md; Bown Hill (*Bownehill, Bound Hill* 1608, perhaps from bune 'reed'); (Be)hind Boyt(')s house (cf. Morgan *Boyt(e)* 1608); Branscombe (1608, *v.* cumb; the first el. may be the ON pers.n. *Brandr* found in Bransbury Ha (DEPN) and as a Do surname (*Brond*) in 1332 SR); Brest croft (*Briscrofte* 1608, possibly (ge)byrst[1], -brist 'a landslip', or brēosa, brīosa 'a gadfly'); Brewery Yd; Bridgestone; Bubble Beach; Building Grd; Bumble gdn croft (*Bumbles Crofte, — Lane, Bambells Crofte* 1608, perhaps from bum 'buttocks' and hyll, or a surname, cf. Bombs Lane *supra*); Bunns Cl (cf. Robert *Bunn* 1664); Bussells Cl (cf. *Bushills Crofte* 1608); Camble Stile (*v.* stigel); Cames Cl; Castle Lawn, — Lodges (cf. *Castle Haie* 1608, from Rufus Castle *supra, v.* (ge)hæg); ('bove) Castles (*close called Castles* 1608, cf. *pastur'...in la Bredecastel* 1324, *close called Bussecastles, pasture called Narrowe -, Wester -, Williams Castles, Hixe Castle* 1608, *v.* castel(l) perhaps in the sense 'earthwork'; *Brede-* may be an error for *Brode-* and mean 'broad' from brād, cf. *Narrowe-* from nearu (wk. obl. *nearwan*); *Busse-* is perhaps from busc 'bush', *Wester-* is westerra 'more westerly', *Williams-* is from Sir John *Williams* 1608, *Hixe-* is from the surname *Hick*); Chilmarke 1861 (cf. *Chilmer Hurne, Chillmans Horne* 1608, possibly to be compared with Chillmark in Langton M. par. *supra*, though *Chilmer, -man* may be a surname, *v.* hyrne, horn); Close (cf. *the lower-, the Middle-, Overclose* 1608, *v.* uferra); Coal croft, Lane, Lands & Lawn (*Co(a)le Crofte(s), Co(a)le Lane, Colane, Coale Landes* 1608, *v.* col[1] 'coal', perhaps with reference to the 'stone coal' found in Portland (Hutch[3] 2 810)); Thomas Combens Wear; Common (*The —* 1710); Coney Croft (*v.* coni; there is mention of a coney-warren in Portland in 1382 Fine); Coopers Rd; Court Barton & Lds (cf. (*the*) *Courte Feild* 1608, *v.* court, barton); Cowcroft; Cox's Cl; above Croft; Curl(e)s Croft (*Corles —* 1650); Dobbins door (*Dolphins Dore* 1608, the surname *Dolphin, v.* dor or duru); Dowers Well (*Dowres —, Dooreswell* 1608, the surname *Dower, v.* wella); Down (*Doune* 1321, (*upon*) *Downe, Easter Downe* 1608, *v.* dūn, ēasterra); Down end (*Downend* 1608, *v.* ende[1], cf. prec.); Droop fd (*Dro(o)pefeild* 1608, perhaps from þrop 'a hamlet, an outlying farm'); (N) Duckstile (*Ducke Stile* 1608, cf. *Duckes thearne* (sic) *ib*, perhaps the surname *Duck* with stigel and (?) þyrne 'thorn bush'); Dungeness (possibly from dynge 'dung-heap' and næss 'promontory', but perhaps a transferred name from Dunge Ness K); Durants Wear (cf. Edith *Durrant* 1608); Eals Croft ((*under*) *Eale(s) Crofte* 1608, cf. William *Elis* 1324); East Cl (cf. *Eastmost Close* 1608, *v.* ēastmest); Everys croft; E Furland (cf. *Westerforlong* 1324, (*Wester*) *Vorland, Forland,* (*Easter-, Wester*) *Furland, Furlandes Wall,* (*Easter*) *Fur(r)longe, v.* furlang, with ēasterra, westerra, wall); Fishes croft (*Fishers Croft(e)* 1608, cf. John *le Fysshare, — le Vishare* 1323[1]); Footlands ((*plott...called*) *Foot(e) Land* 1608, *v.* fōt); 4 Acres (*Foure —, Fouer Acres* 1608); Franks House; (W) George(s) Cl (*St George Close* 1608; according to Hutch[3] 2 816, lands in Portland were given to 'the guild of St George in Waymouth' in the time of Hy 6); Gilberts Wear (cf. John *Gilbert* 1323[1]); Gill croft (*G(u)ill-, Guyl-, Guelcrofte* 1608, perhaps

goyle 'ravine', but cf. John *Raw als. Gyle* 1417 DorR); Gore (bars) (*Go(o)re,
Littlegore, Goare* (*Meade*) 1608, *v.* gāra, barre); Goslands end (*Gocelyns
Londe* 1321, *Gosselines-* 1323², *Gosselyneslond* 1397, *Gosland(es Wall*) 1608,
Goslings (*Green*) 1788, 1812, cf. *Gospittes* 1608, the ME pers.n. or surname
Goscelin of which *Gosse* was a pet-form, cf. *John Gosselyn* 1385 (Weymouth),
with land, pytt, wall; cf. *Goose land, -Hill* 1608 which may belong here or
contain gōs 'a goose'); Gowks hill (ME go(w)ke 'cuckoo' or a surname from
it); Grammers Ld (perhaps to be connected with *Germans-, Germersland*
1608, from the surname *German*, the modern form having metathesis of
-*r*-); Grams croft (*Graines-, Grange Crofte* 1608); Under Great Beach;
Great Cl (*Great(e)-* 1608); Green Cl (*a close called Grene* 1608, cf. *terr'
above La grene* 1323¹, *v.* grēne²); Greencroft; Green Hill (*Greenehill* 1608);
Greenhole (*v.* hol¹); Greenways end; Gregorys Wear; Greycroft; Groves
Buoy (near Grove *supra*); G(r)owland(s) (*Gro(w)land(es*) 1608, perhaps
'lands good for growing crops', from eModE grow 'growth', but cf. the
unexplained p.n. Growen D 560 (*Gorwe-, Grouheghes* 14)); Haines Cl;
Hannah's croft (*Hanni(e)s Croft(e* 1608, 1650, probably a diminutive of the
pers.n. or surname *Hann*); Harpland (*v.* hearpe); (Btm) Hayland(s) (*Heyland*
1608, *v.* hēg; *High(e)land* 1608 may also belong here); Heavehay (*v.*
(ge)hæg); Hillyates (*Hill-, Hel(l)yate* 1608, *v.* hyll, geat); Hind(e)s Cl,
Hine's Wear (cf. William *Hine*, Robert *Hinde* 1608); Hogscroft (*Hogges
Crofte* 1608, cf. *Hogges Close ib*, the surname *Hogg*); Inmost acre (*v.*
inmost); Isle (cf. (land) *in Lyle* 1608, which possibly represents ME *l'yle*
'the island', *v.* le, ile); Jackmans croft (— *Crofte* 1608, the surname *Jackman*);
Jacks Cl; Jefferys Cl; (Under) Job Croft (*Job(be) Crofte* 1608, the pers.n. or
surname *Job*); Jordan (cf. *Jordanescroft* 1323¹, 1324, Henry *Jordan* 1323¹);
Killick hill Wear, Killicks Will (*Killickes* —, *Killeys Hill* 1608, the surname
Killick; *v.* hyll, ware, well(a) (WSax will(a))); Kings Arms; 'Bove Knight
Croft, Knights Wear, Nights Cl & Croft (*Knightes Crofte* 1608, cf. Nicholas
Knyȝth, William le *Knyth* 1324); Lane end (cf. Ralph *de la Lane* 1288, (land)
under lane 1608, *v.* lane); Langley (1608, *v.* lang¹, lēah); Larance Cl (cf. John
Laur' 1323¹); Large Lds; Long Cl (1608); Longcroft (*Langcrofte* 1608, *v.*
lang¹); Long flg (*Lang(e)furlonge* (*Headland*) 1608, *v.* furlang, hēafod-land);
Long Hay (*Longe-, Langehaie* 1608); Martin Cl, Martin(')s Croft (*Martins
Crofte* 1608, cf. William *Martin* 1323¹); May —, Mead Bower (*under Meade
bower, Mead bouer* 1608, cf. (*the) Mead ib, v.* mǣd, būr¹ 'cottage'); Meadow
(Cl), Meadwall (cf. prec.); Mid(dle) Croft (*Middlecrofte* 1608); Mile; Monks
Plot (*Monkesplott, Muncke Plott* 1608, *v.* munuc, plot, cf. Priory *supra*);
Mound Knowle (*v.* mound, cnoll); Mouse Plot (*v.* mūs); Nap St (*v.* cnæpp);
Netherfield (*v.* neoðerra); New Cl Corner (*New(e) Close* (*Wall*) 1608, *v.*
nīwe, wall); Nill (*furlong called Above Knill* 1608, *Knill Peece* 1650, *v.*
cnyll(e) 'hillock', pece); Ox Croft; Paddock(s), Parricks, Parrocks ((*pasture
called) Parrocke(s)* 1608, *v.* pearroc); Palmers Croft (— *Crofte* 1608, cf. John
Palmar 1323¹); Pasture; Pauls Mead (Cl) (*Paul(e)s Mead* 1608, the pers.n.
or surname *Paul*); Simon Pearces Wear; Pickers Hay (*Pickard hay* 1608, the
surname *Pickard*); Pitts Grd & Wear (cf. *Pitthaies* 1608, Richard *Pitt ib*);
Pound (*v.* pund); Pump Ld; Redcliffs; Redcroft (1608, *v.* rēad; *Rudd
Crofte(s) ib* may also belong here, in which case the first el. is hrēod); Rip

Croft & Lane (*Reape Lane* 1582, *Rype-, Ripcrofte, Reape Crofte, — Lane,*
Riple lane 1608, *Reep Lane* 1845, perhaps from rip(p) 'edge, shore'; the form
Riple- may be due to metanalysis, but is possibly from the derivative
rip(p)el 'strip of land'); Rods Wear (cf. Isaac *Rodd* 1792); Rolls Croft
(*Rawl(e)s —, Rawes —, Raffe Crofte* 1608, cf. *Thomas Raul* 1323[1], v. Reaney
s.n. *Ralf*); Rottle Wall; Roughbarrow (*Row(e)bar(r)ow(e), -barrie, -borowe,*
-borroughe 1608, v. rūh (wk. obl. *rūgan*), beorg); Roughland (*Ro(w)land*
1608, cf. prec.); Round Well Wear; Rubble Batch & Grd (v. batch; the
'rubble' is from stone quarrying); Ruins; ('bove) Russhetts (Parricks)
(*Richardes Parrockes* 1608, cf. Peter *Ricard* 1323[1], v. pearroc; the Mod form
has been influenced by ryscett 'a rush-bed'); Schollars Cl (cf. Elizabeth
Schollar 1792); Scotland (*-feild* 1608, v. scot 'tax'); 7 Acres (*Seaven —* 1608);
Shaggars —, Shaggers Lawns (v. land or launde); Shankcreat (*Shanke —,*
Shange Crofte 1608, probably the surname *Shank*); Shay ((land) *upon Shey,*
— upon Shie 1608, perhaps from scēo 'shelter'); Shear croft (*She(i)re crofte*
1608, the surname *Shere,* or from scīr[2] 'bright' or sc(e)aru 'a share of land');
Sheepcroft; (W) Shoals, Shoals Pitts (*close called Shoule, Showles, Shooles,*
West Showle(s), -Should, (land) *bewest Showle* 1608, v. scofl 'a shovel',
west; *bewest* means 'to the west of', v. bī, westan; the form *Westshewe* 1608
may also belong here); Shops (from sc(e)oppa 'shed', perhaps as a surname);
Shortbatts (*-battes* 1608, perhaps from ME batte 'stick, lump', v. sc(e)ort);
Shortlands (*-lond* 1324, *-land(es)* (*Corner*) 1608); Silas Cl; Silver Well Wear;
Simple Croft (*— croft(e)* 1608, cf. *Symplehous* 1324, John *Symple, — Simple*
1323[1], v. hūs); Slidcroft (*Sl(e)ad(e) Croft(e)* 1608, v. slæd); Slobs (ModE
slob 'mud, ooze'); South; Southfield (*the Southfeild* 1608); Spencers Cl (cf.
William *Spencer* 1792); Stert Corner (Cmn) (v. steort); Stewards Wear (cf.
Gabriel *Steward* 1790); Stone Hill (cf. *Stone Ways* 1792); Will Stones Cl,
Henry Stone's Wear, John Stones Wear; Store house; Street hill (cf.
Streetend 1608, v. strǣt, ende[1]); Sweek (v. swice 'a trap', cf. Swyke in
Weymouth par. *infra*); Thirtoop (*Durthoope,* (land) *in 30 hoope, Thirtie*
hoope furlonge 1608, perhaps 'dirt(y) inlet' from drit, -ig[3], hōp[2], with
furlang, but the second el. may be the word ope suggested for Church Hope
Cove *supra*; Thirtoop is near to Mutton Cove *supra*); Toby's Cl (cf. Richard
Tobye 1608); Troophay (*Toopes Haie* 1608, the surname *Toop* with (ge)hæg,
but the name may be connected with Thirtoop *supra*); Turn croft ((*West*)
Thorne (*Crofte*) 1608, v. þorn); 2 Acres; Under Bank (v. under); Underhay
(*Under haies* 1608, v. (ge)hæg); Under Hedge (1608); (Upon hole and)
Under Hole ((land) *subter la hole* 1417 DorR, (*beneath hill in*) *Underho(a)le,*
Under Houle 1608, v. hol[1]); Under Lane (1608); Under Weeck 1791 (v.
wīc, cf. *Witch Crofte infra*); Vincents Door (*half a close called Vincentes*
Doores 1608, cf. *close called Buishops Dore* ib, v. dor or duru); Watering place;
Wattle Down (*Waddledowne* 1608, perhaps from wād 'woad' and hyll, with
dūn); West Croft(s) (*Westcrofte* 1608, cf. *Westmost Croft Mead* ib, v.
westmest); Top of Westons, 'Bove Westons Well ((land) *above —, at Westons*
Well, Wessons Well 1608, cf. Weston *supra*, v. wella); Wheat Ld(s) (*Wheate-,*
Wet(t)land 1608, v. hwǣte); Whites Cl (cf. *Whytt's* (a croft) 1582, William
le Wite 1323[1], *— White* 1332, cf. foll.); Whits Cable, *— Coble* (cf. prec. and
Cables Crofte, Edith *Cable* 1608); Woolcombe (1608, *-shard* ib, v. wella

(WSax **wylla**), **cumb**, **sceard**, cf. the following names all of which contain **wella**, **wylla**); Woolland, Wool Lds (*Wool(l)and* 1608); Wool Mdw (-*mead*, *Wellmead* 1608); West Wools (*Westwoole(s)* 1608, cf. *dom'*...*in Wolle* 1324, Reginald *atte Welle* 1323[1], William *Atwooll* 1608, *v.* **wella**, **atte**, cf. prec.); Yeolands (*Yealand*, *Yal(l)and*, *Yalan(e)*, *Yal(l)on* 1608, *v.* ēa-land 'island');

(*b*) *Tom Appleman Place* (*v.* **place**); *Ashe Haie* (*v.* **æsc**, (ge)**hæg** (as freq in this par.)); *Avenhaie*; *Austrowes Haie*; *Byles Close*; *Brimiscome* 1324, *Brims-*, *Brins-*, *Brunscombe* (*feild*) 1608 ('Brȳni's valley', from the OE pers.n. *Brȳni* and **cumb**); *Broken Wall* (*v.* **brocen**, **wall**); *Brushe Crofte* (*v.* **brusche**, **croft** (as freq in this par.)); *Cade Haie* (the surname *Cade*); *Camfeilds Croft*; *Chadland*; *Chappells* —, *Chapers Mead(e)* (*v.* **mǣd**, as freq in this par.); *Chawe Parke* (possibly 'paddock for calves', from **cealf** (gen.pl. *cealfa*) and **pearroc**); *Clapiers*; *Clarkes Crofte*; *Clawpittes* (*v.* **clawu**, **pytt**); *Cleeveland* (*v.* **clif** (nom. pl. *clifu*, *cleofu*)); *Cofer's* (a croft) 1582, *Quaffers Crofte* 1608 (a surname from ME *coyfer* 'maker of coifs'); *Collard* (cf. Collard D 258); *Collowaye*; (land) *in Cooke*, *Cowke*, *Couke*, *Cooke Furlonge*, *Couchaye* (*v.* **furlang**, (ge)**hæg**; Professor Löfvenberg notes that the spellings point to a ME word with *ō*, and suggests that there may have been an OE **cōc* or **cōce* 'lump of earth, hillock', from PrGerm **kōk-* and corresponding to OSwed, Swed *kōka* 'lump of earth', Norw dial. *kōk* 'lump of earth', and that such a word may also lie behind the first el. of Cookham Brk (cf. PNBrk 79–80), which according to DEPN is situated at a hill called *Cocdun* in 1220, cf. also OE *cēcel* 'a little cake' (from PrGerm **kōkila-*), and Flemish p.ns. containing words derived from PrGerm **kōkan-* and **kōkila-* and denoting hills (M. Gysseling, *Toponymisch Woordenboek*, 1960, p. 567); the form *Cockelhaie* 1608 may belong here, but it probably contains **coccel** 'tares'); *Creekes Hill* (possibly PrW *crūg* with explanatory OE **hyll**); *Cullandes*, *Cullens* (the surname *Cullen*, or **cū** 'cow' and **land**); *Dowvyne* (second el. possibly **fin** 'heap'); *Eastcrofte* (cf. West Croft(s) *supra*); *Estfelde* 1321, (*the*) *Eastfeild*, *-field* 1608 (*v.* **ēast**, **feld**); *Easthighe Grove* (*v.* **grāf(a)**); *Escheated Peece* 1650 (one of 'certain lands called Escheated lands' *ib*, *v.* **pece**); *Fall Mead* (*v.* (ge)**fall**); *Fawe Christ*; *Flaxepoke* (*v.* **fleax**, **poke** 'bag'); *Flowers Mead*; *Gaycroft(e)* (*Wall*) (possibly the surname *Gay*); *Gisshaies*; *Goggers haie*'(cf. Henry *Goggar* 1323[1]); *Gowerth* (the second el. is probably **erð** (WSax **ierð**) 'ploughed land' if *pastura in Vrthe* 1321, 1323[2] belongs here, cf. G(r)owland(s) *supra*); *Great Acre*; *Greenehaie* (*v.* **grēne**[1]); *Groane feild*; (land) *above Hayes, pasture under haie* (*v.* (ge)**hæg**; *Headyate* (*v.* **hēafod**, **geat**); *Hormyng* (a croft) 1582; *House Crofte* (*v.* **hūs**); *Justice* (a croft) 1582 (probably a surname); (*close*...*called*) *Kingeslocke* (cf. Ralph *Kyng* 1323[1], *v.* **loc** 'a fold'); *ground called Knapps* 1650 (*v.* **cnæpp** 'hillock', cf. Robert *de la Knappe* 1249 Acct, William *Knapes* 1650); *Knoles Combe* 1582 (probably a surname, *v.* **cumb**); *Lanies* (held by Richard *Lanie* 1608); *Langnope* (perhaps 'long inlet' from **lang**[1] (wk. obl. *langan*) and **hōp**[2], cf. Thirtoop *supra*); *Lang-*, *Longoake*, *Lange-*, *Longe Noxe*, *Lange Noke* (*v.* **lang**[1] (wk. obl. *langan*), **āc** 'oak-tree'); *Litle Close*; *Littlefeild*; *Long Mead*; *Lovells Crofte*; *Lovinges Line* (*v.* **leyne**); *Mackhaye* (perhaps the surname *Mack*, *v.* (ge)**hæg**); *Marchandesforlong* 1323[1] (the surname *Marchand*, *v.* **furlang**); *Middle close*;

Modrie Mead; *Neale's Croft* 1582; *Netherclose*; *Newecrofte*; *Newehaie*; *Newewaye* (*v.* weg); *Normans Crofte*; *Oare* (possibly ōra[1] 'bank', but cf. E & W Weare *supra*); *Overclose* (*v.* uferra); *Overyard* 1650 (*v.* uferra, geard); *Parsons Land*; *Peacockes Crofte*; *Perattesacr'* 1323[1] (the surname *Peratt*, *v.* æcer); *Peverelescroft* 1324 (cf. Thomas *Peverel* 1323[1]); *Pintle Mead* (*v.* pintel); *The Poole* 1710 (in Easton *supra*, *v.* pōl[1]); *Porch Haie* (*v.* porch); *Pountes Close* (cf. *Johanne Pounte preposito de Portlonde* 1322); *Rushwell*, *-will* (*v.* risc, wella, willa); *Sams Crofte*; *Saules Crofte*; *Scottes Crofte* (cf. John *Scot*, — *Skot* 1323[1]); *Sharbardes*, *-bordes*, *Sharbus*, *Sharbut Close* (probably a surname); *Shellmust Horne* (*v.* horn; the first part of the name should perhaps be associated with foll.); (land) *upon Shill* (perhaps from scell (WSax sciell) 'a shell' used in some figurative sense, cf. prec. and *Stonschulye infra*); *Skurle's-* 1582, *Scurles Croft(e)* 1608; (land) *called half a slowe* (*v.* slōh 'a slough'); *Nethere-*, *Overesmalecome* 1323[1], *Smalcombe* 1397, 1582, (*Lower*) *Smallcombe* 1608 (*v.* smæl (wk. obl. *smalan*), cumb, with neoðerra, uferra); *Sprattes Acre*; *Stanewey* 1397 (*v.* stān, weg); *Stephens Haie*; *Stockes Place*; *Stonschulye* 1321 (probably a substantival use of the OE (WSax) adj. stānscilig 'shaly, stony', used in the sense 'stony ground' in OE (BT), cf. the f.n. *Hydiestansilie* in Chaldon H. par. *supra* and the f.n. *Shill supra*); *Strad(d)lehole* (perhaps 'hollow it is possible to stride across', *v.* straddle, hol[1]); *Sutters Crofte*; *Twincroftes* ('(land) between crofts', *v.* betwēonan); *terre super Warledenne* 1324, *Warledowne* 1608 (the first form suggests denn 'woodland pasture', the second dūn 'hill'; but Professor Löfvenberg points out that *-denne* may well be an error for *-doune*, and that the first el. may be an OE pers.n. *Wærla* (cf. DEPN s.n. Warlingham Sr) or a compound of wer, wær 'a weir' and lēah); *Wath*, *Wade*, *South-*, *Westwath*, *-wade* (the word *wath(e)*, probably from OE (ge)wæd, discussed under the f.n. *Bitakewathe* in Langton M. par. *supra*; that it was similar in meaning to the frequent Portland word ware may be suggested by the mention of *comon on Oare & Wath* 1608, *our Commons of worth* (sic) *or ware* 1783, *v.* E & W Weare *supra*); *Wattes Close*; *Wencome* 1323[1] (perhaps from wenn, wænn '(hill shaped like) a wen or tumour', and cumb, cf. *Wandene* 1323[1] (p) which may contain the same first el. with denu 'valley'); (*the*) *West Feild*, *-feeld*; *Westlade* (*v.* (ge)lād 'river-crossing'); *Westyates* (*v.* geat); *Whitmothers*; *Souther Wilslade* (possibly 'valley with a stream in it', from wella (WSax willa) and slæd, with sūðerra); *Witch Crofte* 1608, *Wich Croft* 1650 (perhaps from wice 'a wych-elm' rather than wīc 'dairy farm', cf. Under Weeck *supra*); *Woodland*.

Preston

Preston is in the liberty of Sutton Poyntz, *v.* note under Culliford Tree hundred *supra* and *v.* Sutton Poyntz *infra*. In 1933 part of this par. was transferred to the borough of Weymouth, part to the par. of Bincombe, and the rest to the par. of Poxwell for civil purposes (Kelly).

PRESTON (SY 705832), *Prestun* 1228 Pat, *Preston(e)* 1285 FA, 1291 Tax, 1317 Pat *et passim*, 'priest farm', from prēost and tūn; it was an old prebend of Salisbury cathedral (*Prebend' de Prestone* 1291 Tax, etc.).

STREET-NAMES: PLAISTERS LANE (TPlan), no doubt to be identified with *viam regiam in —, alta via voc' Pleystrete* 1451 *Ct*, 1497–1505 *Weld¹*, *Playstrete* 1465, 1466 *ib*, v. plega 'play, sport', strǣt, cf. *Pleystrete* in Winfrith N. par. *supra*; PRESTON RD, —*St.* 1774 Hutch¹; VERLANDS RD, cf. *Verlings* 1838 *TA*, probably from furlang. Lost st.ns. include *la Blynelane* 1466 *Weld¹* (v. blind 'leading nowhere', lane); (*via regia voc'*) *Port(e)wey* 1461 *Rent*, 1466 *Weld¹* (v. port-weg); *Pulsshelane* 1482 *Weld¹* (cf. Thomas *Pulsshe* 1481 *ib*, v. lane); *la West(st)rete* 1466, 1485 *Weld¹* (v. west, strǣt).

CHALBURY (Camp) (SY 695838), — LODGE, (*terre...subtus*) *Charlebury* 1452 *Ct*, *Cherl(e)bury* 1461 *Rent*, *Chall Brow*, *Under Chall Brows*, *Chalbury Lodge* 1838 *TA*, 'the encampment of the peasants', from ceorl (gen. pl. *ceorla*) and burh (dat. sg. *byrig*); Chalbury is an Iron Age hill fort (RCHMDo 2 486–7).

ESTON (lost), *decenna de Eston* 15 *Digby*, 1451, 1460 *Ct*, 1465–1496 *Weld¹*, 'east farm or village', v. ēast, tūn; this was one of the two tithings into which the manor of Sutton Poyntz *infra* seems to have been divided, cf. *Weston infra*.

HORYFORD (lost), *Horylord* (for -*ford*) 1402 IpmR, *Horiford* 1412 FA, 1456 IpmR, *Horyford(e)* 1431 FA, 1470 *NatT et freq* to 1531 *Weld¹*, *Horeford* 1461 *Rent*, 1462 *Weld¹* (— *iuxta Sutton Poytz*), 'filthy ford', v. horig, ford, cf. Sutton Poyntz *infra*; the exact location of the place is not known, but the ford which gave rise to the name was no doubt on R. Jordan, v. foll.

JORDAN HILL (SY 700822) & HO, *pastur' byestechurdon, Churdoneslade* 1452 *Ct*, (*pastur' super*) *Churdon* 1472–1490 *Weld¹*, 1481 *MinAcct, furlong' voc' Cherdo(u)n, Cherdo(u)nslade* 1461 *Rent*, *Yordon* 1496–1503 *Weld¹*, *Jurdayn(y)s* 1525, 1529 *ib*, *Jordayne* 1531 *ib*, *hill called Jorden* 1617 WeyR, *Jurdens* 1635 *Weld¹*, *Jordens farme* 117 *ib*, *Jordan Beach, Cliff & Hill* 1838 *TA*, also giving name to R. Jordan (RNs. *infra*). The second el. is dūn 'hill'; the first is probably cerr (WSax cierr) 'a turn, a bend', with reference to the course taken by R. Jordan as it rounds the E side of the hill. It is possible that *Chur* or *Cher* from c(i)err was an earlier name for the river itself, in which case the name Jordan may mean 'hill on R. *Chur* or *Cher*' rather than 'hill at the bend', cf. DEPN s.n. Chirdon Nb. *Byeste*- is 'to the east of', v. bī, ēastan, -*slade* is slæd 'valley'. Later forms of the name show association with the pers.n. and surname *Jordan*, itself taken from the river of that name in the Middle East.

LODMOOR (SY 687813)

> (*to*) *lodomor* 978 × 984 (14) *Add* (S 938)
> *Loddemor(e)* Hy 3 (14) Cerne, 1496 *Weld*[1], *Loddemor' ysdych* 1505 *ib*
> *Lodemor(e)* 1297 Pat (p), 1451 *Ct*, 1471 *Weld*[1] (*Warenna domini apud* —), 1496 *ib*, 1503 *ib* (— *Lake*), 117 *ib*, *-moure* 1452 *Ct*, *Lod(e)more(s)mede* 1461 *Rent*, 1465 *Weld*[1], *MinAcct*, 1476 *Weld*[1], *Lodemor ys mede* 1503 *ib*, *Lodymour* 1529 *ib*
> *Lodmore* 1460 *Ct*, *Weld*[1], 1461 *Rent*, 1465 *MinAcct et freq* to 1638 *Weld*[1], *Lodmoresoutlete* 1460 *ib*, *Lodmowr* 1525 *ib*, *-moure* 1541 *ib*, *-moore* 1638 *ib*, *Lodmoor*, *-mere* 1838 *TA*

The first el. is difficult; derivation from (ge)lād 'track' as is proposed for Lodmore Ch 3 97 is precluded by the absence of *Lad*-spellings. It should instead no doubt be related to the names *Lod(e)broke* 1451, 1452 *Ct*, 1461 *Rent*, 1496 *Weld*[1], *firma querri domini super Loddon* 15 *MinAcct*, (*terr' super*) *Loddon* 1451 *Ct*, 1461 *Rent*, 1476 *Weld*[1], *quarret' super Loddon* 1481 *MinAcct*, *Gt & Quarry Lodden* 1838 *TA*, *terr' in Loddynges* 1451 *Ct*, *-yngys* 1461 *Rent*, all of which occur in this par.; *Lod-* in all these names may represent a Brit name from lutā 'mud', a derivative of which is suggested by Ekwall RN 258 to explain the r.n. Loddon Brk, Ha (cf. Jackson 578, PNBrk 13), and which may also lie behind names like Ladford D 108 (*Loddeford* 1244, on a stream called *Loddan broc* 938) and Lodfin D 531 (*Lodefenne* 1288), cf. also Laddingford K 170; the name could have been applied, appropriately enough, to what is now Lodmoor, mōr 'marshland' being an explanatory OE addition. *Lod(e)broke* and *Loddon* may then be interpreted as the same Brit name with the addition of brōc 'stream' and dūn 'hill', and the fact that the f.ns. *Great & Quarry Lodden* are located near Chalbury *supra*, over one mile from Lodmoor, may suggest that the Brit name was once applied to the whole western part of the present par.; the lost *Loddynges* may then represent an -ingas derivative denoting the people occupying this area. On the other hand, as Professor Löfvenberg points out, the first el. of Lodmoor and of the other *Lod-* names in this par. may well be an OE pers.n. *Lod(d)a*, *v.* Forsberg 150–1. The other additions are dīc 'ditch', lacu 'water-course', mǣd 'meadow', and utlete 'outlet, channel'.

RADWAY (lost), (*vill' de*) *Radewey(e)* 1280, 1288 *Ass*, 1311 Ipm, 1315
Cl, 1329 Ipm, 1386 Fine, *Radway(e)* 1549, 1616 Hutch[3], *Rodway*
1649 ib, probably named from R. Wey, cf. Broadwey par. *supra*,
with either rēad 'red', from the colour of soil or foliage, cf. Radeslow
in W Knighton par. *supra*, or hrēod 'reed', denoting a place where
reeds grew, cf. Radipole par. *infra*. However the name may alternatively be from rād-weg 'road suitable for riding'. It is probably to
be associated with *Rodway Mead* 1838 *TA*, which is in the extreme
W of Preston par. near Horse Lynch Plant. *infra*; this part of Preston
borders on Broadwey par. and on a part of Melcombe R. that was
formerly included in Radipole par.

RIMBROW COPPICE (SY 696837), *Rembary, terre bynorthe Remb'y*
1451 *Ct, Rymbury(furlong)* 1461 *Rent*, possibly from rima, rioma,
reoma 'rim, border', perhaps in allusion to the rampart of Chalbury
Camp *supra* which lies immediately NW, with beorg 'hill, barrow';
bynorthe is 'to the north of', *v.* bī, norðan.

SUTTON POYNTZ (SY 706837), *Suttone* 891 (14) *Bodl* (S 347(2)),
Sutone 1086 DB, *Sutona* Exon, *Sutton(e)* 1204, 1208 P, 1218 FF,
1259, 1273 Cl, 1280 *Ass*, 1285 FA *et passim, Sutton(e) Poinz* 1307–14
Ipm, — *Pointz* 1314 Cl, 1348 Pat, 1811 OS, — *Poyntz* 1319 FF,
1342 *Weld*[1] *et passim*, — *Peynz* 1399 Cl, — *Poyn(e)s* 1412, 1431 FA,
1504 Ipm, — *Poynt(e)s* 1524 *Weld*[1] *et freq* to 1l17 *ib*, — *Poyntez* 1531
ib, — *Poynt* 1539 LP, — *Pointes* 1569 *Ct, Suttun* 1212 Fees, *Sotton(e)*
1280 *Ass*, 1285 FA, 1353 *Ilch* (— *Poyntz*), 1399 *MinAcct* (— *Pounsz*),
Soutton 1340 NI, 1393 *MinAcct* (— *Poyntz*). 'South farm', *v.* sūð,
tūn; Sutton Poyntz was a royal manor in DB and 'south' may refer
to its situation in relation to Dorchester, but cf. *Eston supra* and
Weston infra which may be much older than their recorded spellings
indicate. The manor was held by the family of *Poyntz* from the 13th
cent. (Nicholas *Puinz* 1212 Fees, Hugh *Poinz* 1218 FF, Nicholas
Poynz 1259, 1273 Cl, Hugh *Poynz* 1280 *Ass*, etc.). For the liberty of
Sutton Poyntz, *v.* Culliford Tree hundred *supra*; for the former
church or chapel here, *v.* Prospect Ctg *infra*.

WESTON (lost), *decenna de Weston* 15 *Digby*, 1451, 1460 *Ct*, 1465,
1496 *Weld*[1], *Weston Town (Orchard)* 1838 *TA*, 'west farm or village',
v. west, tūn; a tithing in Sutton Poyntz *supra*, cf. *Eston supra*; the
TA fields lie just W of Sutton Poyntz village.

WYKE OLIVER HO (SY 692825), *Wyke* 1327 *SR* (p), 1461 *Rent*, 1482, 1541 *Weld*[1], *Wike* 1332 SR (p), 15 *MinAcct*, 1452 *Ct*, *Westwyke* 1531 *Weld*[1], 1549 Hutch[3], *West-Weeke* 1549 Hutch[1], *Weeke Oliver* 1616 Hutch[3], *Wyke Oliver* 1863 ib, 'the dairy farm', *v.* wīc; 'west' probably in relation to either Preston or Sutton Poyntz *supra*; John *Oliver* held lands in Sutton Poyntz in 1640 *Weld*[1].

BOILING ROCK, *the* — 1863 Hutch[3], no doubt so called from a bubbling spring; Melcombe R. was supplied with water from here until 1857 (Hutch[3] 2 466). BOWLEAZE (COVEWAY), (land) *super lez Bolheys* 1461 *Rent*, *claus' voc' Bolhey* 1479 *Weld*[1], 1481 *MinAcct*, *prat' voc' Bolhaise* 1531 *Weld*[1], *Bolehaies* 1586 WeyR, *Bollhayes* 1617 ib, *Bow Leaze* 1838 *TA*, 'bull enclosure(s)', *v.* bula, (ge)hæg; Bowleaze is now the name of a small bay, *v.* cove. BROADROCK, a coastal feature. CANBERRA RD, from the Australian p.n. COOMBE BARTON & VALLEY (RD), cf. *terre in la combe* 1451 *Ct*, *le Combe* 1461 *Rent*, *v.* cumb 'valley', barton. EAST HILL, cf. *East Down Hill* 1838 *TA*, *v.* dūn; it is E of West Hill *infra*. EWE-LEES (lost), 1811 OS, *Eweleaze* 1838 *TA*, *v.* eowu, lǣs. FURZY CLIFF, cf. *Lytelclyf* 1451 *Ct*, *Litulclyff* 1461 *Rent*, (land) *super le Clif(fe)* 1461 *ib*, 1481 *MinAcct*, *le Clyf* 1479 *Weld*[1], *East Cliff(e)* (*Beach*) 1838 *TA*, *v.* fyrsig, lȳtel, clif, cf. also *jannior' voc' Furses apud Jurdayns et Northedowne* 1525 *Weld*[1], *v.* fyrs, Jordan Hill *supra*, Northdown *infra*. GREEN HILL, GREENHILL BARTON, *Grenehill* 1461 *Rent*, *v.* grēne[1], hyll, barton. HORSE LYNCH PLANT., *Horse Lynch & Plant.* 1838 *TA*, *v.* hors, hlinc. LITTLEMOOR RD, to Littlemoor in Broadwey par. *supra*. MANOR FM. MILL RACE, cf. *molendini aquatici domini voc' Gristmyll* 1461 *Rent* (in Wyke Oliver *supra*), 1465 *MinAcct*, *Mill Plot* 1838 *TA*, *v.* grist-mill, cf. Sutton Mill *infra*. NEW BARN. NORTHDOWN BARN & FM, *furlong' voc' Northdoun*, (land) *apud Nordon* 1461 *Rent*, *Northdon* 1500 *Weld*[1], *North(e)downe* 1525 *ib et passim*, *Northdowne farme* l17 *ib*, *North Down Cowleaze* 1838 *TA*, *v.* norð, dūn, cf. South Down *infra*. OLD KILN, cf. *Middle Fd and Limekiln* 1838 *ib*; the lost names *Lekillane* 1451 *Ct* and *le Kilhay* 1452 *ib* probably also contain cyln 'a kiln', with lane, (ge)hæg. OVERCOMBE BEACH, perhaps uferra 'higher, upper', with cumb. POUND, cf. *punfald domini apud Sutton* 1461 *Ct*, *pratum voc' le Pounde* 1461 *Rent* (in Wyke Oliver *supra*), *v.* pund, pund-fald. PROSPECT CTG (on site of Church), *v.* prospect; a former church at Sutton Poyntz is mentioned as *ecclesiam de Sottone* in 1280 *Ass*, and Hutch[3] 2 835 notes an e15th cent. reference to a

chapel here. PUDDLE DOCK DAIRY HO, a name probably analogous
with the f.n. Paddle Dock in Corfe C. par. *supra q.v.*; the place is on a
small stream, but 'muddy pool where a boat could rest' looks less
appropriate here than for the Corfe name, *v.* **puddel, dock.** ROMAN
BRIDGE (local), from its proximity to the site (marked 6″) of a Roman
villa (Jervoise 88). ST ANDREW'S CHURCH, cf. 'the church of *Preston*'
1358 Pat, *ecclesie Sancti Andree de Preston* 1393 *AD, ecclesie de
Preston* 1461 *Ct.* SHIP INN, *The* — 1838 *TA.* SOUTH DOWN CTG &
DAIRY, SOUTHDOWN ESTATE, *South downe* 1541 *Weld*[1], *Southdown*
1811 OS, *South Down (End)* 1838 *TA, v.* **sūð, dūn,** cf. Northdown
supra. SPRING BOTTOM, *Spring Down and Bottom* 1838 *ib, v.* **spring,
dūn, botm,** cf. foll.; springs are marked here 6″. SPRING HEAD HOTEL,
cf. prec. SUTTON FM, from Sutton Poyntz *supra.* SUTTON MILL, cf.
cursus aque iuxta molendinum domini 15 Digby, *firma molendini aquatici*
1481 *MinAcct,* cf. prec. and Mill Race *supra*; there is also mention of
a mill in Sutton Poyntz in 1640 *Weld*[1]. TOLLHOUSE CTG, on the
Preston–Melcombe R. road, *v.* **toll-house.** TOUT, 1838 *TA, La Toute*
1452 *Ct, le Toute* 1461 *Rent,* a hill-spur over 300′ high with a view
over the low-lying coastal area, *v.* **tōt(e)** 'a look-out (hill)'. WEST HILL,
cf. *la West Doune* 1451 *Ct, pastur' montana voc' le Westdoun* 1461
Rent, West Down 1838 *TA, v.* **west, dūn;** it is W of East Hill *supra.*
WHITE HORSE CHALET, from White Horse (Hill) in Osmington par.
supra. WINSLOW, *Winsload* 1838 *TA,* a small round hill (250′);
second el. perhaps **(ge)lād** or **hlāw,** cf. Winslow Bk 75. WYKE
OLIVER RD, to Wyke Oliver *supra.*

FIELD-NAMES

The undated forms are 1838 *TA* 176. Spellings dated 1327 are *SR,* 1332 SR,
1340 NI, 1395 Hutch[3], 15 Digby, 15[2], 1465[2], 1481 *MinAcct,* 1451, 1452,
1460, 1461[2] *Ct,* 1461 *Rent,* 1664 HTax, 1791 Boswell, and the rest *Weld*[1].
   (a) Barn Cl, Bern Brake (*v.* **bere-ærn, bræc**[1]); Baylis (cf. *prat' nuper
Willelmi Beley* 1482); Bot Hayes (perhaps the surname *Bot(t),* but cf. *prat'
nuper Thome Batte* 1465[1], *v.* **(ge)hæg**); Bottom Md; Brake Orchd (cf. Bern
Brake *supra*); Breach (*furlong' voc' le Breche* 1461, *v.* **brēc**); Briers Cl (cf.
John *Bryer* 1640); Broad Md ((*la*) *Brodemede* 1451 *et freq* to 1541, *v.* **brād,
mǣd**); (N & S) Chalkshill (*Chalkeshill(e)* 1451, 1461, probably from **hyll**
and the surname *Chalk(e),* but possibly from **c(e)alc** 'chalk' and **scell** (WSax
sciell) 'shell', cf. the f.n. *Shill* in Portland par. *supra*); Chapple's Cl (cf.
William *Chappel* 1395); Hr Claylands, Clay Lawns (*lez Cleylondes* 1451,
Cley- 1461, *Claylond* 1475, *v.* **clǣg, land**); (Fore) Cleaves ('(land in front of)
the cliffs', *v.* **fore, clif** (nom. pl. *clifu, cleofu*), cf. Wincleaves, *Vnderclyf infra,*

Furzy Cliff *supra*); Close; Cockleton (*Cokoldon* 1461, *v.* coccel 'tares', dūn 'hill', cf. *fossat' apud Cokelhegge* 15, 1474, 1524, *via reg' apud Coggulhegge* 1460, *v.* hecg 'hedge'); Common Md; Coppice; Corner Cl; Court Cl (*claus' (apud Wyke) voc' Courtclos(e)* 15², 1471, 1481, 1482, *loc' super le Courtclos* 1481, *bosc' apud Courteclos(e)* 1496, 1525, cf. *pastur' super Cur'* 1452, *1 boscus et 1 Witheber voc' le Courtgrove* 1461, *v.* court, clos(e), wīðig, bearu, grāf(a), cf. Wyke Oliver *supra*); Lt & Old Cowleaze; Coxs Orchd (cf. William *Cox* 1664, but perhaps to be associated with *furlong' voc' lez Cokkes* 1461, *v.* cocc¹ 'heap, hillock'); Croam Bags (perhaps from crumb 'crooked' and bagge 'bag-like feature'); Hr & Lr Crocks; Gt & Lt Cuckoo Park (cf. *le Parke* 1460, 1461, *Parkemede* 1461, *claus' voc' Neuparke* 1481, *Newparke* 1525, 1541, *v.* park, cuccu, mǣd, nīwe); E & W Culliver Tree (near Culliford Tree in Whitcombe par. *infra*); Dryer's (cf. *sepes Johannis Dryer* 1460, *tenement' Walteri Dryer* 1486); Eights Cl (perhaps from ēgeð 'a small island' used in a figurative sense, since this field, in the extreme E of the par., is bounded on 3 of its 4 sides by other pars.); 11 Acres; Fore Hill (*v.* fore); Foss Hill ((land) *super —, furlong' voc' Forshill* 1461, perhaps analogous with West Fossil in Chaldon H. par. *supra q.v.*, but the first el. may be fyrs 'furze', *v.* hyll); Gore Md (cf. *prat' voc' le Gore* 1452, *furlong voc' le Gore* 1461, *v.* gāra); Gunville (probably a surname, cf. Tarrant G. par. *infra*); Hams (*lez hammes* 1452, *v.* hamm); Helliers Cl (cf. Robert *Hellyer* 1664); Higher Bridge 1791; Hill Pce; Holes ((land) *apud le Hole* 1461, *v.* hol¹); Holy Lawns (*Holylond* 1461, *v.* hālig, land, perhaps denoting land belonging to the church); Horseman's Bridge 1791; Long Kitchen (*v.* cycene, perhaps in allusion to land for the maintenance of a kitchen); Land; Lawn (from land or launde); Long Cl; Lodmoor Bridge 1791 (*v.* Lodmoor *supra*); Long Lawns (*Langlond* 1461, *v.* lang¹, land); Love Lane Md (*claus' voc' Louelane* 1472, 1481, *aqua apud —* 1496, *v.* lufu, lane); Lower Hill (cf. *Middelhill* 1461, *v.* middel, hyll); Hr, Lr & Old Loynes (possibly a development of leyne); Maiden Hill; Malthouse (cf. *cot'...nuper Johannis Malteman* 1501); Marley Wall; E, W, Hr & Lr Marsh (*le Mers(s)he* 1461, *v.* mersc); (Large) Meadow(s); Middle Cl & Fd; Naps Cl (*v.* cnæpp); New Cl (*Nueclose* 1531, *Newe Close* 1541, *v.* nīwe); New Md (-*mede* 1465¹, *v.* mǣd); New Pce; (Gt) Orchard(s) (cf. *le Brodeorchard, le Orchard apud Wike* 1452, *v.* brād, orceard, Wyke Oliver *supra*); Long Passbury; Plantation; Plot; Old Poorhouse; Preston Bridges 1791 (cf. foll.); Preston (Common) Md (*prat' subtus Preston* 1452, *Prestonmede* 1460, 1461, *Prestonesmede* 1465², *via apud Preston ys mede* 1505, from Preston *supra*, *v.* mǣd); Pulpit (cf. Pulpit Wood Bk 164); Radcliff ('red cliff', *v.* rēad, clif); Red Lawns (*Redelond* 1461, *v.* rēad, land); Reek (*v.* ricke 'a rick', cf. foll.); Rick Yd; Rowdens (*Roudoun* 1461, *v.* rūh (wk. obl. *rūgan*) 'rough', dūn); Rumsey; Sand Pit Fd; 7 & 16 Acres; Slaughter Ho; South Pce; Straights (perhaps to be connected with (*furlong' voc'*) *le Sterte* 1451, 1461, *v.* steort 'tail of land', but cf. the st.n. Straits in Portland par. *supra*); Sutton Bridge 1791; Swan P.H.; Symes' Bridge 1791; 10 & 12 Acres; Two Planks; Vartee; Verless Md; Vine Cl; Wad Brow (perhaps from wād and brū or beorg); West Beach; West Fd (*le Westfild* 1461, *la Westfeld* 1466, *v.* west, feld); West water; White Md (*v.* hwīt); White Roughit (*v.* hwǣte, rūhet, cf. an identical f.n. in Weymouth par. *infra*);

Wincleaves (*terre apud Twynclif(fe)* 1461, 'between the cliffs', *v.* betwēonan, clif, cf. (Fore) Cleaves *supra*); Winlakes (*Twynlake* 1461, *Wynlake* 1461², 'between the streams', *v.* betwēonan, lacu, cf. prec.); Wire Pce; Withy Bed (cf. *le Whitheber* 1481, *lez Wythybers, unu' maresc'. . .voc' Wethybere* 1531, *v.* wiðig, bedd, bearu).

(b) *le Acr* 1525 (*v.* æcer); *le Barys ys Crosse* 1504 (cf. Geoffrey *Bars* 1327, — *le Barys* 1332, *v.* cros); *le Barly feild* 1635 (*v.* bærlic); *Bynehill* 1461 (*v.* bēan, hyll); *Blakelond* 1461 (perhaps to be identified with *Blacklands Yeate* 1649 WeyR in bounds of Melcombe R., *v.* blæc, land (as freq in this par.), geat); *Brodebrygge* 1506 (*v.* brād, brycg); (*le*) *Brodeclos* 1461, 1472, 1481 (*v.* brād, clos(e)); *Castelcombe* 1481 (*v.* castel(l), cumb); *fossat' apud le Causey* 1496 (*v.* caucie); *Chapehey* 1525, *Chaphaye* 1529 (perhaps 'enclosure with a low rental', from cēap and (ge)hæg, cf. *Chep aker* Gl 1 249); *Checks-* 1635, *Chickshill drove* 1638 (perhaps the surname *Chick* with hyll, *v.* drove); *Nyther-, Nether-, Nitherchurchefurlong, -lang* 1451, 1461, 1472, *Overchurchefurlong* 1461 (*v.* cirice, furlang, neoðerra, uferra); *Churcheslade* 1451 (*v.* cirice, slæd); (*mes' voc'*) *Coldeherb(o)urgh* 1475 (*v.* cald, here-beorg); *Cole(s)fursses* 1461 (cf. Thomas *Cole* 1461², *v.* fyrs); *la Combe* 1451 (*v.* cumb); *atte Croch* 1340 (p) (*v.* atte, crūc³ 'a cross'); (*furlong' voc'*) *Culverslade* 1451, 1461, *Colverhey* 1461 (cf. *dom' Columbar'* 1531, *v.* culfre, slæd, (ge)hæg); *terr' super la Dyche* 1451 (*v.* dīc); *le Doun(e)mede* 1452, 1461, 1471 (*v.* dūn or dūne, mǣd (as freq in this par.)); *furlong' voc' Eld-, Oldbury* 1461 ('old fortified place', *v.* ald (WSax eald), burh (dat. sg. byrig)); *terre apud Ellenstuoke* 1451 ('elder-tree stump', *v.* ellern, stocc, possibly identical with the bdy marks *to ellenstubbe, of ellestubbe* 978 × 984 (14) *Add* (S 938), *Ellenestub* Hy 3 (14) Cerne, and (land) *apud E(l)stubbe* 1461, which have the same meaning, *v.* stubb); (*le*) *Estclos* 1452, 1461 (*v.* ēast, clos(e)); (*le*) *Estfild* 1460², 1461, 1481, *Estfeld* 1479 (*v.* ēast, feld); *Estopenvoll, Estopdovoll* 1461 (the final el. is wella); *in la Fenne* 1327 (p), *intheuenne* 1332 (p) (*v.* fenn, cf. foll.); *pons voc' Fennebrigge* 1476, 1482, *fossat' apud Fennehegge* 15 (*v.* brycg, hecg, cf. prec.); *le Vennyclause* 1503, *via reg' apud la Vennydore* 1451, *Fennydore* 1460, *claus' apud Vennyhowse, Wennyhowse* 1505 (*v.* fennig 'marshy, muddy', clos(e), dor or duru 'a gap, a pass', hūs); *Fildesplase* 1461² (cf. John *in the Feld* 1340, ten'. . .*nuper Feldes* 1471, *v.* place); *via reg' apud Fyssherisbrigge* 1451, *Fisherbrigge* 1460, (*pons voc'*) *Fysshern(e)-, Fyschernbrigg(e), -Brygg* 1476, 1485, 1486, 1524, *Fysser'-, Wysser' ys Brygge* 1496 ('bridge of the fisherman, -men', *v.* fiscere, brycg; *-n(e)-* in *Fysshern(e)-*, etc. is probably a wk ME gen.pl., *v.* -ena); *Frog(ge)lond, Frogwell* 1461 (*v.* frogga, wella); *Fulwill* 1461 (*v.* fūl 'dirty', wella); *parcell' voc' Grandise,* — *Brandise* 1461 (the correct form is uncertain); *claus' voc' Greygromes* 15², 1474, 1481 (a ME surname from *grey* 'grey-haired' and *grome* 'serving-man'); *Greyscombe* 15² (grǣg² 'badger', or the surname *Grey*, with cumb); *terr'*. . .*apud le Grette in le Estfild* 1461, *terr'*. . .*in la Gyrt* 1482 (these forms possibly refer to the same place, and, as Professor Löfvenberg suggests, probably reflect an OE **grytte* 'sandy or stony soil or land', cf. John *atte Grutte* 1327 *SR* (Frome St Q.), PNBrk 245); *terr' vac' voc' Hakeneylond* 1482 (*v.* hakeney, perhaps identical with *pastur' equorum* 1487, cf. an analogous lost f.n. in Coombe K. par. *supra*); *terr' in lez Hassok(k)es* 1451, 1461 (*v.* hassuc 'clump of coarse grass'); *Hemphey* 1461 (*v.* hænep, (ge)hæg); *le Hewysh* 1452, *pastur' montana voc' Huysshe* 1461 (*v.* hīwisc); *Hyford* 1474 ('hay ford', *v.* hēg (WSax hi(e)g), ford, cf. Hyford in Winfrith N. par. *supra*); *Hillymede* 1461 (*v.* hyll, -ig³); *Holme Meade* l17 (probably holegn 'holly'); *Holwey* 1466 (*v.* hol², weg); *Houchynscrosse* 1461 (the surname *Hutchin(s)*, *v.* cros); *Kytabriggelond, -hey* 1475, *Kytabryghey* 1481, *Kyttabryglane* 1505 (perhaps 'bridge haunted by a kite', from cȳta (gen.sg. cȳtan) and brycg, with land, (ge)hæg, lane; however, medial -a- in *Kytabrigge*, etc. may rather suggest a personal name *Kyt(t) a brigge*, 'Kit (a pet-form of Christopher or Katharine) at the bridge'); *Langacre* 1461 (*v.* lang¹, æcer); *furlong' voc' Langbittum, -bitton* 1461 (*v.* lang¹, bytme 'valley bottom'); *Larkedole* 1461 (*v.* lāwerce, dāl); *acr' in Lodemore voc' le levery acre* 1452, *Leueryacr* 1461 (*v.* lǣfer 'rush, reed', -ig³, æcer, cf. Lodmoor *supra*); *fossat' apud Lykeplontes* 1471, *-plontes* 1476 (probably a ME surname meaning 'one who likes plants, a gardener'); *acr' apud Lymepit* 1461 (*v.* līmpytt, cf. Old Kiln *supra*); *Longs farme* l17 (the surname *Long*); *Middelmede* 1452 (*v.* middel); *Milwardlond* 1461 (*v.* mylenweard 'miller'); *Moure-* 1451, *Moremede* 1461 (*v.* mōr); *Oxendon* 1481 (*v.* oxa (gen. pl. oxna), dūn); *les Pittes* 1461 (*v.* pytt); *Poleacre(s), -furlong* 1461 (*v.* pāl 'a stake' or pōl¹ 'a pool', æcer, furlang); *Rackeclose* 1502 (*v.* rakke); *Remesclif* 1461 (*v.* hremn 'raven', clif); *bi richte merke* 978 × 984 (14) *Add* (S 938) (*v.* riht², mearc); *le roderlese* 1451 (*v.* hrīðer 'an ox', lǣs); *terre... desuper le Clif voc' Semenlond* 15², *Semanlond(ez)* 1481 (*v.* sǣmann 'a sailor'); *Shepehey (in Wyke)* 15², 1461, 1472, *-hay* 1461, 1531, (*le*) *Shepenhay* 1452, *-hey* 1461, *Shepyn-* 1461, 1481, *Shapenhey* 1471 (*v.* scēap, (ge)hæg, cf. Wyke Oliver *supra*; *-en-, -yn-* probably represent an analogical ME gen.pl. in *-ene, v. -ena*, cf. *Sheponfurlong infra*); *la Shepehous* 1452 (*v.* scēap, hūs); *Shepon-* 1461, *Shepe(n)-* 1476, *Shepynfurlong(e)* 1481 (*v.* furlang, cf. *Shepehey supra*); *le Shete* 1461 (*v.* scēat or scīete); (*land*) *apud* (*lez*) *Shilues* 1451, 1461 (*v.* scelf (WSax sci(e)lf) 'a rock, a ledge'); *Shortlond* 1461 (*v.* sc(e)ort); *Shulbukesbache* 1461 (*v.* bece¹, bæce 'stream, valley'; the first part of the name is probably a surname); *la Slade* 1451 (*v.* slæd); *alta via apud Robyn' Smyth' ys Crosse* 1503 (*v.* cros); *the Somer feild* 1635 (*v.* sumor); *to-, fram Soredich* 978 × 984 (14) *Add* (S 938) (probably 'ditch leading to the shore', from scor(a) and dīc, cf. *Shoreditch* Mx 145); (*pastur' apud*) *le Soure* 1452, 1461 (possibly from sūr 'sour' or sūre 'sorrel', cf. the lost f.n. *Soure* in Bincombe par. *supra*); *terre apud Stonyhipe* 1461 (*v.* stānig, hēap, cf. Stonehips in Steeple par. *supra*); *prat' voc' iii acr'* 1461 (*v.* þrēo, æcer); (*fossat' apud*) *Thursdyche, -diche* 1451, 1461, 1474, 1475, *Thursedyche* 1496, *Fursediche* 1461, (*le*) *Fursediche, -dyche* 1461, 1504 (from þyrs 'a giant, a demon' and dīc, with interchange of *Th-* and *F-*); *Thursteyn(e)swell* 1461 (the surname *Thursta(i)n* from the ON pers.n. Þorsteinn, *v.* wella); *long vitcombe* 1451 (possibly 'wide valley' from wīd, cumb, with lang¹, cf. Whitcombe par. *infra*); (*pastur' voc'*) *Vnderclyf, -clif* 1479, 1481, 1486 (*v.* under, clif, cf. Furzy Cliff *supra*); *terre in unewade* 1451, *furlong' voc' Vnnewode* 1461 (the forms are not certain); *Wex-* 1452, *Waxmede* 1461 (*v.* weax); *atte Welle* (p) 1327, 1332, 1340 (*v.* atte, wella); *prat' voc' Wenyng(')* 15, 1465 *et freq* to 1476 (Professor Löfvenberg suggests this may possibly be from OE wēnung 'expectation, hope', used of land giving hope of a rich yield); *le West droue* 1635 (*v.* drove); *le Whetfeld* 1466 (*v.* hwǣte, feld); *White Wey* 1451, *-wey* 1452, 1461 (*v.* hwīt, weg); *Wymynschete* 1524 (first el. perhaps wīf-mann 'woman', cf. *le Shete supra*); *Wisefurses, -ez* 1461 (first el. possibly wise 'swamp', *v.* fyrs); (*claus' voc'*) (*le*) *Worth(e)* 15², 1452, 1461, 1481, 1531 (*v.* worð 'enclosure'); *Wormestall* 1461 (*v.* worm-stall 'cattle shelter').

Radipole

In 1894 the civil par. of Buckland Ripers was annexed to Radipole, and part of Radipole was added to Melcombe Regis. In 1933 part of Radipole was transferred to the borough of Weymouth and the remainder to the par. of Chickerell for civil purposes (Kelly).

RADIPOLE (SY 667814) ['rædipoul, 'rædipuːl]

Retpole 1086 DB, *-pola* Exon, *Retpol* 1237 Cl
Redpole 1166 RBE (p), 1194 P, 1212 Fees, Hy 3 (14) Cerne, *-pola* 1195 P
Redepoll 1237 Cl, *-pol* 1244 Ass (p)
Radepol 1237 Cl, 1244 Ass (p), 1259 Cl, *-powle* 1393 *AD, -pole* 1429 *Midd et freq* to 1487 *Weld*[1], *-poll* 1457 *Ct et freq* to 1487 *Weld*[1], *Raddepoll* 1460 Ct
Radipol 1237 Cl, *Radyp(p)oll(e)* 1530 *Weld*[1], 1535 VE, 1543 *Weld*[1], *Raddipoll* 1663 *ib*, *Radipole* 1594 *DCMDeed*, 1811 OS
Radpol(e) 1244 Ass (p), 1280 *ib*
Rappele 1280 Pat, Ass, 1318 Ch, *Rappole* 1288 Ass, 1291 Tax, 1311 Pap *et freq* to 1433 *Midd*, *Rappale* 1288 Ass, *Rapely* 1303 FA, *Rappell* 1340 NI
Rippele 1280 Pat
Reppole 1285 FA, 1303 FF
Roddy pole 16 *RoyMap*, *Rody pole* 1594 *DCMDeed*, *Roddipoll* 1664 HTax, *Rode-*, *Rodipoll* 1682 *Weld*[1]

'Reed pool', *v.* hrēod, pōl, with reference to Radipole Lake at the N end of which Radipole is situated; the forms with medial *-e-* (*Rede-, Rade-,* etc.) may be mainly analogical, but those in *Radi-*, etc. probably contain the adj. hrēodig 'reedy'. It might be noted that the reduced forms *Rappele, Rappole, Reppole,* etc. were in almost exclusive use between 1285 and 1428. The bounds of the par. in 1582 are given in Hutch³ 2 483, cf. also Cerne (DoNHAS **29** 202).

BUCKLAND RIPERS (SY 652825), *Bocheland* 1086 DB, *-lant* Exon, *Bokeland iuxta Waymue* 1268 Ass, *Boclande* 1285 FA, *-laund* 1288

Ass, *-londe* 1303 FA, *Bouclond* 1340 NI, 1346, 1428, 1431 FA
(— *Rypers*), *Bok(e)lond(e)* 1359 FF (— *Ripers*), 1375 Pat, 1390 Fine
(— *Riepers*), 1399 Cl ('— *Ryvers* by *Abbotesbury*'), 1412 FA (—
Rippers), 1428 ib (— *Repers*) *et freq* to 1486 *Weld*[1], *Bu(c)k(e)lond* 1425
IpmR (— *Rivers*), 1495 Ipm (— *Rypers*), 1543 *Weld*[1], *Bukland* 1446
Fine, *Buclond* 1461 *Ct*, 'land granted by charter', *v.* bōc-land, cf.
Buckland N. par. *infra*. The family of *de Riuers* or *de Ripariis* (from
Rivière in Normandy) were here in the 13th cent. (Robert —, John
de Riuers 1268 *Ass*, John *de Rypirs*, — *de Ripirs* 1285 FA), cf. also
Fees pp. 93, 426, 605, 753; for the other affixes, *v.* Abbotsbury par.
and Weymouth par. *infra*. Buckland Ripers was a separate par. until
1894. There is mention of a mill here in 1086 DB, *v.* VCHDo **3** 103.

CAUSEWAY FM (SY 661814), *Caucesweie* 1371 AD I, *Caus(e)wey(e)*
1381 ib I, 1412 FA, 1436 FF, 1473 Pat, *-way* 1412 FA, 1774 Hutch[1],
Caxwey 1543 *Weld*[1], *Cawesway* 1570 *AddCh*, *Casewey* (*ground*,
— *Hill*, — *Meade*) 1582 Hutch[3], *Cas(e)way* 1647 SC (*farme house
of* —), 1682 *Weld*[1], 1705 *ib*; a manor on R. Wey (*v.* RNs. *infra*,
Broadwey par. *supra*), and named from John *de Kauz* (als. *le Kauz*)
who held a third of a fee in Rowaldsway *q.v.* in Broadwey par. *supra*
in 1299 Ipm, cf. also Richard *de Kauz* 1249 Drew and Hutch[3] **2** 479.

CORFE HILL, CORFEHILL FM (SY 665818), *Corfhull* 1303 FF (— *juxta
Reppole*), 1431 FA, 1436 FF, *Corshull* 1412 FA, *Corf(f)(e)hill*, *-hyll*
1457 *Ct*, 1511 *Ampthill*, 1705 *Weld*[1], 'hill at a gap', *v.* corf, hyll,
cf. Corfe C. par. *supra*.

HOCKERILL (lost), 1597, 1863, *Hockeryll* 1558, *Hockerhill* 1579,
(*-ground*) 1582 all Hutch[3], 1594 *DCMDeed*, *Hocker Hill* 1840 *TA*,
'hill called *Hocker*' ('the hump'), *v.* hocer[1], hyll, or 'disputed hill',
v. hocer[2], cf. Hockerill Hrt 203; it is described by Hutch[3] **2** 481 as 'a
farm near Nottington' (in Broadwey par. *supra*).

HOLWELL (SY 655832)

    Halegewelle 1086 DB, *Halghewell* 1244 *Ass* (p), *Halghwell juxta
        Brodeweye* 1307 FF
    Holewill 1244 *Ass* (p)
    Hallewill 1268 *Ass* (p), *Brodewaye Hallewolle* 1285 FA, *Halwell
        [Hathewelle]* 1303 ib, *Halwell* 1510 MP, 1544 *PlR*, *Halewell*
        1346, 1431 FA, 1481 *Ct*, 1486 *Weld*[1], *-wolle* 1428 FA, *-wyll(e)*
        1457 *Ct*, 1464 *DCMCt*, 1465 *Weld*[1]

Hellewelle 1327 *SR*, *-woull* 1332 *SR*, *Helewell* 1388 Fine
Holwey 1445 *Rent*, *Holywell* 1530 *Weld*[1], *Hol(i)well or Holeway*
1795 Boswell, 1863 Hutch[3]

'Holy well, spring or stream', *v.* hālig, wella, cf. Broadwey par.
supra; it stands near a small stream an affluent of which rises nearby
(marked 6″); the spellings in *Hel(l)e-* probably show confusion with
Elwell in Upwey par. *infra* which is 1½ miles NE.

REDLANDS (SY 668820), *Radelond* 13 (15) *ChrP*, *(la) Redelond(e)* 1326
Midd, 1445 *Rent*, *-land* 1484 IpmR, *(le) Redlond* 1445 *Rent*, 1478–
1488 *Weld*[1], *Redelondis* 1457 *Ct*, *Ridlands* 1484 Hutch[3], *Rodelond*
('beside *Brodewey*') 1486 Ipm, *Redlands* 1582 Hutch[3], — or
Knacker's Hole 1774 Hutch[1]; the first el. is probably rēad (wk. obl.
rēadan) 'red' rather than hrēod 'reed', cf. par. name *supra*, *v.* land,
cf. Broadwey par. *supra*. *Knacker's Hole* is 'pit used by a knacker',
v. knacker, hol[1].

TATTON FM & HO (SY 631831), *Tatetun* 1086 DB, *Tatentone* 1086
DB, Exon, *Tadeton* 1204 Cur, *Tattun* 1212 Fees, 1285 FA, *Tatton(e)*
1212 Fees, 1262, 1276 FF, 1278 (1372) *ChrP*, 1375 Cl (*North* —,
South —), 1390 Fine (*South* —), 1399 Cl, Eliz ChancP (*West* —),
1795 Boswell (*East* —, *West* —), 'Tāta's farm', from the OE pers.n.
Tāta and tūn, cf. Tatton Ch **2** 64.

ASH BED. BROAD COPPICE, 1837 *TA*. BUCKLAND FM, SOUTH BUCK-
LAND, from Buckland Ripers *supra*. CHAFEY'S LAKE, *Chaffey's Bridge
Lake* 1785 WeyR. COVERWELL COPPICE, *Kuluerwyll* 13 (15) *ChrP*,
Culverwell Coppice & Md 1837 *TA*, *v.* culfre, wella. FIELD BARN.
HARBOUR BRIDGE & HILL, *Cold Harbor (Hill)* 1840 *TA*, *v.* cald,
here-beorg. HIGHER BARN. HYDE COPPICE, *Hyde (Coppice and (Lane)
Plant.)* 1837 *TA*, *v.* hīd. (OLD) LIMEKILN(s), cf. *(Little) Lime Kiln
Cl, Lime Kiln Md* 1837 *TA*. LOSCOMBE WD, *Lostcombe Coppice*
1837 *TA*, probably hlōse 'pig-sty', with cumb, cf. Loscombe in
W Knighton par. *supra*. MANOR HO. THE MEADOWS, cf. *(Long)
Meadow* 1840 *TA*. MOOR COPPICE, cf. *Lr Moor* 1837 *ib*, *v.* mōr.
NOTTINGTON HO (1863 Hutch[3]) & LANE, named from Nottington in
Broadwey par. *supra*. PAYNE'S COPPICE, *Pains* — 1837 *TA*, cf. *Pains
Grd and Drove* 1837 *ib*, cf. William *Payne* 1567 Hutch[3], *v.* drove.
RADIPOLE LAKE, LANE, & MANOR (FM) (*the Farme of Rodipoll* 1648
WeyM). LR RADIPOLE MILL, cf. *the towne Mill, Mr Strangewaye's*

mill 1582 Hutch[3], *Mill Mdw* 1840 *TA*, *v.* myln. St Anne's Church,
cf. *ecclesie de Radepowle* 1393 *AD*, *the church of Radipoll* 1582 Hutch[3];
the church here was until 1605 the mother church of Melcombe
Regis, cf. *ecclesia de Myl-, Melcomb(e) Regis* 1460 *Ct*, *the paroche
chirche of Milton* (sic) 1535-43 Leland. St Nicholas's Church (at
Buckland Ripers). South Hill Estate, *South Hill* 1582 Hutch[3],
1840 *TA*, S of Radipole village, *v.* sūð, hyll. Stone Spring, bdy
stones marked 6″, *v.* stān, spring. Tatton Coppice, from Tatton
supra. Westend Ctgs, at the W edge of Radipole village, *v.* ende[1].

FIELD-NAMES

The undated forms are 1840 *TA* 180 (Radipole) and 1837 *TA* 33 (Buckland
Ripers, marked †). Some fields in Radipole *TA* are dealt with under Weymouth par. *infra*. Spellings dated 13 (15) are *ChrP*, 1276 FF, 1327 *SR*, 1332
SR, 1340 NI, 1346, 1428 FA, 1621 WeyR, 1648 WeyM, 1664 HTax, and the
rest Hutch[3].

(a) Barley Cl (*the Barly Close* 1582) & Mdw (*v.* bærlic); Barn Yd and
Mowhay (the latter is possibly Do dial. mow 'a rick' (*v.* Barnes 83) from OE
mūga, with (ge)hæg); Barrow Cl (cf. *iuxta la berehe* 13 (15), *v.* beorg);
Bishop's Bottom (*v.* botm); †Black lands (*v.* blæc); †Bramble Cl (*v.* brēmel);
†Briscombe Md (perhaps (ge)byrst[1], -brist 'a landslip' or brēosa, brīosa 'a
gadfly', with cumb); †Broad Md; Broom Hill (*v.* brōm); †Butchers Md;
Calves Cl; †Chicken Orchd; Coppice (Cl); Cow Leaze (freq); E & W
Cranborne (*v.* cran, burna, cf. Cranborne par. *infra*); Dock Hill (*v.* docce);
†E and W Down (cf. *cultura voc' Uppedoune* 13 (15), *v.* uppan, upp, dūn);
East Mdw, †East Md and Plant.; †(West) 8 Acres; 18 Acres; †Elce Cl &
Coppice (cf. John *Ellis* 1617 (Weymouth)); Ewe Leaze (freq); Fern Hill
(Creek) (cf. *Ferndun* Hy 3 (14) Cerne, *v.* fearn, dūn, crike); 5 Acres; †Fir
Plant. (*v.* firr); †4 Acres; †Furzy Grd; Garden; Gooding's Plot (cf. Thomas
Godden 1664); Great Md, †— Mdw; †Grove Plot (*v.* grāf(a)); Hanging Cl
(*v.* hangende); Heathentine; Hill; Home Grd & Hill; †Home Mdw; †Horse
Cl (Coppice); Hurst Ld (*Huddy's land alias Hursland* 1582, *v.* hyrst); Jacob's
Plot (cf. widow *Jacob* 1664); †Little Mdw; †Long Md (and Drove) (*la
langemede* 13 (15), *v.* lang[1], mǣd); Marvels Fm 1763 ('probably named after
the Rev. James Marwell' Hutch[3] **2** 479); †Meadow; Middle Hill (*Midelhulle*
1295 Banco, *v.* middel, hyll); Moorhen Hole (*v.* moorhen, hol[1]); Newfield;
†19 Acres; North Hill; Orchard; Parks; †Parsonage Md; †Pigeon Mead
Orchd; †Plain; Plantation; Plot; Pond Cl; Quarry Cl; Rags and Long Cl (*v.*
ragge); Red Post; †Ridge Cl (*v.* hrycg); Salt Marsh; Shepherd's Plot; 6
Acres; †South Fd; South Md (Ewe Leaze); Stones Grd; 10 Acres; †Toads
Md; †Triangle Pce; 12 Acres; †Twenty Cl; Tyler's (cf. J. *Tyler* 1621
(Weymouth)); †Upper Cl; †Wally's Cl (cf. Richard *Wallis* 1664 (Wey-
mouth)); Watering Place; †Watty Cl; West Mdw, †— Md (*la Westmede* 13
(15)); Willow Bed (cf. *ye Willow berry* 1582, *v.* wilig, bedd, beorg or bearu);
Weymhill.

(b) *berfurlang* 13 (15) (*v.* bere, furlang); *broukfurlang* 13 (15) (*v.* brōc); *Crosse Lanes* 1582 (cf. *iuxta viam ad crucem* 13 (15), *v.* cros, cross, lane); *camp' orient'* 13 (15); *florlond* 13 (15) (cf. Flower Lds in Charminster par. *infra*); *atteforde* 1327, *atte Forde* 1332, 1340 all (p) (*v.* atte, ford); *Heuedaker* 13 (15) (*v.* hēafod, æcer); *Kamenakere* 13 (15); *ye market pathway* 1582 (probably to Melcombe Regis); *New Close* 1582; *Pukefurland* 13 (15) (*v.* pūca, furlang); *Radipoll ground* 1582; *Rowe close* 1617 DorR (*v.* rāw or rūh); *Seudun* Hy 3 (14) Cerne (*v.* dūn, cf. Henry *Soydon(e)* 1323 Ct, 1327, William *Seydone* 1354 Pat (all Weymouth)); *Shortlond* 13 (15) (*v.* sc(e)ort); *Tunfurlang* 13 (15) (*v.* tūn); *atte Walle* 1346, 1428 both (p) (*v.* atte, wall); *the West Close* 1582; *camp' occident'* 13 (15), *the West Field* 1582; *Wild Crosse* 1582 (perhaps 'cross in a desolate spot', *v.* wilde, cros, but cf. the f.n. Wyld in Wyke Regis par. *infra*).

West Stafford

Frome Billet was a tithing in the hundred of St George (Hutch³ **2** 514, 533). In 1933 part of W Stafford was transferred to the borough of Dorchester (Kelly).

WEST STAFFORD (SY 726895)

> *Stanford* 1086 DB, 1322 Ipm, 1381 *DCMCt*
> *Staford* 1086 DB, *Stafort* Exon, *Staf(f)ord(e)* 1205 RC, 1212 P, 1227, 1243 Fees, 1244 *Ass*, 1264 FineR *et passim* with additions -*Turberevil* 1243 Fees, *We(st)*- 1285 FA, 1303 Ipm, 1327 *SR*, 1332 SR *et passim*, -*Bingham* 1402 Hutch³, 1682 *Weld*¹, *Stafforde alias West Stafforde* 1619 *DCMCt*
> *West Stanorde* (for -*uorde*) 1320 FF, *Stavord West* 1340 NI, *Stavorde* 1346, 1428 FA, *Westauorde* 1422 DorR
> *Stofford Byngham* 1412 FA, *Stof(f)ord(e)* 1530 *Weld*¹

'Stony ford', *v.* stān, ford, alluding to a crossing of R. Frome, cf. E Stafford in W Knighton par. *supra*. For loss of -*n*- before a labial consonant, cf. Stoborough in Arne par. *supra*. Henry *de Turbervile* held one third of a fee here in 1213 Hutch³ **2** 512, and c. 1243 Robert *de Bingham* acquired this manor and Bingham's Melcombe (in Melcombe H. par. *infra*) by his marriage with Lucy *Turberville* (DoNHAS **22** 136), cf. also Robert (*de*) *Byngham* 1303 FA, 1332 SR, *terr' Roberti Byngham in Staford* 1464 *DCMCt*, and Hutch³ **2** 512. In 1795 Boswell, *Bingham's* and *Everard's* are still named as two farms within this manor; for the latter *v.* foll.

FROME BILLET (Kelly), 1795 Boswell, *Frome* 1086 DB (f. 84b), 1210– 12 RBE, 1236 Fees *et freq* to 1486 *Weld*¹, *From* 1212 Fees, *Froume*

1222 FineR, *Frome Belet* 1268 *Ass*, 1285 FA *et freq* to 1431 ib, — *Bel(l)ett* 1504 *Ampthill* (p), 1582 *DCMCt*, — *Billet ferme* 1615 *DuCo*, — *Belet or Billet* 1863 Hutch³, *Frome Euer-, Everard* 1270 (1372) *ChrP*, 1288 *Ass*, 1306 Pat *et freq* to 1498 *Ampthill* (p). One of several places named from R. Frome (*v.* RNs. *infra*). William *Belet* held this manor and five others in 1086 DB (VCHDo **3** 113, cf. Winterborne Belet in Winterborne Came par. *infra*), cf. also Robert — 1236 Fees, William *Belet* 1268 *Ass*; William *Everard* died seized of *Frome* in 1279 Ipm, cf. William *Everard* 1327 *SR*, — *de Euerard* 1332 SR, *Frome Belet quod Edmundus Everard quondam tenuit* 1346 FA. There was a mill here in 1086 DB (VCHDo **3** 113). According to Hutch³ **2** 514, Frome Billet 'lies on the south side of the river, half a mile north from Stafford', cf. Frome Dairy & Hill, Stafford Ho *infra*.

BUNKER'S HILL PLANT., *Brunkershill Plant.* 1848 *TA*, named from the Battle of Bunker's Hill in 1775; the spelling in *Br-* may be due to the influence of the f.n. Brunkton *infra*. CONQUER BARROW, 1811 OS, *Conquerors* — 1848 *TA*, *v.* beorg; this tumulus is near to the Neolithic 'henge monument' on Mount Pleasant *infra*. COOK'S PLANT., *Cook(')s* (*Down & Plant.*) 1848 *TA*, cf. Robert *Cok* 1327 *SR*, *v.* dūn. FROME DAIRY (— *Dairy Ho* 1811 OS) & HILL (1811 ib), from Frome Billet *supra*. GOULD'S COPPICE, cf. John *Gould* 1653 Hutch³. IVY CTG. MANOR FM formerly MANOR HO. MOUNT PLEASANT, a complimentary name for productive land, cf. Conquer Barrow *supra*. PARSONAGE PLANT., — *Field* (*Plant.*) 1848 *TA*. ST ANDREW'S CHURCH, cf. 'church of *Westaspord*' (for -*stafford*) 1369 Pat, 'the free chapel of *Stafford Bingham*' 1402 Hutch³. SAND PITS. SANDY BARROW (PLANT.), *Sand(y)* — 1848 *TA*; a tumulus is marked 6″. SIXPENNY GATE, — *Gate Cl* 1848 ib, perhaps alluding to a rent or toll. STAFFORD DAIRY, FM (1785 *EnclA*) & HO ('*the chyffe mansion* of Frome' 1531 Hutch³, *Frome Belet house* 1863 ib), from W Stafford and Frome Billet *supra*. TALBOTHAYS (CTGS), *Talbots* 1838 *TA*, cf. William *Talbott* 1664 HTax (W Knighton), *v.* (ge)hæg.

FIELD-NAMES

The undated forms are 1848 *TA* 192 (alt.app.). The spellings dated 1244 are *Ass*, 1315 Hutch³, 1318 *MiltC*, 1327 *SR*, 1332 SR, 1340 NI, 1381, 1582 *DCMCt*, 1405, 1439 *Midd*, 1584 *DCMSurv*, l18 *Weld*¹, 1838 *TA* 192, and 1841 *TAMap* (Fordington).

(a) Aller Bed Plant. and Pleasure Grd (v. alor); Ash Plant.; Brickkiln Plant.; Brunkton (the first el. may be analogous with that of Brownsea in Studland par. *supra*, perhaps with tūn or dūn, cf. Bunker's Hill Plant. *supra*); Calves Plot; Chalk Pit; (W) Chickerell Weir Md (*prat' domini voc' Chiterell, Chyterell* 1439, *Chitterell* 1615, an obscure name, as is Chickerell par. *supra* to resemble which it has been adapted, v. wer; these fields lie alongside R. South Winterborne); Clover Fd (v. clāfre); Common Md (cf. *prat' de Stavorde* 1318, *Stafford Mead(e)* 1584, 1841, John *atte Mede* 1327, 1332, Walter *de la mede* 1327, v. atte, mǣd); Corner; (Long) Cowleaze; Crofts; Crooked Mdw; 18 Acres; N & S Eweleaze; Folly (v. folie); 14 & 40 Acres; French Grass Fd (v. french grass); Hams (v. hamm); Lady's Cl; Lands Grd; Lawn (from land or launde); Manstons (cf. Manston par. *infra*); New Grd; 9 acres md; 19 acres; Gt North Md; North Moor Cowleaze (cf. Robert *atte Mor* 1340, v. atte, mōr); Old Rd; Paddock and Gdn 1838); Paradise (v. paradis); Plot; Rodden hill; Sheeplands; Shepherds house; Short hill; 16 Acres; Gt South Md; Stafford's hill (cf. W Stafford *supra*); Three Corner Cl; Tizards withybed; 12 acres; Vern Barrow (possibly fearn, but cf. Verne Yeates in Portland par. *supra*); Walled Gdn; Water and double hedge, Water mdw (cf. *ij pec' prati iuxta cursum aque*, John *atte Watere* 1381, v. atte, wæter); Willow bed.

(b) *Grenes hayes* 1582 (the surname *Grene*, v. (ge)hæg); *Horssepoul* 1381 (v. hors, pōl[1], cf. the lost *Horspou(y)(l)lake* in W Lulworth par. *supra*); *Nortonesmede* 1381 (cf. Adam *de Norton* 1315, v. mǣd); *ponfald' domini* 1381; *de la Well* 1244 (p) (v. wella).

Upwey

Elwell was in the liberty of Wyke Regis & Elwell, and part of Upwey formed the separate liberty of Wabyhouse, v. note under Culliford Tree hundred *supra*. In 1933 part of Upwey was transferred to the borough of Weymouth, part to the par. of Bincombe, and the rest to the par. of Chickerell for civil purposes (Kelly).

UPWEY (SY 664849)

?*Wai(a)* 1086 DB, Exon, *Waie* 1194 P (p), 1201, 1209 FF, *Wai(a)* c. 1201 Sarum, *Waya* c. 1201 ib, 1225 Pat, l13 *Ilch* (p), 1259 Cl, *Way(e)* 1237 FF, 1244 *Ass* (p) *et freq* to 1363 Cl, *La Waye* 1244 *Ass*, *Wey(e)* 1312-4 Fine, 1315 Cl *et freq* to 1440 *Weld*[1]

Way(e) Ba(y)(h)(o)us(e) 1237 Sarum, 1285 FA, 1288 *Ass et freq* to 1428 FA, — *Baiocis* 1288 Ipm, — *Baihous* 1412 FA, *Weybause* 1291 Tax, *Weye Bayose* 1303 Ipm, — *Bayhous* 1418 *Marten*, *Weybayhouse* 1504 Ipm

Uppeweie 1241 *Ass*, *Upeweye* 1311 Fine, *Upway(e)*, -*wey(e)* 1327 SR, 1329 *Weld*[1], 1332 SR *et passim*, *Ho(w)pweyȝe* 1393 *AD*, *Upway alias Bayhouse* 1566 Hutch[3], *Upwey alias Waybaiouse* 1863 ib

Waye Pigace 1243 Fees, *-pigaz* 1246 FF (p), — *Pagace* 1388 IpmR, — *Pygace* 1392 Pat, *Pygatewaye* 1272 FF

Way(e) Hamundevill 1249 FF, *-henedeford* 1280 *Ass* (sic), — *Hamond(e)vill(e)* 1343 Hutch[3], 1363 Cl, — *Hamundevyle* 1343–5 Ipm, — *Hamondwylle* 1363 ib, *Weye Hamundevile* 1311 FF, *Weyhamondvile, -vyle alias Uppewey alias Weybayouse* 1456 Pat, *Weyhamondevyle otherwise Upwey otherwise Waybayhouse* 1466 Cl, *Weyhamond(es)feld alias Upwey* 1481 Ct, 1486 Weld[1], *Wayhamondville* (a close) 1622 DCMDeed

Waye Raba(y)ne 1288 *Ass*

Named from R. Wey, *v.* RNs. *infra*, cf. Broadwey par. *supra* where some of the early forms in *Wai(e)*, *Way(a)*, *Wey(e)* etc. may strictly belong, and where the DB forms are discussed. *Up-* means 'upper, higher' with reference to its situation, relative to the other manors called *Wey*, on the river, which rises here, *v.* upp, Elwell *infra*. *Bayhouse*, etc. is from the family of *Baieux* (from Bayeux, Normandy), of which Alan *de Bayocis* was here c. 1200 (Sarum) and John *Bayouse* founded a chantry here in 1244 (Hutch[3] 2 840, cf. Chapel Lane *infra*), cf. also John *de Baiocis als. de Bays* 1248 Ipm, Stephen *de Bahus* 1249 FF, — *de Baiocis* 1309 Cl, and Hutch[3] 2 840–1; this affix survives in the name of the liberty of Wabyhouse (*v.* under Culliford Tree hundred *supra*), and in Wabey House (Kelly), a private residence in Upwey, cf. also Bayard Fm *infra*. *Pigace*, etc. and *Hamundevill*, etc. must also be manorial affixes, although no persons so named have been noted in connection with Upwey; Fägersten 160 cites several instances of the surname *Pigace* in mediaeval records (e.g. John *Pygaz* 1272 FF (Do), cf. also *Winterb(o)urn Pygace* for a part of Winterborne Monkton par. *infra*), and plausibly suggests that some member of the family of *Amundevill* (cf. Thorpe Mandeville Nth 61) may have held land here of the Beauchamps just as in Melcombe H. par. *infra* (cf. Hutch[3] 2 841, 4 364 f). *Raba(y)ne* is also manorial; Maud *de Rabayn* held land here in 1259, 1260 Cl, cf. also Ellis *de Rabayn* 1264 Pat, Maud *de Rabayn* 1288 *Ass*, Isabel *de Raban* 1327 SR, and Hutch[3] 2 840–1.

STREET-NAMES: SHORTLANDS RD, cf. *terre voc' Shortlond (butt')* 1445 *Rent*, *Shortlands* 1841 *TA* (Broadwey), *v.* sc(e)ort, land, butte; STOTTINGWAY ST., *venell' voc' Stotynweylayne* 1530 Weld[1], cf. Stottingway *infra*, *v.* lane; this street seems to be that called *Upway St.* 1811 OS.

ELWELL (SY 669849)

Helewill 1212 Fees, *-woll(e)* 1243 (l13) WinchCath, 1332 SR, *-well(e)* 1259 Ch, 1275 RH, 1284 (1285) Ch, 1288 *Ass*

Hellewell(e) 1249 Acct, 1256 (1258) Ch, 1275 RH, 1280, 1288 *Ass*, 1295, 1324 *MinAcct et freq* to 1449 FF, '— *by Upwey*' 1425 Cl, *Hellewull(e)* 1249 Acct, 1288 *Ass*, *-wyll* 1280 *ib*, *-wolle* 1285 FA, 1322, 1328 *MinAcct*, *Ellewyll* 1376 Misc, 1457 *Ct*, *-well* 1464 DCMCt, 1465, 1481 *Weld*[1], *Ct*

Elwell 1460 *Ct*, 1464 DCMCt *et passim*, *Helwell* 1492 Pat, *Elwell or Ridgeway* 1795 Boswell

Elway alias Stotingway 1643 Hutch[3]

'The sound, healthy spring', or 'the spring which heals or gives good health', from **wella** (WSax **willa, wylla**) and either **hǽle** adj. 'hale, safe', or **hǽlu** 'health, healing' (thus Fägersten 160); alternatively 'the wishing well', with **hǽl** 'omen, good fortune' as first el. (thus Ekwall DEPN). The reference is probably to the spring called Wishing Well *infra* where R. Wey rises ½ mile WNW from here, but the reference could be to a different spring (e.g. that marked 6″ just W of Elwell). Cf. foll. and Ridgeway *infra*.

STOTTINGWAY (local, about SY 668843, cf. Upwey st.ns. *supra*)

Stottingewaie 1212 P, *Stotingeweye* 1288 *Ass*, *Stottyngewey* 1486 *Weld*[1]

Stokingway 1236 Fees, *Stokkyngweye* 1361 Cl

Scottingesweye (probably for *Stottinges-*) 1249 FF, *Stottyngeswey(e)* 1457 *Ct*, 1464 DCMCt, 1465 *Weld*[1]

Stoting Waye 1280 *Ass*, *Stotyngweye* 1399 Cl, *Stotynwey* 1530 *Weld*[1], *Stotingway vulgo Stotton* 1774 Hutch[1], 1863 Hutch[3]

Stottyngetone 1285 FA, *Stottynton* 1445 *Rent*

Stottynways 1285 FA

Stotting-, *Stottyngway(e)*, *-wey(e)* 1288 Ipm, *Ass*, 1346 FF, 1348 Ipm, 1392 Pat, 1481 *Ct*, 1664, 1682 *Weld*[1], *Stottynwaye* 1288 *Ass*, *Scottingwaye* (probably for *Stotting-*) 1305 FF

Statting(e)way 1649 SC, 1664 HTax

The final el. is the r.n. *Wey* as in Upwey *supra*, although there is some early alternation with **tūn** 'farm, village', surviving as the later *Stotton*. The first part of the name is difficult. Only two of the early forms point to OE **stoccing** 'a piece of ground cleared of stumps'

(tentatively suggested by Fägersten 161 but accepted by Smith EPN
2 157), and it does not look likely; the base was almost certainly
Stotting-, the two forms in -*k*(*k*)- being perhaps due to dissimilation
t-t > *t-k* or more probably, as Dr von Feilitzen points out, to scribal
association of the first el. with stocc. One possibility is that *Stotting-*
is a manorial affix (cf. Creketway in Broadwey par. *supra*, Causeway in
Radipole par. *supra*, etc.); this could be from an OE pers.n. *Stotting*,
a derivative with -ing[3] of OE stott 'an inferior kind of horse, an ox'.
Alternatively *Stotting-* could represent an earlier p.n. from the same
el. stott (or a pers.n. *Stott* formed from it, cf. Reaney s.n. *Stott*) and
-ing[2], which would have meant something like 'place where horses
or oxen are kept' (or 'Stott's place'). Cf. the f.n. *Stotingmede* in
Owermoigne par. *supra*.

WESTBROOK DAIRY, FM & HO (SY 667844), *Westebroke* (*Ospitalis*)
1285, *Weywestbrok* 1303, *Wey Westbrook* 1428 all FA, *Westbrok*(*e*)
1318 FF (— *juxta Waye Nichole*), 1342 Pat (p), 1456 ib ('—by
Brodewey), 1457 *Ct et passim* to 1863 Hutch[3], -*brouk*(*e*) 1431 FA,
1440 *Weld*[1], -*brooke* 1795 Boswell, *Westbroke Farm* 1863 Hutch[3],
'(place) to the west of the brook', *v.* westan, brōc, describing its
situation on R. Wey, cf. Eastbrook Ho *infra*, Broadwey par. *supra*.
In 1285 FA it belonged to *prior ospitalis Sancti Johannis Jerusalem*,
cf. Fryer Mayne and E Stafford in W Knighton par. *supra*, VCHDo
2 90–2.

BAYARD BARN, FM & HILL, *Bayard's Fm* 1774 Hutch[1], probably to
be associated with the surname and manorial affix *Bayhouse, v.* par.
name *supra*. CHAPEL LANE, cf. the chantry founded in Upwey in 1244
by John *Bayouse* (Hutch[3] **2** 840, cf. Upwey *supra*), perhaps that
referred to as *capell' de Waye* 1244 *Ass*. COMBE BOTTOM, *v.* cumb,
botm. DOWN FM, near Bincombe Down in Bincombe par. *supra*.
EASTBROOK HO, probably '(place) east of the brook', cf. Westbrook
supra. GIPSIES' CORNER. GOULD(')s BOTTOM & HILL, from the *Gould*
family who held the manor of Upwey in the 17th and 18th
centuries, *v.* Hutch[3] **2** 841–4, cf. John *Gould* 1664 HTax. HEWISH
COPPICE (1840 *TA*) & DAIRY, cf. *Sycamore and Hewish Md* 1840
ib, from Hewish Hill in Portisham par. *infra*. ICEN DAIRY, called
Thornhill 1811 OS perhaps showing confusion with Thornhill Fm
in Broadwey par. *supra*; Icen is obscure but īse(r)n 'iron' is possible,
cf. Icen Way in Dorchester par. *infra*. ICEN LANE, near prec. THE
KNOLL, cf. *Knoll Cl* 1840 *TA, v.* cnoll. MANOR FM & HO. MASON'S

ARMS (P.H.). MILL, cf. *Robert Freeke Esqr' in his Mill house* 1664
HTax, *Mill Md* 1840 *TA*, and a mill in Stottingway *supra* in 1305 FF,
v. **myln**; for possible mills in Upwey in 1086 DB, *v.* Mill in Broadwey
par. *supra.* PROSPECT PLACE, *v.* **prospect.** RIDGEWAY, *Rigd(e)way* 1670,
1671 *Sheridan, Ridgway* 1674 *ib*, 1838 *TA* (Bincombe) (*The Royal
Oak Inn and Bowling Alley at* —), named from the Roman road from
Dorchester to Weymouth (*the way at Rigdeway* 1670 *Sheridan, Ridge
way from the bridge upward to the top of the hill* 1680 *ib, Ridge Way*
1811 OS, marked 6″), *v.* **hrycg, weg,** cf. Elwell *supra*, Ridgeway
Hill in Bincombe par. *supra.* THE ROOKERY. ST LAWRENCE'S CHURCH,
cf. 'the church of *Waye*' 1237 FF, *eccl. St. Laurenti de Wai* 1267
Hutch[3], *ecclesia de Howp Weyʒe* 1393 *AD.* SHIP INN, 1840 *TA.*
UPWEY HO, *Upway-House* 1774 Hutch[1]. WINDSBATCH, 1840 *TA*,
the end of a prominent ridge, perhaps from **batch** 'hillock' with
wind[1] 'wind' or **(ge)wind**[2] 'a winding path' (a path climbs the hill
from the village). WISHING WELL, *v.* Elwell *supra*.

FIELD-NAMES

The undated forms are 1840 *TA* 236. Spellings dated 1249 are FF, 1287
Ipm, 1327, e18, 1863, 1867 Hutch[3], 1376 Misc, and the rest *Weld*[1].

(*a*) Allotment; Ardens Cowleaze (cf. Daniel *Arden* e18); Barn Fd; Batch
(*v.* **batch,** near Windsbatch *supra*); Bathays (Md & Nursery) (second el.
probably **(ge)hæg**); Bazell (cf. Matthew *Beselle* 1327); Bridport Rd; Brook
Md; Bull Cl; Cheese Lane; Close; Common Md; Corner Plot; Cothays (*v.*
cot, (ge)hæg); Cowleaze (freq); Gt, (Millers) Lt, & N Down (cf. John
Miller 1867, *v.* **dūn**); East Fd; 8 Acres; Elwell Fd, Elwell Down 1863 (cf.
Elwell *supra*); Eweleaze (freq); 4 & 14 Acres; Hilly Furzeland (*v.* **fyrs**);
Gore Md (*v.* **gāra**); Great Md; The Grove (*v.* **grāf(a)**); Hill side; Home Cl
and Gdn; Horse Cl; Hundred Acres (here ironically applied to a very small
field); Hurdle Md (*v.* **hyrdel**); Kitchen Plot 1863; Lt Coppice; Hr & Lr
Marsh (*v.* **mersc**); Meadow; (Head of) Milden (perhaps to be identified with
Middeldon 1287, *v.* **middel, dūn**); New Cl; The Orchard; Patched Md;
Plantation; Plot; Plowed Fd; Poor Altmt (cf. 'the Poor's Plot...on which
the poor...exercise the right of cutting furze for fuel' 1863); Popes Cow-
leaze; Puddle Coppice (near Puddle Hole in Broadwey par. *supra*); Rough
Grds; 7 Acres (Coppice); Shearing Cl (*v.* **shearing**); 6 Acres; Slip (*v.*
slip(p)e); Small Mds & Plot; Snag Coppice & Md (*v.* **snag**, cf. Snag Fm in
Corfe C. par. *supra*); South Fd (next the Glebe); South hill; 10 Acres; Three
Corner Down; Tumbledown (cf. an identical f.n. in E Stoke par. *supra*);
Field next the Turnpike; 12 Acres; (North) West Fd; Willow Bed; With(e)y
Bed.

(*b*) *Blyndewell* 1376 (*v.* **blind** 'hidden', **wella**; at Elwell *supra*); *Courtclos*
1481 (*v.* **court, clos(e)**); *La Cresseye* 1249 (*v.* **cærse, ēg**); *La Culverheye* 1249

(v. culfre, (ge)hæg); *Le Heldelond* 1287 (v. ald (WSax eald), land, but first el. possibly helde); *Hemplond* 1478 (v. hænep, land); *Hoghey* 1481 (v. hogg, (ge)hæg); *Leyforlang* 1287 (v. lǣge, furlang); *La Westdon* 1287 (v. west, dūn); *Weyhamondesfylde* 1530, 1543 ('Upwey field', v. feld).

Weymouth & Melcombe Regis

Melcombe Regis, originally a separate borough, was united with the borough of Weymouth in 1571. The joint borough was extended to include parts of the parishes of Radipole and Wyke R. in 1895, and parts of the parishes of Bincombe, Broadwey, Chickerell, Preston, Radipole, Upwey and Wyke R. in 1933 (Kelly).

WEYMOUTH (SY 679786)

   (*of*) *Waimouþe*, (*on ðan*) *Waymouþe* 843 for 934 (eME) ASCharters
   (*apud*) *Waimudā* 1130 PR, *Waymue* 1152–8 Mont, 1244 *Ass*, 1249 Acct (*portus de* —) *et freq* to 1293 Cl, *-mud* 1243 Pap, *-muth(e)* 1252 Cl, 1290 Fine *et freq* to 1382 ib, *-mo* 1282 Cl, *-moth* 1288 *Ass*, 1348, 1411 *AD*, *-mouth(e)* 1322 Cl *et freq* to 1565 *SPDom* (— *Porte*), *-mewe* 1322 Pat, *-meuth* 1323 *Ct*, *-meth* 1327 *SR*, *Waigmouth* 1535–43 Leland
   Weymue Hy 3 (14) Cerne, 1225 ClR *et freq* to 1308 Cl, *-muth(e)* 1248 Ch, 1258 Pat *et freq* to 1408 ib, *Burgus de Weymuth* 1275 RH, *Weymuwe* 1280 *Ass*, *-mouth(e)* 1290 Cl *et passim*, *-moth(e)* 1296 Ipm, 1383 Cl, 1389 AD I, 1539 LP, *Weyemouthe* 1371 AD II
   Wymue Hy 3 (14) Cerne, *-muth(e)* 1256 (1258) Ch, 1317 Cl, Fine, 1395 Pat, *-mouth* 1360 Ipm, 1420 Pat, *Wyemue* 1293 ib
   Wemue 1268 *Ass* (p), 1275 Fine

'The mouth of R. Wey', v. mūða, RNs. *infra*, cf. Broadwey par. *supra*; *-mue*, *-mewe*, etc. are AN spellings, v. Zachrisson ANInfl 82 f, 93 f; *Porte* 1565 is from port[1] 'harbour', cf. Harbour *infra*. The old town of Weymouth lay to the south of R. Wey, Melcombe Regis *infra* to the north, cf. the use of the phrases *Waymouthe side*, *Melcombe side* in 1625 WeyM; the (spurious) OE charter claims that Athelstan granted to Milton Abbey *al þ water binne staþe of Waimouþe, and half strym on ðan Waymouþe out on see* ('all the water within the shore (i.e. inshore) from the mouth of the Wey, and half the river in the Wey estuary out to sea'). For the bounds of Weymouth in 1252, v. Hutch[3] 2 429. According to DBGazetteer 117,

(at least) one of the eight DB manors of *Wai(a)* is to be identified
with Weymouth, cf. Broadwey par. *supra.*

MELCOMBE REGIS (SY 680790)

   Melecumb(e) 1100–7 (l13) WinchCath, 1223, 1225 FF, 1238 Cl,
      1249 (14) Cerne, 1268 *Ass*, 1280 Pat, Ch, *Ass et freq* to 1340 NI
      (— *Regis*), *-comb(e)* 1268 *Ass*, 1280 Pat *et freq* to 1391 Fine,
      -com 1290 ib, *-coumbe* 1322 Cl *et freq* to 1341 Fine, *-cum regis*
      16 *RoyMap*
   Mellecumb 1244 *Ass*, *-comb(e)* 1366 Pat
   Melcoumbe 1280 *Ass et freq* to 1375 Pat with *-Regis* from 1336
      ib, *-comb(e)* 1285 Ch *et passim* with *-Regis* from 1371 Cl,
      -cumbe 1314 Ch, 1350 Cl, 1381 AD I, 1407 Pat, *-cum* 1539 LP,
      New-Melcombe 1774 Hutch[1]
   Meldecombe 1322 *MinAcct*
   Melchecombe 1366, 1401 Pat
   Milcombe 1436 Pat, *Mylcomb Regis* 1460 *Ct*
   Milto(u)n (sic) 1535–43 Leland

Probably 'valley where milk was got, fertile valley', from **meoluc**
and **cumb** (DEPN, EPN), cf. the bdy point *meoluccumb* BCS 620
(Ha) and Melcombe Horsey par. *infra*; the forms in *Melche-* seem to
show alternation of the first el. with **melce** 'milch, yielding milk'
(a derivative of **meoluc**), but they are too late to be of certain
significance. Melcombe Regis was anciently a royal demesne (Hutch[3]
2 446 ff, Eyton 82 f), *v.* **rex** (gen. sg. *regis*). For the bounds of
Melcombe R. in 1649, *v.* WeyR 116, cf. also Cerne (DoNHAS **29**
202).

WEYMOUTH & MELCOMBE REGIS STREETS & BUILDINGS

AUGUSTA PLACE, 1824 Pigot. BANK BLDGS (TPlan), 1824 ib. BELLE VUE, 1824
ib. BOND ST., 1824 ib. LR BOND ST., on the site of *a lane called Cuniger Ditch*
1617 WeyR, *Coniger Lane* 1642 ib, *Coneygar Ditch* 1774 Map, *Conygar Lane*
1805 Hutch[3], *-st.* 1824 Pigot, named from 'the king's warren at *Melcombe*'
1392 Pat, *ye Cuniger* c. 1540 RCHM, *all that theyre Conynger and warren of
Conyes* 1563 WeyR, *(Melcombe) Conigeare* 1579 ib, 1581 Hutch[3], *v.* **coninger**,
dic. BOOT HILL (TPlan), probably named from *The Boot* (an inn) e18 WeyR,
earlier *Leech Lane called also Symes Lane* 1650 WeyR, *Leach Lane* 1774 Map,
perhaps from **lece** 'stream, bog' and the surname *Syme(s)*. BUXTON RD, *the
Lr Wyke Rd, otherwise called Buxton's Lane* 1861 Hutch[3], cf. Wyke Rd *infra.*

OLD CASTLE RD, *the Highway goeing to Sandfoote Castle* 1652 WeyM, *v.* Sandsfoot Castle *infra.* CHAPELHAY ST. (TPlan), *Chapel-street* 1824 Pigot, named from *the Chaple hay* 1554 (18) *Ilch,* *(the) Chapel Hay(e)* 1653 WeyR, 1824 Pigot, *Chapel-Hays* 1774 Hutch[1], the site of *capella Sancti/Beati Nic(h)olai de Weymuth,* —*Waymowth* 1361–1393 *AD, capelle de Weymuth* 1379 *ib,* 'the chapel of St Nicholas' 1455 Pat, *Waymouthe Chaple* 1621, converted into a fort during the Civil War (Hutch[1] **1** 408), *the Chappell* —, *the Church Fort* 1644 Hutch[3], *the Chappill Fort* 1653 WeyR, cf. also *Le Chapplestayers* 1628 WeyR, *the Chappell stayres* 1638 WeyM, *Chappell Closes abutteing upon ye chappell* 1652 *Weld*[1], *the Chappell ground* 1658 WeyM, *Chapelry Gdn, Burial Grd* 1839 *TA, Chapelry Md* 1841 *TA* (Wyke R.), *v.* chapel(e), (ge)hæg, stæger[1]; according to WeyR 70 there was a St Nicholas St. in Weymouth in 1626, no doubt named from this chapel, cf. Nicholas St. (in Melcombe R.) *infra.* CHARLOTTE ROW, -*st.* 1824 Pigot. CHESTERFIELD PLACE, 1824 ib. CHURCH PASSAGE (TPlan), 1824 ib, cf. *the Churchway* 1646 WeyR, St Mary St. *infra.* CLARENCE BLDGS, 1824 Pigot. COVE ROW & ST., *v.* Hope Sq *infra.* CUSTOM HO QUAY, named from CUSTOM HO, *(the) Custom(e) House* 1617 WeyR, 1657 WeyM, cf. *la Keye* 1379 *AD,* 1391 AD I, *a kay and warf* 1535–43 Leland, *the Towne Key* 1579, *le towne kaye* 1582, *le Wharfe* 1616, *Marbell's Quay* 1646, *West Key* 1654 all WeyR, *Melcomb Key* 1679 Hutch[3], *v.* key, hwearf, Harbour *infra.* DORCHESTER RD, —*way* 1653 WeyM, *the way that ledith from Dorchester to Waymouth* 1535–43 Leland. EAST ST., *(the) East Street* 1604 Hutch[1], 1617 WeyR, *the East Lane* 1620 ib. EMBANKMENT BRIDGE (TPlan), cf. *Embankment* 1842 *TAMap.* ESPLANADE, *the Wall called the* — 1785 WeyR. FAIRCROSS AVE, *(land at) Fair Cross* 1582 (18) *Ilch, Faircrofts* 1841 *TA* (Wyke R.), *v.* fæger, cros. FRANCHISE ST., *le Franchise strete* 1413 AD I, *Franchis* —, *Franches Street* 1617 WeyR, *Francis Street* 1774 Map, probably named from Little Francis in Wyke R. par. *infra.* FREDERICK PLACE (TPlan), 1824 Pigot. GREAT GEORGE ST., 1820 DCMDeed, cf. *Little George St.* 1820 ib, named from George 3 who visited Melcombe R. in 1789. GLOUCESTER MEWS, Row (1797 WeyR) & ST. (1863 Hutch[3]), cf. *Gloucester Lodge* 1811 OS, 1863 Hutch[3] *(the Gloucester Hotel, formerly* —), named from the Duke of Gloucester who had a house here in 1789 WeyR. GOVERNOR'S LANE (TPlan), 1774 Map. GREENHILL, 1685 WeyR, *Green Hill* 1840 *TA* (Radipole). GROSVENOR RD, cf. — *place* 1824 Pigot. HELEN LANE, *Hell Lane* 1620, 1646 WeyR, 1774 Map *(Healing or* —), named from *the house called Hellhouse, tenement called Hell* 1617 WeyR, cf. *Hell Doore* 1651 ib, a derogatory name, or referring to a lower room, *v.* hell, cf. a lost p.n. *Helle* in Dorchester par. *infra.* HIGH ST., 1368, 1370 AD I, 1617 WeyR, *alto vico* 1457 *Brid,* cf. *High West St.* 1779 WeyR. HILL LANE, 1650 ib. HOPE SQ (1824 Pigot) & ST. (1774 Map, *a streete called Ye Hope* 1652 *Weld*[1]), named from *la hopehuse* 1252 Hutch[3] (in bounds of Weymouth), *le* —, *la Hope* 1364, 1401 AD I, *(the) Hope* 1617, 1620 WeyR, 1633 WeyM, cf. William *atte Hope* 1323 *Ct, Hope Mead* 1582 (18) *Ilch, Hope Quay* 1824 Pigot, *v.* hōp[2] 'inlet', hūs, atte, mæd; there is a small bay here which also gave name to Cove Row & St. *supra.* HORSFORD ST., —*Ctg* 1841 *TA* (Wyke R.), *v.* hors, ford. KING'S RD, KING ST., cf. *venellam Regiam* 1416 DorR. LOOK OUT, named from *the Looking Place* 1582 (18) *Ilch,* 1618 WeyR, 1652 *Weld*[1], *the worke at Lookout*

1612 WeyR, *Platform atye Look out* 1774 Map, *Look Out (Md)* 1841 *TA* (Wyke R.), *the Look-out* 1863 Hutch[3], cf. *Lookout Ho* c. 1825 Map, *v.* look-out. LOVE LANE (TPlan), 1634 WeyR, *Lovelane* 1399 AD III, 1617 WeyR (*-end*), *v.* lufu. LYDWELL CLOSE (TPlan), named from *Lydwell* 1841 *TA* (Wyke R.), perhaps from hlȳde 'noisy stream', and wella. MAIDEN ST., 1396–8, (*le*) *Mayden Streete* 1617–1620 all WeyR, 'street frequented by maidens', *v.* mægden. MARKET ST., *Markett Streate* 1642, cf. *locus ferianus*, *Anglice the Markett Place* 1617, *the Markett* 1634, *The Corn Market Place* 1658, *the Market Cross* 1705 all WeyR, *The Fish Market* 1863 Hutch[3], *v.* market; according to Hutch[3] 2 465, markets were held in St Edmund St. and St Mary St. before the erection of 'a commodious market-house' in 1855. MARSH RD, named from *the Marsh* (*in Waymouth-syde*) 1635 WeyR, 1636 WeyM, *Waymouth Marsh* 1651 ib, *Marsh* (pasture) 1839 *TA*, cf. *the Marsh Lake* 1785 WeyR, *v.* mersc. NEWBERRY GDNS, *Newberry* 1582 (18) *Ilch*, 1635 WeyM, 1841 *TA* (Wyke R.), *Newbury* 1617 (a street), 1620 WeyR, cf. *Newbery Close* 1627 ib, *v.* nīwe, burh (dat. sg. *byrig*). NEW ST., 1617 WeyR, 1774 Map, cf. *novam viam* 1379 *AD*. NICHOLAS ST., 'St Nicholas Street' 1371 AD II, *vico Sancti Nicolai* 1393 *AD*, *St Nicholas Streate*, — *Street* 1578, 1617 WeyR; for a lost St Nicholas St. (in Weymouth), *v.* Chapelhay St. *supra*. NORTH QUAY, *Quay* 1842 *TAMap*, cf. *la Keye*, *la Kay* 1367 AD I *et freq* to 1391 ib, *Waymouth Key* 1618 WeyR, *v.* key, Harbour *infra*. PARK ST., cf. *Parcum ville* 1635 ib. PULTENEY BLDGS (TPlan), *Pultney* — 1824 Pigot. RADIPOLE PARK DRIVE, cf. *Rodipoll Way* 1649 WeyR, Radipole Park Gdns *infra*. RODWELL RD, 'the *Caseway* to *Rodwell*' 1624 ib, *v.* caucie, Rodwell *infra*. ROYAL CRESCENT (1824 Pigot) & TERRACE (1824 ib), cf. ROYAL HOTEL (1824 ib), near KING'S STATUE (George 3), cf. Great George St. *supra*. (LR) ST ALBAN'S ST., cf. *St Alban's Row* 1824 Pigot, probably named from the Duke of St Alban's who had a house in Melcombe R. in 1790 (WeyR 126); earlier called *Petticoat Lane* 1684 ib, 1774 Map, 1824 Pigot. (LR) ST EDMUND ST., 1617 WeyR, 'St Edmund's Street' 1280 (1318) Ch, *St Edmond Streate* 1578 WeyR, *St Edmunds Street* 1774 Map. ST MARY ST., 'St Mary Street' 1280 (1318) Ch, *Sent Mariestrete* 1365 AD VI, *vico Sancte Marie* (*prope ecclesiam*) 1393 *AD*, *St Mary*('s) *Street*(*e*) 1543 WeyR *et freq* to 1774 Map, named from 'the chapel of *Melecomb*' 1301 Hutch[1], 'the Chapel of St Mary' 1365 AD VI, *capell' de Melcombe* 1393 *AD*, *the Chapel of St Mary* 1543 WeyR, *Melcombe Chapel* 1595 ib, rebuilt as *Melcombe Church* 1621 ib, called *templum* 1646 ib, cf. *Churchyard* 1652 WeyM, Church Passage *supra*; up to 1605 the mother church of Melcombe R. was the church at Radipole, *v.* St Anne's Church in Radipole par. *supra*. ST THOMAS ST., 1456, 1583 WeyR, 'St Thomas Street' 1280 (1318) Ch. SPA RD, cf. *Spa Ctgs, Fd and Plant*. 1840 *TA* (Radipole), *v.* spa. VICTORIA TERRACE, 1863 Hutch[3], cf. VICTORIA HOTEL, named from Queen Victoria. WATERLOO PLACE (TPlan), 1863 Hutch[3]. WEST ST., 1617 WeyR. WYKE RD, *the Highway leading to Weeke Church* 1652 WeyM, *the Upr Wyke Road* 1861 Hutch[3], leading to Wyke R. par. *infra*, cf. Buxton Rd *supra*. YORK BLDGS, 1796 WeyR.

Lost street-names include *the Back Lane* 1648 WeyR (*v.* back); *The Back Street* 1654 ib; *Bakerestrete* 1280 (1318) Ch (cf. Thomas *Pistor* 1332 SR); *Blockhouse Lane* 1617 WeyR, 1861 Hutch[3] (named from 'the blockhouse of

Weymouth' 1541 RCHM, *the Blockhouse* 1625 WeyR, *Block House Fort* 1774
Map, described in Hutch[1] **1** 414 as 'east of the town. . .a square fort, built of
stone'); *Buckler Lane* 1727 WeyR; *Butt's Lane* 1620, 1654 ib (perhaps from
The Butts which were 'deficient' in 1582 ib, *v.* butt[2]); *Mr. Channing's walke*
1721 ib (cf. *Channyns worcke infra*); *Cobourg-place* 1824 Pigot; *Ebenezer
Place* 1842 *TAMap*; *Hynes his Lane* 1649 WeyR; *New Key Streete* 1648 ib
(cf. Custom House Quay, North Quay *supra*); *Little Lane* 1646 ib; *Little
Street* 1646 ib; *Marlbrough-row* 1824 Pigot; *Meechers Lane* 1627 WeyR;
Rogers' Lane 1655 ib; *Rosemarie Lane* 1642 ib; *venella ducens versus le
Seaside* 1617 ib; *Silver Street* 1774 Map, — *Lane* 1784 WeyR; *Simon's Lane*
1654 ib; *Somerset Bldgs* 1824 Pigot; *South Parade* 1824 ib; *Stephen Streete*
1633 WeyR; *Terrace* 1824 Pigot.

Buildings include *The Alms House* 1774 Map, *Alms Houses* 1839 *TA*; *the
Ammunition House* 1654 WeyR; *domos Braxator' in Hope* 1618, *lez Brewhouses*
1619 WeyR, *the widow Knights Brewhouse* 1648 WeyM; *Bridewell* 1658
WeyR (a women's prison, *v.* bridewell); *the Bul(l)wor(c)k(e)(s), -workk,
-wa(r)ck(s), -warkes* 1582 Hutch[3] *et freq* to 1648 ib (*v.* bulwerk); *Burdon Hotel*
1863 Hutch[3]; *le* —, *the Checker* (*House in Hope*) 1646 WeyR (*v.* cheker, Hope
Sq *supra*); *Cold Harbor Fort* 1653 WeyM (*v.* cald, here-beorg); *Cotton fort*
1774 Hutch[1] ('north of the town'); *the Guardhouse* —, *the Gunners Roome at
the Widow Dayes (fort)* 1653 WeyM; *Delamottee's Publick Rooms* 1774 Map;
Dissenter's Meeting 1774 ib; *Dock-Fort* 1774 Hutch[1] ('under the hill, west of
the two Jettys'); *a fair house of Freres* 1535–43 Leland, *the late Fryerie* 1585
WeyR, *the ground and buildings called the Friery lying ruined* 1650 Hutch[1], *the
Schoole in the Fryery* 1651 WeyM, *the Priory* 1774 Map (cf. *frat' intat' Beate
Marie de Melcombe Regis* 1457 Ct, *the Fryery land* 1616 WeyR, *The Friary
Garden* 1646 ib, *the Friery Yard* 1651 ib, *the Fryery greene* 1653 WeyM, *v.*
friary; for this Dominican Friary, established in Melcombe R. in e15, *v.*
VCHDo **2** 92–3); *Holy Trinity Church* 1861 Hutch[3] (erected 1836); *Horse
Barracks* 1811 OS (cf. *Barrack Fd* 1840 *TA* (Radipole)); *Ice House* 1839 *TA*;
Ionss New Ho c. 1825 Map; *the (Grand) Jury Chamber* 1640, 1641 WeyM;
the Long(e) Seller 1587, 1617 WeyR; *the Maine Guard* 1652 WeyM; *Mountjoy
Fort* 1653 ib, 1774 Map; *the New Fort* 1653 WeyM; *the Poor-house* l18 WeyR,
Old Poor House 1839 *TA*; *Radipole Villa* 1840 *TA* (*v.* Radipole par. *supra*);
St John's Church 1861 Hutch[3] (erected 1851); *Salthouse* 1645 WeyM, *the Old
Salt House* 1721 WeyR; *the Shambles* 1633 ib (*v.* sc(e)amol); *le slaughterhowse*
1616 ib; *The Theatre* 1774 Map; *the town gaol* 1774 Hutch[1]; *the Towne House*
1578 WeyR, *the Gui(l)hald of Melcombe Regis* 1625 WeyM, *the Towne hall (of
Melcombe Regis)* 1625, 1645 ib (cf. *the walke* 1640 ib, *the Town(e)(hall) Walk*
1727 WeyR); *Waymouth Townehall* 1685 ib, *Town Hall* 1842 *TAMap*; *Union
Ho* 1839 *TA*, *the Union Workhouse* 1863 Hutch[3] (cf. 'T. Wallis' house, called
the working house' 1633 WeyR); *the watchehouse* 1631 WeyM; *a Watter mill*
1618 WeyR (cf. Robert *atte mille* 1323 Ct, *v.* myln).

Inns (forms from WeyR unless otherwise stated) include *the Anchor* 1659;
Antelope l18; *The Bay Tree* 1703; *the Beare* 1685; *Black Dog* l18; *the Black(e)
Rodd* 1646, 1649; *The Blew Anchor* 1725; *The Boot* e18; *the Bull* 1666; *The
Compass* e18; *Cooper's Arms* l18; *Crown* l18; *the Crown and Sceptre* 1704;
Cutter l18; *ye Dolphin* 1652 Weld[1]; *Duke of Cumberland* l18; *The Fox* e18;

the George 1668; *the Globe* 1658 WeyM; *The Golden Lion* e18; *Hotel* l18; *the New King's Armes* 1691; *the King's Head* 1646 Hutch³; *Lion* 1824 Pigot; *Lyon's Head* l18; *Nag's Head* l18; *Old Rooms* l18; *Portland Arms* l18; *The Queen's Head* 1726; *the Red Lion* 1649; *Richard's Inn* 1621; *Royal Oke* l18; *the Ship* 1649; *the Star* 1659; *the Sun* 1694; *the Thistle and Crown* 1726; *Three Tuns* l18; *Turk's Head* l18; *Union Arms* 1840 *TA* (Radipole); *the White Hart* (in St Thomas St.) 1648; *the White Hard Inn in Waymouth* 1776; *White Horse* l18; *the White Lion* 1658.

ABBOTS COURT, probably a surname, cf. *ten' Johannis Abbot* 1379 *AD*; however the abbey of Cerne held the manor of Melcombe R. in the 13th cent. (Hutch³ 2 448), cf. also 'the house of the abbot of *Lattele*' 1280 Pat, *v.* court. ALEXANDER BRIDGE. ALEXANDRA GDNS, thought by WeyR 117 to be the site of *the void place by the Jutty* where refuse was to be taken in 1650, cf. The Mixen, Pile Pier *infra*. BACKWATER, *Back Water* 1774 Map, the part of the estuary and harbour behind the town, *v.* back, wæter. BELFIELD FM, *Belfield* 1811 OS, *Bellefield Hall* c. 1825 Map, perhaps to be associated with the family of Robert *Belle* 1428 DorR. BINCLEAVES BARRACKS & GROYNE, *Bincliffs* 1554 (18) *Ilch*, *Binkleaves* 1582 (18) *ib*, *Bincleaves* 1665 WeyR, 1841 *TA* (Wyke R.), *Bencliff Point* c. 1825 Map, cf. *le Cleffe* 1401 AD I, *Cliff* 1841 *TA* (Wyke R.), *Barracks* 1842 *TAMap*, '(place) within the cliffs', *v.* binnan, clif; for the elliptical use of binnan, cf. Bindon in Wool par. *supra*. CASTLE COVE, — Grd 1841 *TA* (Wyke R.), from Sandsfoot Castle *infra*. CONNAUGHT HO. GLEBE HO. GLENTHORNE. GREENHILL GDNS, from Greenhill (st.n.) *supra*. HARBOUR, 'the harbour of *Waymethe*' 1100–7 (l13) WinchCath, *the harbor* 1629 WeyM, cf. *aque de Waymuth* 1280 *Ass*, 'the water of *Waymuth*' 1342 Pat, *la commune Huthe* 1368 AD I, 1398 ib III, *one porte or creeke called...Waymouthe Porte* 1565 *SPDom*, *Weymoth haven* 16 *RoyMap*, *the haven mouth* 1535–43 Leland, *le Chan(n)el(l)* 1620 WeyR, 1658 WeyM, *v.* harbour, comun, hȳð, port¹, hæfen¹, channel, cf. Custom House Quay, North Quay *supra*; part of the Harbour 'below the bridge' is called *the Hole* 1617 WeyR, *the Hold* 1639 WeyM, *the Outer Hole* l17 WeyR, *The Hole, now Saumarez Hole* 1883 ib, cf. John *Somer* 1332 SR, -*Summers* 1618 Hutch³, f.ns. *infra*, *v.* hol¹ 'deep place'. JUBILEE WALK. THE MIXEN (an offshore ledge or bank), *Ye Towne Myxon* c. 1540 RCHM, (the) *Mixon* 1774 Hutch¹, c. 1825 Map, from mixen 'dung-hill'; in 1620 WeyR it is presented that 'the dung-heap called *le Towne Mixon* is situated in *le Channel*, and thence is much carried away by storms of rain into the port', to avoid which there are various regulations for the disposal of dung and refuse at other places in 1635, 1650 WeyR, 1648 WeyM, etc., cf. Alexandra Gdns *supra*. MOUNT PLEASANT FM, a complimentary name. NETTLECOMBE. THE NOTHE, NOTHE GDNS & POINT, *Waymouthe('s) North(e)* 1604 WeyR, 1614 DorR, 1618 WeyR, *(ground att) the North(e)* 1622, 1627 ib, *the North end* 1650 ib, *Nose* 1753 Collins, *North Point* c. 1825 Map, *the (North or) Nothe, the Nothe peninsula, -point* 1861 Hutch[3], cf. *the Harbour or Roade commonly called the North Rhoade* 1668 WeyR, *(the) North Fort* 1653 WeyM, 1774 Hutch[1], *the Nothe Fort* 1861 Hutch[3], also called *Queen Elizabeth's Fort* 1774 Map, *Jetty Fort* 1811 OS; derived by Zachrisson EPP 22 from an OE hnoþ 'knoll, hill' connected with Norw *nod(a)* 'lump', etc., cf. also Nath Point in Corfe C. par. *supra*, White Nothe or Nose in Owermoigne par. *supra*, v. road, fort. PILE PIER, 1863 Hutch[3], built c. 1840 'of loose rocks secured with piles' (Hutch[3] 2 465). There were various earlier piers at the entrance to the harbour: *le Jety* 1446 Pat, *the olde Juttie* 1578 WeyR, *ye gitty* 1597 Hutch[3], *(le) Jetty(e)* 1616, 1620 WeyR, *the Jetty hedd* 1629 WeyM, *the Gittye* 1634 ib, *the Jutty* 1648 ib, *the New Jetty* 1774 Hutch[1] ('a mould or pier of stone...at the end of which was formerly a fort or battery', cf. *the Jutty Fort* 1657 WeyM), *v.* jetty, jutty, *the piere* 1586 WeyR, *the Peere or harbor* 1646 WeyM, *the Peerehead* 1658 ib, *the Grand Piere* 1685 WeyR, *the Little Pier, the New Pier* l17 ib, *v.* per, cf. South Pier *infra, the Mo(u)ld(e)head* 1611–1620 WeyR, *Molehead* 1641 WeyM, *v.* mole. RADIPOLE PARK GDNS, cf. *Park Hotel & Mdw* 1840 *TA* (Radipole), from Radipole par. *supra*. ROCKY KNAP, *v.* cnæpp. RODWELL, 1624 WeyR, 'reedy spring or stream', *v.* hrēod, wella. SANDSFOOT CASTLE, 1811 OS, *Sandfot castel, Sandfett castill* 16 *RoyMap*, *Sandys-, -es-, -is-, -fo(o)t(e)* 1553 WeyR *(the Castell of —) et freq* to 1623 ib *(— Castle), San(s)foot(e) Castle* 1646 SC, *Weymouth Castle* 1710 Map, 1774 Hutch[1] *(— called also Sandesfoot or Sandesfort)*, cf. *Castle (Ground)* 1841 *TA* (Wyke R.), *v.* sand (here alluding to the sandy shore), fōt, castel(l); the castle, built c. 1539, is described by Leland (I 250) as 'a right goodly and warlyke castel...having one open barbicane'. SLUICE GDNS, named from *the Sluce leading to Sutton* 1656 WeyM, *the old Sluice on the Wareham Rd* 1861 Hutch[3], also probably referred to in *lez Grate iuxta Gutair' versus le Chesyll'* 1531 *Weld*[1], *v.* scluse 'a sluice', grate 'a grate', gotere 'a gutter', cisel 'shingle', cf. Sutton Poyntz in Preston par. *supra*; the shore here is again called *the Chezill* in 1582 Hutch[3], *the Chessell* 1618 WeyR. SOUTH PIER, *the south pier or old jetty* 1861 Hutch[3], cf. 'at the entrance of the harbour, on the S side are two jetties, the higher and the lower...these seem to have been the old pier' 1774 Hutch[1] 1 408; for other piers at the harbour entrance, cf. Pile Pier *supra*. SPRINGFIELD, near Rodwell *supra*, *v.* spring. SWANNERY. TOWN BRIDGE (built 1930), replacing earlier bridges across the estuary of R. Wey referred to as *The Timber Bridge* 1597 Hutch[3], *the Bridge* 1629 WeyM *et freq* to 1774 Map, *the Towne Bridge* 1648 WeyM, *Weymouth Bridge* 1791 Boswell, *the Old Bridge* 1824 Pigot, cf. *the Bridge Pier* 1688 WeyR; the first bridge in 1597 replaced the *ferry* mentioned in 1535–43 Leland, cf. *the passage boat(e)* 1582, 1585 WeyR, *v.* passage. UNDERBARN WALK. WESTERN LEDGES, a coastal feature. WESTHAM, *v.* hamm; 'west' in relation to Melcombe R. WEYMOUTH BAY, 1811 OS, cf. *the Roade of Waymouth* 1587 WeyR, *Weymouth Road* c. 1825 Map, *v.* road; the sea here is referred to as *in þare æst Sæ* 978 × 984 (14) *Add* (S 938), *v.* ēast, sǣ.

FIELD-NAMES

The undated forms are 1840 *TA* 180 (Radipole) and 1841 *TA* 268 (Wyke R., marked †). Spellings dated 1252, 1398, 1400, 1549, 1582[2], 1617[2], 1665, 1679, 1716, 1861, 1863 are Hutch[3], 1252[2] Cl, 1288 *Ass*, 1323 *Ct*, 1332 SR, 1348, 1379, 1393 *AD*, 1389, 1420, 1421 AD I, 1398[2] AD III, 1418 Pat, 16 *RoyMap*, 1554 (18), 1582 (18) *Ilch*, 1566 *Comm*, 1626, 1633, 1648[2] WeyM, 1664 HTax, 1774 Hutch[1], c. 1825 Map, 1839 *TA* 243 (Weymouth), and the rest WeyR.

(a) the Outer Bar 1774 (a 'bar of sand' near the harbour entrance, *v.* barre); †Barns Md; †Blackland(s); Black Rock (*-rocke* 1649, in bounds of Melcombe R., *v.* blæc, rokke); Brickkiln Fd (cf. *Brick Kiln* c. 1825); Brick Yd 1839 (cf. *land...formerly called Gulleshays, and afterwards Brickfield* 1716, the surname *Gull, v.* (ge)hæg); Broad Mdw; Building Grd 1839; Bush Rods; †Carrington Cl; Clark's Hill (*Clarke Hill* 1617, cf. William *Clerk* 1400); ground called the Cove 1787 (*v.* cove); Cow Leaze; Cow Moor; Cow Willow Beds; †Drove (*the Drove* 1604, *le Towne(s) Drove* 1617, 1618, *the Long Drove* 1659, *v.* drove); Front Fd and Willow Bed; Furzy Point; †Home Md; Hooker's Dock 1792; Horsemoor; †Little Fd(s) ((*common called*) *Littlefield* 1582 (18)); †Longhill (Ctg) (*Longhill* 1582 (18)); Lovel's Fm 1861; †Hr & Lr Marsh; Meadow 1839; †(Lt) Middle Hill (*Middlehill* 1582 (18)); the —, Melcombe Narrows 1770, 1797 (*v.* narrow); †New Cl; New Mdw; †Nine Hedges; †Northover (1554 (18), 1566 (tithing of —), named in contradistinction to *Southover* in Wyke R. par. *infra*, *v.* norð, ōfer[1] or ofer[2]); Open Grd 1839; †Pond Cl; †Pyehill (from pēo 'insect' or pie[2] 'magpie'); Quaker's Grove 1863 (Quaker burial ground); †Rocks (cf. *vie apud lez Rocks* 1623, *v.* rokke); †Ropewalk; Sheep Moor; Shilley 1774 (a sand bank in the harbour); Shipwrights Yds 1839; the Shrubbery 1800; South Mdw; †Summers Hole (a field, cf. *Saumarez Hole* under Harbour *supra* and *Samwaie's Hole* 1753 DorB); †Swyke (*Sweek* 1582 (18), *v.* swice); †Syke (*v.* sīc); †T Close (so called from its shape); †Three Cornered Cl; Three Corners; †12 Acres; †Wall Md(w) (cf. 'the wall' 1582, 'the Town Walls' 1650); Washford (1649 ('an *old elderne stubb* at —', in bounds of Melcombe R., *v.* ellern, stubb), near Backwater *supra*, *v.* (ge)wæsc, ford, cf. Washford D); †Whatcomb(e) (*Wodcumb* 1252 (in old bounds of Weymouth), *Watcom*(b) 1582 (18), *Watcombe Drove* 1655, first el. probably wād 'woad', *v.* cumb, drove); †White Roughit (*common called Wheat Rowett* 1582 (18), *v.* hwǣte, rūhet 'rough ground', cf. an identical f.n. in Preston par. *supra*); †Williams's Line (probably from leyne, cf. John *Williams* 1549); Windmill Fd 1839, †Windmill Pit (cf. *the Windmill* 1582 (18), 1646).

(b) *Beneton by Weymoth* 1418 (perhaps from beonet and tūn); *Blake-manneslond, Blakemanneston* Hy 3 (14) Cerne '(Blæcmann's land and farm (or stone)', *v.* land, tūn, stān, cf. Blackmanston in Steeple par. *supra*; perhaps to be associated with the f.n. *Blakelond* in Preston par. *supra*); *the Broadstone* 1621; *Brook's Drawbridge* 1654, *a marsh at Brookes bridge* 1665 (cf. J. *Brooke* 1570, *Drawbridge infra*); *Channyns worcke* 1590, *the Marsh called Chaynes Work* 1650, cf. *Chanel's Works Lane* 1646 (from Raynolds *Channynge* the elder who in 1590 WeyR sold to his son a 'plat pece of grounde, and Arme of the Sea Milles thereupon erected', *v.* (ge)weorc, cf. *Mr. Channing's walke supra*); *Charrell's hyve* 1595 (thought by WeyR 133 to be for *hythe*, *v.* hȳð); *Colehey* 1393 (*v.* (ge)hæg; *ten' vocat' Est Cowes Hows* 1393 (probably from cū and hūs, with ēast, but *Cowes* may be a surname); *crucem de Waymoth* 1348 (cf. the cross mentioned in the bounds of Weymouth 1252 Hutch[3]); *the Cross* (in Melcombe R.) 1635; (*the Bridge at) Dodderell's Throng end* 1658 (cf. W. *Doth*(e)*rell* 1570, 1579, *v.* drong); (*the) Drawbridge* 1638, 1649 (*the West-*, *Royes-*), 1653 (*the Sally Port at the Middle-*) (*v.* draw-bridge, cf. J. *Roye* 1616, *Brook's Drawbridge supra*); *Elliot his drong* 1654 (*v.* drong); *the Fish Stone* (*by the Towne Pumpe*) 1656, 1691, *the Firsh Stone* 1666 (no doubt where fish was sold, cf. an identical lost name in Dorchester par. *infra*); *Fleetfurlanges dich* 1252 (in the bounds of Weymouth, *v.* flēot, furlang, dīc); *Ford's Drong* 1648 (cf. *ten' Will' forde* 1393, *v.* drong); *the George stairs* 1679 (in bounds of Melcombe R. quay, named from *the George* (inn) *supra*); *Gowerys-place* 1405 DorR (the surname *Gower, v.* place); *terre in le grene* 1578, *meadow called Greene* 1646 (near East St., *v.* grēne[2]); *at the Halle* (p) 1420, 1421 (*v.* hall); *Attehepe* (p) 1252[2] (*v.* atte, hēap); *la Heye* (p) 1288 (*v.* (ge)hæg); *Hodges' Corner* 1646; *Knaplock's Corner* 1654; *Knight's Corner* 1642 (cf. Robert *Knight* 1617); *atte Lane* (p) 1323, 1332 (*v.* atte, lane); *la Leye* 1398[2] (*v.* lēah); *unam placeam...vocat' le Lern* (probably for *Leyn*) 1393, *a place called Lyne or Lynd* 1651, *the Line* 1655 (*v.* leyne, cf. Williams's Line *supra*); *fontem vocat' Longwell* 1619, *the Long*(e)*well* 1635, 1650 (—*or Common well of the Towne*) (*v.* lang[1], wella); *in loco ubi le Maypole antehac stetit* 1625; *quandam marleram* 1288; *Martell's Corner* 1648; *Melcomb*(e) *Com*(m)*on* 1617, 1653; *Melcombe Sande* 1617 (the beach, *v.* sand); *Mersdich* Hy 3 (14) Cerne (*v.* mersc, dīc); *Mowetecombe* 1393 (*v.* cumb; Professor Löfvenberg suggests that the first el. may be an OE *māwett 'mowing', a derivative of OE *māwan* 'to mow', perhaps used here in a concrete sense of land on which grass is grown for hay, i.e. 'hay field');

atte Nasche (p) 1398[2] (*v.* atten, æsc); *the Narrowe Cont* (or *Cout*) 1619 (probably ME c(o)unte 'the female private parts', used to describe a cleft or gap); *the Pown* 1726 (*v.* pund); *Raymond's house* 1687; *the shelf* 16, *the Strend* 1635 (the shore at Melcombe R., *v.* scelf, strand); *atte Slo* (p) 1332 (*v.* atte, slōh); *the Stayres* 1619 (near quay, *v.* stǣger[1]); *Tems Well* 1582[2] ('the well called —'), 1597, 1618, *Tim(e)swell* 1648, 1648[2], *Thames Well* 1663 (possibly a form of the pers.n. or surname *Tim*, *v.* wella); *Tewss or Tewses* 1624 (probably a surname); *opposit ad angustiam, Anglice against the thronge* 1624 (*v.* drong); *the Townesend* 1626, *Melcombs townesend* 1633, *Waymouth Townend* 1685, *Townsend's ground* 1770 (*v.* toun, ende); *the Towne Grounds* 1620; *the Townewell* 1624 (cf. *the Longewell supra*); *fontem qui appellat' Tunne* 1252 (in bounds of Weymouth, perhaps from tunne 'cask, tun'); *Wade bridge* 1665 (probably (ge)wæd 'ford', cf. Wadebridge Co (DEPN)); *Wayman's corner* 1658 (cf. *ten'*...*Waremannys* 1379); *atte Welle* (p) 1323 *et freq* to 1389, *atte Wolle* (p) 1332 (*v.* atte, wella); *the West Gate* 1655; *Westland* 1617[2]; *Wilcher's Bridge* 1651; *Wilson's Well* 1646, 1727.

Whitcombe

WHITCOMBE (SY 717882)

(*at*) *Widecome* 843 for 934 (eME) BCS 738, *Wydecombe* 843 for 934 (17) ib 739

Widecome 1086 DB, *-coma* Exon, *-cumb(e)* 1198 P, 1212 Fees, 1288 *Ass*, *-cume* 1285 FA, *-combe* 1310 Inq aqd, 1461 *Ct*, 1487 *Weld*[1], *-coumb* 1339 Cl (p), *Wydek(o)umbe* 1280 *Ass*, *-cume* 1285 FA, *-cumb(e)* 1288 *Ass*, 1291 Tax, 1421 DorR, *-comb(e)* 1311 Pat *et freq* to 1487 *Weld*[1]

Widicumbe 1212 P

Whydecumbe 1288 *Ass*

Wytecombe 1291 Tax, 1428 FA

Wyt-, Witcombe 1460 Fine *et freq* to 1682 *Weld*[1]

Watt-, Wette-, Vettecomb(e) 1460 *Ct*, *Wettcombe* 1461 *ib*

Wydcombe 1461 *Ct*, 1559 DCMCt, *Widcombe* 1486 *Weld*[1]

Whitcombe 1573 DCMCt, 1795 Boswell

'Wide valley', *v.* wīd (wk. obl. *wīdan*), cumb, cf. Witcombe Gl 2 158. The 15th cent. spellings in *Watt-, Wett(e)-* may suggest that the first el. was thought to be from OE wēt (WSax wǣt) 'wet, damp'.

CULLIFORD [ˈkʌlived] TREE, lı8 *Weld*[1], 1811 OS, *Colifordestre(e)* 15 *MinAcct*, 1454–1460 *Weld*[1], one of a linear group of barrows on the high ground (called *Culliford Down* lı8 *ib*, *v.* dūn) in the S of the par., and giving name to the hundred of Culliford Tree *q.v. supra* which had its meeting place here, cf. the f.n. Culliver Tree in Preston par. *supra*. LONG BARROW, cf. *Barrow close* l18 *Weld*[1], *v.* beorg. WHITCOMBE BARN (PLANT.), cf. *Barn Down* l18, *v.* dūn. WHITCOMBE FM, l18 *ib.* WHITCOMBE HILL, cf. Alice *at hulle* 1318 *MiltC*, *40 Acres over Hill* l18 *Weld*[1], *v.* hyll.

FIELD-NAMES

The undated forms in (*a*) are l18 *Weld*[1] (E19/19), those in (*b*) are 1318 *MiltC*. Spellings dated 1280 are *Ass*, 1318 *MiltC*, 1321 *Winch*, 1327 *SR*, 1332 SR, c. 1550 *DCMSurv*, and 1664 HTax.

(*a*) Brick Kilns; Browns Ctg (cf. William *Browne* c. 1550); Clam Barrow (probably to be identified with *Clovebergh, Biesteclovenberg* 1318, 'cloven or split hill or barrow', from (ge)clofen and beorg with bī, ēastan, cf. Clannaborough D 364); Clavells; Cooks; Cowlaize; Crate (*v.* croft); Mr Damer's Plant. (for the *Damer* family, *v.* Hutch[3] 2 518); Ewelaize; French Grass (*v.* french grass); Great Md; Green Barton; Long-halves (*v.* half); Midlands (*v.* mid, middel, land); New Grd; Nursery Gdn; Robin's Ho; Running Md (*v.* running); (The) Shepherds Gdns & Ho; Spratts Orchd (cf. John *Spratt* 1664 and Hutch[3] 2 518); Stony Cl.

(*b*) *Algaressitte* (the surname *Algar* (from OE *Ælfgār* or *Æðelgār*), probably with (ge)set 'dwelling'); *cultura Bovebury* ('furlong above the fortified place', *v.* bufan, burh (dat. sg. byrig)); *Brokfurlang* (*v.* brōc, furlang (as freq in this par.)); *Bromaker* (*v.* brōm, æcer (as freq in this par.)); *Chelkhulle* (*v.* calc (WSax cealc), hyll); *Cutteforlang* (*v.* cut); *camp' oriental'* ('east field'); *Eldelee* (*v.* ald (WSax eald), lēah); *Forlond* (*v.* fore, land); *Bytwunefursledde* ('(land) between the furze valleys', *v.* betwēonan, fyrs, slæd); *Guldevelond* (possibly the OE fem. pers.n. **Goldgifu* (Feilitzen 273), although *Guldeve-* could be an error for *Guldene-* from OE gylden 'golden', with land); *la Hamme, Hammaker, Hommor'* (*v.* hamm, æcer, mōr); (*Est-, West*)*hevedlond* (*v.* hēafod-land, ēast, west); *atte Heuedstokk* (p) (*v.* atte, hēafod-stocc); *Atte Hole* ('(land) at the hollow', *v.* atte, hol[1]); *Knapfurlang* (*v.* cnæpp); *Lynchaker* (*v.* hlinc); *Middelforlang* (*v.* middel); *camp' borial'* ('north field'); *Nottefurlang* (perhaps hnott 'bare'); *Ocslad* (*v.* āc, slæd); *atte Putte* 1321, 1327, *atteputte* 1332 all (p) (*v.* atte, pytt); *Rynglynch* ('circular ridge or bank', *v.* hring, hlinc); *Risschiaker* (*v.* riscig); *Schiterlynch* (*v.* scitere 'a sewer', hlinc); *Shortaker* (*v.* sc(e)ort); *camp' austral'* ('south field'); *Stanfurlang* (*v.* stān); *atte thorne* (p) (*v.* atte, þorn); *campo de Wydekoumbe* 1280; *atte Woude* (p) (*v.* wudu).

Winterborne Came

Winterborne Came is in Frampton liberty, but part of the present par. was a tithing in Culliford Tree hundred (*v.* note under hundred name *supra*, Cripton *infra*).

WINTERBORNE CAME (SY 705883)

> *Wintreborna* 1129 CartAnt, 1190 (1332) Ch, *Wittremburna* 1174–82
> France, *Wynterbourn* 1362 Pat, *-borne* 1447 *HarlRoll*
> *Winterb(o)urn Caam* 1280 *Ass*, *Wynterbo(u)rn(e)-*, *-burne Ca(a)m*
> 1288 *Ass*, 1340 NI, 1373 Pat, 1439 *Midd*, — *Cham* 1291 Tax,
> — *Caan* 1348 Pat, — *Came* 1437 ib *et freq* to 1489 *Midd*,
> *Winter-*, *Wynterbo(u)rne Ca(y)ne* 1552 *DCMSurv*, 1564 *DCMCt*,
> — *Came* 1559 *ib*, *Winterborne Came als. Winterborne Cayne*
> 1685 *Batten*, *Came Winterborne* 1795 Boswell
> *Came* 1575 Saxton, 1586 *Batten*, 1664 HTax, 1811 OS, *Cane als.*
> *Come als. Wynterborne Billett* 1596 *AD*

One of the several places named from R. South Winterborne, a tributary of R. Frome, cf. *Winterborne Belet infra*; *Came* from the possession of this manor by the abbey of St Stephen at Caen from the time of William I (*v.* Hutch³ **2** 289 and Fägersten 162 note 2). This Winterborne is apparently not mentioned in DB (it is probably included with Bincombe par. *supra*, *v.* Eyton 121–2, cf. RCHMDo **3** 383), but there were no less than thirty-five DB manors in Do called *Wintreburne*, some of them named from this river, some of them from the more north-easterly R. Winterborne which is a tributary of R. Stour; although it is probable that most of the places later called Winterborne are represented somewhere in this number, only nine of the thirty-five can be identified with certainty, in spite of the attempt to identify the rest by Eyton 115–124, cf. DBGeography 74 ff, VCHDo **3** 147 fn. 67, DBGazetteer 129.

CRIPTON BARN, SPINNEY & WD (SY 702868), *Cribbeton* 1457 *Ct*, *Crib-*, *Crybton* 1460 *ib*, 1464 *DCMCt*, 1465 *Weld*¹ *et freq* to 1502 *Eton*, *Krib-*, *Krybton* 1461 *Ct*, *Crypp(e)-*, *Crypton* 1530 *Weld*¹, *Cripton* 1543 *ib*, 1637 *DCMSurv* (— *als. Winterburne Billett*), 1648 SC (— *farme*) *et passim*, *Crippen* 1682 *Weld*¹, cf. *Gupton Hill* (for *Cripton-*) 1843 *TA*. The first el. is probably ME cribbe (< OE *crib(b)*) 'a manger, an oxstall', the second is tūn; the meaning of the compound may be 'farmstead with a crib, cattle farm', cf. Barnes 105 s.v. *stall* 'a cowstall or cribhouse'. The *alias* form from 1637 shows that Cripton was a (later) alternative name for Winterborne Belet *infra* (cf. Hutch³ **2** 289, Eyton 121–2, VCHDo **3** 113, 147); in fact the tithing in Culliford Tree hundred called *Cripton* in 1664 HTax and *Cripton & Farringdon* in 1795 Boswell is almost certainly identical with that called *Wynterborne Belet* in 1332 SR and *Hundyngtone* in 1327 *SR*, *v*. foll., Winterborne Farringdon and *Winterborne Hundyngton infra*.

WINTERBORNE BELET (lost), *Wintreburne* 1086 DB (f. 84b), *Winterburn* 1224 FF, 1225 Pat, 1288 *Ass* (— *Belet*), *Winterborne Belet* 1285 FA, *Wynterbo(u)rn(e) Belet* 1332 SR *et freq* to 1461 *Rent*, — *Ben(n)et* (sic) 1443 *HarlRoll*, 1454 *Weld*[1], *Winterborne Bylett* 1502–4 BM I, — *Billett* 1685 *Batten*. Like Winterborne Came *supra*, named from R. South Winterborne; in 1086 DB this manor was held by William *Belet* (VCHDo **3** 113, cf. Frome Billet in W Stafford par. *supra*), cf. also Robert — 1224 FF, Ralph — 1225 Pat, William *Belet* 1332 SR. Fägersten 253 note 1 takes it to be an alternative name for Winterborne Steepleton par. *infra*, but this is unlikely; on its alternation with (and probable location near) Cripton in this par., *v*. prec.

WINTERBORNE FARRINGDON (SY 695882)
?*Wintreburne* 1086 DB (f. 79)
Winterborn Gemain 1242–3 Fees, *Wynterburne-*, *Winterburn(e)-*, *-bo(u)rn(e) Germayn* 1268 *Ass*, 1285 FA, Ipm, 1288 *Ass et freq* to 1428 FA, — *Germeyn* 1285 ib, 1329 FF, 1348 Pat, — *Germani* (possibly for *-main*) 1286 Cl, — *Germyn* 1343–5 Ipm
Wynterborn Faryngdon 1431 FA, *Winterborne-Faringdon alias Saint Germans* 1774 Hutch[1], *Farringdon Winterborne* 1795 Boswell
Faryngdon 1457 *Ct*, 1464 *DCMCt et freq* to 1530 *Weld*[1], *Faringdon* 1486 *ib*, *Farrindon* 1575 Saxton, *Ferrington* 1664 *Weld*[1], *Farringdon als. Winterborne Farringdon als. Winterborne Germayne* 1685 *Batten*

Named from R. South Winterborne, *v*. RNs. *infra*. For the possible identification of this place with one of the DB manors called *Wintreburne*, *v*. Eyton 121–2, cf. VCHDo **3** 147, Winterborne Came par. *supra*. The earlier affix *Germayn*, etc. is from the dedication of the former church here to St German according to Hutch[1] **1** 439, *v*. St German's Church *infra*, but a manorial affix is also possible, cf. Philip *Germeyn* who held land in the nearby *Wynterburn Pygace* in 1280 *Ass* (*v*. Winterborne Monkton par. *infra*). The later affix *Faryngdon*, etc. is from the family of this name here in the 14th and 15th centuries: Robert *de Faryndon* held $\frac{1}{4}$ of a fee here in 1346 FA, cf. also John *de Farendon* 1348 Pat, John — 1363 Cl, Thomas *Faryngdon* 1464 *DCMCt* (the surname is from a p.n. meaning 'fern hill', *v.* fearn, dūn). Even in 1774 (Hutch[1] 1 437) it is stated that the place 'is entirely depopulated, and has been so beyond the memory of man'; according to Kelly it was destroyed in the plague of 1666. Other forms that may refer to part of this Winterborne or to one of the Winterbornes in this par. are *Wynterburn(e) Gaugy* 1268 FF, 1312 Ass, — *Gauge* 1329 FF, named from Richard —, Thomas *Gaugy* 1268 ib.

WINTERBORNE HUNDYNGTON (lost), *Winterburn Hundington* 1292 Coram, *Wynterburn-, -bo(u)rn(e) Hundynton*, — *Huntindon* 1303 FA, — *Hundingdon* 1305 Abbr, — *H(o)undyngton* 1344 Pat, 1345 FF, — *Huntington* 1344 Inq aqd, — *et Huntyngton* 1346, 1428 FA, — *Hon(n)yngton* 1346 ib, 1397 Pat, — *Houndyton* 1348, 1353 ib, — *Hondeston* 1405 Fine, 1416, 1434 Cl, — *Homyngton* 1428 FA; *Houdyngton* (for *Hond-*) 1323 Pat, *Hundyngtone* 1327 *SR*. Like Winterborne Came *supra*, named from R. South Winterborne. Fägersten 163 may be correct in supposing that the affix is from the earls of *Huntingdon* who had a grant out of the manor of Frampton in 1413 (Hutch[3] 2 297), and who may have had some concern here at an earlier date since Winterborne Came was in Frampton liberty. On its alternation with (and probable location near) Cripton in this par., *v. supra.*

BRICK HILL PLANT. CAME DAIRY, DOWN (1811 OS, cf. *montes voc' le Downes, le Downe (ende)* 1581 *DCMSurv, Lr Down* 1843 *TA, v.* dūn), FM (*Hr Came* 1811 OS), HO, LODGE (cf. *Lodge Plain* 1843 *TA*), PARK (cf. *Horse Parks* 1843 *ib*), WITHY BED, *&* WD, all named from Winterborne Came *supra*, cf. *Middle Came* 1811 OS; both Middle *&* Higher Came are mentioned as hamlets in 1939 Kelly. CHAPEL HILL (COPPICE), from St German's Church *infra*. COLE HILL WD, *Cold(e)hull* 1406 Midd, *Coal Hill and Mds, Cold Hill Plant.* 1843 *TA*, 'cold hill', *v.* cald, hyll. DOWN WD, cf. *Down Cl & Plant.* 1843 *TA*, from Came Down *supra*. HOME WD, near Came Ho *supra*, cf. *Homeclose* 1552 *DCMSurv, v.* home. NORTH *&* SOUTH PLANT. ST GERMAN'S CHURCH (remains of), 'the church of *Wynterburn-, -borne Germayn*' 1397, 1410 Pat, *v.* Winterborne Farringdon *supra*. ST PETER'S CHURCH, cf. *le Churchehowsse* 1552 *DCMSurv*. WARREN BARN. WELL PLANT., cf. *Well Bottom, v.* wella, botm. WITHY BED.

FIELD-NAMES

For some fields in Winterborne Came *TA* but now in Winterborne Herringston, *v.* under that par. *infra.* The undated forms are 1843 *TA* 256. Spellings dated 1405–1407, 1439 are *Midd,* 1440–1447 *HarlRoll,* 1559, 1564, 1573 *DCMCt,* 1649 WeyR, 1841 *TAMap* (Fordington), and the rest *DCMSurv.*

(a) Great Barn Cl; New Breach Cl (*v.* brēc); Burnt Beat Cl (*v.* burnbeat; now called Burnt Bit (B.K. 254)); Church Md; Copse Cl; 18 Acres; Eweleaze; 15 & 14 Acres; E & W Hobbles (cf. Edith *Hoble* 1649 (Weymouth)); Hog Cl; Lr & Upr Hundred Acres (these fields are neither very small nor very large); Lime Kiln Cl; Lower Mds (cf. *Estmede* 1440, 1447, (*Little*) *Meade Close* 1552, le —, *the Mead Close* 1564, *the Comon meade* 1579, *Came Meade* 1612, *v.* mǣd, ēast); North Field Md, Moor & Plant.; Osmington Gate Cl (from Osmington par. *supra*); Pigeon Hole Cowleaze; Pit Fd; Plantation; 17 Acres; Shepherds Lodge (cf. *falda Walteri Sheperde* 1405); 16 Acres; Smithy Gdn; Taningdon Md; 30 Acres; Three Score Acres; 12 Acres (*lez twelfacris, twel(fe)acres* 1439, *v.* twelf, æcer); Wagon Rd 1841; Yeaning Closes (*v.* yeaning).

(b) *pastur' voc'* le —, *the backe* 1564 (probably back 'lying behind' used substantively or elliptically, cf. foll.); (*claus' voc'*) *le backside, le bakesyde* 1552 (*v.* backside); *prat' voc' Bourdelandes* 1559, *Bourdlonde* 1564 (*v.* bord-land); *Cambickes Close* 1552, 1581 (a surname); *ten' voc' Chippers* 1442 (a surname); *lapid' voc' the Bonde stones apud Cokes* 1581 (the surname *Coke, v.* boundstone); *le Combe* 1407 (*v.* cumb); *the Common feyldes* 1579; *le Courte hayes* 1581 (cf. *le Towne house als. le Court house* 1581, *v.* court, (ge)hæg); *prat' apud Cowbroke* 1439 (*v.* cū, brōc); *Deverells House* 1582 (cf. Avice *Deuerell* 1552); *oriental' campo* 1584 '(east field'); *Furshull* 1405 (*v.* fyrs, hyll); *Harryesacre* 1439 (cf. Andrew *Harrys* 1447, *v.* æcer); *le Hencote* 1439 (*v.* henn, cot); *Knollwalle fylde* 1584 (*v.* cnoll, wall); *le (Lytell)mershe* 1439 (*v.* lȳtel, mersc); *the Newe fylde* 1581 (*v.* nīwe); *ponfald' domini* 1447 ('the lord's pound'); *le Risshiham* 1439 (*v.* riscig, hamm); *Rowemeade* 1573 (*v.* rūh (wk. obl. *rūgan*), mǣd); *Shortlond* 1405 (*v.* sc(e)ort, land); *the Somer fylde* 1581 (*v.* sumor); *Southecombe* 1439 (*v.* sūð, cumb); *the Sowthe felde* 1579; *alt' via apud la strete Uppyntowne* 1439 ('the street higher up in the village', *v.* strǣt, upp, in, toun, cf. *alta strata de Wynterborne* 1443); *past' in la Waterruyne* 1405 (*v.* wæter, ryne); *Westburie* (*close*) 1552, *claus' voc' Wes(t)bury* 1564 (*v.* west, burh (dat. sg. *byrig*)); *the West Close* 1579; *occidental' campo* 1584 ('west field'); *Wynterborne Forde* 1406 (a ford across R. South Winterborne).

Winterborne Herringston

It is ecclesiastically incorporated with Winterborne Came (Kelly).

WINTERBORNE HERRINGSTON (SY 690880)

?*Wintreburne* 1086 DB (f. 79), *Wynterbourne* 1336 Pat

Winter-, Wynterborn(e)-, -burn(e) Harang 1242–3 Fees, 1268

FF, 1270 Cl, 1285 FA, Ipm, — *Haring* 1288 *Ass*, *Wynter-bo(u)rn(e) Heryng(e)* 1327 *SR et freq* to 1435 *Weld*[1]
Wynterburn Beuchamp 1243 FF
Wynterborn(e)-, -burne Heringeston 1288 *Ass*, — *Heryng(e)ston* 1288 *ib*, 1431 FA, 1529 *HarlCh, Winterborn-Herringston* or *Winterborn-Herring* 1774 Hutch[1]
Heryng(e)ston 1464 *DCMCt*, 1465 *Weld*[1], 1481 *Ct*, 1486 *Weld*[1], *Her(r)ing(e)ston* 1575 Saxton, 1615 *DuCo*, 1863 Hutch[3]

Named from R. South Winterborne, *v*. RNs. *infra*. For the possible identification of this place with one of the DB manors called *Wintreburne*, *v*. Eyton 121–2, DBGeography 74 ff, cf. VCHDo **3** 147, Winterborne Came par. *supra*. The affix *Harang*, etc. is from the family of this name; Philip *Hareng, -ang* was here in 1243, 1268 FF, Walter *Heryng* in 1327 *SR*, 1332 SR, 1336 Pat, cf. Chaldon Herring par. *supra*; tūn 'village' is added from 1288. The affix *Beuchamp* is also manorial, from the chief lords of the manor during the 13th cent., cf. Robert *de Bello Campo* 1242–3 Fees, *v*. Hutch[3] **2** 521.

CHAPEL (site of), still in use in 1795 Boswell. CLAPCOTTS (lost), 1795 Boswell, 'Clapcott's tenement' 1677 Hutch[3], cf. John *Clappecote* 1332 SR, William *Clapcote* 1490 Hutch[3]; according to Hutch[1] **1** 437 it consisted of 'some grounds in the farm of Winterborne-Faringdon' (in Winterborne Came par. *supra*), cf. the f.n. Clapcot's House Close in Bincombe par. *supra*; a p.n. Clapcot(e) such as would have given rise to this surname occurs in W 79 and Brk 536. CONYGAR HILL, *Conygore Hill* 1811 OS, *v*. coninger. HERRINGSTON (formerly MANOR HO), *Herringston-House* 1774 Hutch[1], *The Mansion House* 1863 Hutch[3]. HERRINGSTON BARROW (tumulus marked 6″, *v*. beorg), DAIRY HO, & FM. WELL HO.

FIELD-NAMES

The undated forms are 1843 *TA* 256 (Winterborne Came).

(*a*) Barn Grd; Bottom Grd; Carrion pit Grd (*v*. carrion); Cowleaze; Down (*v*. dūn); 40 Acres; Haning Grd; Horse Cl; Gt & Lr Hydes ('a ground called *Hydes*' 1607 Clegg, *v*. hīd, but possibly a surname); Gt, Hr & Lr Mead; Middle Fd; 19 Acres; Paddock Fd; Three Corner Cl; 20 Acres; Willow Bed.

Winterborne Monkton

WINTERBORNE MONKTON (SY 676878)

Wintreburne 1086 DB (f. 85), *-borna* Exon, *Winter-*, *Wynterburn(e)*
1212 Fees, 1228 Ch, 1270 AD III, 1290 Fine, *Wyntirburne*
1269 AD III
Wynter-, *Winterburn(e)-*, *-bo(u)rn(e) Wast(e)* 1244 *Ass* (p), 1291
Tax, 1297 Pat *et freq* to 1501 DorR, 1655 DCMDeed ('-other-
wise *Munckton*'), *Winterburn Sancti Michaelis de Vasto* 1269
Pat, *Winterborn Wast* (*de Wasto*) 1286 AD III
Wynter-, *Winterb(o)urn(e) Moneketon(e)* 1268, 1280 *Ass*, *Wynter-*,
Winter-, *Wyntreburn-*, *-bo(u)rne Munketon* 1288 *ib*, 1464
DCMCt, 1465 *Weld*[1], 1481 *Ct*, — *Monketon* 1397 Cl, 1406 Pat,
1544 PlR, — *Mounketon* 1486 *Weld*[1], *Munckton Winterborne*
1795 Boswell
Moneketon(e) 1285 FA, 1327 SR, 1332 SR, *Monke-* 1457 *Ct*, 1493
Ilch, *Moun(c)k(e)-* 1460 *Ct*, 1486, 1530 *Weld*[1], *Mownck(e)-* 1543
ib, *Munke-* 1464 DCMCt, 1465, 1481 *Weld*[1], *Ct*, *Munckton* 1530
Weld[1], 1575 Saxton, *Monkton* 1811 OS
Wynterborn-, *-b(o)urn(e) Monachorum* 1291 Tax, 1311 Cl, 1405
Pat
Moneken Wynterburne 1331 Pat

Named from R. South Winterborne, *v.* RNs. *infra*, cf. Winterborne
Came par. *supra*. It belonged to the Cluniac priory of Le Wast (*de
Wasto*) near Boulogne from the early 13th cent., *v.* Hutch[3] **2** 530.
Moneketon, etc. means 'village of the monks', and *Moneken-* in the
1331 form is a new ME wk. gen. pl. 'monks" (cf. *-Monachorum*),
v. munuc, tūn, -ena. Another form that probably refers to this
Winterborne (or some part of it) is *Wynter-*, *Winterb(o)urn Pygace*
1280 *Ass*, — *Pygaz* 1329 FF; for the affix, cf. *Waye Pigace*, etc. for
the formerly adjacent Upwey par. *supra*. On the identification of the
DB form, *v.* Eyton 121–2, VCHDo **3** 114, 147.

CHURCH, cf. 'the church of *Wynterbourn(e) Wast*' 1348, 1349 Pat,
'the church of *Wynterbourne Monachorum*' 1405 *ib*, *the cemetery of
All Saints church of Wynterborne Waste* 1501 DorR, *Church Yd*
1839 *TA*. LAMBING YD. MONKTON HILL. PENWITHEN, a house.
WEST FD PLANT., *the West fd* 1839 *TA*. WINTERBORNE MONKTON
FM, *Farm house* 1839 *ib*.

FIELD-NAMES

The undated forms are 1839 *TA* 252. Spellings dated 1327 are *SR*, 1332 SR, 1340 NI, 1438 Hutch³, and 1841 *TAMap* (Fordington).

(*a*) Gt Barrow Green 1841 (cf. Gt Barrow Flg and Muncton Barrow Cmn in Dorchester par. *infra*); Castle Fd 1841 (from Maiden Castle in Winter-borne St M. par. *infra*); Coppice; the Down (*v.* dūn); Drove Cmn 1841 (*v.* drove); the Great Md; Hams Mdw (*v.* hamm, or a surname); The Moor, Common Moor (*v.* mōr); the North Fd; Parsonage Ho; Pummery Fd 1841 (from Poundbury in Dorchester par. *infra*).

(*b*) *in la Hurne* 1327, *intheurne* 1332, *in le Hurn(e)* 1340 all (p) (*v.* hyrne); *le Landshare* 1438 (*v.* land-sc(e)aru); 'a hill called *Westbergh*' 1438 (*v.* west, beorg).

Wyke Regis

Wyke Regis (together with Elwell in Upwey par. *supra*) is a liberty, *v.* note under Culliford Tree hundred *supra*. In 1895 part of Wyke Regis (Westham, etc.) was transferred to Weymouth par., and in 1933 part of it was transferred to the borough of Weymouth, the remainder to the par. of Chickerell for civil purposes (Kelly).

WYKE REGIS (SY 661775) [waɪk]

> *Uuike*, (*to*) *Wike* 978×984 (14) *Add* (S 938), *Wik(e)* 1212 Fees, 1221 Cur, 1237 Cl *et freq* to 1566 *Comm*, *-juxta Porland* 1249 Acct, *Wika*, *Wica* Hy 3 (14) Cerne, 1223 Cur, *Wick* 1220 ib, 1243 Pap, *Wyk(e)* 1100–7 (l13) WinchCath, 1237 Cl, 1244 *Ass et freq* to 1431 FA, *Wyka* 1236 Cl, (*la*) *Wyk' iuxta Weymue* 1288 *Ass*
>
> *Kingeswik* 1242 Cl, *Kyngeswyk(e)* 1309 FF, 1365 AD I
>
> *Wykes* 1244 *Ass*, *Wikes* 1263 Pat
>
> *Wyke Regis* 1407 Cl, 1442, 1455 Pat, *Wicke Regis* 1570 *AddCh*, 1652 *Weld*¹
>
> *Weke* 1525 AD II, 1539 LP, 1575 Saxton, *Weeke Regis* Eliz ChancP, 1664 HTax, 1675 *Salkeld*, *King's Weeke* 1689 Hutch³

v. wīc. The meaning may be '(dependent) farm' (perhaps originally with reference to dependence on Portland), or 'harbour, fishery' (cf. the four fishermen at *Brige* in 1086 DB, one of only two references to fishing in Dorset DB, *v.* Bridge Fm *infra*, VCHDo **3** 100, 111–2, and cf. VCHDo **2** 353 for the fishery at Wyke in the 14th cent.). It was anciently a royal demesne (Hutch³ **2** 850, VCHDo **3** 27), *v.* cyning, rex (gen. sg. *regis*), cf. Portland, Weymouth *supra*. For the *We(e)ke* spellings, *v.* EPN **2** 261. The bounds of Wyke (including also parts

of Weymouth and Melcombe R., cf. Grundy **7** 66) are given in
978 × 984 (14) *Add* (S 938). For the liberty of Wyke R. *&* Elwell,
v. under Culliford Tree hundred *supra*.

STREET-NAMES: BROADMEADOW RD, named from *Brade-, Bredemede* 1322
MinAcct, Brodemed(e) 1322, 1328 *ib, common called Broad Mead, West Broad
Mead* 1582 (18) *Ilch, (West) Broadmead, Broad Mdw* 1841 *TA, v.* brād, mǣd;
CAMP RD; HIGHER RD, *the Upper Wyke Road* 1863 Hutch³; LONGCROFT RD,
named from *Long Craft, Longcrofts* 1582 (18) *Ilch, Longcroft* 1841 *TA, v.*
lang¹, croft; PARK MEAD RD, named from *prat'* in *Park* 1322, *prat' vocat' le
Park* 1323, *Park(e)-* 1326, 1327, *Parcmede* 1329 all *MinAcct, Park Mead(e)*
1582 (18) *Ilch,* 1622 WeyR, 1841 *TA,* cf. *Park-Mead House* 1774 Hutch¹,
Parkmead Fm 1863 Hutch³, *v.* park, mǣd; RYLAND'S LANE, named from
Rilond 1322, 1323, *Rylond* 1324, *Rilondmede* 1329 all *MinAcct, Ry(e)lands*
1582 (18) *Ilch,* 1622 WeyR, *Ryeland(s)* 1841 *TA, v.* ryge, land, mǣd; the f.n.
also gave rise to a surname, cf. Ralph *Ryland* 1581 WeyR; SHIRECROFT RD,
named from *common called Shir Craft, Shee Craft* 1582 (18) *Ilch, Shearcroft
(Bottom)* 1841 *TA,* the first el. may be a surname, *v.* croft. A lost st.n. is
Langton(s) Lane 1582 (18) *Ilch,* probably 'lane leading to Langton Herring'
(*v. infra*).

BRIDGE FM (SY 653777), 1863 Hutch³, *Bridge* 1581 (18) *Ilch* (land
at —), (— *Cl & Ho*) 1841 *TA,* probably preserving the name of
the manor(s) called *Brige* 1086 DB (2 ×), *(ad) Brigam* 1086 DB,
Exon, '*Bruge(s)* near *Waymue*', *Brugi* 1152–8 MontC, *Brugg(e)* 1268
Ass (p), 1324 *MinAcct, Brigg(e)* 1268 *Ass* (p), 1322, 1326 *MinAcct,
Bryges* 1288 *Ass* (p), *Brygge* 1295 *MinAcct, v.* brycg, cf. Weymouth
par. *supra*; the term was perhaps used of some early crossing place to
Portland near Small Mouth *infra*, cf. Leland's description of a
'causeway' there in the 16th cent.

LITTLE FRANCIS (SY 665783), *Franches barn* 1554 (18) *Ilch, Franches,
Easter & Northern Franches Close, Franchis Drove, the Easter —,
the Wester Close at Frances* 1582 (18) *ib, le Franches* 1620 WeyR,
(Great) Franches 1841 *TA, Francis* 1774 Hutch¹, 1811 OS, *Francis's*
1795 Boswell, no doubt to be associated with *la Fraunchise* 1322
MinAcct, la Fraunchice 1327 *ib* which is from ME fraunchise
'district over which the privilege of a corporation extends' (from
1486 NED), perhaps with reference to the liberty of Wyke R. *&*
Elwell, *v.* ēasterra, westerra; it probably gave name to Franchise St.
in Weymouth par. *supra* (only just outside the old par. of Wyke R.),
which has forms from 1413.

LANE HOUSE FM (SY 657785), *Lanhows* 1348 *AD* (p), *-hous Mower* 1582 (18) *Ilch*, *-house* 1676 *Salkeld*, *Lanehous(e)* 1365, 1370 AD I both (p), 1675 *Salkeld*, — *House* 1774 Hutch¹, (— *Md(w)*) 1841 *TA*, *Lanehowse Moore, Easter Lane Howse* 1623 DorR, probably 'house in the lane', *v*. lane, hūs, with mōr, ēasterra; the lane in question is probably the Wyke R.–Chickerell road now called LANE HOUSE ROCKS RD (6″), and it may have given name to Robert *atte Lane* 1332 SR, — *Attelane* 1365 AD I, *v*. atte; the lost names *Lanheye* 1322, 1323, *-hay* 1327, *-hei* 1329, *Lanehey* 1328, and *Lammede* 1322, *Lannemede* 1323, *Lanmede* 1324, *Landmed* 1326 all *MinAcct*, which seem to have the same first el. lane with (ge)hæg and mǣd, may also have been near here.

SMALL MOUTH (SY 668762), 1811 OS, *Smalemue* Hy 3 (14) Cerne (p), 1244 *Ass* (p), 1249 Acct, *Smal(e)mouth(e)* 1328 *MinAcct*, 1332 SR (p), 1387 *Ilch* (*passeg' apud* —), 1391 AD I, 1420 ib ('ferry of —'), 1421 ib ('the passage of —') *et freq* to 1570 *AddCh*, *passagii mei iacent' apud* —, *domum meam super Smalemuth* 1379 *AD*, 'ferry of *Smalemothe*' 1419 AD I, *Small(e)mouth* 16 *RoyMap*, 1526 AD VI, *Smalmoythe* 1539 LP, *tenement called Smalemouthes howse*... *together with the passing and passinge boote of Smalemouth* 1570 *AddCh*, *Small Mouth Mower* 1582 (18) *Ilch*, 'the narrow mouth', *v*. smæl (wk. obl. *smalan*), mūða, alluding to the estuary of East Fleet (*v*. Fleet par. *infra*), with hūs, mōr, passing. The house and ferry are described in 1774 Hutch¹ I 601 as 'the passage house called Smallmouth where is the ferry into the isle of Portland', cf. *The Passage Houses* 1710 Map, *Passage Close*, (*Moor and*) *Passage Lawn* 1841 *TA*, *v*. passage; there was a ferry here until 1839 when a bridge was built, *v*. Ferry Bridge *infra*; the reference to *Lyme Howsse, wher passage ys to Portlande* 1539 LP may also belong here. The ferry would seem to have been here quite early, but at one time there was also a 'causeway' here; Leland (I 250) must be referring to this place when he writes of 'a point of land wher a *trajectus* is into Portland by a long causey of pible and sand', cf. Bridge Fm *supra*.

ALL SAINTS' CHURCH, cf. 'church of *Wyke*' 1172 (l13) WinchCath, *ecclesie de Wyk(e)* 1252 Hutch³, 1361 *AD*, 'church of *Wikes*' 1263 Pat, (*cimiterio*) *ecclesie Omn' Sanctorum de Wyke* 1361 *AD*, 1379 *ib*, *Weke churche* 1539 LP; the present church was built in 1455 (Kelly). THE BEACON, (land) *North of the Beacon* 1582 (18) *Ilch*, *Bicken* 1753 DorB, *Beacon* 1841 *TA*, *v*. (ge)bēacon 'a signal, a beacon';

there is a hill here. CACIQUE, a house, cf. *cacique* 'a native chief...in the West Indies' (NED). FERRY BRIDGE, FERRYBRIDGE COTTAGES, from the former ferry here marked as *Portland Ferry* 1811 OS, *v.* Small Mouth *supra*. GOLDCROFT FM, *Gold Craft* 1582 (18) *Ilch*, *Goldcroft* 1841 *TA*, *v.* croft; the first el. may be gold 'gold', golde 'marigold', or a surname, cf. *John Golde of Waymuthe* 1382 Fine. LYNCH FM, LANE & RD, *Linch* 1774 Hutch[1], *Lynch* 1841 *TA*, *v.* hlinc 'ridge, bank'. MANDEVILLE, *Manwell* 1582 (18) *Ilch*, *Manwells*, *Manvelle* 1841 *TA*, perhaps 'common well or spring', *v.* (ge)mǣne, wella. MARKHAM HO, cf. *Markhams* (*Green Ditch Pound Flg*) 1841 *TA*, cf. *port' iuxta ponfaldum* 1322 *MinAcct*, *Greenditch*, *Pound Furlong* 1582 (18) *Ilch*, perhaps from mearc and hamm, or from a surname, *v.* pund. MARQUIS TERRACE, from the Marquis of Granby (P.H.) in Chickerell par. *infra*. ROUNDHAM NURSERY, *Rown(h)am*, *Roundhams* 1582 (18) *Ilch*, *Round Hams* 1841 *TA*, from rond 'round' or rūh (wk. obl. *rūgan*) 'rough', and hamm, cf. foll. which is near by. ROUNDHAYES, *v.* (ge)hæg, probably with same first el. as prec., cf. Roundhay Nt, YW. WESTDOWNE. WEST VIEW. WYKE CASTLE & HO.

FIELD-NAMES

For some fields in Wyke R. *TA* but now in Weymouth, *v.* Weymouth par. *supra*. The undated forms in (*a*) are 1841 *TA* 268; the undated forms in (*b*) are 1582 (18) *Ilch*. Spellings dated 978 × 984 (14) are *Add* (S 938); 1244, 1268 are *Ass*, 1415, 1584, 1730 Hutch[3], 1554 (18), 1581–82 (18) *Ilch*, 1566 *Comm*, 1620–1622 WeyR, 1623 DorR, 1664 HTax, c. 1825 Map, and the rest *MinAcct*.

(*a*) Abergavenny Ctg; Adlands (*common called* — 1582 (18), possibly from hēafod-land); Angel Gdn; Barn Fd (cf. *Barnfurlong* 1582 (18)); (Small) Barrow (1582 (18)), Barrow Cl (*v.* beorg); Bowditch (probably 'land above the ditch', *v.* bufan, dīc, cf. foll.); (Little) Bowhays (*above Hays* 1582 (18), *v.* bufan, (ge)hæg, cf. prec.); E & W Burdon ((*East* & *West*) *Burden* 1582 (18), *Burden Point* c. 1825); Butts ((*ye*) *Butts* 1582 (18), *v.* butte); Carrion Pit (— *Pitts* 1582 (18), *v.* carrion); Catherine's Cl; Chaphays (cf. *Chapehey* in Preston par. *supra*); Church Naps (— *Knap* 1582 (18), *v.* cnæpp); Claylands (possibly to be identified with *Cleverlands* 1582 (18), *v.* clǣfre 'clover', land, but the first el. may be clǣg, cf. *Klei-*, *Clei-*, *Cleyput*(*te*) 1322–1328, *Cleipette* 1326, (*common called*) *Claypitts* 1582 (18), *v.* pytt); Cobourg Ctg and Gdn; Cockle (*close called* — 1582 (18), — *Drove* 1623, *Cocwellesforlang* 1295, *Kokewellemede* 1322, *Cokwel*(*le*)*mede* 1323, 1328, *Cokwel*(*le*) 1326, 1327, the first el. may be cocc[1] 'hillock', cocc[2] 'a (wood)cock' or the OE pers.n. *Cocca*, *v.* wella, furlang, mǣd); Crab('s) Md(w) (*Crabs Mead* 1582 (18), cf. Nicholas *Crabb* 1398); Crooked Thorn (1582 (18), *v.* croked); Davis Cl (cf.

Abraham *Davis* 1730); Down (Coppice), (Little) Down Cl, Dunclose (*v.* dūn); Drove Cl (cf. *The Droves* 1582 (18), *v.* drove); Ebb's Fleet (*Ebe Fleet* 1582 (18), *v.* ebba, flēot, cf. Fleet par. *infra*); Elver Oaks Bottom (*Elver* may be a reduced form of *Alford-* in *Alfordesmede* 1460, '(mead at) eel ford', from ǣl, ford, mǣd); Fisherman's Arms Inn; Gentleman's Furze (*v.* fyrs); Georgecrofts (cf. Richard *George* 1664 (Melcombe R.); Gibbon's Cl (cf. Owen *Gibbons* 1664); Goose Lease (*common called —* 1582 (18), *v.* gōs, lǣs); Gower Hill (*Gorehill* 1582 (18), *v.* gāra); Green Down; Herring (possibly to be identified with *Hearne* 1582 (18), *Herne* 1753 DorB, *v.* hyrne); Home Cl; Homer's Cl (cf. Agnes *Holmer* 1664 (Weymouth)); Lines (possibly to be identified with *the Layns* 1582 (18), *v.* leyne, but cf. Ann *Lyne* 1621 (Weymouth)); Little Grd; (Gt & Lt) Long Cl (*Longclose* 1582 (18)); Longlands; Lowell (*Lowell, Lovell* 1582 (18), perhaps from hlēo(w) 'shelter' or hlēow 'sheltered' and wella, cf. Lewell in W Knighton par. *supra*); Meadow Long Cl; Mortcleves (*Mortcleaus, Martcleaves* 1582 (18), second el. is clif, cf. Bincleaves in Weymouth par. *supra*; the first el. may be eModE morte 'a harlot' (cf. *Mortstreyte* Gl 3 52), but cf. Mosterton par. *infra*); Old Hill (*common called —* 1582 (18)); Overlands (*Overlond* 1460, from land with ōfer[1], ofer[2] or ofer[3]); Paddock; Parsonage Cl; Pitt's Cl (cf. George *Pitt* 1664); (West) Reeve Md(w) (*one of the Reeves Meads* 1581 (18), *Reeve Mead* 1582 (18), *v.* (ge)rēfa); Roughwalls (cf. *Roweall* (a close) 1622, *v.* rūh (wk. obl. rūgan), wall); Rye Md; Sea House (*Seahouse* 1582 (18), — *Close* 1753 DorB, *v.* sǣ); Snake Down; South Cl (1582 (18)); South Fd (*Suthfeld* 1322, *v.* sūð, feld); Spice Croft; Stone Quarry; Stone's Cl (cf. William *Stone* 1664 (Melcombe R.), but possibly to be identified with *Stoning Close* 1582 (18), *v.* stānen); Tullidge's Grd (cf. John *Tullage* 1664 (Melcombe R.)); Wall Cl; Withy Bed; Woodlands (1582 (18), cf. John *atte Wode, v.* atte, wudu); Wyld (Mdw) (*pastur'...super Wyl* 1323, 1328, (*common called*) *the Wild(e)* 1582 (18), 1623, *v.* wīl 'a trap, a snare', cf. Monkton Wyld in Wootton F. par. *infra*).

(b) *Alwigs*; *Bat(s)comb(e) Cross* (cf. Batcombe par. *infra*); *locum voc' —, terre quondam Beches* 1460 (cf. William *atte Beche* 1329, *v.* bece[1] 'stream' or bēce[2] 'beech-tree', atte); *pastura...Biwestewike* 1322, — *Bywestwyk* 1324 ('to the west of Wyke', *v.* bī, westan, Wyke R. *supra*); *Blagdo(w)n* (*v.* blæc, dūn); *to blake ston, fram þane stone* 978×984 (14) (*v.* blǣc (wk. obl. blacan), stān); *Broad Close*; *prat' iuxta le Broke* 1323 (*v.* brōc); *Bulworks* (*v.* bulwerk); *Buryrydyng* 1460 (*v.* burh (gen. sg. byrig), ryding); *Chalcotts* 1554 (18) (*v.* cald, cot, but possibly a surname); *Chester[...]lang* 1460 (some letters illegible, possibly from ceaster and furlang); *Collelane* (possibly the surname *Coll(e)*); *the Common* 1581 (18); *Coombs* (*v.* cumb, but possibly a surname); *Corbettys* 1460 (cf. *terre Johannis Corbet ib*); *Cowhes* 1554 (18) (probably for *-les, v.* cū, lǣs); *Deadman* (perhaps where a corpse was found, *v.* dēad); *Estfeld(e)* 1322 (*v.* ēast, feld); *the East Stile* (*v.* stigel); *Fern Close Corner*; *Fisher's Close* (cf. William *Fysschere* 1327 SR (Weymouth)); *Frythwod(e)* 1460 (*v.* fyrhð, wudu); *grangia* 1322; *Heathentine*; *Hyde Harvest Bower* (*v.* hīd); *Hyrudyng* 1460 (possibly 'hay clearing', *v.* hēg (WSax hī(e)g), ryding); *Hilperdonesmede* 1460 (*v.* mǣd); *Holcomb* (*v.* hol[2], cumb); *Intrishins* (perhaps to be associated with *In hethinge* (for *-hech-*) 1249 *Acct, v.* in, hēcing);

pastura in...Lake 1326 (*v.* lacu); *Lea Yards House*; *Leyes* 1323 (*v.* lēah or lǣs); *the West Gate of Long Mead*; *Lopeback*; *Lowsie Bush* (*v.* lousi, busc); *Mayncockes* 1460 (cf. *terre...modo Roberti Mayncok ib*); *Middle Way*; *Myllewey* 1460 (cf. *molend' aquatic' ib*, *Old Mill* 1582 (18), *v.* myln, cf. *Oteruggestenement infra*); *de la Myre* 1322 (p) (ME mire 'a mire, a bog'); *Mogacre* 1460 (perhaps the surname *Mogg*, *v.* æcer); *Mochelmondelyes* 1460 (perhaps from a surname *Mondely(e)*, with mycel 'large'); *inne muledich...andlang þare dich* 978 × 984 (14) (first el. the OE pers.n. *Mūla* or (more likely) myln 'mill', *v.* dīc, cf. *Myllewey supra*); *New Inclosure*; *North Down(e)* (*v.* dūn); *North furlong* (*v.* furlang); *Nourngayng* (a bad spelling?); *Oteruggestenement cum j molendino...pertin'* 1460 (cf. John *Oterugge ib*, *Myllewey supra*); *camp' de Pokulchurche* 1460 ('goblin's church', *v.* pūcel, cirice; for similar names from folklore cf. Gl 4 200, but cf. also Pucklechurch Gl 3 64); *Pothays* (second el. (ge)hæg); *la Rudyng* 1460 (*v.* ryding); *in—, fram Saggelorð* 978 × 984 (14) (probably on or near the shore of Radipole Lake, but the form is almost certainly corrupt; possibly 'promontory marked by a stake' from sāgol 'staff, club' (BT, cf. *hege-sāgol* 'hedge-stake' ib) and ord 'point', with -*gg*- for -*g*- and -ð for -*d* due to scribal error); *Sheephays* (*v.* scēap, (ge)hæg); *Smalemede* 1268 (p), *Small Mead* 1582 (18) (*v.* smæl, mǣd); *the South Down* (*v.* dūn); (tithing of) *Southover* 1566 (*v.* sūð, ōfer[1] or ofer[2], cf. the f.n. Northover in Weymouth par. *supra*); *Staying Cross*; *Sticklands* (cf. Temperantia *Stickland* 1620 (Weymouth)); *(Weymouth) Townsend* (*v.* toun, ende, Weymouth par. *supra*); *Wadoms Lands*, *Woodoms Lownes* (cf. John *Woodham* 1415, —*Wadham* 1584, *v.* land); *the Way* (*v.* weg); *atte Welle* 1324 (p) (*v.* atte, wella); *Attewere*, *de la Were* 1244 both (p) (*v.* atte, wer); *Westfeld* 1322 (*v.* west, feld); *fram þare west Sæ* 978 × 984 (14) (*v.* west, sǣ); *Wheat Field* 1581 (18); *Whytes* 1460 (cf. *terre Roberti Whyte ib*).

V. BERE REGIS HUNDRED

In c. 1086 GeldR this hundred was much larger, including what later became Barrow hundred *q.v. infra* and possibly also parts of Winfrith Newburgh hundred N of R. Frome (Eyton 115f, Anderson 124, VCHDo 3 134). Winterborne Muston in Winterborne Kingston par. was a tithing in Combs Ditch hundred, Hyde and Shitterton in Bere Regis par. were tithings in Barrow hundred, and Chamberlayne's Mill in Bere Regis par. was in Bindon liberty (Hutch[3] 1 140, 160, 204). Milborne Stileham par. has since 1933 been included in Milborne St Andrew par. (Kelly).

Bere hundret c. 1086 GeldR, *Berahdr'* 1170, 1180 P, *uthundredum de Bera* 1180 ib, *Hundredum de Bere* 1230 ib, 1244 *Ass*, Fees, 1249 Ipm, 1265 Misc, 1268 *Ass et freq* to 1316 FA, (*Hundr' de*) *Beere* 1258 *For*, 1428 FA, *Dimidium Hundredum de Bere* 1280, 1288 *Ass*, *Ber'* 1303 FA, (*Hundr' de*) *Byre* 1327 SR, 1332 SR, 1346 FA *et freq* to 1476 Cl, *Byre maner' et hundred'* 1362 Ipm, *hd of Bere Regis* 1542 LP. Named from Bere Regis *infra* which was the *caput* of the hundred and to which manor it was annexed (Anderson 124). The 'half-hundred' (*dimidium hundredum*) perhaps refers to the part left after Barrow hundred *q.v. infra* was taken out of it. There is mention of *Hundredum de Kingeswinterburn* in 1212 Fees, named from Winterborne Kingston par. *infra*, which may be an alternative name for this hundred.

Bere Regis

BERE REGIS (SY 848948)

> *Bere* 1086 DB, Exon, 1202 P (*domorum R. de* —), 1203 (*camere R. apud* —), 1204–1230 ib, 1231 Cl, 1244 *Ass*, 1252 Cl *et freq* to 1575 Saxton, *Bera* 1086 Exon, 1195 P, 1205 (*domorum R. de* —), 1210, 1230 ib, *Ber'* 1231 Cl, 1242 *Salis*, 1273 Cl

> *Beer(e)* 1242 Sarum, 1258 *For*, 1314 Ipm, 1343 Cl, 1371, 1387 Pat, 1428 FA, 1435 Pat, 1617 *Add*

> *la Bere* 1365 Cl

> *Byere* 1259 Pat, 1343 Ipm, 1365, 1411 Cl, *Biere* 1306 Pat, 1313 Ipm, 1386–1410 Pat, *Bire* 1327 SR (p), 1374 Pat, 1412 FA, *Byre* 1332 SR, 1340 Cl *et freq* to 1447 *Weld*[1]

> *Kyngesbyre* 1264 Orig, 14 Mansel *et freq* to 1478 HarlCh, *-bire* 1375 Mansel, *King(g)es-*, *Kyng(g)esbere* 1280 Ch, 1288 *Ass*, 1303 FA *et freq* to 1557 Lane, *Kyngesbur'* 1303 FA, *Kyngesbiere* 1346 Cl, 1399 *AddCh*, *Kinghesberia* n.d. (15) *ShaftR*, *Kynkesbere* 1428 FA, *Kyngesbeare* 1557 Lane

> *Bire-*, *Byre Regis* 1495 Ipm, *Beare Regis* 1549 Lane, *Beere Regis* Jas I *TRMB*, 1617 *Add*

'(Woodland) pasture', *v.* bǣr[2], or 'wood, grove', *v.* bearu, cf. Beer Hackett par. *infra*; for the former royal forest here, *v.* Bere Wood *infra*. Professor Löfvenberg thinks that the name is originally probably from bǣr[2], later confused with bearu as is shown by the ME forms with *-ie-* and *-i-*. The manor was crown demesne, *v.* cyning, rex (gen. sg. *regis*), VCHDo 3 27, 64; for the entries from P referring to the 'houses, and chamber or residence, of the king', cf. the tradition mentioned in Hutch[3] 1 136 that King John had a castle here, and *v.* Chamberlayne's Mill *infra*.

BERE WOOD (SY 868950), 1811 OS, *bosco (regis) de Bera*, — (*la*) *Be(e)re* 1230 Cl *et freq* to 1258 *For*, *foresta de Be(e)re* 1252 Cl, 1258 *For*, 1280 *Ass*, (*for(r)esta regis de*) *la Ber(e)* 1253 Cl, 1255 Pat, 1256 Cl, 'wood of *Bere*' 1276 ib, 1280 Ch, 'wood of *Byre*' 1365 Cl, *Byrewode*

1422 *Midd, Berewode* 1516 *ib, v.* **wudu**; for the former royal forest here, *v.* Hutch[3] 1 136.

CHAMBERLAYNE'S FM & MILL (SY 845928), *Chaumberleynesmylle* 1411 Cl, *molend' de Southbroke vocat' Chamberlain Mill* 1546 *Lane,* (*molend' de*) *Chamberlaynes* 1549 *ib,* Jas I *TRMB,* 1617 *Add, Chamberlains Mille* 1647 *Bartelot, Chamberlynes Mill, lands in Chamberlynes* 1682 *Weld*[1], *v.* **myln,** cf. Southbrook *infra*; probably named from the family of Nicholas *le Chaumberlayn* 1244 *Ass,* John *Cha(u)mberlayn* 1327 *SR,* 1332 SR, 1422 *Midd,* all mentioned under this hundred and perhaps the descendants of the official in charge of the *camera Regis apud Bere* referred to in 1203 P, *v.* Bere Regis *supra*; the mill was on R. Piddle or Trent, cf. *molendin' aquatic'* 1489 *Midd, molend' de Beare* 1546 *Lane, viam...vocatam Milleway* 1516 *Midd, Mill Mead* 1776 *DROMap,* 1845 *TA.*

DODDING'S BRICK YARD & FM (SY 853937), *Bere* 1086 DB (f. 83b), Exon (*v.* Eyton 115–16, VCHDo 3 104–5); *molend' de la Doddingg'* 1268 *Ass,* terre apud *la Doddynge* 13 *Douce,* (land) *apud la Doddinge* n.d. (l13?) Hutch[3]; *Dodingesbere* 1288 *Ass, Dogdyngbire* 1320 Ch, *Doddyngbere* 1327 Pat, *-byre* 1348, 1419 FF, 1422, 1489 *Midd, -birea* 1422 *ib, Dodyngbeare* 1412 FA, *Dodyngs Beare* 1546 *Lane, Dodings Be(e)re* 1549 *ib,* 1617 *Add, -beare* 1617 *DuCo, Dodyngton* 1549 *Lan^, Doddingebere Myll* 1550 *Midd, Dodingswick(e)* Jas I *TRMB,* 1617 *Add, Doddinges-Bere or Doddinge* 1774 Hutch[1], *Dodding Bere* 1811 OS, cf. *Doddings Corner, (Island in) Doddings Lower Md* 1845 *TA.* The place lies on a stream at the foot of a 300′ ridge and the name *Dodding(e)* may be a hill-name, a derivative with *-ing*[2] of the el. represented by ME **dodde** 'a rounded hill-top' (as proposed by Fägersten 69, Zachrisson DTR 144, Ekwall PN *-ing* 195 (cf. RN 210), cf. Duddle in Puddletown par. *infra.* Alternatively *Dodding(e)* may be 'Dodda's place' from *-ing*[2] and the OE pers.n. *Dodda*; one of the two DB manors of Milborne Stileham *infra* was held TRE by one *Dodo* (= OE *Dodda, v.* Feilitzen 224), and this pers.n. also occurs as a surname in this par., cf. *claus' quod fuit Will' Dodde in Suthebrok* l14 *Mansel, v.* Southbrook *infra.* The spellings and forms of the p.n. are discussed by Dodgson BNF 2 (1967) 352, where it is held that the manorial genitive (to which can now be added much earlier forms) and the spelling *Dogdyng-* (which possibly represents metathesis of an assibilated pronunciation [-indʒ]) reveal the presence of an OE sg. *-ing̃* formation based on an original PrOE locative sg. *-ingi,* an archaic form. *Dodinges-*, *Doddyngbere*, etc. probably denote 'the part of Bere at or called *Dodding(e)*', cf. par. name *supra*; the (apparently) late formations with tūn and wīc mean 'the village and the (dairy) farm at or called *Dodding(e)*'. There was a mill here in 1086 DB (VCHDo **3** 104).

HR & LR HOVE WOOD (SY 855946, 855939), *de la Houe* 1244 *Ass*, 1258 *For*, 1268 *Ass*, 1327 *SR*, 1332 SR all (p), cf. *Hove Fds, Grd & Plecks (or Closes)* 1776 Map, *Hove Cl & Fds* 1845 *TA*, *v.* hūfe 'hood-shaped hill' or 'shelter', cf. Hove Sx 293; the two woods lie on the lower slopes of Woodbury Hill *infra*.

HYDE HO (SY 870905), MIDDLE HYDE DAIRY, HR & LR HYDE HEATH, *Hyde* 1285 FA, 1374, 1402, 1404 all Pat *et passim*, *Hide* 1288 *Ass*, 1664 HTax, *Hyda* 1291 Tax, *La Hyde* 1316 FA (— *cum Strafford*), *the Hyde* 1476 Cl, *Hide Stratford* 1696 *DCMCt*, *Upr Hide* 1774 Hutch[1], *Lr & Upr Hyde, Hyde Heath* 1811 OS, *Hyde Green* 1845 *TA*, *v.* hīd 'a hide of land'; *Lr Hyde* is now Hyde Ho, *Upr Hyde* is now Woodlands *infra*. This tithing in Barrow hundred (1285 FA, 1664 HTax, 1795 Boswell, etc.) seems to be identical with that called *Stretford* in 1327 *SR*, 1332 SR, cf. the forms cited from 1316 FA and 1696 *DCMCt*, *v.* strǣt, ford. The ford was no doubt on R. Piddle or Trent, perhaps where it is crossed near Hyde Ho by the Bloxworth–Wool road which may then be the strǣt referred to; the nearest Roman road is four miles NW of Hyde Ho.

WHITE LOVINGTON (SY 847944), *Whytelhoueton* 1525 *Pars*, *White-loving(e)ton* 1626, 1627 *Bartelot*, *Shitterton alias Whete-Lovington* 1774 Hutch[1], *Chitterton alias Shitterton alias White-Lovington* 1861 Hutch[3], probably to be connected with *Wystoueton* 1268, *Wytese-t(t)on(e)* 1280, *Whithoueton* 1288 all *Ass* (under Barrow Hundred, cf. Shitterton *infra* which was a tithing in this hundred), *Wight-*, *Wyghtoneton* (for *-oue-*) 1313 FF, 1344 Cl, Ipm, 1352 FF, 1412 FA, *Wyghtoueton* 1352 *Weld*[1]. The first part of this name is a dithematic OE pers.n. in *Wiht-*, probably either *Wihtlāf* (masc.) or *Wihtlufu* (fem.), the latter perhaps being more likely in view of the absence of gen. -*es* inflection; the forms *Wystoue-*, *Whithoue-* show early reduction of the second theme of the pers.n., and *Wytese-* shows a further stage in this reduction, *Wytes-* being a metathesis of *Wist-* < *Wiht-* (for AN spellings for OE *Wiht-*, *v.* Feilitzen 413); the later metanalysis of the pers.n. shows confusion of *Wiht-* with *white* from OE hwīt. The second el. is tūn 'farm', *-ing(e)ton* in the later forms being analogical. For two somewhat similar names, cf. White Lackington So which is from the OE pers.n. *Wihtlāc* and *-ingtūn* (DEPN), and White Lackington in Piddletrenthide par. *infra*.

PHILLIOLS COPPICE, FM (SY 864916) & HEATH, *Pillol(l)s* Jas I *TRMB*, 1617 *Add, farme called Filloles* 1646 SC, *Filiols* 1774 Hutch[1], (— *Heath*) 1811 OS, *Philholds* 1795 Boswell, *Philiholds Heath* 1826 Gre, cf. *Philliols Mead* 1845 *TA*, from the *Fil(i)ol* family, cf. Hugh —, William *Filol* 1354 FF, *v*. Hutch[3] 3 151 ff.

ROKE BARN & FM (SY 835960), WEST ROKE, *Rokemede* (*in Kyngesbere*) 1478 Cl, FF, *HarlCh, Bere Roke al' dict' Oke Kyngesbere* 1500 *Lane, Rocke* 1549 *ib, Roke Lease* 1589 Hutch[3], *Rooke* Jas I *TRMB*, 1617 *Add, Reake Downe* (sic) 1617 *ib, Roke* 1774 Hutch[1], *Roke* (*Barn*) 1811 OS, *Roke Down, Mead & Moor* 1845 *TA*. Roke probably represents a misdivision of ME *atter oke* '(place) at the oak-tree', *v*. atter, āc, cf. Rock Wo 69; alternatively a misdivision of *Bere Oke* is possible. However if the surname of Walter *de Hoke* 1327 *SR— de la Hok'* 1332 SR, belongs here, the el. would be hōc 'a hook, an angle', topographically possible for Roke either in the sense 'corner or bend in a hill' or 'land in a river-bend'.

SHITTERTON (SY 841950) [ˈʃidəRtn], *?Scetre* 1086 DB, *?Scetra* Exon, *Schitereston* 1285 FA, *Shetereston* 1288 *Ass, Shiter(e)ton* 1300 FF, 1316, 1412, 1431 all FA, 1458 *Weld*[1], *Schitertone* 1327 *SR, Shyterton* 1332 SR, 1420 FF, *Chiterton* 1456 IpmR, *Sheter-, Schyterton* 1525 *Pars, Shuterton* 1546, 1549 *Lane, Chiderton* 1597 PlR, *Shytterton* 1626 *Bartelot, Shitter-, Shetterton* 1687 *Weld*[1], *Shitterton alias Whete-Lovington* 1774 Hutch[1], *Chitterton alias Shitterton alias White-Lovington* 1861 Hutch[3], 'farm at *Shitter'* ('the sewer, the stream used as a sewer'), from scitere, tūn, *v*. Ekwall RN 363, cf. White Lovington *supra*; the place is on a small stream, cf. Southbrook *infra*. For reasons of prudishness the name now sometimes appears as Sitterton (in e.g. Kelly and on local signposts), cf. also pronunciation. For the DB identification, *v*. Ekwall RN 363, Fägersten 70, VCHDo 3 69, cf. Eyton 133–4, DBGazetteer 125.

SNATFORD BRIDGE & CTG (SY 856930), *Snadford* 1258 For (p), 1268 *Ass, Snatford, Snardford* 1268 *ib* both (p), *Snarteforde* 1288 *ib, Snotford* 1749 *Poor*, 1776 *DROMap* (— *Plecks*), *Snetford* 1774 Hutch[1], *Snatford Fds* 1845 *TA*. The first el. is probably snād 'a detached piece of land or woodland', with **ford, plek**; a ford is still marked here (6").

SOUTHBROOK (SY 846945), 1419 FF, 1634 Hutch³ (— *Mills*), 1717 ib ('a moor called —'), *Suth(e)brok* 1300 FF, 1316 FA, 114 *Mansel*, *South(e)brouk* 14, 1375 *ib*, *-broke* 1443 *Weld*¹ *et freq* to 1549 *Lane*, *Bysouthbrouk* 1352 FF, *Weld*¹, *Subbrooke* Jas I *TRMB*, *Sudbrooke* 1617 *Add*, *Sowthbrooke* 1627 *Bartelot*, '(place) to the south of the brook', *v.* **bī, sūðan, brōc**; the brook is that flowing from Shitterton *supra*.

HR & LR STOCKLEY FM (SY 856919), *Stocle* (*juxta Kyngesbere*) 1308 FF, *Stockley* 1403 IpmR, 1557 *Lane*, 1617 *Add*, 1861 Hutch³ (*Hr & Lr —*), *Stokkele* 1415 IpmR, *Stokle* 1422 *Midd*, *Stokeley* 1546 *Lane*, 1557 *ib* (*a lytell medowe in —*), *Stokesley* 1795 Boswell, cf. *Lr Stockley Old Mdw* 1845 *TA*, 'stump clearing', *v.* **stocc, lēah**; if the form *Stocclyue* 1288 *Ass* belongs here, the name may originally have had **clif** 'a cliff, bank' as second el., cf. Catsley in Corscombe par. *infra*.

WOODBURY HILL (SY 856947), 1774 Hutch¹, *Windebyre* (probably for *W(i)ude-*) 1242 Sarum, *Wudebur'* 1254 *Salis*, *Wodeburi, -bury* 1287 Banco, 1337 *Ass*, *-bur'* 1341 *Wim*, *Woudebur'* 1332 *Midd*, *Wodbury* 1456 *Weld*¹, *Wodebery hill* 1476 Cl, *Wodeburyhyll* 1535 VE, *Woodbery(e), -berie Hill* Jas I *TRMB*, 1617 *Add*, 'fortification by the wood' with reference to Bere Wood *supra*, *v.* **wudu, burh** (dat. sg. *byrig*), **hyll**, cf. Woodbury D 601, Woodborough Nt 180; for the earthwork here (called *forte* in 1617 *Add* and marked as Camp 6"), *v.* Hutch³ **1** 135, RCHMDo **2** 485–6, cf. Anchoret's Chapel *infra*. Fägersten 70 identifies (*on*) *windee bergh* 943 (15) *ShaftR* (S 490) with Woodbury Hill, but this is not possible as pointed out by Grundy **5** 100, *v.* under Almer par. *infra*. For the identification of the form *Windebyre*, *v.* Fägersten 70, and for its spelling cf. Woodstreet in Wool par. *supra*.

ANCHORET'S CHAPEL (site of), *capelle de Wodebury* 1422, 1439 *Midd*, within the ramparts of the earthwork at Woodbury *supra*, cf. *capellam de Bere* 1205 P. BACK LANE, cf. *Back Lane Cl* 1776 *DROMap*, *Back Cl* 1845 *TA*, *v.* **back**. BAGWOOD CL (1776 *DROMap*), COPPICE & RD, *v.* **bagga**. BARROW HILL, cf. *Barrow Fd* 1776 *DROMap*, tumulus marked (6"), *v.* **beorg**. BEDLAM, perhaps to be associated with *hospitium d'ni apud Byre, -de Byre* 1436, 1443, 1447 *MinAcct*, *v.* **bedlam**. BERE ARCH, DOWN (BLDGS & LANE) (*Beere*

Downe 1617 *Add*), HEATH (CTG) (*Beere Heath* 1617 *Add*), & LODGE, all from Bere R. *supra*. BLACK CASTLE. BLACK HILL, BLACKHILL BRICK WORKS & CLUMP, *Blackhill* 1811 OS. THE BOG. BOLTON'S BARROW, *Bolton* — 1776 *DROMap*, 1811 OS, tumulus marked (6″), *v.* beorg. BOWCROFT HILL, — *Closes* 1776 *DROMap*, *v.* boga; now known as *Bucket Hill* (B.K.). BROOMHILL, *Broome Hill* Jas I *TRMB*, 1617 *Add*, *Broomhill Fd* 1776 *DROMap*, *Stonehill or Broomhill Common Gdns* 1845 *TA*, *v.* brōm, hyll. BUDDEN'S FM, *South Barn* 1811 OS, cf. Phillip *Buddens* 1664 HTax. BUGBARROW (lost), 1719, 1863 Hutch³, *a feilde called Buckbarowe* Jas I *TRMB*, 1617 *Add*, *v.* beorg, perhaps with bugge 'hobgoblin'; in 1774 Hutch¹ 1 43 it is described as a hamlet which 'adjoins to the N of Bere'. THE BUILDINGS. BUTT LANE HOLLOW, *Butt Lane* Jas I *TRMB*, 1617 *Add*, *v.* butte, butt¹ or butt². CHALK PIT FM, from Chalk Pit marked 6″, cf. *Chalkpit* 1776 *DROMap*. CHAMBERLAYNE'S BRIDGE (*Chamberlain's* — 1791 Boswell), CTGS & HEATH, cf. Chamberlayne's Fm & Mill *supra*. COURT FM, cf. *Court Great Gdn* 1776 *DROMap*, *Court Green* 1845 *TA*, near to Manor Ho *infra*, *v.* court. COW DROVE, 1845 *TA*, — *Fd* 1776 *DROMap*, cf. *a Comon Drove way for the Prince's tenantes leading from the towne to Beere Heath* 1617 *Add*, *v.* drove. CUCKOO POUND, a plantation, cf. the same name in Langton Mat. par. *supra*. CULEAZE COPPICE, FM & HO, *Culies* Jas I *TRMB*, *Culyes* 1617 *Add*, *Culeaze* 1664 DCMDeed, (— *Copse*) 1742 Hutch³, *Cowle(a)ze* (*Spring*) 1845 *TA*, 'cow pasture', *v.* cū, lǣs. DARK LANE. THE DESERT, a plantation. THE DUNGEON, part of Bere Wood *supra*, *v.* dungeon. EAST FIELD FM, *East Fd* 1776 *DROMap*. END BARROW, — *Barrows* 1811 OS, tumulus marked 6″, *v.* beorg. FOX POUND, on the par. bdy, cf. *Fox Barrow* 1777 RCHM. FROOM'S LANE, cf. Thomas *Frome* 1422 *Midd*, George *Froome* Jas I *TRMB*, both mentioned in connection with the nearby Dodding's Fm *supra*. GALLOWS HILL, 1811 OS, *Gallis Hill* 1682 *Weld*¹, *v.* galga 'gallows'. GUDGEON CORNER, perhaps the surname *Gudgeon*. HANGING COVERT, *v.* hangende. HAYWARD'S FM, *Upr* & *Lr Haywards* 1845 *TA*, cf. William *Hayward* 1332 SR. HAZEL COPPICE. HOLLOW OAK, 1811 OS, *Hol(l)y Oak Closes* 1776 *DROMap*, *Hollow Oak Fds* 1845 *TA*. HUNDRED BARROW, — *Four Acres* 1845 *TA*, *a place called Hundredes Barrowe* 1593 *Lane*, *v.* hundred, beorg; this tumulus (marked 6″) was the meeting place of the old hundred of Bere Regis, and gave its name to the new hundred taken out of it now called Barrow hundred *q.v. infra*, *v.* Anderson 125. JENKINS'S FM, cf. *Jenkins Grd* & *Md*

1776 *DROMap*, *Jenkings* 1811 OS. JORDAN'S COPPICE, cf. Richard *Jordan* 1327 *SR*. KIMERLEY WOOD, cf. John *Kynele* 1327 *SR*, — *Kyueley* (probably for *Kyne-*) 1332 SR, 'royal wood or clearing', *v.* cyne-, lēah; for the crown demesne here, *v.* Bere Regis *supra*, cf. the tithing headed *Kings Tenantes* in 1664 HTax and called *Kingshold* in 1774 Hutch[1] (described as 'small parcels of land scattered all over the parish', *v.* hold 'tenure'). LANE END, a hamlet at the end of Miles's Lane *infra*, *v.* ende[1]. LARCH PLANT. LAUREL AVE. LITTLE COPPICE. LITTLE WOOD. LOCKYER'S HILL, cf. Martin *Lockeir* 1664 HTax. LONGLEY LEG, — *Bottom* 1776 *DROMap*, *Langley Bottom* 1845 *TA*, *v.* lang[1], lēah, leg, botm. MAIDENFORD WEIR, — *Water* 1811 OS, *Maiden Ford* 1775 *DROMap*, *Maidensford* 1845 *TA*, 'ford frequented by maidens', *v.* mægden, ford, cf. Maidenford D, Maidford Nth. MALTHOUSE. MANOR HO (site of), called 'the ancient seat of the Turbervilles' in 1774 Hutch[1], at which date it was still standing. MATE'S COPPICE, cf. Mary *Mate* 1664 HTax. MIDDLE HEATH, 1776 *DROMap*, a farm between two areas of heathland. MILES'S LANE, cf. John *Myle de Bere* 1258 *For*. MILL RACE, from Chamberlayne's Mill *supra*. MILLUM HEAD, at the head of the small stream flowing to West Mill *infra*, *v.* hēafod; Millum may be from myln and hamm. MINTERN'S FERRY, probably a surname from Minterne M. par. *infra*, *v.* ferja; R. Piddle or Trent is ¼ mile S. MUDDOX BARROW COPPICE, FM & LANE, — *Closes* 1776 *DROMap*, perhaps the surname *Maddock(s)*, *v.* beorg. NEWFOUNDLAND, a transferred name, probably indicating remoteness; it is a plantation in the extreme S of the par. NEW PLANT. OAK COPPICE & CTG, cf. *Oak Plot* 1845 *TA*. THE PARK, cf. *Parsons Parke* Jas I *TRMB*, 1617 *Add*, Edward *Persone* 1288 *Ass*, *v.* park. PEAT MOOR, cf. Adam —, Hugh *de la More* 1258 *For*, *Middle*, *Short* & *Sweet Moor* 1776 *DROMap*, *Moor Cl* 1845 *TA*, *v.* pete, mōr, swēte. PICKARD'S COPPICE, — *Mdw* 1845 *TA*, from the *Pickard* family who were lords of Bloxworth par. *infra* in 17th cent. (B.K.). THE PLANTATION (2 ×). RAWLES BARROW (local, SY 857962), 1777 RCHM. REDPOOL (lost, SY 853933), 1811 OS, *v.* rēad 'red' or hrēod 'reed', pōl. RIVERIDGE WD, cf. *Reveridge Close* 1776 *DROMap*, situated along the 300' contour of Woodbury Hill *supra*, perhaps 'rugged ridge' from hrēof (wk. obl. hrēofan) and hrycg. RYE HILL, 1811 OS, *Rie-* 1597 PlR, *Ryehill* 1719 Hutch[3], *v.* ryge, hyll. ST JOHN THE BAPTIST'S CHURCH, cf. *æcclesiam de Bere* 1086 DB, Exon, *ecclesie prebendal' de Byre* 14 *Roy*, *ecclesie parochialis de Beere* 1578 *HarlCh*. SHITTERTON BRIDGE (cf. William *de ponte*

1327 *SR*, John *atte Brigge* 1332 SR, *v.* atte(n), brycg), FM & WD, from Shitterton *supra*. SKINNER'S COPPICE, cf. William *Skynner* 1664 HTax. SNOW HILL (LANE), probably 'hill where the snow lies long', *v.* snāw, but cf. Snow Hill Ln 180, Sr 323 (both from snār 'brushwood'). SOUTH HEATH, *South Barn Heath* 1811 OS. SPEAR'S COPPICE & LANE, cf. Edith *Spere* 1586 Hutch[3]. STAND BARROW (local, SY 842953), 1777 RCHM, perhaps from stān 'stone'. STOCKLEY BRIDGE, from Stockley Fm *supra*. STURT LANE, *v.* steort. SUMMER HO. SWANDERBURY, part of Bere Wood *supra* on the lower slopes of Woodbury Hill *supra*, perhaps 'peasants' hill' like Swanborough Sx 317, *v.* swān (gen. pl. *swāna*), beorg. TANPITS BRIDGE & COPPICE, *v.* tanpit. TOWN'S END, *Townsend Close* 1776 *DROMap*, at the N end of the village, *v.* toun, ende[1]. VICARAGE, cf. *the Viccaridge house* 1664 HTax. WAREHAM LODGE, *Hyde Lodge* 1842 *TA* (Wareham St M.), named from Wareham par. and Hyde *supra*. WARREN, 1811 OS, *claus' in Warame* 1546 *Lane, Rabbit Warren* 1845 *TA*, *v.* wareine, cf. foll.; the abbess of Tarrant had a warren in Bere R. in 1402, 1404 Pat. WARREN HEATH (1776 *DROMap*), HO (1811 OS) & RD, cf. *Warren Fds* 1776 *DROMap*, named from prec. WHITE HO. WOODCLOSE, cf. *Wood Fds* 1776 *DROMap*. WOODLANDS, earlier *Upr Hyde*, *v.* Hyde *supra*. WOODSIDE CTG. YEARLINGS' BOTTOM & DROVE, perhaps 'strips used for ploughing', from ere-[3] and land, cf. Yarlands in Chickerell par. *supra*, but alternatively from ModE *yearling* 'animal in its second year', with botm, drove. YON BARROW, *Yarn* — 1777 RCHM, *v.* earn 'eagle', beorg; tumulus marked 6″.

FIELD-NAMES

The undated forms are 1845 *TA* 16. Spellings dated 1244, 1268, 1288 are *Ass*, 1258 *For*, 1316 FA, 1327 *SR*, 1332 SR, 1458 *Weld*[1], 1483 IpmR, Jas I *TRMB*, 1617 *Add*, 1626 *Bartelot*, 1664 HTax, 1688 *PlR*, 1776 *DROMap* (ex. inf. B.K.), 1841 Census Returns (ib), and the rest Hutch[3].

(*a*) Bakers Cl & Md (cf. Daniel *Baker* 1664); Banky Cl (1776); Barn Cl (1776); Beer Marsh 1776 (from par. name *supra*, *v.* mersc); Berrick Plot (*v.* bere-wīc); Biles Plot (cf. William *Biles* Smith 1841); Bitchams Md (1776); Blackford (Long Cl) (*v.* blæc, ford); Blagdon Fd (*Blackdown* 1776, *v.* blæc, dūn, cf. Black Hill *supra*); Bottom Fd (1776); Brick Kiln (1776, remains still visible (B.K.)); Broom Closes (1776, *v.* brōm); Browns Broad & Long Cl, Browns Old Mdw (from the *Brown* family, manorial tenants in m18 (B.K.)); Bull Barrow (*v.* beorg); Bulls Cl (1776); Calves Cl (1776); Chaldcott (cf. Richard *Chaldecote* 1458, *v.* cald (WSax ceald), cot); Cockhams Md; Cock

Row 1776 (perhaps from cocc-rodu 'cock-shoot'); Controversy (*Contravers* 1776, probably a name for disputed land); Copse Cl (1776); Gt Cowsl(e)y; Crooked Mdw (*v.* croked); Dairy Ho Fd; Daw's Md 1742 (cf. George *Daw* 1664); Down Cl (1776, cf. *In Down ib*, *v.* in, dūn); Drove; Dunnings Plot; East Md (1776); (Home) 8 Acres; Elders Md (1776); 11 Acre Md; Ferny Fd (1776); 5 Acres (*Five Acr'* Jas I); Ford Mdw & Pleck (cf. Richard *de la Forde* 1288, *v.* ford, plek); 40 Acres (1776); 4 Acre Mdw; 4 Acres; Front Grd (*Hove Grd* 1776, *v.* front, Hove Wood *supra*); Frys (cf. Elizabeth *Fry* 1664); Great Fd & Md 1776; Great Heath; Green Close (Md) (*Greene closes* 1617, *Greens Closes* & *Md* 1776, *v.* grēne¹); Hr & Lr Ground; Ham Md 1742 (*v.* hamm); Hancocks (Grd & Md) (*Hancocks* 1776); Hawkesbarrow (1776, *v.* hafoc, beorg); Hill Fd (1776, cf. Elias *de la Hulle* 1258, *v.* hyll); Hobeys or Hobbys (*Hobys* 1776, cf. *tenement' Simonis Hobbes* 1626); Home Fd & Plot (— *Grd* 1776); Hungary Ld (probably a name for poor land); Hysams (cf. Thomas *Haysome* 1664); In(n) Md (*v.* in); Keats Fds (cf. Thomas *Keate* 1664); Kingsbury 4 Acres; Knaves Acre (1776); Little Leaze & Md; Long Cl (1776) & Md; Lower Md 1776; Luggs Hedge; Maltkiln Grd (1776); Martins Cl (1776, cf. William *Martyn* 1664); Mead ((*Lr* & *Middle* —) 1776); Meadow; Middle Fd (1776); New Grd (— *Fd* 1776); 9 Acres; No Mans Land (1776, near where the bdys of Bere R., Milborne St A., and Affpuddle meet); North Md (1776); Orchard Cl; Pensby Wd; Piddle Grd (from R. Piddle or Trent, *v.* RNs. *infra*); Pleasure Grd (noted for barley growing (B.K.), so probably a nickname for productive land); Post Cl (1776, *v.* post); Rams Md (1776); Rentcroft (*Runcroft* (*Closes*) 1776); Ropers; Roundabout (now part of Bere Wood, probably a circular plant.); Rush Md (1719) & Moor (*v.* risc); Scratch Alley; 7 & 17 Acres; Shilling Plot (cf. John *Eschelling* 1258); 6 Acre Fds; 6 Acres (1776); Slights 15 Acres (1776, a sheep run (B.K.), *v.* slæget); Smith's Md (1776, cf. Richard *Smyth* 1332); South Md 1742; Spanish Liquorice Grd (from a crop of the plants from which liquorice is obtained); Swangers (Copse, Mdws & 12 Acres); (Gt, Lt, The) 10 Acres; Thrashers Md; Toms Long Grd (1776, from the *Toms* family, manorial tenants in 1776 (B.K.)); Trews Moor or Md, Trews Pce (*Trues* 1776, the surname *True*, *Trew*); Trunk Md; 12 & 20 Acres (both 1776); Two Styles (1776, *v.* stigel); Welches Md (cf. William *Welch* 1664); West Fd (1776); West Md (1776); Whores Md 1776; Williams Cl (1776, cf. Walter *Willam(e)* 1327, 1332, le *Reekebarton M'ri Williams* 1626, *v.* rickebarton); Woolfreys Brake (1776, cf. Thomas *Woolfreys* 1664, *v.* bræc¹).

(*b*) *Base Close* 1688; *Bottum Close* 1688; *Calwode* 1258 (in Bere forest, *v.* wudu); *Chilborough* 17, *Chilbar(r)owes* Jas I, 1617 (probably to be associated with *Chileberch* 1244 (p), *Childeber'* 1258 (p), in which case the first el. may be cild (gen. pl. *cild(r)a*) 'a young person' with beorg); *the comon feyldes of Beere* 1617, *Bere Fds* 1719; 'the Cross of *Bere*' 1535; *la Dene* 1258 (p) (*v.* denu); *Folecome* 1285 Banco, *Fulcume* 1316, *Foulecomb* 1483 ('dirty valley', *v.* fūl (wk. obl. *fūlan*), cumb); *foro de Bere* 1288; *Peaked Closes* 1688 (*v.* peked); *Peake Downe* Jas I (*v.* pēac); *Podeleford* 1268 (p), aquam de *Pydeleford* 1288, *Pudel(e)ford* 1327, 1332 both (p) ('ford on R. Piddle', *v.* ford, RNs. *infra*); *atte Stone* 1327, 1332 both (p) (*v.* atte, stān); *Swynehams* (*Comon*) Jas I, 1617 (*v.* swin¹, hamm, cf. Swineham in Wareham par. *supra*).

Milborne Stileham

Since 1933 included in the civil par. of Milborne St Andrew *infra*.

MILBORNE STILEHAM (SY 804975)

Meleburn(e) 1086 DB (f. 83a), 1199 FF, 1200 Cur (p), 1217 Pat,
FF, 1221 Cur (p), 1225 ib *et freq* to 1325 Pat, *-borne* 1086 DB
(f. 84b), *-bourne* 1305 Ipm

Muleborn(e) 13 *Weld*[1] (p), 1285 FA, 1291 Tax, 1327 *SR*, 1332 SR,
-burn 1258 *For*, 1320 Ch, *-bourne* 1331 Pat (p), *Mulburn* 1327
Pat, *-born* 1364 ib

Moleburne 1268 *Ass*

Mileborn 1268 *Ass*, *Milborne* 1361 Cl

Myleburn Munketon 1292 Ass

Mullebourne Beeke 1326 TopCh, *Milbo(u)rnebek(e)* 1436 IpmR,
1454 *Eton*, — *Becke* 1612 *PlR*, *Milburnbeke* 1442 Pat, *Melburne-
bek(e)* 1450 Fine, 1451 Pat, *Melbornbeke* 1467 ib, *Mylborne beke*
1525 *Pars*

Little Mellburne 1332 Ch, *Parva Melebourn* 1340 TopCh

Milborn(e) Stylam 1431 FA, — *Styleham* 1476 *DCMDeed*,
— *Styleam* 1664 HTax, *Mylborne Styllam* 1512 *Pars*

'Mill stream', *v.* myln, burna, cf. Milborne St Andrew par. *infra*
which takes its name from the same stream and where some of the
forms without affix cited above may strictly belong. There was a mill
at one of the two DB manors of Milborne S. in 1086 (VCHDo **3** 112).
The affixes *Munketon* and *Beek, Bek(e)* are from its possession by the
abbey of Bec-Hellouin (Hutch[3] **1** 141), cf. *Beklond* in Steeple par.
supra, *v.* munuc, tūn; *Little* is in relation to Milborne St A., *v.*
lȳtel; *Styl(e)(h)am* may be from stigel 'a stile, a steep ascent' and
hamm 'enclosure', cf. William *de la Stig(h)ele* 1268 *Ass*, 1285 FA
mentioned under Barrow hundred. Another name for this Milborne
or for a part of it was *Mel(l)eb(o)urneford(e)* 1280, 1288 *Ass*, *v.* ford,
but cf. Milborne Mamford in Milborne St A. par. *infra*.

BLADEN DAIRY (1″). FOXPOUND, a plant., *v.* fox, pund. GOULD'S
FM, cf. John *Gould(e)* 1327 *SR*, 1664 HTax. MANOR FM, from Manor
Ho in Milborne St A. par. *infra*. SNAG LANE, cf. Snag Fm in Corfe
C. par. *supra*. WEATHERBY CASTLE, *Weatherbury Castle* 1811 OS,
— *Camp* 1861 Hutch[3], cf. *Castle Rings, Out Castle* 1845 *TA*, *v.* burh
(dat. sg. *byrig*), castel(l), hring, ūt; the first el. may be weðer 'a

wether', in which case the name would suggest that this Iron Age hill-fort was at one time used as an animal enclosure, cf. Fowberry Nb which contains fola 'a foal'.

FIELD-NAMES

The undated forms are 1845 *TA* 16 (as for Bere R. *supra*).

(*a*) Ashley Fd & Md (from Ashley in Tolpuddle par. *infra*); Bowdens Grd; The Cockpit (*v.* cockpit; there is a shallow depression in this field (B.K.)); The Down, Milborne Down; Flowers Cl (cf. Richard *Flower* 1664 HTax); Furze Croft (*v.* fyrs); Galton's Bridge 1791 Boswell; Gt, Lr & Middle Ground; Green Cl; Highway Fd; Hilly Fd; Hollways Grd; Home Fd; Knoll (*v.* cnoll); Little Lane Grd; Littles Grd & Plain; Long Md; Marwood Bridge 1791 Boswell; Hr, Lr & Middle Mead; Middle Fd; Mowlams Cl (a surname from Moulham in Swanage par. *supra*); The 9 Acres; No Mans Land (on the par. bdy); 17 Acres; Sleights (*v.* slæget); Somerses (the surname *Summers*); The 10 Acres; The 12 Acres.

(*b*) *Pytteclose* 1476 DCMDeed (*v.* pytt); *la Strode* 1285 FA (p) (*v.* strōd).

Winterborne Kingston

Winterborne Kingston (SY 862977)

?*Wintreburne* 1086 DB (2×, ff. 84a, 84b), *Winterburn* 1196 ChancR, *Wynterb(o)urn* 1233 Cl, 1280 *Ass*

Kingeswinterburn 1194, 1195 P, 1196 ChancR, 1212 Fees, 1230 ChancR, 1234 Cl, -*born* Ed 1 *AddCh*, -*wynter-* 1244 *Ass*, *Ginges-* 1230 P, *Kyng(g)es-*, *Kingiswinter-*, -*wynterburn(e)*, -*born(e)* 1261 Ipm *et freq* to 1346 FA, *Kynkes Wynterbourn* 1428 ib

Kingeston 1244 *Ass*, *Kyngeston(e)* 1327 SR, 1332 SR, 1387, 1394 *Midd*, — *iuxta Byre* 1422 ib, 1468 IpmR, *Kingston* 1575 Saxton, 1811 OS

Wynterburn Reg' 1258 For, *Wynterborn Regis* 1312 Ipm

Wynterb(o)urn(e)-, -*born(e) Kyng(e)ston* 1280 *Ass*, 1306 FF, 1311 Pat *et freq* to 1626 Bartelot, '— by Byre' 1416, 1434 Cl, *Wyntreburn Kyngeston* 1316 FA, *Wynterburne Kynkeston* 1337 Pat, *Kyngeston Wynterborn(e)* 1459 Fine, 1462, 1501 Pat, 1512 Pars, *Winterborne Kingston(e)* 1549 Lane *et passim*, -*burne-* 1637 DCMSurv

One of several places named from R. Winterborne, a tributary of R. Stour (*v.* RNs. *infra*). It was held by the king from at least as early as the time of John (Hutch[3] 1 145), *v.* cyning, tūn, rex (gen.sg. *regis*), cf. Bere Regis *supra*. For the possible identification of two (or three) of the many DB manors called *Wintreburne* with Winterborne K., *v.* Eyton 115–6, VCHDo 3 134, DBGazetteer 129, Winterborne Came par. *supra*. In 1774 Hutch[1] 1 45 two (older) alternative names for the place are given as *Winterborn-Whitwell* (cf. Whitwell *infra*) and *N. Kingston* (cf. Kingston in Corfe C. par. *supra*).

ABBOT'S COURT (DAIRY) FM (SY 866979), *Abescourte* 1553 *Cott*, *Abbots-Court* 1774 Hutch[1], cf. *Abbots Court Down* 1842 *TA*, named from the abbess of Tarrant who held the manor of Winterborne Muston *q.v. infra* from the time of Hy 3 (Hutch[3] 1 148), cf. *pastura Abbatisse de Tarent* 1403 *Midd*, *v.* abbesse, court.

WHITWELL (lost), *Whitwell* (*in Kyngeston Wynterborn*) 1459 Fine, 1462 Pat, *Whytwell* 1473 IpmR, apparently a manorial name from the family of *de W*(*h*)*yte-*, *W*(*h*)*itewell*(*e*) which held the manor of Winterborne K. in the 13th and 14th centuries (Hutch[3] 1 145); according to Hutch *loc. cit.* they came from 'Whitwell Gambons, or Uphall Manor, in the parish of Runhall, Norfolk'. Eyton 115–6 identifies *Wintreburne* 1086 DB (f. 79b) with this manor, but cf. VCHDo 3 87.

WINTERBORNE MUSTON (SY 872976)

> ?*Wintreburne* 1086 DB (4 ×, ff. 79b, 82a, 84b, 85a), *Winterburn* 1204 RC, FineR, 1205 P, 1221, 1222 Cur, 1228 FF, *Wynterbourn*(*e*) 1363 Cl, 1374 Pat
>
> *Winterburn*(*e*) *Turber*(*e*)*vill*(*e*) 1242 Sarum, 1275 RH, *Vinterburne et Turberville* 1242 Sarum, *Winter-*, *Wynterborn Turber*(*e*)*vill*, *-uill* 1242 *Salis*, 1242–3 Fees, 1262 FF, 1268 *Ass*, *Turberuil*(*l*)*es-*, *-viles-*, *-vyleston*(*e*) 1288 *ib*, 1316 FA, 1327 *SR*, 1332 SR, 1394 *Midd*, 1431 FA, *Wynterborne Turbervyl*(*e*)*s-*, *-vileston* 1416 Cl, 1422, 1423 *Midd*
>
> *Winter-*, *Wynterborn-*, *-burne Musters* 1242–3 Fees, 1285 Ipm, — *Mosters* 1286 ib, *Winter-*, *Wynterb*(*o*)*urne-*, *-born*(*e*) *Mo*(*u*)*ster*(*e*)*s-*, *-Muster*(*e*)*ston*(*e*) 1310 Inq aqd *et freq* to 1403 *Midd*, — *Musterton* 1396 *ib*, 1403 IpmR, 1535 VE, 1596 *AD*, — *Muster*(*es*)*ton alias* (*Wynterborne*) *Turbervyles-*, *-vileston* 1468 IpmR, 1550 *Midd*, *Wynturbourne Muston* 1477 DCMDeed, *M*(*o*)*uster*(*es*)*ton* 1331 FF *et freq* to 1423 *Midd*, *Muston* 1550 *ib*, 1811 OS

Like Winterborne Kingston *supra*, named from R. Winterborne; the affixes are from the families of *de Turbervill* (Walter — 1204 RC, FineR, 1205 P, Bartholomew *de Turbervill*, *-uill* 1228 FF, cf. Melbury Sampford par. *infra* and Bryants Puddle in Affpuddle par. *infra*), and *de Musters* (Walter *de Musters*, — *de Mustries* 1242 Sarum, — *de Monasteriis* 1244 *Ass*, Robert *de Mousters* 1311 Pat, Roger *de Musters* 1317 *MiltC*, cf. Muston Fm in Piddlehinton par. *infra*), *v.* tūn. On the identification of the DB forms, *v.* Eyton 121–2, VCHDo 3 135 and Winterborne Came par. *supra*. It is possible that the form *Winterborne Willelmi filii Radulphi* Ed I *AddCh* (granted by *Johanna filia Johanne filie Willelmi Radulphi*) refers to part of this manor. In fact Winterborne Muston and Winterborne Turberville were originally distinct settlements, the latter (the more westerly) being now called Abbot's Court Fm *q.v. supra* (RCHMDo 3 300).

THE BUILDINGS. CHALK PIT, 1842 *TA* (freq), cf. *Chalkpit Grd & Mdw* 1842 *ib.* DAIRY HO. ELDERTON CLUMP. GREYHOUND INN. GRIFFITHS' PIT, *Grippitts* 1842 *TA*. HILL BARN, — *Fd* 1842 *TA*, cf. *duas acras super Hullam* Ed I *AddCh*, (common) *supra montem* 1387 *Midd*, *v.* hyll. KINGSTON FM, from Winterborne K. *supra*. MUSTON DOWN (— *in Common* 1842 *TA*), FM (— *Farrme* 1637 *DCMSurv*), FIELD BARN (*Muston Barn* 1811 OS, cf. *camp' de Wynterborn Turberuill* 1268 *Ass*, *Over Muston* (f.n.) 1842 *TA*, *v.* uferra 'higher'), & LANE, named from Winterborne Muston *supra*. NORTH DOWN (BARN), *le Northdowne* 1405 *Midd*, *North Down* 1811 OS, 1842 *TA* (— *in Common*), *v.* norð, dūn, cf. West Down *infra*. NORTH FM, N of Kingston Fm *supra*. NUTLEY CLUMP, probably 'nut wood', *v.* hnutu, lēah. PARSONAGE, 1842 *TA*, cf. *Parson's Close* 1607 Hutch³. PUMP HO. ST NICHOLAS'S CHURCH (Kelly), cf. *terram ecclesie* Ed I *AddCh*, *Church Cl* 1842 *TA*. STONY LAWN (CTGS), *Stoney Lds in Common* 1842 *TA*, *v.* land; *Ston(e)y* may represent stānig 'stony', cf. *Stonye acre* 13 *Salis*, *v.* æcer, but it could be a reduced form of *Stoneshey* 1452 *Midd*, 'Stone's enclosure', cf. John *atte Stone* 1332 SR, Thomas *Stone* 1409 *Midd*, *v.* atte, stān, (ge)hæg. WEST DOWN (BARN), *West Down in Common* 1842 *TA*, cf. North Down *supra*. WHITE LANE, — *Close* 1842 *TA*, *v.* hwīt.

FIELD-NAMES

The undated forms are 1842 *TA* 251. Spellings dated 13 are *Salis*, 1244 *Ass*, 1258 *For*, Ed I *AddCh*, 1310 Hutch³, 1327 *SR*, 1332 SR, 1626, 1627, 1647 *Bartelot*, 1637 *DCMSurv*, 1646, 1652, 1669, 1737 *Salkeld*, 1664 HTax, and the rest *Midd*.

(a) Ash Cl; Bakers Grd; Banky Pce; Bar Cl (*v.* barre); Bicks Cl (cf. (*claus'* *voc'*) *Byke-*, *Bikehey* 1396, 1403, 1423, *v.* bīc 'a bees' nest', (ge)hæg); Bloxworth Shard (from Bloxworth par. *infra*, *v.* sceard); Bottom Fd; Bowling Md (doubtless used for the game of bowls); Breaches (*la breche* Ed I, *v.* brēc); Brewers (Grd & Orchd); Broad Cl; Bullam Grd; Bushy Cl (cf. *Busshelond* 1426, *v.* busc, land); Castle Grd (perhaps to be identified with claus' voc' *Caswell, Caswelle hedge* 1626, which is probably 'cress spring', *v.* cærse, wella, hecg); Chalky Fd; Corner Cl; Cowleaze; Cozards Md; Crockers (cf. Henry *Crocker* 1664 (Bere R.)); Dolesbury; Down Fd; East Md (*le —, la Estmede* 1423, 1452, (*the*) *East Mead(e)*, —*Meadow* 1626, 1646, 1652, *v.* ēast, mǣd); Eight Nine and Ten Acres (sic); Far Fd; Fore Street Eweleaze (so called from the Roman road crossing the par., *v.* fore 'in front of', strǣt, Margary 100); 4 & 14 Acres; Fox Cover (according to Hutch³ 1 150 'about 20 acres of fox cover' belonged to Abbot's Court Fm *supra*); Gayley; Great Fd & Md; Higher Fd & Grd; Hell Grd (cf. *1 acram...* *desuper elle* Ed I, perhaps hell 'hell' used as a term of contempt); Hershells Md; Hoary Ld (*Horeland Close* 1652, *v.* hār² 'grey' or horu 'dirt', land); Home Cl; Hospital; Landshut Fd (Professor Löfvenberg compares He dial. *landshut* 'a flood' (EDD s.v. *land*), the second el. of which is apparently OE scyte 'shooting, gushing', cf. Löfvenberg 186–7); Little Fd (— *feild* 1652); Log Grd; Long Monday (probably a plot worked on Mondays as a service to the lord of the manor, 'long' describing its shape or the amount of work needed, *v.* mōnandæg; for this f.n. type, *v.* Gl 3 108, 4 201); Lower Fd; Man Md (perhaps (ge)mǣne 'common'); Meadow; Mortons Pdk (from the *Morton* family who held the manor of Winterborne K. at the end of the 16th cent, *v.* Hutch³ 1 145); New Cl (1646, —*otherwise Newcrosse close* 1652); 19 Acres; North Fd (*campo boriali* 1550, the *North feild* 1646); Nottings (cf. Thomas *Nottine* 1664); Old Marsh or Cowleaze (cf. (*claus' voc'*) (*le-*, *la*) *Southmer(s)ch, -mers(s)h(e)* 1394, 1396, 1403, 1423, *Marshecrofte end* 1626, *v.* sūð, mersc); Orchard and Gdn (cf. (*claus' voc'*) *la-*, *le Nether-*, *-Over-orchard* 1403, 1422, 1423, *v.* neoðerra, uferra, orceard); Paddock (Nottings) (*v.* pearroc, cf. Nottings *supra*); Parish Pound (cf. *panfald* (sic) *domini* 1392, *v.* pund); Pepper Alley (a common medieval st.n. type, *v.* pepper, aley, cf. 'the tenement of William *Pipercorn'* 1310 and the same man taxed under Winterborne Muston in 1327 and 1332); Pidgeon Md; Poor Altmt; Popes (Nottings & Orchd) (cf. Robert *Pope* 1664 (Bere R.), *v.* Nottings *supra*); Potatoe Grd; Ropers Ld; Round Grd; Samways (Mdw) (cf. John *Samwayes* 1664 (Bere R.)); Old Sand Pit (*le Sandputte* 1402, *v.* sand, pytt, cf. *Sandhelue* Ed I, the second el. of which may be (ge)delf 'a pit'); Selbys Pdk; The 7 Acres; Shepperds; Short Ld; 6 & 16 Acres; Smiths Shop; Snakey Cl; Snooks Orchd; Strap (*v.* strap); (The) 10 Acres; 10 Acre Pdk; 3 Acres;

Tower Hill Grd (*Tower Hill* 1647, cf. John *le Tour* 1332, Andrew *Tour* 1387); The 20 Acres; Upper Fd; Walk Grd and Cow Pasture (*v.* walk); Wantable; Wares (on R. Winterborne, perhaps from wer, wær 'a weir'); Well Grd (cf. *Welforlang* 1402, *v.* wella, furlang); Welsteads Grd (cf. George *Welsteed* 1664 (Bere R.)); West Md (*Westmede* 1452, *the West Meade* 1652, *v.* west, mǣd); Gt & Lt Woor (possibly from ōra¹ 'bank', with prosthetic *w-* before *o*, or a rounded form of ware 'sheep walk').

(*b*) *Basons Tenement* (*now in tenure of widdow Bason*) 1669 (cf. John *Beasaunte* 1550, William *Beasons* 1637); *Blakeford* 1244 (p), (*molend' fullon' domini apud-*) 1452, *ij claus' voc' Blackefordes* 1550 (*v.* blæc (wk. obl. *blacan*), ford); *Blandford way feild* 1652 (with reference to Blandford F. par. *infra*); *pastura in le Boderd* 1422; *Brodemede* 1396 (*v.* brād, mǣd); *brokeresþorne* Ed I (the surname *Bro(o)ker*, *v.* þorn); *Busketyshey* 1423 (cf. Thomas *Busket* 1327, 1332, *v.* (ge)hæg, as freq in this par.); *Colleheywardysclos* 1396 ('Coll Heyward's close' or 'Coll the hayward's close', cf. John *Hayward ib*, *v.* clos(e), as freq in this par.; *Coll* is a pet-form of *Nicholas*); *Crumplers* (*Farme*) 1669, 1737 (cf. *Ric' Crompler...Capital' messuag'* 1550); *Da(u)wes-, Dauwysclos* 1394–1403, *Daweshey* 1423 (the surname *Daw(e)*); *the East Close* 1652; *La Estcroft* 1423 (*v.* ēast); *campus orientalis* Ed I, *the East(e) feild(e)* 1627, 1652; *mor' voc' le Founte* 1550 (*v.* fount 'spring'); *Furseforlong* 1426 (*v.* fyrs, furlang (as freq in this par.)); *Goracram* (acc.) Ed I (*v.* gor 'dirt' or gāra 'gore', æcer); *de La Granette* (for *-Grauette*) 1306 FF (p) (*v.* grāfet); (land) *apud le Greynewale* 1405 (*v.* grēne¹ 'green' with wall 'wall' or walu 'ridge'); *terr' apud le Halfe iuxta Wodeweye* 1402 (*v.* half 'half-acre', *Wodeweye infra*); *Hawkins haye* 1550; *le Hile* 1397 (cf. *le Hyle* in Coombe K. par. *supra*); *Hoggewat(t)esclos* 1396, *-hey* 1423 ('Hogge Watt's close'; *Hogge* is a pet-form of *Roger*); *Huvesclos* 1396, *-hey* 1423 (cf. *claus'...q' Rob't Huve nuper tenuit* 1452); *Langelond* Ed I, 1426, *Langlondesacr'* 1394 (*v.* lang¹, land, æcer (as freq in this par.)); *claus' voc' Latily* 1396 (*claus' nuper Roberti Latyly ib*); (*claus' voc'*) *Le(i)ghton* 1396, *la—*, *le Leyghton* 1403, 1423 (*v.* lēac-tūn); *Longeclose* 1626; *claus' voc' Longlete* 1452 ('long conduit', *v.* lang¹, (ge)lǣt, cf. Longleat W 169); *Med(e)hey(e)(s)* 1394–1423 (*v.* mǣd); *claus' voc' Mereacre* 1452 (*v.* (ge)mǣre 'boundary' or mere 'pool'); *Middelforlangg* Ed I (*v.* middel); *viam qua it' versus Berewode voc' Milleway* 1516 (*v.* myln, weg, cf. Bere Wood in Bere R. par. *supra*); *la More* 1258 (p) (*v.* mōr); *common at —*, *venella apud No mans Oke* 1626 (probably on a bdy, *v.* āc, cf. the f.n. No Mans Land in Bere R. par. *supra*); *the North acre* 1646; *claus' voc' la—*, *le Parke* 1403, 1423 (*v.* park); *Pyreshey* 1423 (the ME pers.n. *P(i)er(s)* (Peter)); (*prat' voc'*) (*le*) *Pleymersch, -mers(s)h(e)* 1396, 1423 (*v.* plega 'play, sport', mersc); *Sevyers Tenement* 1669 (cf. Thomas *Sevyer* 1514); *ten' voc' Sewardesthyng* 1422 (cf. John *Syward* 1327, *v.* þing; *a carte Waye under Shilues* 1627 (*v.* scelf (WSax sci(e)lf) 'a rock, a ledge'); *Smockacram* (acc.) Ed I (*v.* smoca, æcer, cf. *Smokacre* in Coombe K. par. *supra*); *campus australis* Ed I, 1550, *the South feild* 1646; *close-, meadow called Spicers M(e)are* 1646, 1669 (cf. William *Spicir* 1327, *— Spicer* 1332, *v.* (ge)mǣre 'boundary' or mere 'pool'); *Staynesmo(u)reshey* 1423 (cf. *terre Johannis Staynesmore* 1394); *pasturam voc' Stockeley* 1550 (*v.* stocc, lēah, cf. Stockley in Bere R. par. *supra*); *le Stubbymerssh* 1405 (*v.* stubbig, mersc, cf. foll.);

place called Stubbs 1652 (*v.* stubb 'tree-stump', cf. prec.); *Tadds-* 1396, *Taddecroft* 1403 (perhaps tadde 'toad'); *the West Close above Galtons* 1652 (*Galtons* is probably a surname from Galton in Owermoigne par. *supra*); *campus occidentalis* Ed I, *the West feild* 1646; *Wethforlang* Ed I (wēt 'wet' or hwǣte 'wheat'); *camp' de Wynterburn Kinggeston* 13; *Wodeweye* 1402 (cf. *semitem que iacet versus boscum* Ed I, *v.* wudu, weg).

VI. BARROW (or HUNDREDSBARROW) HUNDRED

This small hundred was created out of the DB hundred of *Bere* in the 12th cent. (*v.* Bere Regis hundred *supra*). Hyde and Shitterton in Bere Regis par. *supra*, and Worgret in Arne par. *supra*, were tithings in this hundred in 1327 *SR*, 1332 *SR*, 1664 HTax and 1795 Boswell.

Hundredesberihdr' 1168 P, *Hunderesbergerhundredum* 1178 ib, *Hundredisberga* 1178 ChancR, *-bergh* 1288 *Ass*, *-barow* 1513 *Pars*, *Hundredebergh, Hondresbergh* 1244 *Ass*, (*Hundr' de*) *Hundredesberg(h)(e)* 1244 *ib et freq* to 1376 FF, *-berehe* 1265 Misc, *-ber(e)we* 1275 RH, 1280 *Ass* (*Dimid' Hundr' de* —), *-burgh(e)* 1280 Ch *et freq* to 1414 Cl, *-bury* 1342 ib, *-borgh, -bargh* 1431 FA, *-barugh* 1539 LP, *Hundretheberwe* 1268 *Ass*, *Hundesber(e)gh* 1303 FA, *Hundresbergh* 1340 NI, *-bargh* 1456, 1463 *Weld*[1], *Hondredesberghe* 1361 Ipm, *Hundreddesbarowe* 1542 LP, *Hundredsbarrow* 1687 *Weld*[1], named from Hundred Barrow ('the barrow of the hundred', *v.* hundred, beorg) in Bere Regis par. *supra* which was the meeting place of the old hundred of *Bere*. It is called 'half-hundred' (*dimidium hundredum*) in 1280 because it was taken out of this old DB hundred, *v.* Bere Regis hundred *supra*.

Affpuddle

AFFPUDDLE (SY 805936) [ˈɑːfpidl]
  rus iuxta Pydelan 987 (13) KCD 656 (Finberg 613, S 1217)
  Affapidele 1086 DB, *-pidela* Exon
  Effipidela 1093–1100 (1313) Ch, *Effepidel* 1212 Fees, *-pidela* 1314 (1372) *ChrP*
  Affepidel(e) 1244 *Ass* (p), 1280 *ib*, 1285 FA, *Assepidel(e)* (for *Affe-*) 1268 *Ass*, 1316 FA, *Affi-*, *Affypidele* 1280 *Ass*, *Aftepidele* 1288 *ib*, *Afpidyll* 1428 FA
  Affepud(e)le 1289 Ilch, 1344 (14) Cerne, 1428 FA, *-pudell* 1549 Lane, *As(se)pudele* (for *Af(fe)-*) 1291 Tax, 1346 FA, *Afpud(e)le* 1303 ib, 1332 SR, 1340 NI, 1421 *Weld*[1], 1575 Saxton, *Af(f)t-*

pudele 1327 *SR*, 1400 *Ilch*, *-pudell* 1458 *Weld*[1], *Affpuddle* 1344
(14) Cerne, 1687 *Weld*[1], *Af(f)pudell* 1589 *Feth*
Pudle 1318 Ch
Ediuepudle 1330 Ch
Adpudell 1529 *AD*, *Athpiddell* 1564 *Feth*, *-puddle* 1617 *DuCo*, *Add*

One of several places named from R. Piddle or Trent (*v.* RNs.
infra). The first part of the name *Affa-*, etc. probably represents a
short form (*Æffa*, gen.sg. *Æffan*) of the OE pers.n. *Ælffrið*; according to the charter dated 987 a certain *Ælfriðus* gave to Cerne Abbey
the *rus iuxta Pydelan* 'farm next to the Piddle' of *quatuor cassatos*,
this corresponding with the manor of four hides held here by the
same abbey in DB; the form *Ediue-* shows confusion of the pers.n.
with the OE fem. pers.n. *Ēadgifu*.

PALLINGTON (SY 787912), *Palliton* 1244 *Ass* (p), *Palin-* 1244 *ib*
(p), 1268 *ib* (p), 1288 *ib*, *Palyn-* 1268 FF, 1327 *SR*, *Palyng-* 1316
FA *et freq* to 1428 *Weld*[1], *Pallington* 1589 *Feth et passim*, probably
'farm called after Pælli', from the OE pers.n. *Pælli* adduced by
Ekwall DEPN to explain Palling Nf and Pallingham Sx (cf. PN -ing
59–60, 124), and -ingtūn.

BRYANTS PUDDLE (SY 819932)
Pidele 1086 DB (f. 84b), 1205 FineR
Prestepidel(a) 1093–1100 (1313) Ch, 1220, 1221 Cur, 1225 FF,
1314 (1372) *ChrP*, *Prestpidl'* 1220 Cur, *Prestes Pidele* 1221 ib,
-pidel 1224 ib
Pidel(e)-, *Pydele Turbe(r)(e)vil(l)(e)*, *-uil(l)(e)*, *-vyll(e)* 1238 Cl,
1268 *Ass et freq* to 1373 Cl, *Pudel(e) Turburvile* 1326 FF,
— *Turberville*, *-vyle*, *-uyle* 1370, 1373 Cl, 1390 Fine, 1446 *Weld*[1]
Turberuile Pydele 1268 *Ass*, *Turberuylepudele* 1332 SR, *Turberviles-*,
-vyles-, *-uyles-*, *-uylyspudel(l)(e)* 1412, 1431 FA, 1442, 1443
Weld[1]
Brianis Pedille 1465 IpmR, *Bryans* —, *Brians Pud(d)ell*, — *Puddle*
1480 ib, 1553 *Feth*, 1565 AD V, 1607 *Feth* (— *alias (dict')*)
Pud(d)ell Turbervyle, *-fyld*), *Brians Pyddell* 1564 *ib*, *Bryanspidle*
1606 *ib*, *Brientes Piddell* 1588 ib, *Briantspuddle* 1687 *Weld*[1]
Pudell —, *Pudyll Bryan* 1504 Ipm

Like Affpuddle *supra*, named from R. Piddle or Trent. The affix
Prest(e)(s)- probably derives from the tenure of the DB manor of

Pidele by Godric *presbiter* ('the priest'), *v.* prēost, VCHDo **3** 112, 134. The later affixes are from the family of *de Turbervill* (Hugh *de T(h)urbervill* 1205 FineR, 1225 FF, Robert *de Turbervill* 1238 Cl, cf. Winterborne Muston in Winterborne K. par. *supra* and Melbury S. par. *infra*), and from the first name of one member of this family (*Brian* de Turbervill 1316 FA, 1327 Ch). There is mention of a mill here in 1086 DB (VCHDo **3** 112), cf. *The Mill Farm* 1838 *TA*.

THROOP (SY 826931), *Pidele la Trop'* 1237 Cl, *Thrope* 1268 *Ass*, 1580 *Feth*, *Trope* 1280 *Ass*, *le Thrope* 1386 Cl, *Thro(o)pe als. Piddle* 1554 Hutch[3], *-als. Pudyll, -Pudle* 1580, 1609 *Feth*, *Thorpe als. Thrope als. Pudle* 1594 *DCMDeed*, *Throupe-*, *Throwpe als. Pudle* 1611 *Feth*, *Thorpe* 1649 SC, 1811 OS, *v.* þrop 'outlying farm, secondary settlement', cf. *Throop* in Tolpuddle par. *infra* which is only some 2 miles distant and with which it has sometimes been confused (e.g. by the indexer of 1285 FA, by Boswell 2, etc., cf. Fägersten 168). Throop is situated near the bdy between Affpuddle and T. Puddle par. *infra* on R. Piddle or Trent; it is identified with one of the DB manors called *Pidele* by DBGeography 74 ff.

AFFPUDDLE HEATH, *le heath* 1612 *Feth*, *Affpiddle Heath* 1811 OS. AFFPUDDLE MILL, cf. *Mill Ho & Gdn* 1838 *TA*; there were two mills in Affpuddle in 1086 DB (VCHDo **3** 75). BOSWELL'S MOUNT, 1809 Brock, cf. George *Boswell* 1802 ib. BOUND STONE PLANT., cf. *the boundstone* 1612 *Feth*, *v.* boundstone. BROOK BARN, 1838 *TA*, cf. *Brook (Common) Md(w)* 1838 *ib.* BRYANTS PUDDLE FM (cf. *Briants' Puddle Ctg* 1838 *TA*) & HEATH (*the heathe* 1564 *Feth*, *Bryans Piddle Heath* 1811 OS), from Bryants Puddle *supra*. OLD CHALK PIT, cf. *The Chalk Pitt*, *Chalk Pit Fd* 1838 *TA*. CULL-PEPPERS DISH, *Hurle-Pepper*, or *Cull-Pepper's Dish* 1774 Hutch[1], *Culpeppers Ditch* 1811 OS, the largest of a number of round shallow depressions in the heath caused by faults in the tertiary strata, from the surname *Culpepper* and ModE dish 'shallow vessel' used in a figurative sense; other depressions are known as *Culpepper's Spoon* and *the Devil's* or *Hell's Pit* (Hutchings 90). If the hollows were notable for herbs, the allusions are perhaps to Nicholas *Culpeper*, author of the popular *English Physician Enlarged or the Herbal*, 1653. DEAD WOMAN'S STONE, *The Dead Woman* 1839 *TAMap*, on bdy between Affpuddle and T. Puddle. DOUBLE BARROW, *(Weste)rowbarrow(e)* 1559 *Feth*, *Row Barrow* 1811 OS, 'rough barrow' from rūh (wk. obl. *rūgan*) and beorg, cf. Rowbarrow hundred *supra*; tumulus marked 6".

EAST FM, 1838 *TA*, E of Affpuddle village. GATE BARN, 1811 OS, *Gate* 1580 *Feth*, *v.* geat 'a pass, a gap in the hills'. GRAVEL PITS. HILL (lost, SY 817927), 1811 OS, probably identical with *a hill or heathy ridge called Bladen, Blagden or Blackdown* 1774 Hutch[1], *v.* blæc, dūn. THE HOLLOW, *v.* hol[1]. LANDSHARE COPPICE, cf. *Lanchard hedge* 1559, *Lansher hedge,* — *hyll* 1564, *le Lawndsheere Close* 1580, *the Lanchard Close* 1611 all *Feth*, *v.* land-sc(e)aru 'boundary'; it is close to the Affpuddle–Turners P. bdy. MARL PITS WD, *Marlinge Pitt* 1590 *Feth*, *Marling Pitts* 1838 *TA*, — *Pits Wood* 1861 Hutch[3], cf. *Marlinge Waye* 1590 *Feth*, *Marl Plot* 1838 *TA*, *v.* marling, marle, pytt. NORTH BARN, *The* — 1838 *TA*, N of Affpuddle village. OAKERS WOOD (CTG & HO), *Wolgariswode* 1465 IpmR, *Aulgers Wood* 1694 Brock, *Okerswood* 1795 Boswell, 1838 *TA* (— *Ho*), *Okers' Wood Plant.* 1838 *ib*, the surname *Woolgar* (OE *Wulfgār*), *v.* wudu, cf. Woolgaries Moor in Moreton par. *supra.* PALLINGTON CLUMP, COPPICE, FM (*Palling Fm* 1838 *TA*), & HEATH (1838 *TA*, cf. *in boscis domini...anglice Busshes in Le Heathe* 1590 *Feth*, *v.* busc, hǣð), all from Pallington *supra.* RIMSMOOR POND, 1811 OS, — *Water* 1826 Gre, perhaps from rima 'rim, edge', and mōr. ROGER'S HILL (CTGS & FM), *Roger(e)s Hill* 1504 Ipm, 1553 *Feth*, — *Hyll* 1559 *ib*, *Rogers' Hill Fm* 1838 *TA*, cf. *Joane Rogers house* 1664 HTax, *v.* hyll. ST LAWRENCE'S CHURCH, cf. *ecclesie de Affepudele* 1289 *Ilch.* SARES WD, *Sares'* — 1838 *TA*, cf. *Sares Fd* 1838 *ib*, John *Sare* 1611 Brock, Hugh *Seare* 1664 HTax. SMOKEHAM BOTTOM, (— *Close*) 1838 *TA*, cf. *le Wale apud Smokeley hedge* 1609 *Feth*, probably land held by payment of 'smoke-money', *v.* smoca, lēah, hamm, wall or walu, hecg, cf. Smoakhams in Winfrith N. par. *supra.* SPRING COPPICES, cf. *Springfield* 1838 *TA*, from a spring marked 6″, *v.* spring; the watercress beds here are known as *The Silver Springs* (Hutchings 91). SPYWAY (CTG), *Spyway* 1769 Brock, 1811 OS, cf. *Spyway Md & Pasture, West Cl or Spyway Cl* 1838 *TA*, no doubt analogous with Spyway Barn in Langton Mat. par. *supra*; there is only a gentle rise in the ground here. SQUIBBS BOTTOM, cf. John *Squibb* 1664 HTax. STARMOOR PLANT., 1838 *TA*, *Starmor* 1564 *Feth*, perhaps from stær 'a starling' (cf. Do dial. *stare*, Barnes 105), and mōr. SYMMONDS' FM, cf. *Robte' Symondes house* 1664 HTax. THROOP CLUMP & HEATH (1774 Hutch[1]), from Throop *supra.* TWO GATES, on R. Frome, cf. *les hatches et weare* 1606 *Feth*, *v.* hæc(c), wer. VICARAGE, *Parsonage Ho* 1838 *TA*, cf. *le parishe house* 1592 *Feth*, *the personage grounde* 1593 *ib.* WADDOCK COPSE, CROSS, DROVE & FM, *Waddoke* 1564 *Feth*,

Waddock(e) 1612 *ib*, 1647 SC, (— *Coppice*, — *Fm Ho*, — *Md*, — *Mill*) 1838 *TA*, *Wadduck* 1674 Seymer (p), *Waddick fm* 1774 Hutch[1], perhaps 'oak-tree near the ford', *v.* (ge)wæd, āc; the farm lies beside R. Frome near Hurst Bridges in Moreton par. *supra*, cf. *le Cause Waye inter Waddock et Hurst* 1612 *Feth*, *v.* caucie. WELL HO. WEST FM (2 ×), one is W of Affpuddle village, cf. East Fm *supra*, the other is W of Bryants Puddle village. WILCOCKS' WD, *Welcocks'* — 1838 *TA*, cf. Thomas *Wilcocks* 1687 *Weld*[1]. WOOD BARN, 1811 OS, cf. *le Woode* 1606 *Feth*, *Woode furlonge* 1607 *ib*, *Wood* 1838 *TA*, *v.* wudu.

FIELD-NAMES

The undated forms are 1838 *TA* 2. Spellings dated 1327 are *SR*, 1332 SR, 1546, 1655, 1722 Hutch[3], 1581, 1599, 1629, 1634, 1635, 1642, 1653, 1725, 1759, 1761, 1834 Brock, 1664 HTax, 1774 Hutch[1], 1840 *TA* alt.app., and the rest *Feth*.

(a) Affpuddle Mdw; Arable Fd; E & W Arnolds' (cf. Christine *Ernald* 1327); Ashclose, Ash Plant. (cf. *Asheley* (*Downe*) 1553, 1564, *v.* æsc, lēah); Field by Barcombs'; Barley Bread or Bottom Breach (possibly a field used for barley, but perhaps a derogatory name for poor land, *barley bread* being inferior to *wheat bread* as in *Piers Plowman* B text Passus VI lines 136–9, cf. Little Breach *infra*); Barn (Cl & Fd); Baycerne (perhaps to be connected with *Heron* 1580, *v.* hyrne 'a nook, a corner'; the first part of the name may be a surname, cf. Philip *Beye* 1327); Bestbury (-*bery* 1606, *Beesbury hedge* 1612, perhaps from bēos 'bent grass' and beorg or burh); Bishops' Md; Bottom Md; Bowers'; Braggs' (Orchd); Butts' Cl (cf. John *Butt* 1664); Calves' Plot; Captains' Grd (cf. Captains Fd in Langton Mat. par. *supra*); Chapels' Cl; Clift (*v.* clif); Coles' Fd; (N & S) Common Fd, Common Fd Enclosure (*the common fieldes* 1611); (N) Common Md(w) (cf. *le Comon* 1553, *the north(e) mead(e)* (*barres*) 1592, 1611, *v.* barre); Coppice (Cl & Fd); Corn Fd; Hr Cotlings (*Coltlanes* 1592); Cowleaze (freq); Creech 1759 (*v.* *crūg); Custon Md & Moor, Custom Moor (*le custome meade* 1609, *Costome Mead* 1611, probably to be associated with *Costington* 1580); Dairy-house; Dollings' Fd & Ham (*v.* hamm); Downshill (*Dungshyll* 1592, *Duncksell* 1607); Drakes' (Fd, Lawn Cl, Md(w) & Coppice) (freq); East Fd (*le eystefelde* 1553); 8 & 11 Acres; Eweleaze; Farm Md; Fir-tree plant.; Fishers' (Coppice & Ham) (freq, cf. *le Fysshpol* 1309 Banco, *v.* fisc, pōl[1]); Folletts' 7 Acres; Fowlers' Fd, Great Md & Plat (*v.* plat[2]); Fuel Ho; Furzy Grd; Under Gales' (cf. William *Gele* 1327); Garden; Hr Gatch, Gatches Orchd (cf. John *Gacch* 1327); Great Fd & Orchd; Green Plot; Grove; The Ham (*Hams, the Hampn* 1559, *le hamme* 1593, *v.* hamm); Harbins' Pdk; Hardys'; Hashills', Haskells 1840; Heath Fd (*Heathfeild hedge* 1606); Higher (Home) Fd; Hill Fd 8 Acres (cf. *Hilclose* 1559); Hills (Fd & Md) (freq) (cf. Mrs *Hull* 1664); Home Fd & Md (cf. *ho(a)me close* 1559, 1612); Hookeys Ctg & Fd; Hoopers' Fd, Md(w) & Southam (cf. South Ham *infra*); Hop Yd; Hunger

Hill 1761 (*Homiger* — 1599); Kite Hill (*v.* cȳta); Labourers Gdn; Landerslake Wear 1834 (*Launders-* 1611 Brock); Lane Cl; Lashmoor, -more (1774, first el. possibly læcc 'stream, bog', *v.* mōr); The Lea (*le lee* 1612, *v.* lēah); Little Breach (cf. *Breach*(*e*)*land*(*e*) 1590, 1593, -*lond* 1602, *v.* brēc, land, cf. Barley Bread *supra*); Little Coppice & Fd; Long Cl & Md; Lower Md & Orchd; (Gt & Lt) Marsh (cf. (*Pallington*) *Marshe* 1590, *the* —, *le Mars*(*s*)*he* 1593, 1612, *the*—, *le Marshe Dytche*(*s*) 1591, 1592, *Marshe Barres* 1591, *v.* mersc, dīc, barre, cf. Pallington *supra*); (Gt & Lt) Mead, Mead Gate Grd, Mead Plot, (The Upr) Meadow (cf. *Meade furlong*(*e*) 1580, 1590, *the Meadowes* 1612, *v.* mǣd); Meadens' (Cl) (cf. James *Meaden* 1664 (Bere R.); Meaders' Md (cf. widow *Meader* 1664); Middle Fd (*le Mydle feylde* 1590, *le Mid*(*d*)*le feild*(*e*) 1606, 1612, *Myddle feild hedges* 1612); Middle Grd; Mill Md (from the mill at Waddock *supra*); Mitchells Upr Piece (cf. Osmund *Michell* 1664); New Enclosure, Fd, Md & Plant.; Niprods' (cf. George *Neppred* 1722; both f.n. and surname should possibly be connected with *Newport* 1590, *a lytle parock of ground called Newportes* 1602, *Nipworth* 1606); North Bridge 1791 Boswell; North East (*Northeast Fild*, *Northeyst fylde* 1559, cf. (*le*) *Northwest felde* 1553, -*fild* 1559); North Fd ((*the gate into the*) *North*(*e*)*felde*, -*fylde* 1559, *the northe fielde* 1589); Norton Fd (*Norden* 1653, *v.* norð, denu); Orchard; (Low) Paddock; The Park (cf. Sheep Sleight and South Fd *infra*, *v.* Cantor & Wilson **13** 79 where a connection with the park of the unidentified *Mansham* 1315 Pat (probably from the OE pers.n. *Mann* with hām or hamm) is tentatively proposed); Pasture Fd; Perkins Plant. (cf. Abel *Perkins* 1664); Plantation; Platt (*v.* plat²); Pond Fd; The Portion Fd; Pounds' Corner Orchd & Pdk (cf. John *Pount* 1664); Rick-yard (cf. *le Reek Barton Close* 1580, *v.* rickebarton); Rideouts' Ho; Roling Bridge 1791 Boswell; Saunders' Heath Fd; Scutts' (Fds & Md) (cf. Thomas *Scutt* 1655); Seymours' Md; Sheafhays' Md (*Sevenhaies* 1629, *Shevenhay* 1725); Sheep Sleight (cf. *Shepe parkes* 1593, *v.* slæget); Sheppards' (Md) (cf. Francis *Shepheard* 1664); Simes Clift Pce, Simes Coppice, Fd & Lower Md (cf. Nicholas *Symms* 1664, *v.* clif); Six Acres; Smiths' Shop (cf. *Smethes Close* 1581 and *Smetham* (*Meade*) 1553, *Smitham*—, *Smytham Meade* 1559, the latter containing either smið 'a smith' or smēðe¹ 'smooth', *v.* hamm); Snooks Long Grd & Md; South Ham Common Md (cf. *Sowthmead* 1564, *the southe meade barres* 1592, *le South Meade* 1612, *v.* mǣd, barre, hamm); South East Fd (*le Southe*(*a*)*st f*(*i*)*eld*(*e*) 1553, 1559, cf. (*le*) *Southwestfelde*, -*fild* 1553, 1559); South Fd (Lower Park); Late Standfields; Stoney Croft (cf. *Stoney Slade* 1599, *v.* slæd); (Under) Stourtons' 9 Acres; 10 Acres; (Home) 13 Acres; 2 Acres Md; Waste; West Fd ((*the gate into the*) *Westefelde*, -*fylde* 1559, *occidentali campo* 1580); West Grd; West Md ((*le*) *Westme*(*a*)*d*(*e*) 1559, 1593); Whitles' Md (cf. *Sydrach Whittle* 1664); Withey-Bed (cf. *terr' voc' a withebere* 1588, *le Wythi-*, *Wythyber*(*e*) 1593, 1602, *v.* wiðig, bearu); Woodrows'; N & S Yearlings (possibly from ere-³ and land, cf. Yarlands in Chickerell par. *supra*); Yedlands (*hedlond* 1559, *v.* hēafod-land).

(b) *and*(*ef*)*forde* 1559, *Anderd* 1634 (perhaps 'ducks' ford', *v.* ened, æned, ford); *the Southe Barres* 1591, *le Barres* 1612 (*v.* barre); *beane stiches* 1606 (*v.* bēan, stycce); *pastur' voc' Bellfordes* 1580 (probably a surname); *blynde lane* 1559 (*v.* blind); *Buck-* 1546, 1593, *Bookemead*(*e*) 1589, 1612 (possibly bucca 'he-goat', *v.* mǣd); *Browne Close* (*v.* brūn[1]); (*le*) *Combe* 1553, 1559, 1580 (*v.* cumb); *Cortclose* 1559 (*v.* court); *le Crossediche apud le Woodende* 1553 (cf. a *Dobble or crosse diche at the corner of the wood betwine Athpiddell and Bryanspuddell* 1564, *v.* cross, dīc, *le Woodende infra*); *Cuthedge* 1606; *Dickinges ditch* 1635 (*v.* dīc); *pastur' voc' Englonde* 1580 (probably from inland); *E(a)st Close* 1553, 1564 (*v.* ēast); (*the*) *eyste me(a)de* 1559, *theast meade* 1589, *Eastmeade* (*barres*) 1591, 1592 (*v.* ēast, mǣd, barre); *Endbarrowe* 1642 (*v.* ende[1]); *le fooldes* 1553 (*v.* fald); *le furlond, le furlonge super villam* 1607 (*v.* furlang); *Gore lane end* 1592 (*v.* gāra); *Greneshylle* 1559 (cf. Edward *Grene* 1664, *v.* hyll); *le halfe Aker* 1559; *Hawkhyll* 1564 (*v.* hafoc); *the Pathe Waie adiacen' Hellyars Parrocke* 1591 (cf. John *Hellyer* 1664, *v.* pearroc); *Hickhills* 1602; *Holme Bush* 1599 (*v.* holegn); *Horse Street* 1599; *claus' voc' Hunts* 1591; *Inwood* 1546 (*v.* in, wudu); *Knoll* 1564 (*v.* cnoll); *Lanes dytche* 1589, —*meere* 1606 (probably the surname *Lane, v.* dīc, (ge)mǣre or mere); *Langlond* 1564 (*v.* lang[1], land); *the Lynes* 1611 Brock (*v.* leyne); *Myddle furlonge* 1580; *le* —, *the mo(o)re* 1580, 1592, 1611, *Morehedge* 1553, 1559, *the Morefurlonge* 1589 (*v.* mōr, hecg); *Morow lese* 1559 (*v.* morgen, lǣs, cf. *Morwelese* in Stinsford par. *infra*); *le* —, *the North(e) Close* 1580, 1611; *Pad linch* 1629 (*v.* padde, hlinc); *Paynes tenement* 1602; *Pathfield* 1593 (*v.* pæð, cf. *Hellyars Parrocke supra*); *Purfurlonge* 1559 (perhaps from pūr 'bittern', cf. Isle of Purbeck *supra*); Red Withies 1599 (*v.* wīðig); *Rowmore* 1589 Brock (*v.* rūh, mōr); *Saltmeade* (*Close*) 1590, 1612 (*v.* salt[2]); *Same londe* 1580; *Short londes* 1606; *the Somer feilde* 1612 (*v.* sumor); *ten' voc' Stones* 1611; *Tylers Tenement* 1612; *le Wale end* 1590 (*v.* wall or walu); *atte Watere* 1332 (p) (*v.* atte, wæter); *the* -, *le Weare* 1592, 1612 (*v.* wer); *Westebarrowe* 1559 Brock, *Vestberye lane end* 1592 (*v.* west, beorg); *Whitland* 1564, *Whytelonde* 1580 (*v.* hwīt, land); *Whitlynche* 1606 (*v.* hwīt, hlinc); *le Woodende* 1553 (*v.* wudu, ende[1], *le Crossediche supra*); *Woodfurlong* 1599; *le Woortcloses* 1612 (*v.* wyrt); *the barrowe in the east of the meyre at Yearmesborowge* 1564 (on a bdy, *v.* (ge)mǣre, beorg; the first part of the name may be an OE pers.n. *Earm* postulated for Armley YW 3 210).

Turners Puddle

TURNERS PUDDLE (SY 831935)

Pidele 1086 DB (f. 83b), *Pidela* Exon, *Pydle* 1280 Ch, *Pudele* 1303, 1346 FA, 1384 *Weld*[1]

Tunerepidel 1242 Sarum, *Toner(e)spydele* 1268 *Ass*, -*pudel(l)(e)* 1327 *SR et freq* to 1458 FF, -*pedell* 1428 FA, *Tun(n)ers-, Tonner(e)spuddel* 1457 *Weld*[1] *et freq* to 1484 IpmR, -*pedyll* 1498 Ipm, *Tunneryspidill* 1474 Pat

Pydele-, Pidel(e) Tunere, -tonere, — *Tonere* 1264 Ipm, FineR, 1268 *Ass et freq* to 1316 FA, *Pudell Tuner,* — *Toner* 1264 (e15) MiltRoll, *Pudel(e) Toner(e)* 1335 Pat, 1443, 1445 *Weld*[1], — *Toners* 1361 *ib*, *Pydell Toner* 1457 *ib*

Tournerspedyll 1428 FA, *Turnerspudell* 1535 VE, *-p(p)ud(d)le,
-Piddle* 1625, 1653, 1683 all *Feth, Tornetts Pedill* (sic) 1549
Lane

Like Affpuddle par. *supra*, named from R. Piddle or Trent. The
manor was held by Walter *Tonitruus* in c. 1086 GeldR, 1086 Exon,
by John *Toneyre* in 1268 *Ass*, and by Henry *Tonere* in 1280 Ch,
1303 FA, etc. (the byname is from Lat *tonitrus*, OFr *toner* 'thunder',
v. Tengvik 382).

SNELLING COPSE, DAIRY & FM (SY 812894), *Snellyng* 1415, 1418
Weld[1] (both p), 1420 *ib* (*prat' apud* —), 1445 *ib* (*piscar' domini apud-*),
1475 *ib* (*pontis apud* —), *Snelling(e)* 1533, 1565 AD V, 1564
Feth, 1625 *ib* (*East* —), 1774 Hutch[1] (*East* —, *West* —), 1838 *TA*
(— *Coppice*, — *Heath & Plant*.), situated on R. Frome (a ford is
marked 6″). This is possibly a manorial name from the ME surname
Snelling (< OE *Snelling*, an -ing[3] derivative of the OE pers.n.
Snell) as supposed by Zachrisson DTR 158, cf. also *claus' cum prat'
in Snellyng nuper Clementis Snellyng* 1443 *Weld*[1]. But the name is
more likely to be a p.n. proper meaning 'Snell's place', from the
OE pers.n. *Snell* and -ing[2], an early p.n. type, cf. the occurrence in
the neighbouring par. of Affpuddle of a Walter *Snel* 1327 *SR*; the
p.n. would then have given rise to a surname (*de*) *Snellyng*.

WESTMYNGTON (lost), 1416, 1442, 1445 all *Weld*[1], 1626 *Bartelot,
Westmauston* (probably for *-man-*) 1316 FA, *Westmynton* 1344 Cl,
Ipm, 1352 FF, 1421, 1422 *Weld*[1], *Westmonton* 1457, 1462 *ib*, probably
'farm of the western dwellers', from west, mann (gen.pl. *manna*),
tūn, cf. Westmanton D 180, Westmancote Wo 103. This seems to
have been the name of a farm or tithing in this par., but it is associated
with Shitterton and Southbrook in 1316 FA, and with Shitterton
and White Lovington in 1626 *Bartelot* (all in Bere Regis par. *supra*),
so it is probably to be located to the N or E of Turners Puddle, 'west'
in the name being in relation to Bere Regis.

BROCKHILL (COPPICE), *Brockholes* 1664 HTax, *Brockhall* 1811 OS,
Brockhill Barn Grd & Fm 1838 *TA*, 'badger holes', *v*. brocc-hol.
BUCKSHILL COPPICE, *Bucks' Hill, Buckshill Wd* 1838 *TA*, cf. *pratum
nuper Johannis Bucke* 1430 *Weld*[1], *Joh' Bukke pro 1 molend' fullon'*
1457 *ib, tenura Thome Bukke voc' Allerhams* 1476 *ib*, cf. Alderhams'
Coppice *infra*; the mill would probably have been on R. Piddle or

Trent beside which Buckshill is situated. CECILY BRIDGE, *Cecil's* —
1791 Boswell. CLOUDS HILL, 1811 OS, *Clouds' Plant.* 1838 *TA*, *v.*
clūd 'a rock, a rocky hill', but perhaps a surname. DAIRY HO, 1811
OS. DAMER HILL, DAMERHILL COPPICE & CTG, *Damer Hill Fd*,
Damers' Coppice 1838 *TA*, possibly from a surname, but perhaps to be
compared with Damerham W 400 the first el. of which is dōmere
'a judge'. EAST PLANT., 1838 *TA*, *Eastern* — 1839 *TAMap*. EWE-
LEAZE COPPICE. FOXBURY, part of a plant. near par. bdy, 'fox's earth',
v. **fox**, **burg**. FURZE COPPICE, cf. *Furzy Grd (Coppice)* 1838 *TA*.
GULLY COPPICE, *claus' voc' Gelet* (probably for *Golet*) 1457 *Weld*[1],
Gulletclos 1480 *ib*, *Gully Grd (Brake)*, *Gullys' Cow Leaze* 1838 *TA*,
v. **goulet** 'a gully, a ravine'. HOLY TRINITY CHURCH, cf. 'the chapel
of *Pydele Tonere*' 1309 FF, 'the Free Chapel of Toner's Pudle'
1405 Hutch[3], *Church Croft(s)* 1646, 1662 *Feth*. LONGCROFT COPPICE,
Long Croft 1838 *TA*. MILLICENT'S PLANT., *Mellicents'* — 1838 *ib*.
MORETON DRIVE & PLANT., from Moreton par. *supra*, cf. foll.
NORTH LODGE, *Lodge* 1811 OS, at the end of Moreton Drive which
leads into Moreton Park, cf. prec. PIDDLE WD, (*-mead*) 1838 *TA*,
cf. John *atte Wode* 1361 *Weld*[1], *Tonner(e)s Wodd* 1456 *ib*, *-wod(e)*
1461–1476 *ib*, *bosc' de Tonnerspudell* 1470 *ib*, *v.* **atte**, **wudu**, par. name
supra. TURNERS PUDDLE HEATH, cf. *la Hethfeld (de Snellyng)* 1386,
1475 *Weld*[1], *le heath* 1625 *Feth*, *ye North* —, *ye South heath* 1668 *ib*,
The Common Heath, *The farm heath*, *Heath Grd*, *The Heath Lots'
Plant.* 1838 *TA*, *Toner's Puddle Fm Heath* 1839 *TAMap*, *v.* hǣð.
PURGATORY, heathland near par. bdy. ROUND BARROW, tumulus
marked 6″. SPRING GDN BARN & COPPICE, *Spring Gdn (Barn Grd)*
1838 *TA*, cf. *Spring Bridge* 1791 Boswell, *Springs' Md* 1838 *ib*, *v.*
spring. THROOP HOLLOW, from Throop in Affpuddle par. *supra*.
WOOL CAMP, a modern army camp, from Wool par. *supra*.

FIELD-NAMES]

The undated forms are 1838 *TA* 232. Spellings dated 1244, 1268, 1288 are
Ass, 1285 FA, 1327 *SR*, 1332 SR, 1340 NI, 1607, 1618, 1625, 1646, 1653,
1662, 1668, 1685 *Feth*, 1664 HTax, 1689 Hutch[3], 1791 Boswell, and the rest
Weld[1].

(a) Alderhams' Coppice (*venella que ducit versus Allerham* 1442, 1473,
Alleramlane 1464, *tenura…voc' Allerhams* 1476, *Alleram* 1483, probably a
manorial name from the family of *de Al(e)reham* 1244, 1268, 1288, (*de*)
Alresham 1285, 1327, 1332, 1340, *Al(le)ram* 1384, 1457, though the surname
itself may be a local p.n. from **alor** 'alder' and **hamm**, cf. *Allerclos* 1442 *et
freq* to 1480, *Alreclose* 1445, *Aldermoore* 1625, *lez Alders* 1646, *v.* **clos(e)**,

mōr); Alners' Coppice (the surname *Alner*, cf. Tucking Md Alner *infra*); Bate Fd; Batts' Cl; Berry Cl; Boggy Cl; Bottles Md; Boyts' fd; Brake (*v.* bræc[1]); Brick Cl (Ctg), Brickiln Cl; Bridle Bishops' Ctg; Brushet fd (*v.* brushet); Butts' House fd, Lr Butts'; Calves' Plot; Chilcots' Enclosure (cf. William *Chaldecote* 1416); Cock pit (*v.* cockpit); (Lr) Cockroad (*v.* coccrodu); Coneygare (*v.* coninger); Coppice (Cl & Md) (*Coppice* 1668); Court hays (*v.* court, (ge)hæg); Cow Leaze (freq); Cowlers' Coppice; Cow pasture; Curtis' new md; (Lt) Dry Md; East fd; East Side coppice; The farm mdw; Field between the woods; 15 & 5 Acres; Fords' Home Md & Orchd (cf. *claus' iuxta la-, -le Forde* 1442, 1445, Edmund *Ford* 1689, *v.* ford); 40 acres; Frog Hams' (*v.* frogga, hamm); Hill Cl; Hog Leaze; Horse Cl (cf. *claus' voc' Hors(e)crofte* 1437, 1445, *v.* hors, croft); Island; Knowles' (Plot & 7 Acres) (cf. widow *Knowles* 1664); Lanishay (*Lamesy* 1445); Lears' Cl; Ledgey Platt (*v.* plat[2]); Little Wd; Locks'; Long bridge md (*prat' iuxta Longbrigge* 1473, *Longebridge* 1607, *-brydge* 1618, *Long Bridge* 1791, *v.* lang[1], brycg); Lower Ho & Md; Lumington's md; Main Platt (*v.* plat[2]); Middle Bridge 1791; Mill Md (cf. Bernard *Molendinarius*, Robert *le Muleward* 1327, John *at(t)e Mylle*, — *Mille* 1361, 1443, 1446, *molend' aquatic'* 1361, *Mulham* 1383, (*le*) *Mulleclos(e)* 1424, 1445, (*le*) *Mill(e)clos(e)* 1470, 1625, *v.* myln, atte, hamm, clos(e); there was a mill at T. Puddle in 1086 DB (VCHDo 3 105), cf. also Tucking Md Alner *infra*); Moreton Main Bridge Plant. (from Moreton par. *supra*); Mount Fd; New Inclosure; (Lt) New Md (*Nywe-* 1442, 1457, *le Nuwe-* 1445, *Newmede* 1477, *v.* nīwe, mǣd); New Plant.; 9 Acres; Norden middle & West Grd (*Northdon* 1416, 1417, *Nordon* 1418 *et freq* to 1478, *-mede* 1442, 1445, *Ouer-* 1442 *et freq* to 1480, *Nether-* 1456, *Nithernordon* 1480, *Ouer Northdoun* 1460, *clausuris voc' Northdones* 1461, *v.* norð, dūn, mǣd, uferra, neoðerra); (Old) Orchard (*claus' voc' le Orchard* 1456, *Southorchard* 1475, *v.* orceard); Ox Leaze; Paines' md; Parsonage mdw (cf. *terr' Rectoris ville* 1419, *le parsons close* 1646); Philips' 5 Acres & Md (cf. William *Phelippes* 1327); Pit Cl (*Pitt* — 1662, *v.* pytt); Platt (*v.* plat[2]); Popish hill; Rooted Wood (fd & pasture) ('full of roots', or 'rooted and dug up by swine', *v.* rooted); Rough Grd; Salt fd; Sandy Knap fd (*v.* cnæpp); (Boundary Ash) Sedgey Pce (*v.* secgig); 7 Acres; 6 Acres (*les vj acr'*, *lez vj acres* 1445, *v.* æcer); Strap md (*v.* strap); Tarrow's Lane Bridge 1791; 10 Acres; Thomers' md; Tucking Md Alner (cf. *molend' fullon'* 1361, 1417, 1421 (— *cum prat' que Joh' Symond ten'*), *Symondesmull* 1420, *curs' aque apud la Toukyng Mull* 1428, *molend' fulleretic' voc' Southmyll* 1475, 1478, *prat' nuper Roberti Touker* 1430, *v.* tucking-mill, myln, cf. Alners' Coppice *supra*; for another mill in this par., *v.* Mill Md *supra*); Upper Ho & Md; Warren; The West Fm Ho; West fd (*la Westfeld* 1379, *le Westfild* 1458, 1461; West Grd; Wheat fd (*le Whetefild* 1462, *v.* hwǣte, feld); White ship ctg; Woodrows' fd; Wrackmead (*v.* rakke).

(b) *camp' apud Asshenlynches* 1421 (*v.* æscen, hlinc); *Barne Close* 1668 (cf. *grang' domini* 1456); *claus' voc' Bekkes* 1445, *Beckys-* 1456, *Bekkesclos* 1458, 1480 (cf. John *Bekke* 1327 (Affpuddle), *v.* clos(e) (as freq in this par.)); *Byne(s)-* 1437, 1445, *Benescroft(e)* 1476, 1477 (the surname *Bean* rather than bēan 'a bean', *v.* croft (as freq in this par.)); *Berton* 1361 (*v.* beretūn); *Byreweye* 1445 ('the road to Bere', *v.* weg, Bere R. par. *supra*); *claus'*

Bochard' 1361, 1384, *claus' voc' Bouchard'* 1442, 1445 (the surname *Bouchard*); *pastur' de Bouselak* 1361 (*v.* lacu); *Braggeswode* 1457 (the surname *Bragg, v.* wudu); (*le-, la*) *Breche* 1456, 1457 (*v.* brēc); *Bryggemede als. Burgeyesmede* 1442, *Briggemede als. Burgeiesmede* 1445, *prat' voc' Burges* 1457, *Burge(y)smede* 1458, 1477, 1480 (from brycg 'a bridge' or the surname *Burgess* (cf. Adam *Borgeys* 1340), metathesis of *-r-* having taken place, *v.* mǣd (as freq in this par.)); (*le*) *Brod(e)lond* 1442 *et freq* to 1480, *Brodland* 1646, *Broadlands* 1662 (*v.* brād, land); *Brademede* 1361, 1417, 1421, *Brod(e)mede* 1456, 1458 (*v.* brād, mǣd); *Callings* 1646; *claus' voc' Coddys* 1443, *Goddes-* 1480, 1483, *Coddesclos* 1481 (cf. *terr' que Will' Codde tenuit* 1417); *Coob Tenemt'* 1664; *Crockerys-* 1442, *Crokkeresclose* 1445 (cf. *ten' nuper Joh' Crocker* 1422); *furlong' voc' le Croft* 1458; *Estfurlong* 1464, 1473 (*v.* ēast, furlang (as freq in this par.)); *la Vyfhoke, Vyf-, Vifoke* 1419, *Fyfokes* 1421, *Fyueok* 1456, 1458, *Fiveok* 1461 (*v.* fīf, āc); *Fys(s)h(e)po(u)lemede* 1421, 1424, *hamma prati voc' Vyssh(e)polemede* 1442, 1445 (*v.* fisc, pōl¹, cf. *la Were infra*); *cultur' voc' Flourelond* 1445 (cf. the analogous Flower Lands in Charminster par. *infra*); *hamme prati voc' Fox(is)ham(me)* 1419, 1428 (cf. Edward *Foxe* 1361, *v.* hamm); *Fromemede* 1419 (cf. *prat' apud Frome* 1361, *prat' iuxta Fromewater* 1464, from R. Frome (*v.* RNs. *infra*)); *cultur' super-, claus' voc' Grey(e)s* 1445, *Grey(e)sclos(es)* 1456, 1461, 1480 (the surname *Grey*); *Hakneylond* 1462 (*v.* hakeney, land); *Ham Meade* 1662 (*v.* hamm); *Houdeman(n)esclos* 1416, 1417, *claus' voc' Houdemannys* 1445 (cf. Walter *Hodman* 1327); *Hoggards als. Vivians Tenement* 1685 (cf. Richard *Vivian als. Hoggards* 1662); *Home Close* 1668; *la Hurste* 1417 (*v.* hyrst); *Hymbury* 1442 (possibly 'high hill or barrow', *v.* hēah (wk. obl. hēan), beorg); (*le*) *Knapp* 1456, 1461 (*v.* cnæpp); *Lanclawes* 1417, *-clawyn* 1442, *-claus* 1464, *Landeclawyn* 1445, *Langclaus(e)* 1462, 1480 (perhaps 'long claws of land', from lang¹ and clawu, *-yn* representing a new ME wk.pl.); (*le*) *Le(y)gh* 1456, 1461, 1462 (*v.* lēah); *La Lynch in la Westfeld* 1379 (*v.* hlinc, West fd *supra*); *little Ham* 1668 (*v.* hamm); *Lytel(l)mede* 1437, 1445 (*v.* lȳtel); *Lit(t)el-, Lyt(t)elmo(u)r(e)* 1361 *et freq* to 1457, *Littyl-* 1428, *Litulmore* 1456 (*v.* lȳtel, mōr); *Lordesclos* 1416 (*v.* hlāford); *Lupyate* 1383 (*v.* hlīep-geat); *Marlyngput* 1428 (*v.* marling, pytt); *Medeclose* 1457 (*v.* mǣd); *Merslade* 1383 ((ge)mǣre or mere, with slæd); *la Middeldich* 1361 (*v.* middel, dīc); *le Middelforlong* 1445; *Netelmore* 1476 (*v.* netel(e), mōr); *le —, the Nether garden* 1625, 1653 (*v.* neoðerra, gardin); (*le*) *Northfild* 1456, 1462, 1480, *-feld* 1464 (*v.* norð, feld); *Nottings Tenement* 1668; *Oate Close* 1668 (*v.* āte); *le Ouercroft* 1456 (*v.* uferra); *Paie-, Pathehay* 1416, *Pagehey* 1457, 1462 (cf. John *Page* 1332, *v.* (ge)hæg); *Palfrayhyll* 1475 (*v.* palefrei, hyll); *Peked Close* 1662 (*v.* peked); *le Pyke-, Pikeacr(e)* 1445 (*v.* pīc, æcer); *claus' voc' Potellesplace* 1383 (the surname *Pot(t)ell, v.* place); *Prestham* 1442 (*v.* prēost, hamm); *claus' voc' Puysleys* 1470 (cf. *ten' Johannis Pyseley* 1464); *lez Runninge Hams in East Snellinge* 1625 (*v.* running, hamm, Snelling *supra*); *Shrepeswell* 1445 (possibly a metathesised form of the surname *Sharp*, cf. foll., *v.* wella); *Sharpes otherwise Vincents Tenement* 1662 (cf. prec., John *Sharp* 1664); (*la*) *Southfeld* 1417, 1464, 1476 (*v.* sūð, feld); *Stokemanys-* 1442, *-mannesclos(e)* 1445 (cf. William *Stokman* 1327); *Top(pe)hey(e)* 1442, 1445, 1456, *Toppis-* 1473, *Toppeshey* 1480, *Toppis-, Toppys-* 1456, *Topsclos, Topmede* 1458 (the surname *Topp, v.* (ge)hæg); *hamme prati voc' Trendell*

1419 (v. trendel); *la Were* 1418, *la (Fysh)wer* 1421, *hamme prati voc' Werham*
1419 (cf. *piscar' aque domini . . . de Tonerspudele* 1419, *v.* fisc, wer, hamm, cf.
Fyshpolemede supra); *la Whitedich* 1419 (*v.* hwȳt, dīc); *Wod(e)furlong* 1445,
1457 (*v.* wudu); *Wollakes* 1476 (possibly from wella and lacu); *le yet-* 1361,
1384, *le ʒetcrof(f)te* 1361, *claus' voc' (le) Yat(e)croft(e)* 1442 *et freq* to 1477,
la Gate 1417, 1418, *ate Yate* 1443, 1444 (both p), *Gatefurlong* 1445, *le
Yatehous* 1483 (*v.* geat, atte, hūs).

VII. PUDDLETOWN HUNDRED

In c. 1086 GeldR the hundred included Piddlehinton and Dewlish (Anderson
117, VCHDo 3 130–1); these are both now separate liberties but have been
included again here for topographical convenience. Besides Dewlish itself,
Dewlish liberty contained *Milborne Church(s)ton* in Milborne St Andrew par.
infra (Hutch[1] 1 476).

PUDDLETOWN HUNDRED, *Pideletone hundret* c. 1086 GeldR, *Pideleton'-
hundredum* 1188 P, *hundredum de Pid(d)elton* 1199, 1210 ib *et freq*
to 1428 FA, *hundr' de Pideleton* 1212, 1227 Fees, 1256 FF, 1275 RH,
and spellings as for Puddletown par. *infra*. Named from Puddletown
which was the *caput* of the hundred and to which manor it was
annexed (Anderson 117). For a possible meeting-place of the
hundred, *v.* the lost f.n. *Modbergh* in Puddletown par. *infra*, cf. also
domus vocat' le Hundred House 1625 *Wal.*

DEWLISH LIBERTY, *hundred of Deuelissh, -lysh* 1337, 1354 Pat,
Hundr' de Deulich 1520 PlR, *Leberty of Devl', Liberty of Diulish*
1641 *Ilch*, *v.* Dewlish par. *infra*.

PIDDLEHINTON LIBERTY, 1795 Boswell, *Liberty of Piddle Hinton*
1664 HTax, *v.* Piddlehinton par. *infra*.

Athelhampton

ATHELHAMPTON (SY 771942) ['æþəlæmtən]

Pidele 1086 DB (f. 77a), 1204 Cur, 1212 Abbr, FF, *Pidel'* 1204 P
Pidele Aleume, — *Aloume* 1250 FF, *-aleaum* Ed 1 (1372) ChrP,
    Pudele Aleume 1250 FF
Athel(h)am(e)ston(e) 1270 (1372) ChrP, 1285, 1303 FA, 1332 SR
    et freq to 1502 Pat, *Hathelhamston* 1280 Ass, 1428 FA, *Atheles-
    meton* 1280 Ass, *Athelaneston, Attol(a)meston* 1288 ib, *Ad(e)-
    lan(e)ston* 1288 ib, 1539 AOMB, *Athellamston* 1327 SR,
    Athel(h)amp(e)ston 1346 FA *et freq* to 1757 DCMDeed

(— *otherwise Admiston*), *Adlampston* 1495 Pat, *Adelmyston* 1547
DorR, *Admyston* 1560 ib (p), *Addlemaston* 1575 Saxton
Pidel(e) Athel(h)amston Ed 1 (1372) *ChrP* (p), 1285 FA, 1288 Cl,
-*attelmeston* 1288 *Ass*, — *Athalamston* 1291 Ipm, *Pydele
Athelmeston* 1288 *Ass*, -*athelamston* 1291 Cl
Alamston 1369 Orig
Athelyngton 1428, 1431 FA

'Æðelhelm's farm', from the OE pers.n. *Æðelhelm* and *tūn*, the
earlier name being simply that of R. Piddle or Trent (*v*. RNs. *infra*)
on which it stands; for the DB identification, *v*. Eyton 135–6,
VCHDo **3** 72, 130. The affixes -*Aleume*, -*Aloume*, -*aleaum* are AN
spellings of the pers.n., with reduction of *Æðel*- to *Al*- (cf. also
the later *Alamston*), and vocalization of pre-consonantal *l* in -(*h*)*elm*-
(Zachrisson ANInfl 107 ff, 146 ff, Feilitzen 78, 102). The form
Athelyngton may have been influenced by the spellings for Allington
par. *infra*. The same name survives in a different (perhaps more
popular) form in South Admiston *infra*.

SOUTH ADMISTON, 1863 Hutch³, *v*. par. name *supra*. ATHELHAMPTON
HALL, *Athelhamston Howse* 1637 *Wal*, *Admiston Hall* 1842 *TAMap*;
one room is called *the King's Room* 1774 Hutch¹. CHURCH (Site of),
cf. *the Freechappell of Athelhamstone* 1667 *CH* (also mentioned in
1504 Ipm). CHURCH, built 1862 (Kelly). COWPOUND WD, 1811 OS,
Cow Pound 1842 *TA*, cf. *Cow Lease* 1842 *ib*, *v*. pund. FIR MOUNT.
HENROOST WD, *Henroost* (*Wd*) 1842 *ib*. HIGH WD, 1842 *ib*. LITTLE
KNOLL COPSE, *Lt & Round Knowl* 1842 *ib*, *v*. cnoll. MILOM LANE,
perhaps from **myln** and **hamm**, cf. *Tucking Mill Hams* 1842 *TA*;
there was a mill at Athelhampton in 1086 DB (VCHDo **3** 72). PARK
FM (lost), 1665, 1863 Hutch³, *Park* 1811 OS, from (*fossatum*) *parci
de Athelamstone* 1270 (1372) *ChrP*, *Adlampston Parc* ('100 acres
called —') 1495 Pat, *The Parke* 1667 *CH*, cf. *Park's Bridge* 1791
Boswell, *Park Hill & Mdw* 1842 *TA*, *Hr Park Ctgs* 1860 *TAMap*
(Burleston), *v*. park; this park (on which *v*. Cantor & Wilson **6**
177–180) also gave name to Park Fm in Tolpuddle par. *infra*.
WHITE BRIDGE, *White Rails Bridge* 1860 *TAMap* (Burleston), cf.
pontem de Athelamston 1270 (1372) *ChrP*, *Gt & Lt New Bridge*
1842 *TA*.

FIELD-NAMES

The undated forms are 1842 *TA* 11.

(*a*) Adleys or Abbey Moor (cf. *moram apud Athelhampston* 1462 *Eton*); Broad Fd; The Close (cf. *le Est* —, *le Mydell Closes* 1495 Pat); The Deans; Furzy Plot; Bucklands & Lt Ewe Lease (the surname *Buckland*); Homebush Fd; Homestead; Horse Coppice; Hungry Hill (a derogatory name for poor land); Kings Standing (with reference to wild duck and snipe shooting, *v.* standing); Hr & Lr Meadow; (Old) Orchard(s); Plantation; The Plot; 12 Acres; Wood.

(*b*) *Gaultons Meade* 1637 *Wal*, *Galtons Meadow* 1667 *CH* (cf. Galtons grd in Tolpuddle par. *infra*).

Burleston

BURLESTON (SY 776942)

(*at*) *Burdalueston* 843 for 934 (eME) ASCharters, *Bordelestone* 843 for 934 (17) BCS 739

Pidele 1086 DB (f. 78a), *Pidela* Exon

Burdeleston 1212 Fees, 1280 *Winch*, 1405 *AddRoll*, 1535 VE, 1546 Hutch³, *Burdalston* 1285 FA, *Burdleston* 1383 *AddRoll*, *Burdellaston* 1386 Hutch³, *Burdelston* 1405 *AddRoll*, 1539 *AOMB*, *Burdelleston* 1431 (15) *ChrP*

Burdefueston (probably for -*elues*-) 1280 *Ass*, *Burdolveston* 1292 Banco, *Burdolfston* 1332 SR

Borde(s)leston 1310 Inq aqd, 1311 Pat

Bardalston 1327 *SR*, *Bardolston* 1340 NI

Bourdelston 1354 FF

Burleston 1535 VE *et passim*, *Burston* 1575 Saxton

v. tūn 'farm, estate'; the first el. is a pers.n., possibly *Burdel*; the early form in -*alues*- (in a late copy), as well as the three later forms in -*efues*- (probably for -*elues*-), -*olves*- and -*olfs*-, may be due to confusion of this name with Bardolfeston in Puddletown par. *infra* which lies only ⅔ mile NW. The pers.n. *Burdel*, found in OE only on coins of Athelstan, is taken to be a mistranscription of *Bardel* by Forssner 42, but Mrs V. Smart points out that on the coins in question, four mint-signed coins of Norwich all from different dies, there are three dies *BVRDEL* to one *BARDEL* (with unbarred *A*, perhaps an erroneous inversion), and Mr C. E. Blunt also considers *BVRDEL* the correct form. The pers.n. *Burdel* should perhaps be associated with the pers.n. *Burde* recorded once in DB as the name of the TRE tenant of Rushton in E Stoke par. *supra*, thought by Feilitzen 211 to be possibly from OFr *Burdel* with AN loss of final *l*, cf. Bush-head Gdn in Wareham par. *supra*. Dr von Feilitzen notes: 'The first el. certainly looks like a pers.n. *Burdel* of obscure origin; it is too early for OFr *Burdel* which, on the other hand, may be the etymon of the name on the coins, since moneyers were of course so often foreigners.' However, if the forms from the OE charters (in late copies) are only ME substitutions for OE *Pidele*, Burleston may also contain OFr *Burdel*. Like Athelhampton par. *supra*, Burleston is on R. Piddle or Trent, hence the DB form; for the identification, *v*. Eyton 135–6, VCHDo 3 78, 130.

BURLESTON DOWN, *Burlestone Down & Cliff* 1843 *TAMap*, cf. ½ *acre against* —, *Headland across the Down, Down Cl* 1843 *TA*. BURLESTON DROVE & PLANT. (cf. *New Plant*. 1860 *ib* alt.app.). CHURCH (Remains of), cf. *Church Yd* 1843 *ib*. FRYER'S BRIDGE, *Swires* — 1860 *TAMap*, cf. *Burleston Bridge* 1635 *Wal*. RECTORY, — *Ho* 1860 *TA* alt.app., cf. *Vicarage Ho* 1843 *TA*.

FIELD-NAMES

The undated forms are 1843 *TA* 34. Spellings dated 1280 are *Winch*, 1664 HTax, 1667 *CH*, 1811 OS, 1860[1] *TA* alt.app., 1860[2] *TAMap*. The open fields (Bottom Fd, Home or Hill Fd, & North Fd) were still unenclosed in 1843 *TA*, cf. *RCHM* 3 54.

(*a*) Adam's Batch (cf. Samuel *Addams* 1664, *v*. batch); Barn Grd (cf. *Burleston Barn* 1811); Bottom Fd 1860[1]; Bottom Flg, Flg against Bottom (*v*. botm); Carrion Pit 2 acres (*v*. carrion); Cattle Pond 1860[2]; Chalk Pit 1860[2]; Coits Cl; Dairy Ho 1860[2]; Dewlish Lane (from Dewlish par. *infra*); Dewlish Old Turnpike Ho 1860[2] (cf. prec.); 4 Acres; 1st, 2nd, 3rd & 4th Furlong; Lr & Upr Furlong; Granges md; Green Cl; Grose's Croft, Green & Hegg (Headland Shooting on —) (cf. Thomas *Grosse* 1664); Halls Moor; Hann's Batch (near Adam's Batch *supra*), Hegg, Md & Moor (Md); Hatch 1860[2] (*v*. hæc(c)); Head Acre (*v*. hēafod); The hegg (against Dewlish) (*v*. hecg, as elsewhere in this par., cf. Dewlish par. *infra*); (the) Hill (Flg on —, Flg Shooting across —); Home Fd or Hill Fd 1860[1]; Home Md; Homeplot; Homestead (— Plot 1860[1]); Jesse's Batch (near Adam's Batch *supra*) & Moor; Little Md; Malt Ho; Hr & Lr Mead; The Moor; (Gt) Moor Md; New Cl (Drove); New Grd 1860[1]; North Fd 1860[1]; Orchard; Poor Ho; Priors Upr & Lr Mead (cf. *Priors Mead* 1667, probably the surname *Prior*); Prospect Fd 1860[1]; Road Cl; Shelves (*v*. scelf); Under Acre.

(*b*) *atte Mulle* 1280 (p) (*v*. atte, myln; there was a mill in Burleston in 1086 DB *v*. VCHDo 3 78); *atte Putte* 1280 (p) (*v*. pytt).

Dewlish

Dewlish is a liberty, *v.* note under Puddletown hundred *supra.*

DEWLISH (SY 776983) ['dju:liʃ, 'du:liʃ]

Devenis 1086 DB

Deueliz 1194 P, 1230 Cl, 1244 *Ass*, 1267 Pat (p), 1316 FA,
Deuelis, -lys 1196 ChancR, 1197 P, 1238 Pat *et freq* to 1300
Ipm, *-leis* 1204 ClR, *-lich* 1236 Ipm, 1346 FA, *-l(l)iss(e)*,
-lysse m13 (c. 1447) *Vaux*, 1254 FF, 1264 Ipm, 1428 FA,
-lis(s)(c)h(e), -lys(s)(c)h(e) 1261 (c. 1447) *Vaux*, 1288 *Ass et freq*
to 1575 Saxton, *-liz* 1300 Ipm, *Develysse* 1291 Tax, *-lyz* 1299
Cl, *-lissch* 1340 NI, *-lych, -lyssh* 1501 Ipm, *-leysshe* 1514 *PlR*,
-lishe, -lysshe 1635 *Ilch*, *Deuiliz* 1300 Ipm

Duuelis 1195 P, *-liz* 1195 ib, 1196 ChancR, *Dueliz* 1300 Ipm

Douelis, -lys 1212 Fees, 1244 *Ass* (p), 1268 *ib*, 1325 Pat (*Est-*,
West-), *-lyz* 1244 *Ass*, *-liz* 1300 Ipm, *Doflis, Douyliz* 1244
Ass, Dovelz 1245 FF, *Donelichs* (for *Doue-*) 1248 ib (p), *Douelich*
1303 FA, *-lys(s)h(e)* 1325, 1412 Cl

Divelich 1234 *Cecil, -lish* 1321 FF, 1636 *Ilch, Diuilis, -lys* 1259
(c. 1447) *Vaux*, 1264 Ch, *Dyvelys* 1280 QW, *Diuelissh* 1484 Cl

Dewelisshe 1481 Cl, *Du(e)-, Diulish(e)* 1613, 1637, 1641 *Ilch*,
Dewlsh 1636 ib, *Dewlish* 1641 ib

Named from the stream now called Devil's Brook (*v.* RNs. *infra*)
which runs S through the village to join R. Piddle or Trent. For the
DB spelling, *v.* Zachrisson ANInfl 128.

CHEBBARD FM (SY 762982) & CLUMP ['tʃibəd], *Scaborth(e)* 1335
(c. 1447) *Vaux, Chebbord* 1765 Tayl, *Chebbard (Fm)* 1811 OS,
1844 *TA*, probably to be associated with the bdy mark *be suþe
Scaftesbury* 859 ? for 870 (15) *ShaftR* (S 334), *be suðe ceatwanberge*
? 870 (15) *ib* (S 342), *on shete bergh, of þane berghe* 1019 (15) *ib*
(S 955 (1)) (a point in the bounds of Cheselbourne which belonged
to Shaftesbury abbey, hence the scribal error *Scaftesbury*). The final
el. of the OE name is **beorg** 'hill, barrow', whereas Chebbard itself
would seem to contain **bord** 'board, plank', also 'border, rim' (it is
near par. bdy), cf. Borthwood Wt 53 and the use of the cognate
byrde in Stibbard Nf (DEPN). However, the first part of the two
names may be identical, although its form and meaning are difficult
to establish. Fägersten 173 suggested an OE pers.n. *Ceatwa*, a wk.

form of the pers.n. postulated for Chaceley Wo 192 (*Ceatewesleah* 972 (c. 1050)); however Ekwall (DEPN) thinks that the first part of Chaceley is more likely to be identical with Chittoe W 252 (*Chetewe* 1168), which is probably from PrWelsh *cẹd* 'wood' with the suffix *-iu* or *-öü* (ultimately from Brit **Caitou̯iā*). It should perhaps be noted that there are signs of RB occupation just W of Chebbard Fm (RCHM 3 88, 331).

ALL SAINTS' CHURCH, cf. *capella de Deuelys* m13 (c. 1447) *Vaux*, *capella de Develissch* 1340 NI, *Church Yd* 1844 *TA*. (OLD) CHALK PIT, cf. *Chalkpit Fd* 1844 *ib*. CRAWTHORNE FM, cf. *Crowthorn 3 & 4 acres* 1843 *ib* (Burleston), *Crothern (Barn) Fd* 1844 *ib*, v. crāwe, þorn, cf. Crowthorne Gl 1 47. DENNET'S BOTTOM BARN, *Denners Bottom* 1844 *TA*, v. botm. DEWLISH HR FM, cf. Lower Fm *infra*. DEWLISH HO, 1811 OS, *Mansion Ho* 1844 *TA*. DEWLISH PARK, cf. Park Hill *infra*. DEWLISH MILL, 1811 OS, cf. *molend'...de Deueliz* n.d. (1372) *ChrP*, *Water Grist Mill* 1613, *the bridge in the high way above the Mill* 1635, *the bridge about the Mill* 1640 all *Ilch*, *Mill Hams* 1844 *TA*, v. myln; there is mention of a mill here in 1317 (RCHM 3 88). HAZEL COPSE. JOCK'S HILL. LORD'S DOWN, 1811 OS. LOWER FM, *Dewlish Fm* 1811 OS, cf. Dewlish Hr Fm *supra*. MANOR FM, cf. the f.n. Court Close *infra*. PARK HILL, 1844 *TA* (— *Coppice & Mdw*), from Dewlish Park *supra*. PARSONAGE BARN, — *Ho Barn* 1844 *TA*, cf. *Parsonage Fd & Mdw* 1844 *ib*. SHAILES COPSE, CTGS & FM, cf. *Shail's Hill Cl* 1844 *ib*. WHITELANDS DOWN, 1844 *ib*, from *locum q' vocat' le Whitelond* 1288 *Ass*, *Whytelond* 1335 (c. 1447) *Vaux Whitelands* 1844 *TA*, v. hwīt 'white' (alluding to chalky soil), land, dūn.

FIELD-NAMES

The undated forms are 1844 *TA* 76, Spellings dated m13 (c. 1447), 1335 (c. 1447) are *Vaux*, 1258 *For*, 1340 NI, 1455 *Weld*[1], 1664 HTax, 1667 *CH*, 1766, 1772 DorB, 1774 Hutch[1], 1863 Hutch[3], and the rest *Ilch*.

(a) Ansties Fd & Md (probably a surname from Ansty in Hilton par. *infra*, cf. also Ansty Lane in Milborne St A. par. *infra*); Bakehouse; Barn (Pce); Barns Pdk; Bottom Cl; Bowling Green; Bush Fd; Butts (*ye Buts* 1632, *our Buttes ar in defaute* 1633, v. butt[2]); Calves Plot; Chebbard Bead (perhaps from beat 'turf', cf. burnbeat, Chebbard *supra*); Chinchester (S of Dewlish Ho, known locally as *Chenister* or *Chinister* (ex. inf. Mrs Anne Rainey), and probably the site of the Roman building represented by a mosaic pavement discovered in 1740 (RCHM 3 88); the second el. is ceaster, the first is probably cinu 'a fissure, ravine, chine', with reference to the deep valley of Devil's

Brook, especially to the steep escarpment on the E side); Common Grd (cf. *the Common* 1641); Cotton Barton (perhaps from *cotum* '(at) the cottages', dat.pl. of **cot**, *v.* barton); Court Cl (1635 DCMDeed, *v.* court, probably with reference to Manor Fm *supra*; there are earthworks representing a mediaeval settlement here (RCHM 3 88)); Cowleaze (fd); Crates (*v.* croft); Dairyhouse Md; Derbers Md; Dewlish Down 1863 (cf. *(the) Common Downe(s)* 1633, 1640, *les Downes* 1638, *v.* **dūn**, *Underdoune infra*); Dewlish Ford Bridge 1791 Boswell; Dewlish Wd; Drove Fd (cf. *the Drove* 1639, *v.* drove); Duforling 1772; Durnwood (Down) (*a sheepe slight call'd Thornewood Downe* 1639, *v.* **þorn, wudu, dūn, slæget**); East Fd (— *Feild* 1640); 8 & 18 Acres; Lr Ewelease; Fat Ox (presumably denoting rich pasture, cf. an identical f.n. in Piddlehinton par. *infra*); Fishers Lane; Flippings; 14 Acres; French Grass (*v.* french grass); Graydons; Greatfield; Gundrys Stable Plant. (cf. *Mr Gundrey's Fm* 1774); Hedge Row; Higher Fd; Hollis's; Home Cl, Fd & Plot(t); Hoopers Cl (cf. John *Hooper* 1664); Horse Cmn; Keyles Plott 1772; Kibbeys (Fd & 7 Acres); Kite Hills, Kites Hill Bottom (*v.* **cȳta**); Lanefield; Lillingtons Cl; Long Hill; Longlands (*close called* — 1640); Long Md; (Davis's) Lous(e)l(e)ys (probably from **hlōse** 'pig-sty' and **lēah**, cf. Loseley Sr); Malthouse (Md); Mr Michel's Fm 1774 (from the *Michel* family, here m18, *v.* Hutch³ 2 607, cf. Milborne Michelston in Milborne St A. par. *infra*); Middle Fd(s) & Grd; The Moor (*the Moore* 1631, cf. *Moore Meade* 1633, *v.* **mōr**); (Nanny's) New Cl (*Newclose* 1639); New Md, Orchd & Pce, New Planted Coppice (cf. *the Newe land* 1640); 19 Acres; Nursery; Old Md; Orchard; Paddock (or drying yd); (Green & West) Peak (*v.* **pēac**); Perchard House 1766; Pitts Wd; Plantation (Dogs Kennel); Pond Cl; Poor Ho; (Bulls) Pound (cf. *ye Pownd* 1632, *v.* **bula, pund**); Puddletown Down Grd (from Puddletown par. *infra*); Rookery Hill Coppice, Rookery Md; Rough Cl; 6 Acres; South Down (Coppice & Fd) (cf. *Southwood (Downe)* 1630, 1636, *South Wood Downe & groundes* 1639); Sturts Wd (*v.* **steort**, but perhaps a surname); Tatcombe (*Tadde-, Caddecumbe* m13 (c. 1447), *Catecombe* (probably for *Tate-*) 1335 (c. 1447), probably 'toad-infested valley' from **tadde** and **cumb**, but the OE pers.ns. **Tāda* or *Tāta* are also possible for the first el., cf. Tadnoll in Chaldon H. par. *supra*); 10 Acres; Tideling Down; 20 & 2 Acres; Underwood (Plant.) (*v.* **under**); Water Mdw; West Fd; White's Wd; Wood Cl & Plot; Yardfield (near foll.); Yards (*v.* **gerd** or **geard**).

(b) *Arnoldes tenement* 1638; *Baches* 1639 (*v.* bece¹, bæce); *Balls Cl* 1640; *Mr Baskettes backside* 1640 (*v.* backside; the *Baskett* family had lands in Dewlish from l15, *v.* Hutch³ 2 607); *close called Cliffe* 1640 (*v.* clif); *campis de Deuelissh* 1261 (c. 1447); *Ethersle(y) Wood* 1631, 1638, *Itherlywood* 1667 (probably to be identified with *Edrel, Ederl* 1258, and *bosc' voc' Ederley apud Milborn Sancti Andr'* 1455, possibly from **ēdre** 'stream' and **lēah**, cf. Milborne St A. par. *infra*); *Halls Lane* 1640; *galtons ground called Langdens* 1636 (perhaps a surname *Langden*, cf. John *Gaulton* 1340); *Lowfeldes* 1640; *pasture called Manycraftes* 1636 (*v.* croft); *the Meade Close* 1633; *Underdoune* 1335 (c. 1447), (*close called*) *Underdownes* 1633, 1640 (*v.* under, dūn, cf. Dewlish Down *supra*); *Weythurne* 1335 (c. 1447) ('thorn-bush by the road', from **weg** and **þyrne**).

Milborne St Andrew

The southernmost part of this par. (*v. infra*) was in Dewlish liberty, *v.* note
under Puddletown hundred *supra*. Since 1933, Milborne Stileham par. *supra*
has been included in this par.

MILBORNE ST ANDREW (SY 803975)

> (*æt*) *Muleburne* 843 for 934 (eME) ASCharters, *Muleborn* 843 for
> 934 (17) BCS 739, m13 (c. 1447) *Vaux*, 1285 FA, 1332 SR,
> *-burn(e)* 1288 FF, *Ass* (p), 1293 (c. 1447) *Vaux* (p), 1311 Pat,
> 1334 FF, *Mulborn(e)* 1327 *SR*, 1405 *AddRoll*
>
> *Meleburn(e)* 1086 DB (f. 82b), m13 (c. 1447) *Vaux*, 1254 FF, 1261
> (c. 1447) *Vaux*, 1268 *Ass* (p), 1288 *ib* (p), *-born(e)* m13 (c. 1447)
> *Vaux*, 1263 Misc, *Melleburn* 1244 *Ass* (p), 1254 FF, *Melbourne*
> 1399 Cl
>
> *Milleburn* 1244 *Ass* (p), *-borne* Hy 3 (c. 1447) *Vaux*, *Mileborn(e)*
> 1259 (c. 1447) *ib*, *Milbo(u)rne* 1412, 1428 FA, 1626 *Wal*, 1641
> *Ilch*, *-burne* 1641 *ib*, *Mylborne* 1539 *AOMB*
>
> *Mileburne Sancti Andree* Ed 1 *HarlCh*, *Muleburn(e) St Andrew*
> 1294, 1307 FF, *Mil(e)bo(u)rn(e)-*, *Mylbo(u)rn(e) Seint-*, *-Seynt*
> *Andrewe* 1391 ib, 1514 *PlR*, — (*Sancti*) *Andree* 1410 *Ilch et freq*
> to 1612 *PlR*, — *Sancti Andri* 1451 *Weld*[1], — *Seynt Andrews*
> 1512 *Pars*, — *Sancte Andrie* 1520 *PlR*, — *Saynt Androwe* 1533
> *ib*, — *Androston* 1544 *ib*, — *S'ce Androwes* 1578 *HarlCh*
>
> *Melleb(o)urn Cher(le)ton* (probably for *Cher(che)-*) 1280 *Ass*,
> *Mule-*, *Mileburn Chircheton* 1288 *ib*, *Muleburne and Chercheton*
> 1297 FF, *Milburnchyrcheton St Andrew* 1318 ib, *Myl-*,
> *Milbo(u)rn(e) Church(e)ton* 1417, 1436 ib, 1438 *AddCh*, 1441 Cl,
> 1647 *Bartelot*, — *Chirch(e)ston(e)* 1469 IpmR, 1481 Cl, FF,
> 1703 *PlR*, — *Church(e)ston(e)* 1484 IpmR (— *als. Milborne*
> *Sanct' Andreæ*) *et freq* to 1795 Boswell, — *Chyrcheston* 1512
> *Pars*
>
> *Mylborne Abbottyston* 1512 *Pars*, *Milborne Abbatston* 1611 Hutch[3]
> *Milborne Develish* 1617 *DuCo*, — *Diuelishe* 1617 *Add*

'Mill stream', *v.* myln, burna, cf. Milborne Stileham par. *supra*
and the other Milbornes *infra* in this par. which are named from the
same stream. There was a mill here in 1086 DB (VCHDo **3** 97) and in
1501 Ipm, cf. Corn Mill *infra*. The affixes *-St Andrew*, *-Androston*
and *-Church(s)ton* are from St Andrew's Church *infra*, *v.* cirice,
tūn; the name Milborne St Andrew seems originally to have been

applied only to the S half of the present par. (RCHM 3 175, cf. Hutch³ 2 591, *v.* Deverel Fm *infra*), and the southernmost part of this half seems originally to have comprised the manor of *Milborne Church(s)ton* (probably identical with *Milborne Develish*) which belonged to Dewlish liberty (this settlement is perhaps represented by the medieval remains ¾ mile S of the village, *v.* RCHM 3 178). *Milborne Abbatston* is thought by Hutch³ 2 591 to have been 'probably the same' as Milborne St Andrew, *v.* abbod, tūn; the latter was granted to Milton abbey in 934 (cf. also e15 *MiltRoll* m.4r), and belonged to Cerne abbey in 16th cent (Hutch³ *loc. cit.*).

DEVEREL FM (SY 807987)

> *Muleborn, -burn* 1261 FF, 1264 Ipm, 1303 FA, *Mul(l)ebourne* Ed 2 *HarlCh*, (— *iuxte Middelton*) 1340 *ib*, *Mulborn(e)* 1346 FA, 1356 Ipm
> *Muleburn Deverel(l)* 1316 FA *et freq* with variant spellings *Mil(e)-, Mul-, -bo(u)rn(e)-, -Deuerell* to (— *als. Mil(e)borne Cary*) 1478 Cl, FF, (— *als. Mileborne Cray*) 1478 *HarlCh*, *Mylborne Deuerell' als. dict' Mylborne Carye* 1512 *Pars*, *Milborn-Deverel or Cary* 1774 Hutch¹
> *Deverill Farm* 1839 *TA*

Originally a manor, probably comprising the N half of the present par., *v.* prec., RCHM 3 175, 179, cf. Milton Abbas par. *infra*. It was held by the family of (*de*) *Deverel(l)* (from Deverill W) from m13 (Elias — m13 (c. 1447) *Vaux*, 1261 FF, Ed 2 *HarlCh*, etc., John *de Deverel(l)* 1261 FF) and by Thomas *de Cary* in 1340 *HarlCh*, 1346 FA. Eyton 115–6 identifies *Meleburne* 1086 DB (f. 83a) with this manor, but this form is taken by VCHDo 3 102, 134 to refer to Milborne Stileham par. *supra*.

MILBORNE MAMFORD (lost), 1611 Hutch³, *Mainford* 1795 Boswell, *v.* par. name *supra*. Its location is unknown, but it should perhaps be associated with *Mel(l)eb(o)urneford(e)* mentioned under Milborne Stileham par. *supra*, cf. also Giles *de la Forde* m13 (c. 1447) *Vaux*, *v.* ford. *Mam-, Main-* may represent (ge)mǣne 'communal'.

MILBORNE MICHELSTON (lost), *Mul(e)bo(u)rn(e)-, -burn Michel(e)-ston(e)* 1316 FF, 1325 Orig, 1326 Misc, 1328 FF, 1335 Pat, — *Mychelston* 1392 ib, *Mulbourne als. Milborn Michelston* 1325 Inq aqd, *Michelston* 1412 FA, *Mylbourn(e) Mychel(e)ston* 1417 FF,

1544 *PlR*, *Michaelstone* 1795 Boswell, *v.* par. name *supra*; its location
is unknown, but it is perhaps to be associated with *Michel's farm*
1611 Hutch³ which is said to be in *Milborne Mamford* (*v.* prec.),
Milborne Bek (*v.* Milborne Stileham par. *supra*) and *Milborne
Deverel* (*v.* Deverel Fm *supra*). The affix is no doubt manorial,
cf. John *Michel* 1332 SR (Dewlish), Richard *Michell de Milborne
S'ce Androwes* 1578 *HarlCh*, *v.* tūn; for a later family of this name
hereabouts, *v.* Mr Michel's Fm in Dewlish par. *supra*.

MILBORNE SYMONDESTON (lost), 1611 Hutch³, *Mule-, Mil(e)b(o)urn(e)
Simoneston* 1288 *Ass*, — *Simondeston(e)* 1315 Ass, 1481 Cl, FF,
Mylbo(u)rn(e) Symondeston 1501 Ipm, 1512 *Pars*, *Symondstone* 1795
Boswell, *v.* par. name *supra*. Its location is unknown. The affix is
probably manorial, from the pers.n. or surname *Simon*, cf. *Symon'
Muleborn* Hy 3 Hutch³ (a witness in a Dewlish charter), and tūn.

ANSTY LANE, perhaps 'lane leading to Ansty' (3½ miles NW in
Hilton par. *infra*), but possibly an independent name, *v.* ānstiga.
BREWER'S POND. COLES FM, 1811 OS, from the *Cole* family who
possessed the manor of Milborne St A. from m17, cf. John *Cole* 1664
HTax. CORN MILL, *Devrell Mille* 1647 *Bartelot*, *Deverill Mill* 1839
TA, near Deverel Fm *supra*. DEVEREL BARROW (*the* — 1863 Hutch³)
& DOWN (1811 OS, *The Down* 1839 *TA*), cf. prec. FAIR BARN,
1811 OS, cf. *Fair Pce* 1839 *ib*. FROGMORE HO. GRAVEL PIT. LAWN
BARN, 1811 OS. LITTLE WD. LONGTHORNS (WD), *Long Thorns Cl*,
Longthorns Coppice 1839 *TA*, cf. an identical name in E Stoke par.
supra. MANOR HO (site of), 1839 *TA*. MILBORNE WD, 1811 OS,
— or *Norwood* 1839 *TA*, *Mylbornyswode* n.d. (e15) *MiltRoll*, *North-
wood* 1647 *Bartelot*. THE NURSERY, 1839 *TA*, a small plantation.
ROUGH CLOSE BARN, *Row Cl* 1839 *ib*, *v.* rūh (wk. obl. rūgan). ST
ANDREW'S CHURCH (built from 12th cent.), *ecclesie* (*S'te Andree*) *de
Mileborn* m13 (c. 1447), 1259 (c. 1447) *Vaux*, cf. *Church Cl & Yd*
1839 *TA*, *v.* par. name *supra*. SAND PIT. VICARAGE, *Parsonage Ho*
1839 *TA*. WARREN HILL, 1811 OS, cf. *Out Warren* 1839 *TA*, *v.*
ūt. WEST END BARN, cf. *West end fd* 1839 *ib*, at W extremity of par.

FIELD-NAMES

The undated forms are 1839 *TA* 149. Spellings dated 1459 are *AddRoll*, 1546
Hutch³, 1627, 1647 *Bartelot*, 1636 *Ilch*, 1582, 1637 *Wal*, 1664 HTax, and
1688 *PlR*.
   (*a*) Barns fd; Barton; Black Brake (*v.* bræc¹); Brocklands (cf. *Brookland*

Lane 1637, *v.* brōc, land); Cardinalls Cap Inn; Carters Ho; Chalk Pit; Cliff (*v.* clif); Gt & Lt Common; Coneygar (*v.* coninger); (Lt) Coppice; Copse Ld Pit (cf. *Cops Wood* 1647, *v.* copis); Cowleaze; Down (Fd), (Lr) Downs; Drangway (*v.* drong); Dry Md; (The) Ewe Leaze; The 5 Acres; Foldams; The 4 Acres (hopyard); (Pit in) Foxlinch (*v.* fox, hlinc); (Pit in) Great Fd; The Grove; (Besants & N) Heath Fd (cf. Henry *Bessant* 1664); Heathfield Hopyard; Hogslands; (Pit in) Home Bush (*v.* holegn); (Clump of Firs in) Home Fd; Home Grd; Hop Warehouses & Drying Kilns; Horse Cl; Kite Hills (*v.* cȳta); Launch Grd (*v.* lanch); Hthr & Lr Lime Kilns; Lime pit fd; Hr & Lr Lines (*v.* leyne); Longlands; Long Md; Malthouse; Masons grd; The Mead; Hr, Lr & Middle Mead; Meadow; Milborne Churchstone Bridge 1791 Boswell; Milborne fd (*-towne feild*) 1636; New Cl; North fd (*the Northfeilde* 1627); Oak Tree Grd; (Old) Orchard; Outhouse; Paddock (cf. *little Parrock* 1688, *v.* pearroc); Parish Pit & Pound; The Park, Park Md (*v.* Cantor & Wilson 3 144)); Pasture; Phippets Mdw (cf. Robert *Fippett* 1664 (Dewlish)); Pit fd; Pond; Poor Altmts; Reynolds or Reads Grd (cf. John *Rede* 1459); Royal Oak P.H.; Sawpit (Cl); The 7 Acres (hopyard); The Sheep Down; The 6 Acres Hopyard; Square Fd; Stoney Ld(s Md); 12 Acres; Waste; The Water Mdw; Water Pit; West Cl.

(*b*) *Chipmans coppice* 1546 (cf. Ann *Chipman* 1664 (Puddletown)); *Goreway* 1688 (*v.* gāra); *Grenewaye* 1582 (*v.* grēne[1]); *medius campus* 1688; *australis campus* 1688.

Piddlehinton

Piddlehinton is a liberty, *v.* note under Puddletown hundred *supra*. Little Piddle was transferred to this par. from Puddletown in 1885.

PIDDLEHINTON (SY 716972) ['pidl'hɛːntən]

Pidele called Hinctune (probably for *Hine-*) 1082–4 France
Pidele 1086 DB (f. 79a), 1100–6 France, *Bidele* 1100–4 ib, *Pidle* 1339 Fine
Pidel Hineton 1244 *Ass*, *Pydelinton* 1268 *ib* (p), *-henton* 1440 IpmR, *-hynton* 1449 *Eton*, *Pyddy(l)hynton* 15 *ib*, *Piddlehinton* 1575 Saxton; *Pudel-, Pudylhenton* 1270 (1372) *ChrP*, 1403 Pat *et freq* to 1498 *Eton*, *Pudel(l)(e) Hynton*, *-hynton* 1368 Cl *et freq* to 1480 *Eton*, *-henton* 1544 *PlR*, *Pudylhynton* 1510 *MP*, *Pudehinton* 1569 *Eton*; *Pedyl-, Pedelhynton* 15 *ib*, 1449 *Weld*[1] (p), 1454 *Eton*, *-henton* 1502 *ib*
Hine-, Hynepid(d)el(l)(e), *-pydel(l)(e)* 1244, 1268, 1280, 1288 all *Ass*, 1297 Pat, Cl, 1372 Pat *et freq* to 1423 Cl, — *alias (dict')* *Pydel-, Pidelhington*, *-hyngton* 1438 Fine *et freq* to 1445 (15) *ChrP*, *Hynepide* 1244 *Ass*, *Hynpidel* 1423 Pat; *Hine-, Hynepedel* 1244 *Ass*, 1379 Pat; *Hine-, Hynepudel(l)(e)* 1285 FA, 1291 Tax

et freq to 1431 (15) *ChrP*, — *or/alias Pudel(i)henton* 1427, 1428
Pat, — *alias dict' Pydelhynton* 1445 (15) *ChrP*, *Hynepudle* 1428
FA, *Hynpudel(l)(e)* 1405 *AddRoll*
Hineton 1288 *Ass*
Honi-, Honypedele 1361, 1363 Cl
Hyme Pedill als. Pedillington 1442 *Eton*
Hynnepedyll alias Peydelhynton 1462 Pat

Named from R. Piddle or Trent, cf. Affpuddle par. *supra. Hine-,*
etc. represents the gen.pl. *hīgna* of *hīwan* 'a household (of monks), a
religious community', and *Hineton*, etc. a composition of *hīgna* with
tūn 'farm', cf. Tarrant Hinton par. and Hinton Martell par. both
infra. Piddlehinton belonged to the abbey of Marmoutier in the late
11th cent. (VCHDo **3** 85, 130).

BOURNE FM (SY 730972), *Bourn* 1811 OS, named from the small
stream which flows S from Lyscombe Fm in Cheselbourne par. *infra*
into R. Piddle or Trent; this stream is referred to in the bounds of
Puddletown as *la Bourne* 1270 (1372) *ChrP*, and in other contexts it is
burn 1270 (1372) *ib*, *la bourne* 1306 (1372) *ib*, *v.* burna 'stream'.
Points higher upstream are referred to in the OE bounds of Cheselbourne as *to bur(n)stowe* 859 ? for 870 (15) *ShaftR* (S 334), *to burn-*
stowe (þanen up anlang burnstowe) ? 870 (15) *ib* (S 342), *on burestowe*
1019 (15) *ib* (S 955 (1)), cf. also *anlang burnstowe* 966 (15) *ib* (S 744)
in bounds of *Vppidelen, v.* Piddletrenthide par. *infra*; this is OE
burn-stōw 'place where people assembled at a stream, bathing place',
or perhaps 'watering place for cattle' (Sandred 98).

MUSTON FM (formerly MANOR HO) (SY 724960)

Mostereston 1270 (1372) *ChrP*, 1288 *Ass*, *M(o)usterston* 1303,
1346, 1431 all FA, *Mustreston* 1412 ib, *M(o)usterton* 1428 ib,
1431 (15) *ChrP, Mystereston* 1440 IpmR, *Muserton* 1539 *AOMB*,
Muston 1774 Hutch[1]
Pudele Musterton 1297 Banco, *Pudelemusters* 1339 FF, *Pudel-*
mustreston 1364 Pat, *-musterton* 1365 Cl

A manor on R. Piddle or Trent (cf. Affpuddle par. *supra*), once
held by the family of *de Musters* (Richard *de Musters* 1303 FA,
— *Mosters* 1340 NI, — *Moustrers* 1346 FA; earlier references to the
family in this neighbourhood include Robert *de Must(i)ers*, — *de*
Monasteriis c. 1165 MontC, Richard *de Musters de Pydel* 1244 *Ass*),

v. tūn 'farm, estate', cf. Winterborne Muston in Winterborne Kingston par. *supra.* In 1306 (1372) *ChrP* there is reference to *Musteres-, Mustareslandschare, -schere,* 'Musters's boundary, the boundary of Muston', *v.* land-sc(e)aru.

LITTLE PUDDLE FM (SY 966717) ['lidl 'pidl]
  (*at*) *Litele Pudele* 843 for 934 (eME) AS*Charters,* 1303 FA, *Litele-pidele* 843 for 934 (17) BCS 739, 1212 *Fees, Litelpidele, -pidre* 1086 DB, *Litel Pidel, -pidra* Exon, *litilepedele, lytilpudele* Hy 3 (1372) *ChrP,* 1270 (1372) *ib, Lit(t)le-, Lytel(l)-, Lytle-, Litel-, Litilpidel(e), -pudel(e), -pyd(e)le, -pidle, -pud(d)ell* 1251 Ch *et freq* to 1539 *AOMB, Lutelpudele* 1306 (1372) *ChrP, Litull Pudull* 1428 FA, *Little Piddle* 1811 OS
  Pidre 1086 DB (f. 78a), *Pidra* Exon, *Pydel(e), Pidel* 1261 Cl *et freq* to 1329 ib, *Pydle* 1314 Pat, *Pydyll* 1440 Cl, *Poudle* 1308, 1312 Pat, Fine, *Pud(e)le* 1309 Pat *et freq* to 1324 ib
  Parva Pidele 1235–6 Fees, — *Pudele* 1323 Hutch[3]
  Combe Deverell als. Deverell Combe als. Litilpudill 1456 Pat, — *Lytylpudyll* 1466 Cl, *Deverell(es) Com(b)e* 1495 Ipm, 1539 *AOMB,* cf. *Deverell Combe Bridge* 1791 Boswell

Named from R. Piddle or Trent, cf. Affpuddle par. *supra, v.* lȳtel; for the DB spellings with *r* for *l, v.* ANInfl 142. John *Deverel* held 1/16 part of a fee here in 1303 FA, cf. also Elias *Deverell* 1456 Pat, Hutch[3] 2 619; for other lands held by this family, cf. the f.n. *Deverils infra* and Deverel Fm in Milborne St A. par. *supra; Combe* is cumb 'valley', probably with reference to the valley through which R. Piddle or Trent flows near Little Puddle Fm. There are medieval settlement remains on either side of this valley, *v.* RCHM 3 210. There is mention of a 'free chapel' here in 1323 Hutch[3].

BLACK HO. BOURNE DROVE (*quendam Droue* 1270 (1372) *ChrP,* in bounds of Puddletown par. *infra, v.* drove) & HILL PLANT. (*Bourn Hill* 1839 *TA* (Puddletown)), from Bourne Fm *supra.* CHURCH (St Mary's), cf. *Ecclesiam S'te Mar' de Hynepidele* 1288 *Ass,* 'the church of *Hynepudele*' 1339, 1348 Pat, 'church of *Pudelhenton*' 1403 ib, *cottage called Church Barrow* 1870 Eton; the present church dates from 15th cent. (RCHM 3 207). COOMBE BOTTOM (*Coomb* — 1838 *TA*) & PLANT., *v.* cumb. DOLE'S HILL PLANT. EAST FM, on E bank of R. Piddle or Trent. HEAVE COPPICE, FM (*Heath* (sic) 1811 OS) &

ROOKERY, adjacent to fields called *Heare* (sic) 1837 *TA* (Charminster), *Heave* 1839 *ib* (Frampton), perhaps from ModE dial. *heave* 'a heap, a hillock' (EDD). HILL BARN, 1811 OS. HOLCOMBE BARN (1811 OS), BOTTOM & HEAD PIT, *v.* hol², cumb, botm, hēafod 'head of a valley'. MANOR HO. MUSTON COPSE, — *Coppice* 1838 *TA*, from Muston Fm *supra*. NEW BARN. NEW BLDGS. NEW INN. PARSONAGE BARN, near Rectory *infra*. PEAK COPPICE, cf. *Peake furland* 1652 Eton, *Peak* 1838 *TA, v.* pēac, furlang. LITTLE PIDDLE DOWN, from Little Puddle Fm *supra*. THE PLANTATION, cf. *Plantation* 1838 *TA*. LITTLE PUDDLE BOTTOM, COPPICE (cf. *Coppice Pce* 1839 *TA*) & HILL (FM) (*Piddle Hill* 1839 *ib*), from Little Puddle Fm *supra*. PUDDLETOWN FM, from Puddletown par. *infra*. RECTORY, cf. *Parsonage Ho* 1774 Hutch¹, Parsonage Barn *supra*. SMITHY. WEST LANE, W of the village. WEST LODGE, at the NNW end of the village. WHITEHALL CTGS.

FIELD-NAMES

Fields in Puddletown *TA* but now in Piddlehinton are marked †. The undated forms are 1838 *TA* 167 (those marked † are 1839 *TA* 168). Spellings dated 1285 are FA, 1270 (1372), 1306 (1372) *ChrP*, 1339 Fine, 1405 *AddRoll*, 1608, 1609, 1615, 1630, 1652, 1683, 1865 Eton, 1625 *Wal*, 1664 HTax, 1863 Hutch³, and the rest *Eton*.

(*a*) †Almshouse Mdw (from *Napper's Almshouse* in Dorchester par. *infra* which possessed a farm in Puddletown in 1774 Hutch¹ 1 489); Bank Fd; Barn Hill; Bourn Ash (Md), †Bourn Ewe Leaze & Md (from Bourne Fm *supra*); Butter Md (*v.* butere); The Cleave (*v.* clif (nom. pl. clifu, cleofu)); Coppice; Cowlease Hill, Small Cow Lease (*le Coulese* 1498, cf. *the Cowhouse* 1631); Hr & Lr Crate (*v.* croft); Curclose; Deveril(l)s (Bottom & Md) (*terr' voc' Deuerils* 1625, from the *Deverel* family, cf. Little Puddle Fm *supra*, Hutch¹ 1 578); Dorchester Fd (from Dorchester par. *infra*); E & W Down, Down Altmt & Furze Poor Lot (cf. *le Downe* 1452, *Piddlehinton Down* 1811 OS, 1863, *v.* dūn); Druce Md (from Druce Fm in Puddletown par. *infra*); †Dyle Corner; (Hr) East Fd (*camp' orient'* 1306 (1372), *Estfeld* 1452, *the Lower & Upper East Fd* 1652); East Md; 8 Acres; †Old 11 Acres (*Elleueacres* 1306 (1372), *v.* en(d)leofan); Ewelease, †Middle Ewe Leaze; 15 Acres; Fat Ox (cf. an identical f.n. in Dewlish par. *supra*); Flax Cl (*v.* fleax); †Foder Ho Grd (*v.* fōdor); 4 & 14 Acres; Gaskins (*tenement called Gascoynes* 1609); Gorins Md (cf. William *Goreing* 1664); Grangers Grd; †Great Grd on 26 acres; Hither Fd; Home Fd; Joice Md; †Kite Hill (*v.* cȳta); Lawrence's Md; Little Fd; Long Friday (probably a nickname for unproductive land, cf. Sr 279); Lovard Hill & Md (cf. *the Loffer Barne* 1631, from Lovard in Puddletown par. *infra*; the N part of Lovard was in this par.); Lower Fd; Meadow & Three Orchds; †Meadow under Coppice; Middle Fd; †Middle Grd; Muston Ewelease (from Muston Fm *supra*); New Md; 9 Acres; Oak

Fd; †Orchard; Orchard (*paddocke vocat' the* — 1631); Paines Grd; Peaked Fd (*v.* peked); Pegs Md; Pit; †Hr & Lr Plain; †Pond Cl; Popes Wall (cf. Richard *Pope* 1664); Pound Fd (cf. *clausura pounfaldi domini* 1454, *v.* pund); Randalls 1865 (cf. *Thomas Randall(s house)* 1664); Rick Yd; Romans Md; 6 Acres (Md); Shove Lds (perhaps to be identified with *cultur' voc' Scholdelond* (possibly for *Schowel-*) 1452, *v.* scofl, land); 10 & 13 Acres; Thwart Ld (*v.* thwart 'athwart, lying across', cf. *Burclinch infra*); Town Bridge 1791 Boswell; Townsend Md (*v.* toun, ende); 12 & 20 Acres; Walnut Grove; Well Bottom; West Water; Willow Bed; Yonder Fd.

(*b*) *Acrehay* 1569 (*v.* æcer, (ge)hæg); *cultur' voc' le Breche* 1452, *Breach furland* 1652 (*v.* brēc, furlang); *Bridgmans* 1630; *cultur' voc' (Thurtover) Burclinch(e)* 1452, *Burt Linch* 1652 (possibly from beorc 'birch-tree' with hlinc, *v.* thwart-over, cf. Thwart Land *supra*); *metes iaculares vocat' the Buttes* 1569 (*v.* butt²); *Chelbargh* 1306 (1372) (perhaps from calc (WSax cealc) 'chalk' and beorg); *Cherlokeslandschere* 1306 (1372) (the surname *Sherlock, v.* land-scearu); *la Cnylle desuper Cur', Forther-, Westerknyll* 1306 (1372) (*v.* cnyll(e) 'hillock', furðra, westerra, cf. *le Courtewyke infra*); *les Colkys* (probably for *Cokkys*) 1306 (1372) (*v.* cocc¹ 'heap, hillock'); *the comon feildes* 1571; *le Courtewyke* 1452, *the Court Close* 1683 (*v.* court, wīc, cf. *la Cnylle supra*); *Culuerdyngge* 1306 (1372) (perhaps from culfre 'dove' and dyncge 'manured land', but one of the pers.ns. suggested for Culliford Tree hundred *supra* with -ing² would also be possible, cf. William *Cullyford* 1597); *the dreve* 1652 (*v.* drǣf); *viis infra manerium...vocat' les Droves* 1569 (*v.* drove); *cultura...voc' la Dunye* 1306 (1372) (perhaps 'water-meadow below the hill', *v.* dūn, ēg, cf. Duni Gl 3 163; however Professor Löfvenberg suggests an OE wk. noun *dūni(g)e of obscure origin and meaning, possibly a side-form of the plant-name *dӯnige* which is also obscure, to explain two apparently analogous names, *v.* PNBrk 237); *cultura voc' Elfhede* 1452 (*v.* elf, hēafod); *Elstubbelond* 1306 (1372) (*v.* ellern, stubb, land); *Feldweye* 1306 (1372) (*v.* feld, weg); *cultura voc' Fifacres* 1306 (1372) (*v.* fīf, æcer); *Furshat* 1306 (1372) (*v.* fyrs, hæt(t)); *Galpyns* 1630 (cf. John *Galpyn* 1569); *Ganstede* 1306 (1372) (*v.* gangstede 'walk or pasture for cattle'); *toft' mes' voc' Gerneseys* 1480 (cf. John *Gernessey* 1405); *Gilten acre* 1652 (*v.* gylden); *Greneplekke* 1462 (*v.* grēne¹, plek); *Gurneteresclos* 1306 (1372) (the ME surname *Gerneter* found as *Gurneter* in 1332 SR); *cultura voc' Halfhide* 1452 (*v.* half, hīd); *Hangynglond* 1306 (1372) (*v.* hangende); *la Heuedlond* 1306 (1372) (*v.* hēafod-land); *Hollirodehill* 1609 ('holy cross hill', *v.* hālig, rōd²); *Katherines Place* 1631 (*v.* place); *Dounlangelond* 1306 (1372) ('(place) below langelond', *v.* dūne, lang¹, land); *cultura desuper la Lynch* 1306 (1372) (*v.* hlinc); *Loklond* 1306 (1372) (*v.* loc(a)); *cultura voc' le Longlynche* 1452 (*v.* lang¹, hlinc); *the Lordes mede* 1571 (*v.* hlāford, mǣd); *cultur' voc' Loscombe* 1452 (*v.* hlōse, cumb); *cultura voc' Loweste* 1452 (perhaps the superl. adj. lowest (NED c. 1200)); *le lydie dyche* 1498 (first el. possibly hlid-geat 'swing-gate', or hlǣfdige 'lady'; if the latter, perhaps in allusion to the nuns of the priory of Mortain who had lands here, cf. *terris et ten' Priori de Mortaigne* 1442, Hutch³ 2 803, *v.* dīc); *Lynes* 1569 (probably from the family of Geoffrey *de la Linde* 1285, George *de la Lyne* 1526 who had lands here, *v.* lind, but possibly from leyne); *la Marl, Nyther-, Ouermarle* 1306 (1372), *cultur' voc'* *le Furthe-, Westermarle* 1452, *Higher Marle furland* 1652 (*v.* marle, neoðerra, uferra, furðra, westerra, furlang); *the Mylle Ponde* 1571 (cf. *molend' bladiser'* 1440, *molend' aquatic'* 1462, *v.* mylen, ponde); *la Nywefoundelond* 1306 (1372) (an early instance of this name, *v.* new-found (NED c. 1496), land); *the Northe Tenemente* 1608; *Pacchorn* 1306 (1372) (perhaps an OE pers.n. **Pæcca* as in Patchacott D 131, etc., with horn); *the parish house* 1597; *Piggeshey* 1480, *-haye* 1597, *Pyg(g)ys-* 1498, 1526, *Pyggeshay(e)* 1569 (probably from pigga 'young pig' and (ge)hæg, but the surname *Pigg* is possible); *le posthowsse ten' voc' clavelles* 1569 (*v.* post-house (NED 1645), with the surname *Clavell*); *cultura desuper-, -iuxta Preste(s)he(y)ghe* 1306 (1372) (*v.* prēost, (ge)hæg); *la Rig-, la Rygwey* 1270 (1372) (in bounds of Puddletown, at about SY 730975), *Esterrygwey, Middulriggewey, Normeste-, Southmestryggewey* 1306 (1372) (all in Little Puddle *supra*, *v.* hrycg, weg, ēasterra, middel, norðmest, sūðmest); *le Rotherles(s)e* 1486 (*v.* hrīðer, lǣs); *Seueacre(s)* 1306 (1372) (*v.* seofon); *Sheringhey* 1480 (cf. John *Shering* 1597, *v.* (ge)hæg); *Schyplond* 1306 (1372) (*v.* scēap (WSax scī(e)p), land); *cotag' voc' le Shop* 1597 (*v.* sc(e)oppa); *cultura voc' Shortlond* 1306 (1372) (*v.* sc(e)ort); *cultura voc' Sixlate Furr'* 1452 (the second el. may be (ge)lǣt in the sense 'conduit', or slǣget 'sheep pasture', *v.* sex, furh); *Sladlond* 1306 (1372) (*v.* slæd); *Small Way* 1652; (*domus mansionalis vocat'*) *South Place* 1615, 1631 (*v.* place); *the South Tenement* 1608; *Stonylond* 1306 (1372) (*v.* stānig); *Sunnyclose* 1569; *la Thurne* 1306 (1372) (*v.* þyrne); *claus' voc' le toft* 1569 (*v.* toft); *the Towne house* (or *the Churche house*) 1571, 1597; *domus voc' le Twyne Dores* 1631 (perhaps from twinn 'double' and dor or duru 'door, gate' (here with reference to sluice gates?), but the first el. could be betwēonan 'between'); *Nyther Uplond* 1306 (1372) (*v.* neoðerra, upp, land); *Waddene* 1306 (1372) (*v.* wād, denu); *la Waterlond, Myddel-, Ouerwaterlond, Nytherwaterland* 1306 (1372) (*v.* wæter, land, middel, uferra, neoðerra); *Westfeld* 1452, *Lower & Upper West Fd* 1652; *le —, the West Meade* (*Hedge*) 1569; *semitam pedalem subtus Whitelynche* 1462 (*v.* hwīt, hlinc); *Wydyatham* 1339 (possibly wīd, geat, hamm).

Puddletown

Little Piddle, formerly in this par., was transferred to Piddlehinton par. in 1885.

PUDDLETOWN (SY 758943) (ˈpʌdltɑun, ˈpidltɑun]
 Pi(t)retone 1086 DB, *Pidretone, Piretona* Exon
 Pideltona Hy 2 HarlCh, *-tun* 1219 Fees, *Pidel(e)-, Pydel(e)ton(e)* 1212 ib, 1231 Cl, 1244 *Ass et freq* to 1379, 1495 Pat, *-toun* 1280 *Ass*, 1539 AOMB, *-towne* 1539 *ib*, *Pydeltun, Piddelton* Ed 1 (1372) ChrP, *Piddilton* 1429 Pat, *Pydil-, Pidilto(u)n* 1450 Eton, *Pyteltowne* 1508 DLCt, *Piddle Towne alias Puddle Towne* 1665 Ilch, *Piddletown* 1795 Boswell

Pudel(e)ton 1246 (1372) *ChrP*, 1270 (1372) *ib*, 1280 *Ass et freq*
to 1539 *AOMB*, *-toun(e)* 1270 (1372) *ChrP*, 1280 *Ass et freq* to
1539 *AOMB*, *-tune* 1290 Ch, 1415 Fine, *Pudultoune* 1349 Ipm
Pedeltowne 1462 Pat

'Farm on R. Piddle', *v*. tūn, RNs. *infra*, cf. Affpuddle par. *supra*.
For the DB spellings, *v*. ANInfl 142. DEPN, following Fägersten
175, cites the OE forms (*at*) *Vppidelen*, *uppidele* here, but they belong
under Piddletrenthide par. *infra*. The bounds of Puddletown are
described in 1270 (1372) *ChrP* (f. 119). In 1956, there was considerable local controversy over the name of this village. Dorset County
Council wanted to change its name to Piddletown in order to make it
conform with the other villages in the Piddle valley (*Piddle-* generally
occurring as prefix as in Piddlehinton and Piddletrenthide, *-puddle* as
suffix as in Affpuddle, Tolpuddle and Turners Puddle); but fierce
local protest against the change (mainly on the grounds of the
expense involved, but also because Puddletown sounded 'nicer')
eventually won the day.

BARDOLFESTON (Site of) (SY 767947), BARDOLF MANOR, BASAN HILL
& PLANT.

Pidele 1086 DB (f. 77a, Eyton 135–6, VCHD0 **3** 72)
Pidelebardolveston 1257 Cl, — *Bardolfeston* 1257 Ipm, — *Bardals-
ton* 1285 FA, *Pud(d)el(e) Bardolveston* 1339 Cl, 1385, 1419
IpmR
Pidel-, *Pydele-*, *Pudel(l)(e) Bardolf* 1264 FineR, Ipm, 1264 (e15)
MiltRoll, 1306 (1372) *ChrP et freq* to 1384 Ch, — *Bardalf* 1264
(e15) *MiltRoll*, *Bardolf Pidel* 1342 IpmR
Bardolveston 1264, 1282 Ipm, 1383 *AddRoll*, 1397 Cl ('—by
Pudelton'), *-oluys-* 1264 (e15) *MiltRoll*, *-olues-* 1288 *Ass*,
Bardufueston (probably for *-ulues-*) 1280 *ib*, *Bardolf(e)ston* 1282
Hutch[3], 1303 FA, 1332 SR, 1405 *AddRoll* (p), *Bardals-* 1285
FA, 1327 *SR*, *-ols-* 1303, 1412 FA, *-alves-* 1346, 1428 *ib*,
-el(v)(e)s- 1401 Cl, 1405 *AddRoll*, 1412 FA, 1539 *AOMB*,
-alfston 1431 FA, *Bradolveston by Pudeletune* 1415 Fine,
Bardolphweston 1774 Hutch[1]
Pudel Barston als. Bardolfeston 1594 Hutch[3]
Barson Hill 1627 *Wal* (*via regia apud* —), *Baston* (*Plant.*), *Lower
Basan, Bason Hill or Eighteen Acres*, — *or Seven Acres* 1839 *TA*

A manor on R. Piddle or Trent (cf. Affpuddle par. *supra*) once held by the *Bardolf* family (Ralph — 1244 Ch, Drogo — 1272 ib, Richard —1288 *Ass*, etc.; they were probably descended from *Bardulph* (the OG pers.n. *Bardulf*) *de Chiselburneford* (*v.* foll.), also called *Bussel*, c. 1165 MontC, who was himself descended from the DB tenant of Little Cheselbourne, Roger *Boisell*, *v.* Fägersten 176–7), *v.* tūn 'farm, estate'. *Bardolfueshulle* 15 ChrP no doubt belonged to the same family, *v.* hyll. The 13th cent. Drogo Bardolf probably gave his name to Druce Fm *infra*. For the deserted medieval village here, *v.* RCHM 3 229, cf. Church Knap *infra*.

LITTLE CHESELBOURNE (lost, about SY 771963)

   Ceoselburne 1086 DB (f. 83b), *-burna* Exon, *Cheselbo(u)rn(e)* 1285, 1303, 1346 FA, 1383, 1405 *AddRoll*, 1431 FA, 1539 *AOMB*, *Chesylburne* 1428 FA, *Chesilborne* 1431 (15) ChrP, *Cheselborne* Fm 1839 *TA*

   Chiselburneford(e) Hy 1 (14) *AddCh*, c. 1165 MontC, *-born-* 1332 SR, *Chileborneford* Hy 1 (14) *AddCh*, *Chiseburneforde* c. 1165 MontC, *-borne-* 13 (14) *AddCh*, *Cheseburn(e)ford(e)* 1228 FF, 1244 *Ass* (p), 1288 *ib*, *Chesul-* 1244 *ib* (p), *Cheselbo(u)rn(e)-*, *-burn(e)f(f)ord(e)* 1270 (1372) ChrP *et freq* to 1352 *Weld*[1]

   Little Chesilborne 1477 Hutch[3] (— *als. Chesilborne Ford*), 1863 ib, *Little Ches(s)elborne* 1664 HTax, 1795 Boswell

Named from the same stream as Cheselbourne par. *infra q.v.*, from which 'Little' distinguishes it. The settlement was near the confluence of the Cheselbourne stream and Devil's Brook (RCHM 3 230); at this point, which is on the par. bdy and where several tracks still converge, the ford must have been, *v.* ford; *viam...in Cheselbourneforde* 1270 (1372) ChrP occurs in the bounds of Puddletown. There was a mill here in 1086 DB (VCHDo 3 103). On the early forms *Chile-*, *Chise-*, etc. with AN loss of *-s-* and *-l-*, *v.* ANInfl 54, 146.

DRUCE FM (SY 746953), *terr' Drugon'* 1306 (1372) ChrP, *Drewes* 1431 FA, 1431 (15) ChrP, 1480 Eton, 1565 *Hen*[1], *Druwes* 1447 *MinAcct*, *Drewez* 1539 *AOMB*, *farm of Druce* Eliz ChancP, *Druse*, *Druce farme* 1641 Ilch, *Druce* 1811 OS, cf. *in cultura biesteweye que dicitur Druesgore* 1306 (1372) ChrP. A manorial name from the possessive form of the OFr, ME pers.n. *Dru*, *Drew* from OG *Drogo*, *v.* gāra. The *Drew* in question was probably the 13th cent. *Drogo* (*Drew*) Bardolf mentioned under Bardolfeston *supra*; Druce Fm lies only 1 mile W of Bardolfeston, and the early reference to *Druesgore* is in connection with that manor. However Fägersten 177 notes that land in Puddletown belonged to *Al(u)ina uxor Drogonis de Monte Acuto* in 1219, 1227 Fees, cf. also John *Drewe* 1463 *Ct* mentioned in connection with land in Waterston *infra*.

DUDDLE FM (SY 731907), 1842 *TAMap*, *Doddel* 1270 (1372) *ChrP*, *Duddell* 1459 *AddRoll*, 1539 *AOMB*, *Duddle* 1580 *Wal et passim*, *Dudle* (*pounde*) 1624, 1625 *Wal*, *Duddles* 1811 OS. Perhaps an -el derivative of the el. represented by ME dodde 'hill' suggested as possibly entering into Dodding's Fm in Bere Regis par. *supra*, cf. ModE *duddle* 'a teat, nipple' (NED rec. once 1708) and Do dial. *duddles* 'little dods or dumps' (Barnes 61). The topography of Duddle is similar to that of Dodding's; Duddle Fm itself lies at about 140′ on a subsidiary watercourse of R. Frome, but behind it the ground rises to 300′ at Duddle Heath *infra*, cf. *Duddle Hill* 1839 *TA*.

FROME MEAD (SY 755908), *Fromemede* 1325 (1372) *ChrP et freq* to 1531 *Weld*[1], -*Meade* 1571 *Eton*, 1579 *Wal* (*West* —), *prato de* (*Weste*) *Frome* 1437 *MinAcct*, 1579 *Wal*, *Fromede* 1440 *Eton*, *1 hampma prati...apud Frome* 1459 *AddRoll*, *Frome Medowe, medowe in West Frome* 1539 *AOMB*, *Warde Meade als Frome Meade* 1579 *Wal*, *Fro(o)me Mead(ow)*, *Froome Mead Drove* 1839 *TA*, cf. *prati in Warda de Frome* 1440 *Eton*, (*prat' apud*) *Frome Stathe* 1456 Pat, 1462 *Eton*, 'meadow on R. Frome', *v.* mǣd, RNs. *infra*, stæð 'bank'; *Warde* (Lat *Warda*) may represent warod 'shore-meadow', cf. the f.n. Ward Mdw in Charminster par. *infra*.

HYDE (lost, about SY 735955), *la Hyde* 1270 (1372) *ChrP* (*nouum fossat' de* —), 1306 (1372) *ib* (*terr' de* —), 1390 Fine ('—by *Walsterton*'), 1393 (15) *ChrP* (— *iuxta Waltereston*), *La Hide* 1331 Cl, Fine, Ipm, 1332 Cl, 1378 Hutch[3] (—*juxta Walterstone*), *Pudelhide, -hyde* 1367 (1372), 1393 (15) *ChrP*, *Hide* 1384 Ch, 1431 FA, 1774 Hutch[1], cf. *Hyde Mede* (*als. Long Mede*) 1539 *AOMB*, *v.* hīd 'a hide of land'. The location of this place, on R. Piddle or Trent N of Waterston Ho, is established by the reference to *nouum fossat' de la Hyde* 'the new ditch of *la Hyde*' in the 13th cent. bounds of Puddletown between *aquam torrentem voc' Pudelwater* 'the rapid stream called *Pudelwater*' (i.e. R. Piddle) and *la Bourne*, the small stream

which runs S to join R. Piddle near Druce Fm, v. Bourne Fm in
Piddlehinton par. *supra*, cf. C. C. Taylor in DoNHAS **88** 213.

ILSINGTON (SY 755919)

> *Elsangtone* 1086 DB, (*H*)*elsington*(*e*) Hy 3 (1372) *ChrP*, *Elsindon*
> 1244 *Ass* (p), -*ton* 1260 FF, *Elsyngton* 1332 SR
> (*H*)*ilsington*(*e*) Hy 3 (1372) *ChrP*, *Ilsing*- 1257 FF, 1270 (1372)
> *ChrP*, 1664 HTax, *Ilsyn*- 1280 Ipm, *Ilsin*- 1285 Ch, *Ils*(*s*)*yng-*
> *ton*(*e*) 1306 (1372) *ChrP et freq* to 1539 *AOMB*, *Isyngton* 1405
> *AddRoll*, *Islington* 1795 Boswell

Probably 'farm called after Ælfsige', from the OE pers.n. *Ælfsige*
(WSax *I(*e*)*lfsige*) (as suggested by Ekwall DEPN), and -ingtūn, cf.
Ilfracombe D 46 (*Ælf*-, *I(*e*)*lfrǣd*), Ilsington D 475 (possibly
*I(*e*)*lfstān*); however the name may alternatively be taken to mean
'farm at *Ilsing* (< *Ælf*-, *I*(*e*)*lfsiging*)' ('Ælfsige's place'), *v*. -*ing*[2], cf.
the related *Ilsyngbere*, the old name for Ilsington Wd *infra* which lies
just N of Ilsington itself. Fägersten 178 suggests that the pers.n.
is *Elesa*, but while formally possible (with *e* > *i* before a dental, *v*.
Jordan 54), this OE pers.n. is extremely rare. There was a mill here
in 1086 DB.

ILSINGTON WD (SY 755926), *Ilsyngbere* 1270 (1372) *ChrP* (*fossatum*
bosci (*Prioris...de Twynham*) *voc'* —), 1399 *AddRoll* (*copic' domini*
in —), 15 *ChrP* (*bosci de Pudeltoune voc'* —), *Ilsingbere* 1285 (1372)
ib (*bosco de* —), *Ulsingbere* 1288 (1372) *ib*, *Ylsinbr'* 1289 Cl ('wood
called —'), *Ilsyngber Wode* 1539 *AOMB*, *Isembre* 1540 Hutch[3]
('wood and coppices called —'), *Ilsingbury Wd* 1811 OS, *Ilsington Wd*
1839 *TA*. '(Woodland) pasture, or grove, called after Ælfsige, or at
Ilsing', *v*. -*ing*[4], -*ing*[2], bǣr[2] or bearu, and prec.

LOVARD (lost, about SY 725955)

> *Luveford* 1235–6 Fees
> *Loue*-, *Lovef*(*f*)*ord*(*e*) 1268 *Ass*, 1285 FA, 1288 *Ass et freq* to 1863
> Hutch[3], 1270 (1372) *ChrP* (*South*-), 1285 FA (*Pudele* —), 1404
> Hutch[3] (*North* —), 1409 Cl ('—by *Pudelton*'), 1426 *Weld*[1]
> (*North*-, *South*-), 1487 Ipm (— *als. Lofford*), *Loneford*(*e*) (for
> *Loue*-) 1321 Cl, 1354 AD II, 1379 Pat ('—by *Hynepedel*'),
> *Londford* 1383 *AddRoll*
> *Leford* 1280 *Ass*, *Lefford* 1346 FA
> *Lufford*(*e*) 1303 FA, 1322 *Ext*, 1586 Hutch[3]

Lof(f)ord 1331 Fine *et freq* to 1539 *AOMB*, 1389 Hutch[3] (*North*—), 1412 FA (*Est* —), *Lovord(e)*, *Louord* 1331 Ipm, Fine, 1405 *AddRoll*, 1428 *Weld*[1], 1431 (15) *ChrP*, 1438 *MinAcct*, *Lonord* (for *Louord*) 1331, 1332 Cl, *Louforde* 1374 *ChrP*, *Lovehead* Eliz ChancP, *Lovard* 1622 Hutch[3] (— *als*. *Lufforde*), 1795 Boswell, *farme of Loverd*, *Lovered farme* 1641 *Ilch*, *Loverd* 1664 HTax

Possibly 'Lufa's ford', from the OE pers.n. *Lufa* and ford, or 'ford used as a courting place', from lufu 'love' (cf. Maidenford D 26, Maidford Nth 41 (from gen.pl. of mægden 'maiden') and Playford Sf (DEPN), Plyford D 597 (from plega 'play'), which may have similar connotations). However a topographical el. OE *luf- 'river valley, low wet place' proposed by Zachrisson DTR 146, KockF 407 ff, SNPh **8** 83 (cf. also Luccombe Wt 47, Forsberg 169, Sandred 246) would be a formally possible, and topographically suitable, alternative for the first el. The ford was probably where the Dorchester–Piddlehinton road crosses R. Piddle or Trent (hence *Pudele-* 1285) near Hr Waterston *infra* with which South Lovard has been identified (C.C. Taylor, DoNHAS **88** 212–3, RCHM **3** 222); this identification is supported by the mention of *fossat' de South-loueforde* in the 13th cent. bounds of Puddletown. North Lovard is thought to be represented by the medieval settlement remains at SY 727958 in Piddlehinton par. *supra* (RCHM **3** 210, cf. Piddlehinton f.ns.). Eyton 135–6 may be correct in identifying the 2 small DB manors of *Pidele* (ff. 79a, 79b) with 'Lovard, Puddletonford, and Comb Deverel' (*v*. Little Puddle in Piddlehinton par. *supra*), cf. VCHDo **3** 85.

WATERSTON Ho (SY 735952), HR & LR WATERSTON

Pidere 1086 DB (f. 82b), *Pidra* Exon, *Pidela Walteri* 1212 Fees *Walterton* 1227 Fees, *Walter(r)(e)ston(e)* 1268 *Ass*, 1285 FA *et freq* to 1863 Hutch[3], (— *Farme*) 1626 *Ilch*, *Walster(s)*- 1390 Fine, 1438 *MinAcct*, *Walteris*- 1393 AD V, *Waterlis*- 1422 *Ilch*, *Waltis*- 1428 FA, *Waterston* 1658 *Ilch*, *Walters Toune* 1539 *AOMB*, *Waterson* 1664 HTax, 1842 *TAMap* (— *Farm*), *Higher & Lower Walterstone* 1811 OS

Pydele —, *Pidele Walter(e)ston(e)* 1268 FF, 1280 *Ass*, 1303 FA, 1429 *Ilch*, — *Walstereston* 1429 *ib*, *Pudele Walter(r)eston* 1285 FA, 1319 FF, 1326 Cl, 1346 FA, *Pedel Walteriston* 1492 Ipm

'Walter's farm (on R. Piddle)', from the ME (< OG) pers.n. *Walter* and tūn, v. RNs. *infra*, Affpuddle par. *supra*; no reference to the early owner called *Walter* has been found. Hutch[1] 1 489 mentions a former chapel here; it is referred to as *capelle de Waltereston* n.d. (1372) *ChrP, ecclesie de Walterston* 1412 *MinAcct*. For Hr Waterston, cf. Lovard *supra*.

YELLOWHAM HILL & WD (SY 733935) ['jæləm], *bosc' de Zolwham* 1270 (1372) *ChrP, bosci vocati Yolweham* 1404 *Ilch, Yalwe-* 1427, 1428 *Weld*[1], 1448 *MinAcct, Yelweham* 1427, 1428 *Weld*[1], *Yolu-* 1445 *MinAcct, Yeolo-* 1451 *ib* (— *Throte), Yolowham* 1457 *Weld*[1], *Yolo(w)hamthrote* 1457, 1461 *ib, Yeleu-, Yelew-* 1492, 1494 *Ilch, Yalow-* 1497 *ib, Yeolowham* 1545 *ib, via regia (ducens a capite montis) vocat' Yellow(e)ham(e) Hill* 1579, 1625 *Wal, via apud Yelham Hill* 1625 *ib, Yellowham Wd* 1839 *TA, Yelham Wd & Heath* 1842 *TAMap*. From geolu (wk. obl. *geolwan*) 'yellow', and hamm 'enclosure'. 'Yellow' may allude to the soil (sand and gravel pits are marked 6″) or to yellow flowers. The el. hamm may here mean 'cultivated plot in marginal land' as suggested by M. Gelling, NoB **48** 151–3, for various names in Ha, Brk and D; Yellowham is in high (400′) wooded country on the W edge of the par. 1 mile from the nearest stream (R. Piddle or Trent). *Throte* no doubt refers to the narrow cutting made through the hill by the Dorchester–Puddletown road (*the Wey whych ledyth betwen Pudeltowne and Dorchest'* 1539 *AOMB), v.* þrote 'throat, passage', cf. Snail Creep in Stinsford par. *infra*.

ASH COPPICE. BEACON CORNER, HILL (1811 OS) & PLANT., cf. *le becon apud Whiteborne* 1625 *Wal, v.* (ge)bēacon, hwīt, burna. BIRCH LANE. BLACK BARN. BLACK WD BOTTOM. BLIND LANE, *v.* blind. BOSWELL'S PLANT. CASTLE HILL, just S of a Roman road (Margary 4e), but the significance of the name is not clear, *v.* castel(l). CAUSEWAY WITHY BEDS, *Casway Md & Willow Bed* 1839 *TA*, cf. *Castway Bridges* 1791 Boswell, *v.* caucie. CHARMINSTER LANE, *Charmister* — 1636 *Wal*, leading to Charminster par. *infra*. CHINE HILL (LANE), *Chynhulle* 1306 (1372) *ChrP, -hyll* 1539 *AOMB, Chinehill* 1635 *Wal, Chine Hill* 1839 *TA*, cf. *Chinehill Bridge* 1791 Boswell, possibly from cinu 'chine, ravine', with hyll, but the first el. should perhaps be associated with 'John *Chynne*, styled *atte Mulle*' 1393 AD VI, *v.* atte, myln. CHURCH (St Mary's), cf. *æcclesiam de Pitretone* 1086 DB,

— *Pidretone* Exon, *parochial' eccles' de Pudelton* 1270 (1372) *ChrP*, *eccles' Beate Marie de Pudeletone* 1338 *HarlCh*, *Cherch(e)mede* 1270 (1372) *ChrP*, *(le) Churchewey* 1463 *Ct*, *the Churche waye* 1635 *Wal*, *v.* mǣd, weg; the present building dates from 12th cent. (RCHM 3 222). CHURCH KNAP, 1863 Hutch³, traditionally said to be the site of the church of Bardolfeston *supra*, *v.* cnæpp. COMMON DROVE, *v.* drove. COOMBE BARN & PLANT., *la Combe* 1306 (1372) *ChrP*, *Combe* 1436 *MinAcct*, *Cumbe* 1437 *ib*, *Coombe Acre, Barn & Yd* 1839 *TA*, *v.* cumb. COW LANE, cf. *Cow(e) Close* 1626 *Ilch*. DRUCE HANGINGS, *Hangynglond iuxta terr' Drugon'* 1306 (1372) *ChrP*, *Hangynlond* 1306 (1372) *ib*, 1463 *Ct*, *v.* hangende 'steep', hanging 'steep slope', land, Druce Fm *supra*. DRUCE HR BARN, cf. *Druce barne* 1641 *Ilch*. DRUCE LANE, cf. *via regia a loco voc' druse-yeate* 1626 *Wal*, *v.* geat. DUCK DAIRY HO. DUDDLE HEATH (1839 *TA*) & PLANT., *v.* Duddle Fm *supra*. HR, HOME & LR EWELEAZE, *Hr Eweleaze Clump, Lr or Home Ewe Leaze* 1839 *TA*, cf. *(W) Ewe Leaze, Ewe Leaze Hill & 9 Acres* 1839 *ib*. GADDY'S LANE. (OLD) GRAVEL PITS. GREEN HILL. HASTINGS' FM, *Hastings* 1811 OS, cf. Henry *Hastings* who held the manor of Puddletown in 1612 Hutch³. HELL PIT, *v.* hell. HIGHER BARN. HILL'S COPSE, *Hill Coppice* 1839 *TA*. HOME FM, *Higher Barn* 1811 OS. ILSINGTON DAIRY HO (*Islington* — 1839 *TA*), FM (1842 *TAMap*), HEATH, HO (1842 *ib*), LAWN & RD (*viam regiam que ducit' ad Dorch'* 1270 (1372) *ChrP* ('the road to Dorchester', in bounds of Puddletown), *(via regia vocat')* *Ilsington Lane* 1625, 1637 *Wal*), all named from Ilsington *supra*. KEEPER'S LODGE. THE KENNELS, cf. *Dog Kennel Bridge* 1795 Boswell, *Kennel Plot* 1839 *TA*. KING'S ARMS (P.H.). KITE HILL, 1839 *TA*, *v.* cȳta. LAYCOCK CTGS & DAIRY FM. OLD LIMEKILN, cf. *Lime Pit Cl & Plant., Limepits Clump & Hedge Row* 1839 *TA*. LITTLE WD. LONG LANE, 1839 *TA*. MARTINS RIVER ISLAND, no doubt named from one of the *Martin* family which had lands in various parts of Puddletown from 14th cent. (Hutch³ 2 586, 619). THE MOOR, *le Moure* 1424 *Weld¹*, *le Moore* 1579 *Wal* (*pons desuper aquam in -*), cf. *Broademoore* 1624 *ib*, *v.* mōr. (LR) NORRIS MILL, NORRIS MILL CTGS, *Norris Mill* 1625 *Wal*, *Norris Mill Fm & Moor* 1839 *TA*, cf. *Norris Meade* 1635 *Wal*, Maud *Norris* 1635 *ib*, *Norris Fm* 1811 OS, *v.* myln; there were two mills in Puddletown in 1086 DB (VCHDo 3 66), cf. also *cursum aque de molendino de Pydelton* Ed 1 (1372) *ChrP*, *pons apud la Westmull* c. 1400 *AddRoll*, *Westmyll* 1459 *ib*, *le West Mille* 1582 *Wal*, *pontem apud la Nywemull* 1400 *AddRoll*, *Newmyll* 1459 *ib*, *the —, le New(e) Mill(e)* 1582, 1625

Wal, New Mill Bridge 1791 Boswell, *Mill Md & Plot* 1839 *TA, v.*
west, nīwe. NORTHBROOK, 1579 *Wal*, 1811 OS, *Bynorthebrouk* Ed 3
(1372) *ChrP, Northebrook* 1580 *Wal,* cf. *North Brook Md* 1839 *TA,*
'(place) to the north of the brook', *v.* bī, norðan, brōc; it lies on N
bank of R. Piddle or Trent. POND HO, from Heedless William's Pond
in Stinsford par. *infra.* PUDDLETOWN BRICK WORKS, cf. *(the) Brick
Close* 1623 *Weld*[1], 1626 *Ilch,* 1839 *TA, v.* brick. PUDDLETOWN DOWN,
Piddletown — 1839 *TA,* cf. *the Sheepe downe* 1626 *Ilch.* PUDDLETOWN
HEATH, *(le) Heath(e)* 1579 *Wal,* 1641 *Ilch, Piddletown Heath (Ctgs)*
1811 OS, *Piddletown Cmn & Heath* 1839 *TA, v.* hǣð. PUMP HO.
RAINBARROWS, tumuli marked 6"; the first el. may be hræfn 'a
raven'. RIDGE WAY, runs along Waterston Ridge *infra.* ROBIN'S
BARROW, tumulus marked 6", perhaps an allusion to *Robin Good-
fellow* or *Puck.* ROD HILL LANE, probably to be associated with
cultura bisouthtoun ('furlong to the south of the village') *voc' Rodewey*
1306 (1372) ChrP, *terr' in Southefylde iuxta Rodwayes Hill* 1579 *Wal,*
v. rād-weg 'road suitable for riding', hyll, bī, sūð, toun, cf. f.ns.
infra. THE ROOKERY. SAND PIT. SHEEPWASH, cf. *Sheep Wash Plot*
1839 *TA, v.* scēap-wæsce. SNIPE MOOR, cf. *Snytemede* n.d. (1372)
ChrP, v. snīte 'a snipe', mǣd. STAFFORD PARK COPSE & FM,
Stafford Parkes 1539 *AOMB, copicie voc' Stafforde Parke* 1579 *Wal,*
Stafford Park, Stafford's Park Coppice 1839 *TA; Stamperdespark*
(probably for *-ferdes-*) 15 *ChrP* may also belong here, and cf. *le parc* in
f.ns. *infra*; probably 'stone ford' from stān and ford, with park; the
farm is near R. Piddle or Trent. THREE LANES END, where three lanes
meet. TOLPUDDLE HOLLOW, probably named from Tolpuddle par.
infra although 3 miles from that place. TRAVELLERS REST (lost), 1811
OS. TROY TOWN COPSE (*-Coppice* 1839 *TA*) & FM (1842 *TAMap,*
Troy Town 1811 OS), *v.* troy town 'a maze'. TWO DROVES, a lane,
v. drove. WALTERSTONE CTG (lost), 1811 OS, from Waterston *supra.*
WARREN PLANT. (1839 *TA*), RD & WITHY BED, cf. 'chace of
Pideleton' 1272 (1313) Ch, *(Gt, Green & Lt) Warren, Warren Peak*
1839 *TA, v.* wareine, pēac. WATER BARN, near Devil's Brook, cf.
Water Md (Clump) 1839 *ib.* WATERSTON LANE (cf. *Walterston Waye*
1580 *Wal*) & RIDGE (1811 OS, *Ridge* 1839 *TA*), from Waterston
supra. WELLCLOSE PLANT., cf. *Well Cl (Coppice)* 1839 *ib,* Adam *atte
Wolle* 1340 NI, Richard *atte Wylle, -Welle* 1412 *MinAcct, v.* atte,
wella. WELL HO CTGS, near to Pump Ho *supra.* WHITE HILL, *via
regia voc' Whitehill* 1637 *Wal,* cf. *Whait Hill, White Hill Cl* 1839
TA, v. hwīt, hyll. WHITE MEAD, 1839 *ib, la Wyte-*1270 (1372)

ChrP, Whytmede 1539 *AOMB, Whit(e) Meade, Whitmead bridge* 1579 *Wal*, a water meadow on R. Frome, *v.* hwīt, mǣd, brycg. NEW WITHY BED, cf. *arborem voc' la Wythy* 1270 (1372) *ChrP, (prat' voc') (le) Wythy-, Wethi-, Wetheber(e)* 1443 *MinAcct et freq* to 1457 *Weld¹, (Lt) Withey Bed, Willow Bed* 1839 *TA, v.* wīðig, bearu. WREDEN PLANT., *Hr & Lr Wreydon, Wreden* 1839 *ib*, probably to be identified with *cultura vocat' Wiredon* 1306 (1372) *ChrP, Were-* 1579 *Wal, Wyredowne* 1625 *ib*, which may contain wīr 'bog myrtle' with dūn.

FIELD-NAMES

For some fields in Puddletown *TA* but now in Piddlehinton, *v.* Piddlehinton par. *supra*. The undated forms are 1839 *TA* 168. Spellings dated 1228 are FF, 1288 *Ass*, 1332 SR, 1340 NI, 1346, 1409, 1549, 1561, 1867 Hutch³, 1383, 1399, 1400, c. 1400, 1459 *AddRoll*, 1399², 1412, 1436, 1437, 1440, 1441, 1443, 1444, 1445, 1446, 1447, 1448, 1450, 1451 *MinAcct*, 1404, 1626¹, 1641 *Ilch*, 1423, 1424, 1426, 1427, 1428, 1455, 1457, 1461, 1474, 1531, 1623, 1635, 1638 *Weld¹*, 1440², 1462, 1480, 1483 *Eton*, 1458 *AD*, 1463 *Ct*, 1539 *AOMB*, 1578, 1579, 1580, 1624, 1625, 1626², 1627, 1635², 1636, 1637 *Wal*, 1664 HTax, 1791 Boswell, 1842 *TAMap*, and the rest *ChrP*.

(a) Arable Sheephouse (cf. *the hr, Lr, Midle & West Arrable feild* 1626¹); Ash Cl; Ashley (cf. *Assheleforlong* 1306 (1372), *Aysshleforlang* 1400, *v.* æsc, lēah, furlang); Backwater Bridge 1791; Barn Cl, Fd, Grd & Yd; Bartlett's Cl & Lot (cf. *Barteletes Howse* 1626², John *Bartlett* 1664); Gt Beach; Beat Leaze (*Batlese* 1539, *v.* lǣs; the first el. may be an early example of *beat* 'turf' (1620 NED), *v.* bete², cf. Bourn Beat *infra*); Belbury (*(ten' voc')* *Belbury(e)* 1579, perhaps from bēl¹ 'fire, pyre' and beorg; *Beldene* 1383 may have the same first el. with denu); Bobs Lot; Bottom Grd; Bourn Beat (*v.* burnbeat); Bowling Green; Broad Cl, Fd & Md; Inner Brooklands, Outer Brocklands (*Bro(u)kelond(es)* 1404 *et freq* to 1531, *v.* brōc, land); Lt Broom, Broom Cl (cf. *bromlond* 1306 (1372), *v.* brōm, land); Buddens Plot; Butt Cl (*v.* butte); Buttons 8 & 12 Acres; Carrot Cl; Carters Lawn (cf. John *Carter* 1459); Cayepond Bridge 1791; Cheese Ld; Chequer Cl & Gdns (*v.* cheker); Cherry Orchd; Chubbs Ham (*v.* hamm); Close; Cobbs Cl & Lot, Cobbs Cross or Poor Gdns (cf. Henry *Cobbe* 1270 (1372)); Common Md; Coppice Cl (cf. *The Coppice(s)* 1626¹, 1641); Court Mdw (*Courtemede* 1531, — *Mead* 1626¹, *v.* court, mǣd); Cowleaze (Plant.) (*the Cowlease* 1623); Creeches Md (probably a surname from East Creech in Ch. Knowle par. *supra*); Croads Lot (cf. Joseph *Crode* 1641); Culverhays (cf. *Coluerwell* 15, *the Coulverhouse, a closse called Coulverwell* 1539, *v.* culfre, (ge)hæg, wella, hūs); Long Dance in Froome Md (*v.* Frome Md *supra*; *Dance* is perhaps a surname); Darbeys Ho, Md, Moor & Plot; Dawes Plot (cf. John *Dawe* 1664); Dog Kennel Bridge 1791; Double Ctg; Downtons (Cowleaze, Fm, Ho & 9 Acres); Druce Lot (from Druce Fm *supra*); Drudge Bridge Plot (*dudge bridge* 1580, *druse Bridge* 1626², *Drudge Bridge* 1791, cf. prec.); Dry Plot; Dunditch; East Fd (*campus orientalis* Hy 3 (1372), *Estfelde* 1306 (1372), *le Estfild* 1463, *v.*

ēast, feld); East Hill; Egg Plant.; 8, 18 & 11 Acres; Everlasting Cl; 15 & 5 Acres; Flash Lots (*v.* flasshe); Folliff's Lot (perhaps for *J*-, cf. John *Jolliffe* 1664); 40, 4 & 14 Acres; Foxholes (*v.* fox-hol); Furzy Ball (*v.* ball); Garden (cf. *crofta iuxta gardinum* 1306 (1372), *Gardyn Clos* 1539, *v.* gardin); Gascoins; Gillinghams Ctg; Gilly Croft; Gore (*la Gore* 1270 (1372), *le Gore* 1404, *v.* gāra; *terr' vocat' la Gar'* 1393 (15) may also belong here); Great Md & Moor; Green Cl & Fd; Green Moor (*Greene-* 1624, *Granemoore* 1625, *v.* grēne¹, mōr); Green Sheephouse; Gundries; (The) Ham(s) (in Froome Md, — in White Md, — in West Md) (cf. *le Hammes in prato Occidental'* 1579, *v.* hamm, Frome Md, White Md *supra*, West Md *infra*); Harris's Lot(cf. John *Harris* 1664); Harts Cl (cf. *mes' nuper in tenur' Hugon' Hert* 1455, William *Harte* 1664); Haynes's Bush (cf. John *Hayne* 1867); Heath Grd & Lot (cf. *Hethfeld* 1428, *Hethiknoll* 1404, *v.* hǣð, hǣðig, feld, cnoll); Hedge Row; Hemmington's Lot (cf. John *Henington* 1664); Hems Moor (perhaps hemm 'edge, border'); Higher Grd & Plot; Higher Three; Hills Lot; Hog Plain; Hoggards (cf. Henry *Hoghurd* 1399); Hr & Lr Hollow Way (cf. (*Ouer-, Nether*)*hol*(*e*)*weyscombe, Hol*(*e*)*weysgore* 1404, 1463, *Holloway* 1641, *v.* hol², weg, with uferra, neoðerra, cumb, gāra); Home Fd, Grd & Plot (cf. *Homeclose als. Hilclose* 1531, *v.* home); Hop Yd; Horse Cl & Lot; The Horse Pool (*Horsepoole* 1637, cf. *Horsepool Bridges* 1791, *v.* hors, pōl¹); Hunger Hill (3 ×, a nickname for poor land); Hunt Hay Mdw (*v.* (ge)hæg; first el. perhaps hunte, but cf. *close called Huntes* 1539); Hurds Grd (cf. John *le Hurde* 1270 (1372)); Island in Froome Md, — in White Md (cf. Frome Md, White Md *supra*); Jack the Miller (cf. *claus' nuper Johannis Muller* 1440); Kimber Cl, 4 Acres & Orchd, Kimber Heath Grd (perhaps to be associated with *Cornebary* 1463, which is possibly from corn² 'crane' and beorg); Kings Arms Inn; Knight's Lot; Lains (*v.* leyne); Lanch (*v.* lanch, cf. *landschareknappe, -put* 1270 (1372) in bounds of Puddletown, *v.* land-sc(e)aru, cnæpp, pytt); Land Md; Langford Lot, Lords Cl or Langfords 7 acres (cf. Robert *Langford* 1480); Little Cl, Fd & Heath; Lodge Hay (*v.* (ge)hæg); Long Acre (*longeacre* 1625); Long Cl; Long Friday (cf. Piddlehinton f.ns. *supra*); Long Md (*Hyde Mede als. Long Mede* 1539, *Longmeade* 1623, cf. Hyde *supra*); Lords Weir Cl (cf. *Wereham* (a mdw on R. Frome) n.d. (1372), *les Weres domini* 1400, *la Were* c. 1400, *v.* wer); Lovard Fd (*camp' de Loford* 1399²) & Md (*Loueford*—1623, *Lufford*—1626¹, *Leouard Mead*(*e*) 1641, from Lovard *supra*, *v.* mǣd); Lovelace's Cl & Lot; Lower Fd & Plot; Maggot Md; Malthouse; Mason's Fd (cf. John *Mason* 1459); Meadow Grds; Meagers; Middle Grd; Middle Mart (perhaps to be connected with *mercatum in villa de Pudelton* 1274 (1372)); Milborne Acre (probably from Milborne St A. par. *supra*); Mitchells (cf. Henry *Mychell* 1440² (Piddlehinton)); Mount Hill; Moxey's Narrows (*v.* narrow); Muston Peak (from Muston in Piddlehinton par. *supra*, *v.* pēac); Nathans Fm; New Croft (*Newcroft* 1539); Gt & Lt Newland; New Md(w); Nightingale's (Md) (cf. Benjamin *Nightingale* 1664); Niland Lot & Md (*Nilam, via regia ducens a Nilam yeate, -gate* 1579, *Nilam Moore* 1624, *Nilans, Nilams closes* 1625, perhaps from hamm, *v.* geat, mōr; Professor Löfvenberg suggests that the first el. may be OE igil, il 'a hedgehog, a leech', *Nil-* arising from a ME atten Il-, *v.* atten); 9 Acres; No Mans Ld (at corner of par. near meeting of 3

boundaries); North Fd (*Northfyld* 1539); Oak Cl; The Oak Inn; Orchard
(Plot) (*le Orchard* 1440, cf. *le Brode(h)orchard* 1443 *et freq* to 1457, *v.* brād,
orceard); Ox Grd (cf. *montem voc' Oxefryth* 1270 (1372), *v.* oxa, (ge)fyrhðe);
Parish Md; Parson's Cl (cf. *cultūra biesteprestesthorn* 1306 (1372) ('to the
east of the priest's thorntree', *v.* bī, ēastan, prēost, þorn), *Vycayrs Acr' siue
Priesteacr'* 1531); Pauls Lot (cf. Nicholas *Pawel* 1270 (1372)); Paynes' Lot
(cf. *Pain's Bridge* 1791, Isabella *Payne* 1346); Patten Wd; Peaked—, Picked
Cl (*the peaked close* 1625, cf. (*la*) *Pikedelond(e)* 1306 (1372), *Pyked Halfe acre*
1458, *v.* peked, pīced, land); Piddlehinton Md (from Piddlehinton par.
supra); Pigeon Cl; Pigs Md (cf. *mes'...nuper Joh' Pigges* 1399, *Pygyz Croft*
1539); Pitchers Cl (cf. John *Picher* 1400); Plain; Plot; Pluddy Fd (*v.* pluddy);
Pond Bottom & Cl; Pooks Lot (cf. John *Pooke* 1664); Poor Gdns; Potters
Md; Pound Ash (*v.* pund); Pryers Fd, Priors Md (cf. William *Prior* n.d.
(1372), *Priors Bridge* 1625); Quay; Rick Yd (cf. *Abouerekestygheles,
Abouerekesheigh* 1306 (1372), *la* —, *le Hamreke* 1412, 1436, *v.* hrēac 'rick',
abufan, stigel, (ge)hæg, hamm); Rings in Froome Md (*v.* hring, cf. Frome
Md *supra*); Rough Cl & Pasture (cf. *Rogheham* n.d. (1372), *v.* rūh, hamm);
Rushy Plot; Hr Crofts or Rye Crofts (*closs called Ricroft* 1539); Samways
(Living) (cf. William *Samways* 1549); 7 Acres; Sherrins and Hanging Wall
Pce, The Barn Ho late Sherrins Barn, Town and Sherrins Closes, Sherrins
Md (cf. Thomas *Sherring* 1664); Shilton (cf. Shilton O 328, etc. from scelf
(WSax scylf) and tūn); 6 Acres; Small Fd; Smith's Shop; Snail Fm (*v.*
snægl); South Cl; Spring Orchd; Square (Acre & Fd); Stone Bridge 1791;
Stones Grd (cf. Emma *Stone* 1561, but cf. also *i acr' apud Stone* 1463, *v.*
stān); Gt & Lt Stoney Coombe (*Nether-, Ouer-* 1306 (1372), *Estestoncombe*
1399, *v.* stān, cumb, with neoðerra, uferra); Strap (*v.* strap); Strouds Plot
(cf. *cot' nup' Mich' Strode* 1463); 10 & 13 Acres; 3 Acres (and a half);
Three Corner Moor; Tingleton Hams (from Tincleton par. *infra*); Travellers
Rest 1842; (Lt) Trendle Coombe (Coppice & Pasture) (*Trendelcombe* 1426
et freq to 1463, *Little* —, *Great Trendlecombe* 1623, *the two Trendle Combes*
1626[1], 'circular valley', *v.* trendel, cumb); 12 Acres; 20 Acres (*cultura voc'
Twenty acre* 1306 (1372), *v.* twēntig, æcer); 22 Acres; 2 Acres (on the East);
Under Acre; Upper Moor; Vicarage Ho (*the Church Howse* 1539, cf. Parson's
Cl *supra*); Waterson Drove (*la Dreue apud le Thurne* 1427, *les droue yeate*
1636, *the Drove* 1641, *v.* drǣf, drove, þyrne, geat, Waterston *supra*);
Waterson Heath (cf. prec.); Watery Lane; Way Acre; Welch Md & Moor
(cf. George *Welch* 1664); West Md (*la* —, *le Westmed(e)* 1270 (1372) *et freq*
to 1539, — *Meade* 1579, *v.* west, mǣd, cf. (The) Ham(s) *supra*); Picked
Whatcombe, Whatcombe Coppice (*boscum vocatur Watecumb* Ed 1 (1372),
Whate- 15, *Watcomb(e)* 1539 (*a Under Wode called*—), 'wheat valley', *v.*
hwǣte, cumb, pīced); White Ridge (*la Wytherige* 1270 (1372), *la Wyter(h)ygge*
1288 (1372), 1288, *la White-, la Whyterigg* 1288, *v.* hwīt, hrycg); White's Lot
(cf. John *White* 1459); Whore Md; Withy Hays (*Wythy heys* 1539, *v.* wīðig,
(ge)hæg); Wood Cl (*Wodeclose* 1531); Wopses Castle ('a scrubby plot' B.K.
248) and on par. bdy, *v.* wæsp, castel(l)); The Wood stubbed up; Lr & Upr
Yards (*v.* gerd); Yearnings Bushes; Yonder Lot.

(b) *Abbysch-* 1539, *Abbishlane* 1579 (perhaps abbesse 'abbess'); *Jack
Adams Crose* 1539 (*v.* cros); *Aymstonforlong* 1306 (1372) (*v.* furlang, as freq in

this par.); *le Akerdich* Hy 3 (1372) (*v.* æcer, dīc); *Alneslane* 1579 (cf. Richard *Allen* 1664); *Bagham* 1306 (1372) (*v.* bagga or bagge, hamm (as freq in this par.)); *Ballescroft* 1446, *loco vocat' Bales* 1625 (cf. John *Ball* 1462 (Piddlehinton), *v.* croft (as freq in this par.)); *La Litell Bassehull* 1458 ('Bassa's hill', from the OE pers.n. *Bassa* and hyll, with lȳtel); *Batemanescrofte* 1458 (the surname *Bateman*); *ten' voc' Bernes* 1459 (cf. *ten' Johannis Berne in Loueford* 1404, *v.* Lovard *supra*); *Berton Close* 1531 (*v.* beretūn, clos(e) (as freq in this par.)); *bosco de Blakemore* 1244 (1372), *viam regiam versus Blakemour* 1270 (1372), *Blachemore* Ed 3 (1372) (*v.* blæc, mōr); *Blanford Lane* 1625, *the bridge uppon Blandforde Way* 1641 ('lane, way to Blandford Forum' (par. *infra*)); *le Bottokes* 1404 (*v.* buttuc); *Bradeweyslond* 1404, *Brodeweye* 1426 (*v.* brād, weg, with land (as freq in this par.)); (*claus' vocat'*) *la breche* Hy 3 (1372), 1306 (1372), *fossat' voc' Brechedych* 1270 (1372), *Middel-, Northmeste-, Southmestbreche* 1306 (1372), *le Nether-, le Ouerbrechefurlang* 1404, *Brechtopp,* —*Croft* 1539 (*v.* brēc, dīc, middel, norðmest, sūðmest, neoðerra, uferra, topp, cf. *Brechequart'* 15 which like *Hoggesquart' infra* was one of *Nomina quartiorum bosci de Pudeltoune vocat' Ilsyngbere*, from quart 'a quarter' (NED from 1454) or quarter, cf. Ilsington Wd *supra*); *Broc-* Hy 3 (1372), *Brokefurlang* 1441 (*v.* brōc); *Brode acre* 1458 (*v.* brād, æcer (as freq in this par.)); *Brodelond* 1463; *Brokyndiche* 1463 (*v.* brocen, dīc); *Brunyngescombe* 1306 (1372) (cf. *ten' Roberti Brounyng* 1404, *v.* cumb); *Bullynche* 1424 (*v.* bula, hlinc); *Cadeham* n.d. (1372) (the OE pers.n. *Cada*); *Che(l)fham* 1270 (1372), n.d. (1372) (*v.* calf (WSax cealf)); *Chesberghe* 1306 (1372) (*v.* beorg; Professor Löfvenberg suggests that the first el. is probably an OE **ceos,* a side-form of *cis 'gravel', due to influence from OE ceosol by the side of cisel); *Cheselbournemede* 1270 (1372) (from Little Cheselbourne *supra, v.* mæd (as freq in this par.)); *Clare clos'* 1539 (cf. *ij claus'…nuper Thome Clare* 1455); *Clauhulle* 15 (perhaps from clawu 'a claw' and hyll); *Clerkys-* 1404, *Clerkesplace* 1426 (*v.* clerc); *lez cliuys* 1457 (*v.* clif); *la clouenbergh* 1270 (1372) (*v.* (ge)clofen 'split', beorg); *duos cottag' vocat' Coates* 1624 (*v.* cot); *Cochestubbe* 1292 (1372) (cf. John *Coch* 1340 (Burleston), *v.* stubb); *Colyfordes Closse* 1539 (cf. John *Culiford* 1399); *les* —, *the Cornefeilds* 1635, 1641 (*v.* corn[1]); *terr' iacent' by the croft(e)* 1404, *Croftesclose* 1531; *Crokescumba, -cumbe* Hy 3 (1372), *-combe* n.d. (1372) (the pers.n. *Crōc* (< ON *Krókr*) and cumb, cf. *ten' Johannis Groke* 1483); *at Crosse* (p) 1474 (*v.* cros); *Denewyll* 15 (*v.* denu, wella); *Donfurlang* 1404 (*v.* dūn or dūne); *Durnewey* 15 (*v.* derne, weg); *Edforde Myll* 1579; *le Egras in occidental' prato* 1579 (*v.* eegrass, West Md *supra*); *Elcomb* 1539 (*v.* cumb); *locus vocat' Ellic barrs* 1637 (the pers.n. or surname *Ellice, v.* barre); *Ele-, Hellestub(h)aker* Hy 3 (1372), *Ellestubbe* 1306 (1372) (*v.* ellern, stubb, cf. foll.); (*le*) *Ellynhegge* 1463 (*v.* ellern, hecg, cf. prec.); *Estcumbe* Hy 3 (1372) (*v.* ēast, cumb); (*le*) *Estmede* 1444, 1457; *Estmestforlong* 1306 (1372) (*v.* ēastmest); *Estmeste-, Middel-, Westmesteflourlonde* 1306 (1372), *Flourlond* 1400 (cf. the analogous Flower Lds in Charminster par. *infra, v.* ēastmest, middel, westmest); *Forshulles* 1306 (1372), *Furs(se)dich, -gore* 1424, *Fyrsecloss* 1539 (*v.* fyrs, hyll, dīc, gāra); *Fotte acre* 1458; *la Fryelandshor* 1292 (1372) (probably from frīgland 'freehold land' (cf. Löfvenberg 71) and scoru '(boundary) mark'); *Fries Close* 1580; *Goridge Lane* 1626[2], —*Waye* 1627,

Gorage 1635; *acr' appellatur Gorprode* Ed 1 (1372) (*v.* gār-brǣdu); *Goushey* 1427, -*hay* 1428, (*la* -, *le*) *Gosehay*, -*hey* 1441 *et freq* to 1457 (*v.* gōs, (ge)hæg (as freq in this par.)); *Goseham* 1531; *Gosehill* 1579 (*v.* hyll); *Grodbury* 1424, *Grotbarwe* 1428, *Grotebary* 1463 (*v.* grot(a) 'particle of (sand or gravel)', beorg); *Hageham* 1270 (1372); *Her(r)inge(s) Pitt(e)* 1579, 1625 (the surname *Herring, v.* pytt); *la hevedacre* 1292 (1372) (*v.* hēafod); *heuedlond* 1306 (1372) (*v.* hēafod-land); *Heighewey* 1306 (1372), *Estheywey* 15 (cf. *altam stratam* 1404, *v.* hēah, weg); *Nethere-*, *Ouerehile* 1306 (1372) (cf. *le Hyle* in Coombe K. par. *supra, v.* neoðerra, uferra); *the Hill Topp* 1636; *Hynewill* 1427, *Hynwoll* 1455 (*v.* wella; the first el. may represent the gen.pl. *hīgna* of hiwan 'a household (of monks)', perhaps with reference to the possession of Puddletown manor by Christchurch priory (Hutch³ 2 614), cf. *the Hoppes infra*); *Hoggespoleshurn* 1270 (1372) (*v.* hogg, pōl¹, hyrne, though a surname *Hogg* is possible, cf. foll.); *Hoggesquart'* 15 (cf. prec. and *Brechequart' supra*); (*la*) *Holedich* Hy 3 (1372) (*v.* hol², dīc); *Holrewode* 15 (perhaps for *Holne-, v.* holegn, wudu); *claus' voc' the Hoppes als. Hincrofte* 1579 (*v.* hoppe; for *Hin-*, cf. *Hynewill supra*); (*cultura vocat'*) *Horiforde* 1306 (1372) (*v.* horig, ford, cf. *Horyford* in Preston par. *supra*); *Howletes Ham* 1624 (cf. *1 hampma prati apud Frome q' Joh' Houlat nuper tenuit* 1459); *Hurd(e) acre* 1270 (1372), 1306 (1372) (*v.* hirde); *Jolynes-* 1306 (1372), *Jolycroft* 1539 (the ME pers.n. or surname *Joelin*); *Kallesput* Hy 3 (1372) (cf. *clos' called Calsey* 1539; the first el. of both names may be a pers.n., cf. Walter *Calle* 1332 (Folke), with pytt, (ge)hæg); *Kirshull* 1404 (*Kyrvill* 1463 may also belong here); *la knap up lousedone* 1270 (1372) (*v.* cnæpp, lūs, dūn); (*le*) *Knoll* 1440, 1445, (*lez*) *Knolles* 1427, 1455 (*v.* cnoll); *Knoules* —, *Knowles Meade* 1625 (cf. *domus Nich' Knoles* 1579); *Kotemer(y)sdon* 1404, *Codmeresdowne* 1424, *Cotenersdoun* 1463 (*v.* dūn; the first part of the name may be a surname, or a p.n. from cot and mere¹); *la langelond(a), in longa terra* Hy 3 (1372), *Langelond(e)* 1306 (1372), 1458 (*v.* lang¹); *Langethornesfurlang* 1404, *Langthorn* 1463 (*v.* þorn); *Leperston* 1306 (1372); *Lerkeshey* 1459 (*v.* lǣwerce); *la lynche, abouelynch* 1306 (1372) (*v.* abufan, hlinc); *litelham* n.d. (1372) (*v.* lȳtel); *Locfurlang* 1404 (*v.* loc(a)); *via apud Longe Bridge* 1579; *Longeforlong* 1306 (1372); *Longhey* 1539; *Loscomb(e)* 1404 (*v.* hlōse, cumb); *Louard Lane* (cf. *Lovard supra*); *Mapilfurlonge* 1458 (*v.* mapel); *crucem marmoream* 1270 (1372) (in bounds of Puddletown; no doubt a cross of Purbeck marble, cf. G. D. Drury, "The Use of Purbeck Marble in Mediæval Times", DoNHAS **70** (1948) 94–5); *Marledelond* 1404 (*v.* marlede); *Marlyngputtes* 1306 (1372) (cf. *ii puteos marler' ib, v.* marling, pytt); *Attemede* (p) 1228 (*v.* atte); *le Medecrofte* 1446; (*le*) *Middelcroft(e)* 1443, 1451, -*crafte* 1450 (*v.* middel); *medius campus* 1292 (1372), *Middelfeld* 1306 (1372), *M' Bucklers Midle feilde gate* 1579 (*v.* feld); *Middelforlong* 1306 (1372); *Middelhull* 1404 (*v.* hyll); *Myntylond* 1404 (perhaps minte, -ig³); *Modbergh-furlang* 1404, *Modbargh* 1462, *Motborow* 1531 ('assembly hill or barrow', *v.* (ge)mōt, beorg, possibly the meeting-place of Puddletown hundred, cf. Modbury hundred *infra*); *Mogwelle(slake)* 1270 (1372) ('stream called *Mogwelle*' (possibly 'Mogga's stream'), from an OE pers.n. *Mogga*, cf. *Mogworthy* D 390, and wella, lacu); *le Moore* 1641 (*v.* mōr); *Morehey* 1463; *Nelbowe* 1463 (perhaps from ME *atten elbowe* '(place) at the elbow' (in some topographical sense), v. atten, el(n)boga); *Netelydene* 1270 (1372) (v. netel(e), -ig³, denu); *Newe Ley Moore* 1579 (v. lēah); *Newport* 1579 (v. port²); *loco voc' Nicholes* 1626; *croftam voc' Nythewey, Nytheweyescroft* 1270 (1372) ('(place) beneath the way', v. beniðan, weg); *Northforlong* 1306 (1372) (v. norð); *Binorthewode* (p) 1270 (1372) (v. bī, norðan, wudu); *le Nuwehouse* 1444 (v. nīwe, hūs); *Oldelond* 1306 (1372) (v. ald); *Otresford* Ed 1 (1372), *molend' de Otereford* n.d. (1372) (v. oter, ford); *le parc* Ed 1 (1372), *Parke Clos* 1539 (cf. Stafford Park Copse *supra* and *Wodepark(e)* 15, 1539, v. wudu, park); *Pathefurlong* 1463 (v. pæð); *Penyham* n.d. (1372) (v. pening); *Peuersle* 1270 (1372), *Peueris-* 1539, *Pevysley* 1579 (the ME surname *Peuer*, v. lēah); *angulum ubi situatur tumulus lapidum* 1270 (1372) ('a mound of stones, a cairn', in bounds of Puddletown at 300–400'); *Pyxden* 1306 (1372) (possibly the OE pers.n. *Pīc* (Redin 22), with denu); *Placeclose* 1531; *atte Pleystret* (p) 1340 (v. atte, plega, strǣt, cf. *Pleystrete* in Winfrith N. par. *supra*); *Estore-, Westoreplumle* 15 (v. plūme, lēah, ēasterra, westerra); *ten' voc' Pokeput* 1428 (v. pūca, pytt); *super la Porche* 1437 (v. porch); *campo de Pudelton* 1424; *aulam de Pudeltoun* 1270 (1372); *Pudeltowne Lane* 1635²; *Purforland* Hy 3 (1372) (v. pūr, furlang); *dimidiam acram ad putte* Hy 3 (1372) (v. pytt); *Estredeschute, Westredeschete* 15 (v. rēad, scīete); *la Reuelonde* 1306 (1372) (v. (ge)rēfa); *Riefurlong* 1463 (v. ryge); *Roberdynge-* 1306 (1372), *Robyndyngelond(e)* 1400 (apparently the pers.n. *Robert* (< OG, OFr *Rodbert*), with -ing⁴ and land); *Roddele* n.d. (1372) (v. rodd(e), lēah); *Salisbury Waye* 1625 ('the road to Salisbury W'); *biestesauntheresheigh* 1306 (1372) (the surname *Saunter*, v. bī, ēastan); *Saxcemede* 1270 (1372) (v. mǣd; *Saxce-* may represent an OE **Seax-ēa* 'a stream called *Seax*' ('the sword, the bright one'), v. seax 'knife, sword', ēa, cf. the probable figurative use of the cognate ON *sax* in Scand r.ns. and p.ns. (A. Bjerrum, *Danmarks Stednavne* XII 72–3, S. Benson, SOSÅ (1966) 41–5, J. K. Sørensen, *Dansk Sø- og Ånavne* 2 231), and cf. Saxfield, Saxbroke Ch 1 236; *Saxce-* may however represent the ON pers.n. *Saxi*, cf. Saxeys Ham in Wool par. *supra*); *Boscu' de Seynt Pere* 1458; *Scheplez* 1539 (v. scēap, lǣs); *crofta voc' Shepeorchard* 1404 (v. orceard); *Short(e)-, Chortelond(e), -lande* Hy 3 (1372), 1306 (1372) (v. sc(e)ort); *Schowddon* 1539; *la Sled* Hy 3 (1372), *Sladeacre* 1463 (v. slæd); (*lytel*)*smalwey* 15 (v. lȳtel, smæl, weg); *Sourelond* 1463 (v. sūr); *campo australi* 1292 (1372), *Sowthfylde, — Felde* 1539, *Southefylde* 1579; *Sowthheth* 1539 (v. hǣð); *Middelsoutlond, Northmestesouthlond, Southmestsotlond* 1306 (1372) (from sōt 'soot' or sūð 'south', cf. *Suteput infra*); *Southmest(e)forlong* 1306 (1372) (v. sūðmest); *les Splottes* 1423, *Splattes* 1539 (v. splott); *the Close by the Stable* 1626¹; *Stakedeham* n.d. (1372) (v. staked); *Stanshaue Wode* 1458 (v. stān, sc(e)aga, wudu); *Stapulforlong* 1306 (1372) (v. stapol); *(le) Stodfold* 1292 (1372), 1306 (1372) (v. stōd-fald); *crucem lapideam* 1270 (1372) (in bounds of Puddletown); *Overstonschulye undercome* 1270 (1372) (in bounds of Puddletown, v. stānscilig 'stony (ground)', ofer³, under, cumb); *viam regiam voc' Stretewey, la Gore de la Stretende* 1270 (1372) (in bounds of Puddletown at about SY 697955), *cultura apud la strete* 1306 (1372) (in Bardolfeston *supra*) (cf. *magnam stratam que tendit versus Pideletoun* Hy 3 (1372), v. strǣt, weg, gāra, ende; none of these forms refer to the Badbury Rings–Dorchester Roman road); *Suteput* 15 (perhaps sōt and pytt, but the first el. may be sūð or sūðan 'south'); (*prat' voc'*) (*le*) *Swan(n)esneste* 1444, 1447, 1450 (*v.* swan, nest); *Swenesdenefote* 1270 (1372) (probably to be associated with *terre apud la Swyne* 1400, *v.* swin² 'creek', with denu, fōt); *landschareknappe de la Sweteplek* 1270 (1372) (*v.* land-sc(e)aru, cnæpp, swēte, plek); *Tilers House* 1637 (cf. Christopher *Tyler* 1664); *Tynkkeltons hedge* 1539 (from Tincleton par. *infra*); *Tippelynch* 1306 (1372) (perhaps an OE pers.n. **Tippa,* and hlinc, cf. Tiptree Ess 307); *Totty acre* 1458; *Tounefurlong* 1463 (*v.* toun); *Twynesclose* 1448 (cf. *claus' q' Rob' Twyn' nuper ten'* 1443); *Varsfeld* 1427; *Wadham* 1270 (1372) (*v.* wād); *le Walls places* 1578; *Waterputtefurlonge* 1458 (*v.* wæter, pytt); *la Werawsdich* Hy 3 (1372) (*v.* dīc; first el. possibly wearg 'criminal'); *la Westererode* 1306 (1372) (*v.* westerra, rod¹); *campus occidental'* Hy 3 (1372), *Westfelde* 1306 (1372) (*v.* west, feld); *Westmestforlong* 1306 (1372) (*v.* westmest); *Wetelande* Hy 3 (1372), *-lond* 1306 (1372) (*v.* wēt); *Weteweye* 15 (*v.* wēt, weg); *le Wheatefeild* 1638 (*v.* hwǣte); *Whitebrigg* Hy 2 (1372) (*v.* hwīt, brycg); *White crosse* 1579 (*v.* hwīt, cros); *Wyteham* n.d. (1372) (*v.* hwīt, hamm); *la Wytheghe* (p) 1270 (1372) (*v.* wīðig); (*le*) *Whitelond* 1463 (*v.* hwīt, land); *fontem voc' Whithewell* 1270 (1372) (*v.* hwīt, wella); *Wika de Pudeleton* 1246 (1372), *la Wyke* 1270 (1372), *Wyke de Pudelton, terram de la Wyke* n.d. (1372) (*v.* wīc); (*le*) *Wilde-, Wyldecrofte* 1443, 1444, 1447, *-crafte* 1450 (*v.* wilde); *Willecroft* 1423 (*v.* wella, but possibly identical with prec.); *Wynehill* 1463 (possibly the OE pers.n. *Wina,* hyll); *Wodebroke* 15 (*v.* wudu, brōc); *la Wodecote* (p) 1270 (1372) (*v.* cot); (*la*) *Wodefurland, -furlang* Hy 3 (1372), *-forlong* 1306 (1372); *Wodeham* n.d. (1372); *Wod(e)weyshill* 1463 (*v.* wudu, weg, hyll); *Wodyetes* 1539 (*v.* geat); *la Woghelonde* 1306 (1372) (*v.* wōh); *medow called Worthes* 1539 (*v.* worð); *Wotecrofte* 1461 (*v.* āte); *le Yatehous(e)* 1444, 1450 (*v.* geat, hūs).

Tincleton

TINCLETON (SY 775918)

Tincladene 1086 DB, *Tyncleden* Hy 3 (1372) *ChrP*, 1268 *Ass* (p), 1296 Pat, *Tincledene* Hy 3 (1372) *ChrP*, 1316, 1386 Hutch³, *Hole-* Hy 3 (1372) *ChrP*, 1260 FF, *Uptincleden(e)* 1257 ib, *Tineleden* (for *Tinc-*) 1252 Cl, *Tynkelden(e)* 1270 (1372) *ChrP* (*Hole-*), 1331 FF (*Est—, West—*), 1332 SR *et freq* to 1535 VE, *Tinckledenne* 1280 *Ass*, *Estynkelden* 1304 Orig, *Tinkledene* 1386 Hutch³, *Tinkelden* 1552 (1674) *Mansel*

Tingledon 1201 FF, *Est* —, *West Tyngeldon* 1483 IpmR

Holetuncledene Hy 3 (1372) *ChrP*

Tincledon 1244 *Ass,* 1665 *Ilch, Tyncledon* n.d. (1372) *ChrP*

Hincleden, Ingleden 1244 *Ass*

Holetyngeldene 1270 (1372) *ChrP, Tingledene* 1291 Pap, *Tynglelden* 1405 *AddRoll*

Tinclinden 1288 *Ass*

Tykeldene 1327 *SR*
Tynkelton 1535 VE, *Tinklton* 1575 Saxton, *Tincleton als. West Tincleton* 1594 Hutch³

The second el. is denu 'valley' (in some forms replaced by or confused with dūn 'hill' and (later) tūn 'village'. The first el. is probably OE *tȳnincel 'small farm or estate', a mutated variant of OE *tūnincel* (occurring as glosses for Lat *villa* and *praediolum* (BT s.v.), cf. Fägersten 178); as Ekwall DEPN points out, derivatives in *-incel* do not usually have *i*-mutation, but cf. OHG *gensinklî, eninklî* from *gans, ano*. This manor was in fact assessed at only 2 hides in DB (VCHDo 3 88). The DB form with medial *-a-* and the ME forms with medial *-e-* may suggest derivation from an OE gen.pl. in *-a*, the meaning of the name then being 'valley of the small farms'; on [k] for OE *č* before consonants and back vowels (assuming *tȳninkilo > *tȳnincla > *tȳnncla* through syncopation), *v.* Campbell 174–7. This meaning would seem to be not inappropriate in view of the early divisions of Tincleton suggested by the affixes *Hole-, Up-, Est-* and *West-, v.* hol² 'hollow', upp 'higher', ēast, west. Kökeritz 125 points out that the initial *T-* may be excrescent (from OE *æt-* or ME *Est-, West-*) as suggested by the spellings *Hincle-, Ingleden* 1244, and compares Incledon D 33 (*Hingledon* 1238, *Incledene* 1242, 1244) for which the editors of PND suggest as first el. a pers.n. *Inghild, Ingflæd* or *Incla*; however the *Hincle-, Ingle-* forms, in view of their rarity, are better explained as due to the wrong analysis of *at Tincle-, Esttincle-, Westtincle-* etc., cf. Acton in Langton Mat. par. *supra.*

CLYFFE FM & HO (SY 782922), (*at*) *Clyue* 843 for 934 (eME) ASCharters, (*apud*) *Clyve* 843 for 934 (17) BCS 739, *Clive* 1086 DB, Exon, 1212 Fees, *Clyue, Clyve* 1288 *Ass* (p) *et freq* to 1405 AddRoll, *Clyff* 1535 VE, *Cliffe* 1664 HTax, *Cliffehouse* 1846 *TA*, '(place) at the cliff', *v.* clif (dat. sg. *clife*), with reference to the steep slope on the side of a 300′ ridge, cf. *Cliff Mount* 1811 OS.

OLD CHALK PIT. CLYFFE COPSE & LAUNDRY. DARK LANE. EWELEAZE FM, cf. (*Lt*) *Eweleaze* 1846 *TA*. GAMEKEEPER'S LODGE. GRAVEL PITS, *Heath and* — 1846 *TA*. HOLLAND'S FM. JARVIS'S TENEMENT, cf. Edmund *Gervas* 1664 HTax (Tolpuddle). NAPIER'S COPSE, cf. Nathanael *Napier* 1732 Hutch³. ST JOHN'S CHURCH (built 1849), cf. 'the church of *Tingledene*' 1291 Pap, 'the chapel of *Tincledene*' 1316 Hutch³, *Church and Yd, Church Fd* 1846 *TA*. SKATING POND.

SPRING CTG, spring marked 6". TINCLETON CROSS (*Tinklton Crosse* 1626 *Wal, v.* cros), DAIRY, FM (— *Farme* 1667 *CH*), & HANG (a wood, 1811 OS, cf. *Hanging* 1846 *TA, v.* hanging). VICARAGE, *Parsonage Ho* 1846 *ib.* WATERY LANE, down to R. Frome.

FIELD-NAMES

The undated forms are 1846 *TA* 226. Spellings dated 1270 (1372) are ChrP, 1332 SR, Eliz ChancP, 1626 *Ilch*, 1627, 1635 *Wal*, 1664 HTax, and 1667 *CH*.

(*a*) Abrahams pit; Bottom Grd; Bower; Boyce's Bridge 1791 Boswell; Calves Cl & Plot; Cowleaze; Cow Pound; Dallys md (cf. John *Delly* 1664 (Puddletown)); Drang, Throng (*v.* drong); Drove way; East Moor; 8, 15 & 5 Acres; Fook's Moor; 4 Acres (and half); 14 acres; Gollop's Cl; Green Fd; Hart heath wd (*v.* heorot); Heath (cf. *Mydleheath* Eliz, *v.* hǣð); Hilly grd; Homeplot; Lacy's md; Lawns (pasture, *v.* land or launde); Little moor; Long Breach (*v.* brēc); Long Gdn & Grd; Moor; New Foundland (probably referring to remoteness); Oat cl; (Old) Orchard; Paddock; Peake (*v.* pēac); Plot; Pound Cl; Purse md(w) (cf. *Purse-moore* 1667, perhaps a surname, cf. Henry *Purs* 1332 (Puddletown), Purse Caundle par. *infra, v.* mōr); Rates Cl; Rickhams; Rodney's cl; 7 & 17 Acres; Silver Plot; 6 & 16 acres; South Barrow (*v.* beorg); Stack yd paddock; Stephens md; Strap (*v.* strap); (Moor) 10 Acres; 3 acres; Tincleton Md (*Tinck-* 1626, cf. *at Clyue mid ðare mede þ þereto liþ* 843 for 934 (eME) ASCharters, *v.* mǣd, Clyffe *supra*); (Pit) 12 acres; 28, 27 & 2 Acres; West Pdk; Whithy bed; Willow bed.

(*b*) *Deanes pasture* 1667; *le Hollowe Waye* 1627 (*v.* hol²); *Keates Close* 1667; *Tinklton Lane* 1635 (cf. *venellam voc' Holetyngeldene* 1270 (1372)).

Tolpuddle

TOLPUDDLE (SY 793945) ['toupidl], *Pidele* 1086 DB (f. 78b), *Pidela* Exon, *Tolle-* 1210 P, 1268 *Ass et freq* to 1428 FA, *Tolepidele, -pyd(e)le, -pud(e)le* 1212 Fees, 1291 Pap, 1336 Ch, *Tolpud(e)l(l)(e)* 1270 (1372) ChrP *et freq* to 1626 *Wal, -pidel* 1401 DorR, *-pudull* 1428 FA, *-pydyll* 1441 Pat, *Towpiddle* 1575 Saxton, 'Tola's manor on R. Piddle', cf. Affpuddle par. *supra. Tola* (< ODan *Tola*), widow of *Urc*, Edward the Confessor's *huscarl*, got Edward's permission between 1058 and 1066 to give her lands to Abbotsbury abbey (ASWrits 2, Sawyer 1064, cf. Fees 92); Tolpuddle belonged to Abbotsbury abbey in 1086 DB (VCHDo **3** 80). *Tolleton* 1268 *Ass* ('Tola's farm', *v.* tūn) is probably an alternative name for Tolpuddle but may be a separate place somewhere in this neighbourhood.

ASHLEY BARN (SY 813955), 1811 OS, *Asleg'* 1268 *Ass* (*villa de* —), *Asseleg'* 1268 *ib* (p), *Ayslee* 1270 (1372) ChrP (*terra de* —), *Aschlegh*

1327 *SR* (p), *Asshleye* 1332 SR (p), *Asshele, Eislega, Esseleg(h)* n.d.
(1372) *ChrP, Asslegh(wode), Assle(is)-, Assleyswode* 1400 *Ilch,*
Ashley 1774 Hutch[1], 'ash wood or clearing', *v.* æsc, lēah, with **wudu.**

Southover Fm & Ho (SY 792939), *Southouer(e)* 1400 *Ilch,* 1625
Wal, -over 1546 Hutch[3], 1811 OS, 1841 *TA* (— *Fm Ho*), cf. *via*
regia voc' South over Streat 1579 *Wal,* 'south bank', *v.* sū ð, ōfer[1],
probably with reference to its position on R. Piddle or Trent, cf.
Northouere 1400 *Ilch, -over* Eliz ChancP, 1648 SC. According to
Hutch[3] 2 632, Southover was 'anciently called Thorpe or Throop',
v. foll.

Throop (lost), 1795 Boswell, *Trop* 1280 *Ass (vill' de* —), (*la*) *Throp(e)*
1285 FA, 1288 *Ass,* 1327 *SR,* 1332 SR, *La Thorp* 1288 *Ass, Throup*
1405 *AddRoll, West Throp(p)e* 1545, 1546 Hutch[3], *Thorpe als.*
Park Pale Eliz ChancP, *Throope* 1664 HTax, *v.* prop 'outlying farm,
secondary settlement', 'west' to distinguish it from Throop in
Affpuddle par. *supra q.v.,* cf. prec. and Park Fm *infra.*

(Old) Chalk Pit, cf. *regia via in Southouer ducens ad le Chalkepitt*
1625 *Wal.* Crown Inn. East Barn. Gravel Pit, cf. — *Pits* 1841
TA. Great Copse. Hill Barn. Little Copse. Manor Ho. Park
Fm, *Park(e) Pale (Farm)* 1645 Hutch[3], 1667 *CH,* 1811 OS, *Park(e)-*
pal(l)e 1648 SC (*farme of* —, *lands called* —, *the home medow of* —),
cf. *Park (Coppice & Md*) 1841 *TA, v.* park, pale 'fence', cf. Throop
supra; so called from its situation at the edge of Athelhampton park
for which *v.* Park Fm in Athelhampton par. *supra.* St John's
Church (from 12th cent.), 'the church of *Tolepudele*' 1291 Pap,
ecclesia parochie de Tollepudel 1348 *AD,* cf. *Church Cl* 1841 *TA.*
Southover Heath, 1811 OS, *v.* Southover *supra.* Tolpuddle Ball
(336', *v.* ball 'hillock'), Common (cf. *Poor lot cmn* 1841 *TA*) & Mill
(cf. *molendino d'ni de Tolpudele* 1400 *Ilch, via regia ducens a ponte*
vocat' Tolpuddle Mille Brugge 1579 *Wal, Mill Bridge* 1791 Boswell,
Tolpiddle Mill Fm 1794 Hutch[3], *Water Mill* 1841 *TA, v.* myln,
brycg; there were two mills at Tolpuddle in 1086 DB (VCHDo
3 80)).

FIELD-NAMES

The undated forms are 1841 *TA* 230. Spellings dated 1288 are *Ass,* 1332 SR,
1386, m17, 1794, 1863 Hutch[3], 1399, 1400[2], 1641 *Ilch,* 1400[1] *AddRoll,* 1579,
1627, 1635, 1636, 1637 *Wal,* 1648 SC, 1664 HTax, and 1667 *CH.*
   (a) Ashley Eweleaze & Hills (from Ashley *supra*); Ayres's; Bakers Thorns

(cf. John *Baker* 1400[1]); Barn (grd & md); Barricks Fd; Batters Grd; Bottom (Grd) (*v.* botm); Breech grd (*v.* brēc); Brick pits; Brook dry mdw, Eweleaze & water mdw (cf. *Brooke Lane* 1637, *v.* brōc); Browns Ham (*v.* hamm); Burleston plot (from Burleston par. *supra*); Burnb(r)ake (*v.* burnbake); Burtley; Cake Stones; Carthouse Barton; Catcombe (*a little coppice called Gatcomb* 1648, probably from gāt 'goat' and cumb); Causeway md (cf. *regia via vocat' the Casewaye* 1627, *v.* caucie); Cowleaze, Cowlease Hill; Cross Grd; Dairy Ho Barton; Dogs plot; 8 & 18 acres; Elbrow (cf. *Erthburie infra*); Eweleaze; 5 Acres; Long 14 acres; Furzey grd & Lynch (*v.* hlinc); Galtons grd (cf. Edward *Galton* 1664, *Gaultons Meade* in Athelhampton par. *supra*); bilow Glebe 2 acres (*v.* below); Goulds Cl (cf. William *Gould* 1664); Green fd; Groves's Grd; Halls cl; Hammer hill (perhaps from hamor); Hangings (*v.* hanging); (N)E & (S)W heath grd, Heath 6 acres (cf. *la Hethfeld* 1400[2], *v.* hǣð, feld); Home Md, Orchd & Plot; Horse cl; Island; Kitehills (*v.* cȳta); Knowle Hill (*v.* cnoll); Lambing plot; Land md & 9 acres; Lawrences; Little fd hill; Little grd; Long md; Lovelace's (Mdw & New Cl) (cf. Robert *Louelace* 1664); Lower Fd; Lynch 9 acres (*v.* hlinc); Marling pits (*v.* marling); Meadens (cf. John *Meedens* 1664 (Puddletown), *Meaders Bridge* 1791 Boswell); (Hr & Lr) Mead(ow); Middle Md; 9 & 19 acres; Niprods fd & md; Old Down; Orchard; Oxmoor (and hopyard); Paddock; Parish Md & pound; Parsonage water mdw (cf. Vicarage Ho *infra*); Pollards (cf. John *Pollard* 1400[1]); Rick yd; Rolls's Md & Withey bed (cf. Samuel *Rolle* m17); Sawpit; Sand pits; 17 acres; Shitlocks; Short lds; 6 & 16 Acres; Small plot; Smithey; South mdw; Spear bed (*v.* spear); Stile Cl; Tatcombe (cf. an identical f.n. in Dewlish par. *supra*); 10 & 13 acres; Thornberry 1863 (*v.* þorn, beorg); Tolpiddle East & West Fm 1794; 12, 20 & 2 Acres; Vicarage Ho (cf. *parsonage of Southover* 1648, *the Churchowse* 1667); Warren; Wateredge; Watering pce (*v.* watering); West fd; West Leaze Coppice; Whitehouse grd; Willowbed; Withey bed; Hr & Lr Wood.

(b) *loc' voc' Beare gate* 1636 (*v.* geat, Bere R. par. *supra*); *le butt close* 1635 (*v.* butt[2] or butte); *Doddecrofte* 1399 (cf. William *Dodde* 1332, *v.* croft); *loco vocato antiquitus Erthburie* 1386 (*v.* eorð-burh 'fortification built of earth'); *Forwode* 1399 (*v.* fore, wudu); *la Fremede* 1386 (*v.* frēo, mǣd); *Hussle(y)wode* 1400[2] (first el. probably hys(s)e 'a shoot', with lēah, wudu); *atte Mere* (p) 1400[2] (*v.* atte, mere); *la More* (p) 1288 (*v.* mōr); *Reynesacr'* 1400[2] (the ME surname *Reyne*, *v.* æcer); *Smalcombe* 1400[2] (*v.* smæl, cumb); *le Stone Bridge iuxta Tolpudle* 1627 (*v.* stān); *campo de Tolpudle* 1627; *Tolepuddle Way* 1641 (*v.* weg); *via apud Velle* bridge 1579 (Professor Löfvenberg suggests that the first el. may be eModE *fell* 'a cutting down of timber' (NED s.v. *fell* sb.[4] sense 1b)); *Walkardesham* 1400[2] (a ME surname from the OE pers.n. *Wealhheard*, with hamm); *regia via vocat' Whitewaye* 1627 (*v.* hwīt, weg).

VIII. ST GEORGE HUNDRED

In c. 1086 GeldR the hundred did not include Broadmayne (then in *Celberge* hundred, *v.* Winfrith hundred *supra*) and part of Winterborne St Martin (then in Culliford Tree hundred *supra*) (*v.* Anderson 117–8, VCHDo 3 144). At the same date the borough of Dorchester was within the hundred, and

has been included here for convenience, likewise Fordington which became
a separate liberty containing Hermitage par., Dalwood par. (now D) and
Hartley in Minterne Magna par., etc., besides Fordington itself (Hutch³ **2**
791).

St George Hundred, *Dorecestre hundret* c. 1086 GeldR, *hundredum
Sancti Georgii de Dorecestria* 1166 RBE, (*hundredum*) *Sancti Georgii*
1185 P *et freq* to 1428 FA, — *Georgi* 1244 *Ass*, (*hundredum de*) *Sancto
Georgio* 1212, 1219 Fees, 1244 *Ass*, — *Jeorgio* 1227 Fees, *Sancti
Gregorii* (sic) 1272 Cl, *hd of Seynt George* 1329 Ipm, *Hundredum de
Seint Georg* 1346 FA, *hundr' de George* 1462 *MinAcct*, *George hd*
1539 LP, *hundred of* (*the*) *Georg*(*e*) 1617 *Add*, 1653 *ParlSurv*, 1664
HTax. The GeldR name is from Dorchester par. *infra*; the subse-
quent name seems to be from the church of St George in Fordington
(*v.* Dorchester par. *infra*), which is *eccl. S. Georgii in Dorcestra* 1091
Osm, cf. Hutch³ **2** 533.

Fordington Liberty, *Liberty of Fordington* 1664 HTax, *Forthington
Liberty* 1795 Boswell, *v.* Fordington in Dorchester par. *infra*.

Bradford Peverell

Bradford Peverell (SY 659931)

> *Bradeford*(*e*) 1086 DB, 1196 ChancR, 1197 P, 1200 RC, 1210–12
> RBE, 1219 Fees *et freq* to 1535–43 Leland, *-fort* (?) 1175–6
> France, 1212 Fees, *Bradford* 1402, 1428 FA
> *Bradeford Peuerel*, — *Peverel*(*l*) 1244 *Ass*, 1257 Pap, 1288 *Ass et
> freq* to 1431 FA, *Bradford Peverell* 1352 Midd, 1377, 1382 Pat,
> — *Peverill* 1664 HTax

'Broad ford' (across R. Frome), *v.* brād, ford, cf. *sub ponte de
Bradeford* 1268 *Ass*. The family of *Peverel*(*l*) was here in the 13th
and 14th centuries (Robert — 1200 RC, 1212, 1219 Fees, Andrew —
1236 ib, John *Peverel* 1275 FF, RH, etc.), cf. Newton Peveril in
Sturminster M. par. *infra*.

Muckleford (SY 640935)

> *Mukelford* 1244 *Ass* (p), 1309, 1315 FF, 1402 DorR, *Mukle-*
> 1268 FF (p), *Mucle-* 1268 *Ass* (p), *Mukele-* 1288 *ib*, *Muckil-*
> 1575 Saxton, *Muckleford* 1636, 1662 GW (*common Feilds
> of* —), 1811 OS

Mokeleford 1268 *Ass* (p), *Mokelford(e)* 1327 *SR et freq* to 1504 Ipm
Mukelesford 1288 *Ass*

'Mucel's or Mucela's ford' (across R. Frome), from the OE
pers.n. *Mucel* (Redin 142, cf. Mucklestone St, Muggleswick Du
(DEPN)) or an unrecorded weak form *Mucela*, and ford. Most of the
spellings suggest *Mucela*, but they can also be accounted for as an
uninflected genitive of *Mucel* or by assuming loss of gen. -*s* in the
compound. Kökeritz 125 suggests connecting the first el. with S dial.
muckle '(a heap of) manure', cf. also *muckle* 'furze or heath laid in on
the top of a drain ere the earth is cast in' (Barnes 83). Eyton 123–4
tentatively suggested identification of the small lost DB manor of
Hiwes (f. 80b) with this place, *v.* the f.n. *Hywysshhegge* in the adjacent
par. of Winterborne St M. *infra*.

WHITFIELD BARN & FM (SY 675915), *Whitewell(e)* 1195–1202 P,
1231, 1301 Cl *et freq* to 1615 *DuCo* (—*ferme*), 1664 HTax (—*house*),
Witte- 1195 P, *Witewell* 1196–1202 ChancR, 1205, 1222 ClR, 1227
Fees, -*will* 1212 ib, -*wolle* 1328 *Ct*, *Wytewll* 1268 *Ass*, -*welle* 1335 *Ct*,
Whytewell(e) 1300 Ipm, 1319 Pat, 1650 *ParlSurv*, *Whete-* 1315 FF,
Whittewell(e) 1318 Fine, *Whitwell* 1345 *Rent*, *Frome Whit(e)well* 1774
Hutch[1], 1863 Hutch[3], *Whitfield Fm* 1798 *EnclA*. 'White spring',
from hwīt and wella, in allusion to a spring (marked 6″) 'which
breaks out here at the bottom of a chalky hill' (Hutch[3] 2 415), near
R. Frome. The modern alteration of the name is due to confusion
with Frome Whitfield (in Stinsford par. *infra*) to which manor it
once belonged.

BRADFORD DOWN, 1811 OS, *ye Downe* 1634 *SalisT*, *the Down* 1798
EnclA, cf. *Hr*, *Lr*, *Middle*, *N & S Down* 1798 *ib*, *v.* dūn. BRADFORD
PEVERELL FM & HO. BRIDPORT RD PLANT. BROWN'S COPPICE, cf.
Judith *Browne* 1664 HTax. COMBE BOTTOM, cf. *Great Coombe* 1798
EnclA, *v.* cumb. THE COPPICE. COUX PLANT., -*Fd ib*, perhaps the
surname *Cook* in the possessive case. CUCKOO POUND, 1837 *TA*
(Charminster), an island in R. Frome, cf. the same name in Langton
Mat. par. *supra*. DAIRY HO. FORDINGTON BOTTOM & DOWN
(*Fordyngton Downe* 1607 Clegg, *Le Downe* 1615 *DuCo*, *The Down*
1841 *TAMap* (Fordington), cf. Nicholas *atte Doune* 1332 SR, *v.*
dūn, atte), in the old par. of Fordington, *v.* Dorchester par. *infra*.
FORTY ACRE PLANT. GASCOYNE NEW BARN, from Gascoyne Bridge
in Charminster par. *infra*. GILES CROSS, *Hyles Crosse* 1634 *SalisT*.

GOLDSMITH'S PLANT. GROVE HO., *v.* grāf(a). HALF MOON PLANT., from its shape. HANGING PIECE BELT, a narrow wood on the slope of Penn Hill *infra*, *v.* hangende or hanging, belt. HART HILL PLANT., *v.* heorot. HIGHFIELD PLANT. HILL PLANT. HOME BARN, cf. *Home Fd & Md* 1798 *EnclA*. LONG COPPICE. LONG WALK PLANT. LONGWALLS COPPICE. MANOR FM (formerly MANOR HO). MUCKLEFORD DAIRY HO, HR BARN *&* PLANT., (HR) MUCKLEFORD FM. NEW BARN *&* PLANT. PARK BELT, near to Bradford Peverel Ho *supra*, *v.* park, belt. PENN HILL (1811 OS, 418′), PENNS PLANT., cf. *Hr & Lr Pen* 1798 *EnclA*, *v.* penn[1] 'a hill'. POUNDBURY FM, from Poundbury in Dorchester par. *infra*. PUMP HO. QUATRE BRAS, a house. RECTORY, cf. 'rectory of *Bradeford Peverel*' 1257 Pap, *ye Parsonage house* 1664 HTax, *ye parsons Hamms* 1634 *SalisT*, *v.* hamm. RED BARN. ST MARY'S CHURCH, cf. 'the church of *Bradefort*' ? 1175–6 France, 'the church of *Brad(e)ford Peverel(l)*' 1348–1384 Pat. SEVEN BARROW PLANT., *Seven Barrows* 1798 *EnclA*; there are nine tumuli marked 6″ and twelve are noted by RCHMDo **I** 35; one is called *Sea Barrow* 1811 OS. LR SKIPPET (1811 OS), HR SKIPPET FM (*Hr Skippet* 1811 OS), *v.* Mount Skippet in Owermoigne par. *supra*. SQUARE COPPICE *&* PLANT. STRAP BOTTOM, cf. *Straps* 1798 *EnclA*, *v.* strap. OLD TANYARD. THREE CORNERED PLANT. THREE CORNERS, like prec. a triangular plant. TILLY WHIM (COPPICE), a house named from Tilly Whim Caves in Swanage par. *supra*. TRANCHANT, a plantation. WELL HO.

FIELD-NAMES

The undated forms are 1798 *EnclA* 24. Spellings dated 1335, 1426, 1483 are *Ct*, 1340 NI, 1470 DorR, 1615 *DuCo*, 1634 *SalisT*, 1662 *GW*, 1664 HTax, 1774 Hutch[1] and 1811 OS.

(*a*) Bakers Hedge Flg; Barn Fd; Bartletts (cf. Richard *Bartlett* 1664 (Fordington)); Billings Ditch (*Bills-* 1634); Bradford Cl (First- to Fourteenth-inclusive); Bradforth Heath (*-ford-* 1811); Broaden Hams (*v.* hamm); Broad Flg; Broken Way; Chapel Cl 1774 (the site of a chapel at Muckleford, *v.* Hutch[1] **I** 445); Charminster Mdw (from Charminster par. *infra*); Cow Leaze; Dutch Cap (probably an allusion to shape); East Cl *&* Ctg; Ewe Leaze; 5 Acres; Forge Fd; 4 Acres; Furze Down; Gratton Cl (*v.* grǣd-tūn); Gravel Hill; Green Pale Flg (*v.* pale); Grimstone Lot (from Grimstone in Stratton par. *infra*); Gutt Flg (*Gut-* 1634, *v.* gut 'water-channel'); E *&* W Ham (*Westham* 1662, *v.* hamm); Hardy's Orchd (cf. John *Hardy* 1664); Hog Fd; Hounslow Fd (cf. Hounslow Mx 26); Knowlhill Bottom (*v.* cnoll); Long Cl (1662) *&* Md; Marsh Flg (*Mersh-* 1634) *&* Mdw; Mill Acre (there were two mills at Bradford P. in 1086 DB, *v.* VCHDo 3 91, and a mill is mentioned in

1315 FF); Morass (v. morass); New Fd; 19 Acres; North Md(w) (— *Meade* 1662); Nursery (Cl); Oat Cl; Hr & New Orchard (*ye Lower*—, *the higher Orchard* 1634); Paddock; Pond Cl; Poor Ho; Rue Fd (from Rew in Winterborne St M. par. *infra*); 7 & 16 Acres; South Fd; Stoney Cl (cf. *Stonie furlong* 1634, v. stānig); 10 & 30 Acres; Touches Hedge Flg (cf. John *Touch* 1340); 12, 20 & 27 Acres; Wade Md (v. (ge)wæd); West Ctg & Fd; E & W Willow Hams (v. hamm); Wolfs Hay (*Wolues-* 1335, 1426, *Wulveswere* 1483, *Woulves weere als. Woulves hayes* 1615, *Wolfer Heys* 1634, cf. Henry *Woulfe* 1470, v. wer, (ge)hæg).

(b) *ye com'on meade* 1634; *Culverhill* 1634 (v. culfre); *the East feild* 1634; *ye greene* 1634; *Longlands* 1634; *the middle feild* 1634; *South Close* 1634.

Broadmayne

BROADMAYNE (SY 729866)

> *Maine* 1086 DB, 1236 FF, *Meine* 1200 Cur (p), *Meines* 1204 FF (p), *Mayne* 1236 ib, 1244 *Ass et freq* to 1348 Cl
>
> *Brademaene* 1202 FF, *-meyne* 1244 *Ass*, *Brodemayn(n)(e)* 1288 *ib*, 1297 Pat *et freq* to 1575 Saxton, *-maygne* 1392 *Weld*[1] (p), *Brodmayne* 1297 Pat, *Brodemayne Martel(l)* 1368 FF, 1378, 1387 Cl, *Broadmayne otherwise Mayne-Martel* 1785 *SalisT Mayn(e) Martel(l)* 1244, 1288 *Ass*, 1280 Ipm, 1297 Pat *et freq* to 1450 Cl, — *Martill* 1428 FA, *Meyne Martel(l)* 1268, 1280, 1288 all *Ass*, 1291 Tax, 1428 FA, *Maigne Martel(l)* 1350, 1354 Pat

From PrWelsh main[2] 'a rock, a stone', no doubt with reference to the many large sarsens scattered around Little Mayne Fm ½ mile NE of Broadmayne village (called Stone Circle 6″, but according to RCHM 2 513 'a natural phenomenon...despite alleged arrangements in one or more circles or avenues'). 'Broad' to distinguish it from Little Mayne in W Knighton par. *supra*, v. brād; *Martel(l)* from the family of that name which held this manor from at least as early as the beginning of the 13th cent. (Eudo — 1202, 1236 FF, Helewise — 1268 *Ass*, Roger *Martel(l)* 1280 Hutch[3], v. Hutch[3] 2 539, cf. Hinton Martell par. *infra*). It is referred to as 'the hundred of *Brodmayne*' in 1297 Pat.

MAINE DOWNE (lost, about SY 705853), 1811 OS, *The Down* 1785 *SalisT*, *Broadmaine Down* 1811 *EnclA*, probably identical with *Meurigge* (for *Men-*) 1236 FF, *Meynrugge*, *Manriggia* 1269 Ch, *Maynerig(g)e*, *-rygge* 1436–1477 *Weld*[1], v. hrycg 'ridge', cf. prec.

BLACK DOG (P.H.), — *Inn* 1811 *EnclA*. BROOMHILL DROVE, *Bromhull* 1346 Ipm, cf. *Broomhill Cl & Ditch* 1785 *SalisT*, *Broomhill (Rd & Inclosures)*, *Hither & Yonder Broomhills* 1811 *EnclA*, v. brōm, hyll. CHALKY RD. CHARLMONT HO, *Charlemont Fm* 1863 Hutch³. COLD PARK WD, *Cold Parks* 1811 *EnclA*, v. park. GLEBE FM. HALF MOON COPPICE, now rectangular in shape. HOLCOMBE BOTTOM, v. hol², cumb. MANOR FM. OSMINGTON DROVE, — *Bridle Way* 1811 *EnclA*, leading to Osmington par. *supra*. POOR LOT. RECTORY, cf. *the Parsonage Barn* 1785 *SalisT*, *Parsonage Gdn* 1811 *EnclA*. SOUTH DROVE. WATERGATES CTG & LANE, perhaps with reference to sluices; near the stream rising at Broadmayne which (lower downstream) was called *Mayn(e)water* in the 15th cent., v. the f.n. Main Water Close in Moreton par. *supra* and cf. *aquam de Mayne Martel* 1288 *Ass*. WORKS, cf. *Brick Yard Rd* 1811 *EnclA*.

FIELD-NAMES

The undated forms are 1811 *EnclA* 15. Spellings dated 1327 are *SR*, 1332 *SR* and 1785 *SalisT*.

(a) Behind Town Rd; Bottom Flg; Broadmayne St. 1785; Chip's Cl; the Common Fd 1785; Cooks Cl; Courtlands Corner; Cross Tree Lane; the East Fd 1785; Furze Lott 1785; Gore Flg (v. gāra); Hammonds Barton; E & W Headlands; Hr Her(r)ons (cf. Robert *Hayron* 1327, 1332); Knaps (v. cnæpp); (Head & Long) Langcomb(e) (v. lang¹, cumb); Longhedge (1785); Maine Cmn (v. par. name *supra*); Marblen's Flg; the Middle Fd 1785; the Moor Cmn; North Down 1785; Papern Hill; the Parish common Lott 1785; Pearces (Lane Rd), Pearses Tenement & Rd; Sansom's; Shepherds Flg (cf. John *Shephurd* 1332); Short Bat(t)s (v. batte); South Close(s), South Cl Rd (*South Cl (Ditch)* 1785); Talbot's Rd (cf. the *Talbot* family which bought the manor of Broadmayne in the 16th cent., v. Hutch³ 2 541); Warmwell Rd (to Warmwell par. *supra*); West Fd 1785; West Flg; Weymouth Rd (to Weymouth par. *supra*); Whitcombe Bridle Way (to Whitcombe par. *supra*); Whiteshord (possibly 'white gap' from hwīt and sceard); Woods Rd.

Charminster

CHARMINSTER (SY 681927) [ˈtʃɑːrmistər]

Cerminstre 1086 DB, 1200–10 Osm, *-minister*, *-ministr(e)* 1091 ib, 1212 Fees *et freq* to 1288 *Ass*, *-menistra*, *-menistr(e)* e13 *Salis*, 1223 ClR *et freq* to 1288 *Ass*, *-menstre* 1278 QW, *-myn(i)str(e)* 1288 *Ass*, 1332 SR, *Ceremenstre* 1278 QW, *Chermyn(y)str(e)*, *-mynistre*, *-ministre*, *-minster*, *-mynster*, *-minystre* 1289 *Ilch et*

freq to 1435 Pat, *-munstre* 1330 FF, *-men(i)stre* 1330, 1331 Pat,
1385 Cl, *-mystr(e)* 1407 *Salis*, 1412 Pat, 1428 FA, *Cheremenstre*
1340–1342, 1371 Pat, *-mynstre* 1371 ib
Cerneministr' 1223 ClR, *Chernminstr'* 1291 Tax
Chirmistre 1323, *-menistre* 1330, *-mynstre* 1371, 1386 all Pat,
Chyrmynstre 15 *AD*
Charminstr' 1376 Ilch, *-mynstre* 1386 FF, 1400–1443 Ilch, *-mistr'*
1410 ib, *-mystr'* 1449 Weld[1] (p), *-mester* 1546 Lane, *-myster* 1549
ib, *-mister* 1606 (1770) ib, 1642 Ilch (— als. *Carmister*), *-minster*
1617 Add

'The church on R. Cerne', v. mynster, RNs. *infra*. The prebend
of Charminster was called *the Go(u)lden Prebend(e)* 1549 Lane et freq
to 1619 DuCo, because it was the best endowed prebend of Salisbury
cathedral (Hutch[3] 2 556). The bounds of Charminster are described
in 1606 (1770) Lane (M5, p. 27).

STREET-NAMES: EAST HILL, 1837 *TA*; MILL LANE, named from one of the
two Corn Mills *infra*; NORTH ST., 1617 DuCo, *le Northstre(e)t(e)*, *-streat*
1606 (1770) Lane; POUND CL, 1837 *TA*, Pounde — 1617 DuCo, v. pund, cf.
The Pounde is utterlie ruyned and fit to be spedely repayred 1617 Add; WEST
HILL, 1837 *TA*. Lost street-names include *South Street* 1606 (1770) Lane;
la Weststret 1343 Ilch.

BURTON (SY 687917), HR & LR (2×) BURTON FM, Burton 1204
LibR (— sub *Dorcestr'*), 1212 Fees, 1213, 1222 ClR et passim, Buriton
1258 Ilch, Bourton 1289 ib (— iuxta *Dorchestr'*) et freq to 1497 ib,
Borton 1300 Ipm, Estburton 1453 Weld[1], great(e)-, magn'-, Little
Burton 1546, 1549 Lane, Hr or Lt —, Lr or Gt Burton 1774 Hutch[1],
Middle Burton 1863 Hutch[3], 'farm near the fortification', v. burh-tūn,
with reference to Poundbury Camp in Dorchester par. *infra*.
Estburton was probably an earlier name for Hr Burton, v. ēast. A
bridge here is mentioned as *pontem de Burton* 1345 Ilch, Burton
Bridge 1791 Boswell.

CHARLTON HR DOWN (SY 688955), Cherlton 1226 Cur, Cherleton(e)
1242 Ch, l13 Ilch, 1280 Ass et freq to 1360 Ipm, — iuxta Polayneston
1328 Ilch, Charleton 1303 FA, 1376 Ilch et freq to 1606 (1770) Lane
(villat' de —), — iuxta Charmynstre 1400, 1443 Ilch, — Farme 1637
ib, 1664 HTax, Charlton juxta Charmynstre 1412 FA, Carleton 1409
Ilch, 'farm of the peasants', v. ceorl (gen.pl. ceorla), tūn, cf. Pulston
infra. There was a mill here in 1226 Cur.

FORSTON (SY 666956), HR FORSTON FM, FORSTON GRANGE & HO,
? *Cerne(l)* 1086 DB, *Fos(s)ardeston* 1236 Fees, 1343, 1346 FF, 1344
Pat, *Forsardes-* 1285 FA, 1327 *SR*, 1332 SR, 1371 *Ilch*, *For(e)-
shardeston(e)* 1303, 1346, 1428 FA, *Forston* 1431 ib *et freq* to 1837
TA (— *Fm*), *Furston* 1546 *Lane*, (— *als. Foston*) 1606 (1770) *ib,
For(r)eston* 1553 *PlR*, 1606 (1770) *Lane* (— *als. Forston*), 1617 *Add,
Foston Ferme* 1617 *Add*, 'Fo(r)sard's manor', a post-Conquest name
in tūn like Herrison and Pulston *infra* (*v.* IPN 131). William *Forsard*
held this manor in 1285 FA, but the family must have been here
earlier, cf. William *Fossard* 1244 *Ass* (possibly the same man,
mentioned under this hundred). Forston, like Herrison and Pulston
infra, is on R. Cerne, and like them is no doubt one of the nine
manors called *Cerne(l)* in DB (Eyton 123 f, VCHDo 3 144, DBGazetteer 120; *v.* further RCHMDo 3 71–2 on the probable sites of the
various original settlements). There is mention of a *grangia* here in
1470 *Weld*[1], 1478 *Ct*.

HERRISON (CTGS & HO) (SY 678945), ? *Cerne(l)* 1086 DB, *Harenges-
tun* 1224 ClR, *-ton* 1244 *Ass*, *Haring(e)ston* 1227 FF ('all the land of
Cerne which is called —'), 1236 Fees, *Harangeston* l13 *Ilch* (*semita
que venit de Dorcestra ad* —), 1285 FA, *Her(r)yng(g)(e)ston* 1303 ib,
1327 *SR*, 1332 SR, 1346, 1412 FA (*Lytel*—), 1428, 1431 ib (*Lytel*—),
Northeryngeston juxta Charmynster 1372 Hutch[3], *Heringeston juxta
Cherminstr'* 1416 IpmR, *Hernyston* 1546 *Lane*, *Parva Herriston als.
Parva Hetheringston, Hermston, Hernston* (*als. Herings-, -Harings-
ton*) 1606 (1770) *ib*, Lt or N *Herringston* 1774 Hutch[1], *Herriston Fm*
1837 *TA*, 'Hareng's manor', *v.* tūn, cf. prec. where the identification
of the DB form *Cerne(l)* is also discussed. The *Hareng* family was here
from the 13th cent. (Philip *Hareng* 1224 ClR, 1227 FF, 1236 Fees,
-Harang 1244 *Ass*, Adam *Harang* 1285 FA, etc.), cf. Chaldon
Herring par. *supra*.

PULSTON BARN (SY 667954), ? *Cerne(l)* 1086 DB, *Cerna Pulli* 1166
RBE, *Pulleinston* 1236 Fees, *Pul(l)eyn(e)ston* 1244 *Ass* (p), 1268 FF,
1288 *Ass*, 1319 FF *et freq* to 1462 MinAcct (*Nether-*, *Ouer-*), 1473
ib (*Nither-*), 1470 *Ct* (*Nyther-*), 1475 *ib* (*Over-*), *Polayn(e)s-,
Polaines-, Pole(y)n(e)ston* 1270 (1372) *ChrP*, 1275 RH, 1280 *Ass et
freq* to 1444 *Weld*[1], *Pouleynston* 1330 FF (p), *Pullaynnestone* 1429
Ilch, *Pullyngeston* 1492 Ipm, 1531 *Weld*[1], *Pullingstone* 1653 *ParlSurv*,
Polington 1774 Hutch[1], *Pollingston* 1795 Boswell, *Pollyston* 1546

Lane, Pulston, Poleston als. *Polyston* 1606 (1770) *ib*, *Pulston Fm* 1837 *TA*, 'Pul(l)ein's manor', *v.* tūn, cf. Forston *supra* where the identification of the DB form *Cerne(l)* is also discussed. *Bernardus Pullus* (also referred to in connection with Do as Bernard *Poleyn*, — *Polein*, — *Puleyn* Hy 2 RBE) held one fee here in 1166 RBE, as did John *Pulein* in 1236 Fees, cf. also William *Polein* 1195, 1197 RBE, Richard *Puleyn* 1258 *Ilch* (the surname is from Lat *pullus*, OFr *poulain* 'a colt').

WOLFETON HO (SY 678921) & MANOR ['wulftən, 'wouvətən], *Wlveton* Hy 3 Ipm (p), 1247 FF, 1285 FA, *Wylweton* Hy 3 Ipm, *Wolue-*, *Wolveton* 1231, 1233 FF, 1259 Cl, 1268 *Ass* (p), 1280 *ib et freq* to 1837 *TA* (— *Fm* & *Ho*), — *juxta Dorcestre* 1330 FF, *Wuluuiton* 1236 Fees, *Wulve-* 1236 ib, 1495 Ipm, *Wulue-*, *Wolueneston* 1244 *Ass*, *Wlfre-* 1262 FF, *Wulfeton* 1279 Ipm, *Wolneton* (for *Wolueton*) *juxta Chermunstre* 1285 FF, *Wolfe-* 1303, 1346, 1428 all FA, *Wolver-* 1327 Cl, Ipm *et freq* to 1476 Cl, *Wolfveton* 1412 FA, *Wolton* 1546 *Lane*, 1575 Saxton, *Wotton* (als. *Wolveton*) 1606 (1770) *ib*, *Wulton* als. *W(o)ulveton* 1615 *DuCo*, probably 'Wulfa's farm', from the OE pers.n. *Wulfa* and tūn (DEPN). *Wulfa* is a short form of dithematic pers.ns. in *Wulf-*, and in fact some of the early spellings (*Wuluui-* (? for *Wuluiu-* or *Wuluin-*), *Woluenes-*, *Wlfre-*, *Wolver-*) look like reduced forms of such dithematic names (*Wulfgifu* and *Wulfwynn* (both fem.), *Wulfwine* and *Wulfhere* (both masc.)).

BROOKLANDS, *Brokelond* 1461 *Ct*, *v.* brōc, land. BURTON CTGS (cf. *Hr Burton Ctg* 1811 OS) & MILL (cf. *molend'* in *B(o)urton* 1350 *Ilch*, 1606 (1770) *Lane*), *v.* Burton *supra*. BUSHY EWELEAZE, cf. (*Btm, Gt* & *Long*) *Eweleaze* 1837 *TA*. CHARMINSTER DOWN, (*pastur' super*) *la Doune* 1343 *Ilch*, *les Downes* 1606 (1770) *Lane*, *le downes end* 1617 *DuCo*, *v.* dūn. CHARMINSTER FM & HO. CHURCH (St Mary's), cf. *cimiterio Beate Marie de Chermynstr'* 1338 HarlCh, 'the church of *Charmynstre'* 1423 DorR, *domum parochial' iuxta cemiterium* 1617 *DuCo*, *Parish howse* 1617 *Add*, *Church Bridge* 1791 Boswell. CORN MILL (2×), cf. John *atte Mulle* 1340 NI, m14 *Ilch*, *Mul-* 1350 *ib*, *Mil(l)ham* 1606 (1770) *Lane*, 1617 *DuCo*, *Mill Hams* 1837 *TA*, *Mill Close* 1617 *DuCo*, 1837 *TA*, (*Grist*) *Mill*, *Red Mills* (*Ham*) 1837 *ib*, *v.* myln, atte, hamm; there is mention of a mill at Charminster in 1086 DB (VCHDo 3 70), and of a fulling mill and a water mill in 1343 *Ilch*. COWDON (HILL), *Cowdon* m14 *Ilch*, 1546 *Lane*, 1606

(1770) *ib* (*villat' de* —), — *Bottom & Hill* 1837 *TA*, *Cowden* 1546
Surv, 1615 *DuCo*, 1664 HTax (— *Farme*), 1774 Hutch[1], 1839 *TA*
(Frampton), *Cow-Down Fm* 1863 Hutch[3], *v.* cū, dūn. EAST HILL HO,
from East Hill (st.n.) *supra*. FORSTON BARN (1837 *TA*), CTGS & FD
BOTTOM (—*field* 1837 *ib*), cf. *Forston Bridge* 1791 Boswell, *v.* Forston
supra. FOXBRAKE (WD), *v.* fox, bræc[1]. GASCOYNE BRIDGE & LANE,
Gaskyns— 1606 (1770) *Lane, Gaskins*— 1617 *DuCo, Gascoine's* — 1798
EnclA, Gascoigne Bridge 1837 *TA, Gaston Great & Little Bridge,
Gaston Water Bridge* 1791 Boswell, named from *prat' in Gaskyn als.
Gaston* 1606 (1770) *Lane, prat' voc' Garston,* — *Gaskines* 1617 *DuCo,
Gascoyne* — 1798 *EnclA, Gascoigne Md* 1837 *TA, v.* gærs-tūn
'paddock'. HAYDON CLUMP & HILL, (*camp' voc'*) *Haydon*(*s*),
Heydons, -downe 1606 (1770) *Lane,* (*claus' voc'*) *Haydon, -downe*
1617 *DuCo, -den* 1664 HTax, *Haydon Clift, Fm & Mdw, Hayden
pce* 1837 *TA,* 'hill where hay was made', *v.* hēg, dūn, clif, cf. Haydon
par. *infra*. HIGHER BARN, 1837 *TA*. HILL BARN & COPPICE. HOSPITAL
FM, near to County Mental Hospital (*The Asylum* 1837 *TA*).
IVY CTG. LEAP GATE, 1811 OS, *v.* hlīep-geat. LITTLE COURT, cf.
terr' apud Courtyate 1461 *Ct, Court Close* 1606 (1770) *Lane,* — *Mdw*
1837 *TA, v.* court, geat. LONG COPPICE. LOWER COVERT, *v.* covert.
LYCH GATE, *v.* lich-gate, cf. (*via regia que vocatur*) *Lychwey* 1343,
1345, *Lychweyesforlang* 1346 all *Ilch,* 'corpse way', *v.* līc, weg,
furlang, no doubt the road to the cemetery, cf. Church (St Mary's)
supra. MILL STREAM, named from one of the two Corn Mills *supra*.
NEW BLDGS. NEW INN. PUMP HO. SEAGER'S BARN. SODERN, cf.
Soddern Bridge 1791 Boswell, *Sodom pce* 1837 *TA*, perhaps from
ModE sodom 'a wicked place', but possibly 'south hill' from sūð,
dūn, cf. the f.n. *Newdowne*(*s*), -*dome*(*s*) *infra, Soddon* in E Stoke par.
supra. SOUTHCOT, *v.* cot. SUN INN, 1837 *TA*. VICARAGE, *Le Parsonage
House of Charmyster* 1606 (1770) *Lane*. WALLS COPPICE, cf. John
Walles 1592 Hutch[3]; however the adjacent *Walls Fd* (local) is almost
certainly the site of a Roman villa (RCHMDo **3** 60, 72), so the first
el. may be wall. WATCOMBE BOTTOM (1837 *TA*) & PLANT., cf.
Watcombe(*s*) *Poste* (in bounds of Charminster) 1606 (1770) *Lane*,
1617 *DuCo, Watescombe* 1606 (1770) *Lane, Watcombe* (*foote*) 1617
DuCo, place called Watcombes feete 1617 *Add*, probably 'wheat
valley' from hwǣte and cumb, with post, fōt. WESTLEAZE, *West
Leaze* 1837 *TA, v.* lǣs. WOLFETON BARN, CLUMP, EWELEAZE
(*Wolverton Ewe-lees* 1811 OS) & DAIRY, *v.* Wolfeton *supra*. WOOD
HILL (CLUMP). THE YEWS, a house.

FIELD-NAMES

Fields in Frampton *TA* but now in Charminster are marked †. The undated forms are 1837 *TA* 49 (those marked † are 1839 *TA* 89). Spellings dated 1327 are *SR*, 1332 SR, 1340 NI, 1344 Pat, 1345[2] *Rent*, 1391 *Midd*, 1441, 1449, 1450, 1451, 1452, 1453 *Weld*[1], 1455, 1456, 1460, 1461, 1474[2], 1597 *Ct*, 1457, 1458, 1462, 1474, 1477 *MinAcct*, 1546, 1549, 1606 (1770) *Lane*, 1565 DorR, 1574 Hutch[3], 1617[1] *DuCo*, 1617[2] *Add*, 1650 *ParlSurv*, 1664 HTax, 1791 Boswell, 1826 Gre, and the rest *Ilch*.

(*a*) (Green) Abbey; Alley Bridge 1791; Ayre's Cl (cf. Marie *Eyres* 1597); Balls cl (cf. John *Ball* 1460); Biscuit cl (perhaps descriptive of hard dry ground); Bottom Cl; Bowling Green; Break (*v.* bræc[1]); Broken Cross (— *Crosse* 1606 (1770), *v.* brocen, cros); Bronscombe Flg (perhaps to be associated with *Bronhamp* m14, *a med' y callyd' Borneham* 1493, which may be from brūn 'dark-coloured' and hamm); Buddens Mdw ((*ten' voc'*) *Buttons* (*als. voc' Barryes*) 1606 (1770), *pastur' voc' Buttonsham, ten' voc' Buttons*, — *Barris* 1617[1], cf. *Button Bridge* 1791, Richard *Boton* 1327, 1332, Ralph *Buton*, Robert *Barr'* 1332, *v.* hamm); Burn Beat (*v.* burnbeat); Lt Burton Bottom (*v.* Burton *supra*); Cashiers (cf. William *Catcher* 1606 (1770), —*Cashay* 1617[2]); Hr & Lr Charlton Bottom (*v.* Charlton *supra*); Charminster Cross Bottom & Drove; Chips Orchd (cf. William *Chipp(e)* 1606 (1770), 1617[2]); Cocklands (first el. perhaps cocc[2] 'a cock', cf. *Coc(kes)hulle* l13, *Cocknell(s Furlong)* 1606 (1770) which may however be from cocc[1] 'hillock' with hyll, cnoll); Cothays (*v.* cot, (ge)hæg, cf. *Cote Close* 1617[1]); Cowleaze; Croft (*le Crofte* 1617[1], cf. *Croft(e) Close* 1606 (1770), 1617[1], -*hedge* 1617[1], *v.* croft; now called *Crates* (M.H.)); Dock Acre (*v.* docce); Dry Md; Duntish Fd (perhaps named from, or analogous with, Duntish in Buckland N. par. *infra*); Dyers Plot (cf. (*la*) *Deyerescroft* 1343, 1345, John *Deygher* 1340, *v.* croft); Ebbers Cl; 8, 18 & 11 Acres; Fair Mile; Farm Bridge 1791; 15 & 5 Acres; Five and Twenty Acres; Flower Lds ((*North*) *Florlande* l13, *Florelond* 1345[2], *Flowre-, Flower Land(e)(s)* 1606 (1770) (*v.* land; this f.n., with analogies in several other pars., could be from OE flōr 'a floor, a pavement', but it is perhaps from ME flour 'flower' in the sense 'growing with wild flowers' or 'the choicest, the best'; however, Professor Löfvenberg notes: 'In view of the ME forms with *o*, I am inclined to believe that the first el. is OE flōr, whatever its exact meaning may be in this compound, cf. DEPN s.n. Floore Nth and dial. *floor* 'grass-meadow' in Cornwall (EDD s.v. *floor* sense 6)'); Folly Mdw (*v.* folie); Forston Mdw (*v.* Forston *supra*); 40, 4, Fourscore & 14 Acres; Furzey Cl (cf. *Furscroft, le Furses* 1343, *v.* fyrs); Giddy Cl (*v.* gydig); Gratton (*v.* græd-tūn); Gravelly Knap (*v.* cnæpp); Greens Barton & Plot (cf. John *Grene* 1591); (The) Grove (*v.* grāf(a)); Haggets orchd; Hanging ld (— *Landes*) 1617[1], *Hanginge Land* 1606 (1770), *v.* hangende); Heare (sic), †Heave (*v.* Heave Fm in Piddlehinton par. *supra*); Higher Grd & Pce; Hog Bottom; Home Cl (1617[1]); Horse Cl; Huntsman's Ham (*v.* hamm); Kelloway Cl (cf. Nicholas *Kelloway* 1664); Knights cl (cf. John *Knyght* 1474[2], Hugh *Knighte* 1606 (1770)); Ledmans; Lime Kiln; Linch cl & Hill, Creeper Linch ((*claus' voc'*) *Lynch(e)(s), Linch-, Lynch Close, Lynch(eh)ill* 1606 (1770), *Lynch bottome, — close, Linch comon close*

1617[1], cf. *pastur' de Langelynch* 1343, *v.* lang[1], hlinc; *Creeper* may denote a bird, insect or plant, *v.* creeper); Lines (*v.* leyne); Little Bottom; Locks cl (cf. John *Lokke* 1455, but cf. also *Lokfurlong* 1450, 1461, from loc(a), furlang); Long Cl (*Langclos* 1461); Long Mdw (*Lang(e)-* 1441 *et freq* to 1477, *Longmede* 1458, *v.* mǣd); Long Well (Mdw) (*Longwell* 1574, *Longewill* 1617[1], *v.* wella); Lords Md (*Lordes Meade, the Lords Meadowe* 1606 (1770)); Lower Fd & Mdw; Malthouse; Middle Fd Coppice ((*le*) *Mid(d)le feild(e)* 1606 (1770), 1617[1]); Middle Grd & Pce; New Cl ((*the* —) 1606 (1770)); (Lt) Newland Mdw, Gt New Lds (*Newlandes* 1617[1]); New Md(w); 9 Acres; Orchard Md ((*claus' voc'*) (*le*) *Orchard* 1451 *et freq* to 1474, *v.* orceard); Ox Cl; Park Eweleaze (cf. (*claus' voc-, prat' voc'*) (*le*) *Parke* 1456 *et freq* to 1477, *Parkclose* 1606 (1770), *v.* park, cf. Cantor & Wilson 12 67); Peak (*v.* pēac); Pond Cl; Prigwell Willow Bed (the first el. may be a voiced form of pric(c)a 'prick, prickle', cf. Prickwillow C 222); Punch Crofts (*Bunche* — 1617[1], probably the surname *Bunch*); Rabbit Brake (*v.* bræc[1]); Ram cl; Robert's Bush Pce (cf. Richard *Roberts* 1664); Rough Grd & Pce (the latter contains the remains of four medieval closes, RCHMDo 3 71); Round Hills; Row Cl (cf. *Roudon* m14, *v.* rūh (wk. obl. *rūgan*), dūn); Ryelands (*-landes* 1617[1], *v.* ryge); 7 & 17 Acres; Sheephouse Cl & Grd (cf. *Schepcroft* 1343, *v.* scēap, croft); Shepherds ctg; Shipton md (probably 'sheep farm' from scēap (WSax scī(e)p), tūn); Sideling pasture (perhaps named from, or analogous with, Sydling St N. par. *infra*); 6 Acres (and lambing barton); 16 Acres; South Moor (*South-, Sowthmo(o)re* 1546 *et freq* to 1642, — *Moare* 1617[1], *v.* mōr); Spinnage cl (*v.* spinach); Stares (cf. John *Ster(r)e* 1327, 1332); Long Strap (*v.* strap); 10 & 13 Acres; The Three Compasses Inn; Three Cornered Cl; Tizzard's corner (cf. Joan *Tizer* 1597, —*Tezard* 1606 (1770)); Turkey with the canals (by R. Cerne; perhaps from ME *atte key* '(place) at the quay', *v.* atte, key); 12 acres (*the xij*[e] *acr'* 1493); (Old) 20 & 24 Acres; Turnpike ho; Wanshard Cowleaze (*Wenchyarde, Wensherde Close* 1606 (1770), 'gap fit for a wagon', *v.* wægn, sceard); Lt Warren (cf. 'warren at *Chermenstre'* 1344); Weather cl (*Weter* — 1617[1], possibly weðer); †Ward Mdw, West Ward (Md) ((*prat' voc'*) (*le*) *Ward(e)* (*in prato de Burton*) 1391 *et freq* to 1477, (*le*) *Estwarde* m14, 1549 (— *in Charmyster*), (*prat' voc'*) (*la-, le-, the-*) *Westwarde* m14, 1453 (— *in prato de Estburton*) *et freq* to 1606 (1770), *le weaste warde* 1565, *Westwarde Meade* 1546, *West Ward als. West Meade* 1650, (*the*) *Ward(e) Me(a)de* 1544 *et freq* to 1642, from OE warod 'shore-meadow' (a side-form of waroð, *v.* Löfvenberg 220), with ēast, west, mǣd, cf. the f.n. East Ward (which also lies along R. Frome) in Stinsford par. *infra*, and Frome Md in Puddletown par. *supra*); Willow Bed, Withey Bed (cf. *West Wythebar* 1343, *le Withbargh* 1455, *v.* wīðig, bearu).

(b) *duas acras que iacet in Bache* l13 (*v.* bece[1]); *le Backside* 1606 (1770) (*-sive Barrow Close*), 1617[1] (*v.* backside, cf. foll.); *Barrow(e) Close,* — *hill, claus' voc' Barrey* 1606 (1770), *Barry close,* — *Hill, le Barrowhill* 1617[1] (*v.* beorg, cf. prec.); *le Battes* 1346 (*v.* batte); *terr'-, loc' voc' behind(e) Hay(e)s* 1606 (1770), 1617[1] (*v.* behind, (ge)hæg); *Beneacre* 1492, 1497 (*v.* bēan, æcer); *Berefurlang, -slade* l13 (*v.* bere, furlang (as freq in this par.), slæd, cf. *berton domini* 1456); (*le*) *Bynehey* 1453 *et freq* to 1474 (*v.* bēan, (ge)hæg, cf. *Beneacre supra*); *cultura q' vocat' binetþe weye* l13 (*v.* beneoðan, weg);

Blakenhulle 1346 (*v.* blæc (wk. obl. *blacan*), hyll); *la (Est-, North-, South) Breche* 1346 (*v.* brēc); *La Brodemede* 1343 (*v.* brād, mǣd); *Brockfurlongefeild* 1606 (1770) (first el. perhaps brocc 'badger'); *Brutoneslane* 1343 (cf. *claus' Galfridi Bruton* 1343, *v.* lane); *prat' de Burton* 1455, *B(o)urton Mede* 1456 *et freq* to 1497, *Borton—* 1493 (*v.* Burton *supra*); *cultura que vocatur Buuedih* l13, (*claus' voc'*) *Bowditch* 1606 (1770), 1617¹, *-degg, Boveditch, Buddage, Buddyche* 1606 (1770), *Bawdiche, Budday* 1617¹ ('above the ditch', *v.* bufan, dīc); *Buveheye* l13 (*v.* bufan, (ge)hæg, cf. prec.); *Caleng-* 1452, *Kalengeleyn* 1456 (*v.* calenge, leyne, alluding to disputed land); *Charmister Meade* 1606 (1770); *Chelkweye* 1346 (*v.* calc, weg, cf. *Chalk Pit* 1826); *pastur' voc' Claypitts* 1606 (1770); *lez Cleves* 1460 (*v.* clif, cf. foll.); *terr' apud Clyfes-* 1453, *Cliffesby* 1456 (cf. prec.; the final el. is probably byge¹ 'bend'); *le Combe* 1461 (*v.* cumb); *Le Common Meade* 1606 (1770); *La Conyngere* 1350 (*v.* coninger); *Crawethornesforlang* 1346 (*v.* crāwe, þorn); *le Culuer-* 1492–1497, *Culverclos(e)* 1544 (*v.* culfre); *vnam acram que iacet in Cutebolstre* l13 (perhaps the OE pers.n. *Cūðbeald*, with trēow); *Le forlang de Daundeuyles Thorn* 1346 (cf. *prat' Edwardi Daundeuyle* 1343, *v.* þorn); *Drakecroft* 1343 (first el. draca 'dragon', drake 'drake', or a surname); *Drecchethornesforlang* 1346 (perhaps 'troublesome (i.e. spiky) thorn' if the first el. is ME dreche 'trouble', *v.* þorn); *la Dreue* 1343 (*v.* drǣf); *in campo orientali* l13, (*le*) *Estfeld* 1343, 1346 (*v.* ēast, feld); *Excamb* 1606 (1770) (perhaps from oxa (nom. pl. *exen*) 'an ox', with cumb); *le Fore-, le Forthfeild, -field* 1606 (1770), *Fo(u)rth* (*als. Fore*) *feild(e)* 1617¹ (*v.* fore, forð); *la Gore inter le Westfeld et le Estfeld* 1346, *Gore mede* 1493 (*v.* gāra); *Greteb(er)gesfurlang* l13 (*v.* grēat 'great' or grēot 'gravel', beorg); *atte Haissh* 1332 (p) (*v.* atte, æsc); *le Ham* 1617¹ (*v.* hamm); *Haulfe acre* 1617¹ (*v.* half); *Hegge trendele* l13 (*v.* hecg, trendel); *Heuedacre* l13 (*v.* hēafod); *Heuedlonde* l13 (*v.* hēafod-land); *cultura que vocatur Hile* l13 (cf. Robert *de la Hele* 1258, *v.* halh (WSax dat. sg. *hēale*) 'nook'); *Hokedwale* 1461 (*v.* hōcede 'curved', walu or wall); *Holewey* 1449, *Holway* 1617¹ (*v.* hol², weg); *terr' inclus' voc' Hopyard* 1606 (1770) (*v.* hoppe, geard); *Hotefurlang* 1346 (*v.* āte); *in the Hurn* 1346 (p) (*v.* hyrne); *Inichin* 1606 (1770) (*v.* in, hēcing); *Lamedeneslad* 1346 (lām 'loam' or lamb 'lamb', with denu, slæd); *Langgeheggeweye* 1346 (*v.* lang¹, hecg, weg); *Lang(e)hey* 1453 *et freq* to 1462 (*v.* (ge)hæg); *Langelande, -londe* l13 (*v.* land); *Lecledde* l13 (perhaps from lēac 'leek' with lǣd 'water-course' or hlēda 'ledge'); *Lerkefurlong* 1461 (*v.* lǣwerce); *Le Little Coppice* 1606 (1770); (*prat' voc'*) *Long Reach(e)* 1546, 1617² (*v.* lang¹, rǣc); *Madders Close* 1606 (1770); *Maynshardes* 1617¹ (probably a surname); *cotag' voc' Marchantes* 1606 (1770) (cf. *ten' nuper Henr' Marchant* 1457); *ten' voc' Medyates, -iates* 1606 (1770), *Merdates* 1617¹ (*v.* mǣd, geat, possibly a surname); *Meadlandende, — Lane ende* 1606 (1770) (*v.* mǣd, land or lane, ende); *Melkweyescroft* 1343 (*v.* meoluc, weg, croft); *Middelfurlang* l13, *-forlang* 1346, *Mydle-* 1606 (1770), *Midd(le) furlonge* 1617¹ (*v.* middel); *Molthewrothe-* 1343, 1348, *Moldewrorthecroft* 1350 (perhaps a surname from, or a p.n. analogous with, Mouldsworth Ch 3 279 which is 'enclosure at a hill' from molda and worð); *Mondayes Close* 1606 (1770) (*v.* mōnandæg, or a surname); *le Moreclose* 1606 (1770) (cf. Adam *atte Mo(u)re* 1289, 1343, *v.* atte, mōr); *Nethermancombe* 1461 (*v.* cumb); (*claus' voc'*) *Lower —, Nether —, Over —, Upper Newdowne(s)*,

(*Lower*) *Newdome*(*s*) 1606 (1770), *Nether* —, *Ouer Newdoms* 1617[1] (perhaps 'down newly brought into use', *v*. nīwe, dūn, but possibly a surname); (*le*) *North Close* 1606 (1770), 1617[1]; *the northeast furlong* 1561; *in Boreali campo* l13, (*le*) *Northfeld* 1343, 1345, *le* —, *the North*(*e*) *field*, *-feilde* 1606 (1770), 1617[2] (*v*. feld); *th' Northforlong* 1493; *le Northill* 1449 (*v*. norð, hyll); *pastur' voc' O*(*u*)*ldhayes* 1606 (1770), 1617[1] (*v*. ald, cf. *behinde Hayes supra*); *Peers*— 1606 (1770), *Pearse Furlong*(*e*) 1617[1] (cf. John *Peres* 1460); *le peece* 1617[1] (*v*. pece); *Redelond* 1453 (*v*. rēad, land); *Ridesherde* l13 (perhaps 'gap suitable for riding through', *v*. ride, sceard, cf. Wanshard *supra*); *Riggeende* 1453 (*v*. hrycg, ende[1]); *Schulflond* 1346 (*v*. scelf (WSax scylf), land); *Shelnes wall* 1617[1] (probably a surname, *v*. wall); *Sheryngdon* 1451, 1461 (*v*. dūn; first el. perhaps OE *sciering, scering* 'shearing', as suggested by Professor Löfvenberg, referring to a hill where sheep were sheared); *Shorte acres* l13 (*v*. sc(e)ort); *Shortecumbe* l13, *Shorcombes Heade* 1606 (1770) (*v*. sc(e)ort, cumb, hēafod); *Shortegore* l13 (*v*. gāra); *Shortelonde* l13 (*v*. land); *camp' voc' Sidneham* 1617[1] (*v*. sīd (wk. obl. *sīdan*) 'large', hamm, cf. foll.); *terr' voc' Sidmans, Sidines* 1617[1] (probably a surname, but possibly to be associated with prec.); *Slade* l13 (*v*. slæd); *South Close* 1606 (1770); *Southfeild* 1617[1]; *South*—, *Sowth Furlonge* 1606 (1770), 1617[1]; *Staberwesforlang* 1346 (*v*. beorg, probably with stān); *loc' voc' Stanway* 1606 (1770), *Stonwaye yate* 1617[1] (*v*. stān, weg, geat); *cultura voc' Stiche* l13, *le Stitche* 1617[1] (*v*. sticce[1]); *Stodelond* 1441 (*v*. stōd, land, cf. Studland par. *supra*); *Surelonde* l13 (*v*. sūr); *Sutebarwe* 1343 (perhaps sūð or sūðan, with beorg); *le Thornes* 1343 (*v*. þorn); (*pastur de*) (*le*) *Throte* 1343, 1346, *Throtefurlang* 1346 (*v*. þrote); *M' Trenchard ys mede* 1493 ('Mr Trenchard's mead'); *Ve*(*a*)*lesclose* 1493, 1578 (cf. Robert *Veel* 1400); (*le*(*z*)) *Vernes* 1441 *et freq* to 1455 (*v*. fearn); *le voyde howze close* 1617[1] (*v*. voyde 'not occupied, empty', with hūs 'house', and clos(e)); *ten' voc' Vyncentes* 1554 PlR; *Attewell* (p) 1449 (*v*. atte, wella); *a ham at the Wesshewer* 1493, *le Weare* 1606 (1770) (*v*. wer 'a weir'; *Wesshe-* may be from wæsce 'a place for washing'); (*le*) *Westfeld* 1343, 1346 (*v*. west, feld); *West Slighte* 1617[1] (*v*. slæget); *Le Whytelond* 1346 (*v*. hwīt); *Wodeclose* 1492 (*v*. wudu); *Wdeweies-, Vodeveysfurlang*(*e*) l13 (*v*. wudu, weg); *prat' voc' Wolledge* 1606 (1770); (*claus' voc'*) (*le*) *Worth*(*e*) 1453 *et freq* to 1477 (*v*. worð); *Wulton rayles* 1617[1] (*v*. raile, Wolfeton *supra*).

Dorchester St Peter & All Saints

In 1894 the parish of Holy Trinity was merged in that of St Peter, the borough then comprising for civil purposes the parishes of St Peter and All Saints, but in 1927 these two parishes were united to form one civil parish. The borough was extended to include the parish of Fordington, and parts of the parishes of Bradford Peverell, Charminster, Winterborne Herringston and Winterborne Monkton in 1900, and parts of the parishes of Stinsford and West Stafford in 1933.

DORCHESTER (SY 689906) ['dɔːtʃistə, 'dɔːdʒestə, 'dɑːʀtʃistəʀ, 'dɑːdistəʀ]

Durno(no)varia 4 AntIt, *Durngueir* 893 (e11) Asser
Dornwerecestre 833 (14) *ShaftR* (S 277) (*villa regali qui vocatur* —),
Dornuuarana ceaster 847 (m9) BCS 451, *Dornwaracester* 863
(m12) *Add* (S 336), *-ceaster* 864 (12) *SherC* (S 333), *loco qui
appellatur Æt Dornwara ceastræ* 868 (m12) *Add* (S 340),
Doracestria 843 for 934 (eME) ASCharters, 843 for 934 (17)
BCS 739, *Dorn(e)ace(a)ster* 937 (12) ib 719, 937 (13) ib 716, 718
Do(r) 991–1059 *Coins, Dor(e)c(e)(s)(t)* 1009–1133 *ib, Do(r)i* 1074–
1127 *ib, Dortcei* 1074–7 *ib*
Dorecestre 1086 DB (4×), *-cestra* Exon, *Dorecestr(e)* 1195 P *et freq*
to 1244 *Ass, Dorcestr(e)* 1194 P *et freq* to 1447 Cl, 1275 RH
(*burgus-*), *-cester* 1291 Tax, *burgo Dorcestrie* 1363 *Ilch, libertatem
ville Dorcestrie* 1409 DorR
Dorkecestr' 1210, 1212 P, 1244 Cl, *Dorkcestr(e)* 1261 ib, 1280 *Ass*
(*Burgus de* —)
Dorsecestre 1211 P, *Dors(c)estr(e)* 1244 *Ass*, 1257 Cl, 1268 *Ass*
(*ville de* —), 1439 Pat, *Dorseter* 1268 *Ass*
Dorchester, -chestre 1273 Pat *et passim, -chestur* 1506 ib

Henry Bradley's improbable explanation of this Brit name in E &
S 1 14 as meaning literally 'fist play', from *durno-* 'fist' (cf. Welsh
dwrn) and *war-* (cf. Welsh *gwarae* 'play'), with reference to the
sports carried on at the Roman amphitheatre of Maumbury *infra*,
has been widely accepted (as by e.g. Fägersten 2, Ekwall DEPN,
Gelling NTCB 83, cf. Zachrisson RomK 79 note 1 who suggested
that if *durno-* 'fist' indicated the shape of a hill-fort, *Durnovaria*
may have originally referred to Maiden Castle in Winterborne St M.
par. *infra*). Professor Jackson in *Britannia* 1 72 dismisses the variant
reading *Durnonovaria* and agrees in taking the first el. of *Durnovaria*
(Brit *Durnouariā*) to be PrWelsh *durn 'a fist' (probably also 'a
stone of the size of a fist', and found in Cardurnock Cu 123 and in the
Scottish p.ns. Dornock in Dumfriesshire and Dornoch in Sutherland,
all *durnāco- 'site covered with fist-sized pebbles'); however (*loc.
cit.*) he admits the second el. *-varia* (Brit *uariā*) to be obscure, and
(by letter) totally rejects the meaning 'fist play'.

The Brit name (whatever its meaning, perhaps originally referring
to Maiden Castle as suggested by Zachrisson *loc. cit.*) may have been
adopted by the English in a reduced form *Dorn-* to which was added

OE -ware (gen.pl. -wara, alternative wk. gen.pl. -warena) 'dwellers' and ceaster '(Roman) city', Dornwaraceaster meaning 'city of the men of Dorn', cf. the county name which was OE Dornsǣte 'the Dorn people'. However it is probable that -wara- (-were-) represented in the first place simply an OE sound substitution for Brit -varia which was then treated as the el. ware. On the OWelsh form Durngueir in Asser, v. Jackson 239, and on the Brit change Durn- > Dorn-, v. Jackson 259, 274–5, 278, 681. The forms in Dork(e)- may show influence from or confusion with Dorchester O 152 which has such forms 1086 et passim but which has a quite different origin.

FORDINGTON (SY 698905)
    Fortitone 1086 DB, -*tona* Exon, *Fortintun* 1155 PR, *Fortyngton*
      1378–1404 Pat, -*don* 1404 Cl
    Fordinton(e), -*tun* 1155, 1156 RBE, 1156, 1157 PR, 1160 P *et freq*
      to 1345 Pat, -*en*- 1196 ChancR, -*yn*- 1280 *Ass et freq* to 1397 Cl
    Fordington(e) 1155 RBE, 1200 CartAnt, 1205 RC *et passim*, -*inge*-
      1205 ClR, 1554 DuCo, -*yng*- 1288 *Ass et freq* to 1547 Ct, 1326
      Pat (— *by Dorcestre*), *Fordyngdon(e)* 1291 Tax, 1483 Ct
    Forthington 1242 Cl, -*yng*- 1347, 1358 Pat, *Furthyngton* 1452 ib

Probably 'farm at *Fording*' ('the ford place'), from ford, -ing[2], tūn; the ford was no doubt across R. Frome, cf. Robert *atte Forde* 1335 *Ct*. The rare forms in -*inge*- do not support the presence of gen.pl. -*inga*- or the interpretation 'farm of the ford dwellers' proposed by Fägersten 187, cf. also Ekwall DEPN. The *East & West Tything* 1841 *TA* are mentioned from 1329 *Ct* (*Decen' oriental'*, —*occidental'*), cf. *Upper Fordington* 1863 Hutch[3] (adjoining Dorchester on N and W) and West Fordington (Kelly). For Fordington liberty, v. note under St George hundred *supra*. The bounds of Fordington are described in 1607 Clegg 159–61 and 1615 *DuCo*.

DORCHESTER PARISHES, CHURCHES & CHAPELS (*v.* RCHMDo **2** 105 ff)
ALL SAINTS, cf. *Ecclesia*- 1219 Fees, 1268 *Ass et passim*, *Parochia*-1340 NI, *Cimiterium Omnium Sanctorum* 1348 *AD*, *Churche of All Hallowes* 1555 DorR, *All Hallon parishe* 1562 ib, *Alhaleus church* 1610 DorM, *The Parish of All Saints, commonly called All Hallows, or the Lower Parish* 1774 Hutch[1], v. hālga (gen.pl. hālgena), cf. Church St. *infra*. CHRIST CHURCH, 1863 Hutch[3]. HOLY TRINITY, cf. *Ecclesia Sancte Trinitatis* 1219 Fees, 1268 *Ass et passim*, *Parochia*

Sanctæ Trinitatis 1340 NI, *Trinitie* 1562 DorR (— *parishe*), 1610 DorM, Trinity St. *infra*. ST GEORGE'S CHURCH (Fordington), *eccl. S. Georgii in Dorcestra* 1091 Osm, cf. St George hundred *supra*. ST JOHN'S CHAPEL (lost, N of Colliton Ho *infra*, *v.* Hutch[3] 2 415–6, VCHDo 2 101–3), *Prior hospitalis Sancti Johannis Dorcestr'* Ed 1 (1617) *Add*, 'the chapel of the hospital of St John' 1324 Pat, 'the king's hospital of Dorchester' 1334 ib, 'the hospital (or house) of St John the Baptist' 1351–1467 ib, '— (commonly) called *Saynt-*, *Seintjo(h)neshous'* 1451, 1473 ib, *Hospitale in Dorchestre* 1459 *Eton*, 'the free chapel of St John...alias the priory of St John' 1486 Pat, cf. *parochia Sancti Johannis in Dorchest'* 1547 *Ct*, Loud's Mill *infra*. ST MARY'S CHURCH (built 1911). ST PETER, cf. 'the church of St Peter', *Ecclesia Sancti/Beati Petri* 1233 Pat, 1244 *Ass et passim*, 'the chapel of St Peter' 1363, 1385 Pat, *scalam orientalem Cimiterii ecclesie S. Petri* 1416 DorR, *Saincte Peter's parishe* 1562 ib, *S Peters* 1610 DorM, *the Stayers leading into the east parte of the Churchyard of St Peter's* 1614 DorR, *the parish of St Peeter* 1625 *Ilch*. Lost or unidentified are *aecclesiam de Dorecestre* 1086 DB, Exon; 'the king's chapel of —' 1241 Lib, *capella regis de Dorcestr'* 1259 Cl, cf. *capellani de Dorecestr'* 1206 P; *ecclesiam beate Mar' de Dorcestr'* 1280 *Ass* (cf. 'the burgage of the Fraternity of Blessed Mary' 1396, *Fraternitas Beate Marie in ecclesia Sancti Petri* 1410, *Cantaria beate Marie Sancti Petri* 1426 all DorR, *v.* DorR xlvi); *la Maudelene* 1335 *Ct*, 'the chapel of *La Maudelyne*' 1347 BPR (in Fordington, cf. *montem magdalina* 1615 *DuCo*); 'the sometime chapel (*capellam quondam*) of St Rumwald' Hy 4, 1418 Hutch[3], *capellam quondam Sancti Rowaldi* 1405 DorR, *placiam quondam capelle Sancti Rowaldi* 1420 ib, 'the chapel of St Rumbald' 1576 Hutch[3] (on E side of South St., *v.* DorR xlvii; the saint's name seems to be OG *Rumwold* (Forssner 222)). For the former friary in Dorchester, *v.* Friary Saw Mill *infra*.

DORCHESTER STREETS & BUILDINGS

In the following lists where a date alone is given the reference is DorR.

BARNE'S WAY, cf. *Barnes hedge furlonge*, — *way* 1615 *DuCo*, *Barns Cross Common*, *Barns Hide Way* (*Flg*), *Barns Lane* (*Cl or Days Cl*), *Barns Way Flg & Pce* 1841 *TA*, cf. Robert *Barnes* 1574, Thomas *Dey* 1560; *Hide* may be from OE *hid* or represent the earlier *hedge*. THE BOW, *le Bow* 1617 ('a standing under —'), 'land called *the Bow*', 'messuage called *the Bow or Pentice house*' 1618, earlier *unam placeam que vocatur la Pentys sitam in quodam angulo* 1399, *la Peyntys* 1425, 'burgage called *le Pentice*' 1547, *the Pentice House* 1592, *v.* boga 'a bow, an arch', *pentis* 'a penthouse, an annex'; the Bow (pulled down in 1748) is described by Hutch[1] 1 372 as 'a room or two...built over the street and supported by a large pillar, which made a narrow and inconvenient passage'. BOWLING ALLEY WALK, *the Bowling Alley* 1636, — *Walk(s)* 1779, — or *West Walls* 1780, *Old Walks or Bowling Alley* 1774 Map, following the line of part of the old south wall (cf. South Walks Rd, The Town Walls *infra*) and meeting West Walk *q.v. infra* at right angles; for another bowling green, *v.* Charles St. *infra.* BRIDPORT RD, *Byrtport Waye* 1607 Clegg, *viam duc' versus Bruteport* 1615 *DuCo*, *ground at a place neare Burport highway* 1650 *ParlSurv*, *Bridport Lane, Bridport Rd Little & South Flg* 1841 *TA*, the road to Bridport. LITTLE BRITAIN, *vico voc' Brittanie, Britanie Streete* 1615 *DuCo*, no doubt to be associated with a former mansion in Fordington near R. Frome called *Britain* (Hutch[3] 2 792), cf. the f.n. Britains Cl *infra.* CHARLES ST., 1804, earlier *Bowling Green Lane* 1774 Map, named from *Bowling Green* 1774 ib, cf. Bowling Alley Walk *supra*; Charles St. was called *Back Lane* in 1832 according to Clegg 141. CHURCH ST., 1824 Pigot, *venella que vocatur Durn(e)gate* 1390, *viam regis-, venellam que ducit* (*ab ecclesia omnium sanctorum-, -a vico orientali-*) *versus la Durnegate* 1393, 1396, 1410, (*le*) *Durnelane* 1402, c. 1409, 'a lane on the east side of the Cemetery of All Saints' 1412, *venellam qua ducit versus la Durgate* (sic) 1414, *venella que ducit versus Fordyngton vocata Durnelane* 1431, 'the lane which leads *ab alto vico orientali...in vicum vocatum Durnelane*' 1476, *via regia que ducit a vico orientali usque Forthynton* 1482, *Alhal(l)on* — 1540, 1575, *Alhallen church(e) lane* 1562, (*the*) *Church Lane* 1634 *SalisT*, 1774 Map, named from All Saints (Church) *supra*, cf. Fordington *supra*; the forms in *-hal(l)on-, -hallen-* are from OE *hālgena*, wk. gen. pl. of hālga 'saint'. The earlier names, 'lane leading to *Durnegate*' and *Durnelane*, it seems to have had in common with Durngate St. *infra* which meets it at right angles, though references to All Saints Church and East St., and other contextual descriptions, make it likely that the forms cited above belong here (*v.* DorR xxxix–xli). *Glidelane* 1422 may also be an early name for Church St. according to DorR xlii; Adam *Glide* had property in Church St. in 1401, cf. Glyde Path Hill & Rd *infra*. However *Glidelane*, and also *the Northe lane* 1574, probably refer to lanes running parallel to Church St. rather than to Church St. itself. COLLITON ST., earlier (*la*) *Vlnen(e)lane* 1393–1436 (— *als. Pyzelane*), *Ilnen(e)lane* 1401–1428 (— *als. dicte Puselane*), *Pise-, Pyselane* 1396–1479, *Pisse-* 1396, *Pys-, Pislane* 1410–1461, *Puse-* 1396–1428, *Pusse-* 1402, 1406, *Puzelane* 1404, (*le*) *Peselane* 1540, 1549, *Pease Lane* 1551 DorR, 1774 Map, *Pease or Sheep Lane* 1774 Hutch[1], *Sheep Lane* 1753. If, as seems likely, *Vln-, Iln-* are errors for *Vlu-, Ilu-*, the first of the early names probably means 'elves' lane', either from OE elf (WSax ielf) (if *-en(e)-* represents an analogical ME wk. gen. pl., *v.* -ena), or, as Professor Löfvenberg suggests, from the fem. OE *elfen* (WSax *ielfen*). The alternative early name is 'pease lane', from pise, peosu. *Sheep-* from the sheep fairs held here until 1757 (DorR 503), cf. *Sheepe Markett* 1640. The modern name is from Colliton Ho *infra*, to which the street leads. CORNHILL, 1774 Map, *the Cornehill* 1652, cf. *the corn-market* 1774 Hutch[1]; this name was perhaps

transferred from the London st.n. Cornhill, *v.* Ln 54, 186. DAMER'S RD, cf.
Benjamin *Dam'er* 1664 HTax; for this family, *v.* Hutch³ **2** 375. DURNGATE
ST., 1824 Pigot, (*venella que vocatur*) (*la-*, *le*) *Durn(e)lane* 1394–1492
DorR, 1421–1490 *Lane*, 1578 *Wal*, 1785 *SalisT*, *venella que ducit a vico regio
australi versus la Durnegate* 1395, 'lane which leads from (High) South Street
towards (*la-*, *le*) *Durnegate*' 1401–1432, *venella vocata Durnegate* 1431,
Durn(e)gate lane 1565 DorR, 1841 *TAMap*, *Durn* or *Durngate Lane* 1774
Map, cf. *le Durneʒede* 1381 *Ct*, (*la*) *Durnegate* 1407–1556 DorR, 1436 *Lane*,
'the hidden lane', '(lane leading to) the hidden gate', *v.* derne, lane, geat,
cf. Derngate Np 7. Most of the forms cited probably refer to the lane running
E–W along the line of the present-day Durngate St., but for similar forms
which refer to a lane running S into Durngate St. from High East St., *v.*
Church St. *supra*, DorR xxxix–xli. The *Durnegate* was probably the gate
shown on Speed's plan of 1610 at the foot of Durngate St. and mentioned in
1642 as one of *the two east gates*, *v.* Estgate *infra*; it would have been a back
gate to Fordington. HIGH EAST ST., 1774 Map (— *or All Saints St.*), *vicus
orientalis* (*regius*), *altus vicus* (*regius*) *orientalis* 1395–1476 DorR, 1615 *DuCo*,
via Regia 1409, 'the High Street (*alta strata*) which leads to the East Gate'
1411, *altus vicus vocatus Est strete* 1431, *Este Highe Strete* 1549, *Highe Easte
streat* 1564, *East(e) Streete*, *Eastreet* 1615 *DuCo*, *the High east streete* 1634
SalisT, *the E. street, commonly called the Lower Parish* 1774 Hutch¹, *v.* hēah,
ēast, strǣt, cf. *Back East Street* 1824 Pigot; this is the eastern half of the
main east–west street in Dorchester, the whole length of which is sometimes
referred to as *altus vicus* (*regius*) 1395–1410 DorR, 1489 *Lane*, *alta strata
ville de Dorchestr*' 1438 *Ilch*, cf. High West St. *infra*. The use of *strata* in 1411
has been mistakenly held to imply that the metalling of the Roman road
(roughly aligned with High East St. and High West St.) still remained
(Clegg 15, 127), cf. Icen Way *infra*. For *All Saints St.* and the *Lower Parish*,
v. All Saints (Parish & Church) *supra*. FRIARY HILL & LANE, *Frerene lane*
1310 *Ilch* (*le-*), 1420, *Freren-* 1379 *Ilch et freq* to 1412 *ib* (*venella que ducit
ad fratres minores voc*' —), 1431, *Fre(y)ryn-* 1410–1418, *Freernelane* 1539
(*-que ducit de vico predicto* [East St.] *versus Fratres Minores*), *venella que tendit
ad ecclesiam Fratrum Minorum* 1401, *venella fratrum minorum* 1438 *Ilch*,
Fryars —, *Fryers* — 1556, *le Friers lane* 1564, 'lane leading *versus precinctum
fratrum minorum nuper dissolutorum* 1559, *Priory* or *Fryery Lane* 1774 Map.
'Friars' lane', from frere (with an analogical ME wk. gen. pl., *v.* -ena) and
lane; for the friary in Dorchester, *v.* Friary Saw Mill *infra*. It was called
Brewers' Lane (cf. Thomas Walker, *beer brewer*) in 1665 according to DorR
xxxix; and the north end of Friary Lane, now called Friary Hill, is referred
to as 'the street leading out of the *North Streete* towards the *Friery*' in 1609,
v. North Square *infra*. GLYDE PATH HILL & RD, *vicus borialis qui ducit
versus Glyde-*, *Glidepat(t)h*, — *qui ducit versus la Northgate* 1407, *vicus qui
ducit versus Glydepath* 1417, 'the North Street which leads towards
Glidepatth' 1420, *viam que ducit ad le glyte pathe* 1549, *Glydepath Hill* 1774
Map, probably also identical with *vicus borialis* 1395, *Northstrete* 1401, *High
Northe Strete* 1556 (DorR xxxvi–xxxvii), *v.* norð, strǣt, *Northgate infra*; for
another 'North Street' east of this one and parallel to it, *v.* North Square
infra. *Glydepath* is also *Glydepate* 1349 *Ct*, *Glidepath* 1382 AD I, *Glydepath*

1542, *Glydpath* 1607 Clegg, 1615 *DuCo* (*locum voc'* —), *Gladpath* 1615 *ib*, *Lippath* 1625 Hutch[3], *Glippath* 1636, 1642, cf. *Glippath Bridge* 1634, *Lydepath Hill Bridge* 1791 Boswell; it is probably 'path frequented by the kite or other bird of prey', from glida and pæð, though the first el. could be a surname as is likely in *Glidelane, v.* Church St. *supra*, cf. Adam *le Glede* 1288 Banco, '— *le Glyde* of *Dorcestre'* 1292 ib; part of its course is probably represented by the western leg of the present Glyde Path Hill, called *North Walk* 1774 Map, — *Walks* 1774, cf. South Walks Rd *infra*. An earlier name for the southern leg of Glyde Path Hill was *Colliton Row, v.* Colliton Ho *infra*. Glyde Path Rd was *Shire hall Lane* 1774 Map, named from *Shire Hall infra.* GREAT WESTERN RD, cf. *Great Western Inn* 1877 *TA*, leading to the old GWR station. THE GROVE, called *New Walk* 1774 Map, cf. *Grove Bldgs* 1841 *TAMap, Roger atte Grove* 1381 *Ct, v.* atte, grāf(a). HERRINGSTON RD, cf. *semita que venit de dorcestra ad Harangeston* 113 *Ilch, heringsten Way* 1615 *DuCo*, leading to Winterborne Herringston par. *supra.* HIGH ST. (Fordington), 1863 Hutch[3]. ICEN WAY, a modern name, apparently an adaptation of *Via Iceniana or Icening St.* (1774 Hutch[1], etc., cf. Clegg 15, 127) which is a spurious form of the name *Icknield Way* (cf. PN BdHu 4–5, PN W 16) applied by antiquarians not only to the East Anglian pre-historic trackway but also to the London–Exeter Roman road (Margary 4), the course of which through Dorchester is represented roughly by High East St. *supra* and High West St. *infra*; cf. Hutch[3] **2** 792 who states that 'the easternmost part of Fordington is called *Icen Town*', which he conjectures may be a corruption of *East(en) Town* (cf. East or Ice Hill in Stinsford par. *infra*) or may be so called 'from its proximity to the Icening way, as it almost meets it', cf. also the unexplained Icen Barrow in Ch. Knowle par. and Icen Dairy in Upwey par. both *supra*. The northern end of Icen Way was earlier *the Gaole Lane* 1634 *SalisT, Jail Lane* 1774 Map, *Old Gaol Lane* c. 1832 *DROMap*, named from *County Jail infra.* Further south, Icen Way was earlier *the backlane... towards the Gallowes* 1634 *SalisT, Gallow(e)s Hill* 1642 DorR, 1774 Map, *Gallows Hill Lane* 1774 Hutch[1], *the back Lane...towards Gallows Hill* 1785 *SalisT, Bell St.* 1824 Pigot, *Gallow's Hill or Bell St.* c. 1832 *DROMap*, cf. *the gallo(w)es* 1596–1643, *Gallows Hill Cl* 1749, *Gallows Down Flg, Gallow(s) (Hill) Flg* 1841 *TA, v.* galga; according to Clegg 141, *Bell St.* 'derived its name from the Bell Inn at which condemned men were allowed to have final refreshment before their execution on the gallows at the south end of Icen Way'. MAIDEN CASTLE RD, earlier *Bush(e)way(e), v.* Bush Road Ctgs *infra*, Maiden Castle in Winterborne St Martin par *infra*. MARKET PLACE (TGuide), 1824 Pigot, *locum venalem regium vocatum le merket place* 1551, cf. *mercatum in villa de Dorcestr'* 1274 (1372) *ChrP, forum mercati* 1399, 1417 (near St Peter's Church), *les Fysh(esh)amelles* 1503 (on N side of High East or West St.), *Shambles* 1610 DorM, 1824 Pigot, *the East* —, *the West Row* ('the Butchers' Standings in the north of the Shambles') 1645 (near St Peter's Church), *Sheepe Markett* 1640 (*v.* Colliton St. *supra*), *the Butter Market* 1734, *the corn-market* 1774 Hutch[1], *v.* market, sc(e)amol, rāw, cf. Chepestrete, *the Cupola*, Fair Fd *infra.* MAUMBURY RD, *Mambrey Way* 1615 *DuCo*, cf. *Ma(u)msbury Way East & West Flg* 1841 *TA, Mambury Way* 1877 *ib*, leading to Maumbury *infra.* MILL BANK & ST. (1774 Hutch[1]), leading to

Mill (Fordington) *infra*. MILLER'S CLOSE, cf. William *Miller* 1583 DorR, 1664 HTax, *the Millers house* 1650 *ParlSurv*, near to West Mills *infra*. NEW ST., c. 1832 *DROMap*, cf. *in vico novo* als. *London streete* 1615 *DuCo*. NORTH SQUARE, 1824 Pigot, earlier *vicus qui ducit erga Fratres Minores* 1395, (*altus*) *vicus borialis qui ducit versus Fratres Minores* 1396, 1406, *vicus qui ducit a foro mercati versus Fratres Minores* 1399, *the North Streete* 1609, (*the*) *Bul*(*l*)*stake* 1664, 1762 all DorR, 1774 Hutch[1] (*a little square called* —), 1777 (*a street or place called* —), *North St. or the Bull Stake* 1863 Hutch[3], *v.* bula, staca, cf. Friary Hill & Lane *supra*. The 'bull stake' probably denoted a stake used for bull-baiting, cf. Bulstake Bridge O 35. For another 'North Street', west of this one and parallel to it, *v.* Glyde Path Hill & Rd *supra*. A cross (marked on 1610 Speed) in this street is mentioned in 1396–1429 DorR, and for a pound here, *v.* The Manor Pound *infra*. POUNDBURY RD, cf. *via inter Dorcestr' et Wytewll* 1268 *Ass*, *Pumberry Way* 1650 *ParlSurv*, *Pummery Rd Cmn* 1841 *TA*, leading to Whitfield in Bradford P. par. *supra* and to Poundbury *infra*. POUND LANE, cf. Gilbert *atte Pounde* 1381 *Ct*, *v.* atte, pund. PRINCE OF WALES RD, cf. Prince's Bridge *infra*. PRINCE'S ST., earlier (*the*) *Back West St.* 1757 DorR, 1824 Pigot, *West Back St.* 1774 Map, 1824 Pigot, cf. *the Back Lane part of which is parallel to W. Street, the other to S. Street* 1774 Hutch[1], *v.* Trinity St., West St. *infra*. SALISBURY ST. & WALKS ((*the*) *Walls* 1774 Map, Hutch[1] (a lane)), following the old east wall, cf. The Town Walls, Salisbury Fd *infra*. SOUTH ST., 1774 Map, *haustralis vicus* 1377 Lane, *vicus* (*regius*) *australis* 1395, 1402 DorR, 1477 *Lane*, *viam australis* 1399, *altus vicus australis* (*regius*) 1404, 1409 all DorR, 1475 *Ilch*, *la Southstrete* 1399, 1408, *the* (*High*(*e*)) *South*(*e*) *Streete* 1554, 1567 all DorR, 1625 *Ilch*, *South Stret* 1610 DorM, *Sowth Streate* 1634 *SalisT*, *v.* sūð, strǣt. SOUTH WALKS RD, *the South Walk* 1716, *Chesnut Walk* 1774 Map, cf. *South Walks Common* 1841 *TA*, following the line of part of the old south wall, cf. The Town Walls *infra*; this and the other 'walks' surrounding the town were made in e18 (Hutch[3] 2 337). STANDFAST RD, cf. *terr' vocat' Standfast* 1615 *DuCo*, probably the surname *Standfast*, but possibly a nickname for a muddy place where carts 'stood fast'. THE TOWN WALLS (lost), 1785 *SalisT*, *muros communitatis ville* 1395, *the Towne Walles* 1634 *SalisT*; (*les*) *West Wall*(*es*) (*de Dorchestre*) 1400–1423 ('land lying in —'), (*campum de*) *West Wallys* 1414, 1444, *the we*(*a*)*st walles* 1573, 1668, *The ruins of the ould wall* 1610 DorM, *ripam voc' lez Walls* 1615 *DuCo*; (*terram arabilem de*) *les Estwalles* 1342 FF, 1405, *campum de Estewall* 1411, *la Est Walles* 1412, *les Est Wallys* 1414–1421, (*the*) *East*(*e*) *Wall*(*e*)*s* 1559 *et freq* to 1785 *SalisT* (— *or Walks*), *the east greene walles, tharrable lande commonlye called the towne lande within the west and east walles* 1596; *the South Walls* 1766; *v.* wall. The remains of the walls on west, south and east were made into 'walks' in e18 (Hutch[3] 2 337–8), *v.* Bowling Alley Walk, Glyde Path Hill, The Grove, Salisbury Walks, South Walks Rd *supra*, West Walk *infra*. TRINITY ST., earlier *South Back St.* 1774 Map, *Back South St.* 1824 Pigot, cf. Prince's St., South St. *supra*. HIGH WEST ST., 1774 Map, *Hywesterstrete* 1345 *Rent*, *vicus* (*regius*) *occidentalis* 1395, *altus vicus occidentalis* (*regius*) 1399, 1407, *Westret*(*e*) 1402, 1403, *occidentalis vicus vocatus Heyestret* 1425, *West Stret* 1610 DorM, *v.* hēah, west, strǣt, cf. High East St. *supra*; the earliest form contains the comp. adj. **westerra** 'more westerly'. WEST WALK, *the West Walk (commonly called the Bowling Green)* 1716, 1774, following the old west wall (cf. The Town Walls *supra*) and meeting Bowling Alley Walk *supra* at right angles. WEYMOUTH RD, 1841 *TA*, cf. *the way that ledith from Dorchester to Waymouth* 1535–43 Leland, *Melcombe Way* 1650 *ParlSurv*, leading to Weymouth and Melcombe R. *supra*.

Lost st.ns. include *La Blyndelane* 1335 *Ct* (*v.* blind); *Bro(a)d(e)streete*, *Borestreet als. Brodstreete* 1615 *DuCo* (*v.* brād); *Chepestrete* 1545 *CampbCh* (*v.* cēap 'trade, market', possibly identical with *in vico mercato* 1404, 1426 (which ran N–S according to DorR xliv), cf. Market Place *supra*); *the Church passage* 1791 (near St Peter's Church); *Cow(e) Lane* 1426, 1549 *Ct*, 1615 *DuCo*, 1841 *TA* (*v.* cū; perhaps a drove for cattle, or where they were sold); *crucem in Fordington, A broken crosse* 1615 *DuCo* (cf. William *atte Crouche* 1335 *Ct*, *v.* atte, crūc³ 'a cross'); *Estgate de Dorchestr'* 1330 *ib*, *la Estʒete* ('steps (*scalar'*) at —') 1349 *ib*, *portam orientalem* 1399, 1411, *le Estyate* 1426 *Ct*, *le east yate* 1615 *DuCo*, *the two east gates* 1642, *East Gate* 1841 *TA*, cf. John Jurdan *atteystegate, -yate* 1410, 1411 (*v.* ēast, geat, atte; the main east gate was at the east end of High East St. *supra*; for the other east gate, *v.* Durngate St. *supra*); *the Fish Stones* 1762 (no doubt where fish was sold, cf. an identical lost name in Weymouth par. *supra*); *Glidelane* 1422 (*v.* Church St. *supra*); *Grope Lane* 1741 Clegg (from grōp(e) 'ditch' or grāpian 'to grope'; for an identical name, cf. Moreton's Lane in Wareham par. *supra*; it was near *East Gate supra*); *Lemans Lane* 1615 *DuCo* (cf. Robert *Lemon* 1681); *portam borialem* 1399–1440, *la* — 1407, *le Northgate* 1416 (*v.* norð, geat; this gate is no doubt identical with that said to be at *Glippath* in 1642, *v.* Glyde Path Hill & Rd *supra*); *le Northlane* 1546 (*v.* norð, lane; probably to be identified with *venella que ducit ab alto vico regio occidentali versus portam borialem* 1399, 1410, *venellam que ducit ad vicum borialem* 1416 (*v.* DorR xxxvii–xxxviii), cf. High West St., Glyde Path Hill, *Northgate* all *supra*, and foll.); *the Northe lane* 1574 (not identical with prec., *v.* Church St. *supra*); *a back lane called the Sawpitt* 1669, *Sawpit Lane* 1749 (*v.* saw-pit); *Southihete* 1333 *Ct*, (*le) Southgate, -ʒete* 1382 *ib*, *portam australem* 1402, (*le) S(o)uthyate* (*de Dorchestr'*) 1426 *Ct*, *the three sowth gates* 1642 (*v.* sūð, geat; the main south gate was at the south end of South St. *supra*); (*a passage called) the Thorough Fair* 1721, 1755 (in Holy Trinity par.); *the Twelve Men way* 1551, *the xij men Waye* c. 1594 (in St Peter's par., probably so called 'from the twelve Jurors sworn at the Court of the Town, who went by this way to their place of meeting' (DorR xlii); *la Westʒete* 1345 *Ct*, *Westgate* 1345 *Rent*, *portam occidentalem* 1423 DorR, 1615 *DuCo*, *the two west gates* 1642, cf. Alice *atte Westgate* 1273 Banco (*v.* west, geat, atte; the main west gate was at the west end of High West St. *supra*).

Buildings include (*The) Barracks* 1811 OS, 1863 Hutch³; *Belamys bakehouse* 1540 (cf. John *Belamy* 1499, *the Old Bakehouse* 1821 *DuCo*); *Blindhowse* 1642 ('for confining disorderly people for the night' Hutch³ 2 338); *the Brewhouse & Maulthowse* 1623, *the Towne Brewhowse* 1625; *Brine's house* 1737 DorB; 'house called *Carthous'* 1350 *Ct* (*v.* cræt); *castellum de* — 1200–1210, *castrum de Dorecestr'* 1214 all P, 'gaol of the castle of... *Dorcestre'* 1342 Pat, cf. *domus de* —, *domus R. apud Dorecestr'* 1196 ChancR,

1201–1211 P ('(king's) house(s)') (on Dorchester castle, *v.* King's Works 2 629; the site came into the possession of the friars (*v.* Friary Saw Mill *infra*), hence *castrum fratrum minorum* 1401–1406, *terr' voc' lez Fryers Castle* 1615 *DuCo,* cf. *lands called the Castle als. the higher Castle and the Lower Castle* 1635 *Russ,* 'close called *the Castle'* 1755, *Castle* 1774 Map, *the Castle Mount* 1774 Hutch[1], *the Castle Hill* 1863 Hutch[3] (site of present H.M. Prison), cf. also the f.n. Hators *infra, v.* castel(l)); *Chubbs Almshouse* (*near the Fryery*) 1774 Map, 1793 (founded e17 by Margaret *Chubb, v.* DorR 563, cf. Friary Saw Mill *infra*); (*a place called*) *Clanbulwarke* 1650 *ParlSurv* (*v.* bulwerk; first el. perhaps clǣne 'clean', though in what sense is not clear); *The Corner house in Pease Lane* 1737 (*v.* Colliton St. *supra*); *County Jail* 1774 Map (at E end of High East St., built a1633 (Hutch[1] 1 383) and giving name to *Gaol Lane* now Icen Way *supra*; there was an earlier gaol in Dorchester castle *q.v. supra* and another on the N side of High East St., '(king's) gaol of *Dorc(h)estre'* 1350, 1447 Pat, 'burgage called *la Gaole, -la Gowle* 1458, *Gaolem Domini Regis* 1479, *the jayle of Dorchester* c. 1500 *RoyRoll, the old gaole* 1642, *v.* gail(l)e; the present H.M. Prison built c. 1790 on the site of the castle is *County Gaol* 1840 *TAMap*); *le Court(e) Howse* 1551 *Ct,* 1615 *DuCo, The Court Ho* 1841 *TA; the Cupola* (*or market-house*) 1757 DorR, 1774 Hutch[1] (*v.* cupola 'a rounded dome'); *Dissenters Meeting Ho* 1774 Map; *the Engine House* 1777; *Fre Schole* 1610 DorM, *the Freeschool(e)* 1634, 1785 *Salis, the frescole* 1640, *the Gramer Schoole* 1641, cf. *the scoule howse* 1567, *the Schole Cl* 1694, *the Schoolhouse Cl* 1765 (built 1567, *v.* DorR 563); *the Grand Jury chamber* 1634; *Guild Hall* 1610 DorM, 1774 Map; (*the*) *Hospital or Work(e)house* 1618 DorR, 1774 Map (built p1613 (Hutch[3] 2 341), cf. *The Hospital Gdn* 1840 *TA*); *Hurdle Ho* 1801 (for storing hurdles used at markets); *Napiers Mite & Almshouse* 1774 Map, *Napper's Almshouse or Napper's Mite* 1863 Hutch[3] (founded 1615 by Robert *Napper, v.* DorR 561, cf. Almshouse Mdw in Piddlehinton par. *supra*); *les Nyweshoppes* 1396 (*v.* nīwe, sc(e)oppa); *les Northshoppes* 1474; *The Parsonage Ho* (All Saints) 1737 (cf. *mansio Rectoris ecclesie Omnium Sanctorum* 1550); *the parsonage of Fordington* 1553 *Ilch, the viccaridge* 1664 HTax; *the Pest Ho* 1704; *the Pipekiln* 1749; *the Shyre haale* 1555, *the Sheare Hall or Countie Hall* 1594 *Ilch, the Shirehall* 1634, *the Sheerehall* 1641, *County Hall* 1774 Map (*v.* scīr[1], hall; it gave name to *Shire hall Lane* 1774 ib now Glyde Path Rd *supra*); *Stenyn-* 1406, *le Stenenhous(e)* 1428 (*v.* stǣnen, hūs); 'tenement called *Tanhous* which William *Tanner(e)* holds' 1411, 1416 (*v.* tanhouse); *the Tower* 1643; *the —, le Towne Hal(l)* 1583–1629, — *haule* 1624 (taken down 1793, *v.* Clegg 144); *the schole lately erected in Trynitie parish* 1631, *the English Schoole* 1633, *Trinity School* 1863 Hutch[3] (*v.* Holy Trinity (parish) *supra,* Hutch[3] 2 369); *Whetstones Almshouse* 1774 Map (founded c. 1619 by John *Whettstone, v.* DorR 560); 'house called *Mount Whittle'* 1666 (probably from Whitfield in Bradford P. par. *supra*); *novi hospicii voc' la Wolhous* 1406 *Winch* (*v. New Inn infra*); *Woodhouse* 1848 *DROMap.*

Inns include *Anchor* 1824 Pigot; *the Angel* 1622 Hutch[3]; *The Antelope* 1737; *The Black Horse* 1737; *Bulls Head Inn* 1881 *TA* alt. app.; *Catherine Wheel Ale House* 1821 *DuCo; Chequers* 1824 Pigot; *the Crown Inn* 1737, *Old Crown Inn, New Crown Beerhouse* 1848 *DROMap; Dolphin Inn* 1848

DROMap; *The Exchequer* 1737; *the George* 1620; *Great Western Inn* 1877 *TA* alt. app.; *The Green Dragon* 1737; *The Greyhound* 1737; *The Half Moon* 1743; *Junction Hotel* 1877 *TA* alt. app.; *The King's Arms* 1737; *P.H. the Sign of the Last* 1821 *DuCo*; *The Mail Coach Inn* 1848 *DROMap*; *Mason's Arms Beerhouse* 1848 *ib*; *the Mermaid* 1757; *la Nywehyn* 1398, *nouum hospicium* 1400 DorR, 1406 *Winch* (— *voc' la Wolhous*), 1437, *le Newe Inne* 1548, *The New Inn* 1848 *DROMap* (*v.* nīwe, inn, wull, hūs); *The Phoenix* 1737; *The Plume of Feathers* 1810 *DROMap*; *the Queen's Arms* 1696; *The Queen's Own Beerhouse* 1848 *DROMap*; *The Red Lyon* 1737; *the Royal Oak* 1779; *Ship Inn* 1666 DorB, *Ship Beerhouse* 1848 *DROMap* (cf. *ctg called the Ship* 1821 *DuCo*); *The Swan Ale Ho* 1821 *DuCo*; *The Three Crowns* 1737; *the Three Marriners* 1793; *The White Hart* 1737; *The White Horse* 1737; *Wood & Stone* 1824 Pigot.

COLLITON HO (1863 Hutch³) & PARK (SY 690909), *Colly-*, *Colliton land(e)* 1611 *DuCo*, *Cullen-* 1664 HTax, *Colliton* 1774 Map. An earlier name for the S part of the adjacent street now called Glyde Path Hill *supra*, and also for a tithing in St George hundred, was *Colles Row* 1480 Hutch³, (*vicus vocatus*) *Col(l)yncol(le) Rew(e)* 1542, 1547, (— *streate*) 1559, *Collencollrew* 1547 all DorR, *Colliton Row(e)* 1622 Hutch³ *et freq* to 1863 ib, *Colliten Rowe* 1668 DorR; here *Coll(e)-*, *-col(le)-* represent the ME pers.n. or surname *Col(l)* (often a pet form of *Nicholas*), and *Col(l)yn*, *-en* a diminutive of this, the meaning of the name being '(Colin) Coll's row of houses', *v.* rǣw, rāw, cf. 'the tenement of Nicholas *Cole*' 1399 DorR (situated on the E side of the street later called *Colles Row* near its junction with the lane later called Colliton St. *supra*). *-ton* in Colliton may then simply be a 17th cent. analogical substitution for *-coll*, though of course it is possible that Colliton is an earlier independent formation from the same or a similar pers.n. and tūn.

FRIARY SAW MILL (in ruins) (SY 693909), cf. *the Friery Mills* 1635 *Russ*, *the Friary Mills* 1642 DorR, *the Friery Grist Mill* 1785 *SalisT*, *The Mills* c. 1832 *DROMap*, from the Franciscan friary (founded a1267) to which the mills (built 1485) belonged. References to the friary include *fratres minores Dorcestr'* 1361 *AD*, *ecclesie fratrum minorum Dorcestr'* 1379 *ib*, *the Friars Grove* 1607 Clegg, *le friers grove* 1615 *DuCo*, *the Fryory garden wall* 1634 *SalisT*, *the Friery* 1635 *Russ*, *Priory or Friery* 1774 Map, *the Friery Dwellinghouse*, *Friery Grove* 1785 *SalisT*, *Friary Ld* 1840 *TAMap*, *Friary Md* 1840 *TA*, *Friery Bank* 1841 *ib*, *v.* friary, cf. Friary Hill & Lane *supra*, VCHDo **2** 93–5, and Dorchester castle *supra*.

LOUD'S MILL (SY 709903), *a fulling mill* 1617 *Add, Louds Mill(s)* 1774 Hutch[1], 1841 *TA, Lead Mill* 1811 OS, cf. *pastura qua voc' Grayswick* Ed 1 (1617) *Add, Graswyk* 1300 Ipm, *lowdes ham* 1551 *Ct, Lowdsffylde* 1553 DorR, *pasture then* [Ed 1] *knowne by the name Graiswicke now not to be found within the whole manor* Jas 1 *LRMB, Loweds-, Lowd(e)s Field* 1607 Clegg, *Grays-, Graiswick(e) now(e) Lowdes fielde, -feilde* 1611 *DuCo,* 1617 *Add, St' Johns Lande de Dorchester* 1615 *DuCo, certaine grounde called in auntient Recorde Greiswick latelie Lowdes feilde...in the tenure of John Churchill esq. under the name of St Johns Lande a certaine hospitall as is said in Dorchester* 1617 *Add, Loudsfeilds* 1650 *ParlSurv, Lowds Lds & Orchd* 1841 *TA. Loud* is a surname, cf. the plot granted to Thomas *de Lude* in 1304 Pat, *v.* hamm, feld. *Gray-* in the earlier *Grayswick* may be from græg[2] 'a badger', but is probably a manorial affix; a family of this name has not been noted here so early, but cf. Grey's Bridge *infra* (also on R. Frome, $\frac{1}{2}$ mile upstream), *v.* wīc 'dairy farm, hamlet'. *St Johns Lande* (according to 1617 *Add* a name for only part of *Lowdes feilde*) is so called from its possession by the hospital of St John in Dorchester, cf. *Prior hospitalis Sancti Johannis Dorcestr' un' virgat' terra* Ed 1 (1617) *Add, v.* St John's Chapel *supra.*

MAUMBURY (local, SY 691899), *Memburi, -bury* 1333 *Ct, Mambury* 1382, 1431 *ib,* 1774 Hutch[1] (— *or Maumbury*), (— *Rings*) 1877 *TA* (alt. app.), *-berry* 1650 *ParlSurv, Maumbiry* 1382 *Ct, -bury Ring* 1841 *TAMap, Malmebury* 1553 *Ilch, Amphitheatre* 1773 Bayly, 1811 OS, *Ma(u)msbury* (*Rings*), *The Rings* 1841 *TA,* cf. *Ma(u)msbury 5 Acre Flg & (N) Middle Flg, Maumsbury Cmn & Green, Mamsbray E Flg, Ring Flg* 1841 *ib.* The second el. is OE burh (dat. sg. *byrig*), here in the sense 'pre-English earthwork' since Maumbury is a 'henge monument' of Neolithic date which later served as a Roman amphitheatre, *v.* also hring. The first el. is possibly OE malm (WSax mealm) 'sandy or chalky soil', as proposed by Hutch[3] 2 795 ('Mamebury being derived in the opinion of some writers from malm or mame (as it is called in the Dorset dialects), a kind of earthy chalk, of which it consists'); *Mem-* would then represent WSax mealm, and for the vocalization and loss of pre-consonantal *l* in *Mem-, Ma(u)m-, v.* Zachrisson ANInfl 146 ff, IPN 113, Feilitzen 78. However it is possible, in view of the late appearance of *l* (once, in 1553), that the name contains some other first el. which was only interpreted as malm at this comparatively late date: three out of four of the 14th cent. forms have neither *l* nor *u*, and *Maum-* may simply show AN *au* for *a* before *m*+labial (Jordan 199, Zachrisson ANInfl 153, IPN 105). Professor Löfvenberg suggests that the most likely first el. is OE gemǣne 'common'. Possibly analogous to this name are Membury D 644 (*Man-* 1086, 1238, *Mem-* Hy 2 *et freq*, *Men-* 1238, 1244, 1270, *M(e)yn-* 1270, thought probably to contain PrWelsh main[2] 'a rock, a stone', though DEPN suggests gemǣne 'common' as a possible alternative), and Mambury D 107 (*Mam-* 1330, *Man-* e16, thought possibly to contain main[2] or OE *mamme* 'a teat', cf. PrWelsh mamm with the same meaning). Cf. this comment on Maumbury in Hutch[3] 2 795: 'Roger Gale derived the name from *maen*, a great stone, which lay at the entrance when he saw it in 1719'. For a certain instance of this word (main[2], Welsh *maen*) as first el. in a compound name, cf. Maine Down (probably to be identified with the earlier *Maynerigge* which has 13th cent. forms in *Men-*, *Meyn-* and *Man-*) in Broadmayne par. *supra*.

MILL (Fordington) (SY 700905), probably on or near the site of *Estmull* 1422 *Ct*, *(le) Estmille, -myll* 1435–1552 *ib*, *Eastmill* 1611 *DuCo*, *Luttshill Mill* als. *East Mill, Lutshills mills sive Easte mills, Lutshells mill* 1615 *ib*, *(the) East Mills* 1622 Hutch[3], 1774 Hutch[1], giving name to *le Myll-, Mill close corner, -cornar* 1549 *Ct*, *Fordington Mills Hamlett* 1664 HTax (a tithing in Bindon liberty), and Mill Bank & St. *supra*, v. ēast, myln. 'East' distinguishes these mills from those at West Mills *infra* which were also in Fordington. *Lut(t)shill(s)* is an earlier p.n. occurring as (*pontem apud*) *Lutteshull(e)* 1329, 1335, *Lot(t)es-* 1330, 1349, *Lutheshull* 1330 all *Ct*, probably from an OE pers.n. **Lutt* (v. Reaney s.n. *Lutt*) or **Lott* (v. Ekwall DEPN s.n. Lottisham So), with hyll; the entry for *Lutteshull* in 1329 *Ct* concerns the abbot of Bindon, and it is probable that 'the fulling mill' and 'the abbot of Bindon's mill' mentioned in 1349 *Ct* refer to the mill later known as 'east mill'. Other early references to a mill or mills here (or at West Mills *infra*) include *molendinum de Fordinton* 1199–1230 P, *molendinum extra Dor(e)cestr'* 1204–1230 P, 'the mill which *Aylric Schirewyt* held in *Fordinton*', 'the mill outside *Dorcestre* which Edward *Palmer* held' (given to Bindon abbey) 1280 Ch, and 'the Prince of Wales's mill at *Fordyngton*' 1348 Pat (cf. Prince's Bridge *infra*), whilst one or other of these mills was doubtless the home of Henry *at(t)e Mulle* 1329, Thomas *atte Mulle* 1335 *Ct*, v. atte.

POUNDBURY (CAMP) (SY 682912), *Ponebury* 1333 *Ct*, (*Hysouth*) *Pimbury* 1345 *Rent* (probably for *Pun-*), *Pumrie* 1590 WeyR, *Furlong subtus Pomerie, -rye, Pomeries Bushe furlonge* 1615 *DuCo, Pumberry Feild* 1650 *ParlSurv, the Pombrey* 1653 *ib, Pombry* 1665 DorR, *Pomery or Poundbury* 1774 Hutch[1], *Pummery*(s) *Fd, Pummery Gate Flg, Pummery Rings* 1841 *TA, Poundbury Fm* (*Md*) 1877 *ib* (alt. app.). The second el. is OE burh (dat. sg. *byrig*), here in the sense 'pre-English earthwork' since Poundbury is an Iron Age hill-fort, *v.* also hring. The first el. is probably the OE pers.n. *Pūna* postulated for Poynings Sx 286, cf. John *Pune* 1332 SR (Milborne St A.). *Hysouth-* in 1345 is probably for *Bysouth-* '(land) to the south of', *v.* bī, sūðan, but *Hy-* may represent hēah 'high'.

WEST MILLS (SY 686911), (*la*) *Westmull*(e) 1349, 1426 *Ct*, (*le*) *West Myll*(e), *-Mille* 1431, 1434, 1547 *ib, West*(e) *Mill*(s) 1615 *DuCo et passim*, cf. *terre apud Westgate ex parte boriali Abovethemilne* 1345 *Rent, claus' de Westmylle* 1431 *Ct, West Mill Close* 1650 *ParlSurv,* 1841 *TA, lez hams de Weste mills* 1615 *DuCo, the West mill hams, the West Mill House* 1650 *ParlSurv, v.* west, myln, abufan, hamm, *Westgate supra,* cf. Mill (Fordington) *supra* which was earlier *Eastmill.*

BUSH ROAD CTGS, named from *Bush*(e)*way*(e) 1615 *DuCo,* 1650 *ParlSurv, Bush Way* 1840 *TAMap,* now Maiden Castle Rd *supra,* cf. *Bushe Topp furlonge* 1615 *DuCo, Bush Bottom Flg, Bush Nap Flg, Bushway N & S Flg* 1841 *TA, v.* busc, weg, topp, botm, cnæpp. FAIR FD, cf. *Fair Grd & Plot* 1841 *TA,* where fairs were held, *v.* feire; on fairs in Dorchester, *v.* DorR 501–6. FORDINGTON FD (cf. *camp' de Fordyngton* 1381 *Ct, Fordington Comon feildes* 1617 *Add, Towne feilds of Fordington, Fordington Feilds* 1650 *ParlSurv*), FM (*Fordington Fm* (*Md*) 1877 *TA* alt. app.) & Ho, *v.* Fordington *supra.* GREY'S BRIDGE, 1791 Boswell, *Gregs-* 1840 *TAMap, Grays Bridge* 1841 *ib,* possibly from the *Grey* family of Kingston, *v.* Grey's Wd in Stinsford par. *infra,* cf. *lande of William Graye* 1596 DorR, *Greys Mills* 1774 Hutch[1], *Greys Orchd* 1841 *TA,* and the lost p.n. *Grayswick* discussed under Loud's Mill *supra.* This bridge across R. Frome was built in 1747 to replace another slightly downstream called *Fordington bridge* 1535–43 Leland, *pontem magnum, Greate bridge als. Stockinge bridge* 1615 *DuCo, Stokinge* — 1637 *Wal, Stockin*(g) — 1774 Hutch[1], *Stockham Bridge* 1791 Boswell, *v.* grēat 'large', stoccen 'made of logs', cf. *The Old Bridge* 1841 *TAMap*. LAWRENCE BARROW (lost, about SY 698898), 1650 *ParlSurv*, 1811 OS, *Launce Barrow* 1826 Gre, cf. *Lawrence(s) Barrow Flg* 1841 *TA*, Richard *Lawrense* 1563 DorR, Christian *Lawrence* 1664 HTax, *v.* beorg. LONG BRIDGE, 1791 Boswell, *la Langebrigg* 1349, *Langbrygge* 1435, *Longebrydge* 1552 all *Ct*, *v.* lang[1], brycg. MAEN, a modern house name, no doubt from Welsh **maen** 'stone', an older form of which (main[2]) is to be found in Broadmayne par. *supra*. MAIDEN CASTLE CTGS *&* FM, — *Fm* (*Md*) 1877 *TA* alt. app., *v.* Maiden Castle in Winterborne St M. par. *infra*. MAX GATE (HO), cf. Henry *Mack* 1832 DorR. MIDDLE FM, — *Fm* (*Md*) 1877 *TA* alt. app. GT *&* LT MOHUN'S BRIDGES (local), 1774 Hutch[1], *Moones*- 1607 Clegg, 1631 WeyM, *Mohon(o)es Bridge* 1841 *TA*, *TAMap*, cf. *Moones Bridge River* 1650 *ParlSurv*, no doubt from the family of John *Mone* or *Mohun* who held the manor of Wolfeton in Charminster par. *supra* and lands in Dorchester at his death in 1480 (Hutch[3] 2 415, 546). The references to *magnum pontem vocatum novum pontem* 1565 DorR and to *Great Brydge* 1607 Clegg probably also belong here. NORTHERNHAY, perhaps to be associated with *Northurn* 1280 *Ass* (p) which is from norð 'north' and hyrne 'corner, land in a river-bend', *v.* (ge)hæg 'enclosure', cf. also *la Hurne* 1244 *Ass* (p), John *Inthehurne* 1329 *Ct*; Northernhay lies in a bend of R. Frome. PRINCE'S BRIDGE, cf. 'the prince's wood' 1364 BPR, *Prynce Wood, Prince Woode vel le Princes East Wood* 1615 *DuCo*, *The Princes river* 1617 *Add* (probably R. Frome), Prince of Wales Rd *supra*, all in allusion to the possession of the manor of Fordington by the Prince of Wales. The reference to *pontem borialem iuxta molend' predict' [le Estmyll]* 1549 *Ct* may also belong here, *v.* Mill (Fordington) *supra*. RED COW DAIRY, cf. *Red Cow Cl* 1841 *TA*. RODLANDS, *Middelredelond* 1345 *Rent, Redlandes inferior, Rudlandes superior, media furlong vocat' Rudlandes* 1615 *DuCo*, *Rudlands* 1650 *ParlSurv, Lr, Middle & Upr Redland(s) Flg* 1841 *TA*, *v.* hrēod 'reed, rush', land, middel. SALISBURY FD, cf. Susanna *Salisbury* 1664 HTax, Salisbury St. *supra*. SOMERLEIGH COURT, perhaps named from *the Summerleas* 1650 *ParlSurv*, 'pasture used in summer', cf. *le Wynterlese* 1547 *Ct*, *the Sommer feilds* 1650 *ParlSurv*, *v.* sumor, winter[1], læs. SOUTH COURT. SYWARD ['saiwəd] LODGE, no doubt named from the family of Roger *Syward* who had a tenement in Dorchester in 1363–1379 *Ilch*, cf. also *terram Cantarie Johannis Seward* 1423 DorR (on 'Seward's chantry' in the church of the Holy Trinity, *v.* DorR xlv). TOP O' TOWN (local), the area around the

higher (western) end of High West St. *supra.* TWENTY ACRES ALTMT
GDNS, cf. *Stadium vocat' Over Twentie acres* 1615 *DuCo,* (*The*) *20
Acre Flg* 1841 *TA, v.* uferra. THE TWO BARROWS (site of tumuli), *the
Barrow called Two Barrows* 1832 Hutch[3], cf. *2 Barrow Flg* 1841 *TA,
v.* beorg. VICTORIA PARK. WAREHAM BRIDGE & HO, near road to
Wareham.

FIELD-NAMES

For some fields in Fordington *TA* or Dorchester Holy Trinity *TA* but now
in Stinsford, *v.* Stinsford par. *infra.* The undated forms are 1841 *TA* 88
(Fordington) and 1840 *TA* 77 (Dorchester Holy Trinity) (marked †).
Spellings dated 1234 (1279) are Ch, 1292, 1340, 1585 Hutch[3], 1327 *SR*,
1328, 1329, 1330, 1333, 1335, 1336, 1345[1], 1346–1350, 1381, 1382, 1422,
1426, 1431[2], 1434, 1435, 1437, 1471, 1482, 1483, 1547–1550 *Ct*, 1332 SR,
1342 Pat, 1345[2] *Rent,* m14, 1553 *Ilch,* 1391 *Midd,* 1440 Cl, 1449, 1458 *Weld*[1],
Jas 1 *LRMB,* 1607 Clegg, 1615, 1821 *DuCo,* 1617 *Add,* 1650, 1653 *ParlSurv,*
1664 HTax, 1774 Hutch[1], 1877 *TA* 88 alt. app., and the rest DorR.

(*a*) Ball —, Bull Cross Flg, Ball Cross the Way (cf. *Bolecrouche* 1333, *v.*
bula, crūc[3]); Barn(s) Cl, Barn Croft, Barn Flg (Cmn), †Barn Pce (*v.* bere-
ærn, cf. 'two burgages called *bernys'* 1492 (on E side of South St.)); Barrow
Way Flg (cf. *Barowes Lyne* 1615, *v.* beorg, leyne); Barell —, Bazel —, Bazill
Pit(t) Flg (perhaps ModE basil 'sheepskin tanned in bark'); Upr Bedland
Flg; Beggars Nap Cmn & Flg (*v.* cnæpp); Betters Plot; Birds; Bishops (cf.
Bishop's Court als. Bishop's Hall 1585, *Bushops Lane* 1615, John *Bysschupp*
1391); Bone Mill yd; Britains Cl (cf. John *le Breton* 1292 (Charminster) and
the st.n. Little Britain *supra*); Broad(land) Flg; Buckland Way (possibly to
Buckland Ripers in Radipole par. *supra,* but cf. *acr' iacet in Bokelonde* 1330,
v. bōc-land); Bull Lands (cf. *Bulcroft* 1553, *v.* bula, croft); Bulls; Under
Burlington Flg, Burlington Hill (Cmn & N Side), Burlington Lime Kiln
Flg (*Burledon* 1333, -*ton* 1650, (*The Easte Furlong of* -, *The Midle Furlong
upon*) *Burldon Hill* 1615; the final el. is clearly dūn 'hill'; *Burle-* may mean
'wood or clearing by the earthwork', from burh (gen. sg. *burge*) (probably
referring to Maiden Castle since these Burlingtons are all in Castle Fd *infra*),
and lēah, cf. Bulbury in Lytchett Min. par. *infra*; the medial -*ing-* seems to
be a late analogical development); Came (Hill) Gate, Came Hill E, Middle &
W Flg, Came Rd Cmn (*Came Hill* 1607, *The Wester furlonge upon Came Hill,
Came Yate* 1615, near Winterborne Came par. *supra, v.* westerra, geat);
Carrion Pit (Flg), Cary —, Cory Pit(t) Flg (*v.* carrion); Castle Fd, Castle E
Flg, Castle E & W Middle Flg, Castle Green Cmn, Castle Hole W Flg,
Castle Way or Rd Cmn (*Castle Way(e)* 1615, 1650, all named from Maiden
Castle in Winterborne St M. par. *infra*); Catcham (Flg) (*via apud
Chaccheharme* 1483, probably from ME cacche 'to catch' and ME harm
'evil, injury', either a surname or a fanciful name for a dangerous spot);
Chants; Clanton Bars Flg, Clantons Barn Drove Cmn (cf. *le Drove waye
iuxta fossatum de Clandown* 1615, *v.* barre, drove, Clandon in Winterborne
St M. par. *infra*); Clarks Cl (cf. *cottage called Clarkes* 1650, John *Clerk* 1401);

Close; Collens's, Collen(s), -ins Pit (Fd & Flg) (cf. Isabella *Collyngs* 1404);
Conks Fd (cf. John *Le Konc'* 1335, although this may well be an error for
-*Kouc'*, cf. Cooks *infra*); Constables Flg (cf. John *Conestable* 1332); Cooks
3 Corner Cl (cf. John *(le) Couk* 1327, 1345[1], *le Coukesham* 1391, v.
hamm); Coomb Bottom Flg, — Furlond, Coombs Ditch Cmn, Coomb Ditch Flg &
Pce, Coomb Fd, Middle & W Coomb Flg, Comb Rd Cmn, Coomb Rd
(Bottom, Middle & 9 Acre) Flg, Coomb(e) 10 Acre Flg, Coomb Way Square
Flg, Coomb West Hill Flg (*la Combe* 1382, *Combes ditch, The Hollow of
Combe, Midle Combe furlonge* 1615, cf. Nicholas *atte Combe* 1381, v. **cumb**,
atte); Coombs Half Place; Coopers Ld (cf. Henry *Coupere* 1406); Coxes Nap
Flg (cf. John *Cox* 1621, v. **cnæpp**); Cro(c)kers Cross (E, Middle & W) Flg,
Cro(c)kers Cross Linches, — (Flg) Lanchis (cf. John *Crokker* 1401, v. **hlinc**,
lanch); Ditch End Flg (*terram apud le Dyghend* 1381, v. **dīc, ende**[1]); Doles
Hill, Dolls Hole (cf. Richard *Dowle* 1664); E & W Downs, E Down Flg
(*Easte Downe* 1615, v. **dūn**); Drift Pce (v. **drift**); (The Drove Pce near) Drove
Cmn, Drove Pit Flg (Headland) (v. **drove**); †Dry Md; Eames's (cf. Martin
Eme 1547); East Fd; Long 8 Acres; End Flg; Farthinghold (freq, cf. **terr'**
voc' a *Ferthyngholde* 1548, v. **fēorðung, hold**); Flinty Bottom Flg, Flinty Nap
Flg (v. **cnæpp**); Fordington Green by the Church; Long Fount (Flg) (cf.
(*la*) *Founte* 1350, 1422, v. **funta** 'spring'; the surname of John *de Fonte* 1330
is more likely to be a Latinised form of *atte Welle* (v. Well Bottom *infra*) than
to belong here); Upr Furlong Long & Short 4 Acres; 4 Acres Flg; Glovers
Cl (cf. Benedict *Glovere* 1327, 'the tenement formerly of John *Glouer'* 1411,
cotag' voc' Gloves 1615); E & W Goodforward Flg (*a headlande called good
Forehead* 1615, v. **forehead**); Gt Barrow Flg & Green Cmn (*ground called
Greatbarrow Line* 1650, v. **grēat, beorg, leyne**; a large round barrow is marked
6″); Gt Bottom Flg; Half Place (freq); The Ham (or Lime Kiln Pce) (*le Ham*
1615, v. **hamm**); Hamslade (Hill, Long & Pit(t)) Flg, Little Flg (or)
Hamslade Hill (*Impslade* 1615, v. **impa** 'sapling', **slæd**); Hatchet(t) Ld
(freq), Lane & Pce (probably **hæcc-geat** 'a hatch-gate'); Hators or Caltors
Cl or Castle Orchd (*Caters Close* 1607, 1615, cf. *cotag' iuxta Gladpath voc'
Caters* 1615, the surname *Cater*, cf. Glyde Path Hill and Dorchester castle
supra); (Long) Headland; Her(r)ing(s)ton(e) Gate (Flg) & Way S Flg (cf.
Herringstone Fm (Md) 1877, from Winterborne Her. par. *supra*); Hides Gate
Flg, Hides Middle & N Flg, Hides Way Cmn (*Hides hedge fur'* 1615, from
Hydes in Winterborne Her. par. *supra*); Hiesoms-, -sons-, -some Flg,
Hussoms Flg; Hill Cl (cf. John *Not onthehull* 1381, v. **hyll**); Hitching Edge
Flg (v. **hēcing**); Home Cl, †Home Cowleaze & Pdk; A close originally the
Homestead; Honeycomb (Flg) (v. **hunig, cumb**, cf. *Honymor* 1349 (v. **mōr**),
but perhaps to be associated with *Hungercumbe* 1347, *Hongercombe* 1348, v.
hungor); (the) Huntinghorn Flg (perhaps from its shape); Inches Down Flg;
(Lt) Inn Md (v. **in**); Jackeys; Johnsons; Keepers Cross Flg (*Keepe crosse*
1615, perhaps ModE **keep** 'dungeon'); Laus-, Laws-, Lowsborough (or
Middle Flg) (perhaps **lūs** and **beorg**, cf. Loosebarrow hundred *infra*); Lewell
(Flg), Luewell Corner (*Lewell Hedge* 1650, probably analogous with Lewell
in W Knighton par. *supra*); Limmingtons (cf. John *Lymington* 1621);
Linch(es) (v. **hlinc**); Liscomb (Bottom) Flg, Les-, Liscom(b)e Bottom
(*Luscombe Bottome* 1650, cf. Lyscombe in Cheselbourne par. *infra*); (the

Common) Little Flg (cf. *Parva furlong* 1615); Locks Fm Md 1877 (cf.
William *Loc* 1234 (1279), Richard *Locke* 1664); Longbredy (Pit(t), Short, S
& Way Bottom) Flg, (the) parting Flg Longbredy (from Long Bredy par.,
6 miles W); (Whitewell or) Loops Ld (*Whitewell Lande(s)* 1615, 1617, *Loops
Ld, Loop Grd* 1774, cf. John *Loop* 1750, Whitewell Bottom *infra*); The Manor
Pound (cf. *placeam vocatum le Pount* 1412, *ponfaldum communitatis* 1429 (in
the street now North Square *supra*), *the pownde* 1604, *v.* pund); †Mansion
Ho & Ld; (Cross, E & W) Marle Flg (*Marle furlong* 1615, cf. *A crosse
furlonge* 1615, *v.* marle, cross 'lying across'); Martinstown Path Flg (from
Winterborne St Martin par. *infra*); †Middle Pce S of Barn; Mile —, Mill
Pit(t) (Cmn & Flg); Mile Stone (Flg); Mill Way Cmn & Flg (*Millway
Furlong* 1615); Morgans 4 Acre & Square Flg (cf. Philip *Morgan* 1536);
Muncton Barrow Cmn & (Bottom) Flg (*Munckton Barrow furlonge* 1615, cf.
land at Moncktons Crosse 1553, *a furlonge at Munckton Crose, Munckton
hedge* 1615, all from Winterborne Monkton par. *supra*); Nelsons (cf. John
Nelson 1715); Newland(s) Flg (Gore Pce) (*Newlands* 1650, *v.* nīwe, land,
gāra); 9 Acre Flg; †Nursery Gdns; Parkers Pce (cf. John *Parker* 1327);
†Pasture Pce; Peats Cmn (cf. William *Peate* 1750); †Pet Grd; Picked Flg
(*v.* pīced or picked); Pig Barrow (Bottom) Flg; Pig Stye; †Pitts Mdw (cf.
William *Pitt* 1664); Plot Orchd; Pond Cl & Flg; Rainbow Flg (*v.* rainbow);
Randal(l) Coomb Bottom Cmn & Flg, Randall Coomb Nap Flg, Randall
Down Flg ((*South) Randleton bottom(e) furlonge* 1615, *Radlecombottom* 1650,
cf. Richard *Randolf* 1332, Robert *Randall* 1565, *v.* cumb, botm, cnæpp; the
form in -*ton* suggests a late formation with tūn); Rashers (cf. *William Rasker*
1548); Retham Cl; Old Rd Cmn; Lt & Old Rod Md (*Rodeme(a)de* 1422,
1615, *v.* mæd; first el. perhaps rōd[2] in the sense 'measure of land'); Seagers
(cf. *Segar's orchd* 1774, Roger *Segar* 1547); Shealds Bottom (Flg), Shealds
(E & Middle) Flg, Shealds Wall Cmn; †Sheep Walk; Shepherds Barrow,
Bush & E Flg (cf. Thomas *Shephurd* 1332); Short Acre; Short Breach,
— Bridge Flg (*Short Breach* 1615, — *Breech* 1650, cf. *la Bereche* 1345[2], *v.*
brēc); Short Flg; Shovelling —, Shuffling Flg (perhaps 'shovel piece' from
scofl and -ing[2]); (Under) Six Barrow Flg (*Sixeburrowes furlonge* 1615, burg
'burrow' or beorg 'barrow'); Slade Bottom (Flg), Slade (W) Cross Flg,
Slade (Hill & Long) Flg, Slade Way (Cmn & Flg) (*le* — 1382, *la Slade* 1422,
Slade (*North*) *furlonge* 1615, *the Sleade* 1650, *v.* slæd); Sluggards Cl (Flg);
Smoke Acre Flg (*v.* smoca, cf. foll.); Smoky Hole Cmn, Smoky Hole Middle
& Upr Flg (perhaps ModE smoky in the sense 'smoke-coloured, dark', but
cf. prec.); Smythe —, Smyth(e)y Bottom Flg, Smythe Hill Flg (*Smethenhulle*
1333, probably '(at) the smooth hill', from smēðe (wk. obl. smēðan) and
hyll, later understood as '*Smethe* hill, the hill called *Smethe*', *Smethe* being
then applied also to the adjacent valley bottom); Southfield; Sparrows pce
Flg; Spres(s)bury (Pit) Flg & Path (*Pesberies pit* 1615, perhaps to be
associated with John *Presbro' in venella* 1327); Spy(e) Cross (Long & S) Flg
(the first el. is obscure, cf. Spyway in Langton Mat. par. *supra*); Stafford Md
(cf. W Stafford par. *supra*); Stone Bridge Flg, — furlond, Stone Edge
(Bottom) Flg, Stone —, Stony (H)edge E Flg (*Stone Ridge* — 1615, *Stonebridge Bottom* 1650, *v.* stān, hrycg or brycg, botm); Sull Acre (Nap) Flg, Sull
Acre Way Cmn & Flg (*la Soulhacres* 1348, *Sullacre(s) Bottome), Le topp de*

Sullacres 1615, *v.* sulh 'plough', æcer); Tapps or Bests (cf. Thomas *Tappe* 1547, Hugh *le Beste* 1340); †10 Acres; Thornton Cmn, Thornton (E, Full, Hanging, Hill, S & W) Flg (*Thorndon hill* 1615, *v.* þorn, dūn); (S) Tidden (Bottom & Nap) Flg, Tidden Wall pce (*Tyddene* 1345[1], *Tiddon Wall* 1615, *Tidden Bottome & Hill* 1650, perhaps 'brushwood valley' from tydd and denu, although alternatively the first el. could be the OE pers.n. *Tīda*, with cnæpp, wall); Topath Bridge, Tipoth (sic) Hill Cmn (near R. Frome, *v.* tow-path); Town End, Towns End Flg; Triangle Plot; Old Tucking Mill Wear (near *East Gate supra, v.* wer); 12 Acre Flg (Under Ditch end); Wallcern Flg (*Walyshirne* 1449, *v.* hyrne 'angle, corner', probably with a surname or with walu 'ridge of earth or stone'); Gt Walls Cl; The Ware at Old Red Mill flg (*v.* wer); Waterland(s) (Long) Flg (*Waterland(e)s (furlonge)* 1615, *v.* wæter, land); †Water Mdw; (W) Well Bottom (Flg) (*Well Bottom* 1650, cf. Thomas *atte Wolle* 1328, — *ate Welle* 1329, *communem fontem* 1492, *the comon well* 1573, *v.* wella, botm, atte); Whiffans Ham (cf. Gilbert *Whiffyn* 1664); White fd Gate (probably named from Frome Whitfield in Stinsford par. *infra*); Whit(e)well (†-wall) Bottom, Hill & Hanging Flg (*White-, Whytewell Bottome* 1615, 1650, cf. *Whitwelscombe* 1345[2], *Whitewell Sheepe Downes* 1617, *the Whitwell Sheepslaught* 1653, from Whitfield in Bradford P. par. *supra, v.* botm, hanging, cumb, slæget, cf. Loops Ld *supra*); Whiteway Ditch Flg (*terre apud Whiteweye* 1345[2], *v.* hwīt, weg); †Willow Bed; Wine Street Flg (*terr' apud Twunestret* 1333, *Twynstrete* 1345[2], *Twynnysthrede* 1483, *Wynstreete furlonge* 1615, '(land) between the streets', *v.* betwēonan, stræt, cf. Tweenaways D 518; it lies in the angle of Weymouth Rd and Herringston Rd both *supra*); Winsors (Gore Flg) (cf. *Windesores cross furlonge* 1615, Roger *Wyndesor* 1381, *v.* gāra, cross 'lying across'); E & W Yar-, Garden (Flg) ((*The Easter-, West*) *Yardon* 1615, *Yarden* 1650, probably 'gravel hill' from ēar and dūn); Yard(s) Flg & Headland, The Yards (*v.* gerd); Yeats' Cl 1783 (cf. John *Yeate* 1582); †Yonder Pce W of Barn.

(b) *Abbodesham* m14 (*v acr' Abbatis de Cerne in* —), *Abbotes-* 1426, *Abbotts ham* 1615 (*v.* abbod, hamm (as freq in this par.)); *atte Naysshe* 1395, *atte Aissh* 1396, *Atten Ayssh* 1433 all (p) (*v.* atte, æsc); *the backside* 1553 (*a garden place callid* —) (*v.* backside); *Bagges Crosse (fur')* 1615 (cf. Thomas *Bagge* 1327); *Boldlond* 1333 (*B-* doubtful); *Whidwell Bordelond* 1345[2], *Borde Lands* Jas 1, *Bordlande* 1615 (*v.* bord-land, Whitfield in Bradford P. par. *supra*); *Bottome furlonge* 1615; *Bruers Pitt* 1650; '100 acres of land called *Le Buttys*' 1486 Ipm, *Butt Close* 1615 (*v.* butte); *Byttom Aker* 1471 (*v.* bytme); *Cadmanshire* 1615; *Calysham* 1431[2]; *Campeden* 1400 (perhaps 'valley with enclosures', *v.* camp[1] (gen. pl. *-a*), denu, cf. Campden Gl 1 237); *Can(t)e me(a)de* 1553; *Clyfacre* 1342 FF, *le Cliffe als. Penn* 1615 (*v.* clif, penn[1]); *Col(e)wallys* 1440, 1495 Ipm, *Colewalls furlonge* 1615 (possibly a surname); *Cobteslond* 1335 (cf. John *Cobb* 1621); *the Conigar* 1653 (*v.* coninger); *Corbyns Nyne acres* 1615 (cf. John *Corbyn* 1535); *Courtokeshulle* 1335, *Court Oxhyll* 1434, great —, *litle Curtock(e)s* 1615 (perhaps from court and āc 'oak-tree', with hyll); *Cravellysbern* 1431 (cf. John *Crauel* 1395, *v.* bere-ærn); *close called the Croft* 1650; *Comesham* 1330; 'a place of land called *la* —, *le Dayne*' 1397, 1411, 1483[2], *le Deane* 1545, 'a passage called *the Dane or Dene*' 1585 (these names, all within the old town, probably represent distinct pieces of ground; the same el. occurs in DorR in independent use to denote a measure of land, e.g. *cujusdam Dayne terre* 1423, *vnam quantitatem terre vocate a Dayne* 1444, one *Deane* 1545, cf. Kt dial. *dene* also used of a measure of land (EDD s.v. *dean*), and it is possibly OE denu 'valley' used in some specialized sense; however Professor Löfvenberg considers that the late ME diphthongal spellings tell against this, and that for the present its origin must be left open); *Ledam (aquam abstruxatam in* —) 1330 (*v.* damme); *Doddeston* 1336, *Dodstone furlonge* 1615 (perhaps 'Dodda's stone', from the OE pers.n. *Dodda* and stān, but cf. dodde 'summit of a hill'); *Dolytroppys brygge* 1437 (a surname, with brycg); *le Estbrydge* 1549 (*v.* ēast, brycg); *les Flodeyates* 1422 (*v.* flōd, geat); *Fordington Comon,* — *Meadowes* 1617 (cf. *prat' de Fordyngton* 1458, *v.* Fordington *supra*); *Foxwell's Tenement* 1637 (cf. Nicholas *Foxwell* 1550²); *le frithe* 1615 (*v.* (ge)fyrhðe); *Gentilmannesmede* 1458 (*v.* gentilman, mǣd); *Greynebary* 1348 (*v.* grēne¹, beorg); *una acra iacet By Westegreyne Weye* 1381 ('to the west of the green way', *v.* bī, westan, grēne¹, weg); *(le) Grey(e)ston(e)* 1336, 1382 (*v.* grǣg¹, stān); 'burgage called *(le) Gurnard, -erd'* 1542 (ModE gurnard 'fish of the genus *Trigla*'); *atte Halle* 1335 (p) (*v.* atte, hall); *Helle* 1401 (*placeam Roberti Sutton vocatum* —), 1412 ('a burgage called —'), *Hell Pound* 1737 (*v.* hell, presumably a term of contempt, cf. Helen Lane in Weymouth par. *supra*, with pund); *atte Houke* 1346 (p) (*v.* hōc); *in the hyle* 1327 (p) (*v. le Hyle* in Coombe K. par. *supra*); *Hymbiry* 1345², *Humberry* 1650 (*v.* burh); *montis voc' Iulianes-, Iu Lyanesdowne* 1482, 1483 (the pers.n. or surname *Julian, v.* dūn); *Keporns* 1382 (no doubt a surname); *Kerewere* 1349 (*v.* wer); *le Langacre* 1382 (*v.* lang¹, æcer); *Langebary* 1333, *-bargh* 1349, *Langbary* 1434, *-barowe* 1553 (*v.* lang¹, beorg); *le lawne* 1615 (*v.* launde); *West Lodgate* 1615, 1650 (perhaps analogous with Ludgate Ln 91 which may be from OE ludgeat 'a back door'); *Longelond* 1345² (*v.* lang¹, land); *Maldich* 1350, *-dyche* 1434 (perhaps from malu 'gravel ridge' with dīc); *Midle Close* 1615; *Middelfurlong* 1345² (*v.* middel); *the more* 1553, *le Moare* 1615 (cf. Adam *atte Moure* 1349, *v.* mōr, atte); *the New Close* 1653; *Newdyche* 1434 (*v.* nīwe, dīc); *Newolme* 1431², *Newell hedge,* — *yate* 1615 (*v.* nīwe, welm (WSax wylm) 'a spring', geat); *la Northbern* 1411 (*v.* bere-ærn); *atte Orchard* 1342 (p) (*v.* atte, orceard); *Pakkeberewe* 1330, *Packborow* 1615 ('Pac(c)a's barrow', from an OE pers.n. *Pac(c)a* assumed for several other p.ns. (DEPN), and beorg); *Pesebreche* 1345² (*v.* pise 'pease', brēc); *Pyngysmore* 1483 (cf. John *Pynge* 1540); *Pookes Cottage* 1664 (cf. Robert *Powke* 1429); *Post Furlong* 1615 (*v.* post); *Priersfylde* 1483 (cf. 'the tenement of the Prior of St John of Dorchester' 1395, *v.* prior, feld, St John's Chapel *supra*); *Purfurlonges* 1345² (*v.* pūr 'bittern', furlang; analogous f.ns. occur in Affpuddle par. and Puddletown par. *supra*); *le Rakehay* 1482² (racu 'a hollow' or hraca 'a pass', with (ge)hæg); *Recke-* 1483, *Rackham* 1615 (*v.* rakke); *cotag' voc' Redfords* 1615 (cf. John *Redeforde* 1426); *Rychemansmyll* 1482, *Riche-, Rychemyl(l)* 1483, *cotag' voc' Richemill als. le vayre vel fishing iuxta Pomerye* 1615 (cf. Thomas *Rycheman als. Belhous* 1402, *the Fair and Fishery* 1821, *v.* myln, fishing 'a fishery', Poundbury *supra*; *vayre, fair* probably represent ME weyour 'a fishpond'); *Rydehene* 1333 (*v.* rēad 'red'; *-hene* may be an error for *-hone* from hān 'stone'); *Ropers Stile* 1615 (cf. William *Ropere* 1396, *v.*

stigel); *Rushham, Ruyssham* 1435 (*v.* risc); *Schern-* 1329, *Shern-, Scharnham* 1330 (*v.* scearn 'muck'); *Shurnesbargh* 1431² (*v.* beorg; first el. obscure, perhaps a surname); *Schilves* 1345², *Shelves furlong* 1615 (*v.* scelf (WSax scylf)); 'ground called the *Sley*' 1607, *Le Sleye* 1615 (Professor Löfvenberg suggests that this is probably an early instance of dial. *slay, sley* 'sheep pasture', cf. foll.); *portam (apud) le Sleygate, -le Sleweʒete* 1382, *un' lupeyate voc'-, -apud Sle(y)yate* 1426 (*v.* geat, hlīep-geat; for the first el., cf. prec., *v.* also Sundby, SNPh **27** 106–7, who interprets this compound as 'gate leading to a sheep pasture', or 'swing-gate'); *Slowes gore hedge* 1615 (cf. William *atte Slow* 1327, *v.* atte, slōh 'a slough', gāra); *Smalwayes Cros(s)e* 1615 (*v.* smæl, weg, cros or cross); *ripam de Smalwere* 1382 (*v.* smæl, wer); (*The North-, The South furlonge of*) *E(a)ster Smel(l)ing(e)s, Weston Smellinges* 1615 (cf. Henry *Snellynge* 1465, *v.* ēasterra, westerne); *Sourelond* 1345² (*v.* sūr, land); *the South furlonge* 1615; *a Streame called the Spring* 1650 (*v.* spring); *Stonygore* 1345², 1434 (*v.* stānig, gāra); *atte Strete* 1346 (p) (*v.* atte, strǣt); *Simsput* 1333 (the pers.n. or surname *Sim, v.* pytt); *Twey-* 1336, *Tueygryn* 1345¹ ('watercourse at —') (perhaps from twēgen 'two' and grin 'snare' (for catching fish?), cf. Ekwall, Studies² 154, PNGl **3** 203); *Wasys* 1542 (cf. John *Vase* 1545); *prat' voc' Watringe place* 1615 (*v.* watering); *atte Weye* 1332 (p) (*v.* atte, weg); *la Wendlete* 1350 ('the cross-roads', *v.* weg (analogical ME wk. pl. *weyen*), (ge)lǣt, cf. Wainland Gl **3** 239; Alexander *atte Welle* 1327, — *atte Weyltte* 1332 probably also belong here, though the first form shows confusion with the more common wella, *v.* atte); *le Westfeld* 1431² (*v.* west, feld); *Woodlandes furlonge* 1615 (cf. Roger *atte Wode* 1422, *v.* wudu).

Stinsford

In 1894 parts of Dorchester Holy Trinity (including the once independent par. of Frome Whitfield) and Fordington pars. were added to Stinsford for civil purposes. In 1933 parts of Stinsford were transferred to Dorchester borough and Charminster par.

STINSFORD (SY 712910)

Stite-, Stincteford (for *Stinete-* ?) 1086 DB

Stintesford Hy 3 Ipm, 1244 *Ass* (p), 1286 *AD*, 1306 FF, *Ilch*, 1346 FA, *Styntesford(e)* 1303 ib, 1306 *Ilch*, 1327 *SR*, 1330 *Ilch*, 1338 HarlCh *et freq* to 1446 Pat, 1408 *Ilch* (— *iuxta Dorchestre*), *Stynttesford* 1332 SR

Stinteford 1236 Fees, 1244 *Ass*, 1259 Cl, 1268 *Ass* (p), 1288 *ib*, *Stynteford* 1268 *ib* (p), 1303 FA, 1363 Cl, *-fforde* 1381 *Ct*

Stynsford 1270 (1372) *ChrP*, 1492 *Ilch*, *Stynesford(e)* 1478 *Weld*², 1492, 1497 *Ilch*, *Stynnesforth* 1529 *AD*, *Stynford* 1575 Saxton, *Stynsforde als. Stynesforth als. Stynford* 1591 *Ilch*

Stinchefford 1285 FA

'Ford frequented by the sandpiper or dunlin', *v.* stint, ford, cf. (*on-*, *æt*) *stintes ford*(*e*) 892 BCS 567, 934 ib 699 (in bounds of North Newnton W), Stinchcombe Gl 2 250. The ford was no doubt across R. Frome or some branch of it.

BHOMPSTON CTGS & FM (SY 726907), *Frome* 1086 DB (f. 79a, 2 ×), *Frome Bonevil*(*l*)*eston*(*e*) 1285 FA, 1289 Misc *et freq* with variant spellings *Bon-*, *-vyles-*, *-uyl*(*l*)*es-*, *-uiles-*, *-uylis-*, *-uylys-*, *-vylys-* to 1431 FA, *Frome Bonevile* 1286 Ipm, 1289 Misc, *Bonelis-* 1437, 1439, 1449 *Ilch*, *Boneleston* 1478 *Weld*[2], *Bolmys-* 1492, 1544 *Ilch*, *Bolmes-* 1492, 1495, 1497, 1545 all *ib*, *Bolneston* 1497 *ib*, *Bomson* 1625 *Wal*, *the farme of Bompston* 1641 *Ilch*, *Bomston* 1774 Hutch[1], *Boamstone* 1811 OS, *Bolmston Fm* 1838 *TA*. 'Boneville's manor on R. Frome', *v.* RNs., cf. Frome Whitfield *infra*. William *Bonevyle* was here in 1449 *Ilch* though his ancestors must have been here much earlier, cf. John *de Bonville* 1211–2 RBE, Nicholas *de Bonevill* 1242–3 Fees, and Bredy Fm in Burton Brad. par. *infra*.

LR BOCKHAMPTON (SY 721908), HR BOCKHAMPTON (BLDGS) (726924), ? (*æt*) *Buchæmatune* 1002–12 ASWrits, *Bochehamtone* 1086 DB, *-tona* Exon, *Bocameton* 1212 Fees, *Buchamt'* 1213 ClR, *Boc-* 1228 Ch, 1270 AD I, 1280 *Ass et freq* to 1332 SR, *Bokham*(*p*)*ton*(*e*) 1244 *Ass*, 1327 *SR et freq* to 1407 Pat, *Bukham-* 1244 *Ass*, *Buckhampton* 1244 *ib* (p), *Buketon* 1269 Pat, *Bechampton* 1288 *Ass*, *Bokamp-* 1412 FA, *Bokehamton* 1497 *Ilch*, *Beckinton* 1575 Saxton, *Bock-*, *Book-hampton* 1641 *ib*, *Beak-*, *Boakhampton* 1653 *ParlSurv*, *Bockington* 1664 HTax, *Brockhamton* 1795 Boswell, (*New*) *Bockhampton* 1811 OS. Possibly 'farm of the *Bōchǣme*' ('dwellers by the beech-tree'), *v.* bōc[1], hǣme (gen. pl. *hǣma*), tūn, though the first el. may be an abbreviated form of an older p.n. like *Bocland* from bōcland 'land granted by charter' (DEPN s.n., EPN 1 216). However, if the earliest form does in fact belong here (on the doubtful identification, *v.* ASWrits 484), the first el. may be bucc 'a buck' (cf. also the 13th-cent. spellings in *Buc-*, etc.), but the meaning of *Bucchǣme* would be difficult to determine. The possible presence of, or influence from, OE hām-tūn in the forms is discussed by Tengstrand MN 97, cf. Bockhampton Brk 334, Ha (DEPN), both of which are 'village by the beech-tree' from bōc and hām-tūn.

COKER'S FROME (FM) (SY 698914), 1774 Hutch[1], named from the family of John — 1433, Robert *Coker* 1484 Hutch[3]; it was called

East Froome Whitfield 1607 Clegg, *the farme of East Froome* 1641 *Ilch* (to distinguish it from Frome Whitfield *infra* to which manor it once belonged), and *Culls Frome* 1811 OS (cf. Colliton Ho in Dorchester par. *supra*).

EGLYSHAM (lost, about SY 690911–15), 1607 Clegg, *Eggeles-* 1335 *Ct*, *Eglesham* 1399 DorR, *Eglisham* (*Meadow*) 1409, 1445, 1532 all Hutch³ (2 413–4), 1615 *DuCo*, *v.* hamm 'water-meadow' (on R. Frome). The first el. could be the OE pers.n. *Ecgel* adduced for Eaglesfield Cu 378 and Egglestone YN 301, but Professor Cameron notes that on the evidence now available Eaglesfield Cu almost certainly contains PrWelsh eglẹ̄s 'a church', and this el. is clearly formally possible for this name too. In fact this possibility receives strong support from the location of *Eglysham* near to the former church of Frome Whitfield *infra*, *v.* St Nicholas's Church *infra* (though of course the actual building referred to may have been an earlier one on the same site). Most of the references to *Eglysham* place it in the old manor of Frome Whitfield, but the occurrence of the name in the 17th cent. bounds of Fordington (1607 Clegg, 1615 *DuCo*) establishes its location more precisely: from *Moones Bridge* and *Great Brydge* (across two arms of R. Frome, *v.* Mohun's Bridges in Dorchester par. *supra*) the bdy goes 'along by a ground called *Eglysham*' to *Glydpath* (*v.* Glyde Path Hill & Rd in Dorchester par. *supra*). The name *Eglysham* may well have denoted the river meadows to the S of the church as far as Glyde Path Hill.

FROME CRANCHEN (lost), 1774 Hutch¹, 1863 Hutch³, — *Crauazoun* (for *Cran-*) 1309 FF, — *Cranchyn* 1433 ib, — *Cronchen* 1532 ib, 'a wood called *Frome Kempston or Panters*' n.d. (1774) Hutch¹; like prec. in manor of Frome Whitfield *infra*, named from Robert *le Craneson* n.d. Hutch³, cf. Walter *de/le Cranetun* 1288 Banco, Robert *de Cranestone*, — (*le*) *Cranesson* 1289–1291 ib, Cristine *Cransun* 1327 *SR*, Thomas *Cranthon* 1340 NI (the two last connected with Bradford P. par. *supra*). The form *Panters* (from the surname *Panter*) no doubt survives in PAINTER'S BARN (SY 708932), which bears out the statement in Hutch¹ 1 396 that Frome Cranchen lay near the (old) bounds of Stinsford.

FROME WHITFIELD (FM & HO) (SY 692916), *Frome* 1086 DB (f. 83b), 1236 Fees, 1268, 1280 *Ass*, 1471 *Weld¹* (— *iuxta Styntesford*), *Froma* 1086 Exon, e13 *Salis*, *Froma Witefeld* 1243 Fees, *Frome Wytefeuld*

1264 Ipm, — *W(h)yt(e)feld, -feud* 1268 *Ass*, 1275 RH, 1280 *Ass et freq* with variant spellings — *Whit(e)fe(i)ld(e)* to 1615 *DuCo*, — *Vitefell* 1285 FA, — *Whittefeld* 1455 Cl, — *Whytfyld* 1465 Pat, — *Whitfilde* 1588 DorR, *dom' de Frome Whitefeylde iuxta Styntefforde* 1422 *Ct*, *Wytefeldes-* 1328 *ib*, *Whitefeldes-*, *W(h)itewellesfrome* 1329 *ib*, *Frome Whitfield (Ctg)* 1811 OS. One of several places named from R. Frome (*v.* RNs. *infra*). William *de Witefeld* was here e13 *Salis*, Hugh *de Wytefeld* in 1268 *Ass*, John *de Witefeld* in 1285 FA; their surname may be from Whitfield in Lillington par. *infra* or some other place of like origin. The forms from 1329 *Ct* show confusion of this name with Whitfield in Bradford P. par. *supra*, which belonged to this manor. Part of the manor was known as *Holles Frome* 1774 Hutch[1], 1863 Hutch[3] (named from Denzil *Holles* 1628 ib), which may also be identical with *Froome Farm in manor of West Froome in Whitfield* Eliz ChancP, *the farme of West Froome* 1641 *Ilch* (so called to distinguish it from Coker's Frome *supra*), cf. Hutch[3] **2** 410. There was a mill at Frome Whitfield in 1086 DB (VCHDo **3** 102), cf. *Old Tucking Mill* 1841 *TAMap* (Fordington).

KINGSTON (MAURWARD) (SY 719910), *Kingeston* 1244 *Ass* (p), 1247 FF, 1268 *Ass*, *Kyngeston(e)* 1268 *ib*, 1275 RH *et freq* to 1371 *Ilch*, — *Marlevard*, — *Marlebard* 1280 FF, — *Crubbe* 1285 FA, — *Marleward* 1303 ib, — *Maureward* 1329 FF *et freq* to 1475 *Ilch*, — *Maw(e)reward(e)* 1406 *Midd*, 1434 Cl, — *by Dorchestre* 1415 Fine, *Kynkeston* 1329 FF, *Kynggeston* 1332 SR, *Kingston Maurward or Marwood* 1774 Hutch[1]. 'The king's farm, the royal manor', *v.* cyning, tūn; it was ancient demesne of the crown (Eyton 73, 91). Geoffrey *Mauregard* occurs in connection with Kingston in 1247 FF (for the same manorial affix, cf. the early forms for Shipton G. par. and Winterborne Z. par. both *infra*); Robert *Crubbe* was tenant here in 1285, 1303 FA, cf. John *Groubbe* of *Kyngeston* 1323 Pat, John *Crubbe* 1327 *SR* and Hutch[3] **2** 562.

BADGERS COPSE. BHOMPSTON HEATH, *Bolmston* — 1838 *TA*, cf. Bhompston *supra*. BIRKIN HO. BLACK BOTTOM & HEATH (1838 *ib*). BOCKHAMPTON BRIDGE, CROSS (cf. — *Cross Plant.* 1838 *ib*), DAIRY HO (1838 *ib*) & LANE, cf. Bockhampton *supra*. CHURCH LANE, near St Michael's Church *infra*, cf. *Cherchewey* 1383 *Ilch*, *Church Cl &* Md, *The Church Copse* 1838 *TA*, *v.* cirice, weg. CUCKOO LANE. DRONG, *v.* drong 'a narrow way between hedges'. EAST or ICE HILL,

East Hill 1838 *TA*. EWELEAZE BARN, cf. *Eweleaze* (freq) 1838 *ib*.
FANNY'S LAND PLANT. FIDLER'S GREEN. FISH POND, — *Ponds* 1838
ib, cf. Walter *de la Pole* 1327 *SR*, *prat' iac' inter le Lake et piscariam*
1497 *Ilch*, *v.* pōl¹ 'pond', lacu 'stream' or lake 'lake', cf. foll. and
Weir *infra*. FISHING CTG, near prec. so probably ModE fishing 'a
fishery'. GORSE PLANT. GRAVEL PIT, 1838 *TA*. GREY'S WD, 1811
OS, named from the *Grey* family which held the manor of Kingston
supra from the 15th cent. (Hutch³ **2** 562), cf. Grey's Bridge in
Dorchester par. *infra*. HEEDLESS WILLIAM'S POND, *a place called
Hedles Willam* 1539 *AOMB* (in bounds of Puddletown common),
Heedless [vulgo Headless] William's Pond 1774 Hutch¹, named from
lapidem voc' Heuedles Willam 1270 (1372) *ChrP* (in bounds of Puddle-
town par. *supra*), 'the stone called headless William'; this must refer
to 'the remains of a cross' noted in 1774 Hutch¹ **1** 487 and so marked
6″ just S of the pond on the par. bdy, *v.* hēafod-lēas, cf. Headless
Cross Ch **3** 218; the use of the pers.n. *Will(i)am* here is obscure.
HOLLOW HILL. HOVELS BARN. KINGSTON DAIRY HO & PARK, HR
KINGSTON FM (*Hr Kingston or Grey's Wd Fm* 1838 *TA*, *v.* Grey's
Wd *supra*), cf. *Kingston(e)* (*Home*) *Fm*, *Kingston Moor* (*Plant. &
Withey Bed*) 1838 *ib*, from Kingston *supra*. LIMEKILN COPSE. LONG
COPPICE. MANOR HO, *Kingston Mansion Ho* 1838 *ib*. MELSTOCK
CLUB, from *Mellstock*, Thomas Hardy's name for Stinsford, his
place of birth, in his novels. NORTH LODGE. PAINTER'S BARN, *v. Frome
Cranchen*. PIGEON HO BARN & COPSE. THE PLAIN, *v.* plain. RUSHY
POND. ST MICHAEL'S CHURCH, *ecclesia Sancti Michaelis de Stinteford*
1244 *Ass*, *ecclesia de Stintesford* 1286 *AD*. ST NICHOLAS'S CHURCH
(site of), *Ecclesia de Frome* 1268, 1280 *Ass*, 'the church of *Frome
Whitefeld*' 1360 Pat, cf. *Frome parsonage* 1585 DorR, *the parsenage
of Frome Whitfilde* 1588 ib, *Chapel Cl* 1840 *TA* (Dorchester Holy
Trinity) and *Eglysham supra*; it was 'almost entirely decayed before
1549' (Hutch¹ **1** 398), *v.* RCHMDo **3** 257. SLYER'S LANE, cf. *Sly's
Bridge* 1841 *TAMap* (Fordington). SNAIL CREEP, a narrow plant. cut
through by the Puddletown road; the second el. may be crype
'narrow passage' (cf. ModE *creep* NED sense 4, and the use of *prote*
'throat' in describing Yellowham Hill in Puddletown par. *supra*
which is ½ mile NE on the same road), hence 'passage through
which only a snail can get', or perhaps 'passage negotiable only at a
snail's pace', *v.* snægl. SQUARE COPPICE. STINSFORD FM (*Stintsford* —
1838 *TA*), HO (*Stintsford* — 1838 *ib*) & HILL, cf. *Stynsford Lane*
1607 Clegg, *Stinsford Dairy Ho* 1811 OS. THORNCOMBE WD, 1838

TA, v, þorn, cumb. THREE CORNERED COPPICE. VICARAGE, cf. *parsonage of Stynnesforth* 1529 *AD, Parsonage Ho* 1838 *TA.* WEIR (3 ×), at Fish Pond *supra,* cf. (*prat' voc'*) (*le*) *Wereham* 1492, 1495 *Ilch, v.* wer, hamm. WELL HO. YELLOWHAM BARN, cf. *Yellow Ham* (*Plant.*) 1838 *TA, v.* Yellowham Hill & Wd in Puddletown par. *supra.*

FIELD-NAMES

Fields in Dorchester Holy Trinity *TA* but now in Stinsford are marked†, and fields in Fordington *TA* but now in Stinsford are marked‡. The undated forms are 1838 *TA* 197 (those marked † are 1840 TA 77 and ‡ are 1841 TA 88). Spellings dated e13 are *Salis,* 1270 (1372) *ChrP,* 1327 *SR,* 1329, 1335, 1349 *Ct,* 1332 SR, 1339, 1399 DorR, 1342 Pat, 1379, 1409, 1484, 1532 Hutch³, 1431 FA, 1458 *Weld¹,* 1607 Clegg, 1664 HTax, 1841 *TAMap* (Fordington), and the rest *Ilch.*

(a) ‡Bailys Bed (cf. John *Bailly* 1327 (Dorchester)); Barn Fd, †Barn Pce & Plot; Batch (*v.* batch); Upr Bockhampton Cl Plant., Fd, & Heath Cl, Bockhampton Moor & Sheep Sleight (*v.* Bockhampton *supra*); Brick Grd; Brickkiln Fd; †Broad Cl; ‡Buckington Way Cmn (*v.* Bockhampton *supra*); (Inside & Outside) Bushes; Clump; †Coppice; †Old Cowleaze; The Croft (Plant.); Cupid's Bower (no doubt a courting spot); Dead Well Water 1841 (a branch of R. Frome, running parallel to and just N of that river, *v.* dēad 'disused', wella, wæter); †(the) Down; Drail; Drying Grd; Dry Md (Withy Bed); East Plot; ‡East Ward (*Est-* 1458, 1553, *East Ward*(*e*) 1607, *v.* warod 'shore-meadow', cf. West Ward in Charminster par. *supra;* it is divided into Middle Flg, Gt & Lt North Flg, Long South Flg, & 12 Acre Flg all *infra*); †8, 18, 11, 15, †5, †4, & 14 Acres; ‡Froome Pce (from R. Frome, or from Frome Whitfield *supra,* cf. *Froome Mead* 1607, *camp' de Frome Whytefeld* 1350); Frying Pan Pond Pce (so called from its shape); Furze Brake; Furzey Cl; Great Md; The Green; The Grove; Grove Cl; ‡Little Ham; ‡The Ham; East Hayes or Cowleaze (*v.* (ge)hæg); †Hedge Row; Highest Hill Clump & Plant; †Hog Cl; Home Cl (Clump); Home Fd & Grd; Lanchard Plant. (*v.* lanchet); Little Md; †Little Plot; London Gate Plant. (on the road to London); Long Md; Marles (*v.* marle); Middle Fd; ‡Middle Flg; Mile Tree (Plant.); †New Grd; ‡Ham at New Md Gate; (The) 9 Acres (Plant.); 19 Acres; North Cl; North Fd (Plant.) (*borial' camp'* 1494); ‡(Gt & Lt) North Flg; North Wd; †Nut Cl; Oak Grove; Orchard (Cl); Ozier Bed (*v.* osier); Paddock; The Peak; Pigs Md (*i hamma prati* (*inter ij aquas*) *voc' Pygges-* 1492, 1495, *Peggesmede* 1497, the surname *Pigg* or *Pegg, v.* mæd, cf. an identical f.n. in Puddletown par. *supra*); †Pit Cl, ‡The Pit Cmn (cf. William *in la putte* 1327, Gilbert *in the putte* 1332, *v.* pytt); †Plantation; Plot Hams; Pond Cl; †Ram Cl; ‡Rough Barrow Cmn; †7 Acres; Shaw (*v.* sc(e)aga); Sheep Sleight Plant. (from Bockhampton Sheep Sleight *supra*); †Sideling 5 Acres (cf. the f.n. Sideling pasture in Charminster par. *supra*); †6 Acres; 16 Acres; †Sixpenny Md (*Sexpenny Close & Mdw* 1532, cf. William *Sexpenne* 1379); South Fd; ‡(Long) South Flg; South Plot;

Stafford Rd Plant. (the road to W Stafford par. *supra*); ‡Stynsford Yard (*v.* gerd or geard); 10, †13, 30, & †3 Acres; Triangular Plot; 12 Acres; ‡12 Acre(s) Flg; 20, 21, †23, 22, & 28 Acres; †Two and Twenty Acres; Wareham Gate, — Rd N & S Plant. (near the road to Wareham par. *supra*); Water Md; †Well Cl; †Whistons; Withey Bed (cf. *Watherbere* (sic) 1484, *v.* wiðig, bearu); Gt Wood Fd.

(b) *Bolmes-*, *Bolneston more*, — *were* 1492, 1497 (*v.* mōr, wer, Bhompston *supra*); *Bremlecumbe*, *-combe* 1383 (*v.* brēmel, cumb); *Bro(o)kforlong* 1383 (*v.* brōc, furlang); *Bromlynche* 1383, *brumlynchefelde* 1494 (*v.* brōm, hlinc, feld); *Brownings Close* 1532; *Chantry Close* 1532 (*v.* chantry); *Chipmanthorn(e)* 1494, 1497 (cf. Edward *Chipman* 1664, *v.* þorn); *Dorchester Meadow* 1532 (from Dorchester par. *supra*); *le haut chemyn apelle Dreve* 1383 (*v.* drāef); *Elme Close* 1532 (cf. *Boneliston Elme* 1437, *v.* elm, Bhompston *supra*); *Fippes-place* 1409 (cf. John *Fyppe* 1379); *Florelond* 1383 (cf. Flower Lds in Charminster par. *supra*); *Floteham* 1492, 1497 (the first el. is probably ME flote (< OE *flot*) 'state of floating or flowing, etc.', cf. the verb (< OE *flotian*) which had a trans. sense 'to flood' from 1649 NED, with hamm; perhaps synonymous with foll., for which in any case it may be an alternative name); *Flowen-* 1492, 1497, *Flowne-* 1492, *Flowinham* 1495 ('flooded river-meadow', from OE flōwen, pa. part. of *flōwan* 'to flow' ('to flood' trans. from 1382 NED), and hamm, cf. prec.; no doubt situated near R. Frome); *Foot Meadow* 1532 (*v.* fōt); *Fox Close* 1532; *la Gore* 1383 (*v.* gāra); *la Grange* 1383 (*v.* grange); *Hodders-* 1492, *Hoddesham* 1494 (cf. John *Hodder* 1492, *v.* hamm); *Huddesfelde* 1497 (probably from the same surname as prec., *v.* feld); *Hulvehede, Halfhide* (altered from *Hulfhide*) 1383 (perhaps originally from hulfere 'holly' and hēafod 'headland', though the els. have been confused with half and hīd); *la Leygh* 1383 (*v.* lēah); *Lichforlang* e13 (*v.* līc 'corpse', furlang); *More Mdw* 1532 (cf. John *de la More* 1342, Robert *atte More de Styntesford(e)* 1431, *v.* atte, mōr); *lez pasturez apellez Morwelese* 1383, *Morum-, Morehamlese* 1492 (the spellings for the first el. seem to represent OE morgen (ME *morwe, morun,* etc.) 'morning', which is perhaps a reduction of morgen-gifu 'morning gift', *v.* lǣs, cf. Wa 224, Ess 276); *Quintyneswode* 1270 (1372) (in bounds of Puddletown par. *supra*); Hugh *de St Quintin* held the larger of the two manors of Stinsford in 1086 DB (VCHDo 3 101), and John *Quentyn* held a messuage in Stinsford in 1288 Hutch³, *v.* wudu); *Richardes-place* 1399 (cf. John *Richard* 1332 (Charminster)); *Russhemor* 1349 (*v.* rysc, mōr¹); *Sexhulle* 1383, *terre voc' Syxhyll* 1494 (*v.* sex 'six', hyll); *Sewards Close* 1532; *South(e)mede* 1492, 1497 (*v.* mǣd); *Stynesford(e)felde* 1492, 1494 (*v.* feld); *Waterings Close* 1532 (*v.* watering); *Whitefeldeswere* 1329 (*v.* wer, cf. Frome Whitfield *supra*); *Whitings Close* 1532; *Wruttesford(e)* (*Were*) 1492, 1497, *-ford(es)were* 1494, *Wrotes-, Wryttesford(es)were* 1492, *Wrottesforde* 1497 (*v.* ford, wer; the first el. may be an OE pers.n. identical with or related to the pers.n. *Wrott* proposed by Ekwall DEPN for Wrottesley St).

Stratton

STRATTON (SY 651938), *Stratton* 1212 Fees, 1222, 1226 Osm, 1265 Pat (p), 1268 *Ass*, 1275 RH *et passim*, *Stratone* 1270 AD I (p), 1280 *Ass*, AD I (p), *Strathon* 1291 Tax, *Strattene* 1327 *SR* (p), *Stretton* 1348 Pat, *Strotton* 1546 Lane, *Strayton als. Stratton* 1606 (1770) *ib*, 'farm on the Roman road', *v.* stræt, tūn. The Dorchester–Ilchester road (Margary 47) was here joined by a branch from Stinsford (Margary 470).

GRIMSTONE (SY 640942), *Grimes-* 1212 Fees, 1285 FA, 1288 *Ass*, 1297 Pat, *Grymeston* 1278 QW, 1288 *Ass*, 1317 Pat, 1344 Inq aqd, *Gryms-*, *Grimston(e)* c. 1226 Sarum, 1268, 1280, 1288 all *Ass et passim*, *Grims-* 1226 Osm, *Grym(e)stan(e)* 1324–1409 Pat, *Grummes-* 1275 RH, *Grymmeston* 1288 *Ass*, *Grymstede* 1428 FA, *Gremston* 1546 Lane, *Grymston als. Greemston* 1606 (1770) *ib*, 'Grím's farm', from the ON pers.n. *Grímr* and tūn (in some forms replaced by stān 'stone' and once by stede 'place'). The pers.n. *Grímr* seems to have been common even outside the Danelaw by the time of DB, and there are three examples of its use as a Do surname in 1332 SR, one of them being a William *Grym* taxed in Piddlehinton (five miles NE). For another example of the p.n. Grimston(e) outside the Danelaw, cf. D 316.

LANGFORD FM (SY 638958), ?*Langeford* 1086 DB, *Langeford* 1218 FF, 1220–1224 Cur, 1225 FF *et freq* to 1412 FA, *Langeford Percy* 1275 Banco, *Langford* 1332 SR (p) *et passim*, *Longford* 1811 OS, 'long ford' (across Sydling Water, a tributary of R. Frome), *v.* lang[1], ford. On the slightly doubtful identification of the DB form, *v.* Eyton 111 f, Fägersten 186, VCHDo 3 74, DBGazetteer 122. The *de Percy* family was here from 13th cent., cf. Simon — 1218 FF, Geoffrey *de Percy* 1268 *Ass*, 1275 Banco, 1346 Hutch[3] 2 571.

WRACKLEFORD COPPICE & HO (SY 666932), HR WRACKLEFORD (PLANT.), LR WRACKLEFORD, *Wrakyl(s)-* 1544 Ilch, *Wrekelsford* 1546 Lane, *Wra(c)kleford (Gate & Hedge end), Walkelford, Warkelford als. Wrakle-, Wrakelford* 1606 (1770) *Lane, firmam de Wreckleforde* 1617 *DuCo, the Farme of Wrackleford* 1669 DorR, *E & W Wrackleford* 1811 OS, *Wrackleford Dairy Ho, Lr Wrackleford Eweleaze, Md & Plant.* 1838 *TA*. The first el. may be compared to that in

Wrecclesham Sr 175 (*Wreccles-* 1225, *Wreklesham* 1235) for which Ekwall DEPN suggests an OE pers.n. *Wrǣcwulf* (cf. OG *Wracwulf*). The ford was no doubt across R. Frome, *v.* ford.

CHERRY CLOSE COPPICE, *Cherry Cl* 1838 *TA*, *v.* chiri. CORN MILL, *Grimston Mill* 1838 *TA*. CORONATION PLANT., commemorating the coronation of Ed 7 (B.K. 253). EAST FM, E of the village. THE FIRE DOG (local), the railway bridge (B.K. 248). GREAT WAR PLANT., near Prisoner's of War Plant. *infra*. GRIMSTONE CLUMPS, DOWN (PLANT.) & FDS PLANT. HALF MOON PLANT., from its shape. HOG HILL (BARN), *Hog Hill* 1838 *TA*, *v.* hogg. HOWDES BARROW PLANT., *loc' voc' Howdesbarrowe* 1606 (1770) *Lane*, — *Barrow* 1838 *TA*, the first el. may be the OE pers.n. *Hūd(a)*, cf. Huddington Wo 142, *v.* beorg (tumulus marked 6″). JACKMAN'S COPPICE, CROSS (Remains of) & PLANT. KIDNEY PLANT., from its shape. LACEY'S BRIDGE, cf. Margaret *Lacye* 1664 HTax (Charminster). LANGFORD GATE, PLANT. & WITHY BED, cf. *Langford Bottom* 1838 *TA*, from Langford *supra*. LAWYER'S PLANT., cf. — *Grd* 1838 *ib*. LYCH GATE. MANOR FM, cf. *The Manor Ho* 1838 *ib*. MEADEN'S FM. MIDDLE FM, between East Fm and Manor Fm *supra*. MILL STREAM, near Corn Mill *supra*. NEWLANDS GATE & PLANT. PRISONER'S (sic) OF WAR PLANT., cf. Great War Plant. *supra*; in 1915–16 there was a large camp for German prisoners of war at Dorchester (three miles SE). THE ROOKERY. ST MARY'S CHURCH, cf. *Plot under Church Linch* 1838 *TA*, *v.* hlinc. STRATTON BOTTOM, DOWN (PLANT.) (— *Down and Waste, the Down* 1838 *ib*), MILL (*The Mill* 1838 *ib*, cf. *Mill Hams* 1838 *ib*, *v.* hamm) & PLANT.

FIELD-NAMES

The undated forms are 1838 *TA* 209. Spellings dated 1327 are *SR*, 1332 SR, 1580 *Ilch*, 1606 (1770) *Lane*, 1617 *Add*, and 1664 HTax.

(a) Barn Cl by the Pound; Bottom Grd & Md; Brewers Ash Fd (cf. John *de Fraxino* 1327, — *atte Assh* 1332, *v.* atte, æsc); Bridgeham (Mdw) (*v.* hamm); Broad Md(w); The Bull P.H.; Bushey Cowleaze & Cl; Coppice (or Ash Bed); (The) Cow Cmn; Lt Cowleaze, The Cowleaze; Dole(s) (*v.* dāl); East Fd; Eweleaze (or West Fd); Fields; 15 pieces; 4 & 14 Acres; Furze Parks (— *Parkes* 1606 (1770), *v.* park); Great Mdw; Grimston Bridge 1791 Boswell; The Grove (*v.* grāf(a)); Hay Croft; Higher Mdw & Pce; The Hill, Hr & Middle Hill; Langfords (perhaps a surname from Langford *supra*); Lay Croft (*v.* lǣge 'fallow'); Longham Mdw (*v.* hamm); Lords Md; Lower Md(w); Malthouse; Middle Fd, Mdw & Pce; New Cl, Grd & Mdw; 9

Acres; Oat Cl; The Park (cf. Furze Parks *supra*); Pond Hill; Ricks (cf. John *Reeke* 1617 (Charminster)); Servants Cl (cf. Thomas *Serivant* 1617 (Charminster)); 7 & 6 Acres; Lr & Upr Slight (*v.* slæget); Smetherhams Plot; Stony Cl; Stratton Mdw; 10 pieces; 10, 10 and 4, & 13 Acres; (Slip part of) 30 Acres (*v.* slip(p)e); Thornhams (*v.* þorn, hamm, or a surname); Tibbs Cl (cf. John *Tebb* 1664); Tucking Mill Plot; 12 & 25 Acres; West Fd; Willow Bed; Withey Bed.

(*b*) *viam inter Braynes Dore et Mores Crosse* 1580 (probably surnames with dor and cros); *Lobbe Thorne* 1580 (probably 'thorn with low-hanging branches', *v.* lobb, þorn, cf. Lobthorn Gl 2 226).

Winterborne St Martin

WINTERBORNE ST MARTIN (MARTINSTOWN 1″) (SY 647890)

Wintreburne 1086 DB (f. 83b), *-borna* Exon, *Winter-*, *Wynter-b(o)urn(e)* 1270 AD I, 1280 *Ass*, AD I, 1397 Cl

Wynterburn Sancti Martini 1244, 1268 *Ass et freq* with variant spellings *Winter-*, *Wyntre-*, *-bo(u)rn(e)-* to 1428 FA, *Wynterburn(e)-*, *-born Seynt Martyn* 1280 *Ass*, 1345 Ipm, 1363 Cl, *Wynterbo(u)rn(e) Martyn* 1332 SR *et freq* to 1549 *AddCh*, *Wynturborne Martin* 1428 FA, *Winterborne St Martine* 1640 *Weld*[1], *Winterborn Marten* 1653 *ParlSurv*

Martyn towne 1494 *Ilch*, *Martynyston* c. 1500 *Weld*[1], *Martyn(e)s Towne* 1569 *Ct* (— *als. Wynterbone Martynne*), 1615 *DuCo*, *Martinstown(e)* 1575 Saxton, 1635 *Russ*, 1795 Boswell, *Martens Towne* 1640 *Weld*[1] (— *farme*), 1664 HTax

Named from R. South Winterborne, *v.* RNs. *infra*, cf. Winterborne Came par. *supra*. 'St Martin' from the dedication of the church, *v.* St Martin's Church *infra*. For the alternative modern form Martinstown, *v.* toun. On the identification of the DB form, *v.* Eyton 121–2, VCHDo 3 102, 144, cf. DBGazetteer 129.

ASHTON CTGS & FM (SY 664878)

?*Wintreburne* 1086 DB (f. 83b), *Winterburn*, *-born* 1236 Ipm, 1238 Pat, 1241 Cl

Winterborne Esse 1242–3 Fees, *Winterburn Asshe* 1275 Banco, *Winterborne* (*H*)*asse* 1285 FA, *Winterburn Asse* 1288 *Ass*, *Wynterburn(e)-*, *-bo(u)rn As(s)(c)h(e)* 1288 *ib et freq* to 1428 FA, *Wynterburn Osse* [*Esse*] 1303 ib

Wynterborne Atthenasse 1268 FF

Aschtone 1327 *SR*, 1332 SR, *Esseton by Wynterbourne* 1397 Cl, *Ayssheton* 1457 *Ct*, 1464 *DCMCt*, 1481 *Weld*[1], *Ashdowne farme* 1640 *ib*, *Ashen* 1682 *ib*, *Ashdon Winterborne* 1795 Boswell *Wynterbo(u)rn(e)-*, *-burn A(y)s(s)h(e)ton* 1412 FA *et freq* to 1445 FF, *Weld*[1], *Winterborne Assheton* 1425 DorR, *Winterborn-Ashton* 1774 Hutch[1]

Named from R. South Winterborne, cf. prec. For the possible DB identification, *v.* Eyton 121–2, cf. VCHDo 3 103, Winterborne Came par. *supra*. The early affix is apparently OE æsc 'ash-tree', to which tūn 'farm, estate' was later added. However the 1268 form (from ME *atten ashe* 'at the ash-tree', *v.* atte(n)) might suggest that the affix was manorial in origin, similar to that in e.g. Winterborne Herringston par. *supra* (earlier — *Heryng*) or Winterborne Clenston par. *infra* (earlier — *Clench*). *Atte(n) Ashe* is a common ME surname, cf. John *de Fraxino* 1327 *SR*, — *atte Assh* 1332 SR (taxed under Grimstone in Stratton par. *supra*, 3 miles N).

REW (HILL & MANOR) (SY 637902), *La Rewe* 1283 Ipm, *Le Rawe* 1288 *Ass*, *le Rew(e)* 1288 *ib*, 1435, c. 1500 *Weld*[1], *cursus aque iuxta le Rewes* 1474 *ib*, *Rew(e)* 1528 Hutch[3], 1795 Boswell, *Row* 1587 Hutch[1], *Rew Fm* 1774 ib, *N & S Rue* 1817 Hutch[3], *Rue Hill & Md(w)* (*Plant.*) 1841 *TA*, 'the row (of houses or trees)', *v.* ræw, rāw; houses are scattered along the lane between Rew and Rew Manor which lie ½ mile apart. However, the stream referred to in 1474 is no doubt R. South Winterborne, and this form lends support to the suggestion made in RCHMDo 2 393 that the name refers to a 'long narrow stretch of closes' of medieval date along the N bank of the river.

ALINGTON PLACE, perhaps transferred from Allington par. *infra*. BALLARAT HO, perhaps transferred from Ballarat in Australia. BLAGDON BARN, *Blagdon* 1841 *TA*, from Black Down in Winterborne Steep. par. *infra*. BRONKHAM HILL, *Bromcomb* 1445 *Weld*[1], *Brancombe* 1473 *ib*, (*W*) *Branscombe, Branscombe Plain* 1841 *TA*, 'broom valley', *v.* brōm, cumb. CARRANT'S FM (lost), 1774 Hutch[1], 1863 Hutch[3], *Carrants* 1586 ib, cf. *Carrants Ewe Leaze, Plant. & Ridge* 1841 *TA*, *Canon Ewelees* 1811 OS, from the family of William *de Carente* Ed 3, John *Carant* 1476 both Hutch[3]; it lay 'in the western part of the parish' (Hutch[3] 2 574). CHURCH FM, cf. *Churchefurlang* 1471 *Weld*[1], *le Churchowse* 1635 *ib*, *Church Cowleaze* 1841 *TA*, from

St Martin's Church *infra*, *v.* **furlang, hūs.** CLANDON (BARROW &
HILL), *Clandon* 1594 *Ilch* (*Farme of* —), 1640 *Weld*[1] (— *farme*),
(— *Barrow*) 1811 OS, — *Hill* 1841 *TA*, 'hill clear of weeds', *v.*
clǣne, dūn, cf. Clandon Sr 137. EAST HILL, 1841 *TA*, SE of the
village. EWELEAZE BARN, cf. *Ewe Leaze* 1841 *ib.* FOUR BARROW HILL,
1811 OS, cf. *Four Barrows* 1841 *TA*, *v.* **beorg**; there is a line of five
tumuli marked 6″. GREAT HILL. GROVE HILL (BARN & BOTTOM),
Grove, Grove Hill (*Bottom*) 1841 *TA*, *v.* **grāf(a).** HAMAR'S PLANT.
HOG HILL, 1811 OS, *Hog's Hill* 1841 *TA*, *v.* **hogg.** KIT HILL
(BOTTOM & COPPICE), *Kite Hill* 1841 *ib*, *v.* **cȳta.** MAIDEN CASTLE,
1774 Hutch[1], *Mayden Castell* 1607 Clegg, cf. (*Under*) *Castle, Rings*
1841 *TA*, and the f.ns. Burlington, Castle Fd, etc. in Dorchester par.
supra, *v.* **mægden, castel(l), hring**; the same name is applied to a
number of other prehistoric earthworks besides this Iron Age hill-
fort, cf. Cu 255, R. E. M. Wheeler, *Maiden Castle, Dorset*, Oxford
1943, 6–14; the meaning of the name is probably 'fortification
thought never to have been taken, one that looks impregnable', but
for other suggestions, *v.* EPN 2 31–2. Maiden Castle is probably the
city of *Dunium* referred to by Ptolemy (I, 103); this is from Brit
dūno- 'a fort', probably with the Brit suffix **-ion** or **-ion.** MANOR HO.
NORTH DOWN (lost), 1811 OS, *pastur' voc' Northdown* 1463 *Weld*[1],
cf. *Northdown fd* 1841 *TA*, *v.* **norð, dūn**; it lay N of the village, cf.
South Down *infra.* NORTH PLANT., 1841 *ib.* PARK FM, 1774 Hutch[1],
Park 1795 Boswell, cf. 'a ground called *Parks*' 1607 Clegg, *firm*'...
voc' Parkes 1615 *DuCo, Park Corner* (*Cl*) & *Pce, Parks* (*Ewe leaze*)
1841 *TA*, *v.* **park.** PEN BARN & CTGS, *Penn* (*Cl* & *Barn*) 1841 *ib*,
probably from **penn**[1] 'a hill'; the barn and cottages are at 350′, but
the ground rises steeply to 493′ on N and to over 600′ on S. RIDGE
BOTTOM & HILL, *Ridge Bottom* & *Rd, Furzy Ridge* 1841 *TA*, cf.
the f.n. *Waldonrygge infra, Rudge* 1841 *ib*, *v.* **hrycg.** RYLAND'S BARN,
Ryelands 1841 *ib*, *v.* **ryge, land.** ST MARTIN'S CHURCH, 'the church
of *Winterburn* St Martin' 1263 Pap, *Ecclesia Sancti Martini* 1428
FA, *Cantarie Sancti Martini* 1549 AddCh, cf. *Chapel close* 1841 *TA*,
Church Fm *supra.* SHORN HILL, *Shorne* 1841 *ib*, probably from
scoren[1] 'a steep place', cf. Shorne K 117 explained in this way
by DEPN and EPN 2 113. SOUTH DOWN (lost), 1811 OS, cf. *Southdown fd* 1841 *TA*, S of the village, cf. North Down *supra.* VICARAGE,
cf. *rectoriam ecclesiæ* 1361 Hutch[3]. WEST END HO, on W edge of
village, *v.* **ende.**[1]

FIELD-NAMES

The undated forms are 1841 *TA* 257. Spellings dated 1220 (16) are *DCMDeed*, 1327 *SR*, 1337 DorR, 1540, 1546, 1820 Hutch[3], 1664 HTax, and the rest *Weld*[1].

(a) Abbotsbury Rd fd (*v.* Abbotsbury par. *infra*); Allens Cl (cf. Constance *Allen* 1664); Barn Cl; Bartons Cl; Lr Batts, Hr Butts (*v.* batte or butte); Brake (*v.* bræc[1]); Brewers Md (cf. Henry *Bruere* 1327); Brines Md (*Brynes*— 1546); (Lt, Old & Outter) Broad Fd; Broad Md; Butter Cl & Plant. (*v.* butere); Capon Hays (from capon, or a surname, and (ge)hæg); Chalk pce; Coombe Bottom (*v.* cumb); Cowleaze; Crone tenement 1820; Crow Barrow (*v.* crāwe, beorg, cf. Crowborough Sx 372); Culver Cl (*v.* culfre); Hr & Lr Damery (probably a surname); Dirty Gate; Dry Md; East Pce; 8 & 18 Acres; Ferrie's Pce; 15 & 50 Acres; Five Barrows; Folly Md (*v.* folie); 40 & 4 Acres; Furlong; Further Pce; Furze Hill; Gatecombe (geat 'gap' or gāt 'goat', with cumb); Glide Md (possibly glida 'a kite'); Goblets Hole (*v.* hol[1]); Ham Wd (*v.* hamm); Hanging Md (*v.* hangende or hanging); Higher Pce; Hilly Cl; Hr & Lr Holes (*v.* hol[1]); Home Pce, Plant. & Plot; Horse Cl; Hundred Acres (a small field); Island; Joseph's Fd; Knap Plain & Ridge (*v.* cnæpp); Furze Knowle, (W) Knowles (*v.* cnoll); Lane Gdn; Lawn; Lime Kiln Grd; Little Hill; Long Mdw; Lucas's Cl (cf. Richard *Lucas* 1664); Mallards Green; Middle Pce; Mill Stone Grd (cf. *la Mille-* 1470, *le Milhous* 1474, *v.* myln, hūs; there was a mill at Winterborne St M. in 1086 DB (VCHDo 3 102)); Mowhay (*v.* mow, (ge)hæg); New Grd; 9 & 19 Acres; North Md; Nutt Cl (*v.* hnutu); Paddock; Philips md; Pit Pce; Plantation; Plot; Pound Cl; Old Rick Yd; Rowden (probably rūh 'rough' with denu or dūn); 7 Acres; Share Plot (*v.* sc(e)aru); Shawls Plat (*v.* plat[2]); Shepherd Cl; Silly Hoe (no doubt analogous with Silly How in Portisham par. *infra*); 6 Acres; Smalldon, Small down (*v.* smæl, dūn); Smith's Cl (cf. William *faber* 1327, Richard *Smyth* 1445, and *xx acr' terre voc' Smytthe* 1442, *v.* smiðõe 'a smithy'); Snowdon ('hill where snow lies long', *v.* snāw, dūn); Somers Cl; (Gt) South Grd; Stevens Down & Pond (cf. Ann *Stevens* 1664); Stonken (probably for -den, cf. *Stondon* 1445, *v.* stān, dūn); Stran; (Lamberts) 10 Acres; Thomas's Knap (*v.* cnæpp); Three Corner Pce; N & S Town Fd; (Home) Varnington (possibly 'ferny hill', *v.* fearnig, dūn); West Cl & Pce.

(b) *Brofurlange* 1443 (possibly an error for *Brok-*, *v.* brōc, furlang); *Chalvedon* 1472 ('calves' hill', *v.* calf (WSax gen. pl. *cealfa*), dūn); *le Drove* 1220 (16) (*v.* drāf); 'lands called *Gryd*' 1546 (perhaps from grēot 'gravel', ModE *grit*); *viam iuxta Hywysshhegge* 1472 ('hedge of *Hywyssh*' ('measure of land that would support a family'), *v.* hīwisc, hecg; this should perhaps be associated with the lost DB manor of *Hiwes* (f. 80b, assessed at one hide) which is mentioned after *Bradeford* (Bradford P. par. *supra*) in DB and which was tentatively identified by Eyton 123–4 with Muckleford in that par., cf. VCHDo 3 91, DBGazetteer 121); *pontem voc' Langbrygge* 1456, *-brigg* 1457 (*v.* lang[1], brycg); *la Northfeld* 1470 (*v.* norð, feld); *pastur' voc' Oldehill* 1456 (*v.* ald, hyll); *Otefyle* 1472, *le Ottfeild* 1635 (*v.* āte, feld); *Personyslane* 1468, 1472 (*v.* persone, lane); *Pryerslane* 1443 (*v.* prior; the priory of Merton held lands here in 16th cent., *v.* Hutch[3] 2 573); *La Ridedich* *extra Wynterborne Sancti Martini* 1337 ('red ditch', *v.* rēad, dīc); *Shortlond* 1456 (*v.* sc(e)ort, land); 'lands...called *Silke*' 1540 (*v.* sēoluc 'a gulley'); *Southcombe* 1474 (*v.* sūð, cumb); *de quadam Wala que ducit versus Waldonrygge* 1471 (*v.* dūn, hrycg; in view of the context the first el. is probably walu 'a ridge of earth or stone', the latinised *wala* suggesting that the word was still in independent use in the 15th cent in a topographical sense (according to NED *s.v. wale* sb.[1] this sense is confined to OE), cf. Do dial. *wale, weale* 'a large ridge of hay formed during haymaking' (Barnes 70). However *Waldon-* may be a scribal error for *Waddon-*, in which case the name probably refers to Ridge Hill *supra* which lies just N of Waddon in Portisham par. *infra*); *le Wytheber* 1457 (*v.* wīðig, bearu).

INDEX OF DORSET PARISHES

Parishes followed by **1** and page number are dealt with in this Part; the rest will appear in subsequent Parts. Abbreviated forms of affixes, if used in the text, are given in brackets.